INVENTING FILM STUDIES

Lee Grieveson and Haidee Wasson, editors

INVENTING FILM STUDIES

Duke University Press ■ Durham and London ■ 2008

© 2008 Duke University Press
All rights reserved.
Printed in the United States
of America on acid-free paper ∞
Designed by Amy Ruth Buchanan
Typeset in Minion by Tseng
Information Systems, Inc.
Library of Congress Cataloging-in-
Publication Data and republication
acknowledgments appear on the
last printed page of this book.

*Duke University Press gratefully
acknowledges the support of Fonds
québécois de la recherche sur la société
et la culture (FQRSC), which provided
funds toward the production of this
book.*

For Ava, Lauren, and Riley

CONTENTS

■ MAKING CINEMA KNOWABLE

■ MAKING CINEMA EDUCATIONAL

Acknowledgments

■ Assembling a book of this sort provided a very particular set of challenges. We would first, therefore, like to thank our contributors, who have each graciously accepted numerous editorial interventions and delays, and then more interventions. We have learned a great deal from their inspiring scholarship and the provocative conversations that provide the backbone of this book. For both obvious and sometimes unexpected reasons, this project would simply not have been possible without their varied commitments to this discipline, keeping an eye on its past and its future. Likewise, the readers at Duke—including Eric Smoodin—were smart, thorough, and engaged, thereby helping to improve the manuscript at several stages. We are deeply thankful for their help. Recognition is also due to Jack Ellis for his enthusiasm and support and for his own pioneering efforts to make cinema a complex object of study.

We would like to thank Ken Wissoker for his support, countless insights, and the wise counsel. His patience, humor, and belief in this book kept us going; the cocktails softened the bumpy ride. Courtney Berger has also been wonderfully helpful in ensuring that the final wrinkles were suitably pressed.

We would also like to acknowledge the financial support of the Faculty of Fine Arts at Concordia University, the Social Sciences and Humanities Research Council (Canada), the McKnight Landgrant Foundation, the University of Minnesota, and the Visual and Environmental Studies Department at Harvard University. A sizeable subvention was also graciously provided by le Groupe de Recherche sur l'histoire et l'épistémologie des études cinématographiques, funded by Le Fonds pour La Formation de Chercheurs et l'Aide à la Recherche, Quebec. Thanks also to Charles Acland, Martin Lefebvre, Rosanna Maule, Julianne Pidduck, Eric Prince, Katie Russel, and Tom Waugh, fellow members of the previously mentioned research team on the history and epistemology of film studies based at Concordia University. Special recognition goes to Martin who spearheaded this team, working tirelessly to create the ideal conditions in which the key questions of our discipline can be explored. Fabulous research assistance came from Steve Groening, Bruno Cornellier, Ryan Diduck, Heather MacDougal, and Owen Livermore.

Lee would like to thank Lauren and Riley, as always, for the fun and the constant reminder that life and love is a gift, and Amelie Hastie for more fun and laughter, for smart and helpful interventions, and for the fierce belief that this book, and the attempt to think about the history and organization of disciplines, is worth the effort. Peter Krämer provided characteristically insightful readings and remarks. And, in particular, thanks to Haidee Wasson, who has made editing this book a fabulous learning experience. I consider myself very lucky to have had this opportunity to learn, live, and laugh alongside her. Life is better—funnier, smarter, sharper—with e-mails in your inbox from Haidee.

Haidee would like to thank Lee for providing a working relationship that was dynamic and challenging, and continues to be filled with promise, properly balanced with a healthy dose of mischief. She would also like to acknowledge the limitless generosity of Charles Acland, whose own commitment to and love of academic ideals provides inspiration as well as a steadfast supply of the curiosity, discipline, and joy that help to realize those ideals.

The Academy and Motion Pictures

LEE GRIEVESON AND HAIDEE WASSON

■ What's in a name? Or, put another way, what do names do? Take three examples, three moments of naming, from the central professional organization
for English-language cinema studies. The Society of Cinematologists (soc), set
up in 1959, changed its name to the Society for Cinema Studies (scs) in 1968;
then, in 2003, it changed its name once again to the Society for Cinema and
Media Studies (scms). One way that names work in such contexts is to function
as directives, to exemplify ideals, promises, and ultimately practices for the
study of cinema. Names presuppose frames of reference that limit, just as they
help create, that which is named. The procedures for naming and renaming the
organization for cinema studies and for any other professional organization of
study are also part of a wider configuration in which knowledge is produced
and regulated in order to establish objects of investigation, research methods,
professional standards, and, potentially, disciplines. We understand the term
"discipline" here as a procedure for institutionalizing scholarship and conferring authority that finds its locus in the university.[1] To explore the definitional
chores of one professional organization seeking to confer authority and manage
expertise enables us to think about the dynamics underlying three moments,
or three configurations of study. These names indicate, respectively, a period
prior to full academic institutionalization, characterized by disparate agendas;
the formalization of an academic discipline; and the ensuing transformations
of that discipline into its present multimedia configuration. Taking this one

example, it is clear that the relatively short disciplinary life of film has been, and continues to be, a shifting and adaptive one.

We have two primary goals in this book: to present detailed examinations of the social, political, and intellectual milieus in which knowledge of cinema has been generated, and to consider the historically contingent ways in which these varied ideas and practices of film study came to be assembled into a discipline. To achieve these goals requires attention not only to what has been included within the bounds of the discipline and its conventional narratives but also to what has been left out, for the process of disciplinization is also inevitably one of limitation and exclusion.[2] When one scratches at the surface of disciplinary certainties, as the authors in this book do, then one finds long and often complex histories that have been largely omitted from prevailing accounts of what the study of cinema has been and ought to be.[3] This volume begins the process of properly excavating the varied study of cinema in Anglo-American contexts across the history of the medium and its institutions.[4]

Why, then, was the term "cinematologists" used in 1958? What was the resonance of this name at that moment? To name the society in this fashion explicitly connected the American society's goals and self-image to the preexisting French academic movement of "filmology"—an instance of a trans-Atlantic exchange that has consistently been important to the study of cinema generally. French "filmologists" had proposed to set in place a comprehensive methodological approach to what they termed the "science" of cinema, thereby helping initiate university programs and conferences in France as well as the publication of the journal *La Revue Internationale de Filmologie* beginning in 1947.[5] Similarly, the cinematologists sought a name with the "right scholarly and scientific tone," suggesting, as a founding member of the organization recalled in 1968, "a move in the direction of dignity" for the study of cinema in the United States. It was hoped that this move would help support academic careers as well as bolster the expansion of university programs.[6]

At the first meeting of the society, held in New York at the Museum of Modern Art (MOMA) in 1958, Robert Gessner, the first president of the organization, observed that in "acquiring academic standards" the film teacher, now often "alone and isolated," could "end his second-class citizenship in university faculties."[7] To name the organization thus was intended to produce a model for the study of cinema akin to established academic disciplines. It also helped to create affiliations and interchange among not only faculty but also archivists, audio-visual technicians, librarians, programmers, and film critics located throughout the university. Gessner and the early cinematologists also incorporated existing institutional structures that had previously enabled the serious engagement with cinema but that largely existed separate from or parallel to universities: film societies, archives, distribution networks, journals, and book publishing on cinema. In doing so they systematized the broad currents of film culture that had intensified in the immediate postwar period by routing it through a professional society and its various activities, which included annual conferences and the publication of a journal, the *Journal of the Society of Cinematologists*, from 1961. The organization additionally began to disseminate information about job hires and to articulate "professional standards" for scholarship and teaching that impacted upon the self-definition of those interested in studying cinema. As a result, research and teaching—the basic activities fostered by the modern university—became integral elements of the larger field.[8]

While prior to the SOC the long history of studying cinema had led to some university courses as well as to at least one full program of study, there were subsequent developments in the early 1960s that set the groundwork for the sustainability of cinema's study in academe. In 1968, the SOC changed its name to the Society for Cinema Studies (SCS), thus shifting emphasis from those studying—cinematologists—to the object of their study: the cinema. The renaming of the professional organization better reflected, it was thought, the "wide interests of its membership" and was connected also to the "tidal wave" of student interest in the recent European and American new waves. The new name also clearly signaled the link between studying cinema and the remit of humanities disciplines, jettisoning the scientific tinges of "ology." "We are searching for our best approach, our discipline," wrote the editors of the newly renamed *Cinema Journal*. While the "social implications of cinema" and the "scientific aspects of film production and audience analysis" are, the editors stated, "never far from our thoughts," it was felt that "most of the time" the journal and organization "shall probably emphasize film as an art and the criticism of it as one of the humanities."[9] The study of cinema was diverse, the organization conceded, but increasingly a hierarchy of concerns and methodological imperatives was established.

Other pertinent developments informed the burgeoning growth of cinema study in North American universities. The American Council on Education, for example, assembled a report in 1964 on film study for college teachers and administrators planning to "initiate courses in the history, criticism, and appreciation of motion pictures."[10] Necessary to such courses, the report stated, was a film-study information center, adequate film distribution, and training programs for teachers. The findings of the report were disseminated at a conference in New York City in late 1964, which led in turn to the call for another conference to consider the establishment of film studies programs. Delegates there acknowledged a further need for curricular materials, including a book that would "describe, in detail, a variety of courses in motion-picture history, criticism, and appreciation, [reflecting] the broad range of current film courses of high quality."[11] These declarations provide a fascinating picture of an unformed though vibrant field, anticipating but also lacking some of the most basic building blocks for establishing and sustaining disciplinary viability.

It was not only educators and cinephiles who advocated for university-level film study. Other developments in the mid-1960s connected cinema to academic programs, including a study launched in 1965 by the Motion Picture Association of America (MPAA), the commercial and self-regulatory organization representing the major film concerns in North America. The MPAA set out "to further study, research, and [establish] appreciation of motion pictures at various levels of education."[12] Similar work was conducted also by the National Council of Teachers of English, resulting in the publication in 1965 of *The Motion Picture and the Teaching of English*—a volume that focused on the study and teaching of "the unique characteristics of film as an art form" in schools and universities.[13] Once again, and in both cases, the study of cinema was linked to traditions of humanities interpretation in general, and to new critical techniques of close formal analysis in particular.[14] These reports were largely written by working academics and they index the wide and mounting interest in transforming film into the subject of a particular kind of pedagogical and disciplinary scrutiny.

These pedagogical imperatives, joined with the changing professional organization of film study, pushed the diverse strains of cinema's study further toward the requirements of an academic discipline. Parallel to these developments, university programs and departments began forming. The study of cinema grew not only to embrace particular epistemological dispositions but also to exclude others. Cinema study was increasingly intertwined with the humanities, divorced from the social sciences that provided the model for filmologists, for example, and that also informed some traditions of communication studies, which were particularly important for film before, during, and just after World War II. Likewise, the core of academic film study was gradually differentiated from belletrist appreciation, practices of film reviewing, and developing the skills of film production.[15] This winnowing was concretized with the establishment of graduate programs throughout the 1960s, thus further tethering film study to the standards associated with advanced scholarship. Such programs are especially critical in the formation of disciplinary identities, where they function as socializing procedures to produce scholars shaped by disciplinary norms.[16]

We have identified some of the institutions instrumental in engendering a studious sense of cinema outside of the university and in providing a broader context for what was happening inside the university. Yet, we must still ask: What were the immediate forces acting on and within the university itself that facilitated the widespread institutionalization of cinema? In response, we can briefly delineate two related developments, the first of which involved the shifting structures of higher education, including an emergent ethos of democratic mass education in the postwar period that was bolstered by the baby boomers reaching college age in the 1960s.[17] Young faculty and students frequently had a direct impact on curricular reforms by pushing for new disciplinary divisions and for the formation of subdisciplinary and interdisciplinary fields (for example, women's studies, cultural studies, African American studies, Asian American studies, and Latino/a studies).[18] Second, and closely tied to the first point, was the development of influential social movements—for example, second wave feminism, civil rights, gay and lesbian liberation movements, the protest against the conflict in Vietnam, and so on. Collectively, these events were perhaps most clearly symbolized, in Europe at least, by the events of May 1968 that were initiated by a student radicalism dissatisfied with, among other things, the conservative academy. What Dudley Andrew calls "the Prague Spring of academia" in turn impacted on intellectual practices.[19] The influence of structuralist work in the humanities—psychoanalysis, Marxism, and semiology—inspired an ascendant generation of film scholars to explore the pertinence of cinema to influential concepts such as ideology and power. Film scholarship acquired a new and much broader relevance that further facilitated its migration across disciplinary borders. Film theory and criticism became important to linguistics, comparative literature, and English and other language departments as well as in more interdisciplinary programs such as "critical studies." This only added to the visibility of film study in drama and theater departments, arts departments, and education, communications, and American studies departments.

While the May 1968 period and the intellectual and political contexts from which it grew became crucial for the discipline of film studies, it does not mark the birth of the discipline as is frequently assumed. This assumption has been repeatedly articulated and works effectively in two ways: the first as a celebration of the politically radical nature of the discipline; and the second, in contrast to the first, as a critique of the theoretical work undertaken from the early 1970s onward.[20] We propose that both positions are far too partial to stand in for any adequate understanding of the discipline. Why? To begin, we can and must locate the study of cinema in a longer history, as, for instance, the emergence of filmology and cinematology decades earlier shows. Acknowledging this history requires noting the connections among prior forms of study and also tracking the inescapable sociopolitical questions about cinema that inflect virtually all forms of knowledge about film — even if by their absence. We believe, therefore, that the work on cinema and ideology emerging from the political and intellectual context of the later 1960s marks a continuity with and not a break from earlier traditions of study. In this book we claim that the study of cinema was born in the early twentieth century as a political problem in conjunction with the social turbulence of the 1910s, 1920s, and 1930s. To be sure, 1968 marks an auspicious date. Yet, we maintain that the widely shared sense of the centrality of poststructuralist theoretical work to the foundation and functioning of the discipline of cinema studies is partly a consequence of disciplinization itself, which necessarily creates hierarchies of valued work. Furthermore, it is clear, as the account above has already briefly demonstrated, that studies of film have also — before the Prague Spring and the new wave — long been connected to aesthetic questions and thus to the conceptualization of film as a particular kind of art form.[21] This basic assertion was, for instance, central to the remit of the Film Library at the Museum of Modern Art in the mid-1930s, and it was also critical to the acceptance of film as an object of humanities disciplines in the university before and immediately after World War II. In short, the twin poles of sociopolitical critique and aesthetic analysis that constitute standard maps of the discipline have in fact played themselves out in various ways across a long history of studying cinema.

This question of precisely what tendencies have constituted and should continue to constitute film as an object of study underpinned the third act of naming we want to discuss here. In 2003 the membership of the Society of Cinema Studies, by then numbering approximately 1,850, voted overwhelmingly to change the name to the Society for Cinema and Media Studies. Adding the term "media" was seen to more accurately reflect member research. Longstanding concerns with television and video helped facilitate increasing scholarly attention to a proliferation of moving image forms and cultures. Such shifts occurred alongside corresponding transformations of cinema's technologies, which were attenuated from celluloid and connected increasingly to the digital.

Questions about medium specificity and materiality were reinvigorated as the autonomy and purity of "film," the putative object of the discipline, was fundamentally challenged. The definition of cinema expanded, and often it included phenomena not explicitly linked to celluloid. For instance, the rising interest in so-called pre-cinema and early cinema frequently focused on complementary forms of leisure or related venues of spectacle. Alongside this changing object of study, the name change of 2003 also worked to acknowledge the proliferation of methodologies in the discipline. A widely shared assumption that the theoretical models articulated in the early 1970s were no longer sustainable catalyzed this. Such challenges grew from cultural studies, cognitivism, historical work, transnational theorization, and postcolonial criticism. These critiques and the context for them generated a widespread sense of uncertainty and, in part, insecurity about the future of film study.

Many feared that these changes amounted to a form of "death"; others celebrated a rebirth. Nonetheless, the language of "crisis" rose to the fore. In the late 1990s, for instance, plenary panels at the Society for Cinema Studies conferences were set up to redress the predicament of film studies (in 1999 and 2000); books appeared projecting new versions of the discipline with titles like *Post-Theory: Reconstructing Film Studies* (1996) or *Re-Inventing Film Studies* (2000); and committees in universities charged with developing new programs or transforming existing ones chose titles like "Screen Studies," "Media Arts," and "Screen Cultures." Stepping back, we can see here the proliferation of divergent aims, methods, and goals of disciplinary practice. At its best, this situation provided film scholars with an opportunity to engage in a lively discussion about the significance, coherence, and relevance of their work. At its worst, warring camps emerged and battle lines were drawn.

Despite this prominent debate about the object and methodologies of cinema study, and despite a heightened attention to the history of disciplines in the humanities broadly, there has been little attention to the history of the study of cinema, to the nature of film study's kind of disciplinarity, and to its epistemological technologies.[22] Little work has linked the many intentions and imperatives that have made cinema a contested object of knowledge to its status as an academic discipline. The essays in this collection contribute to the project of historicizing and reflecting upon the material, intellectual, and institutional history of studying cinema. Some of these essays move back beyond the formation of cinema studies as an academic discipline proper by engaging with histories that precede the developments of the late 1960s. Other essays examine more recent histories by considering unfamiliar developments and reconsidering familiar ones. As a whole, then, this book reflects our understanding of film study as a constellation of institutions, technologies, practices, individuals, films, books, governmental agencies, pedagogies, theories, and educational sites. Collectively, the authors ask: What impulses were/are there in culture and academe that have made possible, or indeed necessary, the study of cinema? What has been included in the gradual disciplinization of the study of cinema? What has been excluded? How has the study of cinema changed over time?

We begin to answer some of these questions in the volume's first section, "Making Cinema Knowable." Together, the essays in this section examine the early formations of studying cinema, showing how efforts to study film were initially connected to particular governmental concerns and practices as well as to the needs of a changing university. The chapters document and analyze the production and dissemination of expert knowledge (particularly as it relates to the emergent social sciences), the formation of early institutions, and the gathering of basic material resources, focusing on developments before World War II. The authors work to assess links between early studies of cinema and efforts to understand and also shape the social body. The primary epistemological question attached to film during this period was less about aesthetic innovation and medium specificity and more about influence—both on the mind and, inevitably, the social body. The essays in this section also necessarily discuss emergent fields of inquiry such as communication, urban sociology, advertising, educational psychology, political science, and social psychology. To consider these interconnections, as the authors in this section do, allows us to see film study's formation in other fields; it also allows us to observe paths not taken. During this period, films were conceived less as discrete aesthetic objects and more as one phenomenon among many constituting the urban milieu as a complex social environment.

Lee Grieveson's essay "Cinema Studies and the Conduct of Conduct" focuses on the research in the human sciences beginning in the late nineteenth century that promulgated influential ideas about mimesis, predicated on the newly conceived malleability of the modern subject. Grieveson demonstrates that such ideas underpinned investigations documenting the influence of movies, whose primary goal was to gain control of audiences. Cinema study emerges here as one aspect of the governance of mass publics. Yet the import of ideas about mimesis and the movies, Grieveson contends, extends beyond the initiation of the study of cinema and goes on to shape later configurations of study emerging from within the social sciences and the humanities. Complimenting Grieveson's chapter, Mark Anderson reexamines the urban sociology informing the so-called Payne Fund Studies conducted in the late 1920s and early 1930s that worked to identify the effects of moving pictures on children. In particular, Anderson explores the "media expert"—a figure that consolidated institutional authority and came to serve as an intermediary between film, governing bodies, and universities. The media expert was a new, distinct, and enduring figure, capable of holding forth on matters at first sociological and later also aesthetic.

Zoë Druick's essay "'Reaching the Multimillions': Liberal Internationalism and the Establishment of Documentary Film" further maps the relations between film study and questions of governance. In doing so, Druick focuses on how knowledge of cinema became instrumental to educating modern citizens. Specifically, she investigates the film programs of the League of Nations and the United Nations. These organizations, she argues, found a powerful consort in the cinema, building lasting institutions and shaping foundational ideas that pertain to two key components of film study: educating *with* film and educating *about* film. The first component crafted film as a particularly modern educational tool (i.e., documentary film) and became an integral part of the emergent liberal elite's mandate to balance, on the one hand, the ostensible and rapid erosion of traditional models of culture and, on the other, a world increasingly and unavoidably mediated by information technologies. The second component, educating about film, provided the seeds for what would become the central mission of the discipline. Film study in both senses emerged as an instrument of state but also as a new technology of global governance. A world torn asunder by politics provided a dramatic backdrop.

Dana Polan's essay "Young Art, Old Colleges: Early Episodes in the American Study of Film" concentrates on the connections between the university and the study of film in the interwar period. Polan demonstrates that film courses appeared across the university curriculum, and—like Druick—he highlights the fact that films were often conceived as a way to renew pedagogy and reassert the relevance of prominent institutions. With regard to American universities, film study, in a sense, served as a sort of talisman, a magical object tasked with solving problems incumbent upon the academy to respond to changing technologies, shifting demographics, and new educational and sociopolitical missions. Cinema offered a way to reconcile the seeming divide between the present and the past, between the new machine aesthetic and the traditions of humanist inquiry, and between a set of practical techniques and abstract ideas. Clearly, film's capacity to integrate these varied realms continued throughout the decades. In particular, the fusion of making and thinking—production and critical study—is an issue considered in several of the essays in this volume (notably, those by Hastie et al., Zryd, and Mulvey and Wollen). Polan's essay shows us that film has long served as the bad object and the good across American academe, representing what has been deemed the worst of culture under capitalism but also the best hope for maintaining relevance and establishing harmonies within the complex configurations of the modern.

The issues of education and expertise that weave throughout the essays by Grieveson, Anderson, Polan, and Druick are also taken up by the authors gathered together in the second section, "Making Cinema Educational." The idea that it could be pedagogically useful to watch and then discuss a film—linking vision to mind and to learning—was not born with film itself but instead developed gradually in a variety of settings. Moreover, the precise form taken by this assumption changed tremendously from institution to institution. This section supports one of the volume's key claims: in order to understand the emergence of the study of film one also needs to tend to the politics of the institutions and organizations that foster film knowledge. These essays thus accord attention to particular kinds of spaces in addition to the university, not just for watching films but also for thinking and writing about films: namely, museums, film councils and societies, and national film institutes. These organizations coalesced to provide forms of exhibition and reception alternative to the dominance of commercial forms and institutions; each had its own unique relationship to a larger civic vision for cinema and to cultural networks and social imperatives distinct from Hollywood.

The essays in this second section concentrate less on the connections between the study of cinema and anxieties about audiences—previously figured as childlike, as Grieveson and Anderson show—and more on the way that cinema studies was linked to the pursuit and organization of an adult audience. Over and over we see the importance of harnessing to film the ideals either of sophistication or of lifelong learning (self-improvement, community improvement, social equality). This can be observed readily in the case of MOMA, the Film Council of America, and the film society movement, and also in many postwar university environments. Such institutions easily interfaced with formal programs of adult education in the United States and also in the United Kingdom, where such initiatives provided a key aspect of the early film study efforts of the British Film Institute (BFI).[23]

Building a practical infrastructure for an international and sustainable network of specialized films and film viewers was a basic precondition for what we now know as film study: films must be seen to be known. The early institutionalization of this idea can be seen in the loose associations that developed during the interwar period in the form of film societies and, in particular, as Haidee Wasson shows, in organizations like the Museum of Modern Art, where the logics of the modern art museum provided a pretext and a material infrastructure that corrected for the difficulty of actually seeing films. During the 1930s, this required constructing and coordinating a highly unusual site that circumvented the logics of Hollywood and borrowed not only from so-called nontheatrical film renting agencies but also from active museum programs to circulate their objects far and wide. A distinct kind of circuit had to be built, which introduced a range of questions about film's temporality (what did it mean to watch old films?) and spatiality (what did it mean to watch old films in an art museum?). Of course, with the creation of such viewing programs came the issue of which films to include and which to exclude, thereby enabling on the one hand standardized curriculum and on the other hand restrictive canons.

Other organizations with arguably broader reaches were equally important for expanding film knowledge. The International Educational Cinematograph Institute and later UNESCO's film program inflected film education and study with a particular political ethos of liberal humanism and internationalism. We can add to those organizations the film councils, universities, film libraries, film societies, public libraries, and also a growing body of commercial firms seeking to service the growing market for nontheatrical audiences. Together, these institutions contributed to a technological infrastructure and also to ways of moving films, shifting resources, and directing populations (audiences) toward cinema—that is, toward conceiving of and engaging cinema as a primary interface between viewers and the world. Such institutions also became practical meeting points for individual filmmakers, critics, researchers, and activists by providing a theater for the exchange of ideas and collaborations.

One of the key goals of this book is to explore cultural and institutional developments that have prioritized film knowledge as a foundational mode of organization. In this spirit, Charles Acland examines the formation of the American Film Council movement in the late 1940s and 1950s. Film councils grew out of the war effort to educate and prepare citizens, and they were made possible by a newly expansive technological infrastructure comprised of 16mm projectors. In short, Acland shows that as television and suburbs ascended, films and projectors provided a method by which citizens imagined themselves to participate in rather than retreat from civic life. In addition to the council movement's surprisingly active exhibition schedule, equally influential were its efforts to coordinate and circulate ideas about cinema that helped to situate films at the center of a reinvigorated community politic. The councils not only helped to legitimate a range of film activities (teaching, criticism, programming) but also to assert a particular kind of authority in the context of an increasingly mediated world wherein traditional social institutions were scrambling to adapt. Like the instances detailed in the earlier essays by Grieveson, Anderson, Polan, and Druick, ideals of film knowledge are plainly situated in relation to an ideal of relevance but also a larger—if complex—social project.

The pertinence of the film councils to the genealogy of film studies is considerable. Not only did the American Film Council morph into the American Federation of Film Societies, which flourished on university campuses, but the first generation of film scholars and university teachers were often instrumental to this early film education movement. The activities of the councils were predictably diverse, as were their mandates for viewing and discussion. Councils used film not only to educate about the world but also to educate about film technique and style. In other words, the latter of these ideas—the so-called properly cinematic knowledge that would come to form the core of the discipline—not only owes a sizable debt to the infrastructures set in place by the councils but also was intimately interconnected with, and at some levels indistinguishable from, the instrumentalization of film for other kinds of learning.

Michael Zryd's essay "Experimental Film and the Development of Film Study in America" picks up the threads of the history begun here by Dana Polan by exploring the university as a particular kind of site for film viewing and study. Zryd documents a constitutive and material relationship between the university and the avant-garde, demonstrating that the university as a renter of films has long been the most important financial supporter of experimental film institutions in the United States. He thus documents not only a crucial dependency but also a vibrant link between pedagogy and art, between studying films and making films. Zryd also provides a thorough portrait of the conditions in which film programs formed, showing that—at least in the United States—swelling university enrollments and an ascendant youth culture drove curricular reform. The study of film as technique, explored earlier by Polan, began moving toward a project to coarticulate film to art and hence to individual expression. In the meantime, the number of film courses, film programs, professors, and student enrollments exploded throughout the late 1960s and 1970s, possibly outpacing expansion in all other areas of study across the curriculum. Zryd offers us a view of the university as a site not only of contest but also of change, testing simple formulations of what constitutes a progressive or reactionary institution. His essay also reminds us of the persistent and rich dialogue—and perhaps dialectic—that characterizes the history of film study at universities, linking anti-institutional art with an exemplar of modernist bureaucracy. At least in the case of film study, such relationships have been as mutually beneficial as they have been mutually transformative.

Discussing similar dynamics, Laura Mulvey and Peter Wollen's conversation shows how film study in the United Kingdom became a crucial part of projects to correct class imbalance and thus to rethink both the university and the place of education in sociopolitical change. Here Mulvey and Wollen suggest the centrality of the BFI, the state-funded body that has shaped film culture since its inception in 1933. Yet, like Polan and Zryd, Mulvey and Wollen place considerable emphasis on the varied activities that fed interest in film scholarship and study: 16mm experimental filmmaking, intense cinephilia, and contemporary intellectual shifts. They are also both determined to recognize the other conjunctures that shaped an entire context for the work they and others did at the time. Key here is the figure of Paddy Whannel, the head of education at the BFI from 1957 to 1971. Both Mulvey and Wollen acknowledge the role of figures like Whannel and also that of Stuart Hall, cowriters of *The Popular Arts*. Further, they recognize the influence of institutions like the Centre for Cultural Studies in Birmingham and the *New Left Review* in helping to legitimate the serious study of movies in British universities. Through their conversation what emerges is a highly textured portrait of experimentalists, intellectuals, and activists coming together around a diversity of film types (American film, popular film, European art cinema, and experimental film) to forge a sustained context for a nascent discipline.

The contributors to this book help us to see the similarities and differences between the cultures of film study on both sides of the Atlantic. In Britain, state-funded institutions such as the BFI have had a much more instrumental role to play in founding formal and informal cultures of study. In the United States, this history is predictably more varied and dispersed, and is beholden to the specificities of public and private educational institutions, philanthropy, volunteerism, and a powerful industry. In both contexts, the commercial nature of film culture and the dominant role of Hollywood occupy a central position—either as a negative or positive force. In the United Kingdom, for instance, Hollywood stands as much for the problems of Americanization as it does for the liberating, tradition-busting possibility of popular everyday culture. The development of film studies has always to some degree been a part of the university's own role in addressing the quintessentially twentieth-century condition of culture and capitalism.

All of the chapters in this volume address organizations and individuals that have been instrumental in initiating and distributing knowledge of cinema. Some essays tend to institutions and the discourses they promulgated. Some discuss influential journals and books. Methodologically, our authors also make use of articles in popular magazines, specialized journals, commission reports, and daily newspapers as well as radio shows, television programs, and the ever-proliferating Web-based discourses. Each of these constitutes a mediated site for the generation, circulation, affirmation, and contestation of film knowledge by helping to illustrate the diffuse locations of film culture as well its varied epistemological instruments. In the essays grouped together in the third section, "Making Cinema Legible," we turn our attention specifically to film publishing as a primary mode by which ideas, arguments, histories, and theories germane to film are circulated.

Haden Guest's essay "Experimentation and Innovation in Three American Film Journals of the 1950s" investigates *Films in Review*, *Cinemages*, and *Film Culture*. He argues that each journal supplied a paradigmatic venue for a new generation of film scholars to hone their craft, exchange resources, and comment on other film institutions (film festivals) as well as emergent aesthetic trends (American and European). These publications found national and international readerships, thereby shaping the topography of what we might call film publics. Such journals also constituted specialized networks for critics who were themselves participant in a generative moment: during this period film criticism became a widely influential institution buttressed by its prominent place not just in specialist journals but also in newspapers and television and radio programming. Guest shows that already in the 1950s one can see productive debates and dialectics emerging between critics and historians, and between popular film writing and more rigorous academic writing beholden to standards of evidence and argumentation. Guest also shows that such journals provided critical laboratories for generating enduring instruments of film knowledge and scholarship, such as filmographies. These activities reinsert a specifically American film culture into the history of important writers, critical models, and journals that most likely were as influential during the time for shaping Anglo scholarly practices as were the well-known French journals and critics.[24]

Building on the body of work produced by these journals, but buttressed by the increasingly prominent place of film in English-language universities, a group of more conventionally academic journals emerged in the 1970s. These publications emboldened the field with a new set of pathbreaking intellectual tools, often heavily infused with continental theory, ranging from Marxism to psychoanalysis. A clutch of journals formed including *Cinéthique* in France, *Screen* in the United Kingdom, *Ciné-Tracts* in Canada, and *Wide Angle* and *Camera Obscura* in the United States. Together, they set standards for research and established agendas for debate. These journals spanned geography but also connected different kinds of film institutions, engaging educators, self-styled cinephiles, and unapologetic theorists in discussion that shifted for decades the way cinema would be understood. These debates became paradigmatic for the discipline, providing a certain core identity but also forming the basis of the widespread influence of film scholarship in cognate fields: art history and criticism, literary, linguistic, cultural and aesthetic theory, narratology and semiotics, and feminism(s). The journals accomplished this not only by publishing groundbreaking theoretical work but also by translating select essays into English, thus using their considerable distribution to internationalize further ideas germane to the Anglo film studies scene. As institutions and as widely circulated material objects, film journals played a foundational role in establishing film studies as a major intellectual force across the humanities.

Two essays in this volume concentrate specifically on these dynamics. In "Screen and 1970s Film Theory," Philip Rosen details the key intellectual debates, as well as the national and international contexts, for the British journal *Screen*. He shows that the editors and writers associated with *Screen* sought to reinvigorate a preexisting film culture—exemplified in the United Kingdom by the journals *Sight and Sound* and *Movie*—by drawing on continental, particularly French, intellectual trends. Rosen also demonstrates the interconnections between *Screen* and the proliferating film programs at universities. Many of the individuals associated with *Screen* took up university positions in English, linguistics, and American studies departments. A number worked with the BFI, both as education officers who helped establish university posts in U.K. universities and as part of BFI publishing that—as Mulvey and Wollen and Mark Betz also show in their essays—disseminated scholarly work on cinema.

Concurrently, on the other side of the Atlantic, a feminist collective began to publish *Camera Obscura*, vesting it with an explicitly politicized agenda to explore questions initially of gender and sexual difference, and later of race, ethnicity, nation, and generation. We invited the current editors of the journal to discuss the history of the journal they oversee. Here, in their essay "(Re)Inventing *Camera Obscura*," they look back, but also sideways and forward, by considering on their own terms the significance of the journal's original mandate and context. The editors also discuss the journal's evolution over the years and explore the challenges it has posed to the discipline through its particular intellectual-political research agenda. Also pertinent here is an examination of the journal as a kind of experimental institution, one that attempted to redefine the nature of intellectual work through a model of collective decision making and constant debate. *Camera Obscura* has also expanded not just its theoretical and methodological agenda but also its chosen objects of inquiry. Mirroring and perhaps fueling the wider shifts in the field, what began as a film journal now addresses a wide range of media forms, indicating not only the importance of film's intellectual history for the key debates that enliven the study of other media and their texts but also pressing the limits of film's autonomy across the proliferating sound and image technologies that increasingly constitute our environment. The inclusion by both *Screen* and *Camera Obscura* of so-called other technologies beyond cinema—television, video, the Web, and a range of other imaging technologies (medical, scientific, popular, historical)—should encourage all of us to rethink the historical and presumed coherence of cinema as an object of inquiry, thereby making this a key question for the history as well as the present and future of our field.

Closely linked to the emergence of academic journals is the proliferation of books written and published on cinema, discussed in this volume by Mark Betz. In focusing principally on the publication of a particular kind of book— what he calls "the little book"—Betz charts the shift from a diffuse film culture to a specialized academic discipline. He examines the little book both as a method for the delivery of film knowledge and also as a kind of epistemological technology. Little books helped to organize and execute film courses and to standardize curriculum; in short, they concretized the content of film study. Betz tends to the diminutive book's material specificity by recognizing the functions served by its very smallness—its portability and its low price. He also considers the book's intellectual specificity by examining its contents and its institutional as well as national contexts. The little book has a big message, indicating a certain fluidity and diversity—from popular to academic—in the genres and material forms of the published film writing that has long served as backdrop to the discipline. Today we would add the innumerable Web sites, e-journals, blogs, and DVDs to the growing list of venues wherein academics and fans alike read and often write about film daily.

The history of the circulation of film knowledge indicates a longstanding demand for ideas and talk about cinema in general and films in particular. It also demonstrates the purchase that film and media experts have long exercised in the public sphere, albeit at differing rates and magnitudes throughout the years. That is, cinema knowledge itself has a varied but lasting relationship to concepts of relevance in the wider public sphere, and to commonsense assumptions about why film matters to issues of common concern, whether that means ideals of leisure or the specifics of public policy. We consider the growth of knowledge about film and its purchase in the public sphere and in academe in the final section of this book, "Making and Remaking Cinema Studies." In doing so, the two final essays help us identify what—if any—criteria allow us to differentiate between educating with film, educating about film, as well as the perhaps more crucial question of why we would educate with or about film. To what end do we advocate for the consideration of cinema in the university? The increasingly fluid and mobile nature of the knowledge we produce has not only yielded a series of public and para-public sites for film study (long extant) but also new ones, most notably the home. The domestic locations for film study, explored here by Alison Trope in her essay "Footstool Film School: Home Entertainment as Home Education," require us to think about the many forms that film pedagogy can take and the many ways that the ideals linking film knowledge to public debate are being refigured and sometimes simply eliminated. Trope asks specific questions, including: What is the public function of expert film knowledge? What is the public responsibility of the film expert? What is lost and what is gained as the sites of film study become more diffuse, more readily accessible, and more efficiently commodified?

Trope's consideration of recent technological trends (DVDs, specialty cable channels) continues one of the book's prominent threads. The excitement of new visual technologies has long fueled an entire range of developments in the film educational field, both popular and formal. In the 1930s and 1940s, 16mm enabled a new kind of engagement with images. In the 1950s, television shifted yet again the terms by which film became and retained visibility. Now the computer and the Web are again transforming our interfaces with moving images and sounds. In short, film has long relied on other technologies—visual, print, aural—for establishing and retaining a place in the modern landscape, enabling a complex way of seeing and being seen. By presuming that we might learn simply by watching moving images, the classroom itself has dissipated across a range of other sites. The increased possibilities for film viewing thus presents us with an expanded idea of where and how education takes place—where and how we learn. Film has long been part of this expanded classroom, a site that has proved to be coarticulated with ideals not only of relevance, engagement, and sophistication but also efficiency and instrumentality.

While this book is first and foremost a body of research and a set of questions addressing the history of studying cinema, with both study and cinema broadly conceived, the essays included here collectively make empirical claims about the history of the academic discipline of film studies. Together there is a sense that the discipline is a politically complex, intellectually rich, and dynamic one. Many recent debates about film studies have been flavored with anxieties about the death of film and hence the withering of film studies proper. A wider lens demonstrates that film studies continues to exercise a profound relevance to the modern Anglo university curriculum. Still being renamed, merging with new and old fields and disciplines, the intellectual debates, institutional practices, and cultural activities and objects that have long preoccupied so-called film scholars now form the basis of an increasing not decreasing number of courses, programs, and departments. Part of the resilience of this field is its relevance to a changing technological and cultural world, one wherein moving images and sounds only proliferate and expand their presence and purchase on our social, political, and cultural environment.

In the final essay in this volume, D. N. Rodowick ponders the effects of transformations in the materials of cinema—the replacement of analog technology with digital simulation and processes. Rodowick asks: What is the pertinence of film's intellectual history for our present moment? And, in so doing, he considers the very future of the discipline by examining its past. He argues that disciplinary identity should not be located in a specific object but in a conceptual apparatus that helps us to understand the moving image and our experience of it. Hence the history of, for example, film theory can help us understand emergent forms of moving image culture by helping clarify not only what is new about interactive digital media and computer-mediated communications but also what endures as the core experience of narrative-representational cinema. Rodowick argues that with the multiplication of screens, moving image storage devices (celluloid, DVD, video servers, etc.), and audiences in contemporary culture the discipline of film studies must in turn continue to grow. "Cinema" as an imbrication of visuality, signification, and desire is everywhere—the study of that cinema must in turn be central to the humanities.

Thus the history of film study becomes ever more important for establishing a set of debates, methods, and procedures that help us to understand contemporary technological and aesthetic formations. Key to this continued influence is indeed a practical history of interdisciplinary engagement. That is, despite the ideal of consolidation and clear identity often implied by conventional histories of film studies as a discipline, the coherence of the discipline belies the fragmented nature of the field—one this book suggests is far more constitutive than incidental. This book views this fragmented history and present as a strength. Why? Because this fragmentation is neither simply an effect of the modern university as a technocratic training ground nor simply a consequence of uncommitted or unrigorous practitioners. Instead, it also reflects a will to interface and engage with scholars and institutions representing diffuse interests, diverse political orientations, and changing intellectual formations. The essays here trace out an extreme interdependency with both governmental and avant-gardist organizations, with powerful industries and beleaguered artists, with establishment organizations and emergent technologies, and with an old guard and a youth culture. The longstanding interdisciplinarity of film study is but one manifestation of this; another is its imbrication with filmmakers, cinephiles, artists, collectors, galleries, museums, cooperatives, and marginalized political groups—organizations beyond the university. It is imperative to be aware of the porous nature of film institutions, and the longstanding and productive relations (which includes happy cooperation and charged disagreement) between and among properly academic and nonacademic sites, forces, and individuals.

This book is not a comprehensive history. Its scope is limited to the development of Anglo film study, primarily focusing on the United States and the United Kingdom. Yet, in limiting the book in this manner we in no way want to stabilize the clearly porous boundaries across and within nations, and the importance of the many languages and cultures that have exercised paradigmatic influence on cinema and cinema study. Further, we hope that the polemics in this book will prove adequately productive such that the significantly more complex linguistic and cultural geography of film studies as it has developed elsewhere will be taken up by others. We also hope that the essays in this book will continue to generate discussion about what we do as film scholars, why the knowledge we generate matters, and what the politics of that knowledge is within and outside the university. To do so will enable us to better understand the specificity of film as a field of knowledge and as a discipline.

Notes

1. On the importance of universities for the configuration of disciplinary and ideological legitimacy, see Samuel Weber, *Institution and Interpretation* (Stanford, Calif.: Stanford University Press, 2001), 31–32; and Masali Sarfatti Larson, "The Production of Expertise and the Constitution of Expert Power," in *The Authority of Experts: Studies in History and Theory*, edited by Thomas L. Haskell (Bloomington: Indiana University Press, 1984), 28–80. On the importance of professional associations in conferring authority and creating "realities" for disciplines, see Thomas Bender, "The Erosion of Public Culture: Cities, Discourses, and the Professional Disciplines," in Haskell, ed., *The Authority of Experts*, 84–106.
2. Michel Foucault, "The Discourse on Language," translated by Rupert Swyer, in *The Archaeology of Knowledge*, translated by A. M. Sheridan Smith (New York: Pantheon, 1972).
3. Our reference is to Roland Barthes's observation on the need "to scour nature, its 'laws' and its 'limits' in order to discover History, and at last to establish Nature as historical." Barthes, "The Great Family of Man," in *Mythologies* (London: Vintage, 1993 [1957]), 101.
4. We use the terms "film studies" and "cinema studies" interchangeably. Yet we are mindful that the term "film studies" privileges a particular definition of film that tends to underplay the broader social, cultural, institutional, and political phenomena named by "cinema." The term "cinema studies," then, better reflects the full range of intellectual work done in the discipline, including not only formal analysis but also research on, for instance, the film industry, exhibition, and reception, as well as related visual technologies.
5. Edward Lowry, *The Filmology Movement and Film Study in France* (Ann Arbor, Mich.: UMI Research Press, 1985), 4–5.
6. Jack Ellis, "The Society of Cinema Studies: A Personal Recollection from the Early Days," *Cinema Journal* 43.1 (2003): 106; "Annual Meeting," *Cinema Journal* 9.1 (autumn 1969): 1.
7. "Minutes of the Second Conference on Motion Picture Education," Museum of Modern Art, April 8–9, 1958, in *Cinema Examined: Selections from Cinema Journal*, edited by Richard Dyer MacCann and Jack C. Ellis (New York: E. P. Dutton, 1982), ix. On the significance of the Museum of Modern Art for the generation of film study in the United States, see the essay by Haidee Wasson in this volume and also Wasson, *Museum Movies: The Museum of Modern Art and the Birth of Art Cinema* (Berkeley: University of California Press, 2005).
8. On the state of film study in the university in North America in 1963, shortly after the establishment of the society, see "University Film Teaching in the United States," *Film Quarterly* 16.3 (1963): 37–47; and Michael Zryd's essay in this volume.
9. *Cinema Journal*, 1968, cited in MacCann and Ellis, *Cinema Examined*, viii.

10. David C. Stewart, *Film Study in Higher Education* (Washington, D.C.: American Council on Education, 1968), 1.

11. Ibid., 3.

12. Ibid., 7. The MPAA study clearly connected the study of film to the attainment of a certain cultural capital, a critical issue for the organization as it negotiated the complex regulatory politics of the 1960s that shortly thereafter, in 1968, led to the dissolution of the Production Code.

13. Marion C. Sheridan, Harold H. Owen Jr., Ken Macrorie, and Fred Marcus, eds., *The Motion Picture and the Teaching of English* (New York: Appleton-Century-Crofts, 1965), vii.

14. On similar battles within the discipline of English, see Gerald Graf, *Professing Literature: An Institutional History* (Chicago: University of Chicago Press, 1987); and Julie Thompson Klein, *Crossing Boundaries: Knowledge, Disciplinarities, and Interdisciplinarities* (Charlottesville: University Press of Virginia, 1996), 138–41.

15. On this process, see Greg Taylor, *Artists in the Audience: Cults, Camp, and American Film Criticism* (Princeton, N.J.: Princeton University Press, 1999), 122–49. See also the essay by Zryd in this volume.

16. On this see, for example, Keith W. Hoskin, "Education and the Genesis of Disciplinarity: The Unexpected Reversal," in *Knowledges: Historical and Critical Studies in Disciplinarity*, edited by Ellen Messer-Davidow, David R. Shumway, and David J. Sylvan (Charlottesville: University Press of Virginia, 1993); and David R. Shumway, "Disciplinary Identities; or, Why Is Walter Neff Telling This Story?" *Symploke* 7.1–2 (1999): 103.

17. On these broad developments, see Thomas Bender, "Politics, Intellect, and the American University, 1945–1995," in *American Academic Culture in Transformation: Fifty Years, Four Disciplines*, edited by Thomas Bender and Carl E. Schorske (Princeton, N.J.: Princeton University Press, 1998).

18. We use the term "fields" not as a synonym for disciplines but rather to designate the areas or specialities within and across disciplines.

19. Dudley Andrew, "The 'Three Ages' of Cinema Studies and the Age to Come," *PMLA* 115.3 (May 2000): 341. Philip Rosen delineates some of this intellectual and institutional history in his essay in this volume.

20. On the one hand, a nostalgic history of the discipline begins with this moment as a founding of a radical discipline. Consider, for example, the accounts offered by Janet Bergstrom in "Introduction: Parallel Lines," in *Endless Night: Cinema and Psychoanalysis, Parallel Histories*, edited by Janet Bergstrom (Berkeley: University of California Press, 1999); and by Christine Gledhill and Linda Williams, "Introduction," *Re-inventing Film Studies* (London: Hodder, 2000). On the other hand, this connection of the study of cinema with political goals is criticized for its methodological flaws and its subsequent problematic shaping of scholarship on film. On this see, for example, David Bordwell, "Contemporary Film Studies and the Vicis-

situdes of Grand Theory," in *Post-Theory: Reconstructing Film Studies*, edited by
David Bordwell and Noël Carroll (Madison: University of Wisconsin Press, 1996).

21. Central texts here were Victor Perkins, *Film as Film: Understanding and Judging Movies* (Harmondsworth, U.K.: Penguin, 1972); and David Bordwell and Kristin Thompson, *Film Art: An Introduction* (New York: McGraw-Hill, 1979).

22. For some examples of work on the history of other disciplines, see James Farr and Raymond Sedelman, eds., *Discipline and History: Political Science in the United States* (Ann Arbor: University of Michigan Press, 1993); Lucy Maddox, ed., *Locating American Studies: The Evolution of a Discipline* (Baltimore: Johns Hopkins University Press, 1999); and Ellen Messer-Davidow, David R. Shumway, and David J. Sylvan, eds., *Knowledges: Historical and Critical Studies in Disciplinarity*.

23. On the BFI, see Christophe Dupin, "The postwar transformation of the British Film Institute and its impact on the development of a national film culture in Britain," and Geoffrey Nowell Smith, "The 1970 crisis at the BFI and its aftermath," *Screen* 47.4 (2006): 443–59.

24. On the important journal *Cahiers du Cinéma*, see, for example, Jim Hillier, ed., *Cahiers du Cinéma. 1: The 1950s: Neo-realism, Hollywood, the New Wave* (London: Routledge and Kegan Paul, 1985); and Jim Hillier, ed., *Cahiers du Cinéma. 2: The 1960s* (London: Routledge and Kegan Paul, 1986).

MAKING CINEMA KNOWABLE

Cinema Studies and the Conduct of Conduct

LEE GRIEVESON

■ In his 1916 book *The Photoplay: a Psychological Study*, the philosopher and psychologist Hugo Münsterberg—a leading figure within applied psychology in America—argued that the "relation between the mind and the pictured scenes" is characterized in part by imaginative, emotional, and associative or memorial responses that find their "starting point" in the "outer impressions" of the photoplay and that are thus felt as "subjective supplements."[1] In the photoplay, Münsterberg writes, "the massive outer world has lost its weight, it has been freed from space, time, and causality, and has been clothed in the forms of our own consciousness."[2] Yet perception is not simply subjective, Münsterberg observes in his chapter "Memory and Imagination," for ideas can be "forced on us" through the "mental process" of "suggestion" and hence not "felt as our creation but as something to which we have to submit."[3] Attention is "forced," that is, drawn away from the socially useful attentiveness critical to industrial discipline—and to the discipline of industrial psychology—toward a dangerously absorbed and directed attention.[4] Outer impressions overwhelm the subject-spectator. In this way, film viewing, as an abandoning of conscious mental processes, is akin to hypnosis: "The extreme case is, of course, that of the hypnotizer whose word awakens in the mind of the hypnotized person ideas which he cannot resist. He must accept them as real."[5] Audiences can thus be analogous to hypnotized subjects.

While the balance of this relation between the mind and pictured scenes was, for the neo-Kantian Münsterberg, in favor of the shaping influence of the mind, the converse of this influence, the power of movies over subject-spectators, hovers at the margins of his account of the psychology of the photoplay. In a curious passage toward the end of his chapter "Emotions," for example, he returned again to the example of hypnosis, invoked now as a way of explaining how emotions "take hold of us" in both a psychological and physical sense.[6] To explain this emotional effect, Münsterberg imagines a scene from a film where a man is hypnotized in a doctor's office: "The doctor and the patient remain unchanged and steady, while everything in the whole room begins at first to tremble and then to wave and to change its form more and more rapidly so that a feeling of dizziness comes over us and an uncanny, ghastly unnaturalness overcomes the whole surrounding of the hypnotized person [and] we ourselves become seized by the strange emotion."[7] Although technologically unrealizable, he admitted, the imagined scene of hypnosis was a compelling example for Münsterberg of the connections between "outer impressions" and the movie spectator's "submission" to the power of the other as a "seizure" of the conscious mind and a loss of self.[8]

It was also certainly not a randomly chosen scene. Münsterberg was a trained doctor who had himself practiced hypnotic therapy—following the so-called Nancy school of Auguste Liébault and Hippolyte Bernheim—using the power of hypnosis as "suggestive therapeutics" to seek a cure for physical and psychological illnesses.[9] For the self-confessed cinephile, watching pictured scenes placed Münsterberg on the other side of the doctor/patient and hypnotic relationship, rendering him dizzy with the uncanny and strange emotions dictated by the other.

Yet if this loosening of the connection to the "outer world" and the undermining of rational response was part of the pleasure of cinema for Münsterberg, explaining in part why he was "under the spell of the 'movies,'" it could also have deleterious social and psychic effects on other audience members who were not apparently capable of the self-discipline and absorbed attention of a university professor.[10] Toward the close of his book, Münsterberg returned to the question of hypnotic suggestion, and the "seizing" of the emotions of audiences, to delineate these dangerous effects: "The intensity with which the plays take hold of the audience cannot remain without social effects . . . The associations become as vivid as realities, because the mind is so completely given up to the moving pictures . . . But it is evident that such a penetrating influence must be fraught with dangers. The more vividly the impressions force themselves on the mind, the more easily they become starting points for imitation and other motor responses . . . The possibilities of psychical infection and destruction cannot be overlooked."[11] Minds "forced" and "penetrated" by influences and impressions, hypnotized by the vivid intensity of cinema, were prone to imitative acts and corporeal "motor" responses that were potentially psychically and socially destructive. Watching pictured scenes threatened individual autonomy and civic responsibility for audiences unable to maintain the specular distance necessary for cognitive knowledge.

Written in 1916, Münsterberg's important and now canonical account of the psychology of the photoplay, and particularly his conception of the hypnotized spectator, was consistent with broad currents of thought in the human sciences that conceived of selfhood as fundamentally experiential and as "suggestible" and thus malleable or plastic.[12] The explosion of work on hypnosis in the late nineteenth century that influenced Münsterberg in various ways had, for many others also, shown the suggestible nature of people and the complex imbrication of self and other. In turn, the development of psychology, crowd psychology, psychoanalysis, sociology, and social psychology further challenged the Cartesian ontology of the subject as autonomous, preexisting consciousness to posit a conception of the self as divided, as essentially social, and thus as derived from relationships with others.

In the context of this rearticulation of dominant ideas about selfhood, the question of mimesis became central to the varied sciences of the human and of society: the individual, it was widely argued, develops a self through mimetic contact with others (be that individuals or broad "attitudes" or "folkways"), thus becoming in some respects what the psychologist James Mark Baldwin called a "copying machine."[13] Mimetic contact in turn both underpinned and potentially problematized what was widely called "social control," or the foundations of sociality and social order. In this sense, the human and social sciences, as the quest for knowledge about psychology and social groupings, were connected to the increasingly pressing need to guide "the conduct of conduct" of mass publics in the newly configured *gesellschaft* of urban modernity.[14] Ambivalence about mimesis and the movies—about cinema as what the social reformer Jane Addams called "this mimic stage"—emerged in early-twentieth-century America in the intellectual and social context of work in the human sciences.[15] The initiation of the serious study of cinema as exemplified by the thoughts of Münsterberg was fundamentally shaped by the work on subjectivity, mimesis, and governance that characterized social thought in early-twentieth-century America. Knowing cinema, and what it did to people and social groups, was for a time important to the broader governmental project of knowing people in order to act upon their conduct.

I thus begin this essay by mapping out in some detail the intellectual context that underpinned the emergence of the study of cinema as an object of the human sciences in America in the early twentieth century. I continue by examining the investigations of cinema, including social reform, government, and academic accounts, that emerged most clearly in the post-nickelodeon era and extended to, most famously, the Payne Fund Studies of the late 1920s and early 1930s. My endpoint corresponds with the consolidation of the conception of the study of cinema as a humanities subject. Yet it is worth noting that the historical divide between cinema as an object first of the human sciences and then of the humanities is not an absolute one. Indeed, I conceive of my task here as one of sketching out lines of genealogical descent. In other words, my account of the initiation of the study of cinema is guided also by the belief that the constellation of ideas about cinema, mimesis, and governance has continually and complexly informed the academic study of cinema across the social sciences and humanities, with cinema variously conceived as a form of mass culture and pernicious visual pleasure. I outline some of the parameters of these overlaps in the final section of this essay. I hope in doing so to point to what is recurrent, and in an important sense, structural, in the scholarship conducted on cinema throughout the twentieth century.

"Inter-psychical Photography"

In his 1886 book *De la suggestion et de ses applications à la thérapeutique* (translated in 1889 as *Suggestive Therapeutics: A Treatise on the Nature and Uses of Hypnotism*), professor of medicine Hippolyte Bernheim defined "suggestion" as "the production of a dynamic change in the nervous system of a person . . . by another person by means of the calling forth of *representations* or ideas."[16] It is "suggestion that rules hypnotism," Bernheim argued, making hypnotic phenomena a consequence of "the influence exerted by an idea which has been suggested to, and received by, the mind."[17] Images thus "created" in the minds of people are "like a living memory, which governs them to such an extent as to appear an incontestable reality."[18] Arguing for the importance of suggestion to the formation of subjectivity, Bernheim proposed that the subject was penetrated by the discourse of the other and hence not fully conscious to him/herself—thus functioning as a kind of somnambulist or automaton. We are all open to this power of suggestion, Bernheim proposed, for at base the subject is a highly plastic, receptive material, bearing the imprint of the other as suggestion. Or put another way, as Sigmund Freud observed in the preface to his translation of Bernheim into German: suggestion forms the subject.[19]

The early work on suggestion, hypnosis, and the mimetic relation to others thus effectively offered a model of the mind as doubled or fragmented, leading to a reconceptualization of mental topography, a radical revaluation of the autarchy of the Cartesian subject, and thus to a conception of a lability central to identity. Imitation of others was at the base of the subject and hence the subject was socially formed, given a broad definition of "the social" as the effect of others. The mimetic paradigm was widely influential in the human and social sciences, providing a key structuring principle for the explosion of theories of subjectivity and social order in the disciplines of psychology, sociology, and psychoanalysis in the late nineteenth century.[20]

Ideas about suggestibility and mimesis immediately informed the development of theories of collective psychology in the 1880s and 1890s. In seeking to describe and explain the phenomenon of collective behavior, scholars like Scipio Sighele in Italy, Gabriel Tarde and Gustave Le Bon in France, and Robert Park and Boris Sidis in the United States utilized ideas about suggestion and imitation to argue that collectivities of various kinds were drawn together by the power of suggestion and, furthermore, that the social was itself predicated on mimetic connections.[21] The criminologist Gabriel Tarde in his influential book of 1890, translated into English as *The Laws of Imitation* in 1903, thus utilized ideas of hypnotic relations to develop an account of the interdependency of sociality and mimesis. As Tarde wrote: "Society may . . . be defined as a group of beings who are apt to imitate one another," and thus imitation was "the elementary social phenomenon," the "fundamental social fact."[22] Tarde's account of the importance of mimesis to collectivities and to sociality effectively extended Bernheim's account of the centrality of mimesis to subjectivity. Mimesis stood at the center of subject *and* social formation.

Writing in the context of the perceived social and moral fragmentation of modernity and the attendant social crises, crowd psychologists viewed with considerable alarm the suggestible and irrational nature of collectivities.[23] Tarde and Sighele, both criminologists, connected the heightened suggestibility of individuals in crowds to criminal acts.[24] Crowds were, above all else, incapable of self-government. In his popular 1895 book *La Psychologie des foules*, translated in 1896 as *The Crowd*, Le Bon asserted that the individual in the crowd behaved like "the hypnotized subject" by undertaking the "accomplishment of certain acts with irresistible impetuosity."[25] In this sense crowds were prone to irrational, dangerous, and impetuous *antisocial* acts. Rhetoric about suggestion, imitation, and crowd behavior was closely tied to anxieties about the governance of mass publics, forming one part of the invention of the new epistemological and, in turn, institutional practices to govern individuals and populations flourishing in late-nineteenth-century modernity.

Le Bon argued that crowds were particularly susceptible to the influence of images: "Crowds being only capable of thinking in images are only to be impressed by images. It is only images that attract them and become motives for action . . . Nothing has a greater effect on the imagination of crowds than theatrical representations."[26] He would later go so far as to argue that cinema, the mass distribution of images, should be placed in the hands of government. Likewise, Tarde connected imitation to the power of images. Imitation was, he wrote, "the action at a distance of one mind upon another," or "the quasi-photographic reproduction of a cerebral image upon the sensitive plate of another brain." Imitation is thus "every impression of inter-psychical photography, so to speak, willed or not willed, passive or active."[27] Later, a social psychologist writing on spectatorship would describe processes of suggestibility as like "a motion picture stamped on the film of associative memory."[28] Tarde's account suggested that imitation functioned through images, and that the visual was critical to processes of mimesis. Language about representations, images, photography, and even motion pictures pervaded the rhetoric about suggestibility and imitation. Minds were particularly malleable in relation to images, this work suggested, a malleability that could be socially and politically problematic.

Work on mimesis from Europe, particularly that by Tarde, transformed American social thought from the late nineteenth century, informing the establishment of the human sciences as university disciplines.[29] William James, for example, included a chapter on hypnosis in his extremely influential book *Principles of Psychology* in 1890, in which he observes that hypnotized subjects "repeat whatever they hear you say, and imitate whatever they see you do."[30] Imitation is important to self-formation, James argued, like Bernheim and others, and thus the self is inextricably enmeshed with the social. Likewise, the psychologist James Mark Baldwin utilized Tarde's work on mimesis to develop an account of mental development in children. Imitation and "ideo-motor responses" were critical for the development of selfhood, Mark Baldwin argued, a process that passes through the "projective stage," where the child receives impressions "of a model as a *photographic plate* receives an image," to the "subjective stage," where the child then assumes the movements and attitudes of the model and becomes what Baldwin termed a "veritable copying machine."[31] "The self," Baldwin wrote, "is realized in taking copies from the world."[32] In these important and influential accounts of the functioning of the mind, mimesis—again understood as connected to representations as mediated events—was thus posited as central to subject formation. James and Baldwin understood the mind and self to be a consequence of interaction and imitative responses with, and to, others. Implicit here was the import of thinking carefully about images.

The mimetic paradigm, and its influence over psychology, also informed the establishment of sociology in the United States and the emergence of the discipline of social psychology, both of which gained presence in academia as universities expanded and reorganized disciplinary divisions in the 1890s.[33] Work in sociology developed in the late nineteenth century as one way of understanding the formation of social groups and social order/disorder in the face of anxieties about the breakdown of primary groups and local communities in the context of the emergence of an increasingly industrialized and urbanized culture.[34] Edward Ross's work, bearing a direct relation to that of Tarde, is critical here.[35] Ross published a series of influential articles in the recently formed *American Journal of Sociology*, established out of the University of Chicago, on the subject of "social control." The first of these pieces was published in 1896 and all of the articles were collected together in 1901 as the book *Social Control: A Survey of the Foundations of Order.*[36] Later Ross's work was widely disseminated in popular accounts written for mainstream magazines. His work was premised on the idea that there was a fundamental conflict between individual and social interests and that in order to maintain itself society had to modify individual feelings, ideas, and behaviors to conform to social interests. In reversing the valences of nineteenth-century philosophical liberalism—for it was now social control that was sought and individual autonomy became a subsidiary theme—Ross defined social control as the process by which "an aggregate reacts on the aims of the individual, warping him out of his self-regarding course, and drawing his feet into the highway of common weal."[37] The pressing question of "social control," of how society modifies individual desires to conform to sociality, defined early-twentieth-century American sociology and the quest to, as the philosopher John Dewey framed it, "gain control of the forces forming society."[38] Hence by 1921, in the widely used textbook *Introduction to the Science of Sociology*, Robert Park and Ernest Burgess of the University of

Chicago could simply state that "all social problems turn out to be problems of social control," and thus that the issue of social control should be "the central fact and problem of sociology."[39]

Ross, Park, Burgess, and many others regarded the question of how to bind liberal individuals into a harmonious society as preeminently a psychological one. And here questions of suggestibility and imitation were critical, seen by Ross as central mechanisms by which individuals shaped their conduct in accord with the desires and expectations of others and society, but also potentially as problematic stumbling blocks for the foundation of social order. Thus in his 1908 book *Social Psychology*—a foundational text in the discipline of social psychology in the United States—Ross argued that "suggestibility" could lead to problems mitigating against proper socialization.[40] And this was so particularly in relation to certain groups: "suggestibility is at its maximum in young children," "suggestibility is not a weakness produced by civilization," and "hysteria, the mental side of which is exaggerated suggestibility, is much more common in women than in men."[41] Women would indeed come frequently to stand for "mimeticism itself" in work in the human sciences.[42] All of these groups—made up of those, it is worth noting, commonly regarded as central to moving picture audiences in the early twentieth century—were without the requisite rationality and cognitive distance necessary for self-governance. Ross, following Tarde's work, believed that suggestible subjects would go on to imitate those suggestions. "Suggestion and imitation," he wrote, "are merely two aspects of the same thing, the one being the cause, the other effect."[43] To control those processes, to govern individuals and mass groups, was a critical task, Ross argued, and he called for the establishment of what he described as an "ethical elite" and the development of "the state in its administrative side."[44]

Work in the human sciences, then, connected subject formation to social order, and in the process inaugurated the discipline of social psychology. (Tarde had indeed presciently observed, in his 1890 book on the philosophy of incarceration, that "hypnosis is the point of experimental juncture between psychology and sociology.")[45] The connection between sociology and psychology, through conceptions of mimesis, was, I have maintained, guided by practical concerns in governing individuals and masses. Knowing people, and the behavior of groups, was widely accepted as important to the functioning of liberal democracies.

Cinema, as emblematic of modernity, mass media, and urban experience, would be closely scrutinized by public commentators and scholars well versed in the varied work on mimesis and its importance for understanding individuals, groups, and thus psychic and social order. Mimetic relations at the movies became the central issue animating a sense of urgency about studying cinema. The ensuing studies included efforts to gain knowledge about its existence, its form, and its social and psychic effects. It is toward an account of such studies that I now turn.

"Mimic Stage"

Various kinds of reports about the phenomenon of "nickelodeons"—cheap moving picture shows—flourished in the United States from late 1906 on. Typically these reports appeared in newspapers and magazines or in social reform documents. They generally included statistical information about nickelodeons and audiences (notably enumerating and classifying audience members), and they frequently featured warnings of the social and psychic effects of cinema on vulnerable and dangerous audiences and thus on social order.[46] Identifying potential disorder with the goal of instilling social order was a primary impulse underpinning these studies. Accounts claimed that the audiences for nickelodeons were predominantly children, immigrants, or women—all groups regarded as particularly prone to mimetic tendencies, as we have seen, because of their unstable location as self-aware/governing subjects.[47] The reform journal *Outlook* typically commented, "Undeveloped people, those in transitional stages and children are deeply affected" by moving pictures.[48] Initial studies of cinema often posited the direct impact of moving pictures on the behavior of audiences and thus on what the social reformer Jane Addams called their "working moral codes."[49]

One of the first sustained reflections on the psychic and social effects of cinema was indeed within Addams's 1909 book *The Spirit of Youth and the City Streets*. Addams recounted the story of three boys "who had recently seen depicted the adventures of frontier life including the holding up of a stage coach and the lassoing of the driver," and who subsequently spent weeks planning to lasso, murder, and rob a neighborhood milkman. "Such a direct influence of the [moving picture] theatre is by no means rare," Addams concluded, for the cinema was a "mimic stage."[50] Accordingly, Addams supported the efforts of the Juvenile Protective Association, which conducted critical investigations of the cinema in Chicago in 1909 and 1911.[51]

Countless popular and reform accounts of cinema in this period articulated a similar perspective on the mimetic potential of cinema. As the social reformer John Collier remarked, in a child welfare conference address entitled

"The Problem of Motion Pictures," "Modern thought has been keenly aware that all influences which reach the child, make more than a transitory impression . . . We are reminded that the child is imitative, that he is suggestible."[52] William McKeever, a professor of philosophy at the Kansas State Agricultural College, articulated similar anxieties in *Good Housekeeping* in 1910, contending that cinema had deleterious effects on "plastic youth."[53] Likewise, in a lecture in 1911 to the People's Institute, a progressive reform organization involved in the regulation of cinema, Reverend H. A. Jump asserted that movies operated through "psychologic suggestion."[54] In a 1912 article entitled "Social Psychology of the Spectator," George Elliott Howard argued that sometimes "under the spell" of the motion picture "the 'gash' in consciousness is so deep, the 'mental disaggregation' so complete, the entire obsession of the mind by the momentary suggestion so profound, that the spectator is hypnotized."[55] Time and time again, ideas about "impressionability," "plasticity," "suggestion," and "hypnosis" informed the study of cinema and its psychic and social effects, indicating, I believe, the influence of the work in the human sciences concerning mimesis, subjectivity, and sociality on the popular and reform studies of cinema. The governmental context for the emergence of the human sciences as practical epistemology in managing mass publics also shaped the establishment of studies of cinema and its mimetic effects.

Work on cinema and delinquency clearly exemplified this connection between the human sciences and studies of cinema. A number of scholars have suggested that the "invention" of delinquency as a category of deviant personhood in the late nineteenth century was made possible by new ideas about psychology and about social order and was connected to the social and political crises of modernity.[56] In this context "delinquency" and the person designated as "delinquent" became an object of governmental reflection and action. Accounts of cinema in newspapers, magazines, and reform and scholarly investigations frequently posited a causal connection between cinema attendance and delinquency, as exemplified by the above-mentioned reports in Chicago in 1909 and 1911. "The social mind is . . . beginning to take notice of the great number of juvenile Court cases," noted Reverend John J. Phelan in a 1919 study of moviegoing in Toledo, Ohio, and he added his finding that a "prolific cause is the excessive and non-discriminating patronage of picture houses."[57] William Healy, director of the Psychopathic Institute in Chicago's Juvenile Court, included in his 1915 book *The Individual Delinquent* several case studies concerning the "peculiar plasticity" of children allegedly influenced by "pictorial suggestions" to commit criminal acts.[58] Wary of the "motor consequences of imagery," Healy wrote: "The strength of the powers of visualization is to be deeply reckoned with when considering the springs of criminality . . . It is the mental representation of some sort of *pictures* of himself or others in the criminal act that leads the delinquent onward in his path."[59] Watching criminal acts leads to imitative acts; visualization is a critical component of mimesis, a literal "inter-psychical photography" triggering imitative acts and, crucially, conditions of personhood.

William Healy's book on delinquency emerged the same year as Hugo Münsterberg's *The Photoplay*, a book that was informed, as I noted above, by work on physiological and psychological imitative acts. Münsterberg's account of the psychic and then social effects of cinema was situated at a confluence of practical and now increasingly scholarly concerns, generated from work on corporeal motor responses, hypnosis, and imitation, and from the widely articulated anxieties about the social impact of moving pictures. In this respect *The Photoplay* marks an important moment, joining reform/practical concerns about cinema with a nascent scholarly study of cinema on the terrain of the human sciences on mimesis, subjectivity, and social order.

The imperative to verify the social and psychological effects of cinema on individuals and on society that was important to Münsterberg, himself director of the psychological laboratory at Harvard, also informed the development of empirical psychological studies of reception. In 1917, for example, the French doctors Edouard Toulouse and Raoul Mourgue monitored spectators' changes in breathing at a screening of Abel Gance's *Mater Dolorosa* (1917) in order to chart emotional response. Toulouse and Mourgue believed, like Münsterberg, that the perception of movement gives birth to the beginnings of a corresponding internal movement and, since this was "scientifically proven," they argued that "a phenomenon would take place" when watching moving pictures "of the same sort as hypnotic suggestion practiced on a subject after he has been placed in a given pose."[60]

Later, in 1920, the behavioral psychologists John Watson and Karl Lashley undertook an investigation of the effects of films used in campaigns against venereal diseases. Watson and Lashley showed the film *Fit to Win* (1919) to "many groups of individuals of various economic, social, and educational status" and posed four central questions for the study:

1. The amount, kind, and accuracy of information the films can give;
2. The emotions they arouse;

3. The transitory and permanent effects they produce in the behavior of those who see them;

4. The probable social effects of such permanent modifications in behavior as may be made.[61]

Watson and Lashley conducted a "thorough analysis" of *Fit to Win* and pursued audience research through the observation of audience response, personal interviews, questionnaires, and "inquiries as to results in communities after a lapse of some months."[62] The study was conducted under the aegis of the United States Interdepartmental Social Hygiene Board, a government organization that sought to investigate and ameliorate the problems of venereal diseases. In concluding that cinema should not engage with the problems of venereal diseases in "dramatic form" because of problematic "emotional reactions" with "erethitic effect," Watson and Lashley situated cinema, like sexuality, as a problem of governance.[63]

Watson and Lashley's experiments were conducted in the immediate postwar period and their anxieties about powerful and ungovernable emotional effects were underpinned in part by the intensified recognition of the effects of mass media on society as a consequence of the propaganda activities of governments during the war and the subsequent publicity surrounding these activities. Memoirs, exposés, and commentaries on the effects of propaganda heightened interest in the study of communication.[64] For example, in an important 1920 article entitled "The Psychology of Propaganda," the Yale psychologist Raymond Dodge observed that "it has been discovered by individuals, by associations, and by governments that a certain kind of advertising can be used to mold public opinion and democratic majorities."[65] The study of propaganda emerging in the early 1920s was heavily influenced by the European work on mimesis and its appropriation by American scholars, predicated then on the particular conceptions of subjectivity, social order, and media effects delineated thus far. These were tied directly to anxieties about the sustainability of democracy, further intensified as a consequence of the war.

Work on public opinion, and its shaping by the mass media, developed out of this work on propaganda in the early 1920s, which was connected to the pressing imperative to understand the management of opinion in mass democracies. Walter Lippman's work, for example, set the agenda for the field's development in his widely influential analysis of public opinion in contemporary society in the books *Liberty and the News* (1920), *Public Opinion* (1922), and *The Phantom Public* (1925). Lippman argued that democracy is governable only on the basis of a knowledge of the opinion of the masses. One has to know what people think before one can govern them. Lippman feared that people's thoughts were increasingly shaped by the agencies of mass communication, which molded a society's knowledge and appealed only to "stereotypes" and beliefs rooted in myths, dreams, traditions, and personal wishes, thereby "manufacturing consent" and problematizing the sustainability of democracy.[66] What was needed, Lippman argued, was a scholarly elite to assess and interpret objectively the potentially dangerous public opinion and to work through organizations of independent experts to make "the unseen facts intelligible to those who have to make decisions."[67]

Lippman and others contended that "opinions" or "attitudes" led relatively directly to actions. Attitudes were, it was widely accepted, a principal mechanism underlying social behavior. Harold Lasswell, for example, defined an "attitude" as a "tendency to act according to certain patterns of valuation."[68] Measuring opinions and attitudes was, accordingly, a critical component of managing behavior; an assessment of people's mental attitudes could be useful not only for commercial purposes but also for ensuring the sustainability of democracy and of social order.[69] Philosophical concerns with mass publics, opinions, and mimesis were made empirical.

Watson and Lashley's empirical study of cinema and venereal disease coincided, then, with the intensification of anxieties about media, mimesis, and governance in the immediate post–World War I period. It marked also an increasing attention to the empirical verification of mimetic effects, consistent with a broad shift in the social sciences toward empiricism (an issue that I discuss further below). Other studies also flourished in this context. Thus, in late 1918, immediately after the end of the war, the Chicago Motion Picture Commission was convened to consider the regulation of moving pictures in the city. At the hearings, which ran every Friday until May 1919, testimony was given from exhibitors, producers, social reformers, and social scientists about the effects of moving pictures on audiences. Münsterberg was quoted at length by the film producer and distributor George Kleine, who stated: "No psychologist can determine exactly how much the general spirit of righteousness, of honesty, of sexual cleanliness and modesty, may be weakened by the unbridled influence of plays of low moral standard."[70] Yet beyond these familiar assertions of deleterious effect, the commission sought empirical verification of the effects of moving pictures. Hence it sponsored a survey conducted by the University of Chicago sociology professor Ernest Burgess, coeditor of the influential textbook *Introduction to Sociology*, to quantify the effects of motion pictures on schoolchildren. His report included tabulated responses to questions posed to children and to schoolteachers about the attendance of children, the effects of moving pictures on school work and home life, and the general and specific moral effects of moving pictures. In the responses to Burgess's questionnaires, teachers complained in familiar ways that moving pictures induced in young girls the "vampire attitude," taught young boys "boy bandit games," and stopped children from becoming "good citizens."[71] The efforts of Burgess to empirically measure effects via ethnographic methods reiterated these familiar accounts; the long-standing ideas about mimesis, subjectivity, and social order shaped the efforts to empirically measure audiences.

Other studies emerging from the social sciences followed a similar tack, principally seeking to verify the preexisting models of the mimetic effects of cinema. In a 1923 article entitled "The Effects of the Motion Picture on the Mind and Morals of the Young," for example, the social scientist Joseph Roy Gieger utilized the concepts of imitation and suggestion to argue that moving pictures lead the "individual to experience the emotional states and instinctive behavior" of those "other individuals who come under his observation" and this leads to the implantation of "false standards of value" and, most worryingly, "the ways and means of accomplishing antisocial ends."[72] The Chicago sociologist Frederick Thrasher's ethnographic account of gang culture observed that "many of the exploits of the gang undoubtedly involve imitating the movies," before quoting criminologists and newspapers asserting direct links between movies and crimes of murder, blackmail, and burglary and concluding that movies induce "imitative conduct."[73]

Alice Miller Mitchell, a social scientist affiliated with the University of Chicago, conducted a survey of children attending cinemas in Chicago, the results of which were published in 1929 as *Children and the Movies*. In surveying Boy Scouts and Girl Scouts, children from public schools, "a group which enjoys intelligent adult leadership," and "unadjusted" children confined to juvenile institutions, Mitchell showed that delinquent groups attended the movies most frequently and recounted several stories of young people claiming mimetic effects from movies.[74] One example encapsulates the sense of the mimetic effects of movies articulated in Mitchell's study. While watching a "thrilling underworld picture," a young "delinquent" boy became too involved: as the policeman on the screen chased the criminal, the boy in the audience "whipped his gun from his pocket, fired three shots, and the crook instantly disappeared before the huge slit in the screen." Later, the boy remarked that "this was his last movie."[75]

"Psychogalvonometer"

In the so-called Payne Fund Studies initiated in 1927 we can see most clearly the amalgam of governmental anxieties about cinema combined with the scholarly study of cinema from within the human sciences. The studies emerged from the work of the National Committee for the Study of Juvenile Reading (NCSJR) to develop a program of reading materials promoting citizenship. The committee was funded by the philanthropist Frances Payne Bingham Bolton, who sought to employ her financial fortune to utilize social science in discerning the workings of society. Reverend William H. Short, who had worked briefly with the NCSJR, proposed to establish a Motion Picture Research Council (MPRC) with funding from the Payne Study and Experiment Fund (as the NCSJR was renamed in 1927). The council would conduct a nationwide study to determine the degree of influence and effect of films upon children and adolescents and ultimately to lobby for more stringent forms of legalized social control over the film industry.[76] As part of this project to lobby for the regulation of cinema, Short published in 1927 a work titled *A Generation of Motion Pictures: A Review of Social Values in Recreational Films*, which brought together existing work from sermons, articles, and books on the negative role and impact of films.[77] Yet, conscious of the paradigm shift in the social sciences toward empiricism, Short became increasingly convinced that more precise and empirical work was necessary to generate further measures of social control.

In pursuit of such precision, Short met with social scientists in Chicago in summer 1928, including Jane Addams (a formative influence on the policy activism of social scientists at the university),[78] Alice Miller Mitchell (who at the time was completing *Children and the Movies*), and faculty at the university, including Werret Wallace Charters, a professor in the School of Education, the attitude psychologist Louis Leon Thurstone, and the School of Sociology's Robert Ezra Park.[79] With the help of Charters and Park in particular, Short proceeded to enlist the expertise of a number of social scientists to pursue a precise study of the effects of moving pictures. Members of this group included several scholars associated with the social sciences at Chicago — widely regarded as the nation's most important social science program — along with social scientists at other major research institutions.[80] Together, the scholars gathered worked in the disciplines of sociology, psychology, social psychology, and education; the innovation of the study of cinema grew from the disciplinary imperatives to understand individuals, social groups, and the educability of both the individual and the social group.

At the first meeting of the group of scholars involved in the project, Short presented a document entitled "What We Need to Know as a Basis for a National Policy in Motion Pictures," which listed six categories of research:

1. the number of children reached by the movies;
2. a quantitative measure of their influence;
3. the positive, negative, or neutral qualities of their influence;
4. differentiations of their influence ascribed to gender, age, intelligence, level and temperament;
5. the influence of cinema on children's information processing, attitudes, emotions, conduct, and aesthetic and moral standards;
6. the influence of cinema on "such important matters" as respect for authority, marriage, forms of crime, hero worship and international understanding.[81]

The document formed the basis for the subsequent studies, which were translated into a series of questions articulated by Charters in his preface to the published volumes: "What sorts of scenes do the children of America see when they attend the theaters? How do the mores depicted in these scenes compare with those of the community? How often do children attend? How much of what they see do they remember? What effect does what they witness have upon their ideals and attitudes? Upon their sleep and health? Upon their emotions? Do motion pictures directly or indirectly affect the conduct of children? Are they related to delinquency and crime, and, finally, how can we teach children to discriminate between movies that are artistically and morally good and bad?"[82] When placed together, Short and Charters contended, the individual studies would "provide a composite answer to the central question of the nature and extent of [the] influences" of moving pictures.[83]

In response, the attitude studies carried out by L. L. Thurstone and the University of Chicago graduate student Ruther Petersen sought to measure the "affective value" of a motion picture on "the social attitudes" of high school children "toward nationality, race, crime, war, capital punishment, prohibition, and the punishment of criminals."[84] Thurstone and Petersen measured the attitudes of students to social issues, showed them a film pertaining to particular issues (e.g., *The Birth of a Nation* [1915] for attitude toward black Americans, or *The Jazz Singer* [1927] as a film "which might affect the children's attitudes towards the Jews"), and then remeasured the student's attitudes.[85] "Motion pictures have definite, lasting effects on the social attitudes of children," they con-

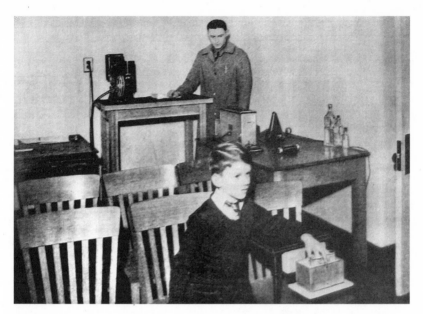

Psychogalvonometer in the "Laboratory Theater." (From Wendell S. Dysinger and Christian A. Ruckmick, *The Emotional Responses of Children to the Motion Picture Situation* [New York: Macmillan, 1933], 17)

cluded, noting further "that a number of pictures pertaining to the same issue may have a cumulative effect on attitude."[86]

Work on the physical and emotional response to moving pictures was carried out by Christian Ruckmick and the University of Iowa psychology graduate student Wendell Dysinger, who used a "psychogalvonometer" wired to children watching moving pictures to measure the galvanic resistance in the skin believed to be connected to "the sympathetic nervous system."[87] Children were shown films such as *Charlie Chan's Chance* (1932), *The Road to Singapore* (1931), and a scene from *The Wanderer* (1925) showing "extravagant scenes of oriental luxury, some debauchery, and occasional love-making" as well as "female figures scantily clad, kissing scenes, and oriental dancing." The investigators concluded that "the moving and talking pictures are a powerful stimulus, especially at certain ages and notably at the pre-adult ages, to conduct and behavior."[88] Likewise, for a study on "sleep motility as an index of motion-picture influence," the psychologists Samuel Renshaw, Vernon Miller, and Dorothy Marquis of the psychology department at Ohio State University wired children's beds with a device called a "hypnograph" to measure how often they tossed and turned at night and whether this was connected to the "strong impression" conveyed by moviegoing.[89] The attempts to render through machines the seemingly invisible—the engagement of individuals with cinema—into a form that could be recorded and classified made clear the way that knowledge about cinema was being inserted into circuits of knowledge and power.

Work on delinquency and behavior once again exemplifies the connections between these studies and long-standing ideas of mimesis and problems of governance. Robert Ezra Park initiated this work. After graduating from the University of Michigan, and working briefly as a journalist, Park conducted graduate work in Germany. There he completed a thesis entitled *Masse und Publikum* in 1904 (translated in 1972 as *The Crowd and the Public*), which surveyed the work on crowd psychology and mimetic effects, including that of Tarde, Le Bon, and Sidis.[90] Later, Park's perspective on collective behavior informed his influential *Introduction to the Science of Sociology* (coedited with Ernest Burgess in 1921), which included work by Le Bon and extensively surveyed work on collective behavior as a critical component of understanding the problematics of social control, defined as the central task of sociology.[91] Park's enthusiasm for the Payne Fund project was important to Short at its inception, and he intended himself to conduct work on cinema as a component of collective behavior and its impact on the creation of delinquency. Granted a fellowship in China, he reluctantly withdrew from the project, passing the study of cinema and delinquency over to his colleague Herbert Blumer, then a young social psychologist at Chicago (and later well known for his work developing "symbolic interactionism," the sociological paradigm examining how individuals and groups interact).[92] Blumer's *Movies, Delinquency, and Crime*, coauthored with the Chicago graduate student Philip Hauser, included data from questionnaires distributed to, and interviews with, male and female prisoners, former criminals on parole, children with school truancy problems, and children who resided in areas designated as high-rate delinquency areas.[93] In developing this work the authors drew precisely on models of suggestibility and imitation to show, using the accounts of their subjects, the "imitation of criminal techniques" that followed from watching movies; how moving pictures "furthered and fortified the development of criminal conduct" and presented "disciplinary problems"; and how movies functioned also as a "sexual excitant" producing "sexual delinquency."[94] Movies, they concluded, have both readily observable effects in producing and contributing to delinquency and also "unconscious" effects, disposing or leading "individuals to various forms of misconduct" and thus "problems of social control."[95]

In another study for the Payne Fund project, entitled *Movies and Conduct*, Blumer conducted interviews with University of Chicago undergraduates, local high school students, and young working women about their cinema-going practices. What Blumer called "emotional possession" was central to spectatorial experience, he asserted, where "the individual loses self-control."[96] Here Blumer's work directly mimicked accounts of suggestibility and imitation, perhaps most notably Le Bon's ideas about "emotional contagion" in crowds.[97] Movies, Blumer concluded, induce "emotional agitation . . . while in this condition the observer becomes malleable to the touch of what is shown. Ordinary self-control is lost. Impulses and feelings are aroused, and the individual develops a readiness to certain forms of action which are foreign in some degree to his ordinary conduct. Precisely because the individual is in this crucible state what is shown to him may become the mold for a new organization of his conduct."[98] In particular, Blumer proposed, observers may be malleable in relation to sexuality. Aiming to "inquire into intimate experience" via confessional-like interviews, Blumer's accounts of the engagement of individuals and groups with cinema was, as the focus on criminal and "sexual delinquency" suggests, inextricably connected to concerns about cinema and social control and thus cinema and the problem of managing individuals and masses.

In arguing for the suggestible and imitative effects of cinema and its position as a problem of social control, Blumer's perspective rhymed precisely with that of Short, who commended his work wholeheartedly. And it was this sense of the mimetic and deleterious effects of cinema that was most widely publicized from the Payne Fund Studies, notably through the publication of a popular summary commissioned by Short and written by the journalist Henry Forman. *Our Movie Made Children*, as the book was called, simplified the complexity of some of the studies, though it was entirely consistent with the preexisting accounts of mimesis and the movies that informed many of the studies and that was most clearly apparent in the work on delinquency. "The conclusion appears inescapable," Forman wrote, "that to show certain types of pictures — so numerous in the current output — in what are known as high-rate delinquency areas, in cities, is in some measure like selling whiskey to the Indians, against which there are quite justly severe laws and sharp penalties."[99] The pressing need to study cinema, as many had argued, was a consequence of the problems it presented of mimesis and, in turn, to the governance of undisciplined subjects (kids, for example, and "Indians"). To innovate the study of cinema thus was a critical task for maintaining social control.

Coda: "A Fundamental Relationship between the Cinematographic Apparatus and the Hypnotic Apparatus"

While not exactly ignored, the Payne Fund Studies, when published between 1933 and 1935, did not become central to a new and as yet unformed discipline of film studies. They did, however, have some impact on pedagogical practices in high schools and universities. Edgar Dale, whose book *How to Appreciate Motion Pictures* was the best-selling volume of the Payne Fund Studies, pursued a program of film education in concert with Ohio State University and the National Council of Teachers of English.[100] Likewise, Mark May, whose volume for the studies was entitled *The Social Conduct and Attitudes of Movie Fans*, set up a program of film education in affiliation with Yale University and the Motion Picture Producers and Distributors of America (MPPDA).[101] On the one hand these programs promoted a sense of film as art and discussion subject, with Dale, for example, commending a canon of approved films such as the adaptations of *A Tale of Two Cities*, *Great Expectations*, *A Midsummer Nights Dream*, *Anne of Green Gables*, and so on. Yet, more substantively, the educational programs were conceived as a way of destroying the mimetic effects of cinema, thereby enabling adolescents to control their response to moving pictures and thus not fall foul of what Blumer had termed "emotional possession." Lea Jacobs rightly observes that the programs Dale and May devised follow from the model of spectatorship advanced by the Payne studies as a whole.[102] Cinema study could become, it seems, a pedagogic administration of psychological and aesthetic disciplines for forming sensibility and managing the self and problematic conducts.[103]

Aside from these programs, though, the studies had a muted impact on the continuing study of cinema, even though they informed the ongoing empirical study of audience effects in other media. One can speculate on the reasons for this limited impact. Certainly the Production Code established by the MPPDA in 1930 had already incorporated in its preamble the logic underpinning the studies, noting the great "emotional appeal" of moving pictures, their "affect [on] moral standards," and the processes of "sympathy" generated for characters or stars.[104] In the code the political goals of the studies were partly realized, or at least deflected (and we can note again that theories about cinema, and the study of cinema, had profound effects on the shaping of cinema itself). The MPPDA also actively sought to undermine the validity of the studies when the organization seized upon a critique of the studies' methodology and findings articulated by the philosopher Mortimer Adler in his 1937 book *Art and*

Prudence. The organization not only promoted Adler's critique but also commissioned Raymond Moley to write a popularized summary of it.[105] One other important potential reason for the eclipse of the Payne Fund Studies is worth briefly considering—notably that cinema itself became less centrally important to practices of governance in line (in part) with the increased importance of other media, starting with radio and later with television, both of which were initially studied in relation to proposed mimetic effects.[106] The Payne Fund, for example, went on to support research in radio.[107] "Communication studies" emerged here—principally aligned with the social sciences then coalescing into a discipline in the 1940s when the term "communication research" first became apparent. The field became established in universities through research institutes funded by private foundations or the government in the 1950s,[108] and it was imagined by some that cinema would be a part of this expansive discipline.[109] Yet cinema came increasingly under the aegis of the humanities— more closely linked to the category of "art," as evidenced most clearly by the developments in the mid-1930s at the Museum of Modern Art—and thus was positioned no longer as a category of "risk."[110] Knowing about this safer form of cinema was a task delegated to the humanities.

While this shift toward the humanities is fundamental and certainly foundational for the discipline of film studies, the connections between research practices and metadisciplinary configurations are a little harder to untangle than the discussion above suggests. We can see, I think, a migration of the governmental anxieties about cinema to another research tradition, not the empirical social sciences but the critique of mass culture emerging from a Marxist perspective associated initially in the 1930s with European émigré intellectuals like Theodor Adorno, Max Horkheimer, Leo Lowenthal, and Herbert Marcuse and later informing (in part at least) American traditions of mass culture critique in the work of scholars like Clement Greenburg, Dwight MacDonald, David Riesman, and C. Wright Mills in the 1940s and 1950s.[111] What Adorno and Horkheimer famously called "the culture industry," or what MacDonald characterized as "the spreading ooze" of mass culture, worked, these scholars asserted, to implement social control by reproducing normative subjectivity and so effectively enslaving people and making totalitarianism possible.[112] Writing in response to the social and political context of the 1930s and beyond (to the failure of socialist movements, the emergence of fascism and communism, and the spread of late-industrial capitalism and mass culture), these scholars saw cinema as *leading to* social control rather than, as others had stated previously, contributing to the breakdown of social control and order. "Critical theory" bypassed the empirical work that had increasingly characterized American social science from the 1920s and drew instead on Marx and Freud to make broad claims about the deleterious effects of mass culture for the establishment of rational citizenries and thus for democracy.[113]

Although at times this perspective merged with older traditions of anxieties about the mimetic effects of cinema—with Theodor Adorno, for example, commending the conception of the effects of cinema articulated in the Production Code—it could be seen to effectively mark an intensification of anxieties about the effects of cinema, for the argument was now that subjectivity itself was constituted by mass media.[114] Here the question was not of immediate mimetic effects—of boys lassoing milkmen—but rather more broadly of the very constitution of subjectivity and class consciousness. Psychoanalysis was critical to this work. Indeed, psychoanalysis was itself complexly connected to ideas about hypnosis and mimesis, as Freud acknowledged in his 1921 book *Group Psychology and the Analysis of the Ego* and as Mikkel Borch-Jacobsen had shown in compelling detail in *The Freudian Subject* and in *The Emotional Tie*.[115] The complex connections of Freud's work to ideas about mimesis informed the articulation of ideas about mass media penetrating the unconscious and shaping malleable subjects in accord with bourgeois ideology. The malleable, mimetic subject of psychoanalysis was a critical precondition for these arguments about the formative impact of cinema on subjectivity and social ordering.

Critical theory, particularly through the work of Adorno, Horkheimer, and Marcuse, would play a major role in the resurgent critique of mass culture—in particular, cinema—conducted under New Left and countercultural auspices starting in the 1960s.[116] The critique of cinema developed from work on psychoanalysis, Marxism, and semiotics in this period is well known. I will thus only very briefly and selectively detail some aspects of this work, drawing it together as a series of responses to the fundamental question about—as David Bordwell has framed it—the social and psychological functions of cinema.[117] One of the central arguments mounted by a number of theorists was that cinema, through a combination of its particular configuration of technology and the establishment of a realist narrative form as hegemonic, appears to spectators as if it were reality and that this is a critical ideological sleight of hand. Jean-Louis Baudry, for example, talked of "representations experienced as perceptions" while Christian Metz argued that the spectator of the "traditional fiction film" drifts into a deceived, dreamlike state, in which the represented world is experienced as a reality.[118] In this projection of an illusion, mainstream cinema works to reproduce normative subjectivity, with this being the central function of ideology (as defined by Louis Althusser, whose fusion of Marxism and psychoanalysis was widely influential). Feminist scholarship became particularly influential here. Identifying the transcendental subject constructed by film with the male subject, feminist film theorists suggested that this was predicated in part on the structures of narcissistic "identification" set in play by mainstream cinema.[119] The concept of "identification" here, drawn from Freud, and in particular from Jacques Lacan's reworking of Freud, took over the work that mimesis and "emotional possession" did for earlier accounts of the impact of cinema on subjectivity.[120]

Mimetic effects, the mistaking of representations for reality, the impact of cinema on acts and conditions of personhood—this perspective, stretching at least from Münsterberg on, informs the continuing study of cinema and its social and psychological effects. To be sure, the accounts offered by contemporary film theorists, as film studies coalesced into a discipline firmly located in humanities departments, went further than those imagined by earlier scholars by situating cinema as a critical mechanism in the constitution and shaping of subjectivity. And indeed there is a radical change of political perspective here, for the work emerging from the humanities, in particular from European philosophical traditions, suggested that cinema *enforced* social control. And, of course, this later work included a much more nuanced approach to the analysis of the cinematic image. Yet, viewed from a slightly different angle, it is perhaps the continuity of these traditions of thinking about cinema that may well be more striking. What the critical theorist Leo Lowenthal described as the pressing need to study "the underlying social and psychological function" of cultural phenomenon like the cinema is consistent with the goals underlying the earliest studies of cinema and the later efforts to study cinema through a fusion of Marxist/leftist critique and psychoanalysis.[121]

Consider, then, one final account of cinema as a hypnotic force. In a conversation between Raymond Bellour and Janet Bergstrom in 1979, Bellour talked of his interest in hypnosis and its relation to the cinematographic apparatus. Motivated in part by certain films—he mentions Fritz Lang and the Mabuse cycle—Bellour proposed that there was in fact a more profound "link between cinema and hypnosis," namely that the "filmic representations of hypnosis are the manifestations, the pre-theorization, of a fundamental relationship between the cinematographic apparatus and the hypnotic apparatus."[122] Referring to Freud's book *Group Psychology and the Analysis of the Ego*—the text influenced by work on collective behavior—Bellour's conception of the connection between "the cinema-effect and the hypnotic process" enables, he suggests, a greater understanding of "how cinema produces a deep identification, both subjective and social," which in turn "explains the very great fascination it exercises."[123] Cinema, in this respect, is like hypnosis.

The effects of critical theory and (so-called) contemporary film theory were not quite as dramatic as the effects of earlier regulatory discourses on the social functioning of cinema and its positioning in the public sphere. Films themselves were not shaped by this work—aside from the production of the avant-garde films aiming to return spectators to a material awareness of the medium, now watched rather reluctantly by students enrolled in film studies courses—but the discipline of film studies itself certainly was. Confirmed as a part of humanities departments starting most noticeably from the 1960s, film studies was shaped by its contact with the poststructuralist theoretical work of (in particular) Althusser and Lacan. Contemporary film theory, and much of contemporary film studies, has its origins in questions about the functioning of cinema that begin with cinema itself. Questions of cinema and its mimetic effects establish a discursive formation that emerges and reemerges in popular, policy, and theoretical debates, and shifts across various registers of discourse and across the social sciences/humanities divide, tied to questions about the constitution of selfhood and governance that have been central to the response to modernity.

Notes

Many people have helped with the research and writing of this essay. I would like to thank, in particular, Charles Acland, Richard Butsch, Kay Dickinson, Amelie Hastie, Peter Kramer, Richard Maltby, Vanessa Martin, Roberta Pearson, and Haidee Wasson.

1. Hugo Münsterberg, *The Photoplay: A Psychological Study* (1916), in *Hugo Munsterberg on Film: "The Photoplay: A Psychological Study" and Other Writings*, edited by Allan Langdale (New York: Routledge, 2002), 96–97.
2. Ibid., 90.
3. Ibid., 97.
4. Münsterberg played a significant role in the development of industrial psychology in America, and his book *Psychology and Industry Efficiency*, published in 1913, is seen by some as the founding work in the discipline. See here, in particular, Mathew Hale Jr., *Human Science and Social Order: Hugo Münsterberg and the Origins of Applied Psychology* (Philadelphia: Temple University Press, 1980); and Merle J. Moskowitz, "Hugo Münsterberg: A Study in the History of Applied Psy-

chology," *American Psychologist* 32.10 (October 1977): especially 834–38. On the problem of determining and disciplining attention in this period, regarded as a critical feature of a productive and socially adaptive subject, see Jonathan Crary, "Unbinding Vision," *October* 68 (spring 1994): 21–44.

5. Münsterberg, *The Photoplay*, 97.

6. Ibid., 108.

7. Ibid.

8. Münsterberg had imagined this scene also in an earlier article, though he concluded it there slightly differently by proposing that the result would be a "kind of hypnotic spell [that] lies over the whole audience" (Münsterberg, "Why We Go to the Movies," *Cosmopolitan* 60.1 [December 15, 1915]; reprinted in Langdale, ed. *Hugo Münsterberg on Film*, 181).

9. Hippolyte Bernheim, *Suggestive Therapeutics: A Treatise on the Nature and Uses of Hypnotism*, trans. Christian A. Herber (New York: G. P. Putnam's Sons, 1889). On Münsterberg's use of hypnosis, see Moskowitz, "Hugo Münsterberg: A Study in the History of Applied Psychology," 829; and David Hothersall, *History of Psychology* (New York: McGraw Hill, 1995, 3rd ed.), 163. On Auguste Liébault and Hippolyte Bernheim, see below and also, for example, Alan Gauld, *A History of Hypnotism* (Cambridge: Cambridge University Press, 1992), especially 334–40.

10. Münsterberg, "Why We Go to the Movies," 172.

11. Münsterberg, *The Photoplay*, 154.

12. I use the term "human sciences" to refer to a broad panoply of disciplines that includes psychology, sociology, psychoanalysis, anthropology, linguistics, economics, and political science. On the configuration of the human sciences, see, for example, Roger Smith, *The Fontana History of the Human Sciences* (London: Fontana, 1997).

13. James Mark Baldwin, *Mental Development in the Child and in the Race* (New York: Macmillan, 1895), 24. On the broad currency of ideas of mimesis for subject formation, see the essays collected in Mikkel Borch-Jacobsen, *The Emotional Tie: Psychoanalysis, Mimesis, and Affect* (Stanford, Calif.: Stanford University Press, 1993). For the central place that ideas of mimesis occupied in social thought in America in the early twentieth century, see Ruth Ley's important essay "Mead's Voices: Imitation as Foundation, or, The Struggle Against Mimesis," *Critical Inquiry* 19.2 (winter 1993): 277–307. Mimesis had a broader cultural centrality also, informing novels (notably George du Maurier's best-seller of 1894, *Trilby*) plays, and vaudeville performances of hypnotism and mimicry. On the latter, see Susan A. Glenn, "'Give an Imitation of Me': Vaudeville Mimics and the Play of the Self," *American Quarterly* 50.1 (1998): 47–76.

14. In this essay I use the concept of "governmentality" as "the conduct of conduct" in the sense in which it is used in Michel Foucault's later philosophy—that is, as a way of conceptualizing and detailing the establishment of various epistemological and institutional practices focused on the management of bodies and

populations so as to shape, guide, correct, and modify the ways in which individuals and groups conduct themselves. On this issue see, in particular, Michel Foucault, "Governmentality," in *The Foucault Effect: Studies in Governmentality*, edited by Graham Burchell, Colin Gordon, and Peter Miller (London: Harvester Wheatsheaf, 1991), 87–104. The connection of work in the human sciences to discourses and practices of governance is important to Foucault's account of disciplinary histories, including that of the human sciences generally in *The Order of Things: An Archaeology of the Human Sciences* (London: Tavistock, 1970), and, for example, psychoanalysis in *The History of Sexuality. Volume 1: An Introduction*, trans. Robert Hurley (London: Penguin, 1990 [1976]). I draw the term *gesellschaft* from the sociologist Ferdinand Tönnies, who argued, in the late nineteenth century, that civilization was passing from *gemeinschaft* to *gesellschaft*—that is, from a community organically evolved and bound together in particular by personal contact to an impersonalized society of interchangeable and contractual relationships. See Ferdinand Tönnies, *Community and Association*, trans. Charles P. Loomis, 1887 (London: Routledge and Kegan Paul, 1955).

15. Jane Addams, *The Spirit of Youth and the City Streets* (New York: Macmillan, 1909), 86.

16. Bernheim, *Suggestive Therapeutics*, 15 (my emphasis).

17. Ibid., 125.

18. Ibid., 164.

19. Freud wrote: "It is worth while considering what it is which we can legitimately call a 'suggestion.' No doubt some kind of psychical influence is implied by the term; and I should like to put forward the view that what distinguishes a suggestion from other kinds of psychical influence, such as a command or the giving of a piece of information or instruction, is that in the case of suggestion an idea is aroused in another person's brain which is not examined in regard to its origin but is accepted as though it had arisen spontaneously in that brain" (Freud, "Preface to the Translation of Bernheim's *Suggestion*," in *The Standard Edition of the Complete Psychological Works of Sigmund Freud*, vol. 1, edited by James Strachey (London: Hogarth Press, 1966]; hereafter cited as *SE*). Freud wrote this passage after visiting with Bernheim on the way to the International Congress for Experimental and Therapeutic Hypnosis in Paris in 1889. On Freud's visit with Bernheim, see Henri Ellenberger, *The Discovery of the Unconscious: The History and Evolution of Dynamic Psychiatry* (New York: Basic Books, 1970), 762.

20. On the broad currency of ideas of mimesis in psychology, sociology, and psychoanalysis, see Theodore R. Sarbin, "Attempts to Understand Hypnotic Phenomena," in *Psychology in the Making: Histories of Selected Research Problems*, edited by Leo Postman (New York: Knopf, 1964), 759–67; Gordon W. Allport, "The Historical Background of Modern Social Psychology," in *Handbook of Social Psychology*, vol. 1, 2nd ed., edited by Gardner Lindzey and Elliot Aronson (Reading, Mass.: Addison-Wesley, 1968); Leys, "Mead's Voices"; and Mikkel Borch-Jacobsen's

books *The Freudian Subject*, trans. Catherine Porter (Basingstoke: Macmillan, 1989), and *The Emotional Tie*. Ruth Leys has shown how this thinking on hypnosis also influenced the emergence of conceptions of trauma; see Leys, *Trauma: A Genealogy* (Chicago: University of Chicago Press, 2000), especially 18–82.

21. Scipio Sighele, *Le Crime à deux* (Lyon: A. Deux, 1893); Gustave Le Bon, *The Crowd: A Study of the Popular Mind* (London: T. Fisher, 1897); Gabriel Tarde, *The Laws of Imitation*, trans. Elsie Clews Parsons (New York: Holt, 1903); Boris Sidis, *The Psychology of Suggestion: A Research into the Subconscious Nature of Man and Society* (New York: Appleton, 1898); and Robert Park, *The Crowd and the Public and Other Essays*, edited by Henry Elsner Jr., translated by Charlotte Elsner (Chicago: University of Chicago Press, 1972; first published as *Masse und Publikum*, 1904). Le Bon, Tarde, and Sidis made the connection between individual hypnosis and social suggestibility apparent in their work. Sidis, for example, simply stated that "social suggestibility is individual hypnotism written large" (Sidis, *The Psychology of Suggestion*, 327).

22. Tarde, *The Laws of Imitation*, 68. Tarde begins with an acknowledgment of his debt to Bernheim. On the reception of Tarde in the United States, see Leys, "Mead's Voices," 278–79; and on the development of theories of collective behavior in the United States and their indebtedness to European thought, see Leon Bramson, *The Political Context of Sociology* (Princeton, N.J.: Princeton University Press, 1961), 57–72; and Eugene E. Leach, "Mastering the Crowd: Collective Behavior and Mass Society in American Social Thought, 1917–1939," *American Studies* 27.1 (1986): 99–115.

23. On the social context of French crowd psychologists and the various social crises of the Third Republic as it was establishing itself as a secular polity, see Russell Nye, *The Origins of Crowd Psychology: Gustave Le Bon and the Crisis of Mass Democracy in the Third Republic* (London: Sage, 1975), 59–190; and Susanna Barrows, *Distorting Mirrors: Visions of the Crowd in Late Nineteenth-Century France* (New Haven, Conn.: Yale University Press, 1981), 7–42, 73–92.

24. Tarde was a judge d'instruction in his native town of Sarlat, Dordogne, in the latter half of the nineteenth century and then became head of the Bureau of Statistics at the Ministry of Justice in Paris. He wrote *The Laws of Imitation* during the latter appointment. See Terry N. Clark, ed. *Gabriel Tarde: On Communication and Social Influence* (Chicago: University of Chicago Press, 1969), 5. Ian Hacking has shown how statistics—literally the science of the state—was developed to transcribe the attributes of people into a form where they could enter into the calculations of rulers. Tarde's practical and theoretical work was driven by questions of governance. See Ian Hacking, "How Should We Do the History of Statistics?" in Burchell et al., eds., *The Foucault Effect*, 181–96.

25. Le Bon, *The Crowd*, 34.

26. Ibid., 68.

27. Tarde, *The Laws of Imitation*, xiv.

28. George Elliot Howard, "Social Psychology of the Spectator," *American Journal of Sociology* 18.1 (July 1912): 36.

29. Leys, "Mead's Voices," 278–79. Overviews of American social thought can be found in Bramson, *The Political Context of Sociology*, and in Dorothy Ross, *The Origins of American Social Science* (Cambridge: Cambridge University Press, 1991). On human sciences and the university, see L. R. Veysey, *The Emergence of the American University* (Chicago: University of Chicago Press, 1965), 73–78.

30. William James, *The Principles of Psychology*, vol. 2 (London: Macmillan and Co., 1891), 598. James was instrumental in bringing Hugo Münsterberg from Germany to Harvard.

31. James Mark Baldwin, *Mental Development in the Child and Race: Methods and Processes* (New York: Macmillan, 1895), 336–38 (my emphasis).

32. Ibid., 487–88.

33. Veysey, *The Emergence of the American University*, 73–78, 117–18.

34. See Bramson, *The Political Context of Sociology*, especially 11–46.

35. On Tarde's influence on Ross, see Bramson, *The Political Context of Sociology*, 58; and on Tarde's influence in the United States more generally, see Clark, *Gabriel Tarde*, 65–66.

36. Edward A. Ross, *Social Control: A Survey of the Foundations of Order* (New York: Macmillan, 1901). On Ross's work, see Julius Weinberg, *Edward Alsworth Ross and the Sociology of Progressivism* (Madison: State Historical Society of Wisconsin, 1972).

37. Edward Ross, letter to Richard Ely, June 12, 1891, cited in Ross, *The Origins of American Social Science*, 231.

38. John Dewey, "The Need for Social Psychology," *Psychological Review* 24 (July 1917): 272.

39. Robert E. Park and Ernest W. Burgess, *Introduction to the Science of Sociology* (Chicago: University of Chicago Press, 1969 [1921]), 785, 42.

40. Ross, *Social Psychology* (New York: Macmillan, 1908); Ross, "The Nature and Scope of Social Psychology," *American Journal of Sociology* 18.5 (March 1908): 577–83.

41. Ross, *Social Psychology*, 13–16. Conceptions of "civilization" were entwined with discourses about racial hierarchy. On this issue, see Gail Bederman, *Manliness and Civilization: A Cultural History of Gender and Race in the United States, 1880–1917* (Chicago: University of Chicago Press, 1995).

42. Ruth Leys, "The Real Miss Beauchamp: Gender and the Subject of Imitation," in *Feminists Theorize the Political*, edited by Judith Butler and Joan W. Scott (New York: Routledge, 1992).

43. Ross, *Social Psychology*, 13.

44. Ibid., 87.

45. Gabriel Tarde, *Penal Philosophy*, translated by Rapelje Howell (London: Heinemann, 1912), cited in Barrows, *Distorting Mirrors*, 124.

46. On these reports, see Alan Havig, "The Commercial Amusement Audience in Early Twentieth Century American Cities," *Journal of American Culture* 5.1 (spring 1982): 1–19; and Lee Grieveson, *Policing Cinema: Movies and Censorship in Early Twentieth Century America* (Berkeley: University of California Press, 2004), especially 11–22 and 58–66.

47. On nickelodeon audiences and the debates about them, see Lee Grieveson, "Audiences: Surveys and Debates," in *Encyclopaedia of Early Cinema*, edited by Richard Abel (London: Routledge, 2004), 45–48.

48. "'Movie' Manners and Morals," *Outlook* (July 26, 1916): 694.

49. Addams, *The Spirit of Youth and the City Streets*, 86.

50. Ibid, 93.

51. Jane Addams, *Twenty Years at Hull House* (New York: Macmillan, 1910), 267.

52. John Collier, "The Problem of Motion Pictures," reprinted by the National Board of Censorship from the proceedings of the child welfare conference, Clark University, June 1910, in box 74, National Board of Review of Motion Pictures Collection, Rare Books and Manuscripts Division, New York Public Library.

53. William A. McKeever, *Good Housekeeping*, August 1910, 184, 186.

54. Reverend H. A. Jump, "The Social Influence of the Moving Picture" (New York: Playground and Recreation Association of America, 1911), n.p.

55. Howard, "Social Psychology of the Spectator," 40.

56. See, for example, Anthony M. Platt, *The Child Savers: The Invention of Delinquency* (Chicago: University of Chicago Press, 1969); and Steven L. Schlossman, *Love and the American Delinquent: The Theory and Practice of "Progressive" Juvenile Justice, 1825–1920* (Chicago: University of Chicago Press, 1977).

57. Reverend John J. Phelan, *Motion Pictures as a Phase of Commercialized Amusement in Toledo, Ohio* (Toledo: Little Book Press, 1919), reprinted in *Film History* 13.3 (2001): 234.

58. William Healy, *The Individual Delinquent* (Boston: Little, Brown, 1915), 307.

59. Ibid, 340.

60. Edouard Toulouse and Raoul Mourgue, "Réactions respiratoires au cours des projections cinématographiques," in *Naissance du Cinéma*, edited by Léon Moussinac (Paris: J. Povolozky, 1925), cited in Rae Beth Gordon, *Why the French Love Jerry Lewis: From Cabaret to Early Cinema* (Stanford, Calif.: Stanford University Press, 2001), 137.

61. John B. Watson and Karl S. Lashley, *Report of the United States Interdepartmental Social Hygiene Board* (Washington, D.C.: Government Printing Office, 1920), 152.

62. Ibid.

63. Watson and Lashley, *Report of the United States Interdepartmental Social Hygiene Board* (Washington, D.C.: Government Printing Office, 1921), 112.

64. Most well known here was George Creel's *How We Advertised America*, 1920 (New York: Arno Press, 1972). Creel had been director of the Committee on Pub-

lic Information. On the publicity surrounding the Creel committee, see, for example, J. Michael Sproule, *Propaganda and Democracy: The American Experience of Media and Mass Persuasion* (Cambridge: Cambridge University Press, 1997), especially 9–16.

65. Raymond Dodge, "The Psychology of Propaganda," *Religious Education* 15 (1920), in Park and Burgess, eds., *Introduction to the Science of Sociology*, 838.

66. Walter Lippman, *Public Opinion* (New York: Macmillan, 1922).

67. Ibid., 18.

68. Harold Lasswell, "Theory of Political Propaganda," cited in Jesse G. Delia, "Communication Research: A History," in *Handbook of Communication Science*, ed. Charles R. Berger and Steven H. Chaffee (Beverly Hills: Sage Publications, 1987), 28.

69. Sproule, *Propaganda and Democracy*, 59–64. "Attitude scales," Sproule observes, "now began to supply the pins by which the old macroscopic notions of public and crowd behavior could be held down for precise analysis and dissection" (63).

70. Chicago Motion Picture Commission Hearings, *Report* (Chicago: Chicago Historical Society, 1920), 46.

71. Ibid., 134.

72. Joseph Roy Geiger, "The Effects of the Motion Picture on the Mind and Morals of the Young," *International Journal of Ethics* 34.1 (October 1923): 78, 80, 81.

73. Frederick Thrasher, *The Gang: A Study of 1,313 Gangs in Chicago* (Chicago: University of Chicago Press, 1927), 107, 108, 111.

74. Alice Miller Mitchell, *Children and the Movies* (Chicago: University of Chicago Press, 1929), xiv, 10.

75. Ibid., 140–41.

76. For the most complete account of the establishment of the Payne Fund Studies on Motion Pictures, see Garth Jowett, Ian C. Jarvie, and Kathryn H. Fuller, *Children and the Movies: Media Influence and the Payne Fund Controversy* (Cambridge: Cambridge University Press, 1996), 17–56.

77. William H. Short, *A Generation of Motion Pictures* (New York: Garland Publishing, 1978 [1927]), 33.

78. On the importance and influence of Addams's work for the development of sociology at the University of Chicago, see Ross, *The Origins of American Social Science*, 226–27.

79. Jowett et al., *Children and the Movies*, 60–61.

80. On the importance of the program at Chicago, see F. H. Mathews, *Quest for an American Sociology* (Montreal: McGill-Queen's University Press, 1977), especially 85–157.

81. Jowett et al., *Children and the Movies*, 64.

82. W. W. Charters, "Chairman's Preface," in Wendell S. Dysinger and Christian A. Ruckmick, *The Emotional Responses of Children to the Motion Picture Situation* (New York: Macmillan, 1933), viii.

83. Ibid.

84. Ruth C. Petersen and L. L. Thurstone, *Motion Pictures and the Social Attitudes of Children: A Payne Fund Study* (New York: Macmillan, 1933), xv.

85. Ibid., 2.

86. Ibid., 38, 66.

87. Christian A. Ruckmick, "How do Motion Pictures Affect the Attitudes and Emotions of Children?: The Galvanic Technique Applied to the Motion Picture Situation," *Journal of Educational Sociology* 6 (1932): 210.

88. Dysinger and Ruckmick, *The Emotional Responses of Children to the Motion Picture Situation*, 118.

89. Samuel Renshaw, "Sleep Motility as an Index of Motion-Picture Influence," *Journal of Educational Sociology* 6 (1932): 226; Samuel Renshaw, Vernon L. Miller, and Dorothy P. Marquis, *Children's Sleep* (New York: Macmillan, 1933).

90. Park, *The Crowd and the Public*. On Park, see Howard W. Odum, *American Sociology: The Story of Sociology in the United States through 1950* (New York: Longmans, Green, 1951), 131–35; Ross, *The Origins of American Social Science*, especially 306–8.

91. On collective behavior, see Park and Burgess, eds., *Introduction to the Science of Sociology*, 865–933 (for Le Bon, see 887–92, 905–9); on social control, see ibid., 27–42, 785–853. On Park's work on crowds, cities, and social control, see also Ralph H. Turner, ed. *Robert E. Park on Social Control and Collective Behavior* (Chicago: University of Chicago Press, 1967); Park, *The City and Other Essays*; and his entry on collective behavior in the 1934 *Encyclopaedia of the Social Sciences*.

92. On Park's reluctant exit from the project, see Jowett et al., *Children and the Movies*, 71. On symbolic interactionism and Blumer's work therein, see, for example, Norman K. Denzin, *Symbolic Interactionism and Cultural Studies: The Politics of Interpretation* (Oxford: Blackwell, 1992), 2–10 (on Blumer and film, see 106–14).

93. Herbert Blumer and Philip Hauser, *Movies, Delinquency, and Crime* (New York: Macmillan, 1933).

94. Ibid., 30, 201, 35, 79.

95. Ibid., 198, 202.

96. Herbert Blumer, *Movies and Conduct* (New York: Macmillan, 1933), 74.

97. Richard Butsch makes this connection also in his essay "Class and Audience Effects: a History of Research on Movies, Radio, and Television," *Journal of Popular Film and Television* 29.3 (fall 2001): 114. Blumer draws explicitly on work on mass behavior in his account of the effects of cinema in "Moulding of Mass Behavior through the Motion Picture," *Publication of the American Sociological Society* 29. 3 (August 1933): 115–27.

98. Blumer, *Movies and Conduct*, 198.

99. Henry Forman, *Our Movie Made Children* (New York: Macmillan, 1933), excerpted in Gerald Mast, ed. *The Movies in Our Midst: Documents in the Cultural History of Film in America* (Chicago: University of Chicago Press, 1982), 357.

100. Edgar Dale, *How to Appreciate Motion Pictures* (New York: Macmillan, 1933); Jowett et al., *Children and the Movies*, 101.

101. For details, see Lea Jacobs, "Reformers and Spectators: The Film Education Movement in the Thirties," *Camera Obscura* 22 (1990): 36–40.

102. Jacobs, "Reformers and Spectators."

103. In *Movies and Conduct*, Blumer had also suggested that instruction could produce emotional distance, thus counteracting the processes of emotional possession. "The more effective and so desirable form of control comes," he wrote, "through instruction and through frank discussion" (Blumer, *Movies and Conduct*, 140).

104. "A code to maintain social and community values in the production of silent, synchronized and talking motion pictures," March 31, 1930, in "Documents on the Genesis of the Production Code," edited by Richard Maltby, *Quarterly Review of Film and Video* 15.4 (1995): 61.

105. Mortimer Adler, *Art and Prudence* (New York: Longmans, Green, 1937), especially 147–212; Raymond A. Moley, *Are We Movie Made?* (New York: Macy-Masius, 1938).

106. On regulatory debates about radio and television, see, for example, Cmiel, "On Cynicism, Evil, and the Discovery of Communication in the 1940s," 88–107.

107. Robert W. McChesney, "The Payne Fund and Radio Broadcasting, 1928–1935," in Jowett et al., *Children and the Movies*, 303–35.

108. Cmiel, "On Cynicism, Evil, and the Discovery of Communication in the 1940s," 88, 95.

109. For example, Paul Lazarsfeld and Frank Stanton called for the integration of work on movies and other media in Paul F. Lazarsfeld and Frank N. Stanton, eds., *Communications Research, 1948–1949* (New York: Harper and Row, 1949), xviii.

110. On the growing distinctions between the social sciences and the humanities in relation to studying communication, see Sproule, *Propaganda and Democracy*, 51, 76–78. On the concept of "risk," and its place in governmental discourses and practices, see, for example, Francois Ewald, "Insurance and Risk," in Burchell et al., eds., *The Foucault Effect*, 197–210.

111. On the Frankfurt school, see Martin Jay, *The Dialectic Imagination: A History of the Frankfurt School and the Institute of Social Research, 1923–1950* (London: Heinemann, 1973). Jay situates this work in the context of prewar studies of mass society, notably those associated with Robert Park and Herbert Blumer (217). On American traditions of mass culture critique, and the complicated connections to critical theory, see Hanno Hardt, *Critical Communication Studies: Communication, History and Theory in America* (London: Routledge, 1992), 143–48; Bramson, *The Political Context of Sociology*, 96–139; T. J. Jackson Lears, "Mass Culture and Its Critics," in *Encyclopedia of American Social History*, edited by M. K. Clayton, E. J. Gorn, and P. W. Williams (New York: Scribner, 1993), especially 1594–1600; and John Durham Peters, *Speaking into the Air: A History of the Idea of Communication* (Chicago: University of Chicago Press, 1999), 22–26. On the reception of

critical theory in the United States, see also Andrew Ross, *No Respect: Intellectuals and Popular Culture* (London: Routledge, 1989), 42–64. On nascent Left critiques of cinema in the 1930s in the United States, in the context of the broad emancipatory social movement of the 1930s labeled "the popular front," see Michael Denning, *The Cultural Front: The Laboring of American Culture in the Twentieth Century* (London: Verso, 1996), 455.

112. Theodor Adorno and Max Horkheimer, *Dialectic of Enlightenment*, translated by John Cumming (New York: Herder, 1972); Dwight Macdonald, cited in Lears, "Mass Culture and Its Critics."

113. On the complex relations of critical theory to empirical communication research, see Hardt, *Critical Communication Studies*, especially 106–9.

114. Commenting on the stereotyping prevalent in television, Adorno wrote: "Here, those who have developed the production code for the movies seem right: what matters in mass media is not what happens in real life, but rather the positive and negative 'messages,' prescriptions, and taboos that the spectator absorbs by means of identification with the material he is looking at" (Adorno, "Television and the Patterns of Mass Culture," in *Mass Communications*, edited by Wilbur Schramm [Urbana: University of Illinois Press, 1960], 610).

115. I mentioned above that Sigmund Freud met with Bernheim on his way to the International Congress for Experimental and Therapeutic Hypnosis in Paris in 1889 and subsequently translated two of Bernheim's books into German. Later, however, Freud would suggest that psychoanalysis developed precisely out of the repudiation of the suggestive method and hypnosis, arguing instead for the primacy of individual psychology over that of a group or social psychology. See, for example, Freud, *Introductory Lectures to Psychoanalysis*, SE 16; and Freud, *Group Psychology and the Analysis of the Ego*, translated by James Strachey (London: Hogarth Press, 1959 [1922]), especially 4–19. Yet the argument that Freud makes for the disciplinary identity of psychoanalysis, and its distinction from the mimetic paradigm, is problematic. Mikkel Borch-Jacobsen's work clarifies this issue. In his book *The Freudian Subject*, as well as in related essays — notably those gathered together in the book *The Emotional Tie* — Borch-Jacobsen has conducted a close reading of a wide range of Freudian texts in order to question this conception of the "birth" of psychoanalysis. He shows in compelling detail the difficulty that Freud experienced in establishing a clear distinction between hypnotic suggestion and the psychoanalytic concept of transference, and thus how the mimetic paradigm continued to serve as a key structuring principle in Freud's thought. While Freud's libidinal hypothesis was predicated on the idea of a monadic subject whom the relationship to others would affect only secondarily, Borch-Jacobsen shows that the whole problem of the social tie, of what bound individuals and social groups together, made it necessary for Freud to imagine an original alteration by others well before any constitution of the "ego" (and thus also well before any oedipal triangle). Hence identification, or what Freud

will call "emotional ties," necessarily precedes any libidinal object. As Borch-Jacobsen writes: "Thus Freud, having attempted at first to exploit the resources of the psychoanalytical concept of identification, ends by making *hypnosis*, in a striking reversal, the paradigm of the relationship to others" (Borch-Jacobsen, *The Emotional Tie*, 42). And the centrality of mimesis to social bonds is clearly seen in the analytic relation as transference. Transference, or suggestibility on the patient's side, and suggestion (even if unintentional) on the part of the analyst, is merely another way, Freud acknowledged and Borch-Jacobsen emphasizes, of describing "suggestibility." Freud, *Introductory Lectures, SE* 16: 446; Freud, *An Autobiographical Study, SE* 20; Borch-Jacobsen, *The Freudian Subject*, 151. In Borch-Jacobsen's explanation, Freud's account of the history of psychoanalysis as one of differentiation from the mimetic paradigm is disingenuous, driven ultimately by anxiety about the ramifications of ideas of mimesis for the autarchic subject. The effect of Borch-Jacobsen's interpretation is thus to propose that behind Freud's apparently radical critique of the authority of consciousness, the schema of the subject continues "silently to command the theory and practice—and even the politics—of psychoanalysis" (Borch-Jacobsen, *The Freudian Subject*, 157). Ruth Leys has extended this account of the anxieties about mimesis in psychoanalysis, showing its provenance across a wide range of social thought, arguing that the mimetic paradigm was initially and simultaneously attractive to a generation of scholars as a way of explaining influence and thus social solidarity but troublesome for "its inability to impose limits on change, its threat to an ideal of individual autonomy, its challenge to an existing social order based on hierarchy and difference" (Leys, "Mead's Voices," 282).

116. Jackson Lears, "Mass Culture and Its Critics," 1599–1603. See also Denning, *The Cultural Front*, 462. Adorno and Horkheimer's *The Dialectic of Enlightenment* was translated in 1972; other work from the Frankfurt school was translated at this moment also, and Martin Jay's book on the Frankfurt school, published in 1973, was important in further generating interest in the school's work. See Jay, *The Dialectical Imagination*; and Martin Jay, *Permanent Exiles: Essays on the Intellectual Migration from Germany to America* (New York: Columbia University Press, 1985), 127–30. The best account of post-1968 film theory is D. N. Rodowick's *The Crisis of Political Modernism: Criticism and Ideology in Contemporary Film Theory* (Urbana: University of Illinois Press, 1988).

117. "The 'New Film Theory,'" David Bordwell writes, can "usefully be understood as asking this question: What are the social and psychic functions of cinema?" (Bordwell, "Contemporary Film Studies and the Vicissitudes of Grand Theory," in *Post-Theory: Reconstructing Film Studies*, edited by David Bordwell and Noël Carroll [Madison: University of Wisconsin Press, 1996], 6).

118. Jean-Louis Baudry, "The Apparatus: Metapsychological Approaches to the Impression of Reality in Cinema," in *Narrative, Apparatus, Ideology*, edited by Philip Rosen (New York: Columbia University Press, 1986), 314; Christian Metz, *Psycho-*

analysis and Cinema: The Imaginary Signifier, translated by Celia Britton, Annwyl Williams, Ben Brewster, and Alfred Guzzetti (London: Macmillan, 1982), 69–74.

119. Laura Mulvey's essay "Visual Pleasure and Narrative Cinema" (*Screen* 16.3 [autumn 1975]: 6–18) is the most well-known articulation of this perspective. Mulvey's famous call for the destruction of visual pleasure and the production of avant-garde films that would return viewers to a material awareness of the medium was widely shared, and was articulated in part through a revalidation of the work of Bertolt Brecht and a modernist counter-cinema exemplified by a figure like Jean-Luc Godard. On the Brechtian tradition in film studies, see Murray Smith, "The Logic and Legacy of Brechtianism," in Bordwell and Carroll, eds., *Post-Theory*.

120. Theodore Sarbin has proposed that "suggestion" and "identification" are closely related concepts. See Sarbin, "Attempts to Understand Hypnotic Phenomenon," 766. Likewise, Gordon Allport observes: "What has been called suggestion, especially in mass situations, is in reality a consequence of identification" (Allport, "The Historical Background to Social Psychology," 38). On Freud's understanding of processes of "identification," see Borch-Jacobsen, *The Emotional Tie*, 59–60. Henri Ellenberger has likewise observed that "what Tarde called imitation, Freud called identification" (Ellenberger, *The Discovery of the Unconscious*, 528). On conceptions of "identification" in contemporary film theory, see Murray Smith, *Engaging Characters: Fiction, Emotion, and the Cinema* (Oxford: Oxford University Press, 1995), 1–7, 222–23, 230–31.

121. Leo Lowenthal, cited in Jay, *Permanent Exiles*.

122. Janet Bergstrom and Raymond Bellour, "Alternation, Segmentation, Hypnosis: Interview with Raymond Bellour," *Camera Obscura* 3/4 (1979): 101.

123. Ibid.

Taking Liberties: The Payne Fund Studies
and the Creation of the Media Expert

MARK LYNN ANDERSON

One of the main functions of teaching was that the training of the individual should
be accompanied by his being situated in society. We should now see teaching in such a
way that it allows the individual to change at will, which is possible only on condition
that teaching is a possibility always being offered.
—Michel Foucault, "The Masked Philosopher"

■ The dramatic broadening of film studies over the last quarter century—or,
what some might think of as its increasing fragmentation—represents something of a return to its institutional beginnings. Investigations into the diverse
social contexts of film receptions, discussions of social policy and motion picture regulation, documentation of amateur and alternative filmmaking practices, studies on audience behavior and psychology, critical interests in the relations between various media, support for interdisciplinary work on motion
pictures, and evaluations of the social significance of media celebrity—in other
words, much of what we tend to think of as relatively new and emerging areas
of film studies research was also the purview of a nascent film studies as it
emerged in the North American academy of the 1920s and early 1930s. However, before any aesthetic, psychological, economic, or sociological inquiries
into motion pictures could properly converge to form a unique area of scholarship, an important institutional condition had to be fulfilled: the creation of
the media expert.

Media expertise in North America was principally founded upon the emergent authority of the human sciences during the late nineteenth and early twentieth century (namely anthropology, psychology, sociology)—disciplines whose application to practical tasks discursively produced various forms of modern expertise as so many sets of power relations (anthropologist/native, psychologist/patient, sociologist/deviant). As Foucault and others have noted, one of the most significant consequences of modern disciplinary power is that various forms of authority are no longer secured solely by the exercise of political position or by the ideological recognition of social entitlement. Instead, authority is now a function of knowledge production, and truth is a form of constraint. Modern scientific disciplines have become sites of power, and they have significantly diminished the possibility of effectively challenging or resisting various forms of authority through political action or alternative social organization alone.

The cultural ascendancy of the modern human sciences coincided with the rise of mass culture. Tradition was losing its preserve as the development of mass communications—the tabloid press, motion pictures, radio—freed culture from geographical and sociopolitical restrictions. When a set of ideas, practices, and peoples formerly separated by a host of social barriers came to share a common space within mass society, the category of "influence" became an area for scientific investigation and social intervention. In the mid-1920s Frederick Thrasher, a doctoral student in the Department of Sociology at the University of Chicago, explained the problem of an unregulated mass society this way:

> Every new invention which facilitates human mobility both as to rapidity and range of locomotion—every new device which increases the vividness, the quickness, and the spread of ideas through communication—has in it the germs of disorganization. This is because such innovations as the newspapers and the movies, as well as the automobile and the radio, tend to disturb social routine and break up the old habits upon which the superstructure of social organization rests.
>
> . . . The Chicago papers have a combined circulation of 4,300,000. They are bound to have tremendous influence, but they cannot be suppressed; that would be like turning out the light. Ordinary individuals are capable of building up a certain amount of resistance to demoralizing suggestions contained in the press. The fact that gang boys seem more suggestible probably does not indicate temperamental variations, but more likely is a conse-

quence of the disorganized state of their social milieu and their own lack of contact with organizing influences.[1]

Here Thrasher describes the mass media as part of a larger social environment, one more or less equally available to all members of society. As a graduate student, Thrasher had studied gang behavior in the Chicago area in order to demonstrate that juvenile delinquency resulted from particular processes of socialization. Controlling mass culture presumed knowing how members of society are differently placed and, therefore, differently affected by these ubiquitous and largely unregulated systems of communications. Thus, the young sociologist sought a means of reintroducing difference into the media's presumed anonymous address by proposing a distinction between "ordinary individuals" who can resist "demoralizing suggestions" and those who are more suggestible. Given the rapid expansion of leisure time and the rise of the mass media during the early twentieth century, media expertise increasingly would become the basis upon which the practices of advertising, public relations, political science, educational psychology, and communication studies flourished.

In this essay I consider the emergence of "the media expert" in North America as a particularly decisive development within modernity and a necessary precondition for consolidating film studies as an academic discipline. The early media expert possessed a high-level professional identity, was typically a university professor or researcher, and worked as part of a larger managerial class whose lower-level technicians and specialists administered educational, recreational, and service programs within a corporately modeled social bureaucracy.[2] While the media expert is related to the general development of bureaucratic forms within monopoly-capitalist society, in this essay I am more concerned with specifying both the socio-philosophical basis of media expertise and its discursive production through sociological fieldwork and the development of audience research methods. The media expert's authority could not simply be claimed; rather, it had to be won. In winning that authority, motion pictures were central to the development of early communication studies. Concerns about the movies made it necessary to create evaluative distinctions between different types of knowledge about motion pictures and between different types of interests in them. The principal means of securing the authority of the media expert and distinguishing it from other types of engagements with motion pictures were the Payne Fund Studies (PFS), a series of film audience studies conducted between 1928 and 1933. While the PFS yielded inconclusive evidence on questions of media influence, they successfully produced the professional distinctions necessary for the media expert's authority, and they determined the ways in which knowledge of the cinema would become part of university research and academic study. Frederick Thrasher's academic career was exemplary of this process.

Chicago School Sociology and the Payne Fund Studies

As a product of the Department of Sociology at the University of Chicago in the 1920s, Thrasher received his field training through a larger theoretical understanding of society that was grounded in Lebensphilosophie. Beginning in 1914, Robert Park began shaping the development of Chicago's sociology program by promulgating ideas he had encountered in Germany, where he had been a philosophy student of Wilhelm Windelband and had attended the lectures of Georg Simmel. In the nineteenth century Lebensphilosophie was a major European worldview shaped by the work of Darwin to the extent that it sought to give a philosophical account of human life in terms of organic processes of development. It was also deeply influenced by Marx, particularly in his conception of human life as a productive material force that underwent dialectical self-estrangement under capitalist relations of production. The sociologists at the University of Chicago adapted biological concepts of growth and decay to describe the rapid rise of the modern industrial city. For them, the city was both a natural environment and a research laboratory where the social scientist might observe and record the forces of organization and disorganization that led to continual social change. For example, Ernest Burgess made quite clear the equation between the biological organism and the industrial city when he considered how "a normal rate of expansion" for a modern city could be determined "by thinking of urban growth as a resultant of organization and disorganization analogous to the anabolic and katabolic processes of metabolism in the body."[3] Social disorganization was seen as an ordinary part of social formation since it is often necessary that older social relations be broken down so that new relations might form; however, if the rate of growth is too rapid, then social and personal disorganization can easily give rise to social ills such as delinquency, poverty, crime, suicide, and disease. Thus, social problems should be understood as disequilibrium and degeneration in the social organism.

For this reason, many of the Chicago school sociologists were interested in what they termed "interstitial areas," or local urban environments defined by their relatively high degree of separation from the rest of the city life, such as warehouse districts, railroad yards, slums, etc. In Thrasher's study of urban gangs, he used the language of decay and disease to describe these disintegrated areas as spaces "intervening" between the more healthy and stable areas of the city: "In nature, foreign matter tends to collect and cake in every crack, crevice, and cranny—interstices. There are also fissures and breaks in the structure of social organization."[4] Thrasher's language reveals the close proximity of early sociology to reform discourses of the period that tended to view social problems as principally about unassimilated foreigners. Despite their stated commitments to scientific objectivity and their celebrated dedication to a socially useful and progressive research agenda, the Chicago school sociologists produced a conception of social hygiene that was often in accord with the discourses of disease, dirt, and degeneration used to represent the urban ghetto by some of the most conservative and xenophobic social movements of the period.

After earning his doctorate and accepting a position in the School of Education at New York University, Thrasher became one of the principle PFS researchers. The film audience studies of the PFS were coordinated by the Motion Picture Research Council (MPRC), an organization founded in 1927 by William Short. Short was a progressive Congregationalist minister who received funding for the research from the Payne Study and Experiment Fund, a granting organization for projects dealing with childhood education. Short was interested in securing scientific evidence for claims that motion pictures were responsible for antisocial attitudes and behaviors, especially in children. The research projects of the PFS were developed and evaluated by a committee comprised of Short, representatives of the Payne Fund, and the researchers themselves. Besides Thrasher at NYU, other PFS researchers held positions in sociology, psychology, and education at the University of Chicago, the University of Iowa, Ohio State University, Pennsylvania State College, and Yale University. In fall 1933, their work resulted in the publication of eight of the eleven selected research projects, as well as a volume on film appreciation and a summary report by the committee chairman W. W. Charters.[5] Despite the fact that the published PFS were not widely read, these research projects were factors in the institutional legitimation of sustained motion picture research. Furthermore, the PFS helped fashion a new professional identity for a particular kind of scholar whose work was centrally determined by investigations into the cinema.[6]

While the researchers who participated in the PFS shared neither a single methodological orientation nor a coherent theory of social organization, they were mutually involved in innovating methods for the study of media influence within their respective disciplines. Their studies ranged from galvanometric measurements of children's sleep after attending the movies, to the development of scales for measuring the influence of motion pictures on young viewers' attitudes about racial prejudice, to the gathering of individual movie biographies from "delinquent" and "non-delinquent" children. This diversity of quantitative and qualitative approaches was an attempt to found scientific media research on the most current and promising approaches to measuring human response, behavior, development, cognition, and communication. Despite the goal of mutual interdisciplinary support and corroboration, however, significant contradictions existed between these approaches, particularly in the ways they conceived of mass culture.[7] Nevertheless, they all sought to construct their own authority and to support the validity of their findings by demonstrating an intimate knowledge of popular moviegoing pleasures and practices.[8] This appropriation of popular knowledge and experience in the creation of communication science marks an important early moment in the formation of film studies by tying it to the development of modern regulatory strategies.

As policymakers and reformers began to turn their attention toward the management of public consumption, there was a growing need for social experts who knew how the public thought and how they were likely to behave. As director of the NMPRC, William Short distinguished himself from earlier reformers by asserting that the new basis of social power lay in the management and deployment of facts and information rather than in any claim to moral or cultural superiority. His support of the university researchers who participated in the PFS was directly in line with the thinking of political scientists and social critics such as Walter Lippmann, one of the most important champions of modern bureaucracy. Lippmann claimed "that representative government, either in what is ordinarily called politics, or in industry cannot be worked successfully, no matter what the basis of election, unless there is an independent, expert organization for making the unseen facts intelligible to those who have to make the decisions."[9] While the PFS mark an early moment in the history of communication science, they must also be understood as a contribution to the development of modern methods of social control. As Robert Park and Ernst Burgess bluntly stated in their 1921 sociology textbook: "All social problems finally turn out to be problems of social control."[10] Emergent sociology was a particularly attractive means of generating useful information precisely because it promised to understand social activity through an interrogation of the individual social actor as a psychological organism whose development and responses might be predictably shaped through environmental changes and education.

The recent discovery of several previously unknown documents connected with the film audience research of the PFS has provided an occasion for reevaluating the development of communication science in the United States. These texts were first published in 1996 as part of a larger critical history that reinterpreted the contributions of the PFS to our current understanding of the mass media and to the development of communication studies.[11] Garth Jowett, Ian Jarvie, and Katherine Fuller maintain that the rapid disappearance of the PFS from both popular memory and scientific attention was due less to the conflicted and inconclusive nature of the studies' findings than to reformers' careless appropriations of the studies and to the ascendancy of statistical methods in media research. Jowett maintains that the MPRC's decision to have Henry James Forman write a popularization of the research, one that clearly took a position of social advocacy, made it difficult for the PFS to be taken seriously as social science,[12] and he quotes PFS research chairman Charters as having arrived at a similar conclusion. Charters wrote, "I am personally of the opinion that we would have been better off if we had rested the case without this attempt at popularization. It would have been wiser to publish the studies and thereby make them available for journalists and publicists without the implied sponsorship of the popularization of the Forman book."[13] Here, in an effort to claim an exclusive authority over mass cultural communication, the social scientist feels compelled to introduce differences — differences between objectivity and social engagement, between scientific knowledge and public policy, and between technical specialists and ordinary citizens. The necessity for maintaining objective neutrality for the PFS was not incidental to the demands of a centralized bureaucracy operating through principles of nonpartisan and rationalized efficiency but rather was premised directly upon and anticipated such an application.[14]

The place of the PFS within a history of social struggles over knowledge was largely shaped by the urban sociological theories of Park and Burgess at the University of Chicago. Fully one-third of the PFS researchers were either members of the faculty at the University of Chicago or were recent graduates, with Herbert Blumer, Paul Cressey, Philip Hauser, and Thrasher directly connected with the Department of Sociology. Not coincidentally, these particular researchers were interested in social deviance and juvenile delinquency. Their work has been the most often cited of all the PFS monographs, and they are sometimes viewed as exhibiting some of the most progressive tendencies of early media research. In fact, the authors of the recent reevaluation of the PFS refer to Cressey as the "unsung hero of the Payne Fund project," with Jarvie claiming that Cressey's unpublished research "promised to be the most fruitful of all the studies, and . . . might have provided continuity with media research to come."[15] The authors praise Cressey for his attempt to study "the movies as one part of a total 'social situation' or 'configuration' in which they are experienced" rather than as an isolated phenomenon.[16] Katherine Fuller describes Cressey as having had an "intellectual epiphany" when coming to the realization "that movies should not be linked to boys' delinquency, but must instead be viewed as a powerful source of 'informal education' that served boys in a far more direct and practical way than did schools or the Boys' Clubs."[17]

Boys, Movies and Streets was to have been coauthored with Frederick Thrasher, who, in 1929, proposed to the PFS Educational Research Committee a study of the moviegoing habits of the boys and young men of the Jefferson Park neighborhood of East Harlem, a neighborhood with high rates of delinquency. At NYU, Thrasher was already directing a larger study of Jefferson Park for the Boys Club of America, funded by the Bureau of Social Hygiene. Cressey, who had recently earned his master's degree in sociology from the University of Chicago, did not join the Jefferson Park study until quite late, but he clearly steered the motion picture portion of the research away from a circumscribed attention to movies in the lives of Jefferson Park boys to a consideration of the boys' total social environment and the role that motion pictures and the movie houses played in that environment. While such an approach differed in scope from the more atomistic projects of the PFS, it only attempted to extend and intensify the area of authority claimed by the media researcher whose work was still dictated by a practical need to produce that very authority. If the original PFS projects sought to define specific areas and objects of research capable of rendering verifiable results for public opinion purposes, Cressey's broadening of the object of study represents not so much a reversal of the bureaucratic impetus of the original studies as an elaboration on and extension of the sites of observation and of social control. Unregulated spaces were increasingly brought under his surveillance. "In the darkened theater there is an opportunity for the individual to make contacts and to engage in activities which he would not countenance were there probability that he would be identified. The contacts and activities may vary greatly, but they are all products of these opportunities for clandestine contacts afforded in the unsupervised movie house."[18] Cressey cited the gang rape of a young woman whose entrapment began through an unsavory contact she made in a movie theater. He continued by recounting an interview with a boy who had been approached by homosexuals at the movies and who had agreed to be fellated as long as he "got paid for it." While the individual child as biological organism, psychological personality, and social being was still an object of investigation, Cressey was now also interested in the child as inextricably linked to his or her social circumstances. Such environmental analyses, however, tended to create problems of adequate empirical evidence. Yet Cressey did not propose an environmental analysis against or in lieu of other scientific approaches to the study of youth; instead, he based his study upon a presumed natural correspondence between the individual organism and the social processes that produce and reproduce the individual. If anything, it is Cressey who most fully articulates the Chicago school principles of social development in relation to the movies. From the perspective of social control, Cressey's work is less of an individual epiphany than it is the practical articulation of a disciplinary ideal about total information.

Training Media Experts

Cressey's broadening of the Jefferson Park study to include the movie house and the street as important sites of disorganization is consistent with the portrayal of that neighborhood as an interstitial area. For Cressey, motion pictures were only one of many influences on neighborhood children, albeit a particularly powerful one that provided them with an informal education about the larger world. Cressey felt that commercial films ought not to be judged as harmful apart from an evaluation of the other forces at work in the child's world. In fact, he viewed Hollywood products as more or less positive social influences in this neighborhood of "conflicting and contradictory social patterns" since cinema was a "second schoolhouse" that provided members of the community with a common, shared experience and a uniform subject of conversation. Unlike the relatively unregulated, anonymous, and culturally fragmented spaces of the cheap movie houses, candy stores, and city streets, the fictional worlds presented by motion pictures provided for a relatively stable and standardized set of experiences for mass audiences. By presenting "whole patterns of life" previously unknown or unobserved, motion pictures facilitated a "psychological mobility" with distant ways of life.[19] For Cressey, the overall effect of Hollywood motion pictures seems to be culturally assimilative and, therefore, socially progressive.

Cressey's attempt to situate motion picture attendance within the larger social milieu of the boys and young men of Jefferson Park was entirely consistent with the larger goals of the study that Thrasher proposed to the Bureau of Social Hygiene back in March 1928. Thrasher had claimed that his study of delinquency was unique because it dealt with "the problem from the standpoint of *the total situation*, rather than any one phase or aspect of it," and because the project provided "the opportunity to use the Jefferson Park Boys Club as a laboratory to observe and measure the outcomes of this particular boys' work program" over a three-year period. Thrasher further proposed that his study would combine different research approaches—"medical, psychiatric, psychological, and sociological techniques"—in order to "*study the whole child.*"[20] While Thrasher had described his approach to "the total situation" as a "new type of research," he and Cressey had already been thoroughly schooled in this type of fieldwork during their graduate studies. Instead of founding a radically new research orientation to social problems, the Jefferson Park study allowed Thrasher the "opportunity *to train experts for this type of study.*"[21]

Cressey and Thrasher, as well as the other PFS researchers, were only a small part of a general historical tendency toward the adaptation of the applied human sciences to strategies of corporate bureaucracy. For instance, Cressey's observation that motion pictures provided for a type of psychological mobility of significant educational value to members of local, impoverished, and socially disorganized groups was, also, by no means an original idea. The industrial psychologist Hugo Münsterberg had written in 1916 about the importance of motion pictures for the project of social stability and assimilation: "The fact that daily millions are under the spell of the performances on the screen is established. The high degree of suggestibility during those hours in the dark house may be taken for granted. Hence any wholesome influence emanating from the photoplay must have an incomparable power for the remolding and upbuilding of the national soul."[22]

Park had studied with Münsterberg at Harvard in 1898, and Münsterberg's ideas about attention and suggestibility remained an important intellectual influence on Park throughout his life. Cressey and Thrasher most likely encountered Münsterberg's work as graduate students of Burgess, who included portions of Münsterberg's *The Photoplay: A Psychological Study* as required reading in Sociology 34, "Play and the Social Utilization of Leisure Time," a course Burgess taught regularly at the University of Chicago throughout the 1920s. Münsterberg's ideas provided the theoretical basis for the course's unit titled "The Commercialization of Recreation." This unit began with an excerpt from a 1911 Russell Sage Foundation publication, *The Exploitation of Pleasure*, a study of New York that catalogued the city's "unorganized or commercialized recreative provisions" according to the age groups each one served, and then compared these "laissez faire" cultural industries with both the "fundamental institutions" of home, street, school, and factory and the "public or philan-thropic recreative provisions" of playground, settlement, library, museum, and YMCA. The study proposed that civic recreational projects are successful to the extent that they seek to counteract the disorganizing influences of commercial-ized recreations by offering "counter attractions."[23]

The remainder of Burgess's course unit on commercialized leisure consid-ered other important sites of amusement (the movie house, the public dance hall, and the cabaret), the concentration of recreations in "bright light areas," and the problem of urban anonymity and sexual promiscuity. Burgess saw his own students as pioneering fieldworkers in urban sociology, and he often in-corporated recent work by graduate students into his curriculum. According to his outline and his notes for this course in the mid-1920s, the section on motion pictures included portions of Lois Kate Halley's 1924 master's thesis, "A Study of Motion Pictures in Chicago." Halley had surveyed and categorized the various types of theaters in Chicago and traced the history of their development, noting the increasing concentration of the control of exhibition in the large theatrical chains, a development she relates to "a tendency towards concentration that is being found in many kinds of business." She, too, proposed that the mass address of motion pictures promised a means for "influencing people toward better citizenship."[24]

The readings for Sociology 34 included journalistic pieces on the dance hall and the cabaret from progressive publications such as the *American Mercury* and the *Survey*, as well as from Chicago newspaper columnists such as Ben Hecht. These journalists practiced a type of popular ethnography that delighted in describing the stratifications of urban culture, and particularly in describing what they saw as the psychological, moral, and cultural regressions character-istic of the lowest forms of popular amusement. Hecht describes the surren-der of cabaret dancers to the music as a surrender of cognition itself: "Thus the thoughts of the dancers dance—dead hopes, wearied ambitions, vanishing youth do an inarticulate can-can in the heads on the cabaret floor."[25] Again, the dialectic here is that of life falling toward death, of meaning falling toward nonmeaning, and of autonomy falling toward automation. Sociological ideas about the biomechanical nature of culture and about the disorganizing or even annihilating potential of mass amusements and commercialized leisure were not simply of interest to specialists and academicians but rather already part of the general culture, and they were assiduously promulgated by many liberal progressives with elite pretensions.

Finally, "The Change in Role from the Participator to the Spectator in Modern Society," an excerpt from a 1918 article by Robert Park on public opinion, concluded the course unit on commercial recreation. What is particularly striking about this excerpt is the way it articulates one of the central contradictions of Chicago school sociology and, by extension, of the PFS. A recurring problem for Park is that traditional community life is now administered and "taken over by professionals," leaving the masses "no longer actors, but spectators." The incessant search for stimulation through commercial recreation is for Park not some new, socially meaningful activity but a symptom of the deprivation "of most of the natural outlets for the expression of our interests and our energies." The solution is, of course, more careful planning of recreational forms and institutions according to "some method by which the individual can regain a sense of personal participation in the institutional life about him."[26] For Park, democracy can only exist in a society that shares a common identity and a common sense of purpose. Those who have been isolated or alienated by modernity are, by definition, incapable of adequately defining their own interests since their ability to produce accurate knowledge about the world or themselves has been usurped by a set of stimulation apparatuses or by deviant cultural formations such as the delinquent gang. Yet by studying and understanding these subcultures, the sociological researcher can come to understand those compensatory benefits that particular individuals derive from participation in a subculture, so as to develop effective social policies for integrating the individuals back into a healthy community. If the integrated community is proposed as the definition of democracy, then democracy in the rapidly expanding metropolis will have to be carefully administered. Park's analysis points to the political need for professionals trained in securing the data necessary for effective social administration; it also provided an ethical justification for the types of research that followed.

The Importance of the Case Study

One of the most important tools of the Chicago sociologists for studying social groups in situ was the collection of individual life histories. The usefulness of the case study had already been demonstrated in the study of juvenile delinquency by criminologists such as William Healy, who argued in 1915 that the law would "be vastly more curative if understandings of beginnings and foundations of misconduct in general, and knowledge of them as existing in the individual career, were made the business of those who administer treatment under the law."[27] For the sociologists at the University of Chicago, the work of compiling detailed information about social groups through collecting statements in their own words became one of the principal methods of empirical investigation.[28] The depth of information provided by such documents, while unwieldy and next to impossible to summarize, provided social scientists with a glimpse into the lived experiences of social groups and the categories through which those groups understood the world — a sort of practical phenomenological description that could approximate the "vagrant and suppressed impulses, passions, and ideals [that] emancipate themselves from the dominant moral order,"[29] and that subtended urban deviance for these researchers. If the new sociological project was to understand the individual in her or his 'total situation,' this psychological depth was crucial for understanding the relations between individual behavior and social forms. Such intimate information could be obtained from interviews, questionnaires, written or spoken life histories, found or solicited letters, newspaper reports, and the case files of social welfare agencies.

One of the problems Cressey and Thrasher faced in the Jefferson Park study was that their reliance upon such vast and disparate bodies of data, as well as their commitment to preserving that data's richness of detail in reporting their research, required an extended period of careful analysis. Such research also entailed more and more involvement in the lives of the boys and young men being studied. These were surely some of the factors in Cressey's failure to complete the motion picture study before the MPRC's publication deadlines. At the 1930 annual meeting of PFS researchers — before Cressey became involved with the PFS — Thrasher had already reported that questionnaires and daily diaries were supplementing the solicited autobiographies. He also reported on "the recording of overt behavior responses in the actual movie situation, [with] the researcher taking two boys to the movie theater and recording each instance of spontaneous conversation, applause, or laughter and noting on previously prepared sheets the point in the movie story where such responses occur." Researchers kept stenographic records of controlled interviews with these boys and young men, while some of their statements were also recorded by a dictation machine. When asked by Charters how many more controlled interviews would be required to support "statistical validity," Thrasher ventured that approximately only a hundred more were necessary. Robert Park, however, who was at that time still involved with the research committee of the PFS, suggested that the gathering of personal information "should proceed until it was clear that no new types of experiences were likely to be discovered."[30]

Park's support of further data collection and his interest in searching for new experiences among the delinquent populations of Jefferson Park would have been appreciated by his ex-student Thrasher, who had demonstrated his own commitments to exhaustive data collection in his doctoral research on Chicago gangs. Park's comments at the annual meeting may have also been an indirect recommendation to the PFS for Cressey to take over the motion picture research at the Jefferson Park Boys Club. Cressey was amply suited to the type of life-experience research that Thrasher was conducting and that Park was encouraging. Cressey had just completed his master's thesis on Chicago's closed dance halls—the cheap "dancing academies" where only male patrons were admitted in order to buy tickets to dance with female "instructresses." The written thesis had proven him to be an unconventionally skillful researcher of disorganized social milieus, and his work was slated for publication by the University of Chicago Press.[31] In his thesis, Cressey sought to describe the closed dance hall as a particular social world that, while a highly disorganized commercial space of anonymous encounters and exchanges, provided both the dancers and the patrons certain necessary compensations lacking in their impoverished or marginalized lives outside the dance hall.[32] Cressey spent long hours in these establishments masquerading as an unexceptional patron, buying tickets to dance with the young "nickel dancers" and eavesdropping on conversations. Cressey's aim was "to see effects of the life at dance pavilions and halls . . . by studying life histories as far as possible." He also wished "to study the dance hall as a sociological institution indicating its relationship with the immediate neighborhood and the larger communities from which it draws."[33] Thus, Cressey's familiarity with gathering life histories made him an ideal candidate for the type of exhaustive contextual research that Park was urging the PFS to support. Burgess would eventually refer to Cressey's unpublished "The Social

Role of the Motion Pictures in an Interstitial Area" as a pioneering qualitative study of "the relationship between motion picture experience and criminal behavior."[34]

Methods of Appropriation

The advancement in knowledge that such investigations were to achieve rested in their ability to deliver a picture of a particular social milieu from the perspectives of its inhabitants. In other words, social science was seeking to reproduce the lived experiences of those it studied; and those lived experiences, in passing from the immediate orientation of the subjects under investigation to the meditative attention of the social scientists, became, by virtue of this change of possession, scientific knowledge of social processes. Perhaps Burgess described this goal most succinctly in his introduction to Cressey's monograph on the closed dance hall: "The reader is given an entrée into the social world of the taxi-dance hall such as the casual visitor never gains. Vicariously, he may imagine himself in the place as a taxi-dancer or her patron, participating, as it were, in their experiences, and getting some appreciation of their outlook and philosophy of life."[35]

While such research appears to have functioned as entertainment for the student of social processes, the methods employed by Cressey, Thrasher, and other Chicago sociologists were crucial to the social science project of regulating mass society by "sympathetically" appropriating the understandings, ideas, and discourses of particular marginal communities or of the individuals found in various disorganized social milieus. In order to produce a new professional discourse on social deviance, their research methods exploited the social mobility and anonymity indicative of rapid urban development. Similarly, their use of individual life histories as interpretive data was central to the project of fashioning social scientists intimately familiar with and inhabiting organic social processes (as anonymous researchers and as caseworkers), but somehow able to separate themselves from these same processes (as scientists) in order to understand them. These researchers' claim implied that while the various processes, practices, and sites of mass society could function as a laboratory for investigative fieldwork, actual knowledge of that society could not be entrusted to the people who constituted the new masses.[36]

Familiarity with a particular social world and the ability to claim a type of insider status within it was, in the late 1920s, a key to the production of the social expert who could lay claim to an authentic appreciation of the lives of those she or he studied, a claim that simultaneously worked to deauthorize those who had made available to the scientist their own expertise and knowledge of the social worlds in which they traveled. For example, Cressey continually borrowed the terminology and categories used by the inhabitants of the social institutions he studied, but he modified them in such a way so as to claim them as adequate scientific description when used by the more cautious and thoughtful sociologist. In his field notes for the dance hall study, Cressey is quite candid about this process:

> One of my informants, a young man of Polish extraction, now running a store of his own [but] who frequented Gaelic Park several years ago said, "As I size it up there are three types of girls at every dance hall. There are the ones who come just because of novelty. Then there are the ones who come hoping to meet a man whom they might marry. Finally, there are those who come for the business. They are the ones who come across easily but demand a good time and some money if possible. I call them 'foul-balls.' You will find that about two-thirds of the girls out at Gaelic are 'foul-balls.'" While it seems to me that my informant just quoted a good classification, I am disposed to believe that a larger share of the girls who attend come with normal desires for response and are only forced into abnormal types of behavior because of attitudes and forces to which they seem to have to adapt themselves. They are more creatures of the environment than creators of it.[37]

While Cressey accepts this man's conventional understanding of dancer "types" to describe the motivations and desires of the female employees of the dance hall, he must "correct" his informant's allegedly unsophisticated understanding of the "foul-ball" character as a congenital identity. Cressey constructs himself as considerably more knowledgeable and reflective than this Polish-American merchant by providing an explanation of identity as developmental and conditioned by social forces. Yet the merchant's definitions appear to be functional to his own (male) interests rather than diagnostic, and despite the term "foul-ball," there is little evidence that the merchant considers these women in any way "abnormal" as does Cressey. Indeed, one could argue that the merchant has a more properly sociological understanding of the dancers' identities as relational and as shaped by modern contradictory social forces: the dancers' need for excitement ("the ones who come just because of the novelty"), their need for economic stability and social prestige ("the ones who come hoping to meet a man whom they might marry"), and their need for money and independence ("those who come for the business"). Similarly, Cressey might be considered as far too concerned with delineating the behavior of the mercenary dancer as indicative of a particular type of social deviant. The point, of course, is the manner in which various people's everyday experiences and knowledge of modernity were taken over by a corrective discourse that claimed access to those very experiences through sympathetic identification while simultaneously claiming an external unifying authority over them. This process of correction entailed that the emerging social sciences of this period would claim to both speak the voices of the new masses as well as speak about them. As Robert Park earlier described the political problem of social knowledge in his doctoral dissertation, "At the very point . . . where individual interests and viewpoints diverge, practical life demands a definition and interpretation of objects and events in the outer world acceptable to all. Thus the need for a purely theoretical interpretation of things arises, one that is free from individual values."[38] Not coincidentally, Park's argument serves as a fairly succinct statement of the philosophical basis for modern corporate bureaucracy.

Anonymous Authorities

In producing their expertise, a problem that many early media researchers faced was adequately differentiating themselves from their objects of study by fashioning a "purely theoretical interpretation" of media effects. At one point in his work on the Jefferson Park neighborhood, Cressey mentions that although "certain movies may be used *by those interested in delinquency and crime* as a means of self-instruction in crime, the major 'contribution' of the movie to youth is as an agency, presenting patterns of life and personal conduct of which children of all types may avail themselves, which conveys to all types . . . impressions of the *larger world beyond their immediate experience*."[39] Like Cressey himself, the youth of Jefferson Park were interested in criminal behavior as a compelling, modern way of being in the world. Their interest in motion pictures might be, then, properly sociological. However, unlike the scientific researcher, the boys and young men of East Harlem lacked direct access to these modern life patterns except through the commercial cinema — an institution that, for Cressey, was a source of distortion and misinformation about modern life. Nevertheless, urban sociologists of the 1920s not only shared the same objects of knowledge with their subjects but, more significantly, their investigations also relied upon the very same conditions of modern urban life that were seen as contributing to the disorganization of experience for social deviants: that is, anonymity.[40] In Cressey's research on urban dance halls in Chicago, he continually exploited the lack of organic social relationships that obtained in the dance halls: "By trying to appear as a transcent [*sic*] who 'happened in' to the dance hall I succeeded in securing much information concerning the general activities and attitudes of the patrons. By appearing as a prospective renter of the dancing pavilion I secured much information concerning the way in which the Park is controlled . . . By appearing *incognito* in groups of people at the dance, I was able to overhear conversations which aided me in making my judgments."[41]

Cressey's field notes also discuss how he often asked dancers out on dates in order to gauge their moral standards, and, on one occasion, how he accidentally encountered a dancer after hours on a commuter train and surreptitiously followed her home in order to establish her address, even after she pleaded with him not to accompany her.[42] Yet in studying the movie habits of young men in the Jefferson Park neighborhood, Cressey held that the very same conditions of anonymity that allowed him to collect scientific data were "a major factor explaining not only the unusually high rate of emotional instability among boys of the area, but also the community's record in delinquency and crime." As Cressey explains: "Another very significant aspect of the boy's street world contributing to his delinquency is the possibility for him at anytime to move quickly from one social group to another and to become wholly different personalities in the different groups . . . On his 'home block' he may be for a time known as a wholesome, well-mannered boy, yet on another at the same time be a predatory young gangster, or even a major criminal."[43]

Duplicity was an index of social disorganization, except when used toward the ends of bureaucratic social investigation and control. Dissembling for the purpose of official social science was a socially responsible practice precisely because the double lives led by the juvenile delinquent, the taxi dancer, the prostitute, the kleptomaniac, the sexual deviant, and many others are all efforts to avoid traditional social accountability. The ultimate regulatory aim here is to establish control over those new urban social environments that allowed individuals to learn about the modern world through the testing of various identities and through experimenting with various cultural practices *by which those individuals refused to be defined*. Motion pictures provided some of those unregulated social environments — most dramatically the cheap movie house;

yet it was also the "alien" worlds and adult patterns of life presented on the screen and in advertising that Cressey believed facilitated the harmful production and circulation of unsanctioned knowledge.

Cressey theorized the anonymous researcher in counterdistinction to Georg Simmel's conception of "the stranger"—that individual who becomes part of a social group by being physically present within the group while remaining, nonetheless, culturally distant. Park and Burgess made much of Simmel's description of the stranger, offering it as a model of objectivity for sociological research. The stranger's special relation to the group, being simultaneously of the group and outside it, made the stranger a special individual who could be both sympathetic to the group's concerns and, since the stranger's prospects were not tied to the destiny of the group, objective in the assessment of the group's problems.[44] As an addition to the "sociological stranger" Cressey proposed the "anonymous stranger," who he related to those impersonal relations "fostered by the growth of the capitalist spirit" that allow entrepreneurs to "drive harder bargains" by gaining intimate knowledge of local conditions without any of the sentimental attachment or responsibility to the local community that had defined the stranger for Simmel. If the sociological stranger appeared in the social group as social scientist, bureaucrat, or caseworker, the anonymous stranger was nobody in particular. Yet, the purpose of this new research identity was the extension and amplification of the same types of information about personality sought by more traditional means. As Cressey explains: "The sociological stranger is conceived of as belonging to the group and yet having a differential status within the group. The anonymous stranger is in reality 'merely one of the group.' He has no status distinct from the others attached to the same aggregation. Yet in this very fact of uniformity as well as anonymity the unidentified person has an opportunity for securing a more comprehensive revelation of the personalities of the others in the group."[45]

While they might be considered idiosyncratic, Cressey's forays into anonymous surveillance are not marginal to the development of film and media study. His work fully articulates, in a rather dramatic fashion, two interrelated phenomena: first, the main purpose of early communication science—the exhaustive cataloging of audience experiences for purposes of social control; and second, its means of professionalization—the creation of the media expert by the appropriation of mass cultural knowledge obtained by occupying various positions within mass society in order to claim epistemological authority over its inhabitants.

Film Studies at NYU, 1934–1936

Although the motion picture research undertaken by Cressey and Thrasher came to light only in recent years, their work helped define the curricular terrain of early film studies in the 1930s. While Cressey was writing the PFS manuscript, Thrasher spoke in several public forums on motion picture influence as a central problem of mass communication, and, on at least one occasion, he was identified as "director of motion picture study at New York University."[46] In 1933, Thrasher joined the Executive Committee of the National Board of Review (NBR) with whose assistance, during the 1934–1935 and the 1935–1936 academic years, he designed and taught one of the first film courses at New York University. "The Motion Picture: Its Artistic, Educational, and Social Aspects" was a two-semester course taught once a week on Thursday evenings at the School of Education. At least 130 students registered for the course the second year it was offered.[47] The first semester of the course was primarily devoted to studying the historical development of the motion picture, as well as its current technical, industrial, and aesthetic aspects; the second semester gave more consideration to the educational uses of motion pictures, as well as to questions of film regulation and social hygiene. Each week a different representative or professional from some aspect of film culture lectured and usually screened representative or illustrative motion pictures. According to the final syllabus for the 1935–1936 course, Terry Ramsaye lectured on film history; Iris Barry discussed film aesthetics; Joris Ivens talked about documentary and screened his films *Rain* and *New Earth*; Wilton Barrett, the executive director of the NBR, screened *Lot in Sodom* as an example of the experimental film; Pudovkin's film *Mechanics of the Brain* was shown by the renowned psychiatrist and alienist A. A. Brill; the director of the American Social Hygiene Association presented "a private showing of a film originally banned by the New York Board of Censors"; the film critic Evelyn Gerstein lectured on "the social film" at a presentation of René Clair's *À nous la liberté*; the national director of the American Civil Liberties Union spoke on film censorship; representatives from the New York Zoo and the American Museum of National History conducted a class session on science museums and visual education; Max Fleischer discussed animation; and so on. Students in the course also attended conferences conducted by film education societies and reform groups, and they visited a major East Coast film studio.[48]

Thrasher's course had been much the same the year before, with many of the same or similar speakers presenting on the same topics, and with optional student fieldtrips to Warner Bros.' Vitagraph Studios and to Radio City Music Hall. Each year at the beginning of the second term, students were required to purchase a paperback edition of Charters's summary of the PFS. During the 1934–1935 course, the first three weeks of the second term were devoted to questions of media influence, beginning with Cressey and Thrasher presenting on "research into the effects of motion pictures and the Payne Fund Studies." The following week, Thrasher and others lectured on "the motion picture as an instrument of cultural transmission" and discussed "motion picture publications, advertising, and advertising films," and finally a third class was conducted by Thrasher alone and devoted to the "social aspects of motion pictures" and "illustrated by a socially significant film," the 1931 Soviet feature *Road to Life*.[49] Students in the course completed either one or two term projects each semester, depending on the number of credits for which they had enrolled. Students were given five alternatives for the completion of term projects: creating an extensive scrapbook of movie reviews and other film-related articles accompanied by source notations for each item; writing a term paper on any one of fifty-eight suggested topics ranging from problems of film aesthetics to questions of film education and media influence; organizing a student photoplay club and keeping a detailed written account of the club's activities; shooting an amateur film after submitting an original scenario; or writing a motion picture autobiography.[50]

For the latter project, Thrasher distributed a five-page mimeographed description of the assignment that gave detailed directions for writing "a motion picture life history." This description placed a premium on truthfulness, advising students to "write only when you feel in the mood," reassuring them that they need not concern themselves with proper English prose. Students were "to write freely and naturally, telling your experiences, the way you felt about them then, and the way you feel about them now." The life history was to begin with a general description of the student's family and its interrelations as well as the family's relation to the neighborhood. Students were encouraged to begin with their earliest memories—"Since we are just now beginning to realize the meaning of childhood experiences in a person's life"—and to create a linear narrative of friendships, daydreams, play activities, reading habits, role models, and any particularly unforgettable experiences. After this psycho-sociological self-portrait, the student was then required to detail the role of motion pictures in her or his life. Again, students were encouraged to begin with their earliest memories of motion pictures and to write about their evolving interest in films, their behavior and experiences in the movie theater, their favorite stars (describing when and how each star became a particular favorite), their emotions and moods in relation to remembered screenings (including any ideas about fashion and comportment they gained from watching motion pictures), their experiences with love and romance pictures, their experiences with crime films, and their changing understanding of the relation between motion pictures and reality.[51] The project presented these various life history topics to the students as a series of questions. For example, the section on crime films asked the following: "Do you feel that motion pictures have developed in you an[y] ideas favorable toward crime? As a child did you ever take the part of a robber in your games? Did you ever imagine yourself doing a crime? Did you ever feel like committing a crime after seeing a motion picture experience? What kind of crime? Did you ever experience the wish to become an honorable criminal like Robin Hood? Do you believe that the 'thrillers' and serials ever taught you moral lessons and feelings of justice? Tell about these."[52]

If not identical, then the motion picture life history assignment at NYU was closely modeled on the Jefferson Park research and was, in a very real sense, a continuation of it.[53] The principal motivation of the assignment was clearly Thrasher's desire to compile further personal data about media influence, psychological development, and social processes. Despite the fact that the assignment description begins by informing students that the life history is a process of rewarding self-discovery, the assignment was essentially an instrument for gathering sociological data. The only mention of the assignment's usefulness to social science occurs briefly in its second paragraph: "We are asking you to think about the influences which motion pictures have had upon you, your likes and dislikes, your ideas on life and your beliefs. Writing your motion picture biography will not only be a fine experience for you, but will also be valuable in helping to understand movies."[54] Of all of Thrasher's term projects, the life history description's repeated use of the pronoun "we" is unique to that assignment. However, what is far more interesting here is the disappearance of any and all pronouns in the last clause: "but will be valuable in helping understand movies." This clause marks the way that Thrasher was able to overcome the division between the sociological stranger and the anonymous stranger, as the unstated pronoun masks both the agency and the agenda of the social scientist. As a college professor teaching film and a new educational professional, Thrasher had found a way to claim the identity of a media expert while remaining nobody in particular—the bureaucratic ideal.

Film entered the academy as a worthy object of study because of the determining role it played in modern life. The audience research of the late 1920s and the early 1930s made possible a new objectivity for the study of motion pictures as a social phenomenon, one premised upon the need to thoroughly document all the various types of experiences and behaviors made possible by motion pictures. While never fully commensurate, nascent film studies and communication studies overlapped considerably during the period of the PFS. They would soon, however, go their separate ways by adhering to a now familiar division between the arts and sciences. Both, however, sought to distance themselves from the research of the PFS—seeing in that research, perhaps, an embarrassing proximity to the very subjects that the PFS researchers sought to study: those portions of the mass audience who were socially marginalized by age, ethnicity, social class, and sexuality, but who were, nevertheless, a visible presence in the nation's movie houses. The very people who had made motion picture expertise possible by sharing their own knowledge and experiences about modern society have become, in a sense, a repressed other within the disciplinary histories of film and communication studies.

Institutionally and ideologically, Thrasher's course cleared the way for "History and Appreciation of the Cinema," Robert Gessner's more text-centered film appreciation course at NYU in the latter half of the 1930s. Even if forgotten, Thrasher's earlier course represented a necessary step in proposing popular film as an object of special intellectual inquiry. His research and his pedagogy during the late 1920s and early 1930s helped to instantiate within the academy the figure of the media expert whose authority rested upon ethnographic knowledge about the diversity of cultural receptions occasioned by Hollywood films and the motion picture theater, as well as upon the promise of continually pressing that knowledge into the service of practical and socially constructive activities, such as the burgeoning film appreciation movement.[55] As Anne Morey has recently noted with respect to the latter, Thrasher's commitments to film education in the early 1930s clearly represented a version of social Taylorism, with Thrasher supporting highly centralized film educational programs designed and supervised by trained media and educational specialists.[56] Such programs meshed easily with the increasing corporatization of education that intensified during the 1920s union school movement, a national initiative to combine smaller independent schools into larger units under the administrative supervision of district school boards and state departments of education.

The effect of placing increasingly more aspects of public life under the purview of middle-class professionals and experts served as an effective way to make the ideas and interests of an elite managerial class available to the public as a means of self-improvement and professionalization.[57] The creation of the media expert also had the benefit of pulling the epistemological rug out from under those social groups that had had some success seeking reform though agitation and organizational means. Women's organizations, citizen groups, labor unions—in short, all those who had long-standing political stakes in motion picture regulation now took on the hue of "special interests" in the light of an objective and disinterested social science. Film education thus helped narrow the terrain of practical cultural politics. The relatively recent return by film scholars to documenting the diverse ways in which people make use of the cinema is often championed as a progressive project, one more responsive to those interests and identities elided by the hegemony of doctrinaire political analyses of the institution. The last twenty-five years of film and media studies has, undoubtedly, created a critical environment with more possibilities for contesting master narratives. Yet, in the light of its own disciplinary history, film studies might benefit from a thorough interrogation of its present expansiveness. The early motion picture researchers of the PFS believed that they were engaged in work that finally conferred respect on previously marginalized communities, and many of them saw their research and teaching as practical interventions promoting social justice. Yet, the working methods they pioneered and the types of expertise they were able to realize contributed to the expansion of corporate power. Those of us who work as professionals in film and media studies need to consider the types of authority on which our work might ultimately depend and promote them, and we need to continually evaluate whose interests are ultimately served through the exercise of that authority. In short, film and media studies must be fully engaged with questions of its own disciplinary history.

Notes

1. Frederick M. Thrasher, *The Gang: A Study of 1,313 Gangs in Chicago*, 2nd ed. (Chicago: University of Chicago Press, 1936), 114–15.
2. For an extended study of corporate bureaucratic forms during the twentieth century, see John McDermott, *Corporate Society: Class, Property, and Contemporary Capitalism* (Boulder, Colo.: Westview Press, 1991).
3. Ernest Burgess, "The Growth of a City: An Introduction to a Research Project," in *The City*, edited by Robert Ezra Park, Ernest W. Burgess, and Roderick D. McKenzie (Chicago: University of Chicago Press, 1925), 53.
4. Thrasher, *The Gang*, 22. Paul Cressey uses this same quote in his unpublished PFS manuscript. See Garth Jowett, Ian C. Jarvie, and Katherine Fuller, *Children and the*

Movies: Media Influence and the Payne Fund Controversy (New York: Cambridge University Press, 1996), 158.

5. All of the studies were published in 1933 by Macmillan Company, New York, and included P. W. Holaday and George G. Stoddard, *Getting Ideas from the Movies*; Ruth C. Peterson and L. L. Thurston, *Motion Pictures and the Social Attitudes of Children*; Frank K. Shuttleworth and Mark A. May, *The Social Conduct and Attitudes of Movie Fans*; W. S. Dysinger and Christian A Ruckmick, *The Emotional Response of Children to the Motion Picture Situation*; Charles C. Peters, *Motion Pictures and Standards of Morality*; Samuel Renshaw, Vernon L. Miller, and Dorothy Marquis, *Children's Sleep*; Herbert Blumer, *Movies and Conduct*; and Herbert Blumer, *Movies, Delinquency and Crime*. The volume on film aesthetics, *How to Appreciate Motion Pictures*, was authored by Edgar Dale, and W. W. Charters's overview of the PFS was entitled *Motion Pictures and Youth: A Summary*. Two additional studies were published in 1935, both by Edgar Dale: *The Content of Motion Pictures* and *Children's Attendance at Motion Pictures*. The eleventh study, *Boys, Movies, and City Streets*, by Frederick M. Thrasher and Paul G. Cressey, was never published.

6. Both Dale and Thrasher continued to write about motion pictures throughout their careers. See Edgar Dale, *Audio-visual Methods in Teaching*, rev. ed. (New York: Dryden Press, 1954); and Frederick Thrasher, *Okay for Sound: . . . How the Screen Found Its Voice* (New York: Duell, Sloan and Pearce, 1946).

7. Quantitative approaches tended to view individual receptions as idiosyncratic data to be overcome, while more qualitative investigations valued the details of individual experience as desideratum. For example, compare Dale's "Methods for Analyzing the Contents of Motion Pictures" with Philip Hauser's "How Do Motion Pictures Affect the Conduct of Children?" both in the *Journal of Educational Sociology* 6.4 (December 1932). While it is true that each of these researchers is investigating different objects — Dale, conventions of motion picture narration, and Hauser, deviant readings of motion pictures — their respective methods betray radically different understandings of the masses and their organization.

8. For example, Dale explained how he fashioned a method for the classification of motion pictures: "Our next problem was to discover the classes into which these pictures might logically fall. We adopted for this purpose what might be termed a common-sense classification which is similar to that which lay adults commonly use for the description of motion pictures" (Dale, "Methods for Analyzing the Contents of Motion Pictures," 246). Compare with Hauser's discussion of "very carefully selected investigators" to report on the activities of delinquent gangs (Hauser, "How Do Motion Pictures Affect the Conduct of Children?" 242).

9. Walter Lippmann, *Public Opinion* (New York: Macmillan Company, 1922), 31.

10. Robert E. Park and Ernest W. Burgess, *Introduction to the Science of Sociology* (Chicago: University of Chicago Press, 1921), 785.

11. Jowett, Jarvie, and Fuller, *Children and the Movies*.

12. Henry James Forman, *Our Movie Made Children* (New York: Macmillan Com-

pany, 1933). See also articles by Forman, including "To the Movies—But Not to Sleep!" *McCall's*, September 1932, 12–13, 38–39, "Movie Madness," *McCall's*, October 1932, 14–15, 28, 30, and "Molded by the Movies," *McCall's*, November 1932, 17, 54–57.

13. Charters quoted in Jowett, Jarvie, and Fuller, *Children and the Movies*, 111.

14. See Garth Jowett's discussion of the coordination of financial, legal, and academic authorities that made the PFS possible (Jowett, Jarvie, and Fuller, *Children and the Movies*, 17–56). Despite the fact that Jowett sees William Short as "the Machiavellian mastermind who kept the organization going," the whole story of the PFS and the MPRC is typical of modern bureaucratic formations and rational planning.

15. Jowett, Jarvie, and Fuller, *Children and the Movies*, 125, 115.

16. Ibid., 126.

17. Ibid., 86.

18. Ibid., 173.

19. Paul G. Cressey, "New York University Motion Picture Study—Outline of Chapters," in Jowett, Jarvie, and Fuller, *Children and the Movies*, 235.

20. Frederick Thrasher, "Proposal to Bureau of Social Hygiene," March 19, 1928, National Board of Review of Motion Pictures (NBRMP) Collection, New York Public Library (NYPL), Box 45, Thrasher, 1928–1936 (Thrasher's emphases).

21. Ibid. (Thrasher's emphasis).

22. Hugo Münsterberg, *Hugo Münsterberg on Film: "The Photoplay: A Psychological Study" and Other Writings*, edited by Allan Langdale (New York: Routledge, 2002), 155.

23. "Sociology 34/Chapter VI, The Commercialization of Recreation," The Ernest W. Burgess Collection, Special Collections, The University of Chicago Library, Box 31, Folder 4, 2–7.

24. Ibid., 15.

25. Ibid., 21.

26. Ibid., 25.

27. William Healy, *The Individual Delinquent: A Text-book of Diagnosis and Prognosis for All Concerned in Understanding Offenders* (Boston: Little, Brown, and Company, 1915), 8.

28. The highly celebrated five-volume study of Polish immigrants by the Chicago sociologist W. I. Thomas made extensive use of personal letters and autobiographies. See William I. Thomas and Florian Znaniecki, *The Polish Peasant in Europe and America*, vols. 1–2 (Chicago: University of Chicago Press, 1918); vol. 3–5 (New York: Knopf, 1919–1920).

29. This is Park's phrase for the latent psychological forces that find expression in subcultural forms and practices. See Robert Park, "The City: Suggestions for the Investigation of Human Behavior in the Urban Environment," in Park, Burgess, and McKenzie, eds., *The City*, 43.

30. "Annual Conference on Motion Pictures of The Educational Committee of the

Payne Fund," Columbus, Ohio, June 13–14, 1930, New York State Archive, Records of the Motion Picture Division, A1429, Box 4, Folder 21, 10–11.

31. Paul G. Cressey, *The Taxi-Dance Hall* (Chicago: University of Chicago Press, 1932).

32. The dance hall study was begun when Cressey went to the University of Chicago in summer 1925 and was appointed a graduate assistantship to work with the Juvenile Protective Association. Letter from Burgess to Cressey, April 18, 1925, Ernest W. Burgess Collection, University of Chicago Library, Box 7, Folder 3. Dance halls were a regular topic of study for Burgess's sociology students, but Cressey distinguished himself as both deeply interested in problems of data collection and innovative in his methods of investigation. For examples of other students' work on Chicago dance halls, see Steven C. Durbin, "The Moral Continuum of Deviancy Research: Chicago Sociologists and the Dance Hall," *Urban Life* 21.1 (April 1983): 75–94.

33. Paul Cressey, "A Study of Gaelic Park," Ernest W. Burgess Collection, University of Chicago Library, Box 130, Folder 7, 6, 3.

34. Ernest Burgess, "Motion Pictures and Delinquency," Ernest W. Burgess Collection, University of Chicago Library, Box 37, Folder 2.

35. Ernest Burgess in Cressey, *The Taxi-Dance Hall*, xii.

36. See Jennifer Pratt, "The Development of the 'Participation Observation' Method in Sociology: Origin Myth and History," *Journal of the History of the Behavioral Sciences* 19.4 (October 1983): 379–93.

37. Paul Cressey, "A Study of Gaelic Park," 33.

38. Robert Park, *"The Crowd and the Public" and Other Essays*, edited by Henry Elsner Jr., translated by Charlotte Elsner (Chicago: University of Chicago Press, 1972), 60. Compare with Park's discussion of assimilation and Americanization in Park and Burgess, *Introduction to the Science of Sociology*, 762–69.

39. Paul Cressey, "New York University Motion Picture Study—Outline of Chapters," in Jowett, Jarvie, and Fuller, *Children and the Movies*, 231 (my emphases).

40. James Bennett, in his history of the development of research methods in criminology, has pointed out that while Thrasher saw urban gangs "as transitional, interstitial, and marginal groups," those gangs were "not unlike the Chicago sociologists who were trying to establish knowledge about them—and not unlike the human documents that assisted in expanding the boundaries of inquiry" (Bennett, *Oral History and Delinquency: The Rhetoric of Criminology* [Chicago: University of Chicago Press, 1981], 160).

41. Paul Cressey, "A Study of Gaelic Park," 6.

42. Katheryn Fuller reports on several accusations of impropriety made in Chicago against Cressey and his research assistants. These charges made Cressey's candidacy as a PFS researcher problematic, with Charters claiming that Cressey was "someone who had something wrong with him sexually," a perception that may explain the necessity for Robert Park's indirect support of Cressey at the 1930 meeting of the research committee. See Jowett, Jarvie, and Fuller, *Children and the Movies*, 85.

43. Cressey, "The Community—A Social Setting for the Motion Picture," in Jowett, Jarvie, and Fuller, *Children and the Movies*, 156.

44. Georg Simmel, "The Stranger," in *On Individuality and Social Forms*, edited by Donald N. Levine (Chicago: University of Chicago Press, 1971), 143–49. See also Park and Burgess, *Introduction to the Science of Sociology*, 286.

45. Paul Cressey, "A Comparison of the Roles of the 'Sociological Stranger' and the 'Anonymous Stranger' in Field Research," *Urban Life* 21.1 (April 1983): 102–20.

46. "Publicity Hailed as Curb on Movies," *New York Times*, April 8, 1935, 23. See also "Catholics of City to Take Film Pledge," *New York Times*, December 10, 1934, 1, 7.

47. Letter from Thrasher to Wilton Barrett, October 11, 1934. NBRMP, NYPL, Box 45, Subject Correspondence, Frederic Thrasher, 1928–1936, June. Dana Polan has established that the course was advertised in the 1933–34 university catalog, but without NBR involvement. See his chapter on Thrasher's NYU course in *Scenes of Instruction: The Beginnings of the U.S. Study of Film* (Berkeley: University of California Press, 2007), 299–343. Polan demonstrates how Thrasher's pedagogy moved increasingly toward aesthetic appreciation and away from sociological analysis. I am emphasizing the institutional necessity of the latter for the realization of the former.

48. Frederick Thrasher, "Final Outline of the First Term, 1935–36, Course 110, 11, 12," and "Tentative Outline of the Second Term, 1935–1936," NBRMP, NYPL. Box 40, NYU.

49. Frederick Thrasher, "Tentative Outline, Courses 110, 11, 12. The Motion Picture: Its Artistic, Educational, and Social Aspects," n.d. [fall 1934]. NBRMP, NYPL, Box 45, Subject Correspondence, Frederic Thrasher, 1928–1936, June.

50. Thrasher, "Tentative Outline of the Second Term," 2–4.

51. Frederick Thrasher, "Suggestions for Writing a Motion Picture Life History," NBRMP, NYPL. Box 40, NYU.

52. Thrasher, "Suggestions for Writing," 5.

53. Around this time, Burgess also sought to add to the data collected by Cressey and Thrasher on delinquent motion pictures reception when he outlined a proposal to add a motion picture component to three Chicago neighborhood studies being conducted by Clifford Shaw in conjunction with the Behavior Research Fund and the Institute for Juvenile Research. See Ernest Burgess, "Motion Pictures and Delinquency."

54. Thrasher, "Suggestions for Writing," 1.

55. For an analysis of the influence of the PFS on the film education movement, see Lea Jacobs, "Reformers and Spectators: The Film Education Movement in the 1930s," *Camera Obscura* 22 (January 1990): 29–49.

56. Ann Morey, *Hollywood Outsiders: The Adaptation of the Film Industry, 1913–1934* (Minneapolis: University of Minnesota Press, 2003), 180–81.

57. McDermott, *Corporate Society*, 151.

"Reaching the Multimillions": Liberal Internationalism
and the Establishment of Documentary Film

ZOË DRUICK

Every relationship of "hegemony" is necessarily an educational relationship and occurs
not only within a nation, between the various forces of which the nation is composed,
but in the international and world-wide field, between complexes of national and continental civilizations.
— Antonio Gramsci, "The Study of Philosophy"

The contrast is striking between utopian discourse on promises for a better world due
to technology, and the reality of struggles for control of communication devices and
hegemony over norms and systems.
— Armand Mattelart, *Networking the World*

■ Of all film forms, documentary is perhaps the most ambivalently situated
in film studies. Simultaneously inside and outside discourses of film aesthetics, documentary is a marginal genre that is also a mainstay of television fare,
and a truth-telling form whose style can be easily "mocked." Documentary is
at once the type of film most readily associated with Western state education
and the one traditionally championed by oppositional political movements.
"Documentary" potentially refers to so many different things that more than
one commentator has advised jettisoning the name altogether.[1] In any genre,
dominant definitions tend to flatten and elide the tensions and contradictions
that characterize a group of films and the complex practices that shape them. In
this essay I focus on one particular facet of documentary that has great residual

force: the historical formation of documentary as educational cinema in the West between the advent of sound (1929) and the emergence of cinéma vérité around 1960. As part of this study, I will investigate how documentary assumed its ambivalent position in film studies.

Specifically, I will sketch the connections between a Western liberal elite working in the ambit of two international organizations—the League of Nations and the United Nations Educational, Scientific, and Cultural Organization (UNESCO)—and the formation of "documentary" as an educational instrument for modern nation building. This group of educators, civil servants, film producers, and technical innovators were motivated by anxiety about the erosion of culture by modern life. Their work gives us some sense of how the emergence of film was made palatable to a well-educated international elite, a transformation that encompasses both *documentary's* absorption by national educational hegemonies discussed by Gramsci during this period and *film's* subsumption into an international struggle about the role of technology in the formation of political utopias, as Mattelart defines it.

The scope of this study is as potentially vast as its conclusions are preliminary. Nevertheless, it remains important to begin making the historical connections hitherto overlooked between documentary film and educational tasks that might be termed, following Foucault, "governmental."[2] Indeed, the encouragement of citizen formation through the use of film in classrooms as an alternative to Hollywood fare was part of the self-conscious efforts that helped to usher in the documentary film as a form widely studied and used by educators. This makes the form's relative marginality within film studies doubly ironic, given that many of the names associated with documentary's rise occupy central positions in the canons and key institutions of film study, including John Grierson, Paul Rotha, Forsyth Hardy, Iris Barry, Rudolf Arnheim, Béla Balázs, Sigfried Kracauer, Arthur Knight, Roger Manvell, and André Bazin. Thus, the history of documentary film is intimately tied to the history of the field of film study.

The account that follows is neither linear nor univocal; it maps a complicated network of ideas, people, and institutions. Like the wonderful paradox at the heart of documentary's birth—John Grierson coined the adjective "documentary" in 1926 to describe *Moana*, a hybrid documentary-fiction film made by Robert Flaherty for Joseph Lasky at Paramount[3]—what follows rejects the idea that the history of something such as documentary film can de adduced to the genius of just one person. The term "documentary" was rapidly adopted by a wide range of commentators as well as institutions, and clearly it filled a need: it was seen to crystallize an alternative to Hollywood that might be developed outside of theatrical circuits for what were deemed serious purposes. The need for cultural and political opposition to the commercial film industry's overwhelming force was widely considered important. In this sense, the form of documentary may be said to have followed its function.

As would happen later to American political filmmaking of the 1930s, the nonfiction work of artists in various 1920s European avant-garde movements was absorbed and depoliticized by Western governments.[4] Hence the rapid institutionalization of documentary owed a good deal to the political configuration of the interwar period. I have no desire here to overstate the power of these institutions. Rather, against wishful histories that focus on film aesthetics as an autonomous or purely oppositional political category, the liberal bureaucracy that supported documentary film must be seen as a constitutive and normalizing force. It coordinated some interests while suppressing others; it paid lip service to certain ideals, while entrenching far-reaching policy. The byproduct was to forge a common sense about documentary's content and form, yielding lasting effects on film production and film study. Just as Serge Guilbault demonstrates the depoliticized institutionalization of abstract expressionist painting in New York in the late 1940s, the notion of documentary was similarly consolidated, tied to a discourse of neutrality seemingly outside politics.[5] This is not to propose that the League of Nations and UNESCO were fully responsible for creating the official liberal ethos of the documentary tradition. However both organizations provided important institutional spaces for the emergence of discourse about educational film that would set the terms for discussions of documentary—not as film, but as education—for many years to come. Yet even while documentary film was discussed differently from fiction, these discussions and the policies and productions they enabled initiated a widespread international dialogue about film and politics that both included many of the most active film theorists of the day and helped to formulate terms used for the legitimation of film festivals, the construction of national film archives, and the integration of film into education that would have a lasting impact on film studies.

In what follows, I trace the development of film policy and theory in the League of Nations as well as in some of its member nations, primarily Britain. Next, I examine the League's most important contribution to film discourse, the International Educational Cinematograph Institute (IECI). Finally, I consider the legacy of these interwar debates and conventions in the formation and operation of film-related aspects of UNESCO up to 1960, at which point the cold war order began to fray and documentary was taken up and challenged in political ways by an emergent postcolonial Third Cinema movement, as well as by a revitalized Western avant-garde. My aim is to stay away from a technologically determinist story about film, education, and politics. Instead, I try to emphasize the political forces that helped to shape the unpredictable direction of educational documentary film as a core part of liberal internationalist education and cultural policy in this formative period.

The League of Nations and Its Committee for Intellectual Cooperation

Some background on the League of Nations provides context for the use of film in international governance. The League of Nations was established in the wake of World War I to provide a new organ of diplomacy for the six major world powers, also known as the "concert of Europe": Russia, Austria, Germany, France, Britain, and Italy.[6] Not incidentally, the latter four nations, along with the United States, also led the world in the number of theatrical and nontheatrical projection facilities they marshaled.[7] The history of the League is too complex to be completely summarized here. However, the fact that the League was a bridge between nineteenth-century international voluntary organizations and twentieth-century international relations is significant.[8] International organizations proliferated during the nineteenth century, and in 1909 there were 37 intergovernmental organizations and 176 international nongovernmental organizations.[9] Unlike Marxist and feminist internationalist movements predicated on Enlightenment universal humanism,[10] the focus of liberal internationalism was mainly on free trade—both in the economic sphere and in other spheres, which might, as a byproduct, increase trade. Whereas in *The Communist Manifesto* Marx and Engels called for the workers of the world to unite, liberal internationalists had less revolutionary and more pragmatic aims, calling for the international standardization of money, time, weights and measures, and communications infrastructure such as railways and telegraphs. Given the League's consolidation of liberal international principles, it was perhaps inevitable that it would get around to applying similarly instrumental and pragmatic principles to the production and distribution of the new international communication medium of film.

Although the plethora of international organizations was effectively suspended by World War I, the emergence of the League in the immediate aftermath of the conflict consolidated many of the previously amateur and voluntary organizations into the first formal intergovernmental institution. The

League continued to reflect the European character and interests of the earlier international organizations. The United States, which during the war years had made great leaps in many areas of domestic production, including film, refused to participate in the League despite the foundational role of Woodrow Wilson in conceptualizing the organization.[11] Whereas the international organizations of the prewar days reflected European imperial dominance, the pan-European League began to take on the tone of a collective defense against the growth of the United States and, later, the Soviet Union as world powers. In particular, the League idea was taken up with enthusiasm by the governments of Britain and France, two dominant international powers whose empires were beginning to fracture.

At the first meeting of the League in 1919, a proposal was put forward to establish a technical committee for culture such as those being set up in economic and social spheres: child development, international drug and prostitution morality squads, labor (the International Labor Organization), transit and communication, and health and hygiene (especially mental hygiene).[12] In September 1921, the French representative Leon Bourgeois submitted a report on intellectual organization, "urging improved and fuller exchanges of documents in all branches of knowledge and calling upon the League to fortify its ideals through the intellectual life uniting the nations and favor educational enterprises and research study as important influences on opinion among peoples."[13] The result was the 1922 meeting of an international roster of celebrated intellectuals that included such luminaries as Henri Bergson, Albert Einstein, and Marie Curie, as well as Mussolini's minister of justice and public worship, Alfred Rocco.[14] In 1924 the French government, which took an intense interest in its nation's role in international cosmopolitan culture, offered to permanently house the commission in an institute in Paris. By 1926 the International Institute of Intellectual Cooperation (IIIC) had begun operations, associated in the decade to come with thirty-five national groups.[15]

The term "film" quickly became shorthand for a series of things with which the League, in conjunction with modern administered societies, was concerned. Indeed, film seemed to be a technological manifestation of the concerns embodied in each of the committees sponsored by the League, affecting health, morality, social conditions, labor, communication, and the shaping of public opinion. Regulating film through production, censorship, and exhibition became a way to address these larger social issues. Because film was closely associated with education, both formal and informal, it was also soon absorbed into debates about child development and welfare and the burgeoning field of adult or continuing education. Yet discussions of film as a purveyor of knowledge were inextricable from discussions of the medium itself. This perspective was summed up by the German educator Walter Günther: "The educationalist may hope to achieve two things from the film—a new and closer acquaintance with what is known and also fresh knowledge of the film itself. The film becomes more than a means of culture, it is itself educational matter."[16]

League Policy and National Film Policies

Film was seen to be a way to either harm or help youth and, closely connected to this, as a way to protect or erode national identities. Because the profile of its viewers was primarily young and working class, film was regarded as an exceptionally strong social and educational force. In the United States, anxiety about this fact was reflected in a number of developments in the interwar period. The establishment of Hollywood's self-regulatory body (the Motion Pictures Producers and Distributors Association [MPPDA]) in 1922 under the direction of the former postmaster general Will Hays was meant to alleviate concerns about Hollywood film content. The Payne Fund Studies of the 1920s and 1930s examined the effects of movies on children, and the results were widely disseminated. The inauguration of the strict Production Code Administration under Joseph Breen in 1934 was designed to police Hollywood film content during the various phases of production.[17] Religious communities and educators in the United States took their social anxieties out on film.

In Europe such anxieties were manifest in concerns over the erosion of national high cultures. The rapid shift of power in film production and exhibition had been undeniable. In 1914, 90 percent of films shown worldwide were French but, by 1928, 85 percent were American.[18] Having taken over world screens, Hollywood films were seen to be dangerously seductive to populations in both Europe and the colonies. The introduction of synchronized sound in 1929 resolutely ended the utopian discourse of the silent film era, which held that film's predominantly visual character made it a universal art form. According to many commentators, the sound of language worked at cross purposes to the League's universalism and made film "national again."[19] In Europe, the possible influence of American commercial cinema and, later in the decade, Soviet art film, came to be an important motivator for League members in formulating policies for alternative national film cultures as well as film studies.

Initially, at least, film studies was closely associated with government film censorship, as both relied upon cultural authorities to prescreen films to determine quality and appropriateness.

While American film presented a threat to European cultural sovereignty, Soviet film policy and the production of the revolutionary masterworks of the silent period were, for a different reason, important spurs to the film policies of Western countries. The explicitly communist content presented a political threat quite distinct from that of American cinema. By 1925 the Soviet Union was exporting films by Sergei Eisenstein, Vsevolod Pudovkin, Dziga Vertov, and Aleksander Dovzhenko to eager audiences throughout the Western world. These innovative and inspired films could not be dismissed in the way that American films were on the basis of their lack of aesthetic quality. Because of the large number of communist sympathizers in the West, high-quality Soviet film output walked precariously the line between art and politics.[20]

In Britain, film was considered in a variety of official contexts that added a nationalist dimension to the international film work promoted by the League. Film was discussed at the Imperial conferences of 1923 and 1926, and a number of studies of cinema and education were undertaken, such as the "Report of the National Council of Public Morals" in 1917 and James Marchant's 1925 edited collection, *The Cinema in Education*.[21] The establishment of the Empire Marketing Board in 1926 to publicize British products and culture both at home and abroad has been linked to the British government's desire to produce equally distinctive film propaganda to fight the Soviet and American influences simultaneously.[22] In 1927 Britain tabled its Cinematograph Act and in 1930 the Colonial Films Committee, appointed by the colonial secretary Leo S. Amery, reported on the situation in the Dominions with special reference to questions of education, culture, and censorship.[23] Britain still had an interest in maintaining a cultural presence in the colonies and dominions. In 1936, John Grierson, Paul Rotha, Julian Huxley, and Ivor Montagu gave evidence to the Board of Trade in reference to the revision of the 1927 Cinematograph Films Act. These studies and policies most often concerned youth, but they were also directed toward the anxiety about colonial subjects, members of the newly enfranchised working classes, and women. As I show below, the establishment of the British Film Institute was inspired in part by the League's work in film.

How did the League make itself relevant to the various independent governmental activities related to film and culture? On the most basic level, it quickly became a forum for international discourse about cultural film; over time it presented itself as an extragovernmental (and therefore non-self-interested) support for a variety of protectionist and educational film policies mobilized by member nations. The League of Nations itself sponsored three conferences over the course of the 1920s in which film was considered in the broadest possible way.[24] These conferences paved the way for more formal consideration of educational film at an institute established in Rome (discussed further below). The tone for League work was set early on by Julien Luchaire, the director of the International Institute of Intellectual Cooperation. In 1924 Luchaire submitted a report titled "Relations of the Cinematograph to Intellectual Life," in which he asserted that "only the Bible and the Koran have an indisputably larger circulation than that of the latest film from Los Angeles."[25] He tied film to an international humanist project: "This new and extraordinarily efficient instrument of intellectual action is intrinsically international. . . . The mere possibility that the cinema might become a great new universal art should earn it the attention of all who have the intellectual future of humanity at heart."[26] At the Paris congress of 1924, the subcommittee for University Relations adopted Luchaire's resolution to recommend "the organization of an international exhibition of scientific pictures and pictures for other educational purposes, both fixed and moving."[27]

Resolutions with similarly vague humanist principles circulated at congresses on film held in the years to come. For example, at the International Motion Picture Congress, held in Paris in 1926 under the auspices of the International Committee on Intellectual Cooperation, it was resolved that,

> whereas the film could be the source not only of the amusement but also of the culture of the masses, and could therefore serve to bring about a better understanding between the different nations of the world and whereas, by the intermediary of the film, East and West might be brought into contact with one another, since the film is a means of explaining the history, customs and traditions of the different peoples of the world, this Congress recommends that Western films shall portray in a simple, romantic, ethical and entertaining manner the history, culture, science, and powerful industrial development of the Western nations—the heritage of humanity—and that the film should likewise serve to reveal the ancient culture, and all the wonders of the East.[28]

This fundamentally orientalist framework reflected the League's conceptualization of film as an instrument of colonization and promotion of European culture. The emphasis on educational films borrowed from European humanism, a high cultural concept that was seen to be a means of eroding prejudices against film by elites concerned about the destruction of cultural standards by film's popularity.[29]

Once it became clear that film had a part to play in League policy, further conferences refined the discussion about the role of national and educational film. At a 1928 meeting, a resolution was taken to make cinema a more effective form of popular education:

> That the producers of films should make documentary and scientific films as interesting as possible; that public administration encourage either by granting subsidies or facilitating distribution, or by the purchase of collections, the production of those films which for the moment is, and which for some time probably will be[,] less remunerative than the production of amusement-films. That the organizations for popular education by means of the cinema, compose cinema-programmes of proper length, and of sufficient variety, so that the worker may find in them the relaxation which he needs and at the same time the culture which he demands.[30]

In the 1930s, League conferences emphasized the issue of the enhanced training of filmmakers outside of commercial production. The establishment of courses teaching film production in national design schools was encouraged,[31] as was the development of nontheatrical forums for film art: "International stimuli to develop cinematographic art (prizes, scholarships, International Cinema Museum, establishment of film-libraries, catalogues, etc.)."[32]

Even though the United States was officially boycotting the League and its organizations, many Americans were active participants in League initiatives. For instance, Carl Milliken, the secretary general of the MPPDA, sat on the board of the International Institute of Educational Cinematography. William Marston Seabury, an American lawyer and social reformer and one time general counsel to the Motion Picture Board of Trade and the National Association of the Motion Picture Industry, published two books on the topic of international film in the 1920s. In the first, *The Public and the Motion Picture Industry*, Seabury cavils against the low tone of American film products, linking film and the welfare state directly through the notion that like gas, running water, or electricity, film should be considered a "public utility."[33] Seabury distributed the book widely at the League of Nations conference on film held in 1926.[34] His second book, *Motion Picture Problems: The Cinema and the League of Nations* (1929), reviews the American and international responses to Hollywood, maintaining the view that unchecked free trade would be detrimental to international relations. Seabury was certainly not alone in these views. Despite the official American line against participation in the League, in 1934 the American Institute of Cinematography was founded in part "to cooperate with ... the International Institute of Educational Cinematography of the League of Nations and the agencies of the Government of the United States dealing with films and with visual education."[35] Outside of Hollywood, there were many liberal social reformers in the United States who were allied with the internationalist ideology of the League. Alongside government, industry, and educational representatives from Britain, France, and Germany, these social reformers all utilized the League to promote theories of social reform through film production, regulation, exhibition, and preservation policies.

The International Educational Cinematograph Institute in Rome

The International Institute of Intellectual Cooperation was most directly involved with film through its association with the IECI based in Rome (1928–1938). The IECI played a key role in establishing documentary as the preeminent form of educational film. It was under its aegis that Rudolf Arnheim wrote early portions of his influential and canonical book *Film as Art* for a projected encyclopedia of film initiated by the institute.[36] The IECI sponsored a monthly multilingual cinema studies journal, the *International Review of Educational Cinematography* (1929–1934), followed by *Intercine* (1935), both of which were published in English, French, Italian, German, and Spanish. It also formed a substantial library of its film publications collection. Throughout its brief existence, several international film congresses were also realized. The biggest of these, with seven hundred delegates from forty-five countries, took place in Rome in 1934 and was devoted to the topic of educational and instructional cinematography.[37] Spearheaded by Laura Dreyfus-Barney of the International Council of Women, the conference endorsed a declaration that "an entirely free and unencumbered circulation of the largest possible scale, of educational films from one country to another, remains one of the best means to reach the goal of international amity and understanding."[38]

The five volumes of *The International Review of Educational Cinematography* are an important archive of the diversity of writing on educational film during this period. The journal may still be found in many university libraries and it remains a testament to its own goal of producing an alternative international film discourse. Articles by a range of writers—from academics to politicians and technical innovators—debate the role of film in modern life. Protracted studies of the effects of films on children are found side by side with reviews of documentary films, reports on international film conferences, surveys of educational film policies around the world, pragmatic studies on the use of film in programs of workplace efficiency, personal hygiene, and national health, and general philosophical speculation on topics relating to visual education.

In general, articles published in the journal demonstrate the formation of a notion of "documentary" film as "educational." Yet there remain many examples of a wide-ranging debate, illustrating discrepancies among authors' views of film's role in modern life. Claims are made for the special role of women as moral agents and early childhood educators. Women's organizations are frequently linked to discussions of the importance of sober educational films for the young. The journal provided a space for the discussion of the need for teacher training in the use of visual aids, and it advertised university and adult education courses on "cinema culture," such as a proposal by James Marchant to build a "cinema university" in London. A conference titled "The Problem of Cinematograph Archives," chaired by Louis Lumière, was reported on in the February and March 1932 issues. All film-producing countries were encouraged to create national archives and to cooperate in forming an international archive to preserve cinema history, which would include both films and film-related paraphernalia such as projectors and posters. All of these discussions demonstrate a blurring between the desire to integrate film into education and the need to make film itself an object of study.[39]

The journal also catalogued exemplary educational films. The first film produced for the League was *Star of Hope* (1925), a twenty-minute piece on the evils of war and the benefits of the League, which was shown widely to schoolchildren in 1925–26. The film was then remade and expanded in 1926 as *The World War and After*.[40] A 1929 article on the working relationship between the IECI and the International Labor Organization provides a catalogue of educational films relating to "scientific management," many of which are in the collection of the Federation of British Industries. Titles for these obscure films from the 1920s include *Baby's Birthright* (about breastfeeding), *The Magic of Nitrate of Soda*, *Reinforced Concrete*, *Underwear and Hosiery*, *Modern Lighting*, *The Romance of Oil*, *Apple Time in Evangeline's Land*, and *Fresh from the Deep* (on fishing).[41] A film about the eastern opium trade, *Drowsy Drugs*, was circulated to support the work of the League's antidrug squad.[42] Another film, *Motherhood*, received favorable mention for the emphasis it placed on the responsibility of modern women to reproduce. Setting a tone for educational films to come, these short didactic pieces were made to support specific governmental (and intergovernmental) objectives.

As this synopsis of the work of the IECI demonstrates, educational documentary film was closely linked to the development of noncommercial film, both as a form and as a mode of exhibition. The IECI contributed to the latter as well as the former. Although the extent of their participation is hard to discern, members of the IECI sat on the selection committee for the first international Venice Film Festival in 1932.[43] In addition, the journal ran repeated advertisements for the festival and supported its work in a variety of notices and reviews. The Venice festival's fascist and nationalist framework, not to mention its track record of preferential judging, provided a counterbalance to the strong communist film movements of the 1930s, both inside and outside of the Soviet Union. This in turn created the conditions for other European film festivals, such as Brussels (1935) and Cannes (1938), which formed—at least in part—in response to Venice. Whatever else film festivals were to become, they were initially an important strategy for distributing films outside the structures of commercial distribution, and they provided a space in which such films could be seen and discussed.

Fascism, in general, made a more concerted commitment to national culture than did liberalism, and thereby it provided an important motivational force for Western liberals. Italian fascist nationalism, in particular, was an inspiration for emergent forms of British film culture. According to the contemporary writer Amedeo Perna, the British Film Institute (along with other national film institutes) was modeled on the Italian film production unit, L'Unione Cinematografica Educativa (LUCE), established in 1926.[44] Once the BFI was established in September 1933, it became instrumental in centralizing British national film activities by taking over the publication of *Sight and Sound* from the Institute of Adult Education and also publishing *Monthly Film Bulletin*.[45] Moreover, the emphasis by fascist governments on cultural exchange, as evidenced by the film and cultural treaties signed by Germany and her allies, Italy, Japan, and Spain and even France, set the stage for liberal internationalism to make similarly exceptional agreements around the question of culture.[46] While Soviet attention to film experimentation challenged the West to think about film and politics in a new way, the fascist states raised the specter of popular nationalist culture, stimulating liberal states to do the same.

In favoring national participation in international cultural discourse the IECI tacitly supported the establishment of national institutions such as film archives, film societies, and film festivals. At the IECI's initiative, the League was also responsible for the establishment of a significant agreement concerning the international circulation of film, the 1933 Convention for Facilitating

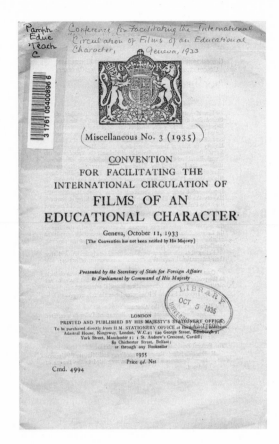

Miscellaneous No. 3 (1935)

CONVENTION
FOR FACILITATING THE
INTERNATIONAL CIRCULATION OF
FILMS OF AN
EDUCATIONAL CHARACTER

Geneva, October 11, 1933
[The Convention has not been ratified by His Majesty]

Presented by the Secretary of State for Foreign Affairs
to Parliament by Command of His Majesty

LONDON
PRINTED AND PUBLISHED BY HIS MAJESTY'S STATIONERY OFFICE
To be purchased directly from H.M. STATIONERY OFFICE at the following addresses:
Adastral House, Kingsway, London, W.C.2; 120 George Street, Edinburgh 2;
York Street, Manchester 1; 1 St. Andrew's Crescent, Cardiff;
80 Chichester Street, Belfast;
or through any Bookseller

1935
Price 4d. Net

Cmd. 4994

The cover of the *Convention
for Facilitating the International Circulation of Films
of an Educational Character*
(Geneva, October 11, 1933).

the International Circulation of Films of an Educational Character. Signed by
representatives of governments from twenty-three states, the Convention ex-
empts from customs duties films intended for use in education and research.
The preamble to this three-year Convention states, somewhat ironically given
the political conflicts that were brewing, that the various representatives are
"convinced that it is highly desirable to facilitate the international circulation
of educational films of every kind, which contribute towards the mutual understanding of peoples, in conformity with the aims of the League of Nations and
consequently encourage moral disarmament or which [sic] constitute especially effective means of ensuring physical, intellectual and moral progress."[47]
Andrew Higson, in his study of the formation of Film Europe in the 1920s,
notes that, as with much of the League's film work, the convention served to
identify international cinema with educational cinema, a move that both ceded
to American pressure for free trade on cultural products and began to eke

out an alternative distribution network for films with national and educational benefits.[48]

Richard Maltby in "The Cinema and the League of Nations" parses the Convention for the contradictions it balances between the free trade agenda of the Americans, a profit-driven strategy, and Europe's attempt to exempt "educational" films, a more liberal project to increase exchange across borders.[49] This desire to placate American trade objectives would continue to shape international policy in the postwar period. National culture and humanism alike were used as framing discourses for policies that were fundamentally about the trade of cultural products. Arguably, the League discussions helped to formulate the language in which culture and politics would be exchanged for decades to come.

The Legacy of the League of Nations

Despite many assessments of the League's futility in dealing with the political unrest of the 1930s, it did not decline into irrelevance in the years leading up to World War II. Indeed some argue that as it became less functional as a political body, it became more successful on the social and cultural front.[50] Even after Italy's withdrawal from the League in 1937 and the closing of the IECI in 1938, the IIIC continued its study of film in a number of conferences and reports, including the 1937 *Report on the League of Nations and Modern Methods of Spreading Information Utilised in the Cause of Peace*. This report, drafted by the British professor Gilbert Murray with input from people as diverse as Germaine Dulac and Edward Murrow, states "the documentary film is one of the best means of information at the League's disposal, provided always that the material is up to the standard of modern technique and kept up to date."[51] The report condones "commercial" films of "high artistic and cultural value" and reiterates the need for national film institutes as "clearing houses" for educational films, especially documentaries on "foreign countries and their folk traditions." Setting the agenda for UNESCO, the report calls for "appropriate colonial films," national film archives, education in film criticism, and support for film clubs, and it endorses the importance of international networks for film organizations. Many of these institutions were already forming and would proliferate in the late 1930s and after the war.

The most lasting effect of the League's work in film was the establishment of the need, if not always the requisite national funding, for catalogues of educational films and the encouragement of film libraries, film archives, and film festivals at the national level. The establishment of the International Federation of Film Archives in 1938 by the Museum of Modern Art Film Library (New York), Cinémathèque Française (Paris), Reichsfilmarchiv (Berlin), and the National Film Library (London), was an international venture to facilitate the sharing of noncommercial films that was very much in the spirit of the League and also directly benefited from the League's established agreements. In their mandate to preserve national film history, these archives provided a material basis for future study, for repertory, and for generating national film cultures, as well as for early studies of "world cinema." In the years to come, educational media in general, and the documentary film in particular, would take on an even more central role in international affairs. The generative seeds laid by the League continued to grow, despite the outbreak of war. Also crucial for what came after World War II was the fact that the League's mechanisms for the international organization of intellectual cooperation provided the groundwork for the fundamental role of culture as part of the United Nations' mandate from the outset.

UNESCO *and Documentary Film*

The United Nations' cultural committee, UNESCO, continued the work of the League's Institute of Intellectual Cooperation in formalizing the place of documentary film in international education and culture. The emphasis by UNESCO on film as a means of "fundamental education" (teaching basic skills of literacy), its insistence that member nations form national commissions, and its cold war strategy of East-West dialogue to dissipate political tensions all had considerable impact on the postwar film landscape. I will focus here on the first fifteen years of UNESCO's existence (1945–1960), in which its activity in film and mass communications was most extensive.[52]

As with the League's continuation of nineteenth-century liberal international projects, UNESCO was a clear continuation of projects and ideas found in the League's Committee on Intellectual Cooperation and other interwar cultural organizations, especially those devoted to education. The preamble to UNESCO's charter claimed a clear place for education, setting out its tendentious syllogism that "since wars begin in the minds of men, it is in the minds of men that the defenses of peace must be constructed." There were other connections as well. Alfred Zimmern, Henri Bonnet, and Gilbert Murray, all prominent members of the League's Committee for Intellectual Cooperation, were involved with UNESCO.[53] The first chairman of UNESCO, the prominent scientist Julian Huxley, had been an early participant in the London Film Society.[54] In 1947 John Grierson, a prominent player in the interwar British documentary film movement, was hired as head of the film division of UNESCO's Mass Communications Department.[55]

One obvious difference between the cultural activities of the League and those of UNESCO was the active participation of the United States. In the interwar period, the United States had resisted explicit participation in the formal structures of the League, partly because of the fact that the output of Hollywood was one of the overt causes of Europe's cultural anxiety. In the late 1930s, the United States changed tack and became a proponent of cultural relations, making activities in the arts and sciences, according to a State Department release, "an integral part of the nation's foreign-policy program."[56] The United States absorbed the moral authority of the League discourse on culture and used it to legitimize American cultural exports, including those from Hollywood.

The name UNESCO reflects the several areas it combined: education, science, and culture. The mass media were at the core of its mandate. The conglomerate name represented international pressures. France wanted to reinstate some version of the Committee for Intellectual Cooperation and insisted that if *intellectual* were unacceptable, then at least *culture* be included in the title. Significantly, while the UN set up headquarters in New York, UNESCO continued the tradition of housing the cultural organization in Paris. The Allied ministers of education, who had been meeting in Britain since 1942, insisted on the word *education*, which the United States initially opposed. Meanwhile, the International Council of Scientific Unions pushed for inclusion of the term *science*. The Americans pressed for the emphasis on popular education and ordinary people rather than advanced scholarship or science. As a predominantly educational medium, documentary films were understood as a superior method by which to showcase national cultures through popularizing scientific and social science observations. As such, documentary film uniquely embodied each of UNESCO's defining terms.

Film and other media were granted a central role in the new organization's sprawling mandate. In reporting on the first meeting of a planning commission for an educational organization, the political scientist Ritchie Calder situates the integral role of mass media in connecting the mandates of the organization: "It was obvious . . . that the liveliest concern of the nations was less with the E and the S and the C of UNESCO than with the invisible hyphens between them — the films, the radio, and the press. They are the means of popular expression of all three, Education, Science, and Culture. While their instruments and techniques can be adapted to the classroom and laboratory, their main interest to UNESCO is their use, for good or ill, in reaching the multimillions. . . . UNESCO, if it is to achieve its objects, has to claim and hold the interest of a world-audience before it can indoctrinate."[57] This notion of media as the "hyphens" connecting people to ideas as well as to each other is a succinct restatement of the American position on film and other media in the postwar world as the paramount means of popularizing their own ideas. As one commentator put it in 1947: "To drop the mass communications activities would be for UNESCO, and for the United Nations, to turn their backs on one of the greatest, potentially most useful and most dangerous centers of force in the modern world. It would mean the renunciation of a world mission for the agency and its parent body. Since the forces of the mass media are so unmistakably both international and supernational in character, an attempt to harness and use them is an unavoidable function of a world agency which pretends to concern itself with the forces which make for war and peace."[58]

With the establishment of national television broadcasting in the postwar period, documentary's star continued to rise: in the classroom, at film festivals, and on the airwaves into living rooms. And still, the meaning of documentary continued to expand. In 1948 the World Union of Documentary defined the genre as "all methods of recording on celluloid any aspect of reality interpreted either by factual shooting or by sincere and justifiable reconstruction, so as to appeal either to reason or emotion, for the purpose of stimulating the desire for, and the widening of[,] human knowledge and understanding, and of truthfully posing problems and their solutions in the spheres of economics, culture, and human relations."[59] Clearly, documentary was still functioning as a category of difference from the artifice and amusement that Hollywood had come to represent (although even Hollywood made a turn toward documentary realism in this period). Films about everyday life were described as documentaries. In 1946, as Hollywood aggressively fought to get its films into the theaters of every nation through the argument that any restriction on the free flow of information was tantamount to fascism, UNESCO tacitly supported a range of alternative spaces for film.[60] Following up on the work of the League, UNESCO sponsored an agreement for facilitating the distribution of educational films and audio-visual materials, thus maintaining the complementary circuits for noncommercial cinema that the League had established.

Film festivals burgeoned throughout this period.[61] Those such as Venice that

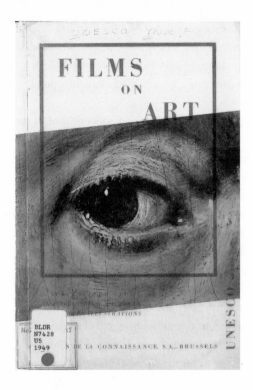

The cover of the inaugural *Films on Art* catalogue (1949).

had ceased during the war now recommenced. New festivals began emerging all over Europe, with some taking over where film societies had left off: Cannes, Berlin, Venice, and Edinburgh were some of the most high-profile venues.[62] For many festivals during the 1940s the dominant concern was realism. The Edinburgh Film Festival, after picking up the war-interrupted work of the London Film Society in distributing noncommercial film, began in 1947 with a mandate as a primarily documentary festival.[63] Venice, which had acted as a "joint Nazi-Fascist celebration" during its last years (1940–42) was reinstated in 1946 with a new policy of giving "exceptional attention to artistic, cultural and scientific documentaries."[64] As a result the Italian neorealist films became the darling of film festival audiences and critics alike.[65]

Following the example set by the League, UNESCO continued to craft a template for national media and cultural policy. Yet, as with the League, UNESCO struggled to accommodate American free trade and free flow policies. Through the General Agreement on Trade and Tariffs (1947), the United States lobbied against what it termed "trade barriers to knowledge,"[66] an effort resisted most vehemently by France.[67] Whereas the League encouraged the establishment of national committees, UNESCO made them a prerequisite of membership. As with the League, UNESCO did not attempt to provide a supranational site of media production so much as to orchestrate a symphony of quasi-independent national commissions.

Some of the film-related projects with which UNESCO was engaged in the 1950s include the organization of conferences and even the production of films. *The Task Ahead* (1951) was a 16mm documentary, released in eight languages, on the activities of UNESCO.[68] Starting in 1951, UNESCO coordinated the international annual meeting for the study of ethnographic films, which brought together experts to discuss subjects such as the place of the filmic reconstruction and the role of entertainment in ethnography.[69] In addition, UNESCO encouraged cooperation between "films and television at the international level" at a series of conferences held in 1955 through 1957. As part of the Major Project on the Mutual Appreciation of Eastern and Western Cultural Values (the East-West project), UNESCO coordinated international exchanges between organizations of creative producers, teachers, and philosophers and released a film, *Orient-Occident: Images d'une exhibition*, which was exhibited at Cannes in 1960.[70] Recommendations were made to set up international clearinghouses of films and other materials to share information about different nations and civilizations,[71] and UNESCO also sponsored the publication of film catalogues such as *Films on Art* (1949).

Although UNESCO did not sponsor a single institution on the scale of the IECI, immediately following the war it did underwrite an extensive series of media studies. The first of these was an in-depth analysis of media resources in countries whose infrastructures had been affected by war (1947); subsequent editions extended this evaluative work to "underdeveloped" nations.[72] If media were to serve as the "hyphens" of the new information order then networks had to be in place. This effort was followed by a series of publications released under the rubric of *Press, Film and Radio in the World Today*, which began appearing in 1949. Demonstrating a profound belief in film as a tool of modern education, the studies include *Use of Mobile Cinema and Radio Vans in Fundamental Education* (1949), *The Entertainment Film for Juvenile Audiences* (1950), *The Film Industry in Six European Countries* (1950), and *Professional Training of Film Technicians* (1951). The studies highlight the use of film to modernize national cultures by either former colonial powers or national government representatives. The preamble to the series justifies the need to examine media in

Daylight mobile cinema van (with shaded screen) in use in Turkey. (*The Use of Mobile Cinema and Radio Vans in Fundamental Education*, UNESCO, 1949)

An amphibious cinema developed for use in tropical areas by the Bell Division of the Thomas de la Rue Company. (*The Use of Mobile Cinema and Radio Vans in Fundamental Education*, UNESCO, 1949)

the modern world as a matter of national public policy: "Surveys of the press, film and radio in the world have shown that side by side with purely material needs, which are linked up with the economic and technical development of each country or region, there exists a wide need for knowledge of the use that can be made, and the abuses that must be avoided, of these powerful means of reaching the mind, and of influencing the opinions and the way of life, of modern man."[73]

Throughout the 1950s, UNESCO published a series entitled *Reports and Papers on Mass Communication*, many of which concerned film as an educational tool. From *Bibliography on Filmology as Related to the Social Sciences* (Jan Bouman, Institute of Psychology, University of Stockholm, February 1954) to *The Kinetescope and Adult Education* (Joffre Dumazedier and Barbro Sylwan, 1958) to *Film Production by International Co-operation* (edited by H. J. L. Jongbloed, 1961), these publications enlisted international experts in the field of film and popular education. Rather than fund film education or production directly, UNESCO continued in the tradition of the League by restricting its influence to applying international pressure to establish national educational and cultural organizations with international standards. In creating forums such as publications and conferences, as well as endorsing educational and film exchanges and film festivals, UNESCO continued the work of accommodating commercial cinema by creating a nonthreatening and ostensibly nonpolitical alternative.

The rift created between education and entertainment films in the late 1920s grew wider as documentary was institutionalized throughout the 1950s. By this point, educational films had been relegated to nontheatrical circuits so as not to compete with entertainment films. They were made with the aim of citizen building, with monies provided by government agencies, schools, churches, industrial sponsors, and community groups. In order to be deemed acceptable to the international conventions and trade regulations that had been negotiated to accommodate cultural concerns during the 1920s and 1930s, they acquired a certain style. Filmed in the nonstandard and nontheatrical 16mm format, these films were short, low-budget, and clearly identifiable in both form and content as national and didactic. The need for a substantial number of educational films in the postwar world meant the standardization and economizing of the pedagogical documentary. Documentary's status as a nonartistic, predictable form of education was cemented; resistance, in the form of direct cinema and mock documentary, would follow soon after.[74]

Conclusion

In this essay I have sketched some of the ways in which two major twentieth-century organizations of international relations have been important contributors to the establishment of the documentary form of educational film and the naturalization of a national framework for film studies. In these organizations' emphasis on national (film) culture within an international community, they gave international endorsement to the idea of national film societies, film journals, film schools, film prizes, film archives, and film catalogues. Through their international trade policies, they also directly helped to affect some of the ways in which both noncommercial and documentary films were distributed. Both organizations placed a great emphasis on film education in its connection to educational film. A byproduct of this emphasis on education by means of film was the emergence of significant discourse on educational film, which was to be instrumental in establishing the standardization of documentary film as short, national, and didactic. Whatever their direct effect, the League's Committee for Intellectual Cooperation, the IECI, and UNESCO were undeniably important organizations for encouraging the thinking and writing about film as an indispensable "visual sensory aid" for modern life.

Finally, and perhaps most important, these organizations helped to push issues about education and film into an institutional setting where, for better or worse, they gained the credibility required to emerge as a fully fledged area of study. The fact that by means of institutions of international relations the banal and instrumental documentary film was forged out of the exciting nonfiction work done in the European avant-garde movements during the 1920s is an irony of film history that remains to be fully savored. In any case, writing about film and education associated with the League and UNESCO merits further attention as utopian discourses thoroughly enmeshed in the hegemonic political struggles underway in the first half of the twentieth century. The development of documentary film's hegemonic form seems to have been the result, in part, of extensive international theorizing on techniques of education in a polarized international context and a new commitment by Western elites to administer mass liberal democracy.

Notes

1. John Corner, "Visibility as Truth and Spectacle in TV Documentary Journalism," in *Moving Images, Culture and the Mind*, edited by Ib Bondebjerg (Luton, U.K.: Luton University Press, 2000).

2. See Graham Burchell, Colin Gordon, and Peter Miller, eds. *The Foucault Effect: Studies in Governmentality* (Chicago: University of Chicago Press, 1991); and Zoë Druick, "Documenting Government: Re-examining the 1950s National Film Board Films about Citizenship," *Canadian Journal of Film Studies* 9.1 (spring 2000): 55–79.

3. Richard Barsam, *The Vision of Robert Flaherty* (Bloomington: Indiana University Press, 1988), 28.

4. For further discussion, see Charles Wolfe, "The Poetics and Politics of Nonfiction: Documentary Film," in *Grand Design: Hollywood as Modern Business Enterprise*, edited by Tino Balio (New York: Charles Scribner's Sons, 1993), 351–86; and Bill Nichols, "Documentary Film and the Modernist Avant-Garde," *Critical Inquiry* 27.4 (summer 2001): 580–611.

5. Serge Guilbaut, *How New York Stole the Idea of Modern Art* (Chicago: University of Chicago Press, 1983).

6. J. P. Dunbabin, "The League of Nations' Place in the International System," *History* 78.245 (October 1993): 422.

7. *International Review of Educational Cinematography* 4.3 (March 1932): 306.

8. Martin H. Geyer and Johannes Paulmann, "Foreword," in *The Mechanics of Internationalism: Culture, Society, and Politics from the 1840s to the First World War*, edited by Martin H. Geyer and Johannes Paulmann (Oxford: Oxford University Press, 2001), v.

9. Clive Archer, *International Organizations*, 2nd ed. (London: Routledge, 1992), 13–14.

10. Geyer and Paulmann, "Editors' Introduction," in *The Mechanics of Internationalism*, 13.

11. Carol Fink, "The League of Nations and the Minorities Question," *World Affairs* 157.4 (spring 1995): 197–98.

12. Geyer and Paulmann, "Editors' Introduction," in *The Mechanics of Internationalism*, 14.

13. Malcolm W. Davis, "The League of Minds," in *Pioneers in World Order*, edited by Harriet Eager Davis (New York: Columbia University Press, 1944), 242.

14. Harold Greaves, *The League Committees and World Order: A Study of the Permanent Expert Committees of the League of Nations as an Instrument of International Government* (London: Oxford University Press, 1931), 118.

15. League of Nations, "International Committee on Intellectual Cooperation," C.I.C.I. 156 (1). Geneva, December 8, 1926.

16. Walter Günther, "Cinematography and Culture," *International Review of Educational Cinematography* 3.4 (April 1931): 324.

17. Douglas Kellner, "Hollywood Film and Society," in *The Oxford Guide to Film Studies*, edited by John Hill and Pamela Church Gibson (New York: Oxford University Press, 1998), 354–64; Leonard J. Leff and Jerold L. Simmons, *The Dame in the Kimono* (New York: Grove Weidenfeld, 1990).

18. Stephen Crofts, "Reconceptualizing National Cinema/s," in *Film and Nationalism*, edited by Alan Williams (New Brunswick, N.J.: Rutgers University Press, 2002), 26.

19. G. Moulan, "The Cinema and International Amity," *International Review of Educational Cinematography* 4.12 (December 1932): 908; see also "Art Technique and the Internationality of the Sound Film," *International Review of Educational Cinematography* 4.12 (December 1932): 958–59.

20. See William Alexander, *Film on the Left* (Princeton, N.J.: Princeton University Press, 1981), 9; and Jonathan Buchsbaum, *Cinema Engagé: Film in the Popular Front* (Urbana: University of Illinois Press, 1988), 24.

21. James Marchant, ed., *The Cinema in Education* (New York: Arno Press, 1978 [1925]).

22. Margaret Dickinson and Sarah Street, *Cinema and State* (London: British Film Institute, 1985), 27.

23. Ibid., 47–48.

24. For a complete discussion, see Andrew Higson, "Cultural Policy and Industrial Practice: Film Europe and the International Film Congresses of the 1920s," in *"Film Europe" and "Film America": Cinema, Commerce and Cultural Exchange, 1920-1939*, edited by Andrew Higson and Richard Maltby (Exeter, U.K.: University of Exeter Press, 1999), 117–31.

25. Quoted in William Marston Seabury, *Motion Picture Problems: The Cinema and the League of Nations* (New York: Arno Press, 1978 [1929]), 236.

26. Seabury, *Motion Picture Problems*, 237–39.

27. Ibid., 263.

28. Ibid., 361.

29. Eva Elie, "The Reign of the Documentary Film," *International Review of Educational Cinematography* 4.5 (May 1932): 348.

30. Twenty-third resolution of the third commission, in Seabury, *Motion Picture Problems*, 368.

31. Ibid., 377–78.

32. Ibid., 379.

33. William Marston Seabury, *The Public and the Motion Picture Industry* (New York: Macmillan, 1926), 160–70.

34. Alvin LeRoy Bennett, "The Development of Intellectual Cooperation under the League of Nations and United Nations" (Ph.D. diss., University of Illinois, 1950), 23.

35. John Eugene Harley, *World-Wide Influences of the Cinema: A Study of Official Censorship and the International Cultural Aspects of Motion Pictures* (n.p.: Jerome S. Ozer publisher, 1971 [1940]), 213.

36. The encyclopedia was incomplete when the institute folded in 1935. "The articles written in 1933 and 1934 in Rome for the projected *Enciclopedia del Cinema* are printed here for the first time," Arnheim wrote in the 1957 edition of *Film as Art* (Berkeley: University of California Press, 1966 [1957], 1). See also Elaine Mancini, *Struggles of the Italian Film Industry during Fascism, 1930–1935* (Ann Arbor, Mich: UMI Research Press, 1985), 123.

37. Harley, *World-Wide Influences of the Cinema*, 234.

38. Ibid.

39. "The Problem of Cinematographic Archives," *International Review of Educational Cinematography* 4.2 (February 1932): 94–96; Walter Gunther, "The Cinematographic Archives of the City of Berlin," *International Review of Educational Cinematography* 4.2 (February 1932): 97–106; "Towards the Creation of an International Cinema Archives," *International Review of Educational Cinematography* 4.4 (April 1932): 303–4; "Cinema Aesthetics," *International Review of Educational Cinematography* 4.7 (July 1932): 55–64.

40. C. M. Wilson, "The League of Nations on the Screen," *International Review of Educational Cinematography* 2.6 (June 1930): 717.

41. "The Cinema as an Auxiliary to the Scientific Organization of Labour," *International Review of Educational Cinematography* 1.3. (Sept. 1929): 338–41.

42. "'Drowsy Drugs': Educational Film," *International Review of Educational Cinematography* 4.11 (November 1932): 883.

43. Flavia Poulon, "History," in *Twenty Years of Cinema in Venice*, edited by Antonio Petrucci (Rome: International Exhibition of Cinematographic Art, 1952), 17.

44. Amedeo Perna, "The State and the Scholastic Cinema," *International Review of Educational Cinematography* 6.4 (April 1934): 221.

45. Dickinson and Street, *Cinema and State*, 52.

46. Harley, *World-Wide Influences of the Cinema*, 262–63.

47. *Convention for Facilitating the International Circulation of Films of an Educational Character (1933)*, (London: His Majesty's Stationary Office, 1935), 2.

48. See Higson, "Cultural Policy and Industrial Practice."

49. Richard Maltby, "The Cinema and the League of Nations," in *"Film Europe" and "Film America*," 99.

50. Martin David Dubin, "Transgovernmental Processes in the League of Nations," *International Organization* 37 (summer 1983): 492.

51. League of Nations, *Report on the League of Nations and Modern Methods of Spreading Information Utilised in the Cause of Peace* (Geneva: A.18, 1937), 8.

52. More could be written on the role of UNESCO with regard to film production and film culture after the 1961 emergence of the Non-Aligned Movement by leaders of twenty-five newly independent nations in Africa, Asia, and Latin America and the

relationship to emerging Third Cinema discourse (William Preston, Jr., Edward S. Herman, and Herbert I. Schiller, *Hope and Folly: The United States and UNESCO 1945–1985* [Minneapolis: University of Minnesota Press, 1989], 295).

53. Jan Kolasa, *International Intellectual Cooperation: The League Experience and the Beginnings of UNESCO* (Warsaw: Prace Wroclawskiego Towarzystwa Naukowego, 1962), 158.

54. See Jamie Sexton, "The Film Society and the Creation of an Alternative Film Culture in Britain in the 1920s," in *Young and Innocent? The Cinema in Britain 1896–1930*, edited by Andrew Higson (Exeter, U.K.: University of Exeter Press, 2002), 293.

55. Jack C. Ellis, *John Grierson: Life, Contributions, Influence* (Carbondale: Southern Illinois University Press, 2000), 229.

56. "Proposed Educational and Cultural Organization of the United Nations: Draft Constitution and Explanatory Statement Issued by the Department of State," *International Conciliation* 415 (November 1945): 730.

57. Ritchie Calder, "UNESCO's Task," *Political Quarterly* 18 (April 1947): 132–35.

58. Brian Dexter, "UNESCO Faces Two Worlds," *Foreign Affairs* 25.3 (April 1947): 402.

59. Cited in Richard Barsam, *Non-fiction Film: A Critical History* (New York: Dutton, 1973), 1.

60. Herbert Schiller, "Genesis of the Free Flow of Information Principles," in *Communication and Class Struggle. Volume 1: Capitalism, Imperialism*, Edited by Armand Mattelart and Seth Siegelaub (New York: International General, 1979), 345–53.

61. Julian Stringer, "Global Cities and the International Film Festival Economy," in *Cinema and the City: Film and Urban Societies in a Global Context*, edited by Mark Shiel and Tony Fitzmaurice (Oxford: Blackwell, 2001), 135.

62. "After the war, no-one felt the need to revive [the film society] — its work was done. As [Ivor] Montagu remembered in 1975, 'there were fewer unshown worthwhile films to hunt. Already the last two seasons before the end had cut down the regular eight performances to six. What need of the Film Society when so many of its aims had been attained, so many reinforcements had arrived to take over?' The BFI, the NFA, the BFFS, the emerging film festivals had all taken up the banner" (quoted in British Film Institute. *The Film Society, 1925–1939*. Guide to Library Information Services/Special Collections, No. 1. London: British Film Institute).

63. Forsyth Hardy, *Slightly Mad and Full of Dangers: The Story of the Edinburgh Film Festival* (Edinburgh: Ramsay Head Press, 1992), 7.

64. Poulon, "History," 30.

65. See, most famously, André Bazin, *What Is Cinema?*, 2 vols., translated by Hugh Gray (Berkeley: University of California Press, 1967).

66. Julian Behrstock, "The Free Flow of Information: UNESCO's Programme and Methods," *UNESCO Chronicle* 11.3 (March 1956): 83.

67. Jean-Pierre Jeancolas, "From the Blum-Byrnes Agreement to the GATT Affair," in

Hollywood and Europe, edited by Geoffrey Nowell-Smith and Stephen Ricci (London: British Film Institute: 1998), 47–60.

68. *A Chronology of UNESCO, 1945–85* (Paris: UNESCO, 1985).

69. UNESCO *Chronicle* 3.12 (December 1957): 333.

70. UNESCO *Chronicle* 6.6 (June 1960): 243; UNESCO *Chronicle* 3.11 (December 1957): 302–3.

71. UNESCO *Chronicle* 3.12 (December 1957): 338–39.

72. UNESCO, Department of Mass Communications, *World Communication: Press, Radio, Film* (Paris; UNESCO, 1950); UNESCO, Statistical Division, *Film and Cinema Statistics: A Preliminary Report on Methodology with Tables Giving Current Statistics* (Paris: UNESCO, 1955).

73. Robert W. Desmond, *Professional Training of Journalists* (Paris: UNESCO, 1949), 5.

74. Even Alain Resnais's *Hiroshima Mon Amour* (1959), a film initially funded with international money to be a documentary about the anniversary of the bombing of Hiroshima, contains a self-conscious reference to a UNESCO-type film: the seemingly incomprehensible "peace" film that the actress is purportedly in Hiroshima to make. As John Francis Kreidl put it, "*Hiroshima* turned out to be a film about the impossibility of making a documentary about Hiroshima" (Kreidl, *Alain Resnais* [Boston: Twayne Publishers, 1977], 54).

Young Art, Old Colleges: Early Episodes
in the American Study of Film

DANA POLAN

■ The title of this essay paraphrases a headline—"Young Art, Old College"—
that ran in the *Boston Transcript* in April 1927 to announce two events at Harvard University: the conclusion of a lecture series by luminaries of the film
industry as part of a business policy course in the University's School of Business and the announcement of an annual award to the best American films
to be sponsored by the Fine Arts division. Through its headline, the Boston
newspaper set out to indicate as noteworthy the fact that the most seemingly
venerable of American educational institutions had welcomed into its hallowed
halls the new cultural form of the movies. Significantly, though, the *Transcript*
was reporting on this conjunction of modern popular art and academic tradi-
tionalism as a *positive* step—a laudable means by which a university founded
on classical precepts could keep up with the new concerns of twentieth-century
modernity. Harvard was welcoming the movies into its midst, and this was
presented as a good thing.

Harvard was not, moreover, alone in this respect. From 1915 on, a number
of colleges and universities tried to introduce film courses into their curricula.
Paradoxically, one of the most curious aspects of the initial entrance of film
study into institutions of higher learning in America is that it seemed not to be
curious to most people at the time. Quite the contrary, there was little outcry as
film courses entered into the system of higher education as it was constellated
early in the twentieth century.

To be sure, it is easy to overestimate the significance of the fact that a few scattered film ventures found a home in some institutions of higher learning in the first decades of the century. For instance, for all its initial promise, the Harvard initiative didn't go very far. With financial support promised by Joseph P. Kennedy, who was using the School of Business lecture series to network among industry leaders and gain prestige for himself as a budding film producer, administrators at Harvard had hoped that a course on the business of film would become a regular part of the curriculum. But when Kennedy decided to leave the film business, and consequently seemed to have no further interest in such a course, his withdrawal of financial aid meant that administrative interest in film pedagogy began to wane. There would be no follow-up to the 1927 offering.

Up through the 1930s, pedagogy about cinema—whether as a cultural, social, or economic phenomenon—was sketchy and somewhat random. Not merely should we not overestimate the significance of any particular venture—such as Harvard's ill-fated plans around film in 1927—but we should also avoid imagining that the scattered array of initiatives around film pedagogy formed any sort of discipline of film made up of common methods, common objects, and common purposes. Nonetheless, the varied and random attempts to imagine that film might serve as object for academic attention are significant in their very randomness. That is, the lack of consensus about the ways to study film and, more than that, the lack of any dialogue among academic institutions out of which such consensus might have grown, means that we can find in these early ventures a range of possible ways in which film was imagined to be an object worthy of study. For example, the Harvard initiatives themselves—a lecture series centered on the *business* of film, along with awards and archive activity centered on the *art* of film—suggest that academic interest in film could range from the moment of production (film as a result of industry) to that of reception (film as a result of an act of appreciation by the spectator). These might easily have constituted different paths toward film study. But as different as these approaches were, it is noteworthy that, as the *Boston Transcript* announcement of them as a joint enterprise bears witness, Harvard saw them as conjoined. There was a link between the business of film and the awarding of cultural distinction among films. As I show later in this essay, this assertion of film as both commerce *and* art could have its advantages. If, for example, for the School of Business the paramount concern was to promote rationalized training in commerce, especially in light of business-community suspicion of academic intrusion in its practical endeavors, then a no less important concern was to show the academic community that the professionalization of business did not have to involve the surrender of traditional academia's concern with humanities and aesthetic value. To the extent that film, so obviously the product of business, could also be demonstrated to offer artistry and uplift, it might serve as a propitious mediator of the various missions of the university between spiritual quest and practical service.

It may be a bit misleading, then, to assert—as I have done in the subtitle of this essay—that the early history of film pedagogy occurred as a series of disparate and isolated *episodes*. It is true, like the Harvard initiative that began with great fanfare only to die out quickly, that very few of the beginning ventures in cinema study endured to create direct legacies for later academic work in the area. True, too, most of the early enterprises were undertaken with little interaction with, or even acknowledgment or awareness of, what was being attempted elsewhere around film in the academy. Endlessly, in fact, many of the early professors of film declared themselves to be the first in the field often in blithe or deliberate ignorance of earlier attempts.

But for all their disparateness, randomness, and isolation from each other, the various attempts to constitute film as a legitimate object of study appear to derive from common wells of inspiration. Here, film's potential role in the Harvard initiative as a mediator of art and commerce provides the important clue. How to maintain moral and aesthetic value in the machine age was a central intellectual dilemma of the American university as it entered the twentieth century, and while some traditional humanists tried to confront that dilemma by a fervent fetishizing of the past, others moved more directly into modernity and tried to find a bearable path within it. Film might be attacked by the traditional intellectual, but it might also be welcomed by a new sort of academic cultural custodian who would see that its status as an art of mechanical reproducibility posed an interesting challenge: if a product of the machine age could be found to offer something more than crass standardization—if from within mass production aesthetic value could be born—then there would be every possibility of humanism and aestheticism showing that they had their necessary, inevitable place within modernity.

Perhaps the most striking example of such an early attempt to make film serve the higher humanistic mission of the university by employing it as a mediator of the practical and the spiritual came from a surprising direction. In 1937, a proponent of great books education, Scott Buchanan, was asked to come up with a plan for the transformation of a failing liberal arts college, St. John's in Annapolis, Maryland, into the first modern academic institution to base its curriculum directly on the canon of great books. Buchanan imagined a curriculum wherein all students would read the same works at the same moment in their education, starting with the Greek classics and moving up through a predictable succession of dead white males that constituted the standard canon of great names. Stunningly, Buchanan also argued fervently that a great books curriculum should be capped by a pedagogy in film. In a long study, "In Search of a Liberal College: A Program for the Recovery of the Classics and the Liberal Arts" that was supposed to serve as the blueprint for St. John's, Buchanan called for the establishment of an Institute of Cinematics that would offer both practical work in filmmaking and instruction in film aesthetics and appreciation.[1] He argued pointedly that film was an appropriate culmination of a great books curriculum, and he even declared film to represent the synthesis of the impulses and ideas that ran through the great humanistic tradition. If the great books moved knowledge into the realm of spirit, the fact that cinema was an art requiring very practical labor—all the techniques and chores of filmmaking—meant that it caused abstract notions to be regrounded in worldly activity. The lessons of the great books would thereby be given relevance and made pertinent to the everyday tasks of the modern world. Simultaneously an art and a set of practical techniques, cinema represented a mediation of the mental and the manual fully appropriate to the contemporary world. Significantly, Buchanan proposed that the famed sociologist of the machine age, Lewis Mumford, be recruited as director of the Institute of Cinematics. Buchanan declared that he had found in Mumford's major opus of the 1930s, *Technics and Civilization*, which included discussion of the beauty that the mechanical art of cinema could produce, an inspiration for his own understanding of cinema as a cultural form that reconciled the practical and the philosophical. Buchanan's was a grand scheme in which the canon of great books found its triumph in the popular art of film.

To be sure, like other initiatives around film, Buchanan's Institute of Cinematics never was put into practice, but its very existence even as a dream is a useful indication of the extent to which even the most seemingly traditional of academic ventures could seek to come to grips with the mass culture of cinema.

The episodic early history of film study is, then, one in which a series of instructors attempted to find a pedagogy adequate to the new demands of a modernity marked not only by massification but also the possibility of resonant mass culture.

What were these early efforts in film pedagogy? First, starting in the middle of the first decade of the twentieth century there was an ongoing course in photoplay composition in Columbia University's extension program, which was taught initially by Victor Freeburg and then by Frances Taylor Patterson. The specific placement of that course in an outreach program for nonmatriculating students meant that the course would hover at the edges of the standard curriculum. Likewise, when in 1926 Terry Ramsaye presented a general survey of film history and aesthetics at the New School for Social Research, his offering was also noncredit and constituted more of an evening lecture series for purposes of cultural enrichment than a bona fide course. More rigorous and more academically promising in fact was a deeper version of the New School course offered by Harry Potamkin in 1932, but Potamkin's early and tragic death cut short that pathway into a serious study of film.

Three initiatives relating to for-credit instruction had longer staying power, however, and they demonstrate that major universities early on found places for film. First, the University of Southern California entered into an agreement with the Academy of Motion Picture Arts and Sciences to develop a program of professional instruction in film as a means of training industry practitioners. The USC/AMPAS initiative began in 1929 with a survey course in which luminaries of the industry lectured on their business. The success of this course led to an expansion of the curriculum, and by 1932 USC was offering the first bachelor's degree in film. However, there were conflicts over the purpose of the degree. Clearly, the original intent had been to develop a professional program serving the industry. But for credential purposes the university had been forced to appoint a traditional academic with a doctorate to head the program, and the available choice, a sociology and comparative literature professor named Boris Morkovin, wanted the program to be less utilitarian and more fully integrated around liberal arts mandates. The USC program thus remained torn between goals of practical training in film production and more abstract instruction in film appreciation/history/analysis until World War II resolved the issue by making it necessary for a film program like that of USC to devote itself to practical issues of instruction in filmmaking in the service of the war effort.

A second initiative found its home at Syracuse University where a theater arts professor, Sawyer Falk, began offering a course in his department in Cinema Appreciation (and did so until his death in 1961). Falk's concern was to establish film as an independent art form—not only independent of other arts such as literature or drama but also even of narrativity. Falk was a strong proponent of abstract or pure cinema. His course was filled with analysis of the medium-specific techniques of film such as montage and dynamic composition. Falk is rare among the early film professors in elaborating so complete an aesthetics of film as an art in its own right, but off in the western reaches of New York state his one course on film could not really serve to establish a general *discipline* of film studies. His greatest influences on the field would be indirect: one of his first students was the future great figure of the American avant-garde, Maya Deren. It seems that Deren did take from Falk's class a devotion to an idea and ideal of cinema as an independent art form in its own right.

Another course based in New York also dealt with the art of cinema. At the beginning of the 1930s in New York University's School of Education, Frederick Thrasher started teaching a media effects course that focused on film as one of the most socially consequential of popular communication forms. Thrasher's concern with the social impact of movies—something he had already dealt with in his 1920s doctoral thesis on leisure and juvenile gangs—was widely known and respected. This led to his recruitment by the organizers of the Payne Fund Studies—that infamous attempt by religious leaders and moralizers to turn to university professors for media effects research that would (so they hoped) provide concrete and academically legitimated proof of the deleterious effects of the movies. Thrasher, however, came increasingly to see no direct and inevitable causal relationship between film viewing and delinquency. Quite the contrary, he began to believe that film could be used as a form of social good, and his media-effects course mutated into one that combined the study of the social impact of film with the aesthetic *appreciation* of it. Again, however, the impact of Thrasher's course was limited. In this case, the fact that the course found its home in NYU's School of Education meant that it did not have the same visibility that film appreciation courses would have later (in, say, the 1960s) when they began to sprout up in humanities areas.

Although these early and sporadic investments in film instruction did not soon coalesce into a discipline with rules, rituals, and transmittable canons of knowledge, they did show that there were conditions under which academia accepted the viability of film instruction. Far from appearing as a scandalous turn of events in which a low art assailed the heights of academic respectability and profound mission, film instruction came quietly but steadily into academia. At the very least, we need to realize that the increasing bureaucratization of higher learning—the multiplication of divisions and departments and the corresponding fragmentation of oversight among a variety of managers (deans, department chairs, etc.) delegated by the central administration—meant that ventures that did not necessarily fit the mainstream of canonic notions of education could still sneak by at the margins. In a famous phrase from his classic history of the modern American university, Laurence Veysey notes that "the university throve, as it were, on ignorance"—by which he means that the new bureaucratic structure could work only if centralizing forms of administration came to know less and less about everything that was being done at the university. It may well be the case that film could enter the academy precisely because of its marginal status, shrouded as it was in ignorance of a very fundamental sort.[2] Offered in the nether region of extension programs, noncredit lecture series, and professional divisions that were removed from the mainstream humanistic mission of institutions of higher learning, film courses came into existence and, in some cases, endured likely by exploiting the benign neglect that frequently results from bureaucracy.

It is striking to note the extent to which in the beginning decades of the century various institutions of higher learning readily absorbed into their curriculum attention to the new cultural form of cinema (and, as we see, "absorb" is a good word to describe the ease by which film found its way into academia since the bureaucratic structure works by benign accretion). It is especially noteworthy that the academic sites that most welcomed film were often those seemingly staid institutions that we most associate with the Ivy League.

For example, Harvard University—seemingly the most venerable and even staid of academic institutions—welcomed cinema into its halls in a big way. From March to April 1927, the Harvard School of Business (hereafter HSB) hosted the aforementioned series of lectures by top luminaries of the American film industry. Will Hays, Jesse Lasky, Adolph Zukor, Cecil B. DeMille, William Fox, Marcus Loew, and Harry M. Warner, among others, each came to talk on the business of film in a special version of the HSB's required upper-class course on business policy. But for one letter of protest from a Boston schoolteacher imputing a lack of morals in some of the invited speakers and a crazed rant from the Payne Fund proponent William Seabury, the lecture series appears to have caused no outcry or sense of scandal that a staid and traditionalist institution of higher learning was opening its doors to the serious study of the entertainment industry and a form of popular culture. Rather than controversy, there was, at the very least, an acceptance of the fact that popular culture could have its place in a university world.

Elsewhere I trace out the details of early film courses, like that at the HSB, and I establish much of their curricular content.[3] Here, I want to pinpoint the preconditions in early-twentieth-century higher learning that enabled such courses to come into being: Just what epistemological presuppositions were necessary for American academia to entertain the idea that cinema could be a legitimate object of study?

Given our standard conception of the history of higher education in America, the early entrance of film into the academy might at first seem surprising. In the "culture wars" of the 1980s, neoconservatives relied in large part on a narrative that imagined the early history of academia as a golden age of devotion to high culture with no place for the scandalous corruptions of mass entertainment. Theirs was a jeremiad that critically took our contemporary moment to represent a fall from the great ideals of the past. Predictably, the neoconservatives tended both to imagine that the emergence of popular culture study was a recent phenomenon and that it came as a dangerous detour from the humanities curriculum's true and traditional devotion to a great tradition of high literature and art.

The neoconservatives perceive, and lament, an ostensible lack of rigor that besmirches academia when it becomes caught up in "fads" of theory, postmodernity, and popular culture appreciation. But they themselves demonstrate a lack of rigor in the very ways they fictionalize American culture and education's historical trajectory. For example, against their bad historiography, Lawrence Levine's research on nineteenth-century cultural production and reception in the United States trenchantly showed how everyday life and leisure necessarily revolved around a blend of seemingly high and seemingly popular cultural forms in ways that make the very distinction between the forms a tendentious and anachronistic projection from the values of a later period.[4] In rewriting the past to their own advantage, the neoconservatives give evidence of their own relativistic disrespect for historical record.

A useful corrective to the neoconservative jeremiad about an academic golden age fallen into mass cultural decadence is the English professor Gerald Graff's genealogy of his discipline, *Professing English: An Institutional History*. In this volume a number of Graff's points provide a context for understanding how film, like the modern literature that Graff deals with, could find a place in early-twentieth-century academia.[5] To begin, Graff challenges the assumption that American higher learning was in its very foundation establishing doctrine devoted to the teaching of a great tradition imagined as a radiant fount of higher value (and in challenging this, Graff by extension then also challenges the narrative that sees later academic history as a reaction against great tradition). In nineteenth-century colleges, for instance, classic books were studied not for their messages, themes, artistry, and so on. Instead, in an academic system dominated by grammar, rhetoric, and logic, great works were studied simply as examples incarnate of well-shaped discourse. Nineteenth-century higher education was driven by a philosophy of "mental discipline": the mind had to be taught the hard work of logical thinking, and the study of well-honed literary language could aid in this instruction. Consequently, there was a strong emphasis on memorization, language drills, sentence parsing, grammatical declension, and so on. There was little concern for great books as repositories of humanistic value, other than the value of good grammatical form. Classic works were examined formally as grammatical structures whose slow and careful study encouraged a salutary self-discipline. The supposed golden age of the great tradition did not recognize the same sort of greatness that later writers attribute to the works of the so-called great tradition.

Several implications follow from this, as Gerald Graff notes. First, to the extent that the modernizing curriculum in the first decades of the twentieth century served as a revision of older academic tradition, what was being revised was not a great tradition imagined to be aesthetically superior to the mass culture around it. Rather, the so-called great tradition concentrated on a set of dry texts assumed to be of interest primarily as examples of rhetoric, logic, and grammar (the famous trivium of classical education) and not as embodiments of any deeper and radiant humanism. At the very least, a revisionist attention to something else — modern literature, everyday culture, problems of contemporary society — was thought to be more exciting and beneficial to learning insofar as its content and teaching was less caught up in dull memorization, rote analysis, formal detail, and so on. In this respect, it is interesting to note that, when Harvard introduced film into its business school curriculum, some of its press releases lauded the ways in which such a contemporary topic could help revitalize a moribund curriculum and make Harvard seem up to date and in touch with the modern age. Here, too, there was recognition that a modern subject matter could revitalize staid academia. (Of course, as today's film professors are aware, cinema studies are still often welcomed as a "sexy" topic that invigorates older programs and boosts enrollments.)

And here we touch upon a second implication in the very way that the modern university regarded the classical curriculum and sought to bring it into line with the needs of a modern utilitarian society. Insofar as the so-called great works were studied not for any ostensible aesthetic greatness but for their formal nature as logical structures whose rigorous study could encourage "mental discipline," there was always the possibility, as Graff notes, of imagining that any work — whether classical or not, whether canonic or not — could fit the bill as an object of study. In other words, to the extent that what the mental discipline tradition called for was the study of grammar, rhetoric, and logic, and the technical ways in which works were put together, there was no need to limit the study to supposed great works. The study of any well-constructed work, classic or not, could fit the bill. In the latter part of the nineteenth century, there were claims, for instance, that modern languages demanded as much effort, as much "mental discipline," as the classical languages of Greek and Latin and could lead to the same overall benefits for the mind.[6]

In an important way, the notion of "mental discipline," for all its original designation as a skill to be inculcated in a ruling class granted its title through imperious legacy, already contained within it the seeds of modernity that anticipated the new context of the twentieth century. In particular, the concomitant notions that texts were to be studied for their formal structures *and* that such study granted students the skills useful in their management of the social world easily fed an established American pragmatism. After all, the study of rhetoric and grammar—even in its most classical manifestations in nineteenth-century American education—was fundamentally technicist, and thus easily could fuel the modern American investment in engineering and craftsmanship. Sentence parsing, for example, was a concrete and immediate skill, and the assumption of the philosophy behind the idea of "mental discipline" was that this skill could usefully be applied to other arenas of social life than the merely linguistic. Seemingly a spiritual alternative to the utilitarian bent of the twentieth century, nineteenth-century classical education actually left much of the concern with spirituality behind and flowed easily into the modern age with its go-getter emphasis on utility.

Now, obviously, the first instruction on film in the American university does not transfer nineteenth-century procedures of mental discipline to this new art form in any direct or literal fashion. The first courses on film did not, for instance, offer an equivalent of sentence parsing by elaborating models for close textual analysis of cinematic works. This would come systematically into film analysis only later—in the semiotic and structural moments of film studies. In this respect, film represented an object of study for the early twentieth century that was somewhat different from the modern literary works studied by Graff that, at the very least, shared the medium of written language with Greek and Latin and that could be broken down easily into their constituent parts. But the idea, underlying the philosophy of "mental discipline," that one hones skills of interacting with the world by pragmatically taking apart an object of study, easily found in film a propitious example of such an object. Indeed, in the books of cinema's first professor, Victor Freeburg, we can find a certain degree of close engagement with the textual makeup of film in ways that resemble grammatical and rhetorical analysis. In, for instance, his first film book, *The*

Art of Photoplay Making, which served as the standard textbook for Photoplay Composition even after Frances Patterson took over the course, Freeburg called for detailed study of film's visuality in both its static and kinetic aspects. Whether the idea of "composition," and of the photoplaywright as composer, took inspiration from music or from literature (and in fact Freeburg did use both arts as an analogy for cinematic creation), the impulse behind the notion was the insistence on film's constructed and authored nature—constructed and authored at the level of individual shots as well as their arrangement into larger narrative form. Freeburg even hinted at an understanding of cinema as a linguistic medium that could potentially inscribe film analysis in the grammatical tradition of mental discipline. In Freeburg's words,

> The cinema composer ignores word language and uses instead the language of countenance and mien, the language of aspect and bearing and demeanour, of gesture and movement, the language of inanimate objects, of furniture and setting, of position and grouping and physical circumstance, the language of light and shadows, and the magic of mechanical devices. This new language has syllables and phrases of a new texture. And the artist writer who would rise above mediocrity must combine these syllables and phrases so deftly that among and beneath them may be found a treasure trove of subtle suggestion, of things unformulated and unexpressed which shall quicken and vivify the imaginations of the multitudes of grateful spectators.[7]

Several aspects of this description of cinema as a form of writing—and of the cinema composer as a type of writer—are worth noting. First, the very comparison of cinema to a language with syllable- and phrase-like components that build up into an overall texture inscribes cinema as merely the latest part of a longer cultural history. Cinema becomes a new manifestation of classic literary arts (rather than their betrayal or bastardization). Second, the emphasis on individual grammatical elements that can be composed into an overall texture enables an understanding of film as a humanly constructed form, a built thing. Third, and consequently, there can be the possibility of film *study*—of an articulated investigation of the art—insofar as cinematic works can be analyzed into their component parts and insofar as the logic of their composition can be specified. Fourth, moreover, the very reach of film—the multitudes of those grateful spectators—may make it even more important a language to learn than the literary languages of the past. And in this respect, not merely can film be studied but it must be studied. It is too consequential a part of democracy to be left alone. And it can be studied not only in its effects, in its resonances for spectators, but also in its making. Not for nothing is Freeburg's *The Art of Photoplay Making* both a guidebook in film appreciation for potential spectators *and* a manual of instruction for potential filmmakers. At Columbia, both Freeburg and Frances Taylor Patterson taught the circulation of film from production to consumption as a singular process in which each phase flowed into the next and in which instruction in any one phase would offer practical tools for intervention at other stages in the process.

And in suggesting that spectatorship and cinematic composition alike were active skills that could be learned by students, Freeburg and Patterson participated in a very American and very modern concern to valorize arts of making (as the very title to Freeburg's *The Art of Photoplay Making* itself implies). Even more than the great books of the past, film presented the advantage of requiring mental *and manual* discipline in a direct, emphatic fashion. After all, even more than literary works—which could still be imagined as organic unities generated from the inspiration and intuition of creative artists—film was from the start a technically complex object, one whose very creation required both a considerable amount of skill and a sizable degree of material provision. Film was a tool-heavy form of production, mechanically and technologically dependent in a way foreign to literary creation. Made through systematic, complex, and concerted material effort, films were the perfect pragmatic object. Given the extent to which it was both labor intensive and technology intensive, film was a quite appropriate object for a mode of study that was concerned with the appreciation and analysis of human achievement in crafting things. Insofar as it resulted from precise procedures of construction, the built object that is a movie was propitious for mechanically inclined and pragmatic analysis.

It is appropriate, for instance, that one of the very first instructors of a film course in American academia—Frances Taylor Patterson, who, as noted above, took over the "Photoplay Composition" course from Victor Freeburg in 1917—wrote a manual (used also as a textbook) for photoplay writing with the title *Cinema Craftsmanship.* "Craftsmanship" is indeed a word that circulates widely through the first decades of the twentieth century, referring to a seemingly indigenous American concern with skilled acts of making, with a manual labor that is overlaid with mental talent and insight. (In Thorstein Veblen's influential texts of the time the comparable word is "workmanship," and it signals a pride in creation—a sense of the job well done and not given over to the empty ostentatiousness of conspicuous consumption.) Revealingly, while Patterson's teaching clearly intended to help those students who were specifically searching for a profession in film, she also assumed that there were educational advantages to the study of film even for those students who did not plan to work in the film industry. To the extent that films exhibited a constructedness that could be broken down into its constituent elements, film study could teach generalizable skills that would be of value even for students whose interest in film specifically was only nominal.[8]

Here, we might remember that the very idea of "industry," as Raymond Williams's investigations of key words in our culture remind us, had originally to do with personal capability in work, a capacity for creation that was fully localized in the individual person.[9] Patterson wanted to inculcate in her students a useful industriousness, whether or not they would end up in the film industry. Interestingly, in her efforts to promote a know-how set of skills in her students, and in her specific promotion of photoplay composition as a meritorious and trainable talent, Patterson frequently contrasted industry at the personalized level to industry as the activity of organized businesses (the American motion picture industry, for example). The individual, according to Patterson, needed to eschew industry in this larger sense in order to find a fully personalized industriousness. The title of Patterson's book indicates another key facet of her approach to teaching film. The term "photoplay *composition*" radiated her conviction that the writer rather than the director or producer was a total artist, properly in charge of composing film narrative, visual style, and tone alike. Patterson frequently pictured the film business as a force of the miscomprehension of, and crass resistance to, the fundamental artistry and personal skill that went into cinematic invention. For her, the personal talent that is required for making a well-shaped photoplay or simply for appreciating the construction of one is a bulwark against the crush of commercialism. In this way, Patterson's investment in the teaching of photoplay composition inscribes her in that modern antimodernist strain in early-twentieth-century life that T. J. Jackson Lears delineated in his classic *No Place of Grace: Antimodernism and the Transformation of American Culture, 1880–1920*.[10] For Lears, the onslaught of modernity—of increasing urbanization, massification, technologization, and so on—resulted in a number of artists, intellectuals, and cultural producers turning to a mythic past in which they imagined that older, simpler, and purer virtues could be cultivated. One form of this antimodernism was the reinvigoration of an arts and crafts tradition in which people could ostensibly discover anew the values of direct creation and of their own capacities of inventiveness in an age increasingly given over to the alienation of Fordist production. In these terms, photoplay construction can be seen as an act of deep-felt personal composition. Its skills were also those that enabled the individual to navigate modernity while never losing sight of pride in one's own work, thus valorizing the act of writing as a source of profound value. From one perspective, instruction in the mechanics of the contemporary art of cinema was in its own way modernizing. For example, as Mark Lynn Anderson shows in his essay in this volume, the sociological study of film in the late 1920s and early 1930s was a means by which professional academics like Frederick Thrasher at NYU could update their careers to the needs of the modern age. The content of the instruction that these film academics enacted offered students a way to negotiate a modernity that was increasingly mass mediated. But the case of Patterson shows that even though her course dealt with a very contemporary cultural and technological form — the machine art of cinema — film study was also in key ways backward looking, tapping into a very American nostalgia for the simplicity of a time in which citizens could be veritable pioneers who would hew their own artful constructions from the raw material of their experience.

Contrary to the view that America is preeminently a pragmatic nation, much of the act of making and doing that its citizens engage in has been nonutilitarian. That is, it has often been the case that craftsmanship in the American context has been valued for its own sake rather than for any imputed usefulness of the things crafted. America is a country of tinkerers, gadgeteers, and hobbyists who labor away at gizmos that are often beautiful objects in their own right but that have little value other than the admirable labor that went into them. Is there anything more quintessentially American than the Rube Goldberg device — that great gadget in which a complicated set of operations are undertaken to achieve the most banal of results? The device fascinates in and of itself, embodying an excess of engineering skill over any use to which that skill may be employed.

This curiously nonutilitarian pragmatism that underlies the American obsession with craft can help explain two important aspects of a photoplay course such as Patterson's and of the many other screenwriting courses conducted by mail that proliferated in the private sector throughout the 1910s and 1920s. First, as Kristin Thompson's studies of continuities in screenwriting pedagogy over the decades remind us, there is the clear acknowledgment in so many screenwriting manuals of a debt to Aristotelian poetics.[11] Here, the important inspiration is not merely the specific form of plot construction — the logical conjoining of beginning, middle, and end to create meaningful and consequent narrativity — but the very fact of construction itself. Aristotelian poesis bequeaths to aesthetic inquiry a fundamental concern with art as something made, crafted, and put together as an activity of engineering rather than brought into being by magical fiat or divine inspiration. The photoplay courses of the 1910s and 1920s do at times make reference to some ultimate and ineffable talent that one either has or not; but, more often, they emphasize that writing derives from hard work, careful application of rules, and a rigorous appreciation of the pieces that go together to make up a well-shaped narrative. Second, there is in many of the photoplay writing manuals a noteworthy admission by the instructor that the pedagogy provided within the lessons is no guarantee of success in the film industry. On the one hand, such caveats no doubt had an immediate legalistic side to them: the schools did not want to find themselves in the position of promising more than they could deliver. On the other hand, there was a more theoretical and positive justification for not guaranteeing photoplay writing as an automatic path to pecuniary success. The philosophy of craftsmanship that underlay so many courses in areas of personal creativity meant that the first benefit to be had from such courses was its refining and honing of craft skills independent of any ulterior motive or even immediate financial gain. Again, it is worth noting that Frances Patterson assumed that not all of her students would become photoplaywrights—or even had such a career in mind by taking her course. Yet she did assume that her course would provide skills that could be transferred in myriad arenas of social life.

In *Professing Literature*, Gerald Graff notes one essential restriction on the idea that the close study of any humanly created object whatsoever provided beneficial forms of mental discipline. Specifically, even as it moved beyond the nineteenth-century canons of classic Greek and Latin texts, and even as it opened up to the study of contemporary texts, the modern university of the early twentieth century nonetheless still required that these less venerable works be in their own way classical—that is, perfectly shaped, harmonious, and balanced models distinguished by decorum, evident structure, graceful symmetry, and so on. Of necessity, the philosophy of mental discipline could be extended to modern works only if they maintained many of the qualities of classicism that the old classics possessed. To put it bluntly, the modern work was always in danger of being too modernist and thus not serving as a viable model of textual perfection.

As Graff thus notes, academic literary study had a hard time finding a place for high modernism and for the experimentation that seemed beyond the sway of grammatical rules. As he puts it in a discussion of the period from 1915 to 1930: "Though 'contemporary literature' was coming to mean two different kinds of things depending on whether 'highbrow' or 'lowbrow' taste was at issue, most professors distrusted both kinds—popular entertainment for its superficiality, the more serious literature for its immorality, materialism, and pessimism. The issue was not whether the literature was contemporary so much as whether it reinforced traditional literary idealism—as less and less current literature seemed to do."[12]

It might be thought that a double suspicion of this sort against modern culture as either too lowbrow or too highbrow would have caught film, as well as modern literature, in a catch-22 of pedagogical inadequacy. Film, after all, was an eminently modern form, one distinguished moreover by divisions between popular entertainment and aspirations toward art. But I want to suggest that for the modern university at the beginning of the twentieth century, cinema could be distinguished from modernist literature in ways that rebounded to the benefit of those pedagogues who wanted to make a place for film as a teachable subject.

Here, an important clue is provided by the fact that when Harvard University announced its 1927 initiatives to welcome film into the academic context, part of the plan included setting up an annual award for best films specifically centered on *American* works. Film's first advantage over literary modernism, then, was that it did not bear the taint of European culture—of a supposedly decadent, effete, even corrupt culture that traded classical harmony for brooding psychologism, cynical relativism, sickly perversity, and so on. Film was not predominantly part of high modernism. To the extent that the movies could be claimed as quintessentially American, they would serve well as a mark of the country's achievement of a valid, vital indigenous art.

It is not insignificant, then, that the very first large-scale survey course on film offered in an American institution of higher learning was that of the historian Terry Ramsaye since he was in many ways one of the key proponents of a specifically Americanist view of cinema history. Ramsaye's twelve-lecture series, "The Motion Picture," offered at the New School for Social Research in fall 1926 appears to have been designed as a promotional tie-in to his massive and massively influential history *A Million and One Nights*, which also appeared that fall. The breakdown of the course, as listed in the New School catalogue, shows that it was very much a condensation of the overall argument of Ramsaye's book. In *A Million and One Nights*, Ramsaye presented film as the ultimate folk art and structured his history within a multiply overdetermined evolutionary framework. There was first of all the evolution of the arts out of an original primitive wish to commemorate pleasurable experience through representational means. For Ramsaye, the history of the arts was primarily the history of progressive refinement—for example, the addition of kinesis to static imagery—of the means of representation in order to make that commemoration all the more potent. Film bypassed the abstractions of words to offer the immediacy of images, but it also bypassed the stasis of drawings and photographs in order to make visuality come alive. For Ramsaye, the evolution of human communication had involved the passage through a stage that we might call, to use a famous phrase, a "dissociation of sensibility." If primitive culture could realize its wishes in the immediacy of action (for example, the caveman who acted on his desires), then subsequent human history had driven a wedge between desire and enactment. For example, the evolution of language might enable new modes of communication, but it also led to indirection insofar as words bore merely a symbolic, ersatz relationship to the things they set out to represent. In its immediacy and vitality, however, film could restore the sensibility that had been dissociated by the abstractions of the verbal. For Ramsaye—and here his theory of visual communication bears interesting comparison with his contemporary Sergei Eisenstein—the cinema was an authentically folk art insofar as it spoke directly in the visceral language of affective inner speech.

But this conception of the large-scale evolution in the mission and medium of the arts in which Ramsaye imagined cinema to be the ultimate realization of an age-old wish was concretized in a second level of evolution, one as much geographical as temporal. For Ramsaye, the history of film is specifically also a movement from Europe to America (and then from East Coast to Hollywood) as filmmakers firmly anchored in the purity of the American new land came to realize cinema's popular potential outside of European refinement. America's pioneer trajectory is replayed in the history of its industry, which moves West to discover fundaments of land, action, direct energy, and vitality. This westward evolution is then itself mimed in the evolution of Ramsaye's own writing. If early chapters of A Million and One Nights give attention to European inventors, then bit by bit they are edged out of the narrative. The bulk of Ramsaye's book is given over to odes to the great American figures, from Thomas Edison to Adolph Zukor, who realize cinema's essential popular and populist potential. Although Ramsaye is at pains in the first pages of A Million and One Nights to give recognition to European inventors and budding film experimenters like Méliès, the evolution of his own tale progressively edges out all but the Americans, and it ends up writing the teleology of an essentially U.S.-governed destiny of cinema.

Here, we can return to the HSB course on film to suggest that it too offered a potentially effective context for understanding and promoting a specifically *American* art of cinema. Off in the land of the Boston Brahmins and of the New England Transcendentalists (who were the figures incarnate of America's "coming of age") and away from the New York melting pot of European-influenced modernisms, Harvard stood for American solidity and tradition. Harvard could venture into new areas of study, but it could do so only from a base point of departure that signaled a fundamental respectability.

Certainly, that film would be studied in a School of *Business* as a commercial product like all others might be taken to mean that there would be no particular endorsement of movies as art. Quite the contrary, in fact, Harvard boldly embraced the idea of film as art. Many of the luminaries from the film industry used their lectures, in fact, to emphasize that theirs was a special commodity distinguished by qualities of aesthetic uplift. In this view they were encouraged by the MPPDA director Will Hays who, along with Joseph Kennedy, was one of the prime instigators of the course and, as such, considered it a public relations mechanism by which film would benefit from Harvard's attention. As Hays saw it, obviously there would be the general legitimation that would derive from the very fact that an Ivy League institution found film an acceptable object of study. But this overall legitimation would gain in detail if it could be shown that film needed to be studied not just as any object of contemporary culture but one of special merit.

Harvard, too, would benefit: if it could be shown that the film industry differed from other American businesses to the extent that its individual products stood out by virtue of aesthetic value (rather than, say, utilitarian ones), then the HSB would be demonstrating its civic ability to cultivate business practice as something worthy in higher, cultural terms. This notion was important to the HSB, which had been caught up in a legitimation crisis of its own. From its founding in 1908 as a branch of the school's Arts and Sciences division, the HSB had to fight for respect from traditional academics who felt that professional training might corrupt the higher mission of the university. On the other hand, the school also required respect from business people who might assume that university education was too abstract and theoretical to have any purchase in the "real world."

Fittingly, the film industry speakers within the HSB course themselves endlessly emphasized that they were doing more than producing a commodity like any other. With whatever degree of honesty, they imagined the cinema as a valuable mass art: valuable both because it was an elevated aesthetic form and because it reached many people. For example, as Jesse Lasky put it in his talk on production problems: "We have a peculiar industry. I call it an industrial art or rather an art industry, for I always put the art first and I am always going to."[13] To be sure, it is not necessary to assume that the studio executives necessarily believed in their own paeans to cinema's potential for uplift. Clearly, there were public relations advantages to be gained for them by these claims of aesthetic value. Their statements of moral responsibility and aesthetic uplift became part of a public record about the cinema that was manifest in their lectures, the newspaper reports about them, and also subsequent publications such as the book-length transcription of the entire lecture series. The inner beliefs of the executives ultimately mattered less than did the regularities of the discourse that they helped construct and that they used to perform a specific image of cinema as art.

In speaking of film as art, the luminaries sought to gain a quite specifically cultural "cultural capital": they created an image of their work as one of value and special merit. But the benefit went also to the HSB and, beyond it, to Harvard. In fact, we might suggest that as an object of study the cinema actually contributed in its own way to the educational mission of the university. First, at a moment when even the most venerable of institutions of higher learning were being forced to demonstrate their relevance to the professional and practical issues of the modern age—rather than to luxuriate in an increasingly outdated commitment to a classical education centered on the great books—the cinema brought a certain hipness, a certain newness, to the academic environment. Endlessly, the carefully orchestrated press releases published in numerous periodicals at the time of the HSB course laud the fact that the oldest of academic institutions would be studying the youngest of arts. Second, by offering a course in the *business* of film that was inextricably linked to awards for the *art* of film, the HSB could claim its own commitment to issues of aesthetic value while not having to deal with them in its own area of specialization. That is, the HSB could maintain its image as a training ground for cool-headed professionalism while accruing an important veneer of cultural sophistication. In this way, the HSB might mediate the contrary criticisms that it faced in its early years. On the one hand, intellectuals committed to the older notion of the university as above professionalism had attacked the HSB as a crassly pecuniary betrayal of the university's essential and disinterested humanistic mission.[14] On the other hand, businesspeople had been wary of the HSB because they worried it might be too intellectual, too disinterested, and not able to bring down to Earth the abstractions of the ivory tower. In combining art and commerce, creativity and practical craftsmanship, cinema was the perfect mediator.

To be sure, what was to be mediated was a vulnerable and volatile coalition of diverse forces—the film industry, the HSB, and the higher university administration—each with their own needs and interests. And each of these forces was itself torn by contradictory impulses and ideologies. There was no guarantee that the mediation of art and industry, academia and popular culture, would work. So many elements in the equation were fragile. For example, as the American studies scholar Michael Augsburger suggests for the specific case of the business culture in the 1920s—and as is also suggested by the broader theorization by the American studies scholar T. J. Jackson Lears of the new entrepreneurial culture of the time—there was always a set of tensions and risks in the drive to argue the higher aesthetic values of business.[15] An example of such tension was the idea that the need to cultivate refinement might lead to an impression of feminization, which then might sit uneasily with the sense that business required forceful figures of effective masculinity. Thorstein Veblen provides a further case. Even as he argued for workmanship and personal investment in craft as an alternative to the alienations of mass production, Veblen also—in his infamous critique of "conspicuous consumption"—inveighed against craft that became too caught up in aesthetics for its own sake, thereby sacrificing virile utility for useless ornament. Yet he also attacked the university for sacrificing higher value to mere pecuniary advantage. There needed to be a careful mediation of—or balance between—work as pragmatic and work as aesthetic. Too much of the former led to crassness and an image of the market as a Hobbesian battle for personal financial benefit; too much of the latter led to inefficient waste and fears of feminine passivity in which inactive aesthetic contemplation took precedence over active doing. As Michael Augsburger states in reference to *Fortune*, a magazine for businessmen that was as much about the aestheticized lifestyle that could and should be cultivated as about specific strategies for immediate business profit, "The magazine offered business people art that was neither aristocratically anticommercial nor professionally exclusive. It stressed instead experience, objectivity, and pragmatism—the values of business—and expressed each of these values in opposition both to what Luce called 'significant snobberies' of outmoded aristocracy and to the intellectualism and self-exclusion of academics."[16]

And in this respect the movies as American art may have offered similar values. To refer to Augsburger's terms, they too "stressed instead experience, objectivity, and pragmatism." The movies may not have been as much a form of high culture as other ventures in art (whether cinematic or otherwise) but that might have been their advantage. They avoided the associations that European art had with elitism, dilettantish connoisseurship, even overly refined and overly civilized aestheticism. Like the case studies addressed in the HSB business policy course—in which pragmatic solutions were sought for concrete problems—American movies offered hard-hitting narratives in which strong-willed heroes faced adversity and used resilience to triumph. Movies and business practice were both offered up as seductive stories of American accomplishment.

But the very tensions in such projects may have made them vulnerable to the vagaries of history. For example, in Augsburger's account the fragile and risky linking of business and aesthetics in the 1920s came apart in the moment of the Depression. If the liberal approach to business as an activity that added quality to life was intended to revise a stereotype of industry as cutthroat competitiveness, the Depression resurrected business practices of rivalry and self-interestedness. The idea and ideal of business as an aesthetic realm and as a site in which personal aggrandizement would give way to beneficent cooperation fell apart. As Augsburger notes, *Fortune* soon gave up on its attempts to elevate cultural taste and increasingly devoted itself to extolling the colder virtues of naked profitmaking. Likewise, what might have seemed an appealing mediation of art and commerce to the Hollywood industry luminaries in 1927 may have appeared more to them as a dispensable luxury just a few years later. For the next decade at the very least, there would be no further ventures by the film industry into the hallowed halls of the Ivy League.

Eventually, and perhaps inevitably, the alliance of industry and academia came undone. For instance, while it is clear that the HSB hoped the course would continue (and hoped as well to have industry support for it), it should be as clear to anyone who knows how Hollywood functions that there was every probability that industry support would soon vanish. It has been a regular and recurrent aspect of the fraught history of Hollywood's interaction with academia that promising initiatives die out. Indeed, it is often the case that the important thing is not the fulfillment of an initiative but its mere announcement. Just as the signing of a deal is news in Hollywood and can make (or break) a career, so too is there cultural capital to be gained in the simple declaration of a will to ally with academia. In this respect, it may well be the case that, for Hollywood at least, the HSB course did not need to continue beyond 1927. To take just one example, Joseph P. Kennedy had clearly used the course as a way both to give himself legitimacy as he began a film production career as head of a somewhat lowbrow studio and to network with more established industry heads who themselves would be grateful to him for the chance to have spoken at Harvard. But within only a few years, Kennedy had gone as far as he wanted in the world of film. He both left that business and became unavailable to the Harvard administrators who had been promised his support. For all its promise, the HSB course would also be one that established no disciplinary legacy.

The success of early film study—the easy entrance of courses into the academy, the extent to which such courses fit a panoply of Americanist needs around curriculum at the beginning of the century—was also then its failure. The beginnings of the American study of film were the mere stutterings of a field that had not yet found its voice. But if the Harvard case suggests that we need to be attentive to local and contingent issues—such as the withdrawal of financial support—that spelled failure for this or that initiative, it is also the case that there were broader structural factors that linked the diverse ventures in film in their moments both of success and of failure. For instance, where the Harvard initiative turned out to be a one-shot deal, a number of the other courses, such as Patterson's at Columbia or Falk's at Syracuse or Thrasher's at NYU did endure and took up a regular place in their university's curricula. These courses benefited from the increasing bureaucratization and curricular expansion of the modern American university, which meant that any singular venture could always find a safe harbor somewhere in the vast complexity of university curricular structure. But the benefit was a limited one: certainly, the individual and isolated course offerings of Falk or Thrasher or Patterson might enter in the academy without outrage or outcry, but in exchange they were often met with that neglect or ignorance that Laurence Veysey sees as central to modern university operation.

Here, we might note one of the key conclusions of Graff's *Professing Literature*: namely, that curricular innovation in the twentieth-century university came to be dominated by a model of simple accretion in which new courses were to be added on with little overall discussion by the university as a whole of the implications of this form of slow, additive expansion. For Graff, accretion allowed the modern university a way to innovate and to invigorate curricula. But it also meant that the university would change bit by bit and without larger dialogue on the meanings of that change. Accretion allowed film courses to enter quietly into the academy, but it also meant that the impact of such courses—whether positive or negative—would be relatively muted.

But beyond the structural factors of the university as a benign and expansive bureaucracy, there were other extra-academic cultural factors that may have prevented the early film courses from coalescing into a full-fledged discipline of film study. Throughout this essay, I've been arguing that, however different their individual concerns, the diverse film courses taught between 1910 and the late 1930s shared an Americanist ethos of craft as the union of mental and manual discipline and of popular culture as a potential mediation of art and commerce. As the case of Scott Buchanan's proposal for an Institute of Cinematics as the capping stone for great books education most boldly shows, these decades offered the possibility of alliance between high and popular culture, between literary art and visual expression, and between works of spirit and works of everyday practicality. And although it is beyond the specific concerns of this essay, it might be worth noting that the 1930s were also the culmination of an ideal and an idea of a common culture — or what Michael Denning has referred to as the "cultural front" in which artists and critics saw the arts along a continuum so that high art and modernist experimentation could find compatibility with democratic popular culture across a range of media forms.[17] The analysis of film could flourish in such a context.

But it may also be the case that as the decade of the 1930s drew to its end, the alliance of popular culture and high culture came apart. A growing chorus of cultural critics began to see in mass culture a cause of the problems of massification rather than the popular or populist crafting of innovative answers to it. One important signpost was the widely discussed 1939 essay by Clement Greenburg, "Avant-Garde and Kitsch," where the then-still-Marxist art critic turned against Stalinist-realist popular aesthetics to argue for anti-representational art as the only effective political art. Another signpost was Theodor Adorno and Max Horkeimer's 1945 essay "The Culture Industry," which likewise found in democratic culture the marks of a degradation of a true aesthetic dimension. Having fled Nazism and its coldly calculating methods of extermination, Adorno and Horkeimer found themselves in the heart of American popular culture, Los Angeles, and they saw there an instrumental reason that for them was potentially no less destructive of rarified spirit than the barbaric world they left behind.

As Andrew Ross notes in *No Respect*, his study of postwar intellectual attitudes toward popular culture, the postwar period is ever more about disdain by cultural custodians toward everyday arts. For Ross, there is increasingly a "failure" (his recurrent word) of encounter between intellectuals and popular culture.[18] In such a context, any study of the mass arts in a form that is other than denunciatory finds difficulty of expression. Thus, as Greg Taylor shows in *Artists in the Audience*, his history of postwar film criticism, the serious analysis of film is forced to go underground as a few isolated writers (for example, Robert Warshow, Parker Tyler, and Manny Farber) are impelled increasingly to treat even the study of popular film as rarified, even avant-gardist activity.[19]

Such a context is one not propitious for large-scale developments in film curricula. Announced with great fanfare at the beginning of the 1940s, Robert Gessner's plans to create a film study program out of a literary background are stymied by the coming of war and then disappear for decades. In contrast, as I've already noted, USC's film program survives, but only by bracketing out cultural and critical issues and turning itself for decades into a service program of film production (and also of film distribution: through the 1950s, USC's film school became one of the country's biggest providers of educational films). The University of California, Los Angeles, began a filmmaking program at the end of the 1940s but like USC's program it emphasized production at the expense of criticism. Only at the end of the 1950s as the intellectuals' cold war critique of mass culture began to calm down and higher education began to confront the McLuhanite explosion of new media did film studies find fertile ground in higher education. New curricula came into existence, dissertations were written, a professional society for film was created (the Society for Cinematologists in 1959), and scholarly books and book series began to appear at a regular rate. A discipline begins. That, however, is a story for another time.

Notes

1. Scott Buchanan, "In Search of a Liberal College: A Program for the Recovery of the Classics and the Liberal Arts," archives, St. John's College, Annapolis.
2. Laurence Veysey, *The Emergence of the American University* (Chicago: University of Chicago Press, 1965), 337.
3. Dana Polan, *Scenes of Instruction: The Beginnings of the U. S. Study of Film* (Berkeley: University of California Press, 2007).
4. Lawrence Levine, *Highbrow/Lowbrow: The Emergence of Cultural Hierarchy in America* (Cambridge, Mass.: Harvard University Press, 1988).
5. Gerald Graff, *Professing Literature: An Institutional History* (Chicago: University of Chicago Press, 1987). To be fair, Graff relies heavily for his overall understanding of the history of higher education on Veysey's *The Emergence of the American University*, but for us his volume has the specific advantage of focusing on the particular area of curricular change in the area of narrative forms of cultural production. His comments on literature make useful points of comparison and contrast to the cultural work of cinema.
6. One result of this assertion that modern languages could serve as well as the classic

ones in the inculcation of "mental discipline" was the foundation of the Modern Language Association in the 1880s. Whereas today the MLA has come to stand for anything having to do with narrative arts, its original impetus was to defend the specific integrity of modern foreign languages against the all-consuming veneration for classic Greek and Latin. For useful background on this issue, see William R. Parker, "The M.L.A., 1883–1953," PMLA 68.4, part 2 (September 1953): 3–39.

7. Victor Freeburg, *The Art of Photoplay Making* (New York: Macmillan, 1918), 104–5.

8. See Frances Taylor Patterson, *Cinema Craftsmanship: A Book for Photoplaywrights* (New York: Harcourt, Brace, 1920); and, for her background thoughts on the course and its goals, "A New Art in an Old University," *Photoplay Magazine* (January 1920): 65, 124.

9. Raymond Williams, *Culture and Society, 1780–1950* (New York: Columbia University Press, 1983 [1958]), xiii–xiv; and *Keywords: A Vocabulary of Culture and Society*, rev. ed. (New York: Oxford University Press, 1983), 165–68.

10. T. J. Jackson Lears, *No Place of Grace: Antimodernism and the Transformation of American Culture, 1880–1920* (New York: Pantheon Books, 1981).

11. Kristin Thompson, *Storytelling in the New Hollywood: Understanding Classical Narrative Technique* (Cambridge, Mass.: Harvard University Press, 1999).

12. Graff, *Professing Literature*, 125.

13. Lasky in Joseph P. Kennedy, *The Story of the Films, as Told by Leaders of the Industry to the Students of the Graduate School of Business Administration, George F. Baker Foundation, Harvard University* (Chicago: A. W. Shaw Company, 1927), 115. This volume is a collection of transcripts of the HSB course and obviously provides the clearest sense of the course content.

14. The most famous of these attacks was Thorstein Veblen's *The Higher Learning in America: A Memorandum on the Conduct of Universities by Business Men* (New York: B. W. Huebsch, 1918).

15. Michael Augsburger, "*Fortune*'s Business Gentlemen: Cultural and Corporal Liberalism in the Early 1930s," in *Prospects: An Annual of American Cultural Studies* 26, ed. Jack Salzman (Cambridge: Cambridge University Press, 2001), 423–47; and Jackson Lears, *No Place of Grace*.

16. Augsburger, "*Fortune*'s Business Gentlemen," 436.

17. Michael Denning, *The Cultural Front: The Laboring of American Culture in the Twentieth Century* (New York: Verso, 1996).

18. Andrew Ross, *No Respect: Intellectuals and Popular Culture* (New York: Routledge, 1989).

19. Greg Taylor, *Artists in the Audience: Cults, Camp, and American Film Criticism* (Princeton, N.J.: Princeton University Press, 2001).

MAKING CINEMA EDUCATIONAL

Studying Movies at the Museum:

The Museum of Modern Art and Cinema's

Changing Object

HAIDEE WASSON

■ In 1935 the Museum of Modern Art in New York (MOMA) announced its intention to collect and exhibit not just modern paintings and sculptures but also films. Despite what may seem common sense today, responses to MOMA's then-unusual endeavor varied. Some declared the Film Library, as it was then called, a welcome rejection of the conventionally low cultural status imbued upon the movies. The library was taken as an authoritative announcement that film had finally and rightfully achieved status as an art. Yet, many others simply scowled, grumbling that the New York elites who acted as figureheads for the museum had succumbed to their eccentricity and privilege.

For the naysayers, the fact that MOMA intended eventually to circulate its films to other museums, schools, and universities provided an opportunity to reassert an idealized divide between popular movies and sacred art, main street amusement halls and venerated sites of cultural contemplation. In response to the Film Library's plan, for instance, Emily Grenauer of the *World-Telegram* (New York) wrote simply, "The academic die-hards are cackling."[1] A concurrent article in the *Telegraph* (New York), commenting on the museum's plans to distribute its films widely to "study groups" and to those interested in researching cinema, sneered: "Said research work, of course, [would be] taking the form of a critical examination of Miss Jean Harlow, Miss Marlene Dietrich's legs, and other curious manifestations of motion picture life."[2] Several months later in the same newspaper a similar sense of whimsy continued to resonate.

The paper invited readers to chuckle at the prospect of a Ph.D. dissertation on a popular western, Bill Hart's *Two Gun Hicks*.[3] Other writers used MOMA's announcement as an opportunity to express more sober concern about the sorry state of higher education, lamenting the ease with which the "low art" had supplanted traditional curriculum.[4]

Cinema's threat to established academic subject matter was clearly being exaggerated for either comic effect or to bolster narratives of cultural decline, forwarded by those uneasy with the broader reworking of cultural hierarchies endemic to the period. Yet responses to the Film Library also tell us something about contemporaneous sensibilities specifically regarding film. Beyond the easy acceptance of, or outright disbelief in, MOMA's plans, we can also observe the novelty of a wide variety of now-commonsense ideas about cinema. Prominent among them was that old or aging examples of this ephemeral amusement might be seen again and that they might also be viewed like other museum objects with serious contemplation. By incorporating film, MOMA explicitly proposed that a cultural form largely understood in America as popular, commercial, and disposable was a form of valuable knowledge, a distinct aesthetic expression, and an educational viewing activity. In response, a persistent be-musement—still familiar—over the prospect of studying movies, especially popular movies, also took firm hold.

Mapping the ascendance of the lowly film to its even partial acceptance as a celebrated art is a complicated task, one that logically involves more than the proclamations of one American art museum and also requires consider-ation of other converging and diverging dynamics: namely, changing theories and practices of art, the work of key intellectuals, the publication of important books and essays, the formation of other institutions, the influence of notable filmmakers, the evolution of film style and technology, and the challenging as-sertion that reproducible everyday objects matter. One might also include the dialectical fact of opposition to these ideas—the resistance to and rejection of film's enduring or elevated value. Nonetheless, MOMA's incursions into the film world are indeed important, partly because they either reflect or catalyzed—to varying degrees—each of these phenomena.

In establishing the Film Library as a museum department, MOMA instru-mentalized several basic ideals: first, that the otherwise amorphous phe-nomena called cinema should also be understood as a collection of individual films, *as an assemblage of objects that endured through time*; second, that these selected films *should be seen, requiring a form of distribution and exhibition of*

The image of a pile of 16mm film cans is a recurring one in film culture, suggesting the consistent ways in which the gauge embodied the promise of both increased access to films and a transformed if not transformative exhibition format. (Cover of the Museum of Modern Art Film Library Bulletin, 1941)

films outside of commercial movie theaters; and, third, that viewing such films should be augmented by informed research materials, placing film in pertinent sociological, historical, political, and aesthetic dialogue. This last assertion had implications both for the manner of watching that MOMA sought to instill in its audience, and for the production and circulation of film scholarship itself. Collectively, these three basic premises provided a lasting material and ideological infrastructure for the expansive mandate to save, exhibit, and most of all, to study films. It was also these formative ideas—embodied by the enticing image of a pile of film cans—that made cinema in its broadest sense, and films in their particular form, more material and therefore empirically knowable. Through all of these activities, the library asserted more than the idea that select films were worthy art; indeed, as a museum that was object oriented and pedagogically circumscribed, MOMA ensured that the institution of cinema was now intertwined with the institution of art.

In the United States, this marriage of cinema and art institutions served as a catalyst for facilitating and legitimating a whole range of films (shaping a particular canon) and activities (sanctioning a particular mode of watching). Key among these activities is a foundational set of assumptions about film study. In brief, in this essay I argue that film study owes a debt to the modern art museum. This debt pertains not only to MOMA's complicated idea about film as a modern art, but also to its institutional idea about film viewing as a museological act. Underpinning both of these ideas is a conceptualization of cinema as an assemblage of enduring objects that could and should be seen, and therefore known. That is, much like the museum's impetus to display art objects otherwise unavailable for public contemplation, MOMA employed the logics of the modern art museum in order to effect a new field for film's visibility. As such, MOMA became an influential force not just in forwarding ideas about film viewing but also about film scholarship and film education, thereby encompassing both specialized monographs and also more widely accessible written materials. At MOMA, then, film became not just a form of museum knowledge but also an educational instrument. As a result, the institution of cinema and the conditions in which films were studied changed paradigmatically. In this essay I provide an overview of these shifts by first describing the larger museum home in which the library operated and then detailing the early activities of the Film Library.

Clearly, the idea of studying hicks with two guns or lending academic immortality to a starlet's legs was—and still is—perceived by many as odd. Yet, after MOMA, studying cinema in the United States inside and outside of universities was tenaciously organized around a particular, persistent, and projected celluloid object. That object was in turn shaped by MOMA's efforts to infuse film viewing with museological tendencies, which in the case of film meant grappling not only with film's aesthetic specificity but also its relations to other arts, as well as to sociological and historical considerations. This new kind of film viewing was equally implicated in small and specialized public formations, themselves predicated on the idea of informed spectatorship, discussion, and—crucially—the belief that museum movies could serve as a primary interface between self and world.

The New Museum

The Museum of Modern Art opened on November 7, 1929. It was established by wealthy matrons of the arts with tastes for the paintings and sculptures emerging from modern European art movements. Born of the longstanding pull in American twentieth-century museums between democratic accessibility and high aesthetic concerns, MOMA was chartered as a national educational institution aimed at collecting and exhibiting what its trustees and curators deemed the best of modern art.[5] Yet, spearheaded by Alfred Barr, the museum was run by a new generation of art historians who had equal passions for an expanded idea about the objects and forms germane to thinking about art—an idea that grew to include industrial design, architecture, photography, and film. In practice, then, MOMA early distinguished itself in several ways. It was the first American museum dedicated wholly to the modern. This entailed a broad definition for what objects counted as art; early exhibits predictably included paintings by Van Gogh, Matisse, and Seurat, but also featured machine parts, movie props, and even mixing bowls. The museum was organized from the beginning to aggressively circulate its exhibits nationally to other museums, schools, ladies clubs, and department stores. Closely related to this activity, MOMA thoroughly integrated media both as a means of publicity and as a method of display. Radio shows, monthly bulletins, daily press releases, art and poster design contests, and children's drawing contests, along with a constant flow of illustrated journal, magazine, and newspaper articles, bolstered the museum's reputation. These aspects of MOMA's operation catapulted the museum to international recognition and toward a daily presence in the American mediascape.[6] This highly visible museum also functioned as a mass educator and as a prominent cultural authority. Persistently forging new and adaptable frontiers for its art and influence through an expansive media network, it simultaneously fashioned a place in which something was always happening. In short, MOMA set out to reinvent the art museum by working with and through a range of media to ensure that it served as a living site rather than an irrelevant and decayed place where ancient gewgaws waited out their days. This aspect of MOMA's institutional identity was also strongly aided by the museum's active relationship to consumer culture.[7]

The gradual entry of movies into the sacred art world thus was linked to a double movement. Not only did MOMA incorporate everyday objects into its displays, it also began to actively circulate its more traditional art objects widely, usually in reproduced form. In this regard, MOMA was symptomatic of a change in the structure and operation of other American art museums, which during this period began to turn their sacral spaces inside out, sending objects everywhere, in the attempt to pull more people into museum orbit. Such a move served not only to ameliorate concerns about the museum's looming irrelevance but also to further the mandate to educate as wide a public as possible. Within this broader transformation, then, film served several purposes at MOMA. On the one hand, it functioned as a convenient and mobile form by which educational films about art could be either shown at the museum or distributed for display at other pertinent venues. On the other hand, MOMA's film program also incorporated a plainly popular form into its hallowed halls, thereby exemplifying a will to offer exhibits that reflected changes in the art world and also changes in the museum's ideal audience. The exhibition of films at MOMA thus was part of a broader museum project: to maintain relevance, continue its educationalist goals, and expand its public by adapting to the sweeping changes in public leisure.[8]

Film and West 53rd

From its inception, the Film Library saved and exhibited a wide range of films that had been lost to public view. To be sure, there was a relatively small network of nascent cinephiles, filmmakers, and critics for whom MOMA's experiment was an obvious and necessary undertaking. Film archives were formed concurrently across Europe, and film societies were a prominent feature of urban life in cities such as Paris, Berlin, London, and Moscow. Yet, at this point in American history, few comparable trends existed. Moreover, the lifecycle of a typical film was extremely brief; the bulk of commercial features disappeared quickly from movie screens, never to appear again. Viewing art films and what we today call movie classics was still a highly unusual activity, confined to major urban centers and only a handful of specialized art house and repertory theaters.[9]

Early film screenings at MOMA confirm the peculiarity of the project. Visitors to the museum's auditorium regularly demonstrated uncertainty about very basic things like, for example, how to behave when watching commercial movies in an art museum. Lacking established norms for watching museum movies, film viewers reportedly engaged in shouting matches punctuated periodically by objects thrown in the auditorium (at other spectators or at the screen). Such behavior occurred frequently enough that the library's first curator, Iris Barry, had a slide projector permanently installed in the museum's auditorium, equipped with a slide that read: "If the disturbance in the auditorium does not cease, the showing of this film will be discontinued." If after stopping the film and showing the slide the audience still did not compose itself, the house lights would come up and the show would be declared over. To further ensure decorum, Barry reserved for herself a permanent seat in the auditorium, alongside a phone connecting her instantly to the projectionist. She became a common fixture in the theater, regularly monitoring both image quality and audience comportment.[10] Persuading spectators to watch films seriously—let alone quietly—at MOMA was neither simple nor obvious. They responded variously to old films and their conventions, neglecting standard museum decorum and importing habits from the popular movie house.

Of course, the behavior of MOMA's early film audience also provides a useful index to rapid change. In its short forty-year life, film's form and function had altered considerably, yet there remained a constant and crucial material fact of film culture. Despite the profound influence that cinema exercised on conceptions of time, space, knowledge, industry, state policy, and leisure, most films could not be seen within a year of their initial release. Once a film's initial theatrical run was exhausted, it was commonly recycled for its material-chemical components or simply was dumped into the ocean. The shift to synchronized sound during the late 1920s further spurred the recycling industry, which flourished in the wake of the uncountable silent films deemed more valuable for their silver content than for their stories, styles, or stars.[11] The majority of films that remained were swept into ill-kept studio vaults or stock footage warehouses. The flammability and fragility of the nitrate stock on which they were printed only made their remaining years more perilous.

Despite what seems today the obvious utility of saving and seeing yesterday's films, forty years after the first public projections in North America and Europe the cries and complaints of critics, writers, and fans yielded few results. In short, when the Film Library formed, no sustained American infrastructure had been successfully built to secure lasting and studied attention to films themselves, as had been done for paintings, sculptures, books, music, plays, and even photographs. The early audiences at MOMA were thus participant in a viewing practice that was unusual not only because it merged museum and movie theater, but because it married past with present, the ephemeral with the enduring.

Film had been a part of the museum plan from its founding. Yet when the Film Library formed, Barr's initial idea of a somewhat elite film salon housed within the museum, featuring primarily European films, had changed considerably. The Film Library was designed as a space in which films—popular, American and European, feature and short, old and new—might find a second, third, and fourth life. Mirroring the educational and traveling programs of the larger museum, the Film Library immediately organized circulating exhibits, made almost daily press releases, placed articles in a range of little and mass publications, and scripted and performed radio shows. Library staff not only actively sold MOMA as a site for viewing films but, more specifically, they crafted the museum as a space for learning about cinema.

The Museum and the Film Scholar

Alongside their early collection of films, Film Library staff also gathered a wide range of other resources for film scholars. These materials included film stills, scripts, magazines, journals, pamphlets, books, and the personal papers of filmmakers and stars. This collection then became the primary material from which a formidable amount of secondary scholarship and writing was generated. Some of this work was crafted by individuals directly employed by the museum—for example, the short monograph by Iris Barry, *DW Griffith: American Film Master* (1940), and a similar work by Alistair Cooke, *Douglas Fairbanks: The Making of a Screen Character* (1940).[12]

Equally important was *Film Notes*, a compilation of program notes written by library staff to accompany films shown at the museum and elsewhere. Widely distributed, these items are still available in academic and public libraries across the United States and Canada.[13] An equally influential body of additional literature was generated through special grants provided by the Rockefeller Foundation. Prominent among this oeuvre is the work undertaken by Jay Leyda on Eisenstein and Soviet cinema and by Siegfried Kracauer on German cinema.[14] Still other scholars, not remunerated for their work, benefited from the library's resources, including Lewis Jacobs who wrote *Rise of the American Film: A Critical History*, first published in 1939.[15] The Film Library was, at its very core, organized around the goal of providing the resources necessary to foster film study, which included two complementary ambitions: to generate a body of specialist knowledge and to spread that knowledge widely. The library's status as a producer of knowledge was itself shaped by a museological and empirical ideal presupposing that *objects must be seen to be known*. Yet, their activities were not confined merely to sacralizing the film object or film art but to creating a whole environment in which film knowledge could be created and disseminated.

In addition, then, to the steady stream of scholars who sporadically visited the museum to use its resources, numerous scholars/filmmakers were actively courted either to study Film Library collections or to deliver lectures as part of its public programming.[16] Library staff invited Robert Flaherty along with several key figures in the British documentary movement, including Alberto Cavalcanti, Basil Wright, and Benoit Levy. Though the impending war forced these men to decline the museum's invitation, one key filmmaker and scholar accepted: Paul Rotha—whose book *The Film till Now* was foundational for the library's collection practices—arrived in 1938.[17] Rotha's work at the Film Library was funded by a temporary Rockefeller Foundation grant that aimed to "develop documentary film in the United States" with the goal of producing and distributing films "outside of the amusement field."[18] During his time at the library Rotha performed a range of activities. He delivered public lectures and worked to assist in developing MOMA's film course, first taught at Columbia University in fall 1938 (discussed further below). He also wrote a screenplay for an instructional film about how movies are made, which some at MOMA believed would gain commercial distribution and thus help to fund the library's programs.[19] This idea was initially endorsed by Will Hays but lost support among the other members of the Film Library's industry-based Advisory Board.

Key to many of these invitations and the smaller projects that developed from them was the consistent support of the Rockefeller Foundation, one of several prominent philanthropies funded by the Rockefeller fortune. The foundation provided the bulk of the Film Library's operational funds during its first ten years, and it further supplied a series of one-time grants for such special projects. How to explain the foundation's interest in MOMA and film study? The Humanities Division of the foundation had been recently charged with helping to reorient university-based research away from "cloistered" activity and toward "the obvious sources of influence in public taste today." The foundation was especially interested in research that explored contemporary media and their capacity to promote "a culture of the general mind." With regard to film, the foundation was uninterested in furthering the regulatory and censorship practices that were so heavily publicized by the industry's Hays Office and called for by the Catholic Legion of Decency. The efforts of the foundation should be similarly differentiated from the effects of research growing out of projects such as those popularized by select versions of the Payne Fund Studies. Foundation officers were far more concerned with changing the manner in which people watched and understood movies, seeking to engender discrimination in film viewing. This, it was believed, would provide a defense against the deleterious influences of so-called mass media and act as a corrective to the damaging effects of what was loosely called "propaganda": commercial, foreign, and domestic.[20] A new and informed public also had the benefit of maintaining the structures of ownership endemic to the rising media industries—shining the apples without upsetting the cart.

In short, MOMA's film education work satisfied the foundation's mandate. Efforts to engender a qualitatively different culture for film also paralleled other media projects supported by Rockefeller and similar philanthropies.[21] As the foundation officer John Marshall wrote: "If it succeeds, (MOMA) will organize a new audience for films much as the Carnegie Library organized a reading public which was previously non-existent. And, if such an audience exists for films that cannot now be shown theatrically, its existence should give substantial encouragement to the production of new films of educational and cultural value."[22] In short, the concern of the foundation was to structurally alter the form and function of film away from what was understood as entertaining the masses and toward a progressive model of film as a nexus for specialized publics and civic intervention. This plan entailed changes to dominant forms of theatrical film exhibition and, eventually, to the kinds of films being made. Foundation officers continually expressed admiration for John Grierson's London-based documentary work, which provided an influential model for them. For foundation officers, Grierson's success was in creating a whole cinematic environment, built not just on a particular genre of film but on an infrastructure for viewing and discussion that existed largely beyond the commercial movie house. The officers maintained regular contact with Grierson during these years, hoping that his success could be achieved in the United States.[23]

The Rockefeller Foundation's commitment to MOMA's Film Library, then, was shaped less by an impulse to sanction film art and more to transform American leisure and reform media practice. As noted above, this led the foundation to fund film scholarship and also to support the library's traveling film exhibitions. Jay Leyda is exemplary of the foundation's dual influences on Film Library activities. Iris Barry and her husband John Abbott first met Leyda in 1936 on their initial European film hunt. Leyda was studying Soviet film and working under Sergei Eisenstein in Moscow. He returned to the United States with Barry and Abbott, continuing his research as an employee of MOMA. Despite the library's small operating budget, Barry consistently found ways to keep Leyda on staff. This was accomplished largely through continued appeal to the foundation. For instance, through to 1937 Leyda was funded specifically on several foundation grants with varied goals, including researching and writing program notes to accompany the library's traveling film programs; studying the organization of film materials in the United States and Europe for loan and rental; and developing the library's circulating programs.[24] Yet during this period Leyda also continued his groundbreaking work on Eisenstein and on his English-language history of Soviet film, some of which was published shortly after he left MOMA in 1940. His expertise in Soviet cinema also facilitated the museum's exhibition of pertinent films in the late 1930s, thereby shaping the accompanying notes.[25] Leyda further contributed to some of the small scale but innovative efforts to advocate for film research and publishing initiated by the Film Library. This work included assembling a list of recommended film books entitled "Have You Any Books about the Movies?", which was published in the trade magazine *Publishers Weekly* in 1937.[26]

Funding and facilitating these researchers in this nascent field of film scholarship provided an unprecedented opportunity for both scholar and institution to develop networks of credibility and a lasting record upon which future projects could be undertaken. It provides an early example of scholars actually getting paid to conduct humanistic inquiry into film—a basic shift that is easy to overlook because of the way that it would later be naturalized across humanities-based university programs. The fact that both Leyda and Rotha went on to have influential and productive careers in film and film study further indicates the valuable role MOMA played in helping to plant seeds and catalyze a way of engaging cinema. Among other such contributions worthy of mention is the first index to film literature, which was funded by the New Deal's Works Progress Administration and assembled from 1935 through to 1939 largely using MOMA's resources. *The Film Index* was also actively publicized by library staff, and Barry herself penned a description of it for a flyer advocating its indispensability not just for the specialized researcher but also for the "layman." In this piece she emphasized the diverse assortment of indexed sources, including trade journals, fan magazines, and the catalogues of defunct production and distribution companies, short-lived magazines, and "extinct quarterlies."[27] This first volume of a planned set of three for the index was devoted to a surprising range of literature, organized under the rubric of film as art. Its 780 pages included roughly 8,600 books, periodicals, and film reviews, 4,300 films, 2,100 authors, and 160 major subject classifications. Indexed sources included articles in fan magazines, women's weeklies, and industry press. Specialist and politicized writing such as that found in *Experimental Cinema* and *Close Up* appeared alongside articles published in *Saturday Evening Post* and *Billboard*.

Sustained monographs by Hugo Münsterburg balanced the brief polemics of Harry Alan Potamkin.[28] Such a resource is distinct in this early history of film study by providing a new if complex compass for research.

Library staff also worked to develop other structured modes of scholarship and learning, sometimes in collaboration with established institutions. As noted above, Barry and others, working in conjunction with the Department of Fine Arts at Columbia University, organized and executed a comprehensive film course in 1938 that continued for several years. The class, titled "The History, Technique and Aesthetic of the Motion Picture," was broad in its course coverage and reflects a field in gestation. Individual lectures dealt with film history, industry, censorship, stars, screenwriting, production practices, and sociological concerns. The Film Library mimeographed its lectures, with plans to distribute them to other colleges interested in teaching film.[29] In addition to this formal course, library staff lectured on film to clubs, societies, and in the growing number of university film courses. They also spoke at cognate institutions such as the National Board of Review, the American Association of Museums, the American Library Association, and the Society of Motion Picture Engineers. Such lectures were generally comprised of brief overviews of film history and usually included an explanation about why the library's programs were important.

Overall, MOMA's Film Library served as a kind of American hub for the first generation of film scholars eager to fortify their interests and scholarship with adequate resources. This entailed individuals situated across a range of organizations and disciplines, including filmmakers, educators, newspaper critics, university-based scholars, European and American intellectuals, as well as Hollywood personalities. The fact that MOMA continued to service the expanding film community in this way is evidenced by the fact that meetings hosted at MOMA in the 1950s led directly to the founding of the Society of Cinematologists in 1959. Renamed the Society for Cinema and Media Studies (SCMS) in 2003, this group is now the largest Anglophone organization of college and university educators, filmmakers, historians, and critics committed to advancing film and media scholarship.[30]

Library Screens

Rounding out the Film Library's efforts to produce and circulate film knowledge are the library's film programs. These events occurred nationally (and occasionally internationally) and expanded in number and diversified in content throughout the library's first ten years. The first two major programs were entitled "A Short Survey of the Film in America, 1895–1932" and "Some Memorable American Films, 1896–1934." Each program situated American film history at its center and organized its films into discrete sections covering, among other areas, "The Development of Narrative," "The German Influence," "The Talkies," "The Western," "Comedies," "Screen Personalities," and "The Film and Contemporary History." National cinema continued to be a prominent rubric for the programs that followed: Germany, France, and Sweden each soon after garnered their own retrospectives. And, by 1940, a program of Soviet films was available, as well as a sizable collection of documentaries—many of which were British. Experimental films received a few special screenings and occasionally appeared in larger survey programs, and by the early 1940s the films were available for individual rental in MOMA's catalogues. Yet, overall, there was a clear emphasis on fictional narrative cinema as well as a gravitation toward the now-familiar idea that non-American or foreign films were represented by exceptional and aesthetically innovative films (not necessarily seen or beloved widely in their country of origin), and that, in contrast, American cinema was represented by popular genre films (westerns, slapstick) and stars. There was also a clear sociological interest in American cinema that was manifest in the programming of gangster films, social problem films, and documentary films, as well as newsmagazines such as *The March of Time*.[31]

The programs' accompanying study guides and film notes supplied a range of information about each film shown. Sometimes this information was brief and at other times it was more detailed. A given film note might contain both production information and comments on the film's popularity and its related impact on fashion or social mores. Another might tend more to a film's stylistic or formal innovation. Still another might focus on a film's imbrication in a national film culture or perhaps its link to a particular director. Occasionally, the political controversy generated by a film would be indicated, though it was rarely discussed with any detail.

These notes were an integral element of every program rental. For instance, with its 16mm film programs, two hundred copies of the notes were furnished along with the films automatically, and five hundred copies came with the more expensive 35mm programs. The notes were not optional but rather constitutive of the traveling film program by shaping the discursive context in which a particular film or group of films would be presented.[32] In addition, the films that MOMA circulated were themselves altered to serve MOMA's pedagogical impulse. Library staff condensed the printed film notes and then converted them into filmed text-inserts or intertitles, which were attached to the beginning of library films. These inserts acted as canned or automated lessons in film history and aesthetics, where they complemented and perhaps occasionally stood in for the printed notes.

Also included in MOMA's film packages were other kinds of catalysts to study and discussion. In bolstering the claim that the library forwarded a sociological as much as high-aesthetic interest in its films, amid the consolidated film notes assembled into one volume rests a document entitled "A Short Table for a Study of the Gangster Film, 1926–34."[33] This document is a timeline detailing a chronology of key developments deemed useful for thinking about the much-maligned film genre. Extending far beyond Josef von Sternberg's *Underworld* (1927), the list includes not only a range of films but also key events in the battle against organized crime. The premier of Broadway plays and the publication of key novels also color the list, as does the stock market crash, the repeal of prohibition, and the formation of the Legion of Decency. This document confirms the Film Library's interest in fostering attention to film's complex significance as an aesthetic form entangled in dynamic social, legal, and governmental phenomena.

While the library's exhibition program grew steadily after its initiation, there remained numerous impediments to its full success. The act of coordinating and in some senses creating a distinct extra-theatrical circuit that included Hollywood films proved difficult. Collecting and circulating any kind of film carried significant costs that the library's budget, always precarious, could not entirely cover. In order to survive, user fees of some sort had to be charged. At first, Film Library staff planned to work by annual subscription—charging a membership fee of $250 ($4,000 in 2008) per year for use of its traveling services. Realizing that this amount was prohibitive, they began to charge per program: $25 ($400 in 2008) for a two-hour film program in either 35mm or 16mm if booking the whole series; $40 ($640 in 2008) for the same program if a film were procured individually.[34] Further, the agreement that the Film Library had struck with the industry that governed the exhibition of its films was necessary in order to secure Hollywood's good will and legal sanction. But it was also restrictive, and it proved to have lasting and sizable impact. The agreement stipulated that all user groups must qualify as educational and nonprofit. Further, and crucially, they could charge no individual admission to their film screenings. With regard to the traveling film programs, by far the bulk of library screenings, this left the dispersed and often small groups to find some other mechanism of financial support.

The agreement with the industry also limited MOMA's in-house exhibition possibilities. Like the interested viewing groups across the country, the museum itself could not charge for movie admission. Therefore, anyone who wanted to see one of MOMA's films had to live in the New York area and attend as a museum member or pay museum admission. Or, alternatively, an interested viewer could join some other sponsoring educational organization (a museum, gallery, library) or form an independent study group. These two options entailed paying the rental fees mentioned above and developing some funding structure alternative to pay-per-view admission.

Partly because of these weighty conditions, MOMA's agreement with the industry served as a catalyst for further institutionalizing a particular ideal of cinematic engagement, thereby providing a formative influence on the emergence of an American film society and film study movement. The founding of educational viewing groups, a requirement of becoming a MOMA library user, was actively encouraged in film library catalogues and brochures.[35] This agreement then served to consecrate the sometimes arbitrary divide between watching to be entertained and watching to be educated. The film itself, according to the agreement, did not shape this particular legal category. Rather, it was the intentions and proclaimed raison d'être of the group seeking to watch a given film that determined the legal status of the object-exchange. Counterintuitively, the distinction between these modes of film watching—entertaining and educational—actually better allowed individual films (including Hollywood films) to circulate and be seen at one remove from conventional commodity structures, thus creating a legal haven for a wholly different kind of moving image circulation while discursively ghettoizing the select films as merely educational.

Defined during this period as educational, film societies began forming either under the aegis of established organs of higher education or, more often than not, with some degree of proximity to them. It was these film societies and universities, with their institutional resources, that became crucial to MOMA's early and later success by actively renting films and simultaneously lending legitimacy. In turn, the Film Library programs and film notes fundamentally changed the material conditions in which film watching and both formal and informal film study evolved in the United States. For example, MOMA supplied select films and study materials that were previously unavailable. Its film programs allowed the still-unusual idea that films could be watched studiously to shift from local, specific, and sometimes eclectic projects to a nationally organized, highly coordinated system that could be run with regularity and reliability. Film Library programs offered the advantage of expert curation, consistency, and authoritative sanction; they were based on a standardized set of films and also on preset methods for analysis around which curriculum could be established and maintained.

The number of university-based screenings of MOMA's films is remarkable. Programs were held at Dartmouth, Stanford, Bryn Mawr, Mount Holyoke, Smith, William and Mary, Vassar, and the New School for Social Research.[36] Films were hired by the universities of Chicago, Pittsburgh, Washington, Minnesota, Missouri, California-Berkeley, New York, Princeton, Brown, Cornell, and Colgate. Wayne State and Indiana universities also exhibited MOMA films.[37] It should be noted that library films were used in a surprising range of university departments, including visual education, drama, public speaking, art and archeology, fine arts, economics, and sociology. Library programs were also frequently shown in language departments. Further, it is difficult and sometimes impossible to know what precisely these films were used for or how they were seen. The growth of the visual education movement played an important role in buttressing MOMA's rentals and further blurred the line between education *about* film and education *with* film. Indisputable, however, is that film societies booking MOMA's films proliferated at many of the institutions noted above and were fed almost exclusively by MOMA's programs. Film Library staff claimed success in directly catalyzing film societies in Buffalo, Los Angeles, and Washington, and at Bryn Mawr, Haverford, Harvard, and Dartmouth, among others.[38] Other film societies formed concurrent to the initiation of MOMA's film programs; these groups were not necessarily linked to universities but met museum criteria — for example, the Southern California Film Society.[39]

By actively advocating for the importance of studying movies the staff members of the Film Library also directly implicated themselves and their programs in the burgeoning discourses of film study and appreciation germinating at American universities. The press releases submitted by MOMA, picked up by national newspaper syndicates, persistently reiterated the importance of studying, thinking, and talking about the films it showed. To bolster their claims they named developments at universities; Iris Barry, for instance, gave lectures on film history in courses offered at three New York–area universities: the New School for Social Research, New York University, and Columbia University.[40] Indeed, throughout the late 1920s and 1930s film study at American universities gained noteworthy visibility. Courses emerged at Columbia, Harvard, Stanford, Iowa, UCLA, NYU, the New School for Social Research, Syracuse, and USC.[41] The MOMA film programs were a constitutive component of these courses. Yet it is also necessary to note that many of these courses demonstrate a catholicity in their approach to what constituted the study of cinema, thus indicating a field still very much in gestation. Courses were taught in a range of departments, schools, and faculties, employing a range of categories, methodologies, and pedagogies. Even courses designed expressly as film classes varied dramatically.[42] The study of film had not yet hardened within disciplinary boundaries, as there was no one disciplinary formation or preexisting institutional mold; film had not yet been plainly defined as the study of a fine art or a mass medium or a popular entertainment—despite MOMA's role as an art institution in each of these efforts.

MOMA's approach to film pedagogy, while more focused than the wide range of those extant, nevertheless maintained a certain dynamism and flexibility. While MOMA's notes tended toward a kind of soft formalism (attention to style and especially to national stylistic tendencies), they also continued to call attention to a film's popularity—its relationship to fashion, personalities, and star persona. During the 1940s, MOMA's film catalogue only became more complex, thereby generating even more categories for film rentals and now-counterintuitive arrangements of particular films. For instance, during the 1944–45 season, the Film Library listed individual films and film programs clearly appealing to a diverse rather than narrow constituency. Program titles include those that had been in circulation for several years: "Three French Film Pioneers [Ferdinand Zecca, Emile Cohl, and Jean Durand]," "Georges Méliès: Magician and Film Pioneer," "A Short History of Animation," and so on. Its programs also included "German Propaganda Films, 1934–40" (which included the infamous abbreviated version of Triumph of the Will) and a series entitled "Experimental and Avant-Garde Films."[43] But even more pertinent here is the fact that individual films were also being organized and packaged to service the much broader field of educational film. Titles were listed under headings such as "Conservation and Economic Planning," "Education," "Public Health," "Industry and Crafts," "Travel and Anthropology," and "History in the Making." Many of these subject headings were comprised of American but mostly British documentaries. Some Swedish, German, and French titles also appeared. The Film Library also circulated early on the films by the Office of War Information, including Frank Capra's "Why We Fight" series. Previously, these films had been only available to military personnel.[44]

Furthering MOMA's expansive implication in a range of film educational genres, a catalogue published three years earlier in 1942 was solely dedicated to the "film of fact." Its categorizations were perhaps even more unusual to the contemporary eye. The catalogue included a wide-ranging collection of subject matter: arts, religion, natural sciences, applied sciences, and social sciences. Individual films found their place in some unusual homes, organized by theme and content rather than by author, production interest, or country of production. For instance, Ralph Steiner's abstract study of moving valves and gears, *Mechanical Principles* (1930), was listed under physics, within the larger category of applied sciences. The Douglas Fairbanks film *Around the World in Eighty Minutes* (Victor Fleming, 1931) was listed under "Social Sciences: Travel and Anthropology." Also listed in the social sciences category but within the subheading "Economics and Sociology: Housing and Community Planning" was a supplementary group of avant-garde films, including *Rien que les heures* (Alberto Cavalcanti, 1926), *Berlin: Symphony of a Great City* (Walter Ruttman, 1927), and *A Bronx Morning* (Jay Leyda, 1932). The turn of the avant-garde toward documentary during the 1930s is well known. But MOMA's film categories further blur these experimental documentary forms. In other words, during its first ten years MOMA itself had a rather elastic approach to its own working definition of "film art," "film history," and "film study" by actively shaping its art museum project to include a sizable program in film education and educational film. Library staff openly acknowledged the interrelated and overlapping areas of concern. Fiction films and what they termed "films of fact" were increasingly considered crucial to the library's overall educational mandate. MOMA's literature also explicitly appealed to teachers and the visual education movement. The introduction to the 1942 catalogue acknowledges not only the remarkable growth of visual education but also the pressing need to account for the history and development of the factual film in a "war world." Library staff here expressly linked their scholarly role to the prominent role of cinema in the world political theater.[45] This effort must in part be seen as a response to an inchoate field and an institution struggling to respond to a rapidly changing set of cultural practices linked to cinema.

In addition to the museum's self-conception as a visual educator, the interests of the Rockefeller Foundation continued to shape library programs. Foundation officers (especially John Marshall and David Stevens) consistently encouraged the library to improve its distribution and exhibition as part of their determination to foment what they deemed a desirable link between new audiences and new film forms. In short, foundation officers remained unsatisfied with the comparatively small percentage of the filmgoing audience that MOMA had attracted. Clearly one of the problems facing the library was material. Potential audiences and rental groups lacked some of the most basic requirements for participating in the study circuit. Many simply did not have access to a film projector, and those interested in renting or buying the necessary equipment possessed widely varying kinds of spaces with different seating arrangements as well as unreliable power supplies where voltages, frequencies, and amperages varied.[46] Early on, the Film Library anticipated that such variables would present a problem. In order to manage these complexities, Iris Barry suggested that the library might circulate its own projector and screen with the programs, thereby creating a self-contained theater impervious to constantly changing technologies and high costs.[47] Yet this plan did not come to fruition. Well into the early 1940s, technical problems combined with a general shortage of funds continued to hinder groups interested in library programs.

The vast majority of Film Library programs circulated in 16mm format. Yet despite the growth of the 16mm gauge both nationally and internationally, saturation of the format was by no means complete. Further, the cost of 16mm projectors was still relatively high during this period and thus taxed small groups and institutions with meager and even modest audiovisual budgets. In 1935, for instance, AMPRO sold a silent 16mm projector for $135 ($2,160 in 2008). Victor sold its 16mm sound projector for as much as $395 ($6,320 in 2008). As discussed above, the cost of renting MOMA's programs was exorbitant for many groups. In response, the Film Library generated several different pricing plans for its films and gradually lowered prices throughout the decade. Yet according to internal documents the cost of its programs remained prohibitive.[48]

In sum, the effort to get its films seen was the then-improbable centerpiece of the Film Library's plan to survive as a viable cultural institution. Its challenges were many, including the basic and wide availability of an affordable display system. Nonetheless, with Rockefeller Foundation influence the Film Library persistently worked to create a new film audience buttressed by a steady network of films. While this network was irretrievably shaped by an impulse to reform or even redeem filmgoing with ideals of erudition and productive leisure, it can by no means be limited to this aim. The robust seeds of its project can be witnessed not only in today's healthy state of moving image study but also in the expansive micro-cinemas and personal archives that constitute contemporary film culture. The Web-based labyrinth of the Internet Movie Database, the endless rental catalogues of Netflix, the hand-held archive of the iPod, and the specialized collections of film scholarship widely available in university libraries all to a degree owe a debt to MOMA's efforts.

The development of film circuits outside of commercial movie theaters grew during World War II and, afterward, exploded.[49] Small-gauge projectors were a prominent part of the domestic propaganda machine that effectively used

16mm to create a national network of government-sanctioned films in schools, libraries, and other locations. The war years provided the technological infrastructure that ensured the thorough and penetrating transformation of movies into an integral element of everyday and institutional life. The proliferation of these projectors also created the conditions in which a national network of films and screening spaces grew to constitute innumerable specialized audiences, operating in public, para-public, and private contexts using film as their dominant as well as incidental pretext. Developments in film culture during wartime both vindicated and bolstered projects such as those by MOMA begun years earlier. Soon after the war, the circuits that grew to foster civilian and military education transformed into the basis for the rapid growth of MOMA's lending library, American film councils, film societies, and the increasingly formal networks of film study in American universities.

As for the Film Library, its history helps us to understand a particularly important period in film history wherein lasting changes to ideas and practices pertaining to cinema took hold. The Film Library sought to blend, balance, and further inflect films with the institutional edicts of preceding cultural institutions. It sought to coordinate resources, circulate select films, and advocate for an informed disposition toward interpretation. In doing so, the library disrupted some of the more staid and conventional aspects of traditional cultural institutions. It did so by invoking the relatively novel and modern assertion that in addition to paintings and sculpture the material of everyday life — buildings, photographs, advertising, machine parts — constituted valuable sources of aesthetic, historical, and intellectual contemplation. By situating film within this institutional claim, it contributed directly and indirectly to a national, highly mediated, and modern dialogue on the means by which the elite, middlebrow, populist, and industrial logics of film's value might convene at the sites of art and its institutions.

The Film Library is also crucial, then, for understanding changes to our most basic ideas about, and practices of, film study. In part, this had to do with authoritatively declaring cinema an art. More important than coarticulating "film" and "art," with the founding of the Film Library considerable steps had been taken to alter the ephemeral condition of film's cultural and material life. Film was gradually understood to be more object-like, stored on shelves, and shown because of the interest of smaller and smaller groups. Yet, these objects also traveled in different circuits and were shown in widely varying circumstances under the aegis of an authoritative art institution. The boundaries of the film object became more clearly defined and found a more stable life, stored on shelves but also shown as "old" films, "art" films, "historical" films, and "educational" films. The functions of these newly labeled film-objects were simultaneously being relocated, their purposes redrawn, and their significance both centralized and dispersed.

Under the rubric of an art museum, poised against commercial culture, MOMA's Film Library fed a burgeoning interest in specialized and repeat film viewing. It also became an elaborate exercise in extra-theatrical distribution and exhibition. Relying largely on the emergent network of 16mm projectors, 35mm films were selected, reduced in size, and arranged into programs. Packaged and circulated to national and international educational organizations, or shown at the museum itself, they were accompanied by production information, notes, and lectures. The Film Library at MOMA not only reimagined but also participated in building a national—if occasionally nationalist—film economy, one that etched away at the strong control over film exhibition held by Hollywood and asserted that watching moving images in small, specialized audiences could and should be an integral facet of public life and civic participation. In short, perhaps most significant of the Film Library's interventions was its attempt to extract individual films—American and not—from the commercial, corporate, and official regulatory restraints that limited their movement, their means of expression, and their influence, thereby providing the privileges as well as the prescriptives of art institutions more generally.[50]

The case of MOMA provides a counterpart to one of the key debates that has shaped film studies over the past ten years—namely that cinema is best understood as a modern, ephemeral, and mobile medium that is symptomatic of modernity's obsessions with shock, hyperstimulus, spectacle, and constant change. At MOMA, the modern also meant collecting and storing the symptoms of modernity, making them visible and empirically knowable. In short, the project to transform cinema from its status as a passing and commercial entertainment to an edifying and educational activity grew out of the impulse to arrest the seemingly endless circulation of ephemeral images by securing them in time and space and moving them away from the fairground and the bustling city street. This was neither an ideologically benign nor simple impulse. Instead, it was tied both to class-inflected projects to reform cinemagoers deemed ignorant or dangerous as well as to alternative models for cinema that sought to integrate movie watching with organized modes of cultural engagement that might be critical not just of industry but also of middlebrow and religious moralizing. This included protection from the rising forces seeking to regulate film content according to spiritual and other ostensibly moral dictates, as well as from the raucous frisson of popular movie houses.

Reworking the most basic material infrastructures in which films circulated and were seen was not achieved only by MOMA's efforts but also by an emergent network of individuals and organizations that had long fought to adapt cinema to uses other than those fostered by Hollywood. Yet MOMA became one of the most authoritative and centralized forces seeking to broker this transformation. Its history is an underconsidered element in the history of this shift—a shift that amounts to a fundamental transformation of the conditions in which movies were seen, thought about, engaged, and debated, becoming integral to understanding modern life in universities and just about everywhere else.

As for film studies, MOMA marks one of the paradigmatic sites that constituted the conditions of possibility for an object-oriented discipline—a model derived as much from literary fascination with the book as with art history's approach to the objet d'art. As this celluloid object disintegrates across the field of moving image studies and emergent technologies, it is important for us to look back at the forces that consolidated cinema as celluloid and constituted film as an object in a can, projected in a quiet dark room. We must also think hard about what these early institutions were responding to, and at the same time enabling. The film object was never only a precious and discrete thing but always part of the complex circuits of modernity. The struggle to make cinema an object of study is clearly not just the struggle to reduce a complex set of institutions into a simple material object. Nor is it about newer manifestations of similarly reductive objects such as the DVD or the movie theater. Instead, the more general project to study the moving image, of which studying film and the cinema is clearly a foundational element, is about assessing a range of pedagogical practices and intellectual apparatuses. What can we know from seeing and hearing mediated forms? What are the relations among seeing, hearing, and the rest of the world? The relations of film study to other kinds of study? In other words, the Film Library's history offers an opportunity to recognize some of the compelling forces that made film study possible. It indicates a museological approach to the cinema, conceived as a series of celluloid objects *and* dispersed publics. This museological approach provides an enduring thread in a field still largely oriented around the study of cinema as a series of discrete film objects. Yet, looking at MOMA should also provide a moment in which to reevaluate the very methods by which we continue to assess the status of film as a disciplinary object. This object has long been far more malleable than we tend to acknowledge; it is stretched, spread thin, broken apart, then reassembled and rearticulated across a surprising range of institutional sites, technological networks, and intellectual projects.

As for MOMA's Film Library, a close look at what it did complicates our basic ideas about film art and its institutions, demonstrating how much has changed in a short time and how multivalent and context sensitive were even the most established of film institutions, at least in the period examined here. This points to changing practices of film art and to the fragile material specificities of the medium — a medium shaped during the 1930s in a particularly influential way by authoritative cultural institutions and increasingly centralized organizations. Clearly, with the proliferation of individualized film theaters and many sources of authority now shaping the culture of film, the dynamics of value and materiality in film culture have dramatically changed. Yet I argue that looking back reminds us that these dynamics are indeed persistently diachronic and synchronic. The film object has long been a changing object; this change has long been part of our field and a key element of the debates that have shaped it. This is particularly true in a discipline that has constituted itself as a self-reflexive one that is determined to establish and maintain relevance across a range of cultural and intellectual activity and across the labyrinthine institution we call a university.

Notes

I would like to thank Charles Acland and Lee Grieveson for their valuable commentary on this essay. Funding also came from the Faculty of Fine Arts, Concordia University, Montreal, the Social Sciences and Humanities Research Council of Canada, and the McKnight Landgrant Foundation, University of Minnesota.

1. Emily Grenauer, "A Museum of the Cinema," *World-Telegram* (New York), June 27, 1935, Film Library Scrapbooks, Special Collections, Film Study Center, Department of Film and Media, Museum of Modern Art (hereafter SC-FSC, MOMA).
2. "Movies Museum Born: Harlow's Legs Immortal," *Telegraph* (New York), June 26, 1935, Film Library Scrapbooks, SC-FSC, MOMA.
3. "College Students May Win Degree for Research 'In Cinema,'" *World-Telegram* (New York), October 10, 1935, Film Library Scrapbooks, SC-FSC, MOMA. Sadly, no sustained study of this film has yet to be conducted.
4. John Hobart, "The Movies Crash the Curriculum," *Chronicle* (San Francisco), January 26, 1935, Film Library Scrapbooks, SC-FSC, MOMA.
5. For a general survey history of MOMA, see Russell Lynes, *Good Old Modern: An Intimate Portrait of the Museum of Modern Art* (New York: Atheneum, 1973); for an

overview of MOMA's early history and its relationship to film, see Haidee Wasson, *Museum Movies: The Museum of Modern Art and the Birth of Art Cinema* (Berkeley: University of California Press, 2005).

6. For instance, by 1939 museum officials calculated that news and comment about the museum appeared in an average of 239 newspapers and 24 magazines each month, with an average of 462 total articles per month. See Museum of Modern Art, *The Year's Work: Annual Report to Trustees and the Corporation Members of the Museum of Modern Art, June 30, 1939—July 1, 1940* (New York: Museum of Modern Art, 1940), 4. Russell Lynes has estimated that this amounted to ten times more publicity than for any other American museum. Russell Lynes, *Good Old Modern*, 126.

7. For more detailed discussion of consumerism and MOMA (and other museums) during this period, see Haidee Wasson, "Every Home an Art Museum: Mediating and Merchandising the Metropolitan," in *Residual Media*, edited by Charles Acland (Minneapolis: University of Minnesota Press, 2007); Carol Duncan, "Museums and Department Stores: Close Encounters," in *High-Pop: Making Culture into Popular Entertainment*, edited by Jim Collins (Malden, Mass.: Blackwell, 2002), 129–54; Marilyn F. Friedman, *Selling Good Design: Promoting the Early Modern Interior* (New York: Rizzoli, 2000); and Felicity Scott, "From Industrial Art to Design: The Purchase of Domesticity at MOMA, 1929–1959," *Lotus International* 97 (1998): 106–43.

8. For a discussion of these shifts, see Wasson, "The Mass Museology of the Modern," in *Museum Movies*, 68–109; and also Wasson, "Every Home an Art Museum."

9. For a fuller history of such theaters, see Barbara Wilinsky, *Sure Seaters: The Emergence of Art House Cinema* (Minneapolis: University of Minnesota Press, 2001).

10. Charles L. Turner, "Witnessing the Development of Independent Film Culture in New York: An Interview with Charles L. Turner," interview by Ronald S. Magliozzi, *Film History* 12.1 (2000): 72–96.

11. It is widely assumed that 75 percent of all American silent films are lost and that 50 percent of all films made prior to 1950 are gone (though these figures are not fully supported by systematic research). For more on this issue, see Anthony Slide, *Nitrate Won't Wait: A History of Film Preservation in the United States* (Jefferson, N.C.: McFarland, 1992). For an excellent overview of the various industrial, legal, material, and practical reasons that silent films have disappeared, see David Pierce, "The Legion of the Condemned—Why American Silent Films Perished," *Film History* 9.1 (1997): 5–22. These practices continued well beyond this period. In 1949 Universal burned its entire nitrate holdings from the silent period in order to reclaim the silver. For a brief but useful history of studio relations to archival projects, see Jan-Christopher Horak, "The Hollywood History Business," in *The End of Cinema as We Know It*, edited by Jon Lewis (New York: New York University Press, 2001), 33–42.

12. Each of these was published in conjunction with major film retrospectives. See Iris Barry, *DW Griffith: American Film Master* (New York: Museum of Modern Art,

1940); and Alistair Cooke, *Douglas Fairbanks: The Making of a Screen Character* (New York: Museum of Modern Art, 1940).

13. These notes were continuously updated over the years and are most widely available as *Film Notes*, edited by Eileen Bowser (New York: Museum of Modern Art, 1969). They also formed the basis of notes generated by film societies organized long after the beginnings of MOMA's Film Library. See, for example, Arthur Lennig, ed., *Film Notes of Wisconsin Film Society* (Madison: Wisconsin Film Society, 1960).

14. See Sergei Eisenstein, *The Film Sense*, edited and translated by Jay Leyda (New York: Harcourt Brace Jovanovich, 1942); Sergei Eisenstein, *Film Form: Essays in Film Theory*, edited and translated by Jay Leyda (New York: Harcourt Brace Jovanovich, 1949); and, later, Jay Leyda, *Kino: A History of the Russian Film* (London: Allen and Unwin, 1960). See also Siegfried Kracauer, *From Caligari to Hitler: A Psychological History of the German Film* (Princeton, N.J.: Princeton University Press, 1947).

15. Lewis Jacobs, *Rise of the American Film: A Critical History* (New York: Harcourt Brace and Company, 1939). A sampling of later works includes Bosley Crowther, *The Lion's Share: The Story of an Entertainment Empire* (New York: Dutton, 1957); Arthur Knight, *The Liveliest Art: A Panoramic History of the Movies* (New York: Macmillan, 1957); Arthur Calder-Marshall, Paul Rotha, and Basil Wright, *The Innocent Eye: The Life of Robert J. Flaherty* (London: Hutchinson, 1961); and Kenneth Macgowan, *Behind the Screen: the History and Techniques of the Motion Picture* (New York: Dell, 1965).

16. Fernand Leger delivered a lecture in 1935; Luis Buñuel also worked at the Film Library during the war years alongside enlisted Hollywood directors such as Frank Capra, Anatole Litvak, and John Ford.

17. Alfred Barr reportedly carried a copy with him during his 1932 trip to Europe, where among other tasks he viewed and attempted to collect films. See Paul Rotha, *The Film till Now: A Survey of the Cinema* (London: J. Cape, 1930).

18. "Interview: DHS" re: Paul Rotha RF 1.1 200, Box 250, Folder 2985, Rockefeller Archive Center (hereafter RAC). In his final report, Rotha concluded that the trade would never come around to the distribution of films "outside of the entertainment field." He asserted that some kind of public subsidy would be required to jumpstart educational films in the United States. He identified the Film Library as the obvious distribution mechanism, in part because it was the closest thing to a centralized agency. Rotha later requested further funds on the basis that he believed he could stimulate the making of documentary and educational films and provide expertise to projects currently underway. He also requested financial assistance for an updated version of *The Film till Now*, which was less than eight years old. Rotha cited high demand from universities and colleges that were eager to use the book in conjunction with their courses. See Rotha to John Marshall, February 24, 1938, RF RG 1.1 Series 200, Box 250, Folder 2986, 2, RAC.

19. "Interview: JM," re: Mr. Paul Rotha, 25 January 1938, RF 1.1, 200 R, Box 250, Folder 2986, RAC. Rotha also seems to have transported several GPO films to the library

when in transit, helping them to build their documentary collection and preparing the way for a major nonfiction retrospective launched in November 1939. See Paul Rotha to John Abbott "Letter," July 10, 1937, RF 1.1 200, Box 250, Folder 2985, RAC.

20. Quoted in William J. Buxton, "Reaching Human Minds: Rockefeller Philanthropy and Communications, 1935–39," in *The Development of the Social Sciences in the United States and Canada: The Role of Philanthropy*, edited by Theresa Richardson and Donald Fisher (Stamford, Conn.: Ablex, 1999), 180.

21. Rockefeller philanthropies continued their commitment to realizing this vision. The Humanities division of the foundation also funded the American Film Center (1938), an organization initially committed to fostering documentary film production and distribution, then later also to helping form a national distribution system linking film educators to educational film. The Rockefeller's General Education Board also funded the formation of the Association of School Film Libraries (1937), which was charged with helping to organize film collection, distribution, and use in American schools. See "RF Aid to the Museum of Modern Art Film Library, 1935–1949," RF 1.1 RG Series 200 R; Box 251, Folder 2993, RAC.

22. John Marshall, "Inter-office correspondence," March 28, 1938, RF 1.1 RG Series 200 R; Box 251, Folder 2986, RAC.

23. For more on the Rockefeller Foundation's relationship to film during these years, see Buxton, "Reaching Human Minds," 77–192.

24. These grants totaled approximately $8,500. See "RF Aid to the Museum of Modern Art Film Library, 1935–1949," RF 1.1 RG Series 200 R, Box 251, Folder 2993, RAC.

25. Indeed, it was these notes that led to a mounting controversy over MOMA's relationship to Stalinist policies, thereby leading to Leyda's resignation from the library. For more on this, see Wasson, *Museum Movies*, 81, 272n.85. Leyda's notes for the infamous program "Ten Programs: French, German, and Russian," can be found in the Department of Film Series, SC-FSC, MOMA.

26. Jay Leyda, "Have You Any Books about the Movies?" *Film History* 10.4 (1998): 448–52 (originally published in *Publishers Weekly*, September 1937).

27. *The Film Index* (pamphlet) Museum of Modern Art Archives; Alfred Barr Papers: I (AAA: 2166; 576).

28. Harold Leonard, ed., *The Film Index: A Bibliography. Volume 1: The Film as Art* (New York: Museum of Modern Art; W. H. Wilson Company, 1941).

29. These mimeographed lecture notes are available in the Department of Film Series, SC-FSC, MOMA.

30. For more on the founding of the Society of Cinematologists, see Jack Ellis, "The Society of Cinema Studies: A Personal Recollection of the Early Days," *Cinema Journal* 43.1 (fall 2003): 105–12.

31. For a more complete list of MOMA's early film programs and the films they showed, see Wasson, *Museum Movies* (esp. chapters 4, 5, and the appendix, which lists all known film exhibits from the beginning to 1948–49).

32. These figures are drawn from the *16 and 35mm Circulating Film Program* (New

York: Museum of Modern Art, 1944–45; SC-FSC, MOMA). I have not been able to determine precisely at which point in the Film Library's development the notes were so plentiful and free. There is, however, little reason to doubt that this was not the case from the very beginning of the circulating programs, which began only several years earlier in 1936.

33. *Film Notes* (New York: Museum of Modern Art, 1940), n.p. These early notes were written by Iris Barry, Alistair Cooke, Jay Leyda, and Richard Griffith (some pieces are signed but others are not).

34. Library staff also began to differentiate rental rates by film gauge and made the structure of available programs more flexible. For instance, in 1937 a feature film in 16mm cost $15 ($240 in 2008) while a feature film in 35mm cost $30 ($480 in 2008) ("Annual Report on the Film Library," 1939, Department of Film Series, SC-FSC, MOMA).The high cost of film rentals clearly worked against the rapid audience expansion that the museum hoped to achieve. During these early years it was already evident that film rentals, once held to be the primary method by which the library might wean itself from outside support, could simply never provide a self-sustaining source of income.

35. Such entities satisfied the legal agreement arranged with studios; no other formal institutional affiliation was necessary. See, for example, "Conditions of Rental," *Film Library Bulletin, Museum of Modern Art* (1940): 21–22.

36. The Dartmouth screenings are the one example I have been able to find of an English Department cosponsoring, with the Art and Archaeology Department, MOMA's film programs. See "Cinema Art Will be Studied in New Dartmouth Course," *Union* (Manchester, N.H.), February 17, 1936, Film Library Scrapbooks, SC-FSC, MOMA.

37. I would like to acknowledge Dana Polan for his assistance with sorting through this generative moment in the early history of American film study. For more, see Dana Polan, *Scenes of Instruction*: The Beginnings of the U.S. Study of Film (Berkeley: University of California Press, 2007).

38. *Film Library Bulletin*, 1938–39, Department of Film Series, SC-FSC, MOMA, 4. Interest in forming a film society also appeared in publications in Philadelphia. See Elsie Finn, "Film Fans Here Eager to Form Movie Society" *Record*, July 28, 1935, Film Library Scrapbooks, SC-FSC, MOMA.

39. Philip K. Scheuer, "Town Called Hollywood," *Los Angeles Times*, July 4, 1937, Film Library Scrapbooks, SC-FSC, MOMA. Los Angeles was, of course, an extremely germane site for such screenings, with its own lively film culture. It's also important to note that the first university degree granted for the study of film was given by the University of Southern California only several years earlier. For more on this topic, see Dana Polan's essay in this volume, and also his book *Scenes of Instruction*.

40. Leyda also lectured at New York University during this period. For more on staff activity during this period, see "Film Library Report (1937)," 34–35.

41. There were many projects before the 1930s already in formation, though some never came to fruition. For instance, in 1927 Will Hays and the president of Columbia

University, Nicholas Murray Butler, commissioned a committee to explore the feasibility of a "Motion Picture School of Technology" to assist in training those either already in the industry or those hoping to gain employment in the industry. Studio heads were consulted as the plan developed in order to better serve their interests. The program resembled a production-oriented training school. The committee was headed by Carl E. Milliken (MPPDA) and James C. Egbert (Columbia). See "Proposal for Establishment of a Motion Picture School of Technology," 1927: Colleges: Columbia, Motion Picture Producers and Distributors of America Archive, Motion Picture Association of America, New York. I am grateful to Richard Maltby for supplying me with copies of relevant MPPDA documents.

42. For more on film courses in the early 1930s, see Dana Polan's essay in this volume, and also his book *Scenes of Instruction*.

43. This last program included many of the now-standard elements of the early avant-garde canon, including *Rhythmus 21* (Hans Richter and Viking Eggeling, 1921), *Ballet mécanique* (Fernand Léger and Dudley Murphy, 1924), *Anémic cinéma* (Marcel Duchamp, 1926), and *Un chien andalou* (Luis Buñuel and Salvador Dalí, 1929).

44. All films and programs indicated here are listed in *16 and 35mm Circulating Film Program*.

45. See Iris Barry and Richard Griffith, "The Film Library and the Film of Fact," in *The Film of Fact* (New York: Museum of Modern Art, 1942), 1–5.

46. "General disinterest" was also cited as a fourth reason. Among those interested, a general lack of coordination plagued efforts at forging film art circuits throughout this period (Barry and Griffith, "The Film Library and the Film of Fact," 1–5). The film department's records are filled with Barry's letters to various distributors, collectors, and exhibitors trying to track down prints for library programs.

47. Film Library, Museum of Modern Art, "Cost of Circulating a 16mm Projector," in *Report on the Film Library*, Appendix G, RF 1.1, 200 R, Box 251, Folder 2996, RAC.

48. During this period, Barry estimated that the library was only able to earn back somewhere between 5 and 10 percent of its operating costs through income garnered by film rentals (Iris Barry to Rockefeller Foundation [report], March 1948, NAR 4, Series 111: 42, Box 139, Folder 1367, RAC).

49. See the essays by Acland and by Guest in this volume.

50. Indeed, Alfred Barr took an active role in the controversy over Roberto Rossellini's *The Miracle*, which led to the 1952 Supreme Court ruling granting First Amendment protection to film.

Classrooms, Clubs, and Community Circuits:

Cultural Authority and the Film Council

Movement, 1946–1957

CHARLES R. ACLAND

■ In 1949, Bernard Friend wrote an article for the *New York Times* about the liveliness of French film societies, noting that nothing comparable was evident in the United States.[1] Seymour Stern responded, protesting that indeed there was a good deal of activity though few were aware of it.[2] Amos Vogel seconded Stern's assessment, elaborating that what distinguished the French movement was its more centralized national operations, a feature evident with Canadian film societies as well. Yet while the U.S. scene lacked national coordination, Vogel went on to claim that "there is doubtless a more extensive functional use here of documentary and educational films by clubs and schools than there is in France."[3]

Later that year, updating Friend's article, Thomas Pryor wrote of the explosion of film societies in the United States. Hundreds of societies had appeared in the years following the end of World War II. With the expanding availability and decreasing cost of 16mm film and projectors, these societies helped guarantee broad distribution for nontheatrical film and for the serious treatment of film as a medium of cultural exchange and artistic expression. Significantly, the growth of these societies was far more rapid than the establishment of courses and programs of study in universities and colleges. While film courses remained rare, Pryor claimed that nearly every college had a film society.

Pryor indicated that the absence of a centralized national organization complicated access to prints and information about films. Instead, the numerous film societies relied upon libraries that had begun to handle films, circulating film programs from institutions like the Museum of Modern Art (MOMA) and Cinema 16, and various other community clubs and voluntary societies that offered facilities and audiences.[4] In this portrait, Pryor reiterated the distinction that Vogel had made, writing, "Unlike the far more numerous users of 16mm films for educational and informational purposes—these are known as 'functional pictures'—the film societies are primarily interested in furthering the study of cinematic art."[5]

In their agreement about the well-developed educational circuits, these commentators were tacitly acknowledging the work of the most visible, national, and influential U.S. film education organization of the 1940s and 1950s, the Film Council of America (FCA). What follows is an examination of the formation and ten-year-long operations of this organization, revealing its contribution to the changing nature of educational institutions and the opening up of spaces for film study. Not only did the coordinated and numerous educational film users put in place a technological infrastructure for nontheatrical film by building film libraries, constructing inventories of available films, and arguing for the purchase of projectors, but they equally did the work of establishing and circulating discourses about film. In their purview, even when serving an instructional purpose film was to be debated, assessed, and evaluated. This public and analytical process took place in written form, on television, and in group discussion.

Contrary to the taken-for-granted division between film societies and film educationalist organizations, the membership and operations of the two often overlapped, thereby making a strict delineation between functional and artistic approaches to film somewhat misleading. The emphasis upon, for instance, Cinema 16, the most widely recognized and documented U.S. film society, has served to underplay the presence and contribution of other types of film organizations—ones that were not necessarily urban based and whose primary enterprise was a brand of film activism combined with forms of film appreciation. On the whole, film education has received relatively minor attention from historians.[6] Indeed, instructional film primarily appears today as a kitschy and ironic reminder of an imaginary 1950s, having become fodder for pastiche.[7] Yet its connections to the formation of film studies are substantial, given that the term "film education" has at times designated both *education about film* and *education through film*. From the earliest film education experiments, it was not unusual to see its critics and champions oscillate between film's potential for mass education and the analysis of film in its own right.

The Film Council was a product of widespread interest in the educational

The logo of the Film
Council of America.

uses of new technological forms, an interest that flourished alongside anxieties
about mass society. Many educationalists in the first decades of the last century
embarked upon investigations of the pedagogical potential of motion pictures,
radio, slide shows, stereoscopes, projection technologies, microfilm, and, later,
television for a wide array of contexts. Their efforts had a lasting impact upon
classroom technology and the conceptualization of where education takes
place. The Film Council's work helped to settle decades of attempts to negotiate the educational challenges posed by new media. In general, it assisted in the
establishment of a critical vocabulary for cultural technologies, one that aided
the dispersal of classroom activity into other locations. Whereas much recent
discussion of modernity emphasizes changes in artistic, leisure, and work environments, we must also address the concomitant technological expansion
of the sites of, and language about, education. Acknowledging this dimension
affirms that histories of film education—education about and through film—
have to confront film's complex relationship to disparate instructional sites,
institutions, and objectives.

In addition to the technological and discursive expansion of the sites and
occasions of instructional activity, the modern educational movement had
another dimension: the organization of social and class factions. In the context of a sense of social upheaval, attempts to control and manage the ensuing
change became a matter of urgency. The expanding availability and mobility
of media—that is, sounds and images from elsewhere becoming ubiquitously
evident—destabilized the hold of traditional educational institutions, authorities, and ideals, thus engendering a certain crisis of modernity and calling forth
efforts to navigate and guide a potentially chaotic realm. The activities of the
FCA illustrate these designs, for just as it played a foundational role in the professionalization of film criticism and pedagogy, it equally legitimized a particular configuration of modern education and cultural authority.

Film cultures come into relief not only as a consequence of films produced but also within the context of their use, which includes the energies of critics, censors, policymakers, social progressives, and moral authorities as they argue for particular deployments of film. Film culture is a byproduct of the materiality of writing criticism, constructing arguments, and circulating articles — that is, the brainwork at the root of any discursive enterprise. As Antonio Gramsci elaborated, such activities are part of a dynamic interplay between intellectuals, education, and hegemony; it is here that one sees the emergence of class and national unity, as well as bridges to international contexts. As Gramsci famously wrote: "Every relationship of 'hegemony' is necessarily an educational relationship and occurs not only within a nation . . . but in the international and world-wide field, between complexes of national and continental civilisations,"[8] an axiom worth bearing in mind as we begin our chronicle of the rise of film studies.

Indispensable to Gramsci's analysis is his distinction between organic and traditional intellectuals. The latter are seen as situated in pseudo-classless locations and might be understood as the conventional sources of intellectual activity (artists, teachers, and religious representatives). In contrast, organic intellectuals, as James Joll puts it, "are somehow more closely bound to the class to which they belong."[9] Marcia Landy adds that they "serve as carriers of new ideas and are the legitimizers of [the class's] power."[10] They are implicated in the establishment of that class's character, qualities, and interests. In other words, organic intellectuals, by virtue of their more intricate association, brighten a class's character and boundaries. Classes have their thinkers whose work, however inadvertently, is the cultural and epistemological production and re-production of social factions.

Gramsci did not treat the traditional and the organic as stable categories of different intellectuals. Instead, he saw this distinction as a varying function of intellectual work, characterized by a relative engagement with and recognition of the sensibility of an era. As Joll describes it, "Organic intellectuals seem therefore to be both those traditional intellectuals who have understood the direction in which history is moving and those intellectuals thrown up by the revolutionary class itself to serve as its leaders."[11] How do new factions and their intellectuals emerge? How do traditional intellectuals become organic? Gramsci explained that the transformation occurs when leaders begin to respond to the tempo and conditions of change (or what he called "occasional, immediate, almost accidental" *conjunctural* moments).[12] Organic intellectuals are those who have a feel for that change, for the direction of history. Carl Boggs suggests that "feeling" begins with being "an organic part of a community; they must articulate new values within the shared language and symbols of the larger culture."[13] For Anne Showstack Sasson, this involves "a moral and intellectual reform in which intellectuals 'feel' in order to 'know' and the people are equipped to 'know' as well as 'feel.'"[14] As Gramsci wrote, "The organic intellectuals which every new class creates alongside itself and elaborates in the course of its development, are for the most part specializations of partial aspects of the primitive activity of the new social type which the new class has brought into prominence."[15] This then leads to the question, What new class or what new social type has been shaped and formed by the labor of the connected intellectual? While Gramsci was most interested in identifying the conditions under which an organic intellectual could unite and lead a working-class formation, I remain convinced that his insights offer a way to analyze the reinforcement of social division through the production of ideas—that is, through a new class and its resident intellectuals.

To account for the reconstruction of social factions in the context of historical change, Gramscian theory recommends a study of all levels of cultural practice, especially those producing and circulating ideas. As Renate Holub explains, this includes "newspapers, journals, almanacs, periodicals, parish bulletins . . . Everything which influences or is able to influence public opinion, directly or indirectly . . . libraries, schools, associations, clubs, even architecture, and the layout and names of streets."[16] The forces involved in the shaping of civic discourse and the modern political subject emanate from varied sources, many of which are not traditional places of instruction. The strict boundaries of educational projects have loosened and are porous, a development propelled by the reproducibility and transportability of cultural forms. Sasson asserts that part of Gramsci's insight on this count is that advanced capitalism has led to "the 'massification' and organization of intellectuals, the socialization and specialization of knowledge and the expansion and specialization of the structures for producing intellectuals."[17] As a result, the locations at which we find and might expect to encourage intellectual labor have multiplied.

Though Gramsci wrote very little of cinema, during his time film entered as a motor and emblem of change, in effect offering connection to the tempo of modern life as felt by a broad population. Below I argue that the materials and discourses pertaining to educational media, beginning well before the 1940s, were responsible for a reconfiguration and settlement of the locations of and procedures for mass education in the immediate postwar period. In particular, the organization of ideas about film was burdened with a reconstitution of social factions and the prospects for a response to changes in a mass age. Thus we witness parallel developments in process, with the first displaying a democratic impulse while the second betrays a technocratic one: the new media of the first half of the twentieth century expanded the locations of education and intellectual labor, forcing factions invested in the reproduction and stabilization of social order to work with—and in—those disparate locales to assure their management. This was done by revising traditional educational venues and by organizing new compacts of private citizens to extend the reconstruction of modern social subjects into those new venues. In this way, we witness a renegotiated relation between the state and civil society, with education and media as an especially fraught battleground.

In the first decades of the twentieth century, it was not obvious what sort of pedagogical procedure was most appropriate to new visual technologies. Educators asked, to borrow Charles F. Hoban's phrase, what did it mean to "visualize the curriculum"?[18] Before synchronized sound, one educational application was the lecture film, in which motion pictures operated as illustrated accompaniment to a speaker. Beyond the economic factors, the relatively slow conversion to sound film in educational contexts indicates that this model required reconsideration. The idea took hold that a notable part of film's educational component was in the postscreening discussion. Film would not stand alone but rather would be integrated with the guidance of an authority figure. Though precursors exist, film forums were novel enough in the 1940s to necessitate testing. For instance in 1941 the American Library Association (ALA), the American Association of Adult Education, the American Association of Applied Psychology, and the American Film Center (AFC) jointly ran experiments using film to generate public discussion at Columbia University and at public libraries across the country in the expectation of a subsequent national launch of film programs.[19]

Driving the emerging visual educational procedures were a number of initiatives that took place under the umbrella of philanthropic and industrial support, including several Rockefeller Foundation grants to the Motion Picture Project of the American Council on Education (ACE),[20] as well as to the Joint Committee on Educational Films, formed in 1940, an effort on behalf of the ALA, the Association of School Film Libraries (ASFL), the Motion Picture Project of the ACE, and the AFC.[21] In 1943, the Educational Film Library Association (EFLA) was launched, taking the AFC's publication *Film News* as its house organ. The wave of institutional activity demonstrates the perceived importance of introducing film to instruction, of developing an appropriate pedagogical standard for it, and of founding new agencies specifically charged with this task. Further, as I discuss below, there was a high degree of duplication among the luminaries involved at the executive level across these fledgling organizations, resulting in a tight network of influential individuals.

Despite this surge of activity, nothing compared to the scope and ambition of the Office of War Information's (OWI) plans to mobilize the U.S. population in service of the war effort. One central program relied on film's effectiveness in explaining world events and the patriotic contribution that individuals could make. Promoting the collection of metal and rubber, selling war bonds, and interpreting the U.S. involvement in the war were propagandistic endeavors of the OWI, but ones that would cut across the ideological affiliations of a peacetime context. The wartime film program encompassed the distribution as much as the production of ideologically appropriate informational shorts. Beginning in 1943, the OWI's film objectives were to capitalize upon and expand existing school and community media facilities, thereby helping to orchestrate channels through which government information could reach local audiences. The head of the OWI's National 16mm Advisory Committee was C. R. Reagan, the founder and president of the educational technology firm Visual Education, Inc. in Austin, Texas, and the first president of the National Association of Visual Education Dealers (NAVED). The Advisory Committee coordinated the work, and relied upon the resources, of seven education and commercial organizations active in 16mm informational film.[22] With their assistance volunteers organized film screenings, and war-related film programs reached labor unions, church groups, women's clubs, schools, and other community organizations. The committee achieved this by gaining access to established resources, the most important of which were the over 25,000 16mm sound projectors held in educational and community institutions.[23] In essence, the initiatives opened up both public and private materials to community leaders in the context of a national emergency. By the end of the war two years later, they estimated their total audience to have been 300 million.[24]

After the cessation of hostilities in Europe, the Advisory Committee became the National 16mm Victory Film Committee and launched a five-month campaign to sell victory bonds, closing out 1945.[25] Their success encouraged those at its final meeting, in January 1946, to transform the committee into a civilian operation—one that would continue to promote film as a catalyst to community action and instruction and that could be called upon to mobilize people should the government require it.[26] With the termination of federal support at the war's conclusion, a largely voluntary film education movement stepped in to fill that void. The members formed the Film Council of America on January 17, 1946. The first orders of business were as follows: to encourage and affiliate local film councils as community centers of film information and activity; to document the wartime activities of the National 16mm Advisory Committee; to target larger consumer groups for closer relationships; to assure that the Library of Congress would continue to provide access to wartime films; to support the establishment of an audiovisual (AV) division of the U.S. Office of Education; and to lobby for national support in the free flow of international film.[27]

The Film Council remained a joint effort on the part of the original seven member organizations of the OWI committee, with Reagan still in charge as its elected president.[28] According to its constitution, the Film Council was a non-profit, educational association whose mission was "to increase the information and work toward the general welfare of all people by fostering, improving and promoting the production, the distribution, and the effective use of audiovisual materials."[29] The organization was to pursue these ideals by coordinating and supporting the activities of community-based councils and national AV organizations, whether commercial or educational.[30] Its main function over the years was to be a clearinghouse for information about film's classroom and community use. In this way, the FCA would help address what the 16mm film reviewer for the *Saturday Review of Literature* Cecile Starr later called "the staggering confusion in the distribution field."[31]

Other industry and educational enterprises voiced support for the rumblings of coordination in the nontheatrical field. Backing the Film Council was the Photographic Industry Coordinating Committee, with the manager of the Films Division at Bell & Howell, the president of the Allied Non-Theatrical Film Association, and the FCA member William F. Kruse as its chair. By early 1951, thirty organizations had affiliated with the FCA, including the American Automobile Association, American Jewish Congress, American Nurses' Association, Anti-Defamation League of B'nai B'rith, Boy and Girl Scouts of America, Canadian Film Institute, and International Ladies Garment Workers' Union.

The desire for the continuation of the wartime mobilization was contingent upon an assessment of film's vital place in everyday life. The 16mm format was finally coming into its own as it reached its twenty-fifth anniversary in 1947. With a broader agreement about film in education than had ever existed, and with a reduction in the cost of equipment, more clubs and schools were purchasing projectors and integrating 16mm films into their curricula. The distri-

Volume III Issue 2

July - August 1949

Film Council of America
6 West Ontario Street
Chicago, Illinois

1949 CONFERENCE REPORT

FILMS
for
COMMUNITY
ACTION

Cover of the FCA's magazine *Film Counselor*, July–August 1949.

bution channels, however, were still maturing and had not yet stabilized. They consisted of many small, scattered companies that had little understanding of what films their clients actually wanted. J. R. Bingham, director of the largest nontheatrical enterprise, the YMCA's Motion Picture Bureau, commented at the time that institutions and homes were purchasing projectors at a remarkable rate, and that training for how best to use the technology was now a going concern.[32] These factors bred an enthusiasm for a dynamic industrial sector of manufacturers, film producers, and sundry nontheatrical programs responsive to informational and pedagogical needs. Albert J. Rosenberg of McGraw-Hill's Text-Film Department noted the initial reluctance of most publishers in the 1940s to enter the instructional film business, reckoning that the market was simply still too small. Rapid expansion was now evident. Rosenberg claimed that before the war the best films sold three hundred prints in six or eight years, while the Text-Film Department's films sold over two hundred their first year, in 1948.[33]

For its part, 16mm was creating a degree of turbulence in Hollywood. Some commercial exhibitors considered switching to the cheaper format, reasoning that audiences could hardly perceive the difference from the standard 35mm projections.[34] As a now mature apparatus, 16mm expanded substantially the location and occasion of commercial exhibition. For instance, some major studios saw the lighter and hence more transportable 16mm as the future standard for international markets, and they encouraged exhibitors abroad to invest in the format.[35] During the war, 16mm prints of feature films had been provided for exhibition overseas. These prints were virtually impossible to track down; they remained in circulation and were being smuggled back into the United States. Small distributors apparently approached schools, libraries, and community groups as possible buyers or renters of these bootleg copies.[36] So-called jackrabbit exhibitors appeared who, with the increasingly insubstantial investment in a 16mm projector, could set up a fly-by-night theater featuring major motion pictures.[37] Simply put, the 16mm sector was wildly unorganized, decentralized, and difficult to monitor let alone control. The Film Council's efforts to coordinate and legitimate the 16mm field responded to these and other concerns that the format would destabilize theatrical operations and negatively affect the market. Moreover, what was a black market nightmare for commercial distributors was a chaotic frontier for educational interests. In 1947, Floyde Brooker, head of the AV Division of the U.S. Office of Education (and who was to become chair of FCA Board of Trustees in the 1950s), likened "the educational film field to the Gold Rush of 1849: everyone thinks there is

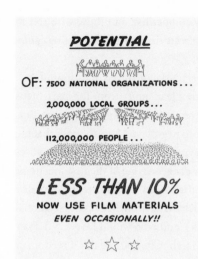

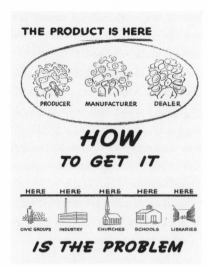

The FCA's understanding of potential audience and distribution challenges as illustrated in *Film Counselor*, June 1952.

THE **FCA** CAN GET USEFUL FILM MATERIALS AND EQUIPMENT TO YOU AND YOUR ORGANIZATION AND HELP YOUR GROUP TO USE THEM EFFECTIVELY...

Because...

FCA is the ONLY agency through which ALL film interests, professional, commercial and general can be co-ordinated in the continuing national emergency.

FCA through mass distribution of subject area film lists, promotional literature about films, and information about film libraries and equipment distributors will create an E-X-P-A-N-D-I-N-G market.

FCA through preview centers, local film councils and film information centers WILL GET THE PRODUCT TO THE CONSUMER.

FCA by aiding national and community organizations to make more effective selection and use of film materials through publications, correspondence and clearing house facilities will help assure a solidly growing market.

FCA by offering publications and instruction on the effective use of films and film equipment will teach the consumer how to use audio-visual materials.

FCA through co-operation with government agencies, U.S. film societies, and international film festivals, will stimulate interest in films among people not now seeing films.

The FCA's pledge to exploit new distribution and market opportunities as illustrated in *Film Counselor*, June 1952.

money to be made in the field; it is highly competitive and those who rise to the top have to be aggressive and therefore create discord; as in a mining camp, there is no law and order."[38]

Organizing the burgeoning nontheatrical market involved questions of censorship, for which the Film Council became a lead entity from the start. Steps to regulate 16mm had been initiated by several states, promising a restrictive, expensive, and uneven field for distributors to negotiate. Many thought that the censorship laws for the mainstream industry, which for all intents and purposes meant 35mm, did not extend to the smaller gauge. At one of the first meetings, David Strom recommended a "Freedom of the Screen" committee during a discussion on pending censorship battles.[39] Richard Griffith, head of the National Board of Review for Motion Pictures (NBR), and who would be elected chair of the New York Film Council (NYFC) in March 1947, became the "Freedom of the Screen" committee chair.[40] He was an obvious choice, given the NBR's longstanding policy of "classification, not censorship." When Detroit announced it would censor all 16mm films, regardless of their use, and Pennsylvania seized prints, imposed fines, and made arrests because the films had not been previewed and classified, alarms sounded.[41]

Griffith expressed the opinion that the FCA would eventually operate like the NBR. He complained that not many nontheatrical films were submitted to the NBR for review, which should not be surprising given that its primary concern was commercial features. Its association with the Film Council offered the possibility of bolstering its responsibility for educational film as well. After all, the NBR already had its own local council structure, with hundreds of chapters. Operating under the auspice of the NBR's National Motion Picture Council (NMPC), these councils dealt with entertainment and theatrical productions.[42] Called the NMPC since 1936, it had its origins in the Federal Motion Picture Council of the early 1920s, which became the Better Films National Council in 1926, with the slogan "mobilize for wholesome motion pictures." As Bettina Gunczy, chair of NMPC, explained, the FCA's purpose was "to foster and promote the production, distribution, and use of the informational film media," while the NMPC's role was "to provide a constructive community program for the study, support, and best use of the motion picture as entertainment and education."[43] Gunczy regularly sent explanations about the differences to both existing and newly created councils, emphasizing that the two were complimentary rather than redundant.

Despite their respective missions, Griffith more boldly felt that the amalgamation of the FCA and the NBR was inevitable. As he put it to the head of

NAVED, Don White: "More and more I am convinced also that the National Board of Review and the Film Council of America are one and the same thing. From now on I'm going to proceed to make that true."[44] He even discussed the idea of combining the two with the Film Council's president Reagan, who was extremely receptive.[45] According to Griffith, it was perfectly consistent with the designs of each operation for the NBR to handle 35mm and for the FCA to focus on 16mm,[46] which would break down into theatrical and nontheatrical respectively, though this ambitious level of coordination never spread beyond Griffith and Reagan.

While 16mm remained the focal point, the Film Council sought a role in the larger field of audiovisual education, promoting the use of filmstrips—lessons consisting of 35mm celluloid strips of still images—alongside motion pictures. The coordination of the 16mm field paralleled similar attempts to streamline all audiovisual services. Precisely a year after the establishment of the FCA, many of the same heads of governmental, industrial, and voluntary societies met to consider creating an all-encompassing national educational media organization, tentatively called the American Visual Council.[47] At the meeting, John Grierson, then chair of International Film Associates, summed up the situation by stating, "The present set-up is unquestionably disorderly yet there is infinitely more vitality in [the] U.S. than in other countries to do the jobs."[48] The state of flux, the ascendancy of the Film Council, and the temporary unsteadiness of the NBR meant that it was not shocking to hear Griffith reiterate that "the NBR is prepared to be liquidated as a separate unit and be absorbed into a National Council."[49] The record of this meeting gives a full indication of the continuity that existed between film and other media, between theatrical and nontheatrical film representatives, between commercial and educational interests, and between the personalities taking leadership roles.

Not all parties were confident about the Film Council's prospects. Roger Albright of Teaching Film Custodians was especially critical of Reagan and saw the FCA as "pretty much a paper organization conceived by C. R. Reagan to promote C. R. Reagan . . . set up primarily for his own prestige."[50] Nor were all parties enamored with the participation of the NBR with the Film Council. To establish its authority on the nontheatrical scene for government, industry, and voluntary societies alike, the Film Council had to appear to operate outside the influence of Hollywood. The NBR, quite simply, was perceived by some as too close to the theatrical industry. The NBR's application to become a member organization briefly stalled as some on the FCA board saw it as a step toward commercialization, prompting Reagan to protest otherwise.[51] This conflict was not an expression of anti-commercialization, and we should remember that the Film Council, as initially conceived, was to represent the interests of the fast-growing nontheatrical industry as much as public educational enterprises, thus billing itself as a legitimate liaison between public and private concerns. For its first three years, the majority of its funds arrived as contributions from companies in the nontheatrical or educational business.[52]

The Film Council's activities echoed the wartime efforts of the Advisory Committee. For the FCA, film could orchestrate the dissemination of information on specified topics and muster participation from a citizenry. The programs linked the education of the population with active community service, even if that service meant involvement with postscreening public discussions. Audiences in dispersed settings confronted carefully rendered ideas, debating their merits with the guidance of a council member, leading to assessments of what can be done in one's immediate community. The Film Council cooperated with the National Committee on Atomic Information in preparing a survey of films on military and civilian uses of atomic power.[53] Similarly, the Film Council coordinated screenings promoting food drives, as requested by the U.S. Department of Agriculture.[54] Even as late as 1950, they passed a resolution to make their services available in light of the "national emergency" of the Korean War, and then they communicated this information to President Truman.[55]

However, over time these initiatives became less central, and their function as a producer and provider of film information rose to be their core activity. Throughout its decade of operations, organizing members wrote and circulated pamphlets to assist local councils in finding and acquiring films, building film information centers, and surveying community resources.[56] Beyond its role as a national information clearinghouse, the Film Council initiated film events that were designed to spark discussions about specific pressing topics as well as about film itself. In addition, the council distributed booklets on these activities.[57] In early 1946, a few weeks after the founding of the Film Council, one of its first branches, the NYFC, was launched (incidentally placing it more than a year and a half ahead of Cinema 16's appearance). By March, Thomas Brandon—head of the prominent nontheatrical distributors, Brandon Films— was elected chair of the NYFC. Other luminaries participating on the board—a lineup demonstrating joint educational, commercial, and artistic representation—included Richard Griffith, Willard Van Dyke (from Affiliated Film Producers, and later the head of MOMA Film Library), Albert Rosenberg (McGraw-Hill), Iris Barry (MOMA Film Library), Bosley Crowther (*New York Times* film critic), Eileen Cypher (Museum of Natural History), Ella A. Marquardt (Films, Inc.), and Elizabeth Florey (EFLA).[58]

Grierson was the featured speaker at the NYFC's first public event. He addressed the audience of more than 250 on the importance of film for public education and on the need for coordination in nontheatrical services.[59] Grierson summed up the U.S. situation as having "not yet arrived at a clear definition of the relationship between private enterprise and public responsibility in the matter of the mass communication, nor specifically have you yet defined where the government's information needs and the interests of the film industry coincide," and he pointed to the new FCA as having begun to address this.[60] In his speech he also succinctly articulated the new educational priorities to which nontheatrical and community organizations were to respond, stating that "a new generation of teachers has to be developed which will more fully understand the *difference between curriculum pedagogy and the larger work of creating a civic imagination fit for the new cooperative world.*"[61]

What followed was a publicity blitz about the Film Council, with articles announcing and encouraging the formation of local film councils appearing in adult education, library, and audiovisual magazines as well as in daily newspapers.[62] Though the idea of educational applications of film was far from novel in the late 1940s, it is worth bearing in mind that the Film Council still had basic work to do in this area. For instance, occasionally it had to reassure its patrons that 16mm was safe and relatively easy to use, and the very idea of the film council required explanation. Glen Burch, the executive director of the FCA from 1948 to 1951, in his contribution to the collection *Ideas on Film* characterized the postwar phenomenon of councils as a response to perceived community problems in accessing and evaluating informational films.[63] In so doing he noted the influence of the Chicago Film Council and its World Festival of 1947, which is described as the first documentary film festival in the United States.[64] Interest in the council movement rested upon a belief that film is a valuable instrument for learning about this "rapidly changing world" and that people "must learn to choose for themselves, from among all the films available." As Burch continued, "The film-council movement might be defined as a growing and determined effort on the part of the people of this country to 1) make good films and other useful audiovisual materials readily accessible where they live, and 2) learn how to select them wisely and use them effectively in programs for the common good. In so far as progress is made toward these goals the ever-present danger that films will become increasingly a medium for mass exploitation and indoctrination will be greatly diminished."[65] Burch's rhetoric lays bare the dominant view that film was either an instrument of or threat to mass democracy. The councils operated to ensure the former by constructing a brand of coordinated liberal civic responsibility about and through motion pictures.

In this and other respects, the concerns of the film council and the film society often appeared to be identical. Amos Vogel, in a chapter following Burch's in the same volume, described film societies as similarly confronting issues of film sources and film evaluation.[66] Like the council, Vogel saw the society as rooted in and responsive to community contexts. In the end, the differences were ones of tone and commitment. The council movement saw itself as especially responsive to community educational needs in contrast to the more avant-gardist interests of the societies. However, even this breaks down upon closer examination, and we see that the films shown and the lead individuals involved were often the same. Indeed, as with other publications, *Ideas on Film* sought to bridge the two operations by advancing the "idea-film," which would include feature, informational, documentary, and experimental films.

In the FCA's first year the Chicago Film Council hosted Thomas Baird, the director of the Films Division of the British Information Service, who gave a speech titled "Film and International Understanding"; the NYFC featured Iris Barry on "Educational Film Industries in Europe"; and the Washington branch hosted Pare Lorentz. The NYFC organized a celebratory luncheon for Robert Flaherty.[67] In New York, the council held and promoted sessions jointly with Cinema 16.[68] In early 1952, together they presented *Valley Town* (Willard Van Dyke, 1940) with Vogel and George Amberg; a session called "New Frontiers of the Cinema" at NYU and one called "Why Experimental Films?" hosted by Edward Steichen at MOMA; and various UNESCO films and the perennial favorites *Night Mail* (Harry Watt and Basil Wright, 1936) and *The River* (Pare Lorenz, 1937).[69]

Activities ran the gamut ranging from organizing film festivals to holding audiovisual workshops for educators. Certification and evaluation committees were a central undertaking, and in 1952 the Film Council promoted its Film Preview Project, which was developed to establish centers for the efficient evaluation and packaging of film programs.[70] As Robertson Sillars put it in his booklet on film evaluation, the purpose "is to weed out the poor and unsuitable films from the ones that are good and meet a real need."[71] He recommended that a preview committee be made up of representatives of community organizations. Their work involved recording details about the film (length, pro-

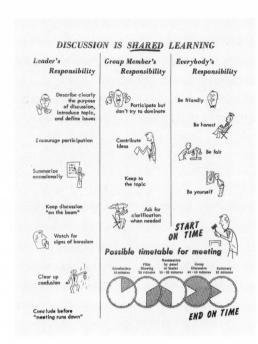

DISCUSSION IS SHARED LEARNING

Leader's Responsibility

Describe clearly the purpose of discussion, introduce topic, and define issues

Encourage participation

Summarize occasionally

Keep discussion "on the beam"

Watch for signs of boredom

Clear up confusion

Conclude before "meeting runs down"

Group Member's Responsibility

Participate but don't try to dominate

Contribute Ideas

Keep to the topic

Ask for clarification when needed

Everybody's Responsibility

Be friendly

Be honest

Be fair

Be yourself

START ON TIME

Possible timetable for meeting

Introduction 10 minutes — Film Showing 20 minutes — Presentation by panel or leader 10-20 minutes — Group Discussion 40-50 minutes — Summary 10 minutes

END ON TIME

Information on the Experimental Film Discussion Project circulated by the FCA, 1952.

ducer, distributor, synopsis, etc.) and judging its value and potential uses. The evaluation included assessments of a film's narrative qualities, its effectiveness and clarity of presentation, and its stylistic merits. These points were to add up to an overall judgment of the film's potential in presenting information, in provoking thought and discussion, and in motivating action, and the judgments were used to make recommendations for the purchase or rental of films.

Typically, film council events combined lectures, discussions, and screenings, with topics covering world peace, various local and international issues, and AV education generally.[72] Popular programs treated mental hygiene, labor relations, atomic power, traffic safety, sexuality, and race relations. Taken together, the defining issues sought to educate audiences in service of a vision of modern citizenship. Importantly, those in attendance were not merely instructed on the topic but also expected to participate, thus enacting an idea of mass democracy in which complex social problems and situations could be encountered in grassroots forums. Beyond recommending topics and appropriate films, the Film Council actively promoted the forum ideal by circulating material on how to run such events. As William Kruse wrote, "The local film council is able to help the individual social units of its town to a constant, effective use of film programs specifically suited to their own normal activities.

Week after week, or at any other desired intervals, films can be brought in to suit the specific purposes of the club, church, school or other group."[73] He saw the councils as modern-day chautauquas, though more stable and responsive to the community.

The coordination of these fields for mass democratic subject formation included cross-media events. For instance, a NYFC talk on educational film use doubled as a televised installment of the Dumont television network's *Serving through Science*, which was broadcast from the Wanamaker Department Store.[74] The Film Council's second annual conference in Chicago included a televised film forum.[75] The Des Moines Film Council conducted televised film discussions at Iowa State College's station WOI-TV in 1950.[76] In other words, this incarnation of the council movement was as invested in ways to disseminate talk as it was in film itself.

To grasp the significance of the council movement, one must note the extraordinary level of activity of even the smallest local branches affiliated with the Film Council. The range of topics, the inventiveness of screening venues, and the sheer number of films remains impressive to this day. In 1952 alone, for example, the council serving International Falls, Minnesota, sponsored 437 film events at seventy-five different venues, with a total audience of 27,679.[77] Expressed as an average, this means that in this remote community there was at least one screening every night of the year, with each event attended by over sixty-three people. These screenings took full advantage of 16mm film's mobility by transforming an assortment of locations, including libraries, department stores, hotels, churches, community halls, and schools, into exhibition spaces.[78] The entire community-based network of roughly one hundred affiliated councils forged a link among these spaces and institutions, thereby effectively constructing a quasi-public educational system. Though much of the Film Council's rhetoric involved a brand of community empowerment in which film forums were driven by grassroots concerns, the organization sought to harmonize these spaces by encouraging, promoting, and providing access to film programs sanctioned by the national executive.

The approach forwarded by the Film Council involved integrating existing institutional life with a system of educational priorities and managed discussion. For instance, representing the Film Council at a conference on juvenile delinquency, Kruse spoke of the place of film in schools, homes, and community centers as a vehicle of citizenship: "Serving rather than competing with existing inter-club and inter-faith movements, the film councils may be able to make the motion picture a sorely needed catalyst for effective, unified, democratic action in every community in which they function."[79] Events were far too numerous for the FCA to exert any kind of total defining influence, and tensions between the local and national levels of organization were evident from the beginning. Nevertheless, the act of constructing the avenues of national coordination, advocating better relations between public and private interests, and occupying leisure spaces and times with a managed educational agenda worked to organize a field of pedagogical investment not singularly tied to schools. Thus, the cultural authorities of the council movement not only selected and publicized the topic and content of films but also operated as organic intellectuals by establishing the procedures of gathering voluntary participation in an idea of modern citizenship, characterized by scattered locations and leisure times molded to act in the service of community and national interest. In short, the *procedures of mobilization* were the defining attributes of this expanded public sphere of screens.

After several years of assessing the educational film scene, the Carnegie Corporation offered support to the Film Council. They saw their 1948 grant of $10,000 per year for two years as complimentary to one given to the ALA, as the latter was aimed at facilitating distribution while the former worked to garner audiences and use film "intelligently."[80] To make a public event of the award, Gloria Waldron of the Twentieth Century Fund asked the actor Eddie Albert to be a "drawing card" at the press conference, to which "he agreed enthusiastically," and Griffith asked Iris Barry for the use of MOMA facilities.[81] The Carnegie grant was to be used for the salary of the executive director, who at the time was the newly elected Glen Burch.[82]

In summer 1948, UNESCO invited Reagan to a meeting of world AV experts in Paris.[83] Unexpectedly, he died at the congress, leaving his wife with the last words, "You finish my speech. Tell them about the FCA."[84] Such evangelical zeal seemed to be shared by other members. Film Council activity was only gaining speed. Local councils met in Chicago in August 1948 for their first annual convention, which was timed to coincide with the meetings of the Midwest Forum on Audio-Visual Teaching Aids, the EFLA, and NAVED, all of which were part of the twentieth-anniversary celebrations of 16mm.[85] In January 1950 at Naval Training Station, Great Lakes, Illinois, the Film Council ran a conference on audiovisual training, at which about forty AV experts were present. As described by the Carnegie Corporation's Florence Anderson, the conference goal was "to make specific recommendations as to what the professional workers in the audiovisual field might do to help the teachers colleges to do a better job, by consultation, preparation of bibliographies, film lists, helping with workshops, etc."[86]

In addition to constructing inventories of materials and methods, one of the Film Council's lasting facets was its commitment to publishing. In fact, the council became a de facto publishing enterprise with members producing their own volumes and contributing essays to collections and periodicals. Thurmon White's *Speaking of Films* was the organization's first in-house publication.[87] Described as a manual for the organization and operation of local film councils, *Speaking of Films* laid out the council idea, specified the likely community and club participants, and promoted the FCA's coordinating role. As White put it succinctly: "Every council meeting will use a film; every meeting will have a current, pertinent common problem; every meeting will have a discussion."[88] In addition to providing guidelines for fund-raising, advertising, and evaluation committees, the publication recommended regular classes to train projectionists. *Business Screen*, the trade companion to *Educational Screen*, provided production support for *Speaking of Films* and several other Film Council publications.[89]

Glen Burch was among one of the most prolific contributors to this emergent discourse.[90] He oversaw the production of eight "how-to" pamphlets, of which the Film Council distributed 13,094 copies in 1948–49 alone. Several of the more popular pamphlets had multiple print runs and stayed in circulation through the mid-1950s.[91] The FCA also conducted surveys of AV activities, distributed 20,000 copies of their promotional leaflet "Films Can Help You—and Your Community," and sponsored the U.S. distribution of *Film and You* (Jean Palardy and Donald Peters, 1948), a National Film Board of Canada (NFB) documentary on the council movement.[92] *Film Counselor* was the Film Council's magazine, with roughly ten issues a year. Beginning in May 1947 as an inexpensive newsletter, it adopted a more expensive, glossy format in 1950, which prompted protests from the editor of *Film News*, Rohama Lee, who worried about splitting the market for an informational film magazine.[93] *Rushes*, the Film Council's weekly newsletter covering educational film news and new 16mm releases, received distribution support from the Arthur P. Sloan Foundation and the Ford Foundation's Fund for Adult Education (FAE) in 1955.[94]

The most considerable of council publications were Charles Bushong's *Community Film Use*, which detailed the running of film discussions, and the two-part "Film Counselor Series" consisting of *Sixty Years of 16mm Film, 1923–*

1983: A Symposium and *A Guide to Film Services of National Associations.*[95] The latter presented 135 profiles of national societies involved with nontheatrical film, and the former looked at thirty years of development of features, shorts, and societies and then projected ahead another thirty years, with the essays focusing on the sites of audiovisual education. To this end the volume did not address films themselves but rather chose instead to devote most attention to institutional uses, including schools, industry, farms, libraries, museums, and churches.

Throughout its existence, the Film Council continued to negotiate its status with respect to the nontheatrical industry. While executive members agreed that it would be detrimental to their objectives if they were perceived to be a trade organization, they nonetheless felt that they were the only national body to communicate interests between manufacturers, producers, schools, community groups, and the general public.[96] Tensions on this point split the membership. At one meeting in 1951, the Carnegie Corporation's Florence Anderson noted that "talk was mostly at cross purposes." The conflict between representing industry or public welfare was such that the chair Floyde Brooker "started by laying down three premises on which he said there was sufficient agreement and suggested going on from there. Unfortunately, no such agreement was present, and none came out of the discussion."[97] The result was a decision not to focus on the promotion of local councils in favor of more effort at the national level—a decision that did not please the membership.[98]

Despite its cozy association with the commercial side of nontheatrical film, the Film Council confronted a nearly fatal financial crisis in early 1951, only to be rescued in the final hour by a grant from the Ford Foundation's FAE, with the personal assistance of the head of the fund, Scott Fletcher, who was president of Encyclopedia Britannica Films and, conveniently, an FCA board member.[99] The FAE announced awards of $20,000 and then $30,000 for 1951 and 1952, respectively; coincidentally Burch, then the outgoing FCA executive director, had been hired to work for the FAE's experimental film discussion project.[100]

With these events yet another branch of the outfit emerged. Tension between community clubs and adult education was added to those between industry and public service and between national and local representation. The FAE's grant to increase local councils, film information centers, and experiments in distribution in the service of adult education came at virtually the same time that the Film Council promised to put its resources at the disposal of training and informing citizens about the looming international crisis, again a holdover

American Film Assembly

GOLDEN REEL
FILM FESTIVAL

Program 1955   THE WALDORF-ASTORIA
                      NEW YORK

SPONSORED BY THE FILM COUNCIL OF AMERICA., 600 DAVIS STREET, EVANSTON, ILLINOIS

Cover for the American Film
Assembly Program, 1955.

activity from its wartime precursor. While the agendas of community service
and adult education are not mutually exclusive, they are not equivalent. In fact,
representatives of some local councils began to complain that there was too
little attention to them, too much attention to adult education, and not enough
"safeguarding against infiltration by undesirable persons."[101]

After Burch stepped down, and before Paul Wagner (Educational and Public Relations Director, Bell & Howell) took his place, the Film Council was
relatively dormant from summer 1951 to spring 1952.[102] In November 1951, the
council directory lists one hundred active councils; a year later, only around
thirty had paid up their dues.[103] Nevertheless, under Wagner, events with national visibility reached a peak with the FCA's American Film Assembly (AFA),
at which it ran the annual Golden Reel Film Festival from 1954 to 1957. At the
first festival, speakers included the NFB chair A. W. Trueman, Gilbert Seldes,
and Jack Ellis.[104] At this time, the Film Council board included such famous
names as the Walt Disney president Roy Disney, the CBS president Frank Stanton, Eddie Albert, and Eleanor Roosevelt. The second AFA had over two thousand participants registered, and it featured James Card, curator of Eastman
House, speaking on the history of 16mm; Bosley Crowther on 16mm's role in

American society; and Paul Rotha on 16mm's role in international understanding.[105] Film award categories included citizenship and government, industrial processes, recreation, visual arts, sound-slide, and avant-garde and experimental film, as well as best classroom film for various educational levels.

These meetings were tangible coinciding moments for the society and council movements. At the first AFA, a Film Society Caucus formed to assist "film societies, film series, film clubs, and film study groups."[106] With this, the Film Council extended its support to the coordination of the still-decentralized film society movement. The first order of business was a survey of existing operations, done with the assistance of Brandon Films, Cinema 16, Contemporary Films, Kinesis, MOMA Film Library, *Saturday Review*, and Trans-World Films.[107] From this initial spark grew the American Federation of Film Societies, in 1955.

One marker of the recognition and efficacy of any national organization is its appearance on the international scene as a legitimate representative of the nation. George Zook encouraged the Film Council to become the Film Panel of UNESCO's National Commission even as the FCA was just getting started.[108] For the next few years, the Film Council sent board members to UNESCO conventions. Edgar Dale, author of one of the Payne Fund volumes in the 1930s, served on the board of the EFLA, acted as chair of the Film Council's International Relations Committee, and was also chair of the Film Panel of UNESCO's National Commission from 1949.[109] The same year, the State Department approached the Film Council to be the responsible body for evaluating and selecting films for international festivals for the United States.[110] The Film Council operated in that capacity for the Venice and Edinburgh Festivals from 1952 to 1957. After the FCA folded, the Department of Audio-Visual Instruction (DAVI) of the National Education Association (NEA) hastily assembled the Committee on International Non-Theatrical Events (CINE) to take over the task.[111]

With the last of the FAE grant spent and no further funds on the horizon, and with other stable organizations taking on what had been council responsibilities, the FCA closed shop in 1957. The EFLA, one of the original seven organizations that made up the Film Council, had dropped its membership, believing that the FCA was no longer a liaison organization and was instead pursuing its own objectives.[112] The EFLA launched the American Film Festival in response to the void left by the termination of the Golden Reel Awards. This festival was an annual event similarly designed to showcase educational film, the first of which took place in New York in April 1959.[113] After the Film Council folded, some local councils continued operation. Under its amended title, the New York Film and Video Council celebrated its sixtieth anniversary in 2006. By the end of the 1950s, the entrenchment of nontheatrical distribution as an informational and community endeavor was indisputable. The EFLA recorded the public library 16mm rentals as 609,355 films shown to 27,590,679 people in 1956, and 721,158 films shown to 36,075,365 people in 1958.[114] At the start of 1959, there were an estimated 595,000 16mm projectors in the United States, or one for every 305 persons.[115]

It is my contention in this essay that progress toward a stable nontheatrical scene equally ensconced ideas about film. These ideas advanced particular modes of serious consideration (e.g., evaluation for social purposes), information exchange, and uses of community space. The work of articulating these concepts of social and media mobilization never let up over the Film Council's ten-year history. Even in 1952, the FCA president Helen Rachford wrote of the necessity of developing 16mm film's use in industry, schools, and community clubs due to "the continuing national emergency"—a reference, no doubt, to the Korean War.[116] So while the organic intellectuals of the councils responded to a perceived condition of emergency, they also acted to manage social and educational reform. In so doing, cultural leaders deployed the mobile media of film to gain access to and influence in locations for molding consciousness and civic participation. In addition to the discourse of democratic life and voluntarism advocated by the movement as a whole came a reconfigured relationship with government (especially in the arena of education and media) as well as an expansion of a nontheatrical market as businesses readied themselves to pry open classrooms and other quasi-educational sites.

It has long been noted that cultural elites elect themselves into positions in which they appear to speak for a national public. Geoff Eley characterizes the nineteenth century as "the age of societies," in which voluntary organizations occupied the better part of public debate on matters of the common good.[117] Even Alexis de Tocqueville wrote of the distinct role of voluntary societies in American political life.[118] The impact of voluntary societies is equally evident with the arrival of motion pictures. This essay has chronicled an episode in the institutionalization of reigning ideas about the role of film in modern life. And throughout these pages it becomes apparent that the formation of film societies and councils bespeaks a struggle over the public and political import of this medium and over the organizations established to solidify the status of authorities and elites, thus reinforcing certain class and social divisions.

Interest in film, at least in part, was a concern about ideas for the masses, and as evidenced by both the society and council movements this was never just a question of how we know film but also how we know people and communities. The brain trust of the council movement treated film as a vehicle of modern citizenship, which involved people's mobilization and preparation for a mediated public sphere of screens. The coordination and clearinghouse functions of film councils, and their interest in educational contexts, became soundly associated with film as a community catalyst, poised against film as a promoter of social malaise and apathy. Patterns of cultural leadership guided this association, with participants working as organic intellectuals to engage people where they live.

Despite the liberal rhetoric of pluralist and community-based participation, theirs was not necessarily a progressively democratic project—perhaps predictably so, given the cold war context in which they operated. As the sites and occasions of education expanded, and as officially sanctioned curricula confronted novel community forms, authorities acting in the name of public interest sought to occupy that new terrain by filling it with what they deemed to be appropriate discussion tactics, subjects, and materials. In effect, the non-theatrical distribution network was also an evaluation network, proposing community leaders as film experts and film experts as community leaders.

Film councils, along with the cultural authorities in the film society movement, comprised a formidable system of film distribution, information, and analytical procedures. Thus film education activities participated in the development of an apparatus of film knowledge. In "inventing film studies" these activities might be easily neglected, for they do not lead without detours to the course outlines and conference debates of today. Nonetheless, they were significant enterprises coordinating, cataloguing, and evaluating the place of film in public life as a modernizing instrument. Moreover, their work helped to buttress a field of authority about matters of the cinema. The coordination of this infant industry of nontheatrical film set in place a technological and discursive infrastructure upon which further types of film analysis would build. This is politically important, especially when we consider the national scope of the FCA's operations. For film education—about and through film—has played a key role in the thinking and enacting of how nations imagine their transformation into advanced capitalist societies, as well as how new factions through their resident intellectuals try to secure a purchase upon the tempo of change and hence upon the ethical state.

Notes

I would like to thank Lee Grieveson and Haidee Wasson for their valuable commentary on this essay. Archival resources and expert assistance at Columbia University, Iowa State University, University of Minnesota, Ford Foundation, Minnesota Historical Society, and the New York Public Library made this research possible, as did funding from the Social Science and Humanities Research Council of Canada.

1. Bernard Friend, "The Cinema Club Flourishes Again in France," *New York Times*, March 27, 1949, X5.

2. Seymour Stern, "Letter—Cine Clubs Here," *New York Times*, April 3, 1949, 2:4.

3. Amos Vogel, "Letter—Audience Clubs," *New York Times*, April 3, 1949, 2:4.

4. C.f. Scott MacDonald, *Cinema 16: Documents Toward a History of the Film Society* (Philadelphia: Temple University Press, 2002); and Haidee Wasson, *Museum Movies: MOMA and the Birth of Art Cinema* (Berkeley: University of California Press, 2005).

5. Thomas M. Pryor, "Film Society Movement Catches On," *New York Times*, September 18, 1949, 2:5.

6. Exceptions to this include Richard DeCordova, "Ethnography and Exhibition: The Child Audience, the Hays Office and Saturday Matinees," *Camera Obscura* 23 (1990): 91–107; Lea Jacobs, "Reformers and Spectators: The Film Education Movement of the Thirties," *Camera Obscura* 22 (1990): 29–49; Eric Smoodin, *Regarding Frank Capra: Audience, Celebrity, and American Film Studies, 1930–1960* (Durham, N.C.: Duke University Press, 2004); Anthony Slide, *Before Video: A History of the Non-Theatrical Film* (New York: Greenwood Press, 1992); Anne Morey, *Hollywood Outsiders: The Adaptation of the Film Industry, 1913–1934* (Minneapolis: University of Minnesota Press, 2003); Ronald Walter Greene, "Y Movies: Film and the Modernization of Pastoral Power," *Communication and Critical/Cultural Studies* 2.1 (March 2005): 20–36; Dana Polan, *Scenes of Instruction: The Beginnings of the U.S. Study of Film* (Berkeley: University of California Press, 2007); Charles R. Acland, "Patterns of Cultural Authority: The National Film Society of Canada and the Institutionalization of Film Education, 1938–41," *Canadian Journal of Film Studies* 10.1 (2001): 2–27; Charles R. Acland, "Mapping the Serious and the Dangerous: Film and the National Council of Education, 1920–1939," *Cinéma* 6.1 (fall 1995): 101–18.

7. C.f. Ken Smith, *Mental Hygiene: Classroom Films, 1945–1970* (New York: Blast Books, 1999).

8. Antonio Gramsci, *Selections from the Prison Notebooks*, translated by Quinton Hoare and Geoffrey Nowell-Smith (London: Lawrence and Wishart, 1971), 350.

9. James Joll, *Antonio Gramsci* (New York: Penguin, 1977), 121.

10. Marcia Landy, *Film, Politics, and Gramsci* (Minneapolis: University of Minnesota Press, 1994), 31.

11. Joll, *Antonio Gramsci*, 122.
12. Gramsci, *Selections from the Prison Notebooks*, 177.
13. Carl Boggs, *Gramsci's Marxism* (London: Pluto, 1976), 76.
14. Anne Showstack Sasson, "The People, Intellectuals and Specialized Knowledge," *boundary 2* 14.3 (spring 1986): 144.
15. Gramsci, *Selections from the Prison Notebooks*, 6.
16. Renate Holub, *Antonio Gramsci: Beyond Marxism and Postmodernism* (New York: Routledge, 1992), 104.
17. Sasson, "The People, Intellectuals and Specialized Knowledge," 143.
18. Charles F. Hoban Jr., *Visualizing the Curriculum* (New York: Cordon Company, 1937).
19. "Film Forums," *Film News* 2.3 (March 1941): 5.
20. See, for example, Edgar Dale, Fannie W. Dunn, Charles F. Hoban Jr., and Etta Schneider, *Motion Pictures in Education: A Summary of the Literature* (New York: H. W. Wilson Company, 1938); and Charles F. Hoban Jr., *Focus on Learning: Motion Pictures in the School* (Washington, D.C.: American Council on Education, 1942).
21. Gerald McDonald, "Libraries and Films," *Film News* 2.6 (June, 1941): 2.
22. The seven participating organizations were ALA, EFLA, National University Extension Association (NUEA), National Education Association (NEA), Allied Non-Theatrical Film Association (ANTFA), National Association of Visual Education Dealers (NAVED), and Visual Equipment Manufacturers Council (VEMC).
23. "Government Influence Dominant in 16mm Field," *Film News* 4.1 (summer 1943): 1, 14; "Advisory Committee Meets OWI," *Film News* 4.3 (December 1943): 6, 7.
24. Stephen M. Corey, "What Is the Film Council of America?" *Film News* 8.5/6 (November–December 1947): 3.
25. "A Brief History of the National 16mm Victory Film Committee," January 10, 1946, National Board of Review of Motion Pictures Collection, Manuscript and Archives Section, New York Public Library [hereafter NBRMPC], box 26 folder 2, 1, 2, 3.
26. Minutes, "Film Council of America succeeding National 16mm Film Committee," January 16, 1946, NBRMPC, box 26 folder 2, 1, 2, 3, 4.
27. Ibid., 2, 3.
28. Other officers were first vice-president David E. Strom (NUEA and AV Aids Center, University of Connecticut), second vice-president Irving C. Boerlin (EFLA), secretary Vernom G. Dameron (NEA), and treasurer Merriman H. Holtz (ANTFA and the Treasury Department).
29. "FCA Constitution," March 4, 1947, Film Council of America Papers [hereafter FCAP], Iowa State University Library, Special Collections Department [hereafter ISU], Ms. 351 box 1 folder 1, 1.
30. Letter, Evans Clark to Carnegie Corporation, March 29, 1950, Carnegie Corporation Grants, Columbia University [hereafter CCG], box 144.12 folder "Film Council of America, 1947–1957," 2.

31. Cecile Starr, "Films, Films, Everywhere . . . ," in *Ideas on Film*, edited by Cecile Starr (New York: Funk and Wagnalls, 1951), 111.

32. Record of Interview, "Educational Films," July 31, 1946, CCG, box 144.13 folder "Film, Radio and Television Education, 1946–1964," 1, 2.

33. A. J. Rosenberg Oral History, vol. 2, part 9, February 1, 1956, 3, 4, 12, McGraw-Hill Oral History Project, Columbia University.

34. "Smallie Exhibs Look with Favor on Commercial Use of 16mm Projection," *Variety*, December 19, 1945, 7; "Hollywood Frankly Watching First 16m Full-Length Feature's B.O. Effect," *Variety*, March 24, 1946, 12.

35. "UA's Foreign 16m Distrib Plans," *Variety*, March 13, 1946, 27; "'Educate' Foreign Exhibs on 16m," *Variety*, March 20, 1946, 22.

36. "Black Market Sales of Majors' 16m Pix Exposed," *Variety*, March 13, 1946, 1, 17.

37. "Bootlegged 16m Versions of Current Features Continues a Major Headache," *Variety*, April 10, 1946, 3, 18.

38. Record of Interview, "U.S. Office of Education," January 15, 1947, CCG, box 144.13 folder "Film, Radio and Television Education, 1946–1964."

39. Minutes, Informal Meeting of the FCA, March 6, 1946, NBRMPC, box 26 folder 2, 3.

40. "Heads Film Council Here," *New York Times*, March 20, 1947, 38.

41. "16m Heads Gird vs. Censorship," *Variety*, March 13, 1946, 27; Letter, William F. Kruse to Richard Griffith, June 15, 1946, NBRMPC, box 26 folder 1, 1, 2.

42. Minutes, Informal Meeting of the FCA, 2.

43. "A Message to the Film Council of America from the National Motion Picture Council," circa December 1947, NBRMPC, box 26 folder 2, 1.

44. Letter, Richard Griffith to Don White, November 26, 1946, NBRMPC, box 26 folder 1, 1.

45. Letter, Richard Griffith to C. R. Reagan, December 2, 1946, NBRMPC, box 26 folder 1, 1–4; Letter, C. R. Reagan to Richard Griffith, December 14, 1946, NBRMPC, box 26 folder 1.

46. Letter, Richard Griffith to C. R. Reagan, April 28, 1947, NBRMPC, box 26 folder 1, 1–4.

47. Notes from a meeting on forming an American Visual Council, January 11, 1947, NBRMPC, box 26 folder 2, 1–6. Along with Reagan and Griffith, the participants were Edward Cheyfitz and Joel Ferris from the MPAA, Paul Howard and Aubry Lee Graham from the ALA, and John Grierson and Stuart Legg from International Film Associates, with Joyce O'Hara observing and George Zook (director, ACE), who was unable to attend.

48. Ibid., 1.

49. Ibid.

50. Record of Interview, "Motion Picture Association," January 13, 1947, CCG, box 144.13 folder "Film, Radio and Television Education, 1946–1964," 3.

51. Letter, C. R. Reagan to Thomas Brandon, March 24, 1947, NBRMPC, box 26

folder 1; Letter, C. R. Reagan to Richard Griffith, March 24, 1947, NBRMPC, box 26 folder 1.

52. For instance, the five largest contributors to the $13,815 total in 1947 were Eastman Kodak ($5,000), Victor Animatograph ($1,100), Encyclopedia Britannica Films ($1,000), Esquire ($1,000), and Ampro ($1,000); others include Radian Manufacturing, Post Pictures, Astor Pictures, United World Films, Burton Holmes Films, Young America Films, Modern Talking Pictures Service, Films Inc., S.O.S. Cinema Supply, Loucks and Norling Studios, Pat Bowling Pictures, Visual Education Inc, A. H. Rice and Co., Calhoun Co., Art Zeiller (Visual Education Service), Brandon Films, Detroit Distributing, and *Time* magazine (Letter, Stephen M. Corey to Florence Anderson, January 8, 1948, CCG, box 144.12 folder "Film Council of America, 1947-1957," 1-4). Industry contributions for 1948-49 were $14,360, and $13,520 for the following fiscal year (FCA, "Progress Report on FCA Activities," circa June 1949, CCG, box 144.12 folder "Film Council of America, 1947-1957," 7).

53. FCA Press Release, May 10, 1946, NBRMPC, box 26 folder 2.

54. FCA Press Release, "Film Council of America to Sponsor Film Drive on Famine Relief," May 16, 1946, NBRMPC, box 26 folder 2, 1, 2.

55. FCA Press Release, August 28, 1950, NBRMPC, box 26 folder 2, 1-3; "Training Movies Pledged," *New York Times*, July 31, 1951, 13.

56. Cecile Starr, *How to Obtain and Screen Films for Community Use* (Chicago: FCA, 1949); Charlesanna Fox, *How to Organize a Community Film Information Center* (Chicago: FCA, 1949); Virginia Beard, *How to Organize a Film Festival* (Chicago: FCA, 1949); and Rex M. Johnson, *How to Conduct a Survey of Community Film Needs and Resources* (Chicago: FCA, 1948).

57. Louis Goodman, *How to Organize and Conduct Film Workshops* (Chicago: FCA, 1948); and Robert H. Schacht, *How to Conduct a Community Film Forum* (Chicago: FCA, 1948).

58. The remaining board members were Louise Condit (Metropolitan Museum), Orville Goldner (Better Business Bureau), A. H. O'Connor (Australian Information Service), and Harold Roberts (National Educational Films). "N.Y. Film Council Sets Its Program," *Variety*, March 20, 1946, 22; "Film Council Elects," *New York Times*, March 14, 1946, 20.

59. "Continuance Urged for Factual Films," *New York Times*, February 14, 1946, 32.

60. John Grierson, "Address — New York Film Council Luncheon," February 13, 1946, Orville Goldner Papers, ISU, Ms. 528 box 12 folder 18, 7.

61. Ibid., 8.

62. "An Opportunity: Organize Your Local Film Council," *NAVED News*, March 1946; Corey, "What Is the Film Council of America?" 1, 3; William F. Kruse, "Film Councils and the Community," *Film News* 8.5/6 (November–December 1947): 4; Rex M. Johnson, "A Film Council in Action," *Educational Screen*, March 1948, 122.

63. Glen Burch, "Film Councils at Work," in Cecile Starr, ed., *Ideas on Film*, 61. It may interest readers to know that Noël Burch is Glen Burch's son.

64. Wesley H. Greene, "Midwest Takes the Lead," in Cecile Starr, ed., *Ideas on Film*, 96.

65. Burch, "Film Councils at Work," 62.

66. Amos Vogel, "The Film Society," in Cecile Starr, ed., *Ideas on Film*, 64.

67. "Robert Flaherty Is Honored," *New York Times*, November 11, 1948, 37.

68. Announcement of Screening, February 24, 1948, NBRMPC, box 26 folder 2.

69. NYFC, "Calendar of Film Events—January 6th to February 4th, 1952," NBRMPC, box 39, 1–3.

70. FCA Press Release, "Film Council of America Announces Plans for a New Program Designed to Serve Community Group Leaders," November 7, 1952, Rohama Lee Papers, ISU, Ms. 354 box 11 folder 48, 1, 2.

71. Robertson Sillars, *How to Evaluate Films for Community Use* (Chicago: FCA, 1949), 1.

72. "Activities of Established Local Film Councils," *Film Counselor* 1, no. 1 (May 1947): 4–7, FCAP, ISU, Ms. 351 box 1 folder 1.

73. Kruse, "Film Councils and the Community," 4.

74. "Writer Hails Use of Teaching Films," *New York Times*, December 4, 1946, 40.

75. FCA, "Program—Second Annual Conference, July 29–August 1, 1949," CCG, box 144.12 folder "Film Council of America, 1947–1957," 1, 2; "Summary Report on the Second Annual Meeting of the Film Council of America," *Film Counselor* 3.2 (July–August 1949), n.p.

76. FCA, "Annual Report of the Executive Director for the Year 1950–51," November 25, 1952, CCG, box 144.12 folder "Film Council of America, 1947–1957," 4.

77. "International Film Council Report—1952," Richard C. Brower Papers, Minnesota State Archives, Minnesota Historical Society, box 105.D.11.9.B folder 1.

78. "Urges Wider Distribution," *New York Times*, November 14, 1946, 40; "Writer Hails Use of Teaching Films," *New York Times*, December 4, 1946, 40.

79. FCA Memorandum from Thurman White, circa October 1947, NBRMPC, box 26 folder 2, 5.

80. "Educational Film Projects," circa March 1948, CCG, box 144.12 folder "Film Council of America, 1947–1957," 14, 15.

81. "Minutes of Meeting, Information Committee, FCA," March 15, 1948, 2, Rohama Lee Papers, ISU, Ms. 354 box 11 folder 45; "Film Council Gets a Grant of $20,000," *New York Times*, April 28, 1948, 33. The actor Eddie Albert had his own educational film company and had recently gained notoriety with a sex education film, *Human Growth* (1946). Gloria Waldron soon released her book *The Informational Film* (New York: Columbia University Press, 1949).

82. "$20,000 Grant to F.C.A.—Glen Burch, New Director," *Film News* 8.11 (May 1948): 1, 9. The Carnegie Corporation followed this with a final grant of $16,000 for 1950–1952.

83. "World Recognition for 'C. R.,'" *Film News* 8.12 (June–July 1948): 1, 35.

84. "C. R. Reagan," *Film Counselor* 2.3 (July–August 1948): 1.

85. "First National AV Convention Marks 16mm's 25th Birthday," *Film News* 8.12 (June–July 1948): 1, 37.

86. Record of Interview, "Film Council of America," January 20–22, 1950, CCG, box 144.12 folder "Film Council of America, 1947–1957."

87. Thurmon J. White, *Speaking of Films* (Chicago: Film Council of America with *Business Screen*, 1946).

88. Ibid., 7.

89. FCA, "Progress Report on FCA Activities," 2.

90. Glen Burch, "Film Councils Meet Living Problems," *See and Hear* (October 1948): n.p.; Glen Burch, "Films and People: The Faith of C. R. Reagan," *Educational Screen*, December 28, 1948, 488; Glen Burch, *How to Form a Film Council* (Chicago: FCA, 1948); Glen Burch, "The FCA and the Film Council Movement," *Hollywood Quarterly* 5.2 (winter 1950): 138–43.

91. "Summary Report on the Second Annual Meeting of the Film Council of America." Other activities for 1948/49 included the preparation and distribution of 1,400 copies of four Film Forum Leader Guides, 1,300 copies of the FCA's own promotional brochure "Putting Films to Work in the Community," and the sponsorship and distribution of 1,000 copies of the lists "Films for Brotherhood Week, 1949" and "Films on Community Problems."

92. FCA, "Summary Report of the Activities of the Executive Director, June 1948–February 1950," 1–6.

93. Letter, C. Scott Fletcher to Rohama Lee, June 3, 1950, Rohama Lee Papers, ISU, Ms. 354 box 11 folder 46.

94. "Of Local Origin," *New York Times*, November 26, 1955, 23. The FCA claimed that *Rushes* would have a circulation of half a million through the thousand-plus film information centers nationwide, though they only guaranteed fifteen thousand to advertisers (FCA, Advertising Rate Card—*Rushes*, 15 July 1955, Rohama Lee Papers, ISU, Ms. 354 box 11 folder 47, 2).

95. *Sixty Years of 16mm Film, 1923–1983: A Symposium*, Film Counselor Series 1, Evanston: FCA, 1954; *A Guide to Film Services of National Associations*, Film Counselor Series 2, Evanston: FCA, 1954; Charles Bushong, *Community Film Use* (Evanston, Ill.: FCA, 1952).

96. FCA Press Release, August 28, 1950, NBRMPC, box 26 folder 2, 1–3.

97. Record of Interview, "Film Council of America," February 18 and 20, 1951, CCG, box 144.12 folder "Film Council of America, 1947–1957."

98. Record of Interview, "Film Council of America," February 21, 1951, CCG, box 144.12 folder "Film Council of America, 1947–1957."

99. Record of Interview, "Film Council of America," May 1, 1951, CCG, box 144.12 folder "Film Council of America, 1947–1957."

100. "Investing in FCA's Future," *Film Counselor* 2.5/6 (May/June 1951): 1, 2. The FCA's

work in promoting film in adult education secured for it the more substantial sums of $75,000 for 1952–53, $180,000 for 1954–55, and $220,000 for 1955–56 from the same agency. Using the FCA to conduct a variety of educational experiments, the total amount of Ford Foundation support for FCA was $738,500. "Summary of Activities, April 3, 1951 to February 29, 1956," Fund for Adult Education, Ford Foundation Archives, box 3, folder 20, April 27, 1956; c.f. Charles R. Acland, "The Film Council of America and the Ford Foundation: Screen Technology, Mobilization, and Adult Education in the 1950s," in *Patronizing the Public: American Philanthropic Support for Communication, Culture, and the Humanities*, edited by William J. Buxton (Lanham, Md.: Lexington Books, Critical Communication Series, forthcoming, 2009).

101. Letter, Tom W. Hope to C. Scott Fletcher, September 11, 1953, Richard C. Brower Papers, Minnesota State Archives, Minnesota Historical Society, box 105.D.11.9.B folder 2, 1, 2, 3.

102. Letter, Paul A. Wagner to Florence Anderson, December 5, 1952, CCG, box 144.12 folder "Film Council of America, 1947–1957."

103. "Local Film Council Directory," *Film Counselor* 2.10 (December 1951): 5, 6, 7; FCA, "Annual Report of the Executive Director for the Year 1950–51," 6.

104. American Film Assembly, *Golden Reel Film Festival Program, 1954*, Rohama Lee Papers, ISU, Ms. 354 box 11 folder 50.

105. "2nd Film Assembly to Open Tonight," *New York Times*, April 4, 1955, 33. The talks by Card and Crowther were published as Bosley Crowther, "The Role of 16mm Film in American Society," *Film Culture* 1.3 (May–June 1955): 12–13; and James Card, "16mm Film in Historical Perspective," *Film Culture* 1. 3 (May–June 1955): 13–14.

106. FCA Press Release, "Film Society Services Available from FCA," October 6, 1954, Rohama Lee Papers, ISU, Ms. 354 box 11 folder 48.

107. Ibid.

108. "Activities of Established Local Film Councils," *Film Counselor* 1.1 (May 1947): 7, FCAP, ISU, Ms. 351 box 1 folder 1.

109. FCA, "Report of Meeting of Board of Trustees," April 11, 1949, CCG, box 144.12 folder "Film Council of America, 1947–1957," 3.

110. Record of Interview, "Film Council of America," July 29–30–August 1, 1949, CCG, box 144.12 folder "Film Council of America, 1947–1957."

111. "FCA to Act as Coordinating Agency for U.S. Entries in Venice, Edinburgh Festivals," *Film Counselor* 3.5 (May 1952): 3; "Film Council of America at Edinburgh and Venice," *Film Counselor* 3.7 (November 1952): 7, 8; "NEA Committee Assures 'First Rate' Films at Venice," *Film/AV News* 17.6 (May–June 1958): 2, 44.

112. "EFLA, 1943–1973," Rohama Lee Papers, ISU, Ms. 354 box 13 folder 29, 6.

113. "Movie Fete Opens Today," *New York Times*, April 1, 1959, 44.

114. ALA, "Public Library Film Statistics," June 1957, Rohama Lee Papers, ISU, Ms. 354

box 1 folder 19; ALA, "Public Library Film Statistics," June 1959, Rohama Lee Papers, ISU, Ms. 354 box 1 folder 19.

115. John Flory and Thomas W. Hope, "Scope and Nature of Nontheatrical Films in the United States," *Journal of the Society of Motion Picture and Television Engineers* 68.6 (June 1959): 388.

116. Helen Rachford, "FCA—Past, Present, Future," *Film Counselor* 3.6 (June 1952): 9.

117. Geoff Eley, "Nations, Publics, and Political Cultures: Placing Habermas in the Nineteenth Century," in *Habermas and the Public Sphere*, edited by Craig Calhoun (Cambridge, Mass.: MIT Press, 1992), 289–339.

118. Alexis de Tocqueville, *Democracy in America*, translated by George Lawrence (Garden City, N.Y.: Doubleday, 1969 [1836]).

Experimental Film and the Development
of Film Study in America

MICHAEL ZRYD

■ This essay takes on two tasks for this volume: first, to chart the development
of film study in the United States during its boom period in the 1960s and 1970s,
and, second, to examine the impact of avant-garde or experimental cinema on
this development, concentrating on its material and institutional history.[1]

Existing accounts of the avant-garde and its impact on film studies have been
discussed mainly in intellectual histories of the field's animating ideas. Three
major aspects of these accounts are noteworthy. First, David Bordwell credits
Annette Michelson's "philosophically informed essays" and her "institutional
situation" at New York University (NYU) for making "the study of avant-garde
film part of modern art criticism and theory" in the 1970s.[2] Second, the avant-
garde was central to 1970s film theory in articulating a radical political and
aesthetic integration of theory and practice, embodied in what Peter Wollen
called "counter cinema."[3] The high profile of 1970s film theory, especially feminist film theory through the circulation of Laura Mulvey's widely anthologized
essay "Visual Pleasure and Narrative Cinema," helped the fledgling discipline
of film studies to raise its academic profile in the 1970s and 1980s and approach
the status of literary, art, and critical studies.[4] Third, many of the founding
scholars of the study of early film, perhaps the most influential branch of film
studies in the 1980s and 1990s, were directly influenced by avant-garde film,
including Tom Gunning (an NYU graduate) and especially Noël Burch (a colleague of Michelson's).[5]

Less discussed and barely documented are the institutional academic formations that arose earlier to provide material support for scholarly and conceptual investigation into avant-garde and experimental film. Although in this essay I will only scratch the surface of this massive material history, I will examine the importance of the broad category of experimental cinema, as a model of both artistic and educational practice, for the enormous and significantly student-driven expansion of film study.[6]

The terms "experimental film" and "avant-garde film" have complex, contested, and ultimately intertwined legacies. The term "avant-garde" has two dominant usages in relation to film. The first identifies specific, often self-identified, film and art movements like the surrealist and Soviet montage cinemas of the 1920s, the praxis of Brechtian or Godardian film in the 1960s, and punk cinema in the 1980s. In the second usage, avant-garde is employed as a descriptor, naming a theory or attitude as "avant-garde," fluctuating between a specific emphasis on political critique and a general celebration of the new (with an attendant critique of the old, the conventional, the established). The new may retain political valence, but not necessarily; indeed, many of the debates surrounding avant-garde films are precisely concerned with the question of whether or not a film is sufficiently "political."

The connotation of novelty and unconventionality is the aspect of "avant-garde" that most overlaps with the term "experimental film." This term usually describes films outside the categories of narrative, documentary, and animation (although "experimental" can be added as a modifier, e.g., experimental narrative, etc.). Even today, as Gary Kibbins avers, the term experimental has been, "whatever its other defects, . . . usefully vague."[7]

Experimental film was the dominant term used during the 1950s and 1960s, and its openness and permeability most accurately names its eclecticism. In the late 1960s and 1970s, "avant-garde" began to be applied by critics like Michelson, Jonas Mekas, P. Adams Sitney, Mulvey, Wollen, and others to describe the American underground, French New Wave, and other European New Wave cinemas. After this point, although the term experimental film was still widely used, avant-garde became the dominant term used in the academy. However, the terms are used interchangeably and are still rarely applied rigorously. In this essay, I will retain the term experimental, although avant-garde will sometimes be used to describe a self-consciously political or "radical aspiration" (to use Michelson's influential formulation).[8]

In the 1960s and early 1970s, two simultaneous phenomena emerge: first, film was the fastest-growing area of arts study in American universities, and, second, experimental film achieved its broadest cultural exposure with the rise to prominence of the New American Cinema, the underground film, and the structural film.[9]

The growth of film study and the visibility of experimental cinema in this period converged in three major ways. First, experimental films helped define the parameters of *alternative cinema*, the foundational object of post-1960s film studies, counterposed to its bad object, Hollywood cinema. The umbrella of alternative cinema covered European art cinema, Third Cinema, and other emerging national cinemas, documentary, and the multiple forms of independent North American film. Experimental cinema was the most radical of these alternative cinemas, and it was an important component of campus film society screenings that was linked closely to their apposite interest in liberatory sexuality and politics. Often overlooked, campus film societies were crucial sites of alternative cinema culture in the 1960s, and they were instrumental in developing student demand for film courses and programs at many universities. Second, experimental cinema suited the powerful and widespread idea that film was *the new mode of individual youth expression.* As *Life* magazine put it, instead of writing the "Great American Novel," students wanted to make the "Great American Film."[10] A "new age" required a new medium of expression, and at its height the "new generation" of late 1960s counterculture proclaimed that film was its true language. Students did not flock to film courses featuring the latest commercial films but rather to see and make alternative films, however vaguely or even naively defined. Third, experimental cinema exemplified a distinctly *artisanal* mode of film production that, for budding university film programs, was the most viable model of filmmaking instruction. Low-budget, hands-on filmmaking invited experimentation with film form and made it possible to make, contra Hollywood, more authentic personal films. This small-scale ethos extended to film exhibition on campus, where 16mm projection (and to a lesser extent 8mm and S8mm) in classrooms and campus film society screening spaces was widespread.

Finally, it is important to emphasize how central the academy has been to avant-garde cinema since the late 1960s: universities became the dominant exhibition site for avant-garde film, sustained its film distribution co-ops, hired filmmakers as faculty and visiting artists, and trained new generations of film artists and audiences.[11] This essay demonstrates that the avant-garde has also had—at least compared to its absolute marginality in both popular and highbrow culture—disproportionate importance for the academy, thus influencing the development of film study in North America both in its familiar role as a conceptual field of modernist investigation defining film's medium-specificity and artistic legitimacy, and more concretely as a model of "experimental"—in its most capacious sense—creativity and educational practice for students.[12]

The Rise of Film Study in the United States

In the United States, the critical study and appreciation of film took place early on in film societies. But in universities, the study of film frequently piggy-backed on production courses, particularly during the first decades of the field's development. After the University of Southern California (USC) pioneered film courses in 1929, it was joined by schools offering a combination of film production and film studies courses such as, in the 1940s, NYU, City College of New York (CCNY), University of California, Los Angeles (UCLA), and the New School for Social Research Dramatic Workshop, and subsequently in the 1950s by Indiana, Boston, Stanford, Columbia, Ohio State, and Northwestern.[13] Bob Jones University was reported to have the most well-equipped film production program in the country.[14] Kenneth Macgowan, writing in 1951, emphasizes the importance of production teaching as he narrates three steps that "forced the motion picture into higher education": "The first step was the study and testing and use of educational films. The second was the setting up of producing units in universities, usually in extension divisions. The third and last has been the creation of courses and departments where the skills as well as the theories of filmmaking are taught on the undergraduate level."[15] That film production paved the way for film studies in the academy is reflected in the history of professional associations. The University Film Producers Association (UFPA), now the University Film and Video Association, primarily composed of film production faculty, was formed in 1947 while the scholarly Society of Cinema-tologists, now the Society for Cinema and Media Studies (SCMS), was founded more than a decade later in 1959.[16]

If the period before the 1960s saw a steady increase in film study programs generally and film production in particular, it was still not an enormously popular course of study. John Tyo's 1961 study notes a crisis in "qualified personnel" for film work; despite a substantial labor market for film professionals in the educational and industrial sectors, "except in a few cases, students are not clamouring for entrance to the film production training programs."[17] The "crisis" of stagnation noted by Tyo parallels other conflicts at this moment in late 1950s and early 1960s film culture. Just as the filmmaker-critics of the

French New Wave were militating against a staid "cinema of quality," so film instructors in the United States were calling for radical changes that would shift film production instruction away from industrial and educational films to documentary, experimental, and narrative forms. An editorial entitled "A Time for Reassessment," reporting on the 1961 UFPA conference, noted the "challenge from abroad" presented by European New Wave cinemas, and posed fundamental questions about "the appropriate form and style of the nonfiction film."[18] Alvin Fiering (a student of Hans Richter at CCNY) writes in terms that reflect what would become a widespread shift in film production teaching:

> It is easy to view film production as a technique and to teach it accordingly, relying heavily upon foot-candles, gamma, and key-light, fill-light ratios for an explanation of the substance of film. This is not only misleading but also unfair.
>
> Students are drawn to study film because of its inherent mystery, the excitement of reproducing, altering, and recreating reality, the fascination at a primitive level that the abstraction of moving pictures has. They desire self-expression, intellectual and emotional stimulation, involvement in art, and through art, a heightened involvement with life.[19]

Fiering's appeal to move from technique to a more holistic notion of art reflects a wider division in the development of film study and higher education in general in the 1960s. The demand for film courses that developed later in the decade grew out of very specific cultural and material conditions: the development of vibrant alternative film cultures on campus, the availability of accessible modes of artisanal film production, and the growth of a media-enthused youth culture, the first generation raised on television. In education generally, a shift toward student-centered models of learning favored participation in the "now" over the passive consumption of the past's seemingly exhausted traditional culture. In the post-World War II period, the GI bill, massive government and private funding, and the demographic bulge of the baby boom increased the size and cultural power of colleges and universities. The class, gender, and racial diversity of both students and faculty slowly increased to make higher education better reflect the demographics of society at large. University culture itself shifted from maintaining classic traditions of knowledge to engaging with contemporary social issues, or what Thomas Bender in *American Academic Culture in Transformation* describes as "the identification of the university with the society in 1968 and afterward."[20] The prominence of student activism, especially around civil rights and Vietnam War protests, is well known;

Faculty member Joseph L. Anderson (with shotgun mic and Nagra III) and student film-makers John Griebsch and David Prince (with Éclair 16mm camera) filming classes at Ohio University, Athens, 1967. (Photo by Carl Fleischhauer)

less acknowledged is the demand for curricular reform voiced by students and sympathetic faculty. As Thomas Hagood notes, "The broad student population pressed for revisions to academic requirements and an expansion in areas of study. Students also wanted a greater say in the organization and governance of the university, desiring input on the range of academic programs, issues of appointment and tenure, and student representation in all aspects of university life."[21] If the university was to be identified with society, then university curriculum needed to reflect "relevance," including an imperative to support new disciplines (like women's studies and African American studies) and respond to the new art of the youth generation, film.[22]

A division also developed between utilitarian and exploratory notions of film study, reflecting differing orientations of sponsoring academic units. For example, James Ackerman's report for the Carnegie Foundation, "The Arts in Higher Education," outlines a distinction between film study as a "vocation" located in communications, radio, and journalism units and film as one of the "liberal arts" located in "humanities, art, theatre, speech, or English" departments.[23] According to Ackerman, "the arts have grown faster than any other segment during the last generation," an upsurge that underlines the shift from vocational to arts-oriented education in the 1960s.[24] The case of film study at NYU is exemplary of this shift. It was part of a Communication Arts Group serving education students in the 1950s and early 1960s before it was transferred in 1967 to a new School of the Arts modeled on a fine art academy, which emphasized film as art in both its filmmaking school and fledgling Cinema Studies Department. The founding statement from the first dean, Robert Corrigan, embodies the utopian strain of art education; in a text entitled "Revolution and the Arts," he writes, "Ours is an age of explosion. There is no escaping the new waves of energy that are reshaping our lives."[25] Not all film production schools turned to NYU's art school model. Indeed, the number of television and communications schools that oriented their students toward careers in broadcast media also grew during this period.[26] Nonetheless, it is clear that film study's inroads in liberal arts and art schools presented options outside its hitherto largely vocational settings.

The main resource for information on the development of film teaching from the late 1960s through the 1970s is the American Film Institute (AFI) series *Guide to College Film Courses*, published from 1968 to 1990 (see table 1).[27] Eight issues surveyed postsecondary institutions teaching film and provide valuable insight into the material conditions bearing on the development of film studies and filmmaking programs. What is most striking is the extraordinary growth of film study in the 1960s and 1970s, which is reflected in all categories measured by the AFI: number of courses, schools offering film courses, instructors, and students majoring in film.

While data comparing film programs with other arts programs is limited, the few accounts that exist corroborate the picture of expansion painted by the AFI guides. Bender notes that overall university enrollments tripled from 1960 to 1980; compared to this overall increase, film enrollments increased almost tenfold.[28] Hagood quotes a study that found that between 1970–71 and 1977–78, "cinematography experienced the greatest overall increase in conferral of degrees with an increase of 830.0 percent, followed by dance (198.3 percent)," photography (101 percent), and music history (76 percent).[29]

One counterintuitive finding in the AFI guides is the emphasis that film production programs put on nonnarrative filmmaking during this generative period. Documentary and experimental filmmaking were consistently emphasized over dramatic fiction, especially in the early guides. The 1970–71 guide indicates that almost 80 percent of production schools emphasized documentary and experimental filmmaking compared to only 6 percent for dramatic fiction (educational film, animation, and TV news were the remaining categories).[30]

Table 1: Film Study Statistics from AFI Guides to College Film and Television Courses

	1963–64*	1968–69	1969–70	1971–72	1973–74**	1975–76	1977–78	1979–80
Total film courses	244	1,233	1,699	2,392	5,889	8,225	9,228	7,648
Number of schools	71	219	301	413	613	791	1,067	1,067
Number of instructors		545	869	627	2,460	2,622	4,220	3,126
Full-time instructors			304	294	966	1,179	2,830	2,034
Student majors and grads		5,300	4,231	6,108	22,466	30,869	40,596	44,183

*Figures quoted in 1968–69 guide
**Television added to survey

Don Staples's 1963–64 survey reports 276 courses in production, and 152 courses in "film history, criticism, and appreciation," at the 100 largest colleges and universities in the United States ("Tables [survey of film courses]," *Film Study in Higher Education; Report of a Conference Sponsored by Dartmouth College in Association with the American Council on Education*, edited by David C. Stewart, Dartmouth College, and American Council on Education [Washington, D.C.: American Council on Education, 1966], 164–167). Although statistics on earlier periods are elusive, Molly Willcox reported that "in 1952, 17 of the 100 largest colleges and universities offered courses in film appreciation, film history, or film criticism" ("Film Education: The National Picture," *Filmmakers Newsletter* 2.2 [1968]: 1).

Later guides ranked documentary first, experimental second, and dramatic fiction third. Given the clear dominance of dramatic fiction (i.e., Hollywood) in the public imagination, the dominance of documentary and experimental film in production teaching requires explanation.

The rise of film study in the academy in the 1960s was neither fostered nor inspired by Hollywood. Students and academics on one side, and Hollywood professionals and studio personnel on the other, largely viewed each other with disdain or simple indifference.[31] Academic film study emphasized "art cinema," however variously defined; select Hollywood films like *Citizen Kane* might qualify but commercial and genre cinema was largely ignored. Hollywood, meanwhile, largely ignored the universities. During the 1960s, Hollywood studios were losing audiences and reducing production. Students trained in filmmaking schools were not welcomed by unions already faced with high unemployment rates, and the fiscal and cultural conservatism of the studios did not make them open to new blood.[32] The AFI guides confirm a long-standing tradition in film production education that serviced the non-Hollywood film industry. As Ackerman notes, "Professionally oriented departments have sought to train film technicians in spite of the fact that the film and television industries and unions have not favored university graduates for employment; they have produced a core of 'audio-visual' experts—essentially equipment specialists—for the entertainment, advertising, and education fields."[33]

Alternative 1960s Film Culture on Campus

For most of the 1960s, Hollywood was the last thing on film students' minds—and vice versa. As Robert Corrigan, the first dean of the NYU School of the Arts, bluntly stated, "Hollywood is a negative force—a model of what not to do."[34] Alternative film, as an inspirational object of study and an artisanal mode of production, was amenable to the spirit and practicalities of emerging film study programs. The fostering of alternative film cultures through the proliferation of campus film societies and film classes increased the range of films to which students were exposed.

But the expansion of film study in the 1960s was largely a student-led phenomenon; universities rarely initiated and only reluctantly responded to student interest. As Corrigan recounts: "The most significant aspect of the college film movement is the fact that its continuing impetus has come from the students themselves. No faculty curriculum committee imposed film courses on the students because it believed such courses should be part of a good education. In fact, just the reverse is true."[35] Dwight MacDonald describes his experience teaching film at the University of Texas at Austin. After noting that "the subject seems to be even more popular in Academe than I had thought," he quotes the film distributor Thomas Brandon, who gives "'primary credit' to 'the youngsters themselves,' and . . . that the faculties 'up to now have done little to stimulate campus excitement in film as art.'"[36] Eventually, the popularity of film study suited the desire of academic administrators to fill seats with tuition-paying students—but whether it was seen in instrumental or idealistic terms, film study was sparked by youth culture in the 1960s and its drive for relevance, innovation, and experimentation.

That Thomas Brandon, owner of one of the largest nontheatrical film distribution companies in the United States, should note the importance of student demand is a testament to the importance of what may be the most crucial para-academic institution in the rise of film study, the campus film society. Campus film societies have existed since the 1920s and have long constituted an important outlet for student and faculty interest in cinema. But their leap in popularity during the 1960s, and their importance in fostering the development of film courses, bears emphasis. The number of campus film societies rose from two hundred in the early 1950s to five thousand by the late 1960s.[37] As early as 1958, Jack Ellis pointed to the "interconnected function" of "film societies and film teachers."[38] Elenore Lester, writing in 1967, argues that the societies substituted for formal instruction: "Film societies, often several to a campus, have arisen to take over the role of education in the cinema that both universities and secondary schools side-stepped until only recently."[39] David Stewart, in his 1966 American Council on Education (ACE) report *Film Study in Higher Education*, states: "It would be too much to say that the establishment of a campus film society always precedes the initiation of a formal film-study course. But there is certainly more than a casual relationship between the two enterprises. Film societies provide, somewhat haphazardly, an extremely valuable source of better-than-average motion pictures (both foreign and domestic) as well as information *about* films."[40]

In 1966, the United States National Student Association (USNSA) issued a "Proposal for a Film Education Program," which notes the key role played by students in developing film programs, usually through a successful campus film society. They quote from the ACE report "The College and Cinema," which stated that "among the activities (on college campuses) currently, the most popular—and for the purposes of this report, the most significant—are the programs of film societies. They represent . . . the intense student interest in the changing characteristics of motion pictures, American and foreign, past and present." The USNSA proposal elaborates on the effect of the societies: "It is significant that such societies are more often than not initiated and improved by students. . . . Students and young faculty members excited by the film society experience are usually the initiators of the college or universities first formal course on film. Students, excited by their experiences in film societies, are those most demanding guidance in experimental films they would like to direct or produce."[41] This narrative recounts how, after registering positive student response to films screened on campus, faculty and/or graduate students initiate courses that in turn provide avenues for students to make "experimental" films. Robert Corrigan repeats the narrative from a student's perspective: "Film had been a regular part of the students' lives. Then they went to college and found that this very real part of their experience had no place. Going to the 'local flicks' once or twice a week wasn't enough, and soon campus film societies began to be formed. Today nearly 5,000 such societies exist, sometimes with several on a single campus. Eventually, such an overwhelming interest couldn't be ignored, and before long a course on film history or appreciation worked its way into the curriculum (almost always at the instigation of the students who persuaded some faculty film buff to teach the course as an overload)."[42] Corrigan also posits an "inevitable" inverse relation, noting a "jump from history to practice" as film study leads students to want to make films.[43]

The network of campus film societies in this period, by providing exhibition sites for alternative cinema, was instrumental in creating regional alternative film culture outside major urban centers. Campus film societies (often more than one to a university) would screen alternative film to both campus and community audiences; anecdotal accounts of experimental campus film screenings place them from California to New York, from Montana to Maine.[44] This wide dissemination is a side effect of the decentralized nature of American university education (there are over thirty-six hundred colleges and universities in the United States). As Thomas Bender has noted, in the postwar period and especially after the 1960s, a conscious effort was made to redistribute funding and research excellence, partly as an effort to make American higher education escape the hegemony of Ivy League dominance.[45] This redistribution of resources did not, of course, eliminate the hierarchies that still characterize American higher education, but regional universities outside New England, Chicago, and California were at least permitted to join the elite. The contrast between American and European models of the film school is informative here. In Europe by the early 1960s, national film academies arose in the Soviet Union, France, Poland, Italy, and Spain.[46] With film study concentrated in these national schools, film was rarely integrated into general postsecondary education. But in the United States and Canada, film study became something that almost anyone attending a college or university could pursue. Because of this decentralization and the large number of schools teaching film, a greater variety of films were screened and made.

The rapid expansion of film programs in the academy did not escape public notice as, between 1965 and 1970, many major U.S. general interest magazines (*Time, Life, Saturday Review, Esquire, Glamour, Newsweek, Variety,* and the *New York Times Magazine,* among others) profiled the new mania for film study. Notably, almost all accounts link or even equate film study with film production. Around the same time, experimental film reached its peak of public visibility: underground film received mainstream press in publications like the *New Yorker* and the *Saturday Evening Post* (1963), the *Nation* (1964), *Life*, *New York Times Sunday Magazine* and *Popular Photography* (1965), *Newsweek* (1966 and 1967), and the *New York Times* (1966 and 1967); *Pull My Daisy* is even satirized in *Mad Magazine* in 1963.[47] The notoriety of underground film made it a staple of many campus film society programs, although its appeal was as much for its depictions of sex and drugs as the films' aesthetic innovations. Jack Kroll explicitly connects underground film to the rise of film on campuses, and he notes a collaboration between the Millennium Film Workshop and the New School for Social Research on a "study of 'alienated youth in the creative arts.'"[48] The demand for filmmakers to screen their work and discuss experimental film at universities was so great that the Film-Makers' Cooperative, the major experimental film distributor of the period, set up a "Lecture Bureau" in 1964 to facilitate campus visits. It published a catalogue in 1969 that featured a wide range of filmmakers and a sophisticated set of lectures, screenings, and workshops.[49]

Rhetoric of Experimentation and Participatory Culture

The convergence of experimental film and the academy can perhaps best be understood as what David James, in his study of independent film in the 1960s, calls a "participatory" cinema that displaced film from its location in mythical Hollywood to a more accessible plane. James speaks of a general 1960s movement toward "new participatory political cultures"—from civil rights organizations to communes to new forms of art making—where "culture was re-created as doing rather than as buying . . . if only for a moment, the concept of popular culture was redefined from one of consumption to one of praxis."[50] Small-scale artisanal film production made this feasible. As Paul Arthur says of the 1960s, it was "a time when anyone could, and it was thought that everyone *should* become a filmmaker."[51] The artisanal mode of image making and the avant-garde idea of transforming social relations, although based less on a collectivist than a personalized politics, are synthesized in the figure of the student filmmaker grasping the means of production to find a mode of self-expression that suits her or his generational conditions.[52] Student involvement in organizing screenings and filmmaker lectures for campus film societies, or simply attending screenings and being part of the film "scene," were also crucial elements of this participatory culture. Arthur is ultimately wary of what he calls "the

David Prince (with Éclair 16mm camera), Joseph L. Anderson (with shotgun mic and Nagra III), and John Griebsch (with cables) filming on campus at Ohio University, Athens, 1967. (Photo by Carl Fleishhauer)

fantasy of film's liberatory potential" but this fantasy nonetheless powerfully motivated participatory cinema culture on campuses.[53] Elenore Lester's 1967 profile of student filmmaking in the *New York Times Magazine* exemplifies the period's utopian rhetoric: "This new age has produced a new crop of creative young people who see an almost magical potential in making films themselves. These embryonic artists speak of their film mission in tones of revelatory rapture. They see the camera as uniquely the instrument of their generation, still rich with unexplored possibilities."[54]

The idealism of the new youth generation and the community of experimental filmmakers and film enthusiasts found shared expression in intense cinephilia, the communication of personal, authentic feelings and ideas, and an opposition to what was seen as an impersonal and orthodox establishment. O. W. Reigel's report on the small filmmaking program at Washington and Lee University in Lexington, Virginia, dryly paints a picture of a typical student filmmaker: "One type of student film maker is the individualist young man, usually with a 'literary' (verbal) orientation, who has an urge to express his personality and ideas. In the absence of the film medium, he would probably be writing stories, novellas and poems. At some point in his life he has been infected by the 'rage for the cinema,' usually as the result of an incandescent emotional reaction to particular films he has seen. He usually views the motion picture as the leading, typical and most authentic, expressive medium of his generation."[55]

Reigel distills the cinephilia of the student film movement: film is enthusiastically held up as the medium of the 1960s youth generation and, it follows, film is the best medium for authentic youth expression. A 1968 story in *Time* observed that "students in college, high school—and now in some cases even grade school—are turning to films as a form of artistic self-expression as naturally as Eskimos turn to soapstone carving. . . . The widespread conviction among young people [is] that film is the most vital modern art form."[56] Robert Corrigan underlines this generation's investment in film: "The film is the medium that students feel they have discovered. It is their baby. They care about it, want to nurture and develop it, and most important, they trust it."[57] Further, as a profile in *Life* magazine a year later states: "The U.S. has bred a generation zonked on films. . . . More and more young Americans are getting behind the camera and expressing themselves as never before."[58]

The rhetoric of the student film movement echoes that of experimental film. Sheldon Renan refers to the personal nature of underground film as "a medium of and for the individual, as explorer and as artist."[59] The emphasis thus is on individual expression and process, with less regard for the quality of the results; student filmmaking, like a certain strain of underground cinema, was less about making great art than finding an authentic voice. As Jonas Mekas said in 1962, the new "independent cinema movement—like the other arts in America today—is primarily an existential movement, or, if you want, an ethical movement, a human act; it is only secondarily an aesthetic one."[60] Personal cinema was not only the province of the then-ascendant auteur theory, which heralded the Hollywood director as artist. Instead, student filmmakers could shoot and edit film with their own hands, thereby making art that was, at least in spirit, expressive, personal, and experimental. Film classrooms and campus film societies became venues where these personal expressions could be experienced, whether in screenings of films by Kenneth Anger, John Cassavetes, and Jean-Luc Godard or by student filmmakers themselves.

Education in the 1960s emphasized personal exploration as a vital part of the college experience. The ethos of career training and its utilitarian conception of education that infiltrated the 1980s and 1990s were largely foreign to the spirit of personal exploration that prevailed, especially at liberal arts colleges and universities. As Lester's profile suggests, the teaching of film in the university was not careerist: "Some of these experimenters are enrolled in film schools and special departments but many come out of places like the psychology department or many [might] even be dropouts. . . . There are plenty of students who do it because it's the in thing and cameras have a way of attracting swinging chicks. Others do it out of the same impulse for fun and self-expression with which they might involve themselves in a play, a musical instrument, painting, sculpture, or poetry-writing."[61]

But the commonalities between 1960s student filmmaking culture and experimental filmmaking culture should not give the impression that the majority of students on campus were grooving to films by Stan Brakhage and Jack Smith—college film students still resisted the most radical forms of this practice. Despite its notoriety at campus film society screenings, the underground was rarely an end in itself for most student filmmakers, and few student filmmakers aspired to, or managed to produce, significant experimental film. The dominant model remained the European art cinema (and the new American directors like Arthur Penn who were influenced by European directors). As one Columbia University film school student stated in 1969, "The underground is no alternative. I'd rather sell insurance. I want to do films that are neither avant-garde nor traditional. I want to do well-structured, serious art movies."[62] Other favored student film genres included satire, parody, symbolic drama, documentary exposés of social inequities, and introspective meditations. In a statement typical of the backlash against the counterculture, O. W. Reigel dismisses "our cultural swingers—that is, underground film makers, hippy, hairy or drug cultures, or anti-Establishment movements of New York and California."[63]

Nonetheless, this resistance to underground cinema did not undermine the overall spirit of openness that characterized alternative film culture on campus. The ethos of experimentation was important to 1960s film study, in part because the category "alternative" was so remarkably heterogeneous, including experimental cinema as well as documentary, European new wave, and radical political cinema. For example, Mekas, writing in 1962, includes under the umbrella of "New American Cinema" not only a category like "Pure Poets of the Cinema" (now canonical filmmakers like Brakhage, Marie Menken, and Robert Breer), but also subgenres like documentary (Richard Leacock), fiction narrative (Shirley Clarke), satire (Stan Vanderbeek), and absurd comedy (Ron Rice).[64] Notably, these were also favored student filmmaking genres, and films by these artists were shown at campus film society screenings. Elenore Lester offers this account of a campus film event in 1967 that, while utopian, captures the spirit of alternative campus film culture: "One day last spring on the prairie campus of Creighton University, a Catholic institution in Omaha, suave, custom-tailored Otto Preminger—maestro of such high-powered movie epics as *Exodus* and *Hurry Sundown*—and explosive, rumpled Stan Brakhage—poet of the 8-mm. camera and creator of the underground opus, *Dog Star Man*—were co-starred in an academic spectacular that drew standing-room-only crowds. Establishment Man and Underground Man, who turned out to be as cozy together as Batman and Robin, talked films and film-making from the way in to the far out before the sea of students."[65]

If the terminological umbrella extending over alternative cinema was large at the beginning of the 1960s, categories began to harden toward the end of the decade. By the late 1960s, experimental cinema became associated mainly with the underground of Andy Warhol, Jack Smith, and Kenneth Anger, now figured as an avant-garde. Gordon Hitchens, writing in 1968, is impelled to insist on the existence of "half a dozen or more" avant-garde film movements— including student filmmaking—against the hegemony of the "underground": "The New Left documentary/newsreel group; the non-Hollywood, even anti-Hollywood feature films; the Pop-Art/collage/TV commercial satirists; the students—subdivided as college-level, teen-level, and, most interesting of all, the Negro/Puerto Rican slum filmmaker; and finally, the *cinéma vérité* social documentarians."[66] Student filmmakers are, in Hitchens's eyes, a significant "avant-garde" group. But they, along with filmmakers like Leacock, Maysles, and Pennebaker are no longer seen as part of the New American Cinema. What is at stake in this constriction is a disincentive for student filmmakers to identify themselves with a rarefied underground avant-garde, a situation that would become more extreme with the rise of minimalist structural film related to the art world.

An instructive site to examine the tension between student filmmaking's simultaneous urge to experiment and conform to mainstream and industry values is the National Student Film Awards. This competition, which began in 1965 at UCLA and continued the next year at the Lincoln Center in New York, received coast-to-coast coverage from newspaper critics like Charles Champlin, Bosley Crowther, John Simon, and Cecile Starr. The National Student Film Awards included experimental film among its four categories (although many reviewers noted that films in the dramatic, documentary, and animated sections were as "experimental" as those in the category proper).[67] Judges for the

Ohio University film students David Prince (camera), Franklin Miller (sound), and unknown student filming child and elder, 1967. (Photo by Carl Fleischhauer)

1966 awards included Nat Hentoff, Joseph Mankiewicz, Arthur Mayer, Willard Van Dyke, Ed Emshwiller, Arthur Knight, Martin Scorsese (the 1965 winner), and Amos Vogel, the last four of whom had significant knowledge of experimental film. If the competition was sympathetic to experimental film, however, the mainstream press was not. The press evaluated student production according to criteria of professional production values, often taking potshots at avant-garde film as the exemplar of failed film. A reporter from *Time* derisively referred to how student films in the experimental category of the National Student Film Awards owe "a debt to the non-styles and non-goals of the cinematic underground . . . Like the products of the underground film world, campus movies are something of an acquired taste—which is one good reason why they have a limited commercial future."[68] The *Newsweek* review of the 1965 festival rejects counterculture, predicting that the new generation of student filmmakers will reform Hollywood from within, foretelling the eventual incorporation of the movie brats: "More than the cool, anti-Establishment hipsters of New York's underground cinema, these new filmmakers do want to be seen and heard."[69] Indeed, the National Student Film Award participants like Scorsese, George Lucas, John Milius, and others would eventually be "seen and heard" by mass audiences even as other award-winning participants like Scott Bartlett remained known only to the experimental film community.[70]

Noted West Coast filmmaker Scott Bartlett talks with students during a guest lecture at Ohio University in 1969. To the right of Bartlett is Joseph L. Anderson, director of the film program at Ohio University. (Photo by Carl Fleischhauer)

The Artisanal Mode of Production

In 1966, for the National Student Film Festival, Amos Vogel wrote a short essay titled "The Camera as Pen," which, in the spirit of Astruc's *camera-stylo* and the auteur theory, made filmmaking analogous to writing. For Vogel, student filmmaking shares writing's expressive intimacy but is more appropriate to a modern, technological historical moment: "In previous times, the young 'took hold' of the pen. Today, they take hold of the camera."[71] Vogel sees student filmmakers as pure, almost naive "explorers": "They take the best and the worst from the contemporary experimentalists and independents. [As] imitators and innovators, they are among the true explorers of our day: and some of their poverty-stricken productions, in a future age, will be viewed by sensitive observers as among the truer representations of the anguished spirit of the Sixties."[72] Vogel here echoes many commentators who link exploration to students' poverty of means and connect alternative film's freedom of expression with its lack of expense, implicitly differentiating this production from Hollywood's heavily capitalized and formulaic style. A *Time* magazine report on student filmmaking quotes Jean Cocteau, who "believed that movies would never become a true art until the materials to make them were as inexpensive as pencil and paper"; this utopian hope relied on the affordability of 8mm and 16mm film production.[73]

The adoption of the experimental artisanal mode by the academy was both idealistic and pragmatic, thus constituting a pedagogically appropriate *and* affordable mode of small-scale film instruction. Since the 1960s, film production instruction has largely taken two forms. First, large university programs with graduate level instruction, especially USC, UCLA, and NYU, developed sufficient infrastructure and funding to claim legitimately that they could train filmmakers for feature narrative filmmaking on 35mm. Although Hollywood resisted absorbing many of those who trained in film school, opportunities existed elsewhere for film graduates in advertising, television, documentary, and educational film, which was a massive billion-dollar industry in the 1960s.[74] The second mode, far more widespread, employed small-scale production as a means for students to make personal films and to aid in the exploration of film aesthetics. The production mode of experimental film suits the scale and temperament of student filmmaking: a small crew (preferably one individual) and an extremely low budget. Limited access to expensive equipment made the availability of cheap 16mm cameras and film, and the simplicity and affordability of even cheaper formats like 8mm and S8mm, a crucial factor facilitating this explosion of personal filmmaking.[75] This personal scale of production also suited the limited budgets of the schools themselves: they could not claim to offer the infrastructure and resources for feature length (or even short) dramatic fiction. As Ernest Rose, the University Film Association president, said in 1969: "An introductory experience in production as well as in film viewing and discussion classes can be accomplished at a relatively modest cost. It is in the more advanced stages of practical training that economics becomes a factor."[76]

Meanwhile, hiring experimental filmmakers as instructors made fiscal sense as they commanded lower salaries and could usually bridge university cultures in the humanities and fine arts better than many industry professionals. As Sally Banes has argued in relation to the hiring of avant-garde theater and performance artists by the academy in the 1960s, "In a crude economic sense, to hire marginalized avant-gardists as faculty or guest artists (whether because that's what they really are by choice or because they haven't yet succeeded in joining the mainstream) is much cheaper for the university administration than to hire established artists."[77] Experimental filmmakers of the calibre of Stan Brakhage (University of Colorado, Boulder) and Leslie Thornton (Brown University) sustained themselves and, in part, their artistic practice through the university. Al-

Abbott Meader, Bruce Williams, and Carolyn Tower filming at Cranbrook Academy, Michigan, in 1978. Meader and Williams were part of a campus film society at Colby College, Maine, in the 1960s, which inspired their subsequent careers as independent filmmakers. (Photo by staff photographer, *Eccentric* newspaper, Bloomfield, MI)

though fiction directors like Martin Scorsese or Spike Lee teach at schools like NYU, they do so only sporadically and rarely take the active role of a full-time faculty member given their opportunities outside the academy. Since the mid-1960s, universities have functioned as a major source of employment, artistic resources, and creative/research time for experimental filmmakers. As Lauren Rabinovitz asserts, "By the end of the 1970s, the university and art school were not only the chief sources for film culture but were the primary economic support and organizational refuge for the avant-garde filmmaker."[78] Experimental filmmakers often found the academy a good fit because the shared principles of artistic freedom and academic freedom protected filmmakers who wanted to explore dissident formal (and even pedagogical) experiments.

Film Practice as Film Study

As mentioned above, the key impact of experimental film on film studies is usually understood to lie in the importance of the concept of the avant-garde in 1970s film theory, specifically in what D. N. Rodowick (following Sylvia Harvey) has called the cinema of "political modernism."[79] The fast-developing new field of film studies was infused with the revolutionary possibilities signaled in the events of 1968 and the impact of radical theories of Marxism, psychoanalysis, feminism, and structuralism/poststructuralism in the humanities and social sciences. The cultural visibility of avant-garde and countercultural projects generally in the 1960s made the avant-garde and other forms of oppositional, non-Hollywood cinema a central (if contested) part of film scholarship, first in the United Kingdom and Europe, and then in North America. As Bill Simon put it, the intellectual excitement of the formation of film studies as a discipline in the early 1970s lay in the modernist investigation of the nature of the medium, a project with which the avant-garde was explicitly engaged.[80] In the germinal essay for Anglo-American film studies, Laura Mulvey's 1975 essay "Visual Pleasure and Narrative Cinema," Mulvey calls for a "politically and aesthetically" radical avant-garde cinema to oppose the "obsessions and assumptions" of mainstream cinema and society.[81] This essay is standard reading in film studies curricula, although it is worth noting that its legacy lies more in introducing psychoanalysis and feminist film theory rather than in popularizing avant-garde cinema.

Mulvey speaks of the importance and interconnectedness of film theory, film viewing, and filmmaking (through access to small-scale artisanal film production) on the development of her and Peter Wollen's work on the avant-garde. She describes herself as part of the "pre-film studies generation" (she studied history at Oxford in the early 1960s) who came to be a film academic first through cinephilia. She has said of the period: "We had both begun to be interested in avant-garde film after spending the 60s—as did so many of our cinephile friends—very absorbed in Hollywood."[82] The love of film turned into involvement in film programming and filmmaking. In 1972 Mulvey helped organize a retrospective of women's films at the Edinburgh Film Festival, "which began to open my eyes to an important if marginal tradition of women's film making." From late 1972 to 1974, Wollen taught at Northwestern University in Chicago, where he and Mulvey were first given the opportunity to make films; there, as Mulvey puts it, "Peter and I discovered another world. . . . The School at Northwestern had a practical film making strand and had the usual 16mm equipment. Peter and I had never encountered the actual equipment or even envisaged the possibility of movie making before. This is where/when we encountered the Lenny Lipton book as it was the 'bible' of the moment and the 16mm film making revolution had spread from artists, and political collectives such as Newsreel to the universities. So we made our first film *Penthesilea*,

Queen of the Amazons in 1973–4, working with students and former students of the Northwestern programme."[83]

Lenny Lipton's 1972 book, *Independent Filmmaking*, was indeed the major filmmaking textbook in the American academy of the 1970s, especially for small-scale instruction. With an introduction by Brakhage, and illustrated for the most part by images and examples from experimental films, Lipton's textbook foregrounded the artisanal mode (although its principles could, of course, be applied to almost any filmmaking tradition). Mulvey and Wollen's experience in the U.S. academy during this period of film study's exponential expansion reflects the energy and eclecticism of the period, especially in the blurred boundaries between criticism, theory, and practice, and it constitutes a concrete link between the artisanal avant-garde mode and the theoretically informed avant-garde practice that arose in the mid to late 1970s.

Indeed, in arts education generally, hands-on practice was seen not only as a way to develop craft but also "as an instrument of criticism." In 1973, Ackerman discussed "practice as an aid to understanding the arts" as one component of "integrated" arts education that emphasized "alternative modes of experience and expression."[84] Haig Manoogian, a central figure in NYU's film production school, argued bluntly: "Film production is an essential part of all film study."[85] Many film instructors in this period understood small-scale student filmmaking as an experimental educational practice. For example, Reigel rationalizes the small scale of production at his institution: "Washington and Lee makes no pretense of being a 'professional' film making school. Our limited purpose is to introduce students to the medium and to show them, through their own experiments, the meaning of thinking visually and kinesthetically."[86] The filmmaker George Stoney, then teaching at Columbia University, wanted his students to "get a feel for the medium. . . . Mostly, I try to help students learn a new way of seeing. It is around the viewfinder that I try to build my course."[87] Students were and are given license to explore the medium in a literally experimental way, learning and thinking about film form by making it.[88]

The 1980s: Retrenchment and Decline

The 1980s began auspiciously for experimental film when the 1980 Society for Cinema Studies conference in New York devoted a third of its panels to the avant-garde. In 1982, a major film theory conference concentrating on the avant-garde, "Cinema Histories/Cinema Practices II," took place at the Center for Twentieth Century Studies at the University of Wisconsin, Milwaukee. But the conference proceedings reflect divisions. As Patricia Mellencamp notes: "A breach between avant-garde practices, academia and politics has grown. . . . It seems that in the academia/avant-garde parry, a circular and mutual defensiveness is in play: preferring narrative, many academics have avoided avant-garde; preferring the ennobling terms of 'high art' to theoretical language, avant-garde artists have benignly scorned academia."[89] Indeed, many experimental filmmakers during the 1980s complained about the importation of theory into film criticism, paralleling an anti-theory backlash generally throughout film studies and popular intellectual culture.[90] By the end of the decade, both the excitement about artisanal avant-garde film practice and the radical avant-garde central to film theory had dissipated (though not expired).

On a material level, by the end of the 1970s the period of expansion and educational experimentation that film study had enjoyed was threatened with contraction and conservative retrenchment. Hagood's analysis of dance applies to film as well: "For dance in higher education, the 1970s ended on a much less promising note than was presaged by the optimism of the beginning and middle years of the decade. By 1978 the nation's economy was pointed toward dramatic change. Throughout the latter 1970s, inflation ran high, and well paid, stable jobs were increasingly hard to find."[91] The massive growth of film programs likewise was halted when economic recession and education cutbacks in the United States led to a slowdown in the expansion of film studies (and other programs), as indicated in the 1979–80 AFI guide. The number of schools offering film or television courses leveled off, and course offerings and faculty complement were reduced. According to Peter Bukalski, director of Educational Services for the AFI, education budget pressures led to a reduction in full-time faculty, an increase in part-time faculty, and resource restrictions on expensive courses: "In screen education, the increasing cost of film rentals and production materials are significant factors in the reduction of film and television programs."[92] But even if resources were strained, student interest in film study, measured both in terms of overall registrations and the number of film and television degrees awarded, continued to rise.[93]

This retrenchment of film studies at the beginning of the 1980s paralleled and contributed to an overall diminishment of experimental film exhibition in the decade. Peter Wollen, speaking in 1982, presents a picture of contraction dictated by the world recession: "Increasingly we're cut off from funding: there is an attrition of money for filmmaking and film distribution. The recession also shows itself in an attrition of money within the academic sector on which avant-garde film has become, for good or ill, very dependent. In the current debate, we must be aware that the period of the Sixties and Seventies, which was one of expansion and consolidation of independent film, has clearly come to an end, as least as far as its economic base is concerned. That doesn't mean, of course, that independent film is going to disappear. But I think economics are likely to have an extremely conservative effect."[94] While schools that specialized in experimental film instruction stayed the course, education budget cuts dictated cutting unpopular courses with "difficult" films and minimizing visiting-filmmaker screening visits requiring honoraria. The gradual trend during the 1980s toward replacing expensive 16mm rentals with video copies, and the drastic reduction in 16mm film purchases by colleges and universities, further contracted academic experimental screenings.[95]

Finally, by the end of the 1970s experimental films almost disappeared from campus film societies; indeed, the decade witnessed the slow decline of the campus film society itself. According to distribution records at the Film-Makers' Cooperative (the major distributor of avant-garde films in the United States), rentals of avant-garde films declined precipitously in the 1970s. In 1970, while 146 checks were deposited from campus film societies, only forty-five were deposited in 1975, thirty-three in 1980, and eight in 1985. Multiple factors are behind the decline. First, with the general slide of student activism and counterculture in the decade, many campus societies folded. Second, it is likely that film classes themselves robbed campus film societies of part of their audience by providing weekly classroom screenings. Third, changes in the economics of nontheatrical distribution made the campus film society less viable for volunteer nonprofit organizations. In 1974, Vincent Canby reported on the difficulties facing campus film societies, citing higher distributor rental costs, lack of publicity, competition from other campus entertainment and noncampus rep houses, and finally, the "liberated commercial product in the theatrical market" facilitated by the relaxing of the rating systems that robbed campus film societies of their more prurient appeal (as Canby notes, for one film society, only a screening of *The Devil in Miss Jones* would guarantee a strong audience).[96]

Legacy

In some ways, there is remarkable similarity between the teaching status of experimental cinema today and that of forty years ago. Whether labeled avant-garde or experimental, films made in the artisanal mode have consistently been part of the film studies curriculum at least since the 1930s, serving as unambiguous examples of film produced as art. Moreover, the ongoing tradition of having experimental filmmakers appear with their films in classrooms goes back to the 1940s. Maya Deren traveled "across the country making personal presentations of her work at colleges and nurturing the environment in which young people began to imagine the possibilities of a film culture outside the studio system."[97] Sidney Peterson taught experimental filmmaking courses in the late 1940s at the California School of Fine Arts while Hans Richter was director of film courses at the City University of New York in the 1950s.[98] In syllabi from the early 1960s, the avant-garde or experimental film was already a set topic, marginal but persistent.[99] In the 1964–65 book *Film Study in Higher Education*, two survey courses are outlined: Jack Ellis lists a week titled "The Experimental Film" (with films by Luis Buñuel/Salvador Dalí, Shirley Clarke, and Arthur Lipsett), and Arthur Knight includes a section titled "The New Avant-Garde" (with films by Deren, Anger, Brakhage, James Broughton, Curtis Harrington, Bruce Conner, Stan Vanderbeek, Norman McLaren, Jim Davis, Ian Hugo, and Warhol).[100]

Experimental film is still taught in four predominant modes. First, introduction to film and film history survey courses often include a one- or two-week unit on "experimental" or "avant-garde" film, usually toward the end of the syllabus, often grouped with documentary, and usually screening canonical films like Fernand Leger and Dudley Murphy's *Ballet mécanique* (1924), Buñuel and Dalí's *Un chien andalou* (1929), Deren's *Meshes of the Afternoon* (1943), Conner's *A Movie* (1958), Anger's *Scorpio Rising* (1963), Snow's *Wavelength* (1967), and a film by Brakhage.[101] The second mode is a semester- or year-long course on experimental film—sometimes under the aegis "Film and the Other Arts"—that examines experimental film in relation to visual art, music, and/or new media. Third, some individual instructors who are well versed in experimental cinema may integrate these films generally into film history, criticism, and theory courses, or teach specialized topics within experimental film studies—e.g., "Found Footage Film" or "Feminist Avant-Garde Cinema." Fourth, there are a handful of universities (many of them art schools) with a tradition of specialization or at least concentration in experimental film study.[102] Experimental film found a stable institutional base at these schools when the cultural and economic contractions of the 1980s threatened the ethos of experimentation in both the arts and education.

The *Time* writer filing the report on the state of student filmmaking in 1968 pointed to an important long-range effect of the ethos of experimentation in film study: the widening of cinematic tastes in the population of cinema-goers exposed to the diversity of film styles and history through film education.[103] In blunt economic terms, university film study created a market for wider defi-nitions of film and film art, even if that art is still being conceived predomi-nantly in mainstream narrative terms. The success of the movie brats and the subsequent music video generation in Hollywood can be traced in part to an acceptance of new cinematic styles developing during the 1960s.[104]

What is more narrowly conceived as the avant-garde has set up modes of discourse and exchange in North America, which have had an important im-pact on film study journals and scholarship. Founded in 1976, *Camera Obscura* was initially dedicated mainly to discussions of feminist avant-garde cinema while *October*, founded the same year, has integrated avant-garde film into wide traditions of art criticism and theory. Key journals like *Wide Angle*, *Screen*, and *Cinetracts* published major essays and special issues on the avant-garde in the 1970s and early 1980s before the avant-garde/experimental film was displaced as a central object of film study.[105]

Within the experimental film world, circuits of exchange continue to thrive. Informally, discussion arises in the community of artists, programmers, crit-ics—and, crucially, students—responsible for setting up festivals and screen-ings, especially the long-standing tradition in which filmmakers present and discuss their work in the circuit of universities, museums, and the media arts centers that grew up in the 1960s and 1970s. Formally, the North American avant-garde has generated a massive if largely unknown literature through newsletters, magazines, journals, small-press books and pamphlets, museum and gallery catalogues, and most recently electronic mailing lists and Web sites, documenting screenings, reviewing films, and providing forums for aesthetic, political, and cultural debate.

Conclusion

The rise of participatory culture in the 1960s was part of a general social movement against large established institutions, rejecting both conventional Hollywood film and conventional university curriculum. Experimental films were showing at university film societies and contributed to the development of university film courses and, more generally, a cinephile culture around a heterogeneous vision of alternative film. Artisanal filmmaking found a crucial institutional site in small-scale film production instruction in colleges and universities, and offered an affordable method by which to integrate film production into meager course budgets. Experimental film as an explicit art practice provided material—celluloid and written—that could be used to legitimate curricular innovation. Meanwhile, mainstream ideas about education were being reformed, working toward facilitating a noninstrumental experience—a "praxis" rather than offering a commodity, in James's terms. Instead of simply learning a set of skills that would replicate, for example, the production values of the film industry, students demanded to be exposed to, and to experiment with, film form. Finally, the intervention of experimental film in the 1960s set the stage for the more visible moment of avant-garde influence on film studies, the development of film theory in the 1970s and 1980s and its radical models of Marxist and feminist cinema, and the early theorization of early cinema.

Notes

This essay has enjoyed substantial contributions from colleagues and research institutions. Haidee Wasson and Lee Grieveson have supported this research by suggesting numerous resources and avenues of inquiry, and with patient and detailed editing. I am grateful to Paul Arthur, James Kreul, Tess Takahashi, Bart Testa, and William Wees, who have read versions of this essay and offered invaluable feedback. The following institutions allowed access to their resources: Anthology Film Archives, New York (Robert Haller); Film-Makers' Cooperative, New York (M.M. Serra); Museum of Modern Art Film Study Center, New York (Ron Magliozzi and Charles Silver); Pacific Film Archives, Berkeley (Nancy Goldman). Assistance with procuring photographs was provided by Carl Fleischhauer, Abbott and Nancy Meader, and Adolfas Mekas. This essay is dedicated to Paul Arthur (1948–2008) whose tragic early death from cancer robs experimental film and media of one of its best critics and historians. Readers interested in a brilliant social and aesthetic history of recent experimental film and media are directed to Paul's remarkable book, *A Line of Sight: American Avant-Garde Film Since 1965* (Minneapolis: University of Minnesota Press, 2005).

1. I distinguish three traditions of the study of film in U.S. universities: "film studies," "film production," and "film study." Scholarly "film studies" existed prior to the 1970s but only then did institutional markers like departmental status and university press publishing become widespread. "Film production" has been taught in a number of institutional contexts including Hollywood studio apprenticeships, nonaccredited workshops and technical institutes, college and university film departments, art institute BFA and MFA programs, and specialized film production schools like the American Film Institute. "Film study" is a more general term that

most accurately describes the eclecticism and overlap of film studies and film production teaching prior to and during the 1960s.

2. David Bordwell, *Making Meaning: Inference and Rhetoric in the Interpretation of Cinema* (Cambridge, Mass.: Harvard University Press, 1989), 60–61. The Ph.D. program at NYU has produced many scholars of the avant-garde (myself included) in part due to its location in New York, the center of the American avant-garde film and art worlds.

3. Peter Wollen, "Counter Cinema: *Vent d'est*," *Afterimage* (U.K.) 4 (1972): 6–17. For a sympathetic critique of 1970s film theory, see D. N. Rodowick, *The Crisis of Political Modernism: Criticism and Ideology in Contemporary Film Theory* (Urbana: University of Illinois Press, 1988).

4. Laura Mulvey, "Visual Pleasure and Narrative Cinema," *Narrative, Apparatus, Ideology: A Film Theory Reader*, edited by Philip Rosen (New York: Columbia University Press, 1986) 198–209; originally published in *Screen* 16.3 (1975): 6–18.

5. Michelson dedicates to Burch the original (1966) version of her germinal essay "Film and the Radical Aspiration" (reprinted in *Film Culture Reader*, edited by P. Adams Sitney [New York: Praeger, 1970], 404–21; revised in 1974). Filmmakers like Ken Jacobs, Hollis Frampton, and Ernie Gehr were investigating early cinema well before the 1978 Brighton Project, which is often seen as the event sparking early film research. In 1979, the Whitney Museum of American Art sponsored a lecture series, "Researches and Investigations into Film: Its Origins and the Avant-Garde," which included Frampton, Jacobs, Burch, Gunning, Thom Anderson, Nick Browne, Regina Cornwell, and Maureen Turim. For an excellent account of the relationship between the avant-garde and early cinema, see Bart Testa, *Back and Forth: Early Cinema and the Avant-Garde* (Toronto: Art Gallery of Ontario, 1992).

6. Primary research for this essay was conducted at the Museum of Modern Art Film Study Center (MOMA), New York University Archives, Anthology Film Archives (AFA), and the Film-Makers' Cooperative, but primary sources like syllabi, curriculum guides to programs, and enrollment statistics are only haphazardly archived. This essay synthesizes and cross-references existing published surveys and essays on film education but the topic requires further research.

7. Gary Kibbins, "Bear Assumptions: Notes on Experimentalism," *Public* 25 (2002): 148.

8. Michelson, "Film and the Radical Aspiration," 404.

9. The New American Cinema Group convened by Mekas and Lewis Allen, modeled on European new wave cinemas, issued in 1961 a manifesto titled "The First Statement of the New American Cinema Group" (see Sitney, ed., *Film Culture Reader*, 79–83). Although its focus was on independent narrative and documentary, New American Cinema later became an umbrella term including experimental cinema. The "underground" emerged as a sexually and aesthetically transgressive cinema associated with films by Ron Rice, Jack Smith, Barbara Rubin, Kenneth Anger,

and Andy Warhol. The promise of nudity and drugs (in the context of widespread film censorship) made the underground a media sensation, but its (rigorous) formal looseness was reviled by many in the experimental—and student—film communities. See J. Hoberman and Jonathan Rosenbaum, *Midnight Movies* (New York: Harper and Row, 1983); and Janet Staiger, "Finding Community in the Early 1960s: Underground Cinema and Sexual Politics," in *Swinging Single: Representing Sexuality in the 1960s*, edited by Hilary Radner and Moya Luckett (Minneapolis: University of Minnesota Press, 1999), 39–74. P. Adams Sitney coined the term "structural" film to describe a reflexively formal film practice associated with the works of artists like Michael Snow, Frampton, Gehr, Paul Sharits, and Joyce Wieland (see Sitney, "Structural Film," *Film Culture* 47 [summer 1969]: 1–10). Structural film briefly enjoyed the attention of the art world and academic film theory, but it was controversial within the experimental film world.

10. Jon Borgzinner, "Made a Good Movie Lately? A Generation That Wants to Say It on Film," *Life*, October 22, 1968, 92.

11. Michael Zryd, "The Avant-Garde and the Academy: A Relationship of Dependence and Resistance," *Cinema Journal* 45.2 (2006): 17–42.

12. I do not claim that experimental film was *the* central project of either film studies or film production. During the 1970s, only approximately 6–7 percent of colleges and universities taught courses devoted to experimental cinema, although introduction to film and film theory courses would usually include experimental films.

13. For early histories of film study in the United States, see Kenneth Macgowan, "Film in the University," in *Ideas on Film: A Handbook for the 16mm User*, edited by Cecile Starr (New York: Funk and Wagnalls, 1951), 28–31; Robert W. Wagner, "Cinema Education in the United States," *Journal of the University Film Producers Association (JUFPA)* 13.3 (1961): 8–10, 12–14; Don G. Williams, "Teaching Programs in Film Production in the U.S.," *JUFPA* 14.4 (1962): 4–7, 17; John H. Tyo, "Film Production Courses in U.S. Universities," *JUFPA* 14.4 (1962): 8–13, 18, 21–22; Colin Young, "University Film Teaching in the United States: A Survey," *Film Quarterly* 16.3 (1963): 37–47; and Raymond Fielding, "Second Bibliographic Survey of Theses and Dissertations on the Subject of Film at U.S. Universities, 1916–1969," *Journal of the University Film Association (JUFA)* 21.4 (1969): 111–13.

14. The prominence of Bob Jones University, a fundamentalist Christian university, in early film production instruction is an example of a long tradition of the early adoption of media technology by Christian evangelicals. On the school's Web site, the following description is provided: "A liberal arts, non-denominational Christian university, BJU stands without apology for the old-time religion and the absolute authority of the Bible" (http://www.bju.edu/index, July 20, 2005).

15. Macgowan, "Film in the University," 29.

16. The Society of Cinematologists grew out of a set of annual conferences of film teachers held by MOMA in New York, beginning in 1957. See Jack C. Ellis, "The

Society for Cinema Studies: A Personal Recollection of the Early Days," *Cinema Journal* 43.1 (2003): 105–12. See also Wasson in this volume.

17. Tyo, "Film Production Courses in U.S. Universities," 13.

18. "A Time for Reassessment," editorial in *JUFPA* 14.1 (1961): 2.

19. Alvin Fiering, "Students of the Film," *JUFPA* 13.4 (1961): 12.

20. Thomas Bender, "Politics, Intellect, and the American University, 1945–1995," in *American Academic Culture in Transformation: Fifty Years, Four Disciplines*, edited by Thomas Bender and Carl E. Schorske (Princeton, N.J.: Princeton University Press, 1998), 33.

21. Thomas K. Hagood, *A History of Dance in American Higher Education: Dance and the American University* (Lewiston, Maine: E. Mellen Press, 2000), 217.

22. For a detailed discussion of the buzzword "relevance" in this period, see Patricia Jasen, "'In Pursuit of Human Values (or Laugh When You Say That)': The Student Critique of the Arts Curriculum in the 1960s," *Youth Education and Canadian Society*, ed. Paul Axelrod and John G. Reid (Kingston: McGill-Queens University Press, 1989), 247–71.

23. James S. Ackerman, "The Arts in Higher Education," in *Content and Context: Essays on College Education*, edited by Carl Kaysen, Laurence R. Veysey, and Carnegie Commission on Higher Education (New York: McGraw-Hill, 1973). Don Williams's 1961 survey of film production programs makes a parallel split between what he calls "Production-Teaching Units" like those at Indiana and Bob Jones and "Academic Programs" like those at USC and UCLA; within "Academic Programs," studies and production coexisted with varying degrees of liberal arts content and approach.

24. Ackerman, "The Arts in Higher Education," 219.

25. Robert W. Corrigan, "A Message from the Dean: Revolution and the Arts," *School of the Arts [NYU], First Bulletin*, 1966–67. New York University Archives, "School of the Arts" file.

26. While television instruction grew, its focus was technical training. As the AFI noted: "In comparison with film, television history/criticism was rarely emphasized" (AFI press release, January 2, 1973, AFA file, Anthology Film Archives Reference Library, "AFI" file). In film programs, production still dominated but was more equitably balanced with film history, criticism, and theory.

27. The 1973–74 edition incorporated television, becoming *Guide to College Courses in Film and Television*.

28. Bender, "Politics, Intellect, and the American University," 25.

29. Robert E. Roemer, "Vocationalism in Higher Education: Explanation from Social Theory," *Review of Higher Education* 23.2 (1981): 23–46, quoted in Hagood, *A History of Dance*, 219–20.

30. *The American Film Institute's Guide to College Film Courses*, 2nd ed. (Chicago: American Film Institute/American Library Association, 1970), ii.

31. The exception lies in the three major U.S. film production schools—USC, UCLA,

and NYU — which cultivated relationships with Hollywood studios. See also Peter DeCherney, "Inventing Film Study and Its Object at Columbia University, 1915–1938," *Film History* 12.4 (2000): 443–60.

32. See Young, "University Film Teaching," 38.
33. Ackerman, "The Arts in Higher Education," 248.
34. Robert W. Corrigan, "Film: The Art That Belongs to the Young," *Glamour*, February 1967, 120.
35. Ibid. See also Thomas Fensch, *Films on the Campus* (South Brunswick, N.J.: A. S. Barnes, 1970), 19.
36. Dwight MacDonald, "Report from the Academy," *Esquire*, November 1966, n.p.
37. Molly Willcox, "Film Education: The National Picture," *Filmmakers Newsletter* 2.2 (1968): 1; and Corrigan, "Film," 120.
38. Jack C. Ellis, "Film Societies and Film Education," *Film Culture* 4.3 (1958): 31.
39. Elenore Lester, "Shaking the World with an 8-mm. Camera," *New York Times Magazine*, November 26, 1967, 59.
40. David C. Stewart, ed., *Film Study in Higher Education; Report of a Conference Sponsored by Dartmouth College in Association with the American Council on Education*, Washington, D.C.: American Council on Education, 1966, 162–63.
41. "Proposal for a Film Education Program," United States National Student Association, 1966, Museum of Modern Art Film Study Center, "Film Education" file.
42. Corrigan, "Film," 120.
43. Ibid.
44. For an account of a film society at Idaho State University in Pocatello, Idaho, see Gene (Moses) Dawson, "Where 'Moses' Was When the Lights Went Out," *Filmmakers' Newsletter* 1.8 (1968); 1–2, 16, 18–19. See also B. Ruby Rich, "Film in the Sixties," in *Chick Flicks: Theories and Memories of the Feminist Film Movement* (Durham, N.C.: Duke University Press, 1998), 13–28; and Lauren Rabinovitz, *Points of Resistance: Women, Power and Politics in the New York Avant-Garde Cinema, 1943–71*, rev. ed. (Urbana: University of Illinois Press, 2003 [1991]).
45. Bender, "Politics, Intellect, and the American University," 17–18.
46. Notably VGIK and All Union Institute of Cinema in Moscow, Institut Des Hautes Études Cinématographiques in Paris, State Higher Film School in Lodz, Poland, Centro Sperimentale di Cinematografia in Rome, and Instituto de Investigaciones y Esperiencias Cinematographicas in Madrid. It was not until 1976 that a national film academy, the AFI, was established in the United States. See Dustin Rawlinson, "A World Survey of Training Programs in Cinema," *JUFPA* 14.4 (1962): 3, 16.
47. See Larry Siegel and George Woodbridge, "A Mad Guide to Art Films," *Mad Magazine* December 1963, 13–18; Pete Hamill, "Explosion in the Movie Underground," *Saturday Evening Post*, September 28, 1963, 82, 84; "Cinema Underground," *New Yorker*, July 13, 1963, 16–17; Ken Kelman, "Anticipations of the Light," *Nation*, May 11, 1964, 490–94; Shana Alexander, "Report from Underground," *Life*, January 28, 1965; Robert Christgau, "The New but Muddy Wave," *Popular Photography*,

May 1965, 118–19, 125–26; Alan Levy, "Voice of the 'Underground Cinema,'" *New York Times Sunday Magazine*, September 19, 1965; Jack Kroll, "Underground in Hell," *Newsweek*, November 14, 1966; Elenore Lester, "So He Stopped Painting Brillo Boxes and Bought a Movie Camera," *New York Times*, December 11, 1966; and Jack Kroll, "Up from Underground," *Newsweek*, February 13, 1967, 117–19. Books on avant-garde film published by trade publishers include Sheldon Renan, *An Introduction to the American Underground Film* (New York: Dutton, 1967); Parker Tyler, *Underground Film: A Critical History* (New York: Grove Press, 1970); Gregory Battcock, ed., *The New American Cinema* (New York: Dutton, 1967); and Jonas Mekas, *Movie Journal: The Rise of the New American Cinema 1959–1971* (New York: Macmillan, 1972). The censorship battles over *Flaming Creatures* in 1963–64 in Knokke-le-Zoute and New York, and *Scorpio Rising* in California in 1964 brought further press attention.

48. Kroll, "Up from Underground," 119.

49. Although as with other Jonas Mekas ventures in this period the popular success of the Lecture Bureau itself is debatable, its existence is testament to the presence of an academic market for experimental filmmakers. Mekas, in his "Movie Journal" column in New York's *Village Voice*, wrote occasional columns on his visits to colleges and universities (see June 6, 1968, 49; July 23, 1970, 48; and May 11, 1972). Despite some ambivalence to how the demands of teaching would affect artists, he celebrated screenings of experimental films on campus. In 1974, reacting against an outcry bemoaning the closing of several "art house" theaters, Mekas said, "I see thousands of 'art' houses in the universities, museums, galleries, etc. More than 600 universities and colleges have film departments today, as against a dozen 10 years ago" ("Movie Journal," *Village Voice*, January 3, 1974, 55).

50. David E. James, "'The Movies Are a Revolution': Film and the Counterculture," in *Imagine Nation: The American Counterculture of the 1960s and '70s*, edited by Peter Braunstein and Michael William Doyle (New York: Routledge, 2002), 275–76.

51. Arthur quoted in ibid., 288.

52. Although filmmaking remained male dominated, universities and film schools gave women more opportunities to make films. Mekas noted the increased participation of women filmmaking students (*Village Voice*, June 6, 1968, 49), and women appear in the popular press accounts of student filmmaking in the period.

53. Paul Arthur, "Routines of Emancipation: Alternative Cinema in the Ideology and Politics of the Sixties," in *To Free the Cinema: Jonas Mekas and the New York Underground*, edited by David E. James (Princeton, N.J.: Princeton University Press, 1992), 18.

54. Lester, "Shaking the World," 45.

55. O. W. Reigel, "Some Thoughts on Student Films," *Film Comment* (winter 1969): 64.

56. "The Student Movie Makers," *Time*, February 2, 1968, 78.

57. Corrigan, "Film," 120.
58. Borgzinner, "Made a Good Movie Lately?" 92.
59. Sheldon Renan, quoted in David E. James, "'The Movies Are a Revolution,'" 281.
60. Jonas Mekas, "Notes on the New American Cinema," in Sitney, ed., *Film Culture Reader*, 104.
61. Lester, "Shaking the World," 47–49.
62. Quoted in R. J. Monaco, "You're Only as Young as They Think You Are," *Saturday Review*, December 27, 1969, 13.
63. Reigel, "Some Thoughts on Student Films," 65.
64. Jonas Mekas, "Notes on the New American Cinema," 87–107.
65. Lester, "Shaking the World," 45.
66. Gordon Hitchens, "Half a Dozen Avant-Gardes," *Film Society Review* (1968): 35, 36.
67. "National Student Film Awards–1966," Museum of Modern Art Film Study Center, "National Student Film Awards" file.
68. "The Student Movie Makers," *Time*, February 2, 1968, 79.
69. "Student Filmmakers," *Newsweek*, October 25, 1965.
70. For a fascinating portrait of Scott Bartlett, who taught film at San Francisco State College, see "San Francisco State College Engulfed in Chaos; Scott Bartlett and the Reno Hotel," in Fensch, *Films on the Campus*.
71. Amos Vogel, "The Camera as Pen," in "National Student Film Awards–1966."
72. Ibid.
73. "The Student Movie Makers," 78.
74. Robert Windeler, "Study of Film Soaring on College Campuses," *New York Times*, April 18, 1968, 58.
75. This moment in the 1960s parallels the early twenty-first century explosion of personal digital video facilitated by affordable, high-quality consumer-grade digital cameras and computer editing systems.
76. Ernest D. Rose, "Problems and Prospects in Film Teaching," *JUFPA* 21.4 (1969): 100.
77. Sally Banes, "Institutionalizing Avant-Garde Performance: A Hidden History of University Patronage in the United States," in *Contours of the Theatrical Avant-Garde: Performance and Textuality*, edited by James M. Harding (Ann Arbor: University of Michigan Press, 2000), 222.
78. Rabinovitz, *Points of Resistance*, 196.
79. Rodowick, *The Crisis of Political Modernism*, 1.
80. In 1973, Bill Simon received the second Ph.D. produced by NYU's fledgling cinema studies graduate program; he was subsequently hired by the department and served as its chair for more than a decade. His perspective on the development of film study at NYU was an invaluable resource for this essay (personal interview with the author, September 5, 2003, New York).
81. Mulvey, "Visual Pleasure," 200.

82. Laura Mulvey, e-mail correspondence with the author, June 16, 2004 (subsequent quotations are from this source).
83. See Lenny Lipton, *Independent Filmmaking* (San Francisco: Straight Arrow Books, 1972).
84. Ackerman, "The Arts in Higher Education," 224–25.
85. Haig Manoogian, "Radical Thoughts for a Radical Art," *JUFA* 23.1 (1971): 5.
86. Reigel, "Some Thoughts on Student Films," 69.
87. Quoted in Willcox, "Film Education," 1.
88. If the discourse of learning by making was pervasive, its actual merits were debated. In the first issue of *Screen Education Notes* (spring 1972), the editorial is skeptical of the "free expression" approach of the 1960s and instead seeks more "structured approaches" (3)—a signal of changes coming in the 1970s.
89. Patricia Mellencamp, "Editorial," *Wide Angle* 7.1/2 (1985): 5.
90. See debates in 1980s experimental film magazines like *Experimental Film Coalition Newsletter*, *Spiral*, and *Ideolects*.
91. Hagood, *A History of Dance*, 242.
92. "New College Guide Shows Screen Education Feeling Money Pinch," American Film Institute press release, 1980, Anthology Film Archives Reference Library, "AFI" file.
93. In a 1995 *New York Times* report on the explosion of interest in film schools in the 1990s, Anita Gates reported that over the period from the late 1970s to the mid-1990s, "film degrees . . . increased nearly 300 percent: 10 times as much as college degrees overall" ("Lights, Camera, Action," *New York Times*, November 21, 1995, C13).
94. Peter Wollen, "Popular Culture and Avant-Garde: Comments," *Wide Angle* 7.1/2 (1985): 103.
95. In 1974, the U.S. Congress cut funding for film purchases by universities, which had the unintentional effect of helping to create a canon of pre-1974 teaching films; see Peter Feinstein, *The Independent Film Community: A Report on the Status of Independent Film in the United States* (New York: Committee on Film and Television Resources and Services, 1977), 48.
96. Vincent Canby, "Who Says College Kids Dig Movies?" *New York Times*, March 24, 1974, 1, 20. Mike Rubin's report, "Film Threat: The Demise of Campus Film Societies," *Village Voice* May 25, 1993, 10–14, extends this narrative of decline into the 1980s and 1990s, blaming home (and dorm) video, education cutbacks, and cultural conservatism.
97. James, "Revolution," 278.
98. Sidney Peterson, *The Dark of the Screen* (New York: Anthology Film Archives/ New York University Press, 1980); Hans Richter, "Hans Richter on the Function of Film History Writing," *Film Culture* 18 (1958): 25–26; and Hans Richter, "Learning from Film History," *Filmmakers Newsletter* 7.1 (1973): 26–27.
99. Robert Steele, "Film Curriculum," *JUFPA* 13.4 (1961): 10–11.

100. In Stewart et al., *Film Study in Higher Education*, 20–30, 66–67.

101. Paul Arthur credits the best-selling textbook *Film Art* by David Bordwell and Kristin Thompson for ensuring a place for avant-garde film in introductory course syllabi in North America. See Malcolm Turvey et al., "Round Table: Obsolescence and American Avant-Garde Film," *October* 100 (2002): 115–32.

102. Schools primarily focused on experimental film in studies and production include Bard, Brown, Cooper Union, Hampshire, Massachusetts College of Art, San Francisco Art Institute, School of the Art Institute of Chicago, School of the Museum of Fine Arts (Boston), SUNY Binghamton, and Wisconsin-Milwaukee. Schools with some concentration on experimental film (with faculty who are scholars and/or makers of experimental film) include SUNY Buffalo's Center for Media Studies, California Institute of the Arts, UC Berkeley, UC Irvine, Colorado (Boulder), Columbia, Concordia (Montreal), Florida, Hartford, Iowa, Ithaca, New School (NYC), NYU, Northwestern, Princeton, Rutgers, Ryerson, San Francisco State, Sarah Lawrence, Simon Fraser, USC, Toronto, Wisconsin-Madison, and York (Toronto).

103. "The Student Movie Makers," 79.

104. See Betsy McLane, "Domestic Theatrical & Semi-Theatrical Distribution and Exhibition of American Independent Feature Films: A Survey in 1983," *Journal of the University Film and Video Association* 35.2 (1983): 23.

105. See *Wide Angle* 2.3 (1978); *Wide Angle* 7.1–3 (1985); *Screen* 25.6 (1984); and *Cinetracts* 17 (1982).

From Cinephilia to Film Studies

LAURA MULVEY AND PETER WOLLEN

WITH LEE GRIEVESON

■ *What follows is derived from two taped conversations between Laura Mulvey and Peter Wollen (the second of which was also attended by Lee Grieveson). All of the material has been edited by Laura Mulvey.*

LM: There are two agendas behind this conversation. First of all, to put on record the crucial contribution made by Paddy Whannel to the establishment of film studies as a recognized discipline in this country [the U.K.] through your [Peter Wollen's] memories of working with him at the British Film Institute's [hereafter BFI] Education Department in the late 60s. Second, I thought it might be interesting to record your own intellectual trajectory from devoted cinephile to film academic. Seeing that Paddy played such an important role in enabling that transformation, the two issues are closely connected.

   PW: Paddy was head of education at the BFI from 1957 to 1971. The policy that he established at the department marked a turning point for the development of film studies in Britain. By and large, there were two related sides to this: it involved creating a productive environment for the development of ideas and projects, a kind of crucible for the future of film theory, while also giving support to existing film education and encouraging its further development. His policy involved bringing ideas out into the world to the department's constituency of teachers. There were the annual summer schools that were incredibly important in spreading the department's work and ideas.[1] Fundamentally,

Paddy's approach was based upon his belief that education involved intellectual work—that is, research and ideas, especially new ideas. It wasn't simply a question of taking established ideas about film and putting them into some kind of curriculum. It was a question of actually coming up with new ways of thinking about cinema. Paddy didn't separate ideas from practical implementation. For instance, he initiated the BFI's projects to further film education at the university level in the U.K. and he started BFI book publishing, both of which I was involved with.

LM: There had, of course, been a couple of earlier instances of film taught at the university level. Thorold Dickinson started a film course at the Slade School of Art [University College, London] and the Royal College of Art had started a postgraduate degree in filmmaking in the early 60s.

PW: But Paddy came from a very different intellectual background. His world was the world of people like Raymond Williams; it was not a nuts and bolts world, it was a structured intellectual world. Most important of all, he was interested in popular, commercial cinema. This was a complete break with tradition. You can see the originality of this kind of approach in the book he coauthored with Stuart Hall in 1964, *The Popular Arts*.

LG: Why was *The Popular Arts* so crucial?

PW: It was the first book to use what you might call a theoretical approach to a subject that had no academic standing, and people like Paddy saw an opportunity to give film studies an academic standing through promoting writing that was theoretical.

LM: I think it's partly because that was Paddy's only publication that his influence has been so forgotten. He was an enabler and organizer. It was his vision combined with everyday management skills that made the Education Department so productive. In some ways, you can see the milieu he created as a kind of precursor to Stuart Hall's Centre for Cultural Studies in Birmingham.[2]

PW: For both of them, their engagement with culture had a political edge. Paddy came from a working-class background and began his career as a projectionist in Pitlochry, Scotland. He had left school at fourteen or fifteen and had further education through the Workers Educational Association.[3] The WEA was his original model of education when he joined the BFI. He wanted to establish film studies in adult education. There was a clear relationship, in Paddy's mind, between film as a popular art and the idea that adult education should include the popular arts, because going to the cinema was part of the people's everyday life.

LG: Initially, working-class education is important, then.

PW: Yes, to a considerable extent. But what differentiated Paddy from, for instance, Richard Hoggart or Raymond Williams was that he loved Hollywood cinema. He also recognized the crucial fact that Hollywood, then as now, dominated the cinema in Britain and other countries. But for Paddy it was not just the appeal of American popular arts but also a will to take them seriously, and to acknowledge their cultural value. This could cause problems with Hoggart, otherwise a good friend of Paddy's, who was horrified by Americanization.

LM: So while [Hoggart's] *The Uses of Literacy* saw American popular culture as the enemy of the English working class, Paddy's project definitely saw Hollywood as a great cinema.

PW: And also, that went with a lack of belief in British cinema. This wasn't confined to the Education Department. If you look at Tom Nairn's piece on the dreadfulness of British cinema (written in 1969) and his incredible diatribe against Richard Attenborough, you see how deeply felt these issues were.[4] Tom, like Paddy, came from Scotland.

LM: That's an interesting perspective on both their anti-Englishness. But anti-Englishness had a more general significance at the time and, speaking for myself, for instance, it affected the English as well as the Scots. There was an intellectual environment that reacted against English complacency and its isolationism and questioned the concept of a Leavisite "great tradition." So to a certain extent this move toward Hollywood was also a symbolic gesture, a provocative stand against dominant cultural values. Perhaps Hollywood, American popular arts, made it possible to think about culture outside the straightjacket of the English class system?

PW: I think that's true. And it's important to remember that Paddy's first love, before Hollywood cinema, was jazz . . . Jazz led him to the movies.

LM: Perhaps we could go back to Paddy's project.

PW: Well, Paddy had a number of different aims. In addition to those mentioned, the Education Department set up a diploma course in conjunction with the University of London Extra Mural Department in the mid-60s.

LM: Yes, that was a great milestone — probably the first university-based film studies program in the U.K. And it gave lots of people of our generation their first teaching experience. I remember giving my first-ever course on melodrama there in the 70s.

PW: And in terms of secondary education, the department ran an advisory service for teachers and supported the Society for Education in Film and Television, which was the original publisher of *Screen*. Then there was Paddy's commitment to screening films. The Education Department built up a study collection of 16mm extracts. They were like quotes you could use in a lecture. This was an attempt to insist that film had its own identity that was different from that of theater or literature. Again this was a break with traditional English film criticism that had tended to be art cinema and script-orientated. We went out to give lectures and had extracts of films on 16mm to take with us . . . Nick Ray, Sam Fuller, Hawks, Hitchcock.

And, of course, probably most important of all from my point of view, Paddy gathered a group of people around him who were as deeply committed to promoting film education as he was, and who also personally loved Hollywood cinema.

LM: And also had an auteur approach to Hollywood?

PW: That's right. But this was the way of thinking about Hollywood that had also come to me through Patrick Bauchau, Eugene Archer, and Andrew Sarris.

LM: We can come back to that and to those people in a minute. One thing I remember very clearly was the seminars in the basement at Old Compton Street, before the Education Department moved into the main BFI offices on Dean Street.

PW: The seminars were the means of getting new ideas articulated and established. The other day I found a copy of *Working Papers on the Cinema,*[5] a pamphlet in which some of the seminar papers were published: Andrew Tudor, "Sociological Perspectives on Film Aesthetics"; Frank West, "Semiology and Cinema"; Peter Wollen, "Cinema and Semiology." The discussions were quite complicated and sophisticated and there was a terminology for thinking about film that was quite new and was beginning to make headway but also of course ran into serious opposition. We also went back to film theorists such as Eisenstein and Bazin.

LM: When I was looking for material for this interview I found, for instance, a note of a paper given by Victor Perkins in February 1967, "Film: Technology and Technique" and Alan Lovell March 1969, "British Cinema: The Unknown Cinema"—both of which formed the basis for future publications; and May 1969, Peter Wollen, "The Concept of Communication(s): A Draft for Discussion."

Another Education Department initiative that was your responsibility was publishing.

PW: The Cinema One series of books were published by the BFI with Secker and Warburg. The series began in 1967 with Richard Roud's book on Godard, and Geoffrey Nowell-Smith's on Visconti, then came Kitses's *Horizons West*, and my *Signs and Meaning* in 1969. Then came Jon Halliday's book-length interview with Douglas Sirk in 1971, and Colin McArthur's book in 1972 on gangster films, *Underworld USA*.[6]

LM: BFI Publishing was originally set up as a collaboration between *Sight and Sound* and the Education Department—though they didn't speak to each other and were at daggers drawn . . . each on a different side of the Hollywood divide.

PW: Let's say we didn't often speak to each other. The meetings were sites for negotiations. The collaboration was a compromise between very different approaches to film criticism in the BFI.

LG: Did you have a vision for what that book series would be, as commissioning editor?

PW: I suppose you could say that the books fell into two categories. One was auteur based, evident in books on Godard, Sirk, Kazan, Visconti, and so on, and then others were more genre orientated—for instance, *Horizons West*.

LM: And *Signs and Meaning*?

PW: *Signs and Meaning* is different because it was not specifically about directors or genres, although they're discussed in the book. It was across the line into film theory.

LM: I think that is the key point about this conversation, to demonstrate the way that the Education Department under Paddy's leadership was the midwife, as it were, to the birth of film theory in this country. Although *Signs and Meaning* had moved toward theory as such, some of the other books you commissioned were certainly theoretically influenced and inflected. Perhaps we could go back to your earlier involvement with film and to why Paddy wanted you there and how you made the transition from cinephilia to academia.

PW: I was introduced to film in the first instance by people I knew at Oxford. Most important of all was Patrick Bauchau, who later became a film actor and is now an actor on American television.[7] Although Patrick is Belgian, he used to spend quite a lot of time in Paris and he introduced the *Cahiers du Cinéma*'s love of Hollywood to his friends in Oxford in the late 50s. That is, between 1956 and 1959.

LG: Were film societies important at Oxford?

PW: No, it was a group of people who were interested in film and who got to know each other but it was not structured, as a society or anything. But it's important to remember that the magazine *Oxford Opinion* was also beginning to take an interest in Hollywood about this time. Victor Perkins was involved with *Oxford Opinion* and it later mutated into *Movie*.

LG: It's quite a curious situation—Paddy coming from workers education and then this bunch of people at Oxford.

LM: I think interest in Hollywood was the crucial link. As Paddy began to look for an intellectual approach to film, writers in two journals, *Movie* and *New Left Review*, were both treating Hollywood cinema as a great cinema. And they were writing about directors who had emerged out of the *Cahiers du Cinema's politique des auteurs.* Paddy picked up on the cinephilia that fed both of these movements.

LG: Marxism provided a connection also.

PW: There was that and the *Popular Arts* connection as well, the idea that just as people in Pitlochry were watching Hollywood movies so were people in Oxford. To go back: Later Patrick introduced me to the American film critic Eugene Archer who was another very important influence.[8] They had met in New York and Gene realized that Paris was the place where Hollywood films were given equal standing with any other great cinema. There was a real film culture there with the Cinémathèque. And by the early 60s, the New Wave was taking off and the *Cahiers* critics who had been responsible for reviving this great enthusiasm for Hollywood had begun to make films themselves.

Gene was fanatical about Hollywood. He was a walking encyclopedia of film lore. I remember him dueling with John Cavell, each coming up with lines of dialogue for the other to identify with increasing obscurity. He knew exactly what film the line of dialogue was coming from and which character in which scene in which film. There was an element in that kind of fanaticism that I wanted to distance myself from because, for whatever reason, I wanted to take a more scholarly, academic approach, although with a journalistic dimension. Andrew Sarris was also a protégé of Gene's, and my bible at the time was the special issue of *Film Culture* on Hollywood that Andrew [Sarris] had done very much under Gene's influence.

LM: That was the issue of *Film Culture* that he [Sarris] later turned into the book *The American Cinema* in 1968.[9] When I started going to the movies with you and Jon [Halliday] in 1963, my ambition in life was to see every movie by the key directors, from "Pantheon" through "The Far Side of Paradise" to "Likeable but Elusive." I've still got the copy of *Film Culture* with the movies marked off. But it might be worth pointing out that in *The American Cinema* there's an acknowledgment of both Gene Archer and Patrick Bauchau. Do you remember where you first met Gene? Was it in Paris?

PW: No it was in London, at the Peploes' [Mark and Clare] house in Chapel

Street.[10] Clare was another Oxford cinephile. Patrick stayed there sometimes when he was in London and Gene used to come over quite often after he moved to Paris. Gene moved to Paris after he lost his job at the *New York Times*. His attempts to become a scriptwriter there never worked out. In the very early 60s, he hired me to write a screenplay of Faulkner's *The Wild Palms* and believed he could sell it to Truffaut. But that didn't work out either and I think that was really depressing for him. While I was working on *The Wild Palms* he took me to Gestaad and locked me in a chalet to write. When he got bored of skiing he'd let me out again. His idea of giving *The Wild Palms* to Truffaut reflects the influence of the New Wave and the way that he saw that the axis of filmmaking was beginning to shift from America to Europe. For someone who wanted to get closer to . . . to get involved with actually making films, Paris seemed to be the place to be.

LG: So Gene's interest was the other way around from yours. He was an American loving Hollywood cinema but who also recognized the importance of the new European cinema and went to Paris in search of it, whereas one of the things you have described is how your cohort of Europeans looked toward America as a way of thinking beyond Englishness.

PW: That's right. And in England, at any rate, this kind of approach to Hollywood could be taken as a provocation—that is, using a theoretical approach to popular cinema. This was one of the reasons for the hostility between the Education Department and *Sight and Sound* that eventually spread to the top of the BFI. Eventually, of course, Paddy was forced to resign. But I don't think it was just Hollywood that was at issue. The struggle that Paddy lost was central to a British—English?—cultural divide. He was absolutely committed to providing the very best service to schools and other areas of education while also believing that the future belonged to film as a discipline in its own right. It was the BFI's philistine attitude that he found so dispiriting.[11]

LM: You first began to write about films in *New Left Review* [NLR] under the name Lee Russell.

PW: I have the list in front of me: Howard Hawks, John Ford, Jean-Luc Godard, Roberto Rossellini, Jean Renoir, Sam Fuller. Geoffrey [Nowell-Smith] did Alain Resnais and François Truffaut.

LM: Would you agree that it [the inclusion of these articles on popular culture] was due to Perry Anderson's complete revision of the journal's policy when he became editor in 1962?[12]

PW: Yes. I had a double role on the NLR. I wrote political articles. I wrote about Iran; I had spent a year in Tehran, probably between 1962 and 1963, which had an important political effect on me. But I also edited the section called "Motifs" that represented the Review's changed approach to culture. My first film article, on Howard Hawks, was published in 1964, the same year as *The Popular Arts*.[13]

LG: It is quite a leap from what you would have done at Oxford, from reading English literature to reading Hawks . . .

PW: I just became more interested in film and there were no options to do that at Oxford.

LM: I remember you telling me that you wrote about Elvis Presley in your Milton paper in finals. The mid-50s was not only the time of Hollywood, it was also when rock and roll arrived in this country. Bill Haley's tour in autumn 1956—around the same time as Suez and Hungary and, incidentally, the first issue of *Universities and Left Review*.[14] Anyway, you joined the editorial board of NLR.

PW: That's right. Again the roots of that are also in Oxford; people I knew there who were interested in leftwing politics rather than the cinema. I was able to serve as some kind of a bridge between those two trends.

LM: I think there's an interesting coincidence between the wider intellectual shift that was taking place with NLR after 1963 and the particular one represented by cinephilia. That trend found American popular cinema through Paris, turning away from Englishness, as we said before. The new NLR rejected traditional English Left politics very vigorously and turned to European Marxism in preference to British Labour politics.[15] Although, looking back, the film pieces seem so important—in fact you were more involved with political journalism at the time, in which European Marxism played a major role. You spent at least a year in Rome working (with Jon Halliday) on Leilio Basso's *International Socialist Journal*. So far as I remember, you came back to London when Paddy appointed you to the Education Department in early 1966, which, looking back, is the moment when your professional life moved definitively from politics to film. But could you say something about the cultural policy of NLR? That is, the "Motifs" section that you were responsible for?

PW: In addition to the articles on cinema there are a number of articles by Alan Beckett on blues, modern jazz and the new wave of pop, the Rolling Stones, for instance.

We also published avant-garde poetry, especially translations of Third World poets—although the great new waves of Third Cinema that were going to have such an impact on film culture hadn't yet reached Britain. It was a period in which the spirit of Bandung was extremely influential on the Left in the First World.[16]

LM: To go back to the particular transformation that happened here, in Britain, which perhaps pioneered the integration of popular cinema into academia. Although, for instance, Andrew Sarris certainly established the idea of auteurism in the United States, I think the first flurry of new theory happened here. We have been suggesting that there was an English eagerness to turn away from its own cultural roots and to embrace French theory and American popular culture. This made *film* theory possible. So what I am trying to say is that the framework that Paddy offered in the Education Department made it possible to bring these kinds of things together—with a professional cadre and institutional support.

PW: Absolutely; that's true. And probably the most important thing that happened was the fusion of auteurism and structuralism, which also originated in Paris in a different context. So the kind of thinking that was then going on in our section of the BFI was dependent on the one hand on people like Jean Rouch and behind that André Bazin, and then on the other hand Claude Lévi-Strauss. Now Lévi-Strauss was not someone who wrote about films but about myths. But anybody can see that there is a certain similarity between the concepts of film and myth—they are both narrative forms and at the same time artistic.

LG: I suppose auteurism was a kind of pivot, moving out of the cinephilia of the *Cahiers* to the kind of structuralist approach you see in the Cinema One books. So could you say that it was this combination of intellectual influences applied to Hollywood cinema that made this innovative approach possible? That it could sidestep the existing film culture [script and character oriented, but also in this country the, by then lost, British documentary tradition]? The theory of myth and narrativity, for instance, made it possible to think in an intellectual way about films made for mass distribution and entertainment?

PW: That's right and it's what enables you, for instance, to think about John Ford in terms of the myth of the west and how the films he made were stories that embodied and reflected on that myth. So the connection with Lévi-Strauss was not arbitrary by any means. Henry Nash Smith's *The Myth of the West*, for instance, had a big impact on the Education Department. Paddy had a particular love of the western and was fascinated by the opposition of the wilderness and the garden. And the influence of Lévi-Strauss is very marked in both *Horizons West* and *Signs and Meaning*.

As well as this idea of films having a similarity to mythical tales there was also, on another level, a similarity to folk and fairy tales, which were the basis for Roman Jakobson's theoretical writings, which had also influenced Lévi-Strauss.

LM: Going back to Paddy's project of "intellectual justification," do you think these kinds of ideas made it possible for the popular cinema to become an object of study in the university? Was this a precondition or just one path? Could there have been other ones?

PW: I am not sure about precondition. But it is more than a coincidence that at the time when film studies was venturing into structuralism that you get a discipline called narratology emerging in universities. Again, ideas reliant upon, or borrowed from, semiotics started showing up in literary criticism. So it was quite logical they would show up in film criticism.

LM: So in a sense this theoretical context was more relevant for the analysis of popular cinema and might be seen as a bridge between film studies and the universities, rather than as a poor relation of "English," for instance.

PW: Yes, certainly in my case it derived from narrative studies. But there were, of course, other pathways that film studies took into universities, and the people who taught there found their own ways to negotiate with different disciplines—including, of course, "English"!

LG: Could you say something about the British Film Institute's funding of film posts?

PW: I don't remember very clearly. I think probably the posts were actually instituted after I left the Education Department at the end of 1968.[17] But my first job in a university was in a linguistics department.

LM: No it wasn't: your first job was with Paddy at Northwestern—autumn 1972.[18]

PW: Oh yes. But I mean in England. My first job in a university in England, which was at the University of Essex, was in the Department of Languages and Linguistics, which goes back to what we're talking about—Jakobson and so on—that's why the people in Colchester were interested in my approach to the cinema. You had a university with a linguistics department that had people who were well aware of Propp already because they were Slavic scholars. Suddenly film studies brought into play the ideas of people like Propp and Jakobson. From this you then had the possibility of film being taught in British universities. None of that could have been predicted.

LM: A series, as you would put it, of knight's moves.

PW: Yes. The other aspect is the birth of *Screen* as a theoretical journal. This is a time of the foundation of a lot of journals. Sam Rohdie was important in engineering the shift of direction in *Screen*. It was modeled on magazines like *Communications* in Paris, which is where people like Christian Metz and Raymond Bellour, a new generation of French theorists, emerged. By the time *Screen* was established you had people who were very opposed to it in a way that had not happened with magazines like *Movie* and *Cinema*. *Screen* hit a raw nerve in British film culture because it was so clearly theoretical and there was a backlash against that.

LM: Was there a backlash because the previous constituency was more involved in teaching in schools or workers education rather than the university?

PW: My memory of working at the BFI, in the Education Department and under Paddy's direct management and influence, was that we thought these different educational strands could coexist, that we could continue with the outreach programs and at the same time have a research component. Within this ethos they were not mutually contradictory. No, the problem was with theory. Film theory was moving into a kind of post-Bazinian world. Bazin was ontology and language and then the influence of structuralism and semiotics opened up new directions and possibilities.

LG: Was the issue about the usefulness of theory itself?

PW: Of course the question of theory led to a lot of discussion, some people disagreeing and not seeing the relevance of it, others defending it and putting forward hypotheses and so on—the discussions were very energetic.

LM: Theory, so called, did cause near apoplexy in the powers that were at the BFI.

PW: It was somewhat alarming to them. This, of course, encouraged people even more! Another point I would like to make is that the influence of French theory was a twofold thing. It was on the one hand Bazin, who had a considerable influence. Even though going back one could think of him as a classical theorist. On the other hand, Christian Metz was also a major influence. Metz was someone who was also interested in semiotics and structuralism. So from France you had two quite different currents.

LG: What was Metz's influence on you?

PW: Encouragement. When I read what Metz was writing, I thought I agreed. I suppose coming from Paris gave it a certain kind of substance, I thought "I am not all alone in this battle," here is Christian Metz arguing along similar grounds with the same interest in semiology, structuralism, and linguistics.

LG: This might be tangential—but what's curious in some respects is that what begins with cinephilia, with the love of Hollywood, and becomes the theoretical study of Hollywood, becomes also a sustained critique of the ideology of Hollywood. So if you were to read some of the early *Screen* pieces, or "Visual Pleasure," for example, you might find it hard to trace back to that love of Hollywood.

LM: But if it had not been for the background of cinephilia, the "Visual Pleasure" critique would never have been possible. It was a critique that was enabled by cinephilia and a deep love of Hollywood.

LG: But it's a rejection of your own cinephilia, of your past.

LM: Yes it was. That's partly because we felt, by the early 70s, that there was a new world beginning in which the Hollywood we had loved no longer existed. Secondly, it was harder to combine a political allegiance to the Left and an allegiance to the culture of the United States. The political spectrum was changing by the late 60s and early 70s. There was the Vietnam War. As our political allegiance shifted toward the Third World there were also more opportunities to see its cinema. And then the idea of a radical avant-garde began to emerge, for instance, at the London Filmmakers Co-op. The actual possibility of making films was appearing on the horizon, a whole new horizon of 16mm.

PW: It is also significant which American filmmakers were picked out at that time—Douglas Sirk, Sam Fuller, Budd Boetticher, Nick Ray—all of them American filmmakers but completely outside the frame of the classical film theory view of American cinema.

LM: And also by the time we were interested in them and writing about them, their world was collapsing around them. As you pointed out, Sam Fuller ended up in Paris. Neither Ray nor Boetticher could find work in Hollywood—or anywhere. Sirk had chosen to end his career and bowed out in 1959 after *Imitation of Life.*

PW: But in 1972 Jon Halliday's book on Sirk came out.

LM: But, if you remember, we all thought Sirk was probably dead and the possibility of doing the interview only emerged after Serge Daney, writing for *Cahiers*, discovered Sirk teaching in a film school in Munich.

LG: Is it possible then to see a trajectory from the interest in figures like Hawks and Ford to Fuller and Ray and Sirk as being one away from mainstream Hollywood?

PW: I think there is a sort of changing of the guard. If you look at the 60s it's all Ford and Hawks but in the 70s it changed, to Sirk and Fuller and Boetticher.

LM: That's in terms of writing—but in terms of actually going to the movies, as we were in the mid-60s, we were certainly chasing around London trying to identify a Boetticher, a Fuller, a Nick Ray movie. We used to spend our Sundays traveling from cinema to cinema to catch the Sunday-only Hollywood double bills. And in those days, the listings didn't name the director. You had to know.

PW: The other important development around this time, in the late 60s and early 70s, was the Edinburgh Film Festival. The festival organized retrospectives and published books. Auteurist directors were invited and there were close connections between people who were involved with the festival and the people in London that we have been talking about.

LM: In terms of the contribution of institutions to the development of film theory, by 1969 the Edinburgh Festival was organizing retrospectives of key auteur/directors. There were publications and symposia. When Lynda Myles was the film festival director she collaborated with *Screen*, I think particularly Claire Johnston and Paul Willemen, and kept the "Paddy Whannel Project" alive with a mixture of cinephilia and theory. She too came in for an enormous amount of criticism, again for introducing theory, for "taking Hollywood seriously," rather like the kind of denunciation that drove Paddy to resign. But at this time Lynda also introduced an avant-garde strand into the festival.

PW: That's a different story. The other side of Edinburgh, the side that led to Douglas Sirk and Samuel Fuller being invited to the festival, plainly related to the arrival of auteurism and its transition into film theory. But the retrospectives at Edinburgh were always a reminder of the films. That it was essential to know the films, in the same spirit as we showed extracts in the Education Department classes.

LG: Another thing Haidee [Wasson] and I were thinking about was the connection between filmmaking and your work. How did that happen? And how did you manage it?

LM: *Penthesilea* was made in '74 at Northwestern. Peter had always been more interested in the avant-garde than me. Hollywood had really been my introduction to cinema until I came under the influence of the Women's Movement and the avant-garde.

LG: And *Riddles of the Sphinx* is '76, after you came back to Britain?

PW: Yes. Just going back a minute to *Penthesilea*. Essentially it's an ultra-Bazinian film. It's a film with five chapters of twenty minutes, each consisting of two ten-minute reels of 16mm film edited together invisibly. So there are no edits in it from beginning to end, which goes much further than many of the films Bazin praised. This is a film built around the sequence shot.

I'd like to end by pointing out that Paddy, as Head of the School of Speech at Northwestern, again played a part in this new development. The film section in the school had been primarily practice based. Paddy was building up its theoretical side, very much in the spirit of his pioneering work at the Education Department—and this was where I came in. The availability of good 16mm equipment and very good students and ex-students to work with and Paddy's support throughout made it possible for Laura and me to make our first film. Paddy was never going to be an enthusiast for the avant-garde but I introduced avant-garde courses to the MA with his encouragement. Paddy was always interested in innovative and new ideas so long as they were rigorous and built on solid intellectual foundations. He was an outstanding example of someone whose enthusiasm and energy was based on principle—and there was no separation between his personal convictions and his professional commitments.

Notes

1. The summer schools were two-week residential courses held at different universities across the U.K. (located at the University of Stirling after 1972). Primarily, but not exclusively, they were directed at teachers interested in developing film studies in secondary schools.
2. This program was founded by Richard Hoggart in 1964; Stuart Hall was appointed as director of the unit in 1968.
3. The Workers Educational Association (WEA) was founded in 1903, and it has since become the largest voluntary adult education program in the United Kingdom.
4. Tom Nairn, "Obituary," *Cinema* 3 (June 1969): 15.
5. *Working Papers on the Cinema* (London: British Film Institute, 1969).
6. Full citations for these publications are Richard Roud, *Jean-Luc Godard* (Garden City, N.Y.: Doubleday, 1968); Geoffrey Nowell-Smith, *Luchino Visconti* (Garden City, N.Y.: Doubleday, 1968); Jim Kitses, *Horizons West; Anthony Mann, Budd Boetticher, Sam Peckinpah: Studies of Authorship within the Western* (Bloomington: Indiana University Press, 1969); Douglas Sirk, *Sirk on Sirk: Interviews with Jon Halliday* (New York: Viking Press, 1972); Colin McArthur, *Underworld U.S.A.* (London: Secker and Warburg; British Film Institute, 1972); Peter Wollen, *Signs and Meaning in the Cinema* (London: Secker and Warburg; British Film Institute, 1969).
7. Patrick Bauchau began his acting career in the films of the French New Wave, later appeared in Wim Wenders's *The State of Things* (1982), and continues to the present day to act in both films and television programs.
8. Eugene Archer died in 1973 at the young age of forty-two. He attended the Univer-

sity of Texas, the University of California at Los Angeles, and the Sorbonne (on a Fulbright). He began working at the *New York Times* in 1958, joining the then-titled Motion Picture Department in 1960. He left the *Times* in 1965 and returned to Paris for several years. He appeared in Eric Rohmer's *La Collectionneuse* and cowrote the script for *Ten Days Wonder* (Claude Chabrol).

9. In the United States this book was published as Andrew Sarris, *The American Cinema: Directors and Directions, 1929–1968*, 1st ed. (New York: Dutton, 1968).

10. After working on Michelangelo Antonioni's *Zabriskie Point* (1970), Clare Peploe worked with her future husband Bernardo Bertolucci as assistant director on *1900* (1976) and on *La Luna* (1979). She also directed a number of feature films, including *2001 The Triumph of Love* (2001). Mark Peploe has worked as a scriptwriter, collaborating with directors such as Bertolucci (with an Oscar for the screenplay of *The Last Emperor*) and Antonioni (*The Passenger* [1975] cowritten with Peter Wollen). He has also directed several films, including *Victory* (1995).

11. Paddy Whannel resigned from the Education Department in 1971 when he felt that the director and the senior executive, with the support of the governors, had made his position untenable. Alan Lovell, Eileen Brock, Jenny Norman, Jim Pines, and Gail Naughton also resigned. For a fuller account of BFI politics, see Colin McArthur, "Two Steps Forward. One Step Back: Cultural Struggle in the British Film Institute," *Journal of Popular British Cinema* 4 (2001): 112–27.

12. Changes to the journal policy included the introduction of European Marxist theory, detailed analyses of the politics and economics of colonial and postcolonial nations, and a notably international rather than exclusively English perspective.

13. Lee Russell [Peter Wollen], "Howard Hawks," *New Left Review* 1.24 (March–April 1964): 82–85.

14. *Universities and Left Review* was founded in 1957 by a number of Oxford graduates including Stuart Hall, Charles Taylor, and Raphael Samuel. In 1960, *Universities and Left Review* and the *New Reasoner* merged to form the *New Left Review*.

15. The contributions of Anderson and Nairn to the *New Left Review* starting in 1964 established an important perspective from the English Left on the history and current state of British society and nationalism. Their collective essays came to be known as the Anderson-Nairn thesis.

16. Bandung refers to the overall optimism surrounding the Asian-African Conference held at Bandung, Indonesia, in April 1955. Government leaders from twenty-nine African and Asian countries met to promote solidarity within the governments of the so-called Third World and in so doing formulate a unified strategy concerning decolonization, ongoing colonial power, and the cold war.

17. The BFI Higher Education Grants Committee had provided funds to establish lectureships in film studies at three universities. These were held by Robin Wood (Warwick, from October 1973), Richard Dyer (Keele, October 1974), and Peter Wollen (Essex, from January 1975). See BFI Education Department, *Annual Report 1973/4* (London: BFI), 10.

18. Paddy Whannel became a professor of film in the School of Speech at Northwestern University after leaving the BFI in 1971. He was invited initially by Professor Jack Ellis who left Northwestern for the University of Texas soon after Paddy arrived. Paddy encouraged Peter Wollen to apply for a position at Northwestern, and Peter joined in autumn 1972. He stayed until autumn 1974. Paddy had just returned to England for his first sabbatical in July 1980 when he died suddenly.

MAKING CINEMA LEGIBLE

Experimentation and Innovation in

Three American Film Journals of the 1950s

HADEN GUEST

> We urgently need schools of criticism—critics and filmmakers writing for themselves.
> We need articulate analysis, debates about theory, controversy over form, greater con-
> cern for tradition. It is only the second rate filmmaker (and critic) who cannot afford
> to give himself to any artistic community of the past or present.
> —Lewis Jacobs, "Preparation for Film"

■ The crucial role played by American film periodicals during the 1950s remains
a largely unwritten, yet absolutely vital, chapter in the history of film studies
as a field. Three film journals in particular need to be recognized for their important role in the profound transformation of American film scholarship and
criticism taking place after World War II: *Films in Review* (1950-present), *Cinemages* (1955–59), and *Film Culture* (1955-present).[1] For the growing community
of critics, scholars, artists, and cinephiles who shared an abiding passion for
the cinema, these upstart and often eccentric publications offered important
forums to debate the latest films and festivals and learn about the art, craft, and
history of film. For film historians today, these journals offer vivid and invaluable primary documents testifying to the aspirations and accomplishments of
a generation dedicated to the advancement of the cinema and a renewed study
of its neglected history. A careful study of these journals' early years also, I
will show, provides fresh insights into the 1950s as a formative period in the
evolution of film study in the United States and the emergence of a distinctly
American film culture.

In the pages that follow, I will look closely at two important trends being explored by film critics and scholars writing for *Films in Review, Cinemages,* and *Film Culture* during their early years. The first of these is the attempt to establish more rigorous standards of film history, which was led by a group of veteran film historians that included Theodore Huff and Seymour Stern — two scholars that I discuss at length later in this essay. Huff, Stern, and their contemporaries saw themselves as members of a highly specialized guild who were beholden to higher standards of empirical research than were the amateur chronicles of movie lore typically featured in contemporary fan magazines and trade publications. A dominant interest and abiding passion uniting this group of film historians was the silent cinema. Together these scholars sought to cast off the distorting myths and legends that clung to the cinema's past by patiently establishing the essential facts and figures of the medium's development from its earliest, obscure chapters through the present day. One question that vexed these historians was how to address, with any degree of comprehensiveness, the vast number of films that had been long overlooked by previous generations of scholars. This quantitative dilemma led postwar historians to experiment with various forms of structuring devices to organize and categorize film history, with the filmography — the listing of full cast and credits — held up as a favorite device.

The second trend that I want to consider is the attempt by postwar film critics to break free from the limitations of the traditional film review and explore film criticism as a type of expansive and deeply personal artistic practice. Following the important precedent of pugnacious and fiercely original critical prose refined by James Agee, Otis Ferguson, and Robert Warshow, rising critics such as Jonas Mekas and Andrew Sarris brought a new intensity and daring to American film criticism by experimenting with vernacular language and poetic forms. The work and career of Agee, the poet-turned-critic-turned-screenwriter, remained an especially important touchstone for the introspective and poetically inflected modes of writing on the cinema explored during the 1950s. The model of the artist-critic so powerfully embodied by Agee was evoked by many postwar writers on the cinema — from critics contemporary to Agee, such as the painter Manny Farber and the poet Parker Tyler, to the younger generation of filmmaker-critics who were closely associated with *Film Culture.*

Rather than parallel developments, the work of postwar film historians and critics remained closely intertwined, engaged in a spirited dialogue that reached across the different factions and generations contained within the burgeoning film community. Indeed, in the postwar journals a strong mutual influence is clearly legible between the careful research of veteran film historians and the artistically inspired criticism being explored by the younger critics. Keeping this in mind, in this essay I seek to reveal postwar writings on the cinema as a rich field of study that has much to say about the general intellectual and philosophical orientation of a vibrant postwar film scene whose full complexity is only just now beginning to draw the attention of scholars and historians.

In recent years, scholars of postwar Parisian film culture have attempted to historicize cinephilia as a specifically French mode of reception and criticism.[2] In a similar fashion, we also need to explore ways to historicize the modes of film study and appreciation being explored in postwar America. And we need to ask if a distinctly American brand of cinephilia can be identified—one specific to the very different film scene emerging in the United States during the 1950s and continuing well into the 1960s. I will return to this question at the end of this essay.

The general methodological principles and assumptions underlying the work of postwar film critics and scholars also, I believe, have much to tell us about the subsequent course of film study in America, as well as about the directions it followed and in turn abandoned in its gradual professionalization into an academic discipline. Rather than simply an exercise in origins, the study of postwar film scholarship can help us understand distinct stratifications within the field and how they interact with one another. Here I focus in particular upon the study of the silent cinema and its relationship to certain strands of avant-garde film scholarship. Instead of a comprehensive survey of writings contained within *Films in Review*, *Cinemages*, and *Film Culture*, in this essay I selectively consider dominant ideas that cut across the three journals to reveal much about how the cinema was perceived and continues to be studied today.

Although I focus on the work of key individual contributors to *Films in Review*, *Cinemages*, and *Film Culture*, I am not claiming that the innovations in film scholarship and criticism discussed here were wholly invented by these writers. On the contrary, I will show that the deliberate turn away from traditional modes of film writing by these individuals was merely one expression of a broader reevaluation of the cinema taking place as a significant cultural movement in postwar America. With this in mind, I want to briefly consider the distinct film culture emerging in the United States during the 1950s before delving into the individual histories of *Films in Review*, *Cinemages*, and *Film Culture*.

The postwar American film scene remains largely overshadowed, in the history books and the popular imagination, by its European counterparts. To be certain, the rich film culture of postwar Europe did exert an indisputable hold over the generation of critics and scholars in the United States who began to write about the cinema in the 1950s. Extended stays in Paris were indelible experiences for such young Turks of American film criticism as Ernest Callenbach, Annette Michelson, and Andrew Sarris. Sarris, for one, has recalled his year in Paris as a "fateful" event that profoundly changed his understanding of the cinema.[3]

Yet Sarris also credits his singular career trajectory to his undergraduate years at Columbia University in the late 1940s where he first discovered his cultist attitude toward the cinema. And Sarris has affectionately recalled how his distinct sensibility toward the cinema and obsessive moviegoing habits were awakened, in large part, by the extraordinary confluence of revival theaters that were centered around Times Square in his home town of New York. It was in these Times Square theaters that Sarris first discovered new constellations in the vast galaxy of studio-era films that he would later trace in his magnum opus *The American Cinema*.[4]

After World War II, French critics and audiences suddenly encountered an unknown chapter of the American cinema in a rush of previously banned films from the 1940s that resulted, among other things, in the now-famous "discovery" of film noir. During the same period a fundamentally different critical project was being explored by American writers like Sarris who sought to reevaluate the achievements and failures of classical Hollywood by selectively revisiting the corpus of studio films. For postwar American critics this task was tinged with a marked nostalgia for the heyday of the Hollywood studio system, which increasingly seemed to be locked into an inevitable decline.

The interests and sensibilities of Sarris and many contributors to the major postwar film journals were directly shaped by the vibrant native film culture emerging in the United States. The growing art house, repertory, and revival theater scenes centered in New York, Los Angeles, and San Francisco offered crucial training grounds for film critics and scholars who came of age in the 1950s.[5] In the Bay Area, Berkeley's popular repertory theater, the Cinema Guild, dramatically exemplified the close relationship between alternative theaters and the rising generation of film critics in America. For, in addition to its regular offerings of the latest foreign films, the Cinema Guild also provided detailed and highly opinionated program notes written by Pauline Kael, who managed

and co-owned the theater during the 1950s.[6] In Los Angeles, the Coronet Theater was unrivaled for its adventurous programming of recent avant-garde,
documentary, and foreign films and for its carefully assembled retrospective
series on master directors such as Chaplin and Pudovkin, and national film
movements such as French surrealist or German expressionist cinema.[7] In
Manhattan, the conversion of numerous prominent newsreel theaters into
art house and repertory theaters in the late 1940s gave New York important
venues for foreign and classic films that remained active throughout the postwar period.[8]

Toward the end of the 1950s, these repertory and revival theaters were com-
plimented by a number of popular television showcases for the libraries of
pre-1948 films recently sold by the faltering Hollywood studios. Television programs such as *Million Dollar Movie* added important new depths to the rising
generation's general knowledge and appreciation of long-forgotten studio films
and genres. Radio also played a minor, yet significant, role in the postwar film
scene, with two pioneering programs devoted to the cinema: Kael's popular
weekly broadcast from the University of California, Berkeley and *Cinemages*
editor Gideon Bachmann's path-breaking radio program *The Film Art*. During
Kael's nine years on the air she established herself as a maverick voice on the
cinema and defined her signature engaged and conversational style of criticism.[9] Bachmann's *Film Art*, an important fixture of America's film scene from
1954 to 1964, helped establish the interview as a powerful tool for film historians and critics alike. In hour-long weekly broadcasts, Bachmann conversed
with a formidable range of directors and artists from the past and present of
American and European cinema—from Lillian Gish, Jerry Wald, and Otto
Preminger to Fritz Lang, Federico Fellini, and Jean-Luc Godard. Bachmann
also frequently spoke with such film scholars and critics as Lotte Eisner, Lewis
Jacobs, and Parker Tyler, and hosted a number of important roundtable discussions with artists and experts on topics from the New American Cinema to
recent European cinema and contemporary film criticism.[10]

One of the more significant developments of the American film scene was
the boom in film clubs and societies that gained momentum after World War II.
Fueled in large part by the circulating library assembled and distributed by the
Museum of Modern Art, membership societies in the model of the French
ciné-clubs began to appear in urban centers and universities across the nation.[11] In addition to the museum-sponsored screenings pioneered by MOMA,
the leading postwar film societies—New York's Cinema 16 and San Francisco's

Art in Cinema—provided important venues for avant-garde, documentary, and foreign feature films and increased awareness of the creative relationships between these different cinematic modes.[12] Indeed, the type of mixed programs presented at Cinema 16—whose first screening in November 1947 offered a scientific documentary, a Martha Graham dance film, and an animated short together with two avant-garde "features"—remained an important model for the provocative eclecticism cultivated by journals such as *Film Culture*.[13]

The diversity of postwar American film culture is suggested by the number of different factions and divisions that quickly emerged within the growing community of committed film critics, scholars, and cinephiles. Among the more outspoken of these groups were the serious devotees to the silent cinema who gathered at specialized venues for silent films—such as the Theodore Huff Memorial Society in New York and the Silent Cinema in Los Angeles—where projection speed was carefully monitored and musical accompaniment, when possible, was historically accurate and appropriate.[14] Members of this group looked with great suspicion at screenings of silent films by other institutions and organizations, like MOMA, where audiences habitually laughed out loud at even acknowledged masterpieces of the silent era.[15] In an irate article on "audience stupidity" written in 1954, one member of the Huff Memorial Society noted with great distress the "giggling idlers ignorant of everything that goes to make up the art of the motion picture" who regularly spoiled screenings of silent classics.[16] For historians of the silent cinema such as Huff, Stern, and William K. Everson, the general audiences' ignorance concerning the silent era remained an important rallying call for their own research.

In close tandem to the widening number and diversity of film screenings in the postwar years was a rapid transformation in the quantity and quality of American writing on the cinema. A groundswell of specialized publications devoted to some aspect of the cinema began to appear in the United States in the 1950s, following a near absence of film periodicals during the previous decade.[17] Most postwar journals were highly ephemeral and quickly fell victim to the same economic travails that continually threatened *Films in Review*, *Cinemages*, and *Film Culture* during their first years. Dedicated film publications became an international phenomenon in the 1950s, with new periodicals launched in almost every country where a film industry existed, from Czechoslovakia and France to Argentina and Japan.

The global reach of the film journal movement was made clear by a remarkably ambitious survey—conducted by Bachmann—that tracked over one thousand publications in more than fifty different countries and was presented in a special issue of *Cinemages* in 1957. The majority of periodicals listed by Bachmann were fleeting presences, with many, in fact, already defunct by the time their name appeared in *Cinemages*. Bachmann's study revealed approximately 173 separate publications in the United States that regularly contained significant content devoted to the cinema. Comprising a large segment of this list were specialized journals such as *Film Music* (1953–1957) and *Church Films* (n.d.), trade publications like *16 mm Reporter* (n.d.), and fan magazines such as *Movie Star Parade* (1940–58) and *Silver Screen* (1930–1954).

Despite the broad range of articles regularly featured within them, *Films in Review*, *Cinemages*, and *Film Culture* were themselves essentially niche publications. Each of the three journals quickly established their own distinct interests and specializations and increasingly appealed to different individual factions of the postwar film community. In this way, *Films in Review* became a home of sorts for critics, scholars, and cinephiles interested in the silent cinema and the more obscure chapters of the medium's history. While *Cinemages* and *Film Culture* immediately defined themselves as international film journals concerned especially with European cinemas, both publications maintained a broad interest in all aspects of the American cinema and welcomed a wide range of writings on both general areas. Despite their many sharp differences, the three journals were, nevertheless, closely intertwined during their early years as contemporary, and essentially rival, publications. Indeed, the broad spectrum of writing on the cinema that stretched across *Films in Review*, *Cinemages*, and *Film Culture* was drawn from the same interlinked constellations of writers and scholars that together comprised the extended family tree of postwar film scholarship and criticism.

Yet the real importance of the postwar journals, I contend, lies less in their individual eccentricities and differences than in their collective attempt to reinvent film scholarship and criticism. Although *Films in Review*, *Cinemages*, and *Film Culture* were perpetually strapped for funds and targeted at an extremely limited readership, they each continued to harbor grand ambitions. "Our objective," *Films in Review* boldly stated, is to be "so authoritative, and so alert, that not only Americans, but people all over the world, will, through our pages, become actively interested in the greatest of arts: the movies."[18] *Cinemages* and *Film Culture* went a step further, dedicating themselves to the shaping of a milieu more appreciative of the cinema as a cultural force and supportive of the medium's advancement toward a "better screen," as *Cinemages'* editor

SHOOTING IN
CINEMASCOPE

THE MAKING OF
MERVYN LEROY

LONG HAIR
FILM GOSSIP

MAY, 35¢

WHAT THE BRITISH
THINK ABOUT 3-D

A MEMORIAL TO
THEODORE HUFF

The diminutive size of *Films in Review*—measuring only 5.5 × 7.5 inches—was echoed in the relatively short length of articles strictly enforced by its notoriously cantankerous long-time editor Henry Hart. Depicted here is the May 1953 Theodore Huff memorial issue, which paid tribute to the recently deceased film historian who was one of the more important contributors to the journal in its earliest years.

Gideon Bachmann phrased it.[19] Calling for a "thorough revision of the prevailing attitude to the function of cinema," *Film Culture*'s editor, Jonas Mekas, stressed the urgent need to "impart depth and vigor to cinematic culture" in the United States.[20]

The extent to which *Films in Review, Cinemages,* and *Film Culture* achieved these lofty goals lies beyond the scope of this short essay. One immediately recognizable achievement is found in the new energy, imagination, and insight that each publication infused into the practice of film history and criticism. The wealth of highly original scholarship and penetrating opinions about all aspects of the cinema contained in their every issue pushed the three journals to the lonely forefront of film study in America. The adventurous exploration by *Films in Review, Cinemages,* and *Film Culture* of different philosophical and historiographic approaches to the cinema allowed the journals to canvas a broad terrain of film-related topics. Rather than a unified territory, however, the range of perspectives on the cinema explored by the journals ultimately, I will argue, reveals distinct stratifications underlying the emergent discipline of film studies that continue to define the work of film scholars and critics today.

Films in Review: *Filmographies, Trivia, and "Long Hair Movie Gossip"*

As the longest continually published film periodical in America, *Films in Review* remains a venerable, although greatly underappreciated, institution in film studies.[21] Founded in 1950 as the flagship publication of the motion picture industry's oldest volunteer censorship organization, the National Board of Review (NBR), *Films in Review* was officially designed to guide movie audiences toward the highest "quality" motion pictures. With this aim film reviews and the regular lists of recommended top ten films long published by the NBR continued to appear in the journal throughout the 1950s and 1960s. Although *Films in Review* thus upheld its official duties, from its very first issues the journal immediately declared film history to be its dominant interest.

The first decade of *Films in Review* is especially notable for the wealth of original scholarship on film history that appeared in its every issue. Within its first year, *Films in Review* established itself as the venue of choice for film historians and scholars such as Lotte Eisner, William K. Everson, and Richard Griffith who were determined to bring a new rigor and authority to the practice of film history. Among the most prominent members of this group were Theodore Huff and Seymour Stern, scholars who were also avid collectors of historical materials on the silent cinema and whose work was frequently inspired by their own remarkable personal archives. The expertise and passion of Huff, Stern, and their contemporaries was aimed predominately toward the silent era, and they dedicated the majority of their work to recovering this chapter of film history that was fading fast from popular memory.

Palpable throughout the writings of these scholars was a profound nostalgia for the silent film that imbued their many contributions to *Films in Review* with a sense of a world irreparably lost. These scholars remained fascinated with tragically fallen figures from the silent era such as Erich Von Stroheim, D. W. Griffith and, to a certain extent, Charlie Chaplin—hugely ambitious directors of the silent screen who had reached a peak of creativity and artistic confidence only to stumble precipitously once they had been banished into the world of sound. For this group of film historians the embattled figures of the silent era embodied a lost art that remained tragically misunderstood and underappreciated.

The sense of loss felt toward the silent cinema by Huff, Stern, and many other writers for *Films in Review* was poignantly evoked by the veteran critic Gilbert Seldes in a passage from an early issue of the journal: "We who lived through the era of the silent film [have] something the present generation lacks. I remember my resentment against people who told me in 1917 that if you hadn't seen Paris before the war, you didn't know what life is, or words to that effect. I hope no one will resent my saying that if you didn't know the silent movie, the excitement of watching it create itself before your eyes, you missed something and, in a sense, you don't know what the movies are. We who went through it know something special: we are, cinematically, a race apart."[22]

As members of the generation who had grown up transfixed by the magic of the silver screen, Huff, Stern, and many of the regular contributors to *Films in Review* clearly belonged to this race apart evoked by Seldes. Indeed, an important wellspring of Huff and Stern's work in particular was formed by their own memories of silent classics such as D. W. Griffith's *Way Down East* (1920) and Charlie Chaplin's *The Gold Rush* (1925), which they had viewed in their original runs. And even more valuable for both historians was the time spent, during their respective youths, at the early New York and New Jersey movie studios where each claimed to have seen silent films in production, including works by Griffith himself.[23] Stern, for one, remained convinced that his own firsthand experience had granted him unique knowledge and insight into the silent era and the American cinema in general. Looking back over his own career in 1965, Stern offered a blistering critique of film scholarship that was not based upon similar firsthand experience: "From [my] total experience, I knew how inadequate and incompetent were the film-history books; where they were in error; and when their authors . . . were falsifying, quite obviously with deliberate intent. . . . No film-history yet written is satisfactory for research and scholarship, to say nothing of insight and interpretation."[24]

The spiritual grandfather of these historians was Terry Ramsaye, the elder statesman of American film history whose late work was published regularly in *Films in Review* until his death in 1954, when he was eulogized in a special tribute article.[25] Despite its many widely recognized inaccuracies and colorful exaggerations, Ramsaye's *A Million and One Nights* (1926) continued in the postwar years to represent a major breakthrough in film scholarship for its extensive use of rarely consulted primary documents and, most importantly, firsthand testimonies of witnesses to the figures and events described in its pages. "Most history is autopsy," quipped Ramsaye, calling *A Million and One Nights* a work of "vivisection" for its close proximity to the lives of historical figures such as Thomas Edison, whom Ramsaye consulted.[26]

Despite Ramsaye's stated belief in the tremendous importance of eyewitness testimony for film history, Huff and Stern in contrast reached for a far greater accuracy of facts and figures than had been achieved by *A Million and One Nights*. Ramsaye's approach to film history was grounded in his work as a popular journalist and was colored by his flair for lively headline-driven narratives. For Huff and Stern, the importance of firsthand accounts lay less in their personal and emotional dimensions than in their ability to reveal or clarify historical facts. In this way, Huff and Stern's work was animated by a type of tactile empiricism in which the film historian's task was deemed to be *archaeological* in principal, an unearthing of historical truths whose true dimensions and meanings could be measured by the expert hand and eye. "In movie history," warned Huff in a 1952 letter to *Films in Review*, "it is extremely dangerous to call anything 'first.' Unless you've seen everything yourself and aren't depending on the statements of others."[27]

Huff and Stern's intimate knowledge and experience of the cinema was the bedrock upon which their scholarship was built. In their writing both historians generally gave pride of place to eyewitness testimony as the best means of establishing accurate historical records. Many of Huff and Stern's contributions to *Films in Review* brought in witnesses from cinema's past in order to debunk the myths and inaccuracies that continued to linger in writings on film history. In an article on Griffith's time in New York, for instance, Stern offered as evidence a letter written to Stern by the famed Griffith cameraman Billy Bitzer that answered questions about the director's use of certain cinematographic techniques.

Huff and Stern's impressive knowledge of the cinema also drew from the two scholars' extensive backgrounds in motion picture production. While Huff had made six short films and an avant-garde feature, *The Uncomfortable Man* (1948), Stern had served as editor on a number of progressive documentaries and avant-garde shorts. Stern had also worked as a technical advisor at several of the Hollywood studios, eventually serving as dialogue director for Preston Sturges's *Lady Eve* (1941). This type of production experience was, in fact, typical for a generation of film historians contemporary to Huff and Stern such as Jay Leyda, Lewis Jacobs, and Herman G. Weinberg, who themselves had all made acclaimed avant-garde films and had diverse motion picture experience.

Huff and Stern's adamant belief that film historians needed to anchor their work with the weight of irrefutable tangible evidence was shared by the regular contributors to the journal who were also active collectors and whose writing frequently drew upon unique objects from their own personal archives. Collecting was a shared hobby, passion, and important research method for Huff,

Stern, and other historians writing for *Films in Review*. During a period in which only extremely limited research facilities existed for the study of film, crucial primary documents and objects related to the cinema—including rare prints of elusive silent films—were often found in private specialized collections. William K. Everson's writing on the silent cinema, the western, and serial film, for example, often centered around rare prints from his personal archives, while George Mitchell's vast collection of cameras and equipment bolstered his expertise on cinematography and historic camera technology during a period when this specialized knowledge was being quickly forgotten. Huff's legendary collection of motion picture related rare film books, stills, and ephemera provided important source material that grounded both his own research and the archives at the MOMA Film Library to which he donated many duplicate stills. In a similar manner, the unfinished multiple-volume study of Griffith, which was Stern's life work and mission, was inspired by the vast trove of documents given to the historian by Griffith himself during the final years of the director's life.

A type of collector's mentality, or archival impulse, was evident in the brief historical essays favored by *Films in Review* during the 1950s. In this way, journal articles generally avoided lengthy critical or theoretical arguments in order to lay down the essential facts and figures for the reader to choose from. Articles that focused upon a given director or performer's career, for example, would typically close with some form of annotated list carefully organizing and summarizing the essential information provided.[28]

The filmographies that remained a popular staple of *Films in Review* during the 1950s directly appealed to readers' evident hunger for vital statistics and arcana about the cinema. In today's digital age it is difficult to appreciate the value of filmographic research. It is difficult as well to realize the formidable challenge of determining credits and vital statistics of films for which scant records were available and about which few reliable sources existed or, in many cases, for which viewable prints were nowhere to be found. Throughout the prewar and postwar years, however, the compilation of filmographies was a high priority of film scholars and considered one of film history's most urgent and important tasks. Without such records, it was rightly feared, important masterpieces might be forgotten and eventually lost forever.

Huff and Stern were at the forefront of those scholars who saw the filmography as a powerful tool for the writing of history. Indeed, the exhaustive "indexes" to the films of Charlie Chaplin and D. W. Griffith carefully assembled by Huff and Stern, respectively, represented the two scholars' most important career works. Both historians similarly offered their filmographies as a crucial intervention designed to reevaluate the larger oeuvres of renowned directors whose achievements had been clouded by the storms of unjust controversy that lingered over their most ambitious works. By accurately mapping the career trajectories of Chaplin and Griffith—and especially their lesser-known early work—Huff and Stern sought to divert attention away from the directors' much maligned off-screen personae and toward the films themselves.[29] The ambitious career biographies of Chaplin and Griffith later taken on by Huff and Stern were logically extensions of their careful filmographic research, with both authors focusing principally upon the films rather than on the personal lives of the directors.[30]

Much of the writing in *Films in Review* during the 1950s was, in fact, directly inspired by the exacting logic of the filmography. Many articles on a variety of topics were, in essence, carefully expanded annotated lists designed to organize essential dates and facts. The range of such articles was quite diverse and increasingly leaned toward bizarre subjects—from Everson's amusing enumeration of badly used stock shots in recent films to macabre listings such as "Death by Airplane: Eight Stars Fell from the Stars."[31]

Despite their frequently irreverent tone, these filmographic articles represented a mode of inventive film scholarship that turned to the patient compilation of lists as a vital form of history writing—a declaration of the filmography as a powerful instrument for, quite literally, sorting through an overwhelming amount of data to distill the facts and figures most essential to film history. At the same time, however, the decidedly offbeat topics frequently explored by the articles in *Films in Review* also suggested the highly quirky and idiosyncratic nature of the list as a historiographic device by revealing the extent to which lists and filmographies are ultimately defined by the compiler's individual predilections and personal whims.

The eccentric and subjective qualities of filmographic research were further explored by two humorous variations on the research method that appeared within *Films in Review*: the "Movie Trivia Quizzes" and the veteran film historian and critic Herman G. Weinberg's "Coffee, Brandy and Cigars." Compiled by John Springer, a successful Hollywood publicity agent, the "Movie Trivia Quizzes" offered monthly tests of film knowledge that called upon the reader to think filmographically. Springer's quizzes challenged readers with a variety of sorting exercises—arranging films into chronological order, for example, or finding the performer who doesn't fit into a given group, or matching a series of film quotes to the scenes in which they appeared. Like the filmographic research articles, the quizzes called for a breaking down of film history into its constituent facts and figures that ultimately revealed distinct patterns and symmetries. Explicitly designed as a form of amusement, the quizzes embraced the more eccentric and obscure interpretations of the filmographic enterprise explored by *Films in Review.*

Weinberg's column "Coffee, Brandy and Cigars," presented another important venue for movie trivia in *Films in Review.*[32] Humorously subtitled "More Things That You Never Knew till Now and Got on Just as Well Without," Weinberg's column was loosely structured as a rambling postprandial monologue about the cinema that strung together esoteric facts and provocative fictions about film history, aesthetics, directors, and stars, thus providing the "long haired movie gossip" promised on many of T. Journey's early covers. Unlike the exacting lists of facts and figures assembled by his contemporaries, Weinberg invented far more ambitious and often provocative categories of film history. In this way, for example, one entry in Weinberg's column wove together skeletal details of ill-fated film projects—Eisenstein's failed attempt to adapt *Ulysses,* von Stroheim's unfinished version of *The Magic Mountain*—with tantalizing evocations of lost alternate versions of classics such as Chaplin's *A Woman of Paris* and Renoir's *Grand Illusion* and then adding rumors of ambitious and most likely unrealizable film projects, such as Billy Wilder's assignment to film *Oedipus Rex.* Weinberg also drew attention to little-known achievements of the cinema, explaining, for example, what was "the most Freudian shot ever made."[33]

While "Coffee, Brandy and Cigars" displayed the same level of knowledge and expertise about the cinema generally found throughout *Films in Review,* Weinberg's column offered a distinctly conditional version of film history, a speculative chronicle that explored the many what-ifs hidden beneath established cinematic milestones. Avoiding any clear organizational structure, "Coffee, Brandy and Cigars" instead favored a stream-of-consciousness narrative animated by a montage logic of sharp juxtaposition between different topics. Like the popular "Movie Trivia Quizzes," "Coffee, Brandy and Cigars" underscored the evocative and poetic dimensions of the film scholarship featured within *Films in Review.* Weinberg's exploration of film history as a type of eccentric curio cabinet also occupies an important pivot point between the idiosyncratically systematic filmographies compiled by the collector-historians

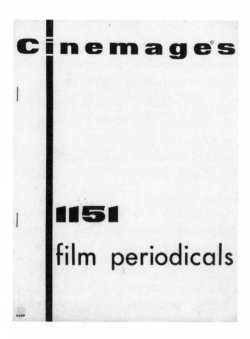

Cinemages

film periodicals

The cutting-edge journal *Cinemages* had perhaps the lowest production values of any of the postwar journals. Indeed, each issue was mimeographed and stapled by the journal's founding editor, Gideon Bachmann. In the April 1957 film periodicals issue Bachmann achieved the remarkable feat of capturing the often fleeting presence of 1,151 international film journals, thereby providing an invaluable and revealing snapshot of global film culture in the late 1950s.

writing for *Films in Review* and the adventurous writings and research projects published in *Cinemages* and *Film Culture*, two periodicals that quickly established themselves as important showcases for the rising generation of American film critics.

Cinemages: *The Voices of Film History*

The history of the postwar American film scene, like that of the avant-garde with which it is closely intertwined, is a history of committed and occasionally visionary individuals who gave of their time, talents, and resources to the cause of the cinema. Faced with a near absence of institutional support for film-related projects of any kind, these individuals increasingly founded their own institutions, often in the form of specialized film societies and periodicals. The history of the short-lived journal *Cinemages* (1955–59) offers an instructional example of how these institutions were formed and were able to flourish. At the same time, *Cinemages* also reveals the extraordinary economy of scarcity that defined all aspects of postwar America's emergent film culture.

Cinemages first began as a series of brief program notes designed to accompany screenings of a fledgling film society, the small but ambitious Group for

Film Study (GFS) that was organized in 1954 by Gideon Bachmann while he was "enrolled" in Hans Richter's filmmaking workshop at City College in New York.[34] Like many of the newly formed film societies emerging at the time in American cities and universities, the raison d'être of the GFS was the access to films provided by its screening activities. The original impetus for the GFS was, in fact, to obtain the official not-for-profit status required for Bachmann and his classmates to rent prints from MOMA's circulating collection.

During its first season, the GFS offered membership screenings of classic films — Von Stroheim's *Greed* (1923–25), Fritz Lang's *M* (1931), and Pare Lorenz's *The River* (1937) — which took place in a Manhattan high school and were accompanied by simple programs that provided accurate cast and credits for that night's films together with a historical introduction and, occasionally, a critical commentary. Describing itself as a "non-profit educational Society dedicated to the study of the film as an art and as a medium of communication," GFS screenings, it was noted, were "held with a view towards arousing audience consciousness to the existence of a cinema of quality." The distribution of "definitive and detailed program notes" was further described as "part of the group's endeavor to create an intelligent film audience."[35] From the very beginning, GFS screenings favored the silent cinema and placed a special emphasis upon the work of European masters of the silent era whose larger oeuvres were little known in America.

The GFS screenings quickly became more elaborate events, culminating in March 1955 in a major two-part retrospective of Jean Epstein's complete films, which was billed as the "first comprehensive presentation" of Epstein's films in the United States. Coming three years after Epstein's death, the memorial retrospective was organized by Bachmann in collaboration with the Cinémathèque Française, which provided several of the prints, and the Museum of Modern Art, which hosted the inaugural screening. Within the same short period *Cinemages* also grew considerably in size and ambition, expanding from skeletal program notes into one of the more innovative film periodicals of its day.

This transformation did not, however, involve any additional funding or resources allocated to the journal. Throughout its four brief years of publication, *Cinemages* maintained the simplest and most economical of formats — typewritten letter-sized sheets stapled into inexpensive paper-stock covers. Like the other publications discussed in this essay, *Cinemages* was a strictly one-person operation, whose founding editor and "Executive Secretary," Bachmann, took responsibility for all aspects of the journal's production and publication. Not only did Bachmann painstakingly edit each issue, writing many of its longest and most important essays, he also ran the mimeograph machine on which the periodical was printed.[36] Despite its miniscule budget, increasingly erratic publication, and narrow circulation, *Cinemages* remained on the cutting edge of American film scholarship and criticism throughout its nine published issues. Most important here is the journal's experimentation with novel approaches to film history and alternate ways to educate the general public about the cinema as an art form and a cultural force.

The experimental nature of *Cinemages* was revealed in its second issue, which was designed as a companion volume to the Epstein series. In *Cinemages* no. 2 Bachmann attempted to reinvent the traditional film society program by abandoning its traditional formula of credits, filmographies, and accompanying critical texts. "This booklet," wrote Bachmann, "contains no program notes in the usual sense. The editors have tried, rather, to present a picture of Epstein the man and the artist as a whole."[37] Toward this goal Bachmann, together with coeditor Jean Benoit-Levy, offered a remarkable compilation of important primary texts related to Epstein, his films, and the milieu in which he worked. In addition to a series of personal tributes by close friends and colleagues of the director—among them Jean Cocteau, Marie Epstein, Abel Gance, Marcel L'Herbier, and Hans Richter—the issue included lengthy critical essays and reminiscences by Henri Langlois and Benoit-Levy, established voices in French film criticism who were also close associates of Epstein. In lieu of a traditional filmography, the Epstein issue interwove fragments from contemporary writings on the individual films with excerpts from Epstein's own writings on the same works. The issue concluded with three translations of essays by Epstein himself discussing his celebrated theories of cinematic realism.

As a work of highly original film scholarship, *Cinemages* no. 2 looked beyond the individual Epstein films screened in the GFS retrospective to offer a composite portrait of the motion picture director as artist. Central to the project of the Epstein issue were the testimonies carefully assembled by Bachmann that each sought to convey the essence of Epstein's cinema through personal reminiscences and reflection. This attempt to craft an intimate mode of film history from personal testimonies and primary documents was explored further in the next issue, *Cinemages* no. 3, which focused upon the German director G. W. Pabst. Entitled "Six Talks on G. W. Pabst: The Man—the Director—the Artist," the centerpiece of *Cinemages* no. 3 was the transcriptions of conversations recorded by Bachmann with five important collaborators of Pabst's, rounded out by a contribution from Siegfried Kracauer. In Bachmann's introduction to *Cinemages* no. 3, he provocatively framed these talks about Pabst as a "new kind of film writing" designed to "capture some of the facts, some of the background, some of the feelings and some of the intimacy that make up [Pabst's] personality."[38] The interviews that followed did, in fact, offer invaluable discussions about Pabst's working methods from individuals well acquainted with the director's editing style, camera work, and direction of performers.

As direct extensions of Bachmann's pioneering radio program, *The Film Art*, the Epstein and Pabst issues of *Cinemages* together signaled the recognition by postwar American film scholarship of the interview as an important tool for historical and critical research. In a similar manner as Bachmann's radio conversations, the talks about Epstein and Pabst published in *Cinemages* attempted to plumb the depths of artistic and creative personality and discover its relationship to a given director's films. In *Film Culture* this strategy took on increasingly avant-garde and experimental directions.

Film Culture: *Avant-garde Film Scholarship*

Film Culture (1955–1996) is best remembered today for its seminal role in chronicling and championing the rise of the New American Cinema during the 1960s. *Film Culture*'s close identification with the avant-garde film movement has, however, largely overshadowed the journal's important contributions to postwar American film scholarship and criticism. Little attention has been given in particular to *Film Culture*'s unique position during the 1950s and early 1960s as a crucial meeting ground for different generations of film scholars and critics. Under the direction of the founding editor Jonas Mekas, *Film Culture*'s contributions were balanced roughly between younger writers such as Andrew Sarris and P. Adams Sitney, and established scholars and critics such as Seymour Stern, Parker Tyler, and Herman G. Weinberg. The highly innovative and often eccentric mode of writing on the cinema defined by *Film Culture* was, I will argue, largely the product of this meeting between vanguard and Old Guard.

Paradoxically, *Film Culture* was initially suspicious of the emergent avant-garde film movement and reluctant to embrace its call for a liberated cinema.[39] Alternate and experimental approaches to the cinema were, however, embraced by the journal from its very first issues. Even before *Film Culture*'s transformation into the official house organ of the New American Cinema, the journal was already keenly aware of innovative currents at work in contemporary film journals such as *Films in Review* and *Cinemages* and, moreover, actively recruited from both publications. The identification of *Film Culture* with Wein-

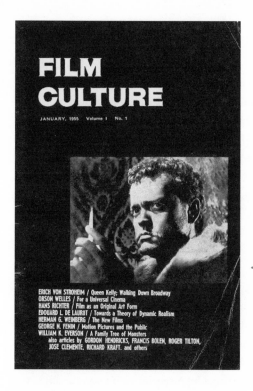

FILM
CULTURE

JANUARY, 1955   Volume I   No. 1

ERICH VON STROHEIM / Queen Kelly; Walking Down Broadway
ORSON WELLES / For a Universal Cinema
HANS RICHTER / Film as an Original Art Form
EDOUARD L. DE LAUROT / Towards a Theory of Dynamic Realism
HERMAN G. WEINBERG / The New Films
GEORGE N. FENIN / Motion Pictures and the Public
WILLIAM K. EVERSON / A Family Tree of Monsters
    also articles by GORDON HENDRICKS, FRANCIS BOLEN, ROGER TILTON,
    JOSE CLEMENTE, RICHARD KRAFT. and others

With its compact size and clean design *Film Culture*'s January 1955 first issue deceptively resembled the literary "little magazines" popular in the 1950s. In keeping with its radical, experimental nature was the frequent change in size and format of the journal, which was designed by the Fluxus founding artist George Macunias (a close friend of *Film Culture*'s founding editor Jonas Mekas). The career of actor-director-writer Orson Welles provided both an important symbol of the ideal of the "complete" artist so cherished by the avant-garde filmmakers associated with *Film Culture* as well a sober cautionary tale.

berg's work was clearly signaled by Mekas's drafting of "Coffee, Brandy and Cigars" from *Films in Review* into *Film Culture* where it remained a regular feature from the journal's second through its seventieth issue.[40]

As a relatively permanent fixture of *Film Culture*, Weinberg's unusual column helped to define the type of introspective and idiosyncratic approaches to cinema cultivated by Mekas's journal. Weinberg's energetic stream-of-consciousness weaving of star-struck movie gossip and trivia into an alternate chronicle of the cinema set an important precedent for the types of experimental modes of film history explored in later issues of *Film Culture*. The montage logic of "Coffee, Brandy and Cigars," with its constant leaps across seemingly unrelated topics, significantly anticipated the type of provocative juxtapositioning that gradually became a signature feature of *Film Culture*. Later issues of *Film Culture* thus increasingly brought together seemingly disparate subjects—an article on the experimental filmmaker Tony Conrad, for example, followed by a history of early surrealist cinema and an essay on Eadweard Muybridge.[41] A type of montage technique was especially apparent in the journal's constant grouping of legendary directors from the past with filmmakers from the rising avant-garde. In this way, for example, Stan Brakhage and Orson Welles were brought together in a single issue, while other unorthodox pairings included George Cukor and Peter Kubelka, on the one hand, and Charlie Chaplin and Andy Warhol, on the other. Throughout, *Film Culture* returned frequently to the same pantheon of actor-writer-directors celebrated in *Films in Review*—Von Stroheim, to whom *Film Culture* dedicated an entire issue in 1959, as well as Chaplin and Griffith—individuals who were increasingly held up as a model for the ideal of total creative independence reached for by the New American Cinema. Implicit in the shock effect created by *Film Culture*'s collision of filmmakers from radically different historical periods and contexts was the suggestion of a deeper continuity and affinity between them—a reinterpretation of film history, then, from the point of view of the avant-garde.[42]

Seymour Stern was another veteran film historian recruited from *Films in Review* whose work was regularly featured throughout *Film Culture*'s first decade. While the steady publication of "Coffee, Brandy and Cigars" in *Film Culture* signaled the journal's receptivity to Weinberg's playful recasting of film history, Stern's work for the journal in the early 1960s further underscored the creative exchange between different sectors of the film community. For although Stern's contributions remained intensely focused upon the silent era and on D. W. Griffith in particular, Stern's writing also took on a new formal complexity and daring fully in keeping with the avant-garde spirit overtaking *Film Culture*. Stern's close relationship with the journal culminated in 1964 in *Film Culture* no. 36, an issue of ninety-five pages (the longest yet for a single issue) that was entirely devoted to his ongoing research on D. W. Griffith's *The Birth of a Nation*.[43] In *Film Culture* no. 36 Stern, like Weinberg, explored montage as a historiographic tool by constantly punctuating his lengthy essays on *A Birth of a Nation* with fragments from a range of primary documents related to Griffith and his film, such as contemporary trade reviews and reproductions of period newspaper articles on Abraham Lincoln and different periods of the Civil War. Calling his technique "literary close-ups," Stern claimed that these inserted quotations—which were set off from the text by a simple black line— were inspired by the early Soviet avant-garde. In this way Stern noted that the "literary close-ups" functioned "much in the manner in which a film-close up . . . objectifies a broader action on the screen."[44] A similar avant-garde impulse is also found in two "interviews" by Stern published in *Film Culture* in 1962. Declaring himself frustrated with traditional interview formats, Stern interviewed *himself* by writing in a spirited monologue about his obsessive research techniques and, inevitably, about D. W. Griffith.[45]

Together with Weinberg's "Coffee, Brandy and Cigars," Stern's contributions to *Film Culture* reveal an active dialogue between the two generations of scholars and artists associated with the journal, which is further underscored by the contemporary work of Andrew Sarris. Take, for example, "Dialogue of a Schizocritic," a piece by Sarris published the same year as Stern's self-interviews. In this work Sarris explores a monologue technique similar to that of Stern in which he offers a humorously rambling conversation with himself weighing the charms and flaws of a series of recently viewed films.[46]

Yet it is Sarris's best-known work *The American Cinema* that furnishes the most convincing proof of a creative cross-pollination between the generations represented by Sarris and Stern. First launched in 1963, in a special expanded issue of *Film Culture*, Sarris's famously bold, and occasionally brazen, categorization of film directors working in the American cinema immediately recalls the audacious pantheons and groups erected by French critics associated with *Cahiers du Cinéma*. Without denying the influence of Sarris's recent time in Paris, *The American Cinema* must be recognized for its roots in a tradition of American film scholarship grounded in patient, evaluative list-making that traces back to the older generation of scholars and critics writing for *Films in Review*. Indeed, Sarris's work is distinguished from contemporary writings in *Cahiers du Cinéma* by the scope and scale of its ambitious attempt to, in Sarris's own words, offer a "systematic reappraisal of the American cinema." Sarris's provocative use of a larger organizational structure—the annotated filmography—as a tool of history writing directly recalls the systematicity that was a dominant concern and methodological principal shared by American film historians.

While *The American Cinema* was clearly indebted to an established tradition of American film scholarship, Sarris's highly idiosyncratic hierarchy fits well within the context of the more personal and introspective modes of writing on the cinema being explored within the pages of *Film Culture*. The journal increasingly explored filmmaking and poetically inspired writing as symbiotic artistic practices. In the early 1960s *Film Culture* began to feature a diversity of personal writings by directors associated with the rising New American Cinema—letters, manifestos, poems and even diary entries by filmmakers such as Bruce Baillie, Stan Brakhage, and Paul Sharits for whom writing was an essential complement to the mode of handcrafted cinema. *Film Culture*'s founding editor, Jonas Mekas, who was himself an established poet, embodied the ideal of the writer-filmmaker through his own diary films and through his appropriately named film column "Movie Diary."

The most important writing by a filmmaker published in *Film Culture* was Stan Brakhage's monumental *Metaphors on Vision*, an intense, sustained meditation on the nature of the cinema and human perception, which in fall 1963 was presented in another stand-alone issue of the journal. The publication of *Metaphors on Vision* signaled the emergence of the American avant-garde filmmaker as an important thinker and writer on the cinema, in a manner that immediately recalled the type of critical and theoretical writing engaged by the Soviet avant-garde in the 1930s. While Maya Deren's influential pamphlet *Anagram of Ideas on Art, Form and Film* (1946) was an important precedent here, it was ultimately *Metaphors on Vision* that really announced the arrival of the filmmaker-theorist as a significant and influential voice. Brakhage's text anticipated the work of other major filmmaker-theoreticians who emerged in the late 1960s and 1970s, such as Hollis Frampton and Yvonne Rainer whose work as filmmakers and writers remained closely intertwined.

These filmmakers are central to this discussion because of the abiding interest in film history, and in the silent cinema in particular, that was shared by members of their group. Like the generation of avant-garde filmmaker-scholars led by Huff, Stern, and Weinberg, many filmmakers of the late 1960s and early 1970s such as Frampton, Ernie Gehr, Ken Jacobs, and Standish Lawder devoted considerable energy to exploring film history guided, like the earlier scholars, by a special attraction to the silent cinema. Yet, even further than the postwar generation, these artists went back to the earliest chapter of American film history—to the era of so-called primitive or early cinema that lasted from roughly 1895 to 1913. And unlike the earlier writers, the filmmakers of the late 1960s and early 1970s also turned to the cinema itself as a tool with which to explore film history.

Two films in particular stand out here: Jacobs's *Tom, Tom the Piper's Son* (1969) and Gehr's *Eureka* (1974). Both films radically slow down or "extend," as Gehr has described his project, a film from the early 1900s—thereby producing, in both cases, an abstraction of swirling grain. As examples of what Scott MacDonald has aptly named "critical cinema," the films of Jacobs and Gehr brought a certain theoretical sophistication into film history by using early cinema to interrogate certain fundaments of cinematic expression such as image, grain, and narrative. Like much of the scholarship explored within the postwar journals, Jacobs and Gehr's projects dealt with materials drawn from the archive—in Jacob's case from the Library of Congress, which had only just recently made celluloid copies of its paper print collection available to the general public as a source of stock footage. And like the earlier scholarship as well, both films made attempts to understand deeper, systematic patterns of film history that are rendered literal in the abstract patterns of grain.

Significantly, Jacobs's and Gehr's structuralist forays into film history point directly toward the subsequent discovery of early cinema by film historians that was unofficially announced by the Brighton Conference of 1979. Indeed, at Brighton film scholars gathered to share their research on the early cinema and to discuss many of the same questions of structure provocatively raised by the films of Jacobs and Gehr. One of the most important scholars to explore the early cinema was, it is important to note, Noël Burch, yet another avant-garde filmmaker who was also predominately interested in questions of form and narrative.

A pattern emerges here that immediately recalls the postwar journals—namely, that of avant-garde film scholarship (meaning work by artists oriented in an avant-garde tradition) that simultaneously looks back at the history of the medium as a way of challenging the assumptions of its present and future. With a striking regularity, the rediscovery of some aspect of the American silent era has continued to bring a new dynamism to the study of the cinema, driving significant breakthroughs that only gradually make their way into the field as a whole. Take, for instance, the recognition of the local as an important research area that was raised by the debates of silent scholars about the Nickelodeon theaters, or the attention to dominant patterns of Hollywood narrative that was first raised not by David Bordwell but by Burch's work on early cinema.

As it was in the postwar period, the silent cinema continues to be privileged as one of the highest priorities of film historians and thus governed by different principles of research and methodology—so much so, in fact, that it has come to resemble a nearly autonomous subdiscipline of film studies. And from the postwar period to the present day, important innovations in the study of the silent cinema have continued to come from outside the academy. The work of the film historians Eileen Bowser and Kevin Brownlow, for example, clearly remains in the tradition of earlier nontenured scholars such as Huff and Stern. Indeed, Brownlow is one of the last of the great collector-historians whose fabled personal archive includes primary materials given to him personally by such luminaries as Abel Gance and King Vidor. In addition, path-breaking scholarship on silent film today frequently comes from motion picture archives and specialized screening venues such as the Italian festivals La Cinema Retrovata in Bologna and Le Giornate del Cinema Muto in Pordenone. Even within the academy, scholarship on the silent cinema continues to deliberately set itself apart from the field of film studies as a whole. Like the historians associated with *Films in Review*, scholars of the silent cinema define their course of study as a more serious and rigorous division of film studies that upholds a higher standard of empirical research and necessitates a fundamentally different perspective than do other modes of film study. Such attitudes are, for example, quite plainly stated in the recent selection of brief essays in *Cinema Journal* focused on issues of archival research.[47]

In order to suggest further continuities between postwar writings on the cinema and the field of film studies today, I want to return briefly to the question of cinephilia that I raised at the start of this essay. Again, the question is this: If scholars have persuasively studied postwar French cinephilia as a means of understanding certain philosophical precepts of Parisian film culture, might we be able to do the same for the contemporary American film scene? Here, this would be accomplished by looking not at patterns of reception or exhibition—a task that certainly needs to be done—but rather at some of the ways in which film was being reevaluated at the time. And I am drawn again to the frequent use of filmographies as a historiographic tool by postwar film historians and the way in which these lists express an overriding concern for the larger underlying structures and patterns of film history. The systematicity reached for by postwar writings on the cinema may suggest one productive way that we might study the general orientation of film scholarship as a starting point for trying to identify and historicize the distinct modes of American cinephilia—that is, of cinema as an object of desire.

Just as French cinephilia works in fragments—fetishizing a punctual detail extracted impulsively from the single frame—so, too, do contemporary writings in *Cahiers du Cinéma* fragment films into telling details and distill director's entire oeuvres into certain intangible essences. For the French, it has been said, the desire was to extract a fragment from a film in order to possess it—just as the boys in *The 400 Blows* snatch a publicity photo from the movie theater lobby.[48] Against the amorous flair of contemporary French cinephilia, the American cinephilia seems, despite all of its obvious eccentricities, to be animated instead by a real pragmatism that seeks to organize and categorize and thus to possess the cinematic object in a very different sense—in fact, quite often in a literal sense in the case of the American historians who were also important collectors.

A similar impulse seems as well to be a major force driving certain structuralist tendencies of the postwar avant-garde that attempt to understand the larger systems—technological, narrative, ideological—by which the cinema operates. The work of Morgan Fisher clearly points in this direction through its constant effort to lay bare the structural logic of the cinema's industrialized grammar. Fisher's most important work, *Standard Gauge* (1984), offers a striking expression of a similar archival impulse that drove postwar film historians as well as other avant-garde filmmakers such as Jacobs and Gehr. For in *Standard Gauge* Fisher quite literally gathers fragments of films, laying strips of 35mm film on a light table before the camera as real objects in his possession, classified and discussed following the rough chronology by which they came into Fisher's possession.

A similar concern for the larger structures of meaning in the cinema also, of course, defines the thriving school of American film historians today led by David Bordwell that is built upon the construction of careful categories, rules, and classificatory systems. And a similar pragmatism to that prevalent throughout postwar writings on the cinema is certainly legible throughout Bordwell's work, which like the writings in *Films in Review* deliberately avoids—and moreover debunks—more abstract, theoretical arguments. Built upon close frame-by-frame analysis, the mode of film study proposed by Bordwell shares the general materialist orientation and concern for systematicity that remains a dominant concern for both postwar film historians and avant-garde film scholars alike.

In much the same way, then, that the "primitiveness" of the early cinema has shed important light upon certain dominant tendencies and patterns of the American cinema, so too do earlier chapters of film study need to be carefully reexamined by looking beyond their frequently obsolete qualities. While at first glance it may be tempting to dismiss postwar film scholarship simply as an early hunting and gathering stage of film history, this essay, I hope, has shown some of the ways in which these earlier writings on the cinema speak directly to the work carried out by film scholars and historians today.

Notes

I am extraordinarily grateful to Gideon Bachmann, Rudy Behlmer, Ernest Callenbach, Andrew Sarris, Anthony Slide, and P. Adams Sitney for generously allowing me to interview them about their careers and about the journals discussed above. This essay could not have been written without the always inspiring assistance and expertise of Ned Comstock at the Cinema-Television Library at the University of Southern California.

1. *Films in Review* became an online publication in 1997; see www.filmsinreview.com. Although the last published issue of *Film Culture* appeared in 1996, the journal's founding editor, Jonas Mekas, has reported that subsequent issues are in production. As of this writing, however, no new issue of *Film Culture* has appeared.

2. For a critical history of French film culture, see Antoine de Baecque, *La cinéphilie: Invention d'un regard, histoire d'une culture, 1944-1968* (Paris: Fayard, 2003).

3. "A long sojourn in Paris in 1961 reassured me that film not only demanded but deserved as much faith as did any other cultural discipline. . . . I have never really recovered from the Parisian heresy (in New York eyes) concerning the sacred importance of the cinema" (Andrew Sarris, "Confessions of a Cultist: A Foreword," in *Confessions of a Cultist: On the Cinema, 1955/1969* (New York: Simon and Schuster, 1970), 13.

4. Andrew Sarris, *The American Cinema: Directors and Directions, 1929-1968* (New York: Dutton, 1968). The frequency with which Sarris attended these theaters in the late 1940s is suggested by his feat of viewing *That Hamilton Woman* (1947) some eighty-three times—a moviegoing adventure he describes in "That Hamilton Woman," in *The Primal Screen: Essays on Film and Related Subjects* (New York: Simon and Schuster, 1973), 265-68.

5. For a general history of the American art house theater, see Barbara Wilinsky, *Sure Seaters: The Emergence of Art House Cinema* (Minneapolis: University of Minnesota Press, 2001).

6. Kael managed and co-owned the Cinema Guild Theater with her third husband, Ed Landberg, from 1955 until 1960.

7. For a comprehensive and insightful history of the film scene in Los Angeles from the 1920s through the 1970s, including the Coronet Theater, see David James, *The Most Typical Avant-Garde: History and Geography of Minor Cinemas in Los Angeles* (Berkeley: University of California Press, 2005).

8. On the conversion of the newsreel theaters, see Douglas Gomery, *Shared Pleasures: A History of Movie Presentation in the United States* (Madison: University of Wisconsin Press, 1992), 184-85, 247-51.

9. Kael's radio program was broadcast on KPFA from 1953 to 1962.

10. Recordings of *The Film Art* are housed in the Cinema-Television Library of the University of Southern California.

11. Haidee Wasson discusses MOMA's circulating film series in her excellent history of MOMA's film library and associated programs, *Museum Movies: The Museum of Modern Art and the Birth of Art Cinema* (Berkeley: University of California Press, 2005), 149-76; see also Wasson this volume.

12. On the rise of the American film societies, see Wasson, *Museum Movies*, 41-44; and William K. Everson, "Film Societies Should Federate," *Films in Review* 4.3 (March 1953): 124-28.

13. For the printed notes that accompanied Cinema 16's first program, see Scott Mac-

donald, ed., *Cinema 16: Documents Towards a History of the Film Society* (Philadelphia: Temple University Press, 2002), 86–89.

14. Originally called "The Film Circle," the Theodore Huff Memorial Society was founded in 1951. On the Huff Society, see Charles L. Taylor, "Witnessing the Development of Independent Film Culture in New York: An Interview with Charles L. Taylor," interview by Ronald S. Magliozzi, *Film History* 12.1 (2000): 72–96, 85–87.

15. According to Wasson, MOMA's silent films generated a nervous and often unpredictable reaction from museum audiences from the very first of the museum programs. Indeed, riotous laughter and boisterous behavior were not uncommon during MOMA screenings. See Wasson, *Museum Movies*, 2.

16. Richard Kraft, "Audience Stupidity: The Pleasure of Looking at Old Films Can Be Spoiled by the Laughter of Empty Minds," *Films in Review* 5.3 (March 1954): 113–14, 134.

17. The only two significant American film journals of the 1940s were extremely short lived and ill fated: *Films* (1939–1940), founded by the film historian Jay Leyda who also served on its editorial board; and *Cinema* (1947), a journal coedited by Lewis Jacobs that lasted for less than a year. For more information on these periodicals, see Anthony Slide, ed., *International Film, Radio, and Television Journals* (Westport, Conn.: Greenwood Press, 1985), 162–63, 50–51.

18. *Films in Review* 3.2 (February 1952): 96.

19. Gideon Bachmann, "Foreword," *Cinemages*, no. 1 (1955): 2.

20. Jonas Mekas, "Foreword," *Film Culture*, no.1 (January 1955): 1.

21. *Film Quarterly* can only be claimed as a longer-running American film journal if it is declared to be an extension of the two journals published previously by the University of California Press—*Hollywood Quarterly* (1945–1951) and *Quarterly Review of Film and Television*. In truth, *Film Quarterly* began as an entirely new publication that was deliberately distanced from both *Hollywood Quarterly* and *Quarterly Review* and modeled instead on the popular literary "little magazines" such as *Kenyon Review*. In sharp contrast, *Films in Review* has maintained a remarkably consistent identity and focus throughout its long lifespan, regardless of changes in editors.

22. Gilbert Seldes, review of *"The Film Till Now," Films in Review* 1.5 (July–August 1950): 29–35.

23. Huff and Stern both claimed to have seen Griffith directing at his Mamaroneck, N.Y., studio. Stern, who was born in 1912, would have been a boy of just nine at the time while Huff, who was seven years older, would have been sixteen. For Stern's account, see Seymour Stern, "Introduction," in "Griffith I: The Birth of a Nation," edited by Seymour Stern, special issue, *Film Culture*, no. 36 (spring-summer 1965): 7–33, 29. Huff's experience at the early movie studios is mentioned in a tribute article in *Films in Review*, which was written after Huff's death in 1953 at the early age of forty-eight. See Charles L. Turner, "Theodore Huff in Memoriam," *Films in Review* 4.5 (May 1953): 209–11. Huff's biography is discussed by Chuck Kleinhans in

"Theodore Huff: Historian and Filmmaker," in *Lovers of Cinema: The First American Avant-Garde, 1919–1945*, edited by Jan-Christopher Horak (Madison: University of Wisconsin Press, 1995), 180–204.

24. Stern, "Griffith I," 30.
25. Henry Hart, "Terry Ramsaye," *Films in Review* 5.8 (October 1954): 385–86.
26. Terry Ramsaye, "Foreword" in *A Million and One Nights: A History of the Motion Picture*, vol. 1 (New York: Simon and Schuster, 1926), xiv.
27. Theodore Huff, letter to the editor, *Films in Review* 3.1 (January 1952): 424.
28. The journal's diminutive size—measuring a mere three by six inches and with a length rarely more than fifty pages—also lent itself to the abbreviated formats favored by the journal's writers.
29. Huff's "index" of Chaplin's films was published in Theodore Huff, *Charlie Chaplin* (New York: Henry Schuman, 1951), 313–34. Stern's index to Griffith's films was published in four parts by the British Film Institute. See Seymour Stern, "An Index to the Creative Work of David Wark Griffith. Part 1: The Birth of an Art, 1908–1915," special supplement, *Sight and Sound*, series no. 2 (1945); Stern, "An Index to the Creative Work of David Wark Griffith. The Art Triumphant: The Triangle Film Period, 1915–1916," special supplement, *Sight and Sound*, series no. 7 (August 1946); Stern, "An Index to the Creative Work of David Wark Griffith. The Art Triumphant: Intolerance," special supplement, *Sight and Sound*, series no. 8 (1946); and Stern, "An Index to the Creative Work of David Wark Griffith. The Art Triumphant: Hearts of the World," special supplement, *Sight and Sound*, series no. 10 (May 1947).
30. See Huff, *Charlie Chaplin*. Stern's biography of Griffith remained unfinished at the time of Stern's death.
31. William K. Everson, "Stock Shots: Potentially of Great Creative Importance, they Now Bolster Inferior Films," *Films in Review* 4.1 (January 1953): 15–20; and Roi A. Uselton, "Death by Airplane: Eight Stars Fell from the Skies," *Films in Review* 7.5 (May 1956): 210–14.
32. "Coffee, Brandy and Cigars" first appeared in *Films in Review* in 1952 and continued in the journal for three years.
33. Weinberg makes this claim for "the dream of the impotent husband with a knife-phobia" in Pabst's *Secrets of a Soul* in Herman G. Weinberg, "Coffee, Brandy and Cigars," *Films in Review* 3.4 (April 1952): 183.
34. On Bachmann's years in New York, see Gideon Bachmann, interview with author, December 18, 2005.
35. Gideon Bachmann, "Foreword," *Cinemages*, no. 1 (1955): 2.
36. On Bachmann's many duties for *Cinemages*, see Gideon Bachmann, interview with author, December 18, 2005.
37. Bachmann, "Program Notes," *Cinemages*, no. 2 (1955): 31.
38. Gideon Bachmann, "Introduction," in "G. W. Pabst:—The Man—the Director—the Artist," special issue edited by Gideon Bachmann, *Cinemages*, no. 3 (May 1955): 3.
39. *Film Culture*'s initially ambivalent attitude toward the New American Cinema dra-

matically changed in 1959, when Mekas instituted the Independent Film Award to honor "American contributions to the cinema," with the first award given to John Cassavetes's *Shadows*. On *Film Culture*'s changing attitude toward the avant-garde, see P. Adams Sitney, "Introduction: A Reader's Guide to the American Avant-Garde Film," in *Film Culture: An Anthology*, edited by P. Adams Sitney (New York: Praeger, 1968), 3–12.

40. Another regular *Films in Review* column was recruited for the first two issues of *Film Culture*—Gordon Hendricks's quirky and often-rambling review of film music, *The Sound Track*. Hendricks continued to contribute occasional articles to *Film Culture* until the mid-1960s.

41. See Toby Mussman, "An Interview with Tony Conrad"; Mussman, "Early Surrealist Expression in the Film;" and Thom Anderson, "Eadweard Muybridge," all in *Film Culture*, no. 41 (1966): 3–4, 5–8, 22–24.

42. The importance of montage to *Film Culture* was also revealed by the journal's original translation and publication of important texts by three masters of the Soviet avant-garde—Dziga Vertov, Slavko Vorkapich, and Leo Kuleshov—who had each brought a new attention to montage techniques in their films. See Dziga Vertov, "The Writings of Dziga Vertov," *Film Culture*, no. 25 (1962): 50–60; Barbara L. Kevles, "Slavko Vorkapich on Film as a Visual Language and as a Form of Art," *Film Culture*, no. 38 (1965): 1–46; and Steven P. Hill, "Kuleshov—Prophet without Honor?" *Film Culture*, no. 44 (1967): 1–41.

43. Stern, "Griffith I."

44. Ibid., 9.

45. See Seymour Stern, "An Interview with Seymour Stern: Part I," *Film Culture*, no. 27 (1962/1963): 66–72; and Seymour Stern, "An Interview with Seymour Stern: Part II," *Film Culture*, no. 28 (1963): 82–96.

46. Andrew Sarris, "Diary of a Schizocritic," *New York Film Bulletin*, May 15, 1962, reprinted in, Sarris, *Confessions of a Cultist: On the Cinema, 1955/1969* (New York: Simon and Schuster, 1970): 44–50.

47. "Film History, or A Baedeker Guide to the Historical Turn," edited by Sumiko Higashi, *Cinema Journal* 44, no. 1 (fall, 2004).

48. On this reading of cinephilia, see Paul Willeman, "Through a Glass Darkly: Cinephilia Reconsidered," in *Looks and Frictions: Essays in Cultural Studies and Film Theory* (London: BFI, 1994); and Christian Keathley, *Cinephilia and History, or The Wind in the Trees* (Bloomington: Indiana University Press, 2005).

Screen and 1970s Film Theory

PHILIP ROSEN

■ In 1971 the British journal *Screen* adopted a new cover format—block
monocolor with the journal's name printed vertically. A transformation in the
English-language study of film and media could also be dated from that moment. *Screen* was descended from the newsletter-become-journal of the Society for Education in Film and Television (SEFT), originally formed by pioneering British film educators after World War II. With the 1971 modification in
cover format, Sam Rohdie assumed chief editorship and announced the urgent
need for profound transformations in film culture and film studies. There were
subsequent changes of the editorial board and chief editors during the 1970s.
But when the cover was again revamped, for the spring 1979 issue, there was a
sense that something had indeed changed during the intervening years. As the
new editor Mandy Merck wrote, since 1971 *Screen* had developed a position and
concepts of extraordinary impact in film and television studies, and it had also
influenced related fields such as fine arts and photography, aesthetic theory,
and cultural and literary theory.[1] However, despite this influence and the fact
that the journal published important work on such topics as television and
British critical thought between 1971 and 1979, its leading object of concern was
film, and its primary intellectual and discursive mode was theoretical inquiry
and reconceptualization. It became one of the most significant journals in the
history of film theory.

Today it is possible to identify something we can call 1970s film theory.
This was a self-conscious attempt at renovation by rethinking the fundamental

terms through which cinema was experienced and understood in classical film theory and in standard modes of film criticism and analysis. The term "1970s film theory" is not only a periodizing label but also a collective one, for it was constituted through a tissue of intersecting, sometimes mutually contestatory, arguments and discourses about cinema written by many individuals. So it was always under development. Nevertheless, its common concerns made it a recognizable intellectual constellation, which set the terms of advanced debate in film scholarship for over two decades, arguably even for those who rejected it. Many of its central concepts and arguments are still felt in the study of film, media, and culture. Examples include the classical cinematic text, structuralist and poststructuralist narratology, textual heterogeneity and excess, ideological contradiction, spectatorship, subject position, Lacanian accounts of filmic identification, and the masculine gaze, to name a few. *Screen* was the most powerful and widely discussed English-language platform for 1970s film theory (some English-language writers have called it "*Screen* theory").[2] Because 1970s film theory was collective, journals were especially important. Many of its originary texts appeared in a troika of leading periodicals: *Screen* and two important French sources, *Cahiers du Cinéma* and *Cinéthique*. These years also saw the founding of additional important English-language journals centered to different degrees on the political and theoretical impulses of 1970s film theory, such as *Ciné-Tracts* in Canada and *Wide Angle* and *Camera Obscura* in the United States.

It is not possible in this chapter to trace every twist and turn of the rich discussions—and disputes and editorial splits—in *Screen*, much less to take into account the subsequent critiques and debates generated by the journal. It is necessary to stick to the pages of the journal and be selective. However, it is possible to gloss some key elements in the formation of 1970s film theory in English as they occurred in the journal. But first it may be helpful to recall something of the context.

In rereading *Screen* and its allies now, one is struck by the extent to which the search for new thinking was in the air at the time. Desires for radical political novelty at the end of the 1960s corresponded with a quest for radical transformation among some intellectual sectors. Notions of fundamental change, epistemological breaks, and, occasionally, revolution were the order of the day. This coalesced with the growing and controversial prestige of theory as a mode by which to renovate Anglo-American critical studies in the academy. All of these fed into ambitions to overhaul film theory along with film culture.

Such ambitions were further overdetermined (a favored term in 1970s theory) by the emergent institutionalization of university film studies in the English-speaking world. A new university discipline needed new concepts to justify itself. When *Screen Education* had been renamed *Screen* in 1969, the editors (Kevin Gough-Yates and Terry Bolas) already proclaimed the need to address controversial issues in the new field of film studies.[3] *Screen* soon became deliberately positional, seeking to develop certain lines of argument and inquiry with political rationales in mind. But to such ends its editorials and articles also called for methodological and theoretical rigor, which, they claimed, was lacking in existing film theory and analysis. Articles often took on a heavily abstract quality unusual in previous English-language writing about film.

A particularly consequential editorial strategy employed in *Screen*'s ambitions to renovate film culture and criticism was the practice of printing translations, most commissioned specifically for the journal. During the 1970s, *Screen* published an extraordinary number of English-language translations of foreign-language texts, especially in the first half of the decade. Before 1975, some issues consisted almost completely of translations and commentaries on them. By 1975 their number was declining, though there were still occasional blockbuster translations such as Christian Metz's "The Imaginary Signifier."[4] Thus, as *Screen*'s project and position became relatively well defined, original contributions came to dominate the journal.

The translation strategy was aggressively polemical. It was intended to implant alternative modes of thought in the midst of British film criticism and culture. But this intervention within British film criticism and culture had the paradoxical effect of internationalizing the journal's audience and its impact. It made *Screen* a unique resource throughout the entire English-speaking world. Translated articles were from European countries with historically vital traditions of filmmaking as well as film theory and criticism—France, Germany, Italy, and the Soviet Union. Some of the translated texts soon became canonical in English-language film studies, so that *Screen*'s positional agenda was rapidly shaping scholarship in many countries. This was probably one reason that, even in some of its earliest issues, the new *Screen* drew authors from North America such as Bill Nichols and Stephen Mamber.

This meant that a relatively new concern was on offer, the history of film theory itself, which contributed to the sense of defining a new discipline. On the other hand, there were clear priorities in the selection of texts for translations. A large proportion of translations emanated from historical moments when revolutionary or Marxist ideas were a premise. Several Russian Formalist and Futurist writings on cinema as well as the 1974 Brecht special issue are examples. *Screen* also translated three Italian articles from the 1960s on popular front Marxism and film aesthetics.[5]

That said, there were more translations from French than any other language. Most of these were contemporary, generally originating after 1968 and usually from *Cahiers du Cinéma* and *Cinéthique*. They engaged cinema with the most current semiotic, textual, and ideological theory. In searching for allies in the project of radically renovating British film culture and English-language film theory, *Screen* found them in a politically, theoretically, and cinematically charged Paris. The translations themselves seemed to establish theoretical self-consciousness and Marxism as the most pertinent starting points.

Screen's Project

One can find two general rationales for new film theory in early writings for the new *Screen*. Many of those on the reconstituted editorial board were associated with the Education Department of the British Film Institute. Some members, exemplified by Alan Lovell, formulated what can be called "educationist" rationales: British film education should be redefined by a new theoretical emphasis that reconceptualized cinema and its analysis. At the same time other members, exemplified by new chief editor Sam Rohdie, articulated goals that can be called "radical materialist": cinema had to be studied as a sector—an especially important one—in the struggle against bourgeois ideology. This required unpacking and theorizing dominant notions and experiences of film and media.

The two rationales overlapped even within the work of individuals. Both promoted reconceptualizations of cinema and British film culture against shared opponents: British film reviews such as *Sight and Sound* and (for different reasons) the influential auteurist journal *Movie* as well as mass culture critiques related to moralizing notions of high art and literature editors associated with the name of F. R. Leavis. In addition, both impulses often involved leftist political tendencies. However, as *Screen*'s theoretical emphases and directions solidified, tensions between the two developed and soon grew into serious rifts. One finds strong traces of this bifurcation in the resignation announcement of several members of the editorial board published in the summer 1976 issue, explained partly on educationist grounds, with rejoinders by those remaining. By then, the debate was posed as one not just over theory but also over the journal's turn to psychoanalytic theories of signification and cinema.[6]

At first, however, it was the shared motivations that were more important. At least three broad interrelated interventions were jointly identified. First, British film education and film culture had to be liberated from a simple, automatic critique of mass culture. Second, film analysis had to become systematic in order to overcome the mystifications of intuitive British criticism, whose most advanced approach was identified as auteur criticism. The third intervention was a grand project that was theoretical and practical, philosophical and political, epistemological and social: namely, promoting alternatives to currently dominant cinemas, in connection with a far-reaching challenge to conceptions of culture and art—conceptions embedded in dominant ideologies of culture, textuality, and society. This last, of course, was central for the radical materialist rationale.

In following years these interventions were not pursued equally. The question of mass culture per se was sometimes taken up, but it was not explicitly central for many major articles and debates in the journal, which increasingly tended to coalesce around issues of textuality and textual form. Auteur criticism was a topic of discussion, but more and more in the context of the third project. In fact, the progressing hegemony of the third intervention can be illustrated by comparing earlier and later discussions of auteurism.

While the new *Screen* was still formulating its position, the autumn 1973 issue included a section of three articles on auteurism. Edward Buscombe reviewed the state of auteur theory, from pre-1968 *Cahiers du Cinéma* through the American auteurist Andrew Sarris and then to so-called auteur-structuralism. This last was a then-recent attempt to depersonalize auteur criticism by deploying selected concepts from Lévi-Strauss's structural anthropology. Buscombe urged that directorial consistencies be understood as effects of society and history rather than personal expression. Stephen Heath agreed. He argued that a "theory of the subject" in relation to ideology could do the job, and he recommended the work of Christian Metz and new psychoanalytic theory for starting points. Geoffrey Nowell-Smith (whose earlier work had been auteur-structuralist) responded to a critique in *Film Comment* by Charles Eckert, arguing that auteur-structuralism was not a rigorous application of Lévi-Strauss but a partly failed contribution toward a radical materialist theory of film. Both Heath and Nowell-Smith pointed toward the theoretical directions that *Screen* was developing. But here note how the section was ordered, beginning with problems raised by the history of film *analysis* and then moving toward calls for new kinds of *theory* as the means of resolving those problems.

In the spring 1979 issue, a discussion of auteurism was ordered in the opposite direction. The issue begins with a reprinted translation of Michel Foucault's

"What Is an Author?" Foucault dissolves authorship into a historical and institutional "author-function" without any reference to film or media. This is followed by a long essay by Sue Clayton and Jonathan Curling. Assuming the perspective of British independent and avant-garde filmmakers, they analyze institutional constructions of filmic authors (author-functions) in practices such as copyright law and state subsidies. Thus, instead of beginning from a problem in film culture or film criticism, the 1979 issue begins with a radical theoretical formulation on authorship and only then does it address cinema. Additionally, the development of a theory of the subject and radical materialist goals, for which Heath and Nowell-Smith had called in 1973, are here taken for granted. In fact, the move toward Foucault is an implicit alternative to the solutions of psychoanalytic theory, which had since come to the fore in *Screen*.

Earlier, it had been deemed necessary to argue explicitly that theoretical reconceptualization would be the basis for renovation in thinking about film and media. Both the educationist and the radical materialist tendencies of the *Screen* editorial board shared this attitude. Within British film culture, this established the journal's opposition to the supposedly unsystematic, impressionistic criticism of *Sight and Sound* and the allegedly romantic expressivist tendencies of the *Movie* group. But by the end of the decade, the necessity of an explicit theoretical framework was taken for granted in *Screen*. This insistence on theory combined with the institutionally and ideologically insurgent tone was influential. It helped determine what counted as leading new work in the growing field of English-language film studies, which was rapidly defining— and legitimating—itself.

The contours of *Screen*'s intervention in film theory seem to have been clearly established by 1975–76. Major articles contested established modes of film analysis and proposed the development of new modes involving a theory of subjectivity in relation to conceptions of film textuality. The most consistent noncinematic foundational theoretical references in this regard would be Saussure and Barthes in linguistics and semiotics, and Freud and Lacan for the theorization of subjectivity. But what linked the concerns with signification and subjectivity was a theory of ideology, which went back to the radical materialist rationale at the beginning of the decade. In what follows, I will construct a kind of framework or logic through which the majority of contributions to *Screen* can be conceived as cohering, even though there were sometimes serious disagreements among them. This is an ex post facto construct, a historical conceit that helps us understand the position of the journal in the history of film theory. It is not a claim about the rationales of any individual author or editor at the time of publication, and I emphasize that it does not cover many important variations, objections, and arguments that appeared in the journal.

Screen's Marxism: Filmic Realism and Ideology

The first steps in establishing the film-theoretical concerns of *Screen* were taken by setting out a new attitude toward a classic issue in film theory: the relation of film to reality. Theoretical critiques of a variety of realist criteria—aesthetic, moral, and epistemological—were part of *Screen*'s insurgent project within British film culture. It was thought that such criteria had informed distortions basic both to existing mass culture critique and to film criticism. Within a year of its "break," *Screen* produced several theme issues explicitly designed to throw a variety of realist premises into question: the first special issue was devoted to Douglas Sirk, the German leftist director who made glossy domestic melodramas in 1940s and 1950s Hollywood that existing realist approaches supposedly could not digest; the second issue was on Soviet Futurism and Formalism; and the third was on realism and technology.[7] Anti-realism soon became a well-established premise, which coalesced theoretically in the summer 1974 special number on Brecht and revolutionary cinema. But first, *Screen* established a Marxist pedigree by insisting that questions of realism should be routed through the concept of ideology.

On the one hand this entailed attacking the strongest realist positions in classical film theory (often that of André Bazin) by insisting that the cinematic pursuit of the real, including technological developments, is ideologically determined. On the other hand, there was attention to earlier anti-realist and realist film and film-theoretical movements with connections to Marxism. *Screen*'s most theoretically intensive recovery of anti-realist predecessors was of 1920s Russian Formalist and Futurist theory bearing on film. The winter 1971–72 issue emphasized the history of politicized avant-gardism in *Lef* and *Novy Lef*, and as late as the autumn 1974 issue *Screen* was still engaging with the Soviet 1920s through translation—notably by publishing recollections by Osip Brik as well as Boris Eikhenbaum's important theoretical essay on cinema and inner speech.[8]

These early Soviet texts seemed to speak directly to *Screen*'s concerns. Several dealt with the relations of artistic to political revolution in the 1920s and could be understood in Marxist theoretical terms as interrogating relations between cultural or ideological superstructure and base. Their focus on theory and on the text as production also made them predecessors of *Screen*'s own emphases. Their discussions of social utility and "production art" often conceived of the artist as one producer among many, a specialist in perception who would help construct a new, revolutionary reality. They therefore broached questions of alternative cinemas, including informational or documentary films as opposed to the "played" or fictional agitprop film. And, of course, they thought in exciting, polemical ways about the idea of reality as a construct and as a construction.

However, the most immediate reference point for *Screen*'s Marxism was not historical and Soviet but contemporary and French. The first two issues of the new *Screen* included translations of several articles from polemical exchanges that had occurred in 1969 between *Cahiers du Cinéma* and *Cinéthique*. The polemics established problems that remained fundamental for *Screen*, both in the kind of Marxism to which they appealed and some of the issues about film and ideology they formulated; as such, they are worth reviewing.[9]

Before doing so, however, the type of Marxist theory should be noted. Both sides in these translated French exchanges made early work by Louis Althusser a primary reference point, as did several subsequent contributions to *Screen*. (In fact, Althusser's translator, Ben Brewster, was on the *Screen* editorial board and for a time served as chief editor.) Throughout the 1960s, Althusser rethought the Marxist thesis of economic determination, with its metaphor of a social formation as a relation between economic base and superstructures (legal/political and ideological practices). Working toward a complex, indirect conception of social determination and causality, he argued that the unity of a society is not organic and immediately centered on the economy. Rather, a social formation is composed of elements or processes that form a whole but also are contradictory, within themselves and to one another. A social formation is the ongoing organization of this contradictory heterogeneity, what Althusser called a complex whole. The emphasis on heterogeneity further entails that every social practice—whether economic, legal-political, or ideological—has its own specificity, its own "relatively autonomous" characteristics and functions. How these relative autonomies operate is determined by the place of any particular practice in the organization of the whole social formation. The economic base ultimately determines the organization of the whole, but it does not directly govern a particular practice at any particular moment. Instead, it functions through the other practices. So the different practices are *different*, and their interrelationships and importance in a social formation shift over time.

For the new *Screen*, Althusser's Marxism seemed enabling for rethinking film and media. For one thing, he emphasized the inescapability and importance of ideology, which implicitly justified research into ideological practices and its central institutions including film, media, and the arts. In some writings, Althusser suggested that artistic form creates ambiguities in the operations or cracks in the facades of dominant ideologies. Furthermore, his emphasis on the relative autonomy of social practices justified attention to the specificity of operations performed by cinema—a concern of film theory. Also, the potential dynamism of social formations theorized by Althusser was undoubtedly attractive for those seeking to envision new and oppositional cultural practices.

There is more of importance to 1970s film theory in Althusser, but this is enough to return to the translated French debates. They were originally written in the aftermath of the quasi-revolutionary moment of May 1968, which shook the French government as well as cultural and artistic sectors. But when translated in the new *Screen* the framework shared by the two French journals was at least as pertinent as their disagreements. They introduced a novel type of theoretical discourse into English-language film culture.

Both agreed that while film is certainly a kind of commodity, its socially specific functioning is in the ideological sphere (including aesthetics), and that cinema's political importance is as ideology. Both conceptualized ideology through Althusser, and many of their disagreements turned on the proper use of Althusserian concepts. They also agreed that the fundamental ideological power of cinema is not just its reproduction of socially dominant ideas but also in endowing these ideas with the force of reality itself. And this endowment, they asserted, operates through a tacit, generally accepted sense, among both audiences and practitioners, of what cinema itself is: a technology with a special capacity to capture reality. The theoretical and practical demystification of the filmic illusion of reality is therefore identified as a political project.

Because the relation of film and the real was already a long-standing central question in film theory, simply by translating these debates, with their shared Althusserianism, *Screen* was taking a position in film theory. Althusser's theory suggests that critique and oppositional art should be in some sense anti-realist, for ideology is said to work precisely by appearing as an unthought, immediate "reality." In the French journals, the powerful impression of reality attributed to cinema gives it a special place in this operation because it lends its sense of reality to other ideological discourses that it carries. While many, ranging from general audiences to sophisticated theorists, treat this capacity as inherent in cinematic technology, the French journals treated the filmic impression of reality as an artificial construct, a bourgeois conception of cinema for a bourgeois-dominated society.

In that case, cinematic "transparency" must operate by masking this artificiality, and therefore *how* meanings are actually produced in film. The French debates associate this aesthetic of masking with the ways that capitalism hides the fact of surplus value and the roots of production in the exploitation of workers. Insofar as working-class audiences, along with those from other classes, accede to cinema's impression of reality, they take the bourgeois "reality" on screen as reality itself; therefore their recognition of the real is tied to mystification or *mis*recognition. Hence, the task of oppositional cinema is to show up this recognition-misrecognition structure.

This has been a lengthy summary of some programmatic, initial formulations. But these translated debates established assumptions, questions, and problems that became central to lines of inquiry for the entire decade in *Screen*. As Comolli and Narboni wrote, in *Screen*'s first translation from *Cahiers*, ideological analysis begins from the "vital distinction," as they called it, between films that "show up the cinema's so-called 'depiction of reality'" and films that do not.[10] Thus, this cinematic politics seemed to militate toward a binary opposition between ideologically complicit films and insurgent films. Crucially, this distinction implies that cinematic illusionism is not simply a matter of cinematic technology—or of cinema "as such"—but of particular filmic strategies. That is, it is a matter of textuality. If textual innovations can unmask cinematic illusionism, could they not then establish a different kind of recognition, one that does not necessarily end in misrecognition or mystification? This in turn suggested the benefits of intensive examination of the implications of diverse forms of textuality. Thus, counterintuitively, theorizing binary political judgments of films could lead toward more differentiated analysis of filmic texts or types of textuality. This tension, between binary definitions and more differentiations was already evidenced in the first translated *Cahiers* piece, "Cinema/ Ideology/Criticism," which proposed a much-discussed seven-category typology of film-ideology relations.

Can political significance be attributed to forms of textuality? In the 1970s *Screen* became a vehicle for working on this question—its implications, its possibilities, and the analyses that flowed from it. In short, the journal's stated concern with ideology and film theory led straight to theorizing film textuality. Within a couple of years, the new *Screen* identified the larger theoretical reference points for this project as semiotics and the theory of the spectator as a relation between text and subject. With respect to subjectivity, *Screen* thus also ended up claiming to move the study of film more toward a theory of the spectator than a theory of the author. In addition, by continually asking how textual characteristics make a difference for ideology and politics, *Screen* opened its doors to contemporary filmmaking and especially avant-garde film culture.

Throughout the decade, *Screen* published articles that theorized dominant or mainstream film, but often it tried to do so from a perspective that supported oppositional cinemas. Within the history of Marxist aesthetics and cultural practices, Brecht served as a historical icon for the politicized theory and practice that opposes standard codes of realism, while implementing an artistic practice that is political and performs work on representation, subjectivity, and pleasure. Certain contemporary filmmakers, such as Godard, Oshima, and Straub and Huillet became some of the more constant reference points. In addition, certain British independent and avant-garde filmmakers came in for special attention in theorized discussions of the politics of representation and oppositional film textuality. Some of them—like Peter Gidal, Laura Mulvey, and Peter Wollen—contributed to theoretical matters in *Screen*. The promotion of British independent, avant-garde filmmaking was a concrete reminder of the intervention being made in British film culture, but the explicit rationale was usually less on grounds of a national cinema, much less a national media educational policy, than on ideological and theoretical grounds.[11]

Textuality in Screen

Screen's argument that conceptions of cinema and film education should be radically transformed thus included a good deal of textual theory; in fact that very notion of film as text, with textuality understood as a complex theoretical concept, became one of its distinctive concerns. In 1973, *Screen* produced its only double issue of the decade—a special number on cinema semiotics and the work of Christian Metz.[12] Previous issues had included some references to Metz as well as to general semiotics and its intellectual lineage, which included Russian Formalism. But the sheer bulk of this issue (258 pages) along with the introductions and translations of both Metz and French commentaries on him, effectively announced that structuralist and poststructuralist semiotics would provide methodological grounds in *Screen*'s drive to transform English-language film culture and criticism. It also announced that Metz would be a key reference.

In his 1971 doctoral thesis, *Language and Cinema*, Metz conceived of a film as a site crossed by a very large number of codes of different orders: first, cine-matically specific codes (existing only in cinema and occurring in all films, e.g., systems of lighting for moving images); second, cinematic subcodes (existing only in cinema but not necessarily present in all films, e.g., certain film genre codes); and third, extracinematic codes (existing outside cinema but suscep-tible to importation through filmic analogy.) A textual system is the particular configuration of relationships among a plurality of codes of all types, which are shaped in the flow of images and sounds of a particular film. In a sense, codes are the "material" of a textual system, which is the overall set of their interrelations. The semiotician abstracts codes from the concrete flow of images and sounds composing a film or films and then abstracts the singular textual system, which is the interrelation of codes as a set in a given film.

Perhaps most suggestive for subsequent discussions of textuality in *Screen* was the way that Metz characterized a singular textual system. The very act of utilizing a code puts it into a unique system of relations with other codes—the *singular* textual system. If a code is always utilized within a unique set of rela-tions to other codes, its force and significance are subject to variation; that is, the code itself is transformed with every use. A textual system does not simply order static, repeated codes, but in that very ordering, which assumes their pre-vious formation, it *deforms* them. For Metz, cinema semiotics now depended on conceiving of a film as an "operation" rather than a structure, as a dynamic signifying *process* involving negation and contradiction as well as repetition and similarity. This emphasis was part of that influential shift in French theory called poststructuralism, and Metz refers to poststructuralist concepts such as intertextuality and textual productivity in Julia Kristeva's work. This notion of a film as a potentially transformative process rather than a structure that re-iterates preexisting ideological codes, became crucial for many of *Screen*'s dis-cussions of textuality and ideology. According to Metz, this process is neither a matter of "pure invention" nor a reorganization of codes arising from reality: "What is called reality—i.e. the different profilmic elements—is nothing more than a set of codes, that set of codes without which this reality would not be accessible or intelligible." Thus, he notes, meaning in film is neither created by an individual nor reflective of a preexisting, perhaps protean reality. This cor-responded with *Screen*'s suspicion of auteurism and realism.[13]

The special number on Metz and the issues immediately following it in-cluded commentaries on *Language and Cinema*, placing conceptions of tex-tuality in the forefront of *Screen*'s concerns. It would be inaccurate to say that after the Metz double issue, *Screen* was single-mindedly preoccupied with semiotics. But from that point, many articles had to do with definitions and analyses of filmic codes and/or textual systems, sometimes in relation to semiotic method and film theory, sometimes going on to emphasize ideological implantation and/or disturbances. The journal regularly published articles probing the nature and operations of codes, often involving close analyses of segments of individual films. Some also interrogated how certain filmic figures or codes operated across several films (for example, point-of-view camerawork and editing). Some sought to distinguish among types of films based on their deployments of codes, which could be understood referring to the opposition between ideologically complicit and oppositional cinemas. At first, articles concerned with codes tended to be translations from French, by figures such as Thierry Kuntzel and Raymond Bellour among others; however, by 1974–75, they consisted mainly of original English-language contributions. Several utilized Metz's categories or addressed his arguments. Some did not share all of the assumptions of *Screen*'s developing position or even utilize the metalanguages of semiotics, but could be read as rigorously and systematically engaging with questions of filmic codification. The most important examples of the last were analyses (many dealing with classical Japanese films) by a formalist-oriented group associated with the University of Wisconsin—David Bordwell, Edward Branigan, and Kristin Thompson. They drew rejoinders from members of the editorial board, which insisted that the theoretical context of such close analyses for *Screen*'s concerns were with ideological and textual theory.[14]

According to Metz, a singular textual system is unique and involves a transformational process of conjoining and thereby deforming codes. Marxist commentators wished to understand how this process was implicated with ideology. Metz's earlier work had emphasized the idea that films codify themselves as segments in the interests of making narrative sense out of the flow of images and sounds constituting a film. Now, partly under the influence of Roland Barthes's book *S/Z* as well as Metz, some contributions to *Screen* dealt with individual films as an internally defined collection of segments through which codes cross and are deformed in the filmic "writing" (and so articles on codes sometimes dealt just as much with textual systems).[15] Some of the most important contributions in this vein linked this conception of textual systems to the operations of ideology. The two key contributions in this regard were probably the collective analysis by editors of *Cahiers du Cinéma*: "John Ford's *Young Mr. Lincoln*" and Stephen Heath's book-length consideration of *Touch of Evil*, "Film and System: Terms of Analysis."[16] The *Cahiers* text was written relatively early in the development of these ideas, and it was translated in a 1972 issue of *Screen*. It did not deal with Metzian categories, though it claimed to be engaged in a new kind of film analysis. It segmented the film in order to argue that its apparent unity was riven with ideological contradictions that were driving it, somewhat like a psychoanalytic symptom. Heath's 1975 tract engaged closely with Metz in a theoretical-methodological dialogue. Heath focused on the systematic way in which a film provokes and contains displacement and deformations of codes, essentially dealing with textual elements in a way that exceeds its own systematicity. The stated *Cahiers* goal was to rethink filmic textuality through ideology, and Heath's stated goal was to engage with Metz through microscopic attention to a single film. Both resorted to psychoanalytic language, though in different ways, to deal with heterogeneity and excess—notions crucial to the conceptions of spectatorship and subjectivity developed in *Screen*.

The Filmic Enunciation and Theory of the Subject in Screen

Realism and ideology, the semiotics of textuality: these were the broad headings developed in *Screen* by 1973–74 for the renovation of film theory and film. But there was a third area through which both were soon developed—an area that was perhaps the most distinctive and influential contribution of *Screen*. This was the psychic position allotted to the spectator by textual systems. Of course, earlier film theorists had included claims about what 1970s film theory soon labeled spectatorship. But there was something different about what transpired in the 1970s.

Conceptions of the spectator in *Screen* appealed to the theorization of the subject or subjectivity as developed in the new poststructuralism. This type of theorization was only partly psychological, if at all, because it was actually based in theories of language and semiotic processes, along with some philosophical argument. The strongest influence in this regard was Lacanian psychoanalytic theory. At this time, the idea of the subject was becoming pervasive in a range of avant-garde continental critical theory. On the one hand, the concept of the subject denotes a philosophical, linguistic, and legal category postulating the human as a coherent agent. The subject is capable of choosing speech and actions, of making coherent meanings in language, and of bearing legal responsibility for its actions. On the other hand, subjectivity also connotes a multilayered, depth model of self-experience as complex and contradictory. In new work Althusser himself had connected this category to his conception of ideology. He redefined ideology as "the imaginary relation of individuals to their real conditions of existence." Previously, Althusser had said that ideological practices produce ideas and concepts; here he added that it is grounded in an "imaginary" *relation*, which is the experience of being a subject. He proposed that when ideology is operating efficiently, institutions construct discourses that "interpellate" or "hail" — that is, address, appeal to — an individual as a free and unified subject.[17] An account of the subject as a social, ideological category fit well enough with critiques of auteurism previously published in the new *Screen*, but, implicitly parallel with Althusser's newer formulation, the subject investigated in *Screen* for film theory was that of the addressee or viewer of a film. This development can be traced back to the recognition-misrecognition structure polemically delineated in the earlier translations from French debates over realism. But now many articles engaged in intense theorization of the textual construction of subjects and, with the growing importance of psychoanalytic theory, subjectivity — though on the basis of the ideological and textual theory already established in the journal. This often came to be posed through a metaphor of positionality, as in what "position" or positions does the text offer to its addressee. All of this defined a whole mode of thinking about film: the study of spectatorship. In the mid-1970s the idea of spectatorial position was institutionalized as a leading area of work in film studies. *Screen* was central to conceptualizing and elaborating this field.

As with most of the journal's forays into semiotics, this kind of move was often explained beginning from terminology of structural linguistics, like *énoncé* (what is enunciated or "said") and *énonciation* or enunciation (the "speech act" that produces meanings, which encompasses the nature of the spectators presupposed by filmic signification). Structural linguistics proposed that all verbal languages include signifiers that refer an utterance (the *énoncé*) to the speech situation in which it occurs (the *énonciation*). Major examples include personal pronouns *I* and *you*, adverbs of time and place, and verbal tense markers. One widely cited linguist, Emile Benveniste, made much of the distinction between a text or utterance that includes marks of the present enunciation and one that suppresses such marks. He called the first one "discourse" and the second one "story" (*histoire.*) Film theorists, including Metz himself, sometimes compared this binary opposition to that between complicit and oppositional cinemas or transparency and foregrounding of the means of signification in films.

At least three claims related to these distinctions were of special consequence for 1970s film theory. First, any semiotic system or code cannot be considered a closed system. It can still be treated as a system, but one that includes indicators of something outside the structure of *langue* or the code, something understandable only in relation to the actual, concrete time and space of *parole* or speech. Second, the utterance (*énoncé*) provides definitions and meanings for that "outside" by employing such textual indicators. Third, such definitions and meanings include subjectivity itself. A commonsense account might have it that language requires a preexisting subject looking to identify with a personal pronoun. However, in structuralism and poststructuralism a radically inverse claim was now common. As Benveniste put it, "'Subjectivity' . . . is only the emergence in being of a fundamental property of language."[18]

By extension, such principles would apply to other semiotic media and signifying systems such as cinema. Yet, as Metz always argued, linguistic categories could not be directly applied to cinema.[19] For *Screen*, then, assumptions were at once more general and more specific: all significations, including films, "address" and thereby offer definitions to a receiver, so there is such a thing as a filmic enunciation. But the film as *énoncé* does this by its own particular means, for its textual systems and the codes take shape in the organization of two-dimensional motion images and recorded sounds.

How does the flow of images and sounds in cinema address and thereby define positions for the spectator? This question led the investigation not to empirical viewers, but to textuality. In a major article synthesizing this approach, Stephen Heath wrote: "Film is not a static and isolated object but a series of relations with the spectator it imagines, plays and sets as subject in its movement."[20] This conceit, in which the film is a process that imagines the spectator rather than the other way around, suggests that the analysis of spectatorship deal with something a little like the ideal reader of narratological theory. It is not a matter of reading the minds of actual audiences, but the construction of a logic conditioning filmic textuality.

But on what grounds would one construct a logic of the enunciation, that is, infer the relations between particular textual procedures or textual systems and the spectator a film "imagines?" Another theoretical framework relating signification to textuality was necessary to justify this inference. From around 1973–74 on, the famous, even notorious answer in *Screen* became psychoanalytic. In one of its most influential contributions to film theory, the journal became an organ that encouraged original English-language work around the pertinence of Freud and Lacan for understanding cinema.[21]

There have been so many accounts of Lacan and Lacan-centered work in critical studies since the 1970s that it seems unnecessary to attempt one here, especially since Lacan's own corpus was constantly growing during this period, and at least some articles in *Screen* continued to elaborate or shift the appeal to his work. But it is worth noting that there were certain basic Lacanian motifs that were always important for developing *Screen*'s project in film theory. Since Lacan conceived of Freud's thesis of the unconscious with Saussurian structural linguistics in mind, psychoanalytic theory could become linked to the journal's ongoing interest in representation, codes, and textuality. Furthermore, Lacan seemed to supply a complex, theoretically radical elucidation of the recognition-misrecognition structures associated with ideology.

In particular, many contributors to *Screen* tended to extract his account of the development of a subject, from prelinguistic and nonsubjective being to a subjectivity in and through language. On that basis, claims could then be made about how cinema and filmic textualities activated the consequences of that process. The major dialectic emphasized in *Screen*'s appropriation of Lacan was that between Lacan's Imaginary and Symbolic Orders. The Imaginary is instituted as the infant develops an image of bodily coherence, which becomes the fundamental model of an early, narcissistic sense of self or ego. The Symbolic is instituted by the introduction of difference or contradiction, which threatens the dispersion of that realm of absolutely secured, unified identity. The Imaginary originates through what Lacan called the mirror phase, the simultaneous identification and misidentification of an infant's bodily image as the self. The Symbolic is accomplished through what Freud identified as symbolic castration, which involved the initiation of the unconscious and repression.

But Lacan associates the sexuality crises of the oedipal period with the child's "entrance" into language, the apprehension of difference as a principle of signification. From then on, the subject is a linguistic being who seeks relationships with others and with objects that could restore the loss of the ego of the mirror phase; that is, the subject seeks substitutes, representations, *signs* that would no longer be signs but the lost thing itself, which would end the trauma of castration. But the individual now exists within language and signification, and no sign can be the object it designates. This Symbolic Order is a universe of language and signification where the subject seeks proof of its secure identity, that is, points of identification. But it is a network of perpetual substitutions, of infinite deferral from one sign to another, of processes of displaced desire as opposed to the static, secure sense of self of the Imaginary. Thus, when a subject recognizes itself as a certain textual position, this is also an Imaginary misrecognition of the ego as central and the self as unified, for subjectivity is internally divided effects of the signifying chains that are the "world."

Theory of the Subject and Cinema: Four Examples

Between 1974 and 1976 several writers in *Screen* engaged in an aggressive exploration of such Lacanian ideas, but aimed them at cinematic signification. The Lacanian implantation became central to the journal's project (though not without controversy). Major articles, often by members of the editorial board, led the way for critical studies in general and film studies in particular in charting discussions of ideology, codes, and textual systems through psychoanalytic accounts of spectatorship. A number of these articles became canonical for film theory. As examples, let us take the widely cited work of just four writers for *Screen* engaged in this project: Colin MacCabe, Christian Metz, Stephen Heath, and Laura Mulvey.

Two essays by Colin MacCabe clearly show how the question of realism and ideology was soon routed through investigations of the spectator conceived as a textually implicated subject. In 1974 MacCabe defined realism and stylistic transparency by the ways a text addresses a spectator as a masterful subject rather than by codes of perceptual verisimilitude. MacCabe associates mainstream cinema with the nineteenth-century classic realist novel, claiming that both consist of a plurality of discourses. A text organizes these hierarchically, with one discourse functioning as a "metalanguage," having the power to judge the truth value of all other discourses. In the novel this metalanguage is the discourse of the omniscient narrator. In classical realist cinema, it is the narration of events as transmitted by the camera. MacCabe particularly stressed a filmic epistemology of mastery through vision: Dominant cinema implements an ideology of vision as truth, in which the image does not lie. This unifies the actual contradictory multiplicity from which filmic meanings are composed.

Thus, the bourgeois transparency attacked by *Cahiers du Cinéma* and *Ciné-thique* is here elaborated as an offer of security to a spectator as the subject of vision. MacCabe even constructs yet another typology of complicit and oppositional films, beginning from the question of whether or not they can evince contradiction, which is associated with the question of whether or not they can embody progressive ideologies and politics. And as with *Cahiers du Cinéma*, his typology includes not only extreme polarities (revolutionary and reactionary texts) but also mixed types (for example, "progressive realist" films and Rossellini). In his logic, the genuinely revolutionary text seems to equalize all discourses of a text, inserting the subject into a network of articulations rather than a transparency and a unity.

On the other hand, MacCabe's use of Lacan leads to radical claims for the transformations of film theory as well as cinema. In his account, a classic real-ist text is sustained through a relation of mutual reflection or specularity be-tween text and spectator, for the two formally echo one another as seamless coherencies. They both exclude heterogeneity and signification. A specularity that constructs a masterful subject position through vision recalls the Lacan-ian mirror phase. In a 1976 reconsideration, MacCabe emphasized even more strongly a Lacanian account of the otherness of the real in relation to the gaze, but the gaze is considered through later Lacan. He now aligns the spectator of all classical realist cinemas with an empiricist epistemology, because of the underlying idea that unmediated evidence of a real is available to perception, which centers all on an unquestioned subjectivity. Furthermore, he subsumes all of classical film theory under this epistemology. His two articles include cri-tiques not only of Bazin's realist theory but even of Eisenstein's montage theory, for presupposing the unifications of text and subject based on the underlying empiricist assumptions of the classical realist text.

MacCabe's work neatly knots three central regimes of the film theory being hammered out in *Screen* by the mid-1970s: a description of the alleged textual transparency of the mainstream or classical text, an account of the relations of subjectivity that textuality supposedly underpins, and a politics of filmic tex-tuality. Some of his claims are not specific to cinema, for example, his concept of the classic realist text and empiricist epistemology. But other claims suggest that cinema has specific social or ideological functions within this constel-lation, for example, the ideology of vision and the cinematic impression of reality.

Perhaps the most cited overview of cinematic specificity and spectatorship during the 1970s was Christian Metz's "The Imaginary Signifier," a translation that seemed an integral part of *Screen*'s theoretical project, for it appeared there almost simultaneously with its French publication.[22] In this article, Metz did not quite focus on cinematic technology as such (though he does assume Jean-Louis Baudry's much-cited ideological and psychoanalytic formulations on the cinematic apparatus).[23] Instead, he starts from a carefully phrased question: What is specific to cinematic signification that psychoanalysis can help ex-plain? Metz mostly treats the cinematically specific signifier as a moving two-dimensional image and then offers an account of the spectator implied by this signifier (though he notes that extracinematic codes may be more important constituents of a filmic meaning than specifically cinematic codes). Agreeing with Lacanians that "the psychoanalytic itinerary is from the outset a semiological one,"[24] Metz explicitly treats his turn to psychoanalytic theory as a continuation of his earlier work.

He proceeds by comparing cinema to major stages in the psychoanalytic history of the subject: first, the originary perceptual drives activated in cinema (seeing/scopic and hearing/invocatory, but the great emphasis is on the visual); second, identification and sameness in cinema; and third, difference and desire. On the drives, he makes a point fundamental to all the rest: The spectator is present in the theater and has a real perception of a field of objects; however, the objects are in fact absent and do not exist in real space and time. Thus, for the impression of reality to be sustained, the spectator must put greater psychic investment into cinema to overcome absence than he or she would in, say, a theatrical performance of the same narrative. Metz calls cinema the imaginary signifier not because it does without the Symbolic and codification (an impossibility) but because it stimulates an extra investment of the Imaginary.

This is the basis for the centerpiece of Metz's psychoanalytic theory of cinematic specificity—his account of identification. It rests on another relation of presence and absence: in the heightened visuality of the cinematic situation, the spectator's body is really present in the theater, yet absent (not visible) on the screen. Now in Lacan's mirror phase, which is supposed to be the primal unconscious model for all subsequent identifications, an image of one's own body is crucial. Since a subject and therefore identification is necessary for any meaningful signification, Metz infers that cinema requires a comparatively more intense identificatory investment to counter the body's absence. At this level also, cinematic spectatorship entails more dependence on the Imaginary than do other media or art forms. Metz then derives much-noted theoretical formulations concerning the organization of cinematic identification. Rather than identifying with an image of oneself, the spectator identifies with the idea of a pure act of powerful perception, manifested in a look whose textual delegate is the camera. Phenomenologically, everything in the film exists for this decorporealized, synthesizing look—a position comparable to philosophy's transcendental ego. Identification with the camera is therefore "primary cinematic identification," on which all films depend. Other identifications (with character point of view or eyelines, for example) are "secondary cinematic identifications." The latter are ways of organizing or vectoring the primary cinematic identification.

With reference to difference and desire, the absence of the object of perception once more governs. The objects to which cinema's impression of reality gives such force are really absent. This suggests that cinema is "infinitely desirable" because it is "never possessible." Metz goes on to compare cinema to a number of perversions highlighted in psychoanalytic theory: the position of the spectator in the theater is compared to voyeurism, to peeping tomism, and to the primal scene described by Freud, for in all the object is elsewhere, therefore supposedly unaware of, the looking subject. Stylization of the image and formal play with it are compared to fetishism, and the cinematic signifier is said to be "more Oedipal" in type than that of other media. Metz argues that the subjective experience of cinema edges onto a regime of mild perversion psychoanalytically speaking, but one that is socially legitimized because it is so widely institutionalized. Yet, he briefly speculates, it is the institutionalization of a more isolated, less communal spectator than that of the theater, and in that is perhaps generated by individualistic ideologies of modern bourgeois societies.

This is a broad Metzian gesture toward possible ideological implications of his account of cinematic specificity. But for writers closely associated with *Screen's* radical materialist project, film theory would have to make ideology central to any appropriation of psychoanalysis and cinema. A crucial figure in this period was Stephen Heath, who served on the journal's editorial board and published extensively in it. For him, psychoanalytic theory was especially germane to understanding the processual, heterogeneous nature of textual systems, in relation to the material organization of films as images and sounds. In several elaborate articles, Heath interrogated Lacanian theory and provided intricate conceptualizations of the semiotics and operations of enunciations in filmic texts. He emphasized filmic textuality as the organization of heterogeneous signifying materials, and he characterized oppositional cinemas as exposure of the productivity of signification, a productivity obfuscated in mainstream cinema.[25]

One major synthesis of Heath's conception of cinema was the lengthy 1975 essay "Narrative Space." In it, photographic and film cameras are treated as extending a Renaissance model of visual representation, identified with central perspective. This *quattrocento* perspective, Heath argues, addresses itself to a single, stable viewpoint outside the picture, in relation to a central vanishing point inside the image. Its ideal of perfect seeing is a subject visually defined as centered, fixed in space, and stable in time. In fact, for Heath this apparently all-seeing centrality is dependent on what cannot be perceived, it is produced in a potentially unstable process, and it is historical. As such it universalizes a sociocultural ideal of visual knowledge as an isolated, individualized, hypostatized gaze that defines a dematerialized subject perfectly situated for direct access to the real outside sociality or contradiction. The subsequent history of Western imaging apparatuses involves innumerable repetitions of this ideological norm, and divergences from it are treated as deviations rather than alternatives.

These claims align Heath with certain French art and film theorists, but for Heath they evince a more fundamental principle underlying *all* representation: representation tries to propose subject positions outside process, but such positions are actually constructed through interminable processes. The representational dialectic between position and process is fundamental to the intertwining of ideology, signification, and psyche. There are parallels with MacCabe's ideology of vision as well as Metz's primary cinematic identification. But Heath placed much more explicit emphasis on examining the excesses, flows, and potential instabilities that subtend the desire for stable positionality. Psychoanalytic theory describes these in relation to the unconscious. In Heath, they are evinced in the microscopic operations of a filmic text, which becomes a dynamic process of mobilizing and organizing these excesses. His characterization of cinema as a "specific signifying practice" led to a sustained examination of relations between textual forms and practices in films, on the one hand, and those excessive processes, which he tended to identify with the specific material characteristics of cinema, on the other.

In "Narrative Space" cinema seems to literalize the dialectic of position and process. The claim of cinema is said to be extending perspectival mastery into movement and time. But since the ideal subject position in this genealogy is fixed and stable, there is a fundamental contradiction within cinema itself. The very mobility that defines cinema as enhancing subjectivity in its supposedly wider access to the real would threaten the perspectival ideal of fixed, powerful subjectivity. On the one hand, then, cinema must contain this threat to sustain its ideological operations around spectatorship and subjectivity; on the other hand, it depends on provoking this threat, because it is defined as a kind of mastery in movement.

Heath decides that this containment works through an enunciation that does not so much suppress excess as aim it at a subject to reassure its mastery. This explains the centrality of narrative to film history and mainstream film especially. Its logic of actions and meaning provide parameters for organizing space. Citing manuals of filmmaking as well as film theory, Heath analyzes dominant filmmaking codes, such as those of invisible editing, conventions of camera placement, looking itself (eyeline matching, point-of-view editing), sound-image relations and so forth. Spectators are presented with not one viewpoint, as in a painting or photograph, but rather with a series of viewpoints centered on narrative events and meanings (shots), which then become inadequate as the movement and change that define cinema take charge. This fluctuation provokes a desire that is then answered by another viewpoint, which is itself soon challenged. Cinema is here a process of perpetual repositioning and perpetually temporary restabilization. This oscillation of decentering-recentering organizes space in the time of the film, and its stabilization is rationalized by narrative.

For Heath subject positioning is interminable, like desire in the strong psychoanalytic sense of the term; it provokes, counters, and then reactivates a subject's inadequacies with respect to meaning and identity. His commentaries on Lacan as well as his work on film consistently treat no textual system and no code as finished or closed in itself, but ideology seeks to obscure this unfinishedness by precipitating a subject position. The pleasure generated by a film's address to the subject is in the dialectic between the flickers of heterogeneity that are evidence of the productivity of the text, and the drive toward homogeneity and meaning through the subject. This is film history's version of the dialectic between position and process. Text and subject, inside and outside, depend on each other, as do the Symbolic and Imaginary. Psychoanalytically, the subject is always produced as a unity or coherence sealing a text or utterance—"stitched" or "sutured" into the fabric of an *énoncé* by the signifier. This theoretical metaphor had previously been imported from Lacanian discourse into film theory, but Heath conceived of it in broader and more thorough ways than had previous English-language appropriations (which tended to equate it with a small number of editing figures, especially the shot/reverse shot).[26]

This led Heath to make important claims and revisions within 1970s film theory. For example, if narrative meaning positions the spectator to overlook materiality, should oppositional cinema be a nonnarrative cinema? In "Narrative Space," Heath argues that the very centrality of narrative means that oppositional film would have to focus on the articulation of narrative, space, and meaning, working on it as the terrain of struggle rather than avoiding it. What of the much-discussed impression of reality as stylistic transparency or "invisibility" as the grounds of ideological subject positioning? For Heath, this is a mischaracterization. Pleasures of mainstream spectatorship consist in a perpetual back-and-forth between lack and fullness, and are dependent on controlled excess. Thus, "classical cinema does not efface the signs of production, it contains them, according to the narrativization described above . . .

what counts is as much the representation as the represented, is as much the production as the product."[27] Heath's elaborate work demonstrates that 1970s film theory was not a unified monolith.

Indeed, another major path in spectatorship studies and psychoanalytic film theory in *Screen* during these years was announced with the publication of Laura Mulvey's "Visual Pleasure and Narrative Cinema" in the autumn 1975 issue. It not only introduced feminism into *Screen*'s theoretical and ideological concerns but also had a remarkable impact throughout film and cultural studies as a foundational text in the appropriation of psychoanalytic theory by feminist film theory, which rapidly became one of the most important approaches in film studies. It has since been explicated, extended, and/or critiqued many times, not least by Mulvey herself. Here, we will simply note certain of its implications for those concerned with psychoanalytic approaches to textuality and cinema within *Screen*'s theoretical project.

Mulvey's much-noted central claim is that the textual norms of classical Hollywood studio cinema systematically construct a masculine spectator position. This is a matter of the hegemony of patriarchal ideology in the aesthetic characteristics of Hollywood studio cinema: mainstream film's "formal preoccupations reflect the psychical obsessions of the society which produced it," she writes.[28] On the one hand, Mulvey agrees that this cinema produces an illusionistic world for the spectator. On the other hand, more elaborately than anyone else in *Screen* at that point she understood cinema as building modes of looking into its presentation of the profilmic or fictional world. In her conception, the cinematic impression of reality or stylistic transparency becomes a system of looks and looking. Mainstream cinema subordinates looks existing in concrete space and time (that of the spectator at the screen and that of the camera at the profilmic) to looks that exist in a fabricated space and time (that of the characters at one another).

So far this might seem simply one emphasis in the theory of cinematic enunciation with which *Screen* was so concerned. However, Mulvey insists that the systematic interrelations of these types of looks in classical cinema imply subject positions, or identifications, organized around ideologically privileged *objects*. Just as "an idea of woman stands as a linchpin to the system" of patriarchal culture,[29] so is an idea of woman the linchpin of the classical cinematic signifying system. The figure of the woman is a privileged object for pleasurable looking and the figure of the male signifies the subject of the look.

Mulvey therefore argues that previous theoretical developments in *Screen* had underplayed the extent to which identification and cinematic enunciation depend on heterosexual, gendered agencies of looking and being looked at. These delimit the formal and stylistic parameters of mainstream cinema, which is defined as a matter of narrative and spectacle. Narrative is organized to provide moments of pleasurable spectacle, and spectacle is organized to articulate with a narrative, but the center of spectacle is the woman. Classical film narrative oscillates between or combines dynamic, fast-moving "sadistic" stories and dilated, slower, less eventful stories. Classical film spectacle correspondingly oscillates between or combines a three-dimensional "voyeuristic" space of action and a flatter, more piecemeal and stylized "fetishistic" space of heightened objects. At the first of these poles on both levels there is a drama of vision and action in which the beautiful female character resists her position as spectacle, and the need to reposition and punish her mandates narrative intensity; at the other pole, the female character accepts her position as spectacle, and this acceptance is stressed by a kind of visual excess around the female body and mise-en-scène, along with an attenuation of dramatic action. In the first case, the spectator's look is offered identification with the agent of punishment—the powerful male character inside the diegesis. In the second case, since the woman does not need to be dramatically controlled, "less" narrative is necessary and the spectator can identify his look more directly with that of the camera at the female, to which the female character can even play directly. Mulvey concluded that oppositional filmmaking must attack this form of pleasure and disarticulate this paradigm, even at the risk of unpleasure. For it depends on the ideological hegemony of the masculinized activity (figured in the look) as the model of a subject.

Many of Mulvey's concerns are recognizable within *Screen*: illusionism and classical cinema, ideology, oppositional cinema, the formal characteristics of textual systems, spectatorship, subjectivity, and psychoanalytic theory. However, she proposes a different emphasis. In the journal there was often something abstractly general about many of the major accounts of spectatorial positioning and ideology, no matter how close the attention to codic or textual systems. Take the examples mentioned above. For MacCabe, the ideology of vision rests on a formal and epistemological hierarchy of discourses, no matter what a film depicts. For Metz, psychoanalytic theory is a matter of signifying structures rather than concrete fantasies or bodies; thus, primary cinematic identification is with a kind of disembodiment, a transcendence that seems implicit in any film, and fetishism is a matter of technology and cinematic style rather than sexual perversion. For Heath, there is always the complex dialectic between position and process, no matter the specific meanings generated.

Mulvey implicitly challenges such abstract functional conceptions of ideology, identification, absence, and lack by asking what it means to think of the image and spectatorship starting from spectacle, which is partly defined by the types of objects it displays. Given Mulvey's view that the most ideologically privileged object of pleasurable looking in patriarchy is the female, this further mandated a greater emphasis on depicted bodies as signifiers for the look. This affects her description of even classical cinema. For example, compare the status of the camera in her account to MacCabe's ideology of vision or Metz's primary cinematic identification. For Mulvey, aligning the spectator's look with that of the camera is just one option for identification, one that occurs paradigmatically in fetishistic narrative-spectacles such as the musical. But in voyeuristic narrative-spectacle such as film noir, the spectator's look is identified with that of a male character. Identification and ideology operate here in an oscillation between camera and character, exteriority and interiority.

Or take the appeal to psychoanalytic theory. If all agree that the subject's anxiety in the face of difference is central to the operations of representation, signification, and therefore social formations, Mulvey insists that if heterogeneity and otherness revolve around a metaphor of castration, this means that they are gendered. The signifier for the foundational threat is the female body as opposed to that of the male. Even if psychoanalysis has its own patriarchal element, this is what makes it useful to her analysis of patriarchal ideology. Mulvey incorporates elements of the Lacanian turn, but she reemphasizes the Freudian point that lack is tied to readings of bodies, sexually differentiated bodies. Her argument becomes that the aesthetics of Hollywood and ideology converge not around the order of signification per se, but around a concrete oppression of an identifiable category of humans — women — and the significations systematically assigned to their bodies underpins that order.

Thus Mulvey's intervention rests on a concrete political perception as a starting point for her theoretical claims. Few other theorists for *Screen*, in spite of their professed Althusserianism and Marxism, were able to achieve such forceful claims for the centrality of, say, social class to systems of signification except through relatively general notions of "bourgeois" subjectivity. While there were many complex achievements in theories of textuality and cinema in the *Screen* of the 1970s, Mulvey's integration of a more concrete political grouping with the new theory was an important achievement and challenge.

Conclusion

This review of a few of the most consequential writers for *Screen* in the 1970s only exemplifies certain nodes in the film-theoretical framework developed in the journal. During these years *Screen* published much more of significance that cannot be discussed in this space, not only in film theory and textual analysis but also in areas such as genre, television, support systems for independent cinema, and even a bit of industrial history. But with Mulvey's article, we at least broach some of the tensions and issues within the terms of *Screen*'s own project. These sometimes led to splits, as we have seen, but could also lead to productive development and critique. Even the tensions helped set the intellectual and scholarly agenda for English-language university film studies as a whole as the field emerged institutionally and defined itself in the 1970s.

In fact, *Screen* in the 1970s arguably included precursors to major critiques of the type of theory that the journal was so instrumental in defining. Feminist film and cultural studies soon found a constant reference point in "Visual Pleasure and Narrative Cinema," thus partaking of the problematics of subjectivity, desire, textuality, and ideology for which the journal became known; and yet this feminism also posed challenges to the emphases of the journal's project that it rarely confronted squarely. At different points and to different degrees, individuals who made important contributions to feminist film scholarship, such as Pam Cook, Christine Gledhill, Claire Johnston, and Annette Kuhn, participated in the journal in various editorial capacities. Nevertheless, even late in the decade feminist work was still the exception rather than the norm in *Screen*.[30]

From another viewpoint and with manipulative hindsight, one might also find premonitions of the later cognitivist critique of 1970s film theory in an exchange between David Bordwell and Ben Brewster about Eisenstein and Vygotsky. More apparent at the time was the opposition between psychoanalytic or textually oriented film theory and cultural studies approaches, which burgeoned in the 1980s. *Screen*'s Marxism was certainly intellectually energetic and decisive about conceptions of ideology, textuality, and subjectivity in cinema. It was also fertile for film theory, beginning from the new ways it foregrounded the very history of film theory. But it was also notoriously vague when it came to matters of class and historical particularity. By 1977 these issues were already a topic of debate within the very pages of *Screen*, between Rosalind Delmar and members of the Birmingham Centre for Cultural Studies. Furthermore, around the same time at least some members of the *Screen* editorial board wished to modify theories of textuality and subjectivity so that they could encompass cultural and historical particularity. The major example is perhaps Paul Willemen, who began pushing toward another conceptualization of psychoanalytic film and textual theory, such that it would open up to political and historical specificity. Willemen thought that this could be done not by rejecting the former but by simultaneously pluralizing and localizing the conception of enunciative structures of texts.[31]

All of this suggests that *Screen* served in part as an agenda-setting platform for the rapid takeoff of film studies as an institutionalized field. The 1970s was a period when critical-historical film and media studies was expanding, establishing its own university departments, its own journals, and its own canonical debates. Within the United Kingdom, the nature of thinking about film was indeed transformed and, furthermore, the impact was international. But whatever the intellectual attractiveness of *Screen*'s work at this point for a new generation of film theorists and scholars, it is finally worth noting that this success was also enabled by a particular infrastructural conjunction.

It is instructive to compare the infrastructural situation of *Screen* to those of its closest French sources and intellectual allies. *Cahiers du Cinéma* had previously been established as the most important film review in the world. It covered current films and was a centerpiece of French film culture, and thus its readership included more general, nonacademic (though *cinéphilic*) interests. It was a major cultural event when *Cahiers* turned to dense politicized theory after the French rebellions of May 1968, and it reverted to its review function before the end of the 1970s. *Cinéthique* was shorter-lived (approximately 1969–85), and it was conceived as a politically radical journal founded by critics and filmmakers to rethink cinema in revolutionary ways after May 1968. A politicized readership was undoubtedly the very basis of its existence. Like *Cahiers*, *Screen* was able to attain relative permanence, and intermittently it sought connection with contemporary British film culture, especially its independent and avant-garde sectors. But it never saw its primary function as comprehensively reviewing current films. Like *Cinéthique*, it sought a radical rethinking of cinema, often with political rationales. On the other hand, throughout this period *Screen* depended on an audience in academic film studies, and it helped establish film studies. Not only was it the official journal of SEFT, it also relied on funding from the British Film Institute.

This meant that, unlike either *Cahiers* or *Cinéthique*, *Screen* constantly had to negotiate its politicized theory and critique with pedagogical commitments and institutional justifications. (One tactic was to try to give *Screen* more freedom by the regular publication of *Screen Education*, a companion journal, published by SEFT between 1971 and 1982, which was concerned more directly with approaches to the study of film and television in the classroom.) In that regard, *Screen* combined the politicized ground-clearing of its radical materialist editorial faction with claims to methodological rigor, as well as claims to academic innovation perhaps derived from the original educationist faction. In the 1970s, when programmatic journals were so crucial to scholarly discourse, this combination may have been most determinative for *Screen*.[32]

This could sometimes make for difficulties in reconciling the new *Screen*'s intellectual ambitions with its financial base and original readership. But it also provided connections and opportunities to disseminate its concerns. Indeed, SEFT itself published a number of books and pamphlets. They included not only occasional anthologies on specific topics from *Screen* but also original books and collections, often written by *Screen* editors and contributors. Furthermore, in the 1970s there were significant conferences and festivals that drew the participation of writers and editors connected to *Screen*. As one important example, at the Edinburgh Film Festival during these years the themes, discussions, and published programs were theoretically informed and involved in debates centered on *Screen*.[33]

Furthermore, many of those associated with *Screen* in the 1970s later gained university posts. But, at the time, stable and permanent academic positions in film were not plentiful, and certain of the editors and contributors were soon working at the British Film Institute as education officers or in publications. BFI publications did not function exclusively in the interests of *Screen*'s theoretical configurations, but the BFI now had editors who were sympathetic to such concerns and spread the demand for rigor, seriousness, and new thinking about film. Thus BFI publications became one of the most important venues for cutting-edge work in film throughout the English-speaking world.

All of this is connected to a general point about the impact of the "new" *Screen*'s original ambitions in the 1970s. The ambitions and the approaches articulated in the journal, along with its internal conflicts and contradictions (as well as externally controversial aspects), were instrumental in shaping debates defining a rapidly expanding film studies. They were all also dependent on an infrastructure of publication and dissemination venues. There was a kind of "expanded *Screen*," a penumbra of activities extending beyond the pages of the journal—conferences, other publications, and articles in other journals. These inserted *Screen*'s concerns into classrooms and continued to foreground its conceptions. In this sense, at least, the negotiation of *Screen*'s political claims with its infrastructural requirements was actually successful. The conception of a textual politics of cinema informed by the theoretical configurations hammered out, attacked, revised, and defended in the journal has become a matter of debate (as it always was). But *Screen*'s position is now widely accepted as a major one within the history of film theory, and it was a crucial implantation at a key moment in the history of film studies.

Notes

1. *Screen* 20 (winter 1979–80): 7–14.
2. See Mark Jancovic, "Screen Theory," in *Approaches to Popular Film*, ed. Joanne Hollows and Mark Jancovich (New York: Manchester University Press, 1995), 123–50. For an early attempt to attribute a theoretical unity to the journal's theoretical project, see Philip Rosen, "*Screen* and the Marxist Project in Film Criticism," *Quarterly Review of Film* 2 (1977): 273–87.
3. For a brief editorial history, see the journal's Web site at http://www.screen.arts.gla.ac.uk/pages/history.html.
4. Important examples of issues composed mostly of translations include the winter 1971–72 and winter 1974 numbers, which were primarily concerned with Russian Formalist and Futurist views of film mostly from the 1920s; a special double issue on the work of Christian Metz (spring-summer 1973); and the first of two special issues on Brecht and cinema (summer 1974). "The Imaginary Signifier" appeared in *Screen* at the same time as the French publication (see the discussion below).
5. Goffredo Fofi, "The Cinema of the Popular Front in France (1934–1938)," *Screen* 13 (winter 1972–73): 5–57; Mario Cannella, "Ideology and Aesthetic Hypotheses in the Criticism of Neo-realism," *Screen* 14 (winter 1973–74): 5–60; Franco Fortini, "The Writers' Mandate and the End of Anti-Fascism," *Screen* 15 (spring 1974): 33–70.
6. See Alan Lovell, "The BFI and Film Education," *Screen* 12 (autumn 1971): 13–25, and "Notes on British Film Culture," *Screen* 12 (summer 1972): 5–15. Sam Rohdie, "Education and Criticism: Notes on Work to Be Done," *Screen* 12 (spring 1971): 9–13; and "Review: *Movie Reader, Film as Film*," *Screen* 13 (winter 1972–73): 135–45. See also Claire Johnston, "Film Journals: Britain and France," *Screen* 12 (spring 1971): 39–46. For the 1976 resignations, see Edward Buscombe, Christine Gledhill, Alan Lovell, and Christopher Williams, "Statement: Psychoanalysis and Film," *Screen* 16 (winter 1975–76): 119–30; and "Why We Have Resigned from the Board of *Screen*," *Screen* 17 (summer 1976): 106–9. Between 1971 and 1982 SEFT also published *Screen Education*, a companion journal with the avowed intention of meeting some of the concerns of the educationists.
7. These issues were, respectively, summer 1971, winter 1971–72, and spring 1972.

8. For Soviet materials, see *Screen* 12 (winter 1971–72). There is a collection of writings of Osip Brik in *Screen* 15 (autumn 1974), along with Boris Eikhenbaum, "Problems of Film Stylistics," 7–32. See also in *Screen* (winter 1974–75), Ronald Levaco, "Eikhenbaum, Inner Speech and Film Stylistics," 47–58, and Paul Willemen, "Reflections on Eikhenbaum's Concept of Internal Speech in the Cinema," 59–71.

9. The exchange discussed here was composed of the following essays as they appeared in *Screen*: Jean-Louis Comolli and Jean Narboni, "Cinema/Ideology/Criticism (1)," 12 (spring 1971): 27–36; Gérard Leblanc, "Direction: Parenthesis or Indirect Route: An Attempt at Theoretical Definition of the Relationship between Cinema and Politics," and Comolli and Narboni, "Cinema/Ideology/Politics (2)," all in *Screen* 12 (summer 1971): 121–55. The confrontation was continued on the different ground of the usefulness of Eisenstein and Russian Formalism in Marcelin Pleynet, "The 'Left' Front of the Arts: Eisenstein and the Old 'Young Hegelians'"; and Comolli and Narboni, "Cinema/Ideology/Criticism (2) Continued: Examining a Critique at Its Critical Point," 13 (spring 1972): 101–31. In other work during this period, *Cahiers* was also intensively recovering and rethinking film culture and theory from the Soviet 1920s.

10. Comolli and Narboni, "Cinema/Ideology/Politics," 1.

11. Scripts for Straub and Huillet's films *History Lessons* and *Arnold Schoenberg's Accompaniment to a Cinematograph Scene* were published in *Screen* 17 (spring 1976); and the script of *Fortini-Cani* was published in *Screen* 19 (summer 1978). The script for Mulvey and Wollen's *Riddles of the Sphinx* was published in *Screen* 18 (summer 1977), and they were also interviewed about an earlier film, *Penthesilea: Queen of the Amazons* in *Screen* 15 (autumn 1974): 120–34. On Peter Gidal, see Deke Dusinberre, "Consistent Oxymoron: Peter Gidal's Rhetorical Strategy," *Screen* 18 (summer 1977): 79–88; and Peter Gidal, "The Anti-Narrative," *Screen* 20 (summer 1979): 73–92, with Stephen Heath, "Afterword," 93–100.

12. *Screen* 14 (spring-summer 1973).

13. Christian Metz, *Language and Cinema*, translated by Donna-Jean Umiker-Sebeok (The Hague: Mouton, 1974), e.g., 70–175, 102–4, 150, 180–82; quoted passages on page 103. There was, of course, also interest in Metz's earlier views and how they had changed. See Christian Metz, *Film Language: A Semiotics of the Cinema*, translated by Michael Taylor (New York: Oxford, 1974), 61–63n, 68n, 111–13.

14. For articles investigating codes in *Screen*, see the following, listed in chronological order: Thierry Kuntzel, "The Treatment of Ideology in the Textual Analysis of a Film" 14 (autumn 1973), 44–54; René Gardies, "Structural Analysis of a Textual System: Presentation of a Method" 15 (spring 1974), 11–31; Raymond Bellour, "The Obvious and the Code," *Screen* 15 (winter 1974–75), 7–17; Kari Hanet, "The Narrative Text of *Shock Corridor*," 15 (winter 1974–75) 18–28; Raymond Bellour, "The Unattainable Text," 16 (autumn 1975) 19–28; Edward Branigan, "Formal Permutations of the Point-of-View Shot," 16 (autumn 1975) 54–64; Peter Baxter, "On the History and Ideology of Film Lighting," 16 (autumn 1975), 83–106. Linda Williams, "Hiro-

shima and Marienbad: Metaphor and Metonymy," 17 (spring 1976) 34–39; Roger Silverstone, "An Approach to the Structural Analysis of the Television Message," 17 (summer 1976) 9–40; Kristin Thompson and David Bordwell, "Space and Narrative in the Films of Ozu," 17 (summer 1976) 41–73; Edward Branigan, "The Space of *Equinox Flower*," 17 (summer 1976) 74–105; Mark Nash, *Vampyr* and the Fantastic," 17 (autumn 1976) 29–67; Bill Nichols, "Documentary theory and Practice," 17 (winter 1976–77) 34–48; Linda Williams, "The Prologue to *Un chien andalou*: the Surrealist Film Metaphor" 17 (winter 1976–77) 24–33; Stephen Crofts and Olivia Rose, "An Essay Towards *Man with a Movie Camera*," 18 (spring 1977) 9–60; Phillip Drummond, "Textual Space in *Un chien andalou*," 18 (autumn 1977) 55–119; John O. Thompson, "Screen Acting and the Commutation Test," 19 (summer 1978) 55–69; Edward Branigan, "Subjectivity Under Siege—From Fellini's *8 1/2* to Oshima's *The Story of a Man Who Left His Will on Film*," 19 (spring 1978) 7–40. The last, relatively late example occasioned the most extraordinary case of a rejoinder to a contributor by an editorial board member, Paul Willemen, "Notes on Subjectivity: On Reading 'Subjectivity Under Siege,'" 19 (spring 1978), 41–69. As noted below, Willemen used the pretext of a response to Branigan for a major theoretical formulation of his own, to argue for his own modifications in the *Screen* line. See also Jacqueline Rose, "Paranoia and the Film System," 17 (winter 1976/7), 85–104, for a reconsideration of semiotic systematicity in terms of psychoanalytic theory, with feminist implications.

15. Some examples include René Gardies, "Structural Analysis of a Textual System," translated by Diana Matias, *Screen* (winter 1974–75): 11–31; Stephen Crofts and Olivia Rose, "An Essay Towards *Man with a Movie Camera*," *Screen* 18 (spring 1977): 9–60; and Philip Drummond, "Textual Space in *Un chien andalou*," *Screen* 18 (autumn 1977): 55–119.

16. Editors of *Cahiers du cinéma*, "John Ford's *Young Mr. Lincoln*," *Screen* 13 (autumn 1972): 5–44. Stephen Heath, "Film and System: Terms of Analysis," *Screen* 15 (spring 1975): 7–77 and *Screen* 16 (summer 1975), 91–113.

17. Louis Althusser, "Ideology and Ideological State Apparatuses: Notes Towards an Investigation," in *Lenin and Philosophy and Other Essays*, translated by Ben Brewster (New York: Monthly Review Press, 1978), 127–86.

18. Emile Benveniste, *Problems in General Linguistics*, translated by Mary Elizabeth Meeks (Coral Gables Fla.: University of Miami Press, 1971), 224, cf. 226.

19. For a more literalistic experiment at finding "filmic shifters" in *Screen*, see Nash, "*Vampyr* and the Fantastic." On Benveniste's terms and cinema, a short, much-cited consideration that turns to psychoanalytic theory is Christian Metz, "Story/ Discourse (A Note on Two Kinds of Voyeurism)," translated by Celia Britton and Annwyl Williams, in Metz, *The Imaginary Signifier: Psychoanalysis and the Cinema* (Bloomington: Indiana University Press, 1982), 89–98.

20. Stephen Heath, "Narrative Space," *Screen* 17 (autumn 1976): 97.

21. The only major translations of psychoanalytic theory are in a special section on the

Lacanian concept of suture and its application to film in *Screen* 18 (winter 1977–78): 23–76, which includes translations of Jacques-Alain Miller, "Suture (Elements of the Logic of the Signifier)" and Jean-Pierre Oudart, "Cinema and Suture," along with Stephen Heath's commentary, "Notes on Suture." This section can be considered a reply to certain less-nuanced articles in *Film Quarterly*, which introduced the Lacanian metaphor of suture into English in Daniel Dayan's summary of Oudart, "The Tutor-Code of Classical Cinema," *Film Quarterly* (fall 1974): 22–31, and a critique by William Rothman, "Against the System of the Suture," *Film Quarterly* (fall 1975): 44–50. As noted below, Metz's "The Imaginary Signifier" was published almost simultaneously in English and French.

22. Christian Metz's "The Imaginary Signifier," translated by Ben Brewster, *Screen* 16 (summer 1975): 15–76, was published as "Le signifiant imaginaire," *Communications*, no. 23 (May 1975).

23. Jean-Louis Baudry, "Ideological Effects of the Basic Cinematographic Apparatus," and "The Apparatus: Metapsychological Approaches to the Impression of Reality in Cinema," from 1970 and 1975 respectively, are both included in *Narrative, Apparatus, Ideology: A Film Theory Reader*, edited by Philip Rosen (New York: Columbia University Press, 1986), 286–318.

24. Metz, "The Imaginary Signifier," 14.

25. See above for some of Heath's articles, including his editorial work on Metz and his book-length analysis of the textual system *Touch of Evil*, published in 1975. In addition, see the following, all in *Screen*: "Lessons from Brecht," 15 (summer 1974): 103–28; "From Brecht to Film," 16 (winter 1975–76): 34–45; "Narrative Space," 17 (autumn 1976): 68–112; "*Anata Mo*," 17 (winter 1976–77): 49–66; "Notes on Suture," 18 (winter 1977–78): 48–76; "Television: A World in Action" (with Gillian Skirrow), 18 (summer 1977): 7–60; "Difference," 19 (autumn 1978): 51–112; and "Afterword" [to Peter Gidal, "The Anti-Narrative"], 20 (summer 1979): 93–100.

26. Thus, Heath's "Notes on Suture," which was a commentary on the concept and various explications and critiques by English-language film scholars, was preceded by translations of non-English-language texts that were sources of the concept in psychoanalytic thought and in film theory: Miller, "Suture (Elements of the Logic of the Signifier)," and Oudart, "Cinema and Suture," *Screen* 18 (winter 1977–78): 23–47. On suture, see also "Narrative Space," 98–100.

27. Heath, "Narrative Space," 97 (see also 90).

28. Laura Mulvey, "Visual Pleasure and Narrative Cinema," *Screen* 16 (autumn 1975): 8.

29. Ibid., 6.

30. Feminism did sometimes affect the work of some of *Screen*'s most prolific theorists, as when Stephen Heath began grappling with the theory and politics of gender and heterosexism not just in film but in psychoanalytic theory—even that of Lacan himself. See Heath, "Difference"; see also Rose, "Paranoia and the Film System."

31. David Bordwell, "Eisenstein's Epistemological Shift," *Screen* 15 (winter 1974–75):

29–46, including the introductory editorial note by Ben Brewster; David Bordwell, "Eisenstein's Epistemology: A Response," *Screen* 16 (spring 1975): 142–43; Rosalind Delmar, "'Class,' 'Culture,' and the Social Formation," *Screen* 18 (spring 1977), and the subsequent exchange between affiliates of the Centre for Contemporary Cultural Studies (Iain Chambers, John Clarke, Ian Connell, Lidia Curti, Stuart Hall, and Tony Jefferson) and Delmar entitled "Marxism and Culture," *Screen* 18 (winter 1977–78): 109–22; Branigan, "Subjectivity Under Siege"; and Willemen, "Notes on Subjectivity."

32. With number 10 (1974), *Screen Education Notes* became *Screen Education*, refurbished its editorial board, and began printing on a more regular basis. There was some overlap in the editorial board and contributors to *Screen Education*. *Screen Education* of the 1970s seems to have taken its name from an earlier incarnation, which from 1959 to 1969 was the direct predecessor to *Screen* itself.

33. John Ellis, ed., *Screen Reader 1: Cinema/Ideology/Politics* (London: SEFT, 1977) was the first of the *Screen* readers, which were published intermittently for the next two decades. The editorial board of *Screen* was asked to organize screenings and presentations on the theme of Brecht and cinema at the 1975 Edinburgh Film Festival. The bulk of the winter 1975/76 issue of *Screen* (16.4) was devoted to the proceedings of this event, but individuals associated with *Screen* had participated in it earlier. When the festival was organized as retrospectives of less-examined Hollywood auteurs (e.g., Sirk, Tashlin, Walsh, Tourneur) the festival publications included major reconsiderations and theoretically informed articles by individuals associated with *Screen* or its approaches, to the point where it might be argued that the theoretical interrogation of auteurism initiated in *Screen* was then carried out through Edinburgh publications. See Laura Mulvey and Jon Halliday, eds., *Douglas Sirk* (Edinburgh: Edinburgh Film Festival, 1972); Claire Johnston and Paul Willemen, eds., *Frank Tashlin* (Edinburgh: Edinburgh Film Festival and SEFT, 1973); Phil Hardy, ed., *Raoul Walsh* (Edinburgh: Edinburgh Film Festival, 1974); and Claire Johnston and Paul Willemen, eds., *Jacques Tourneur* (Edinburgh: Edinburgh Film Festival, 1975). After that the program left auteurism behind for theoretically consequent themes and became *Edinburgh Magazine*, with all of the marks of *Screen* including translations of Metz and Foucault as interviewed in *Cahiers du Cinéma*. See no. 1 (1976), subtitled "Psycho-Analysis/Cinema/Avant-Garde," and no. 2 (1977), subtitled "History/Production/Memory."

(Re)Inventing *Camera Obscura*

AMELIE HASTIE, LYNNE JOYRICH,

PATRICIA WHITE, AND SHARON WILLIS

A man of about thirty strikes us as a youthful, somewhat unformed individual. . . . A woman of the same age, however, often frightens us by her psychical rigidity and un-changeability. . . . It is as though, indeed, the difficult development to femininity had ·exhausted the possibilities of the person concerned.
—Sigmund Freud, "Femininity"

The change seemed to have been accomplished painlessly and completely and in such a way that Orlando herself showed no surprise at it. Many people . . . hold . . . that such a change of sex is against nature. . . . It is enough for us to state the simple fact: Orlando was a man till the age of thirty; when he became a woman and has remained so ever since.
—Virginia Woolf, *Orlando*

■ *Camera Obscura* turned thirty in 2006. The editors eschewed, or neglected, marking the anniversary at twenty-five, a somewhat unformed age, in favor of the celebration of a moment of remarkable potential—perhaps radical change-·ability, as Woolf, if not Freud, would have it. We are marking this historical occasion by writing the history of the journal.[1] This essay therefore reflects on the history, theory, and practice of the journal as it has intersected with the history, theory, and practice of the discipline of film studies.

Most notably, *Camera Obscura* and its history have been unified by the very collective nature of the journal and thus through our shared intellectual curi-

Feminist Looks. *Camera Obscura* issues 2, 20–21, and 54 display the consistency and range of the journal's interest in feminism, media culture, and imagining the various ways that women look.

Camera Obscura issue 2: Hitchcock's *Marnie* and feminist production looms large in the early pages of the journal. (Cover image from *Marnie*, Alfred Hitchcock, 1964)

Camera Obscura 20–21: More than sixty feminist film and television scholars consider the historical and theoretical impact of spectatorship studies in the special double-issue "Spectatrix." (Cover image of Theda Bara, publicity still)

Camera Obscura 54: With a focus on feminist video production, this issue's cover recalls earlier designs and displays the journal's ongoing and widening concerns. (Cover image from *Fountain*, Patty Chang, 1999) osity, theoretical goals, and political investments. In what follows, this unity and our differences are equally apparent. The following sections—each pondering *Camera Obscura*'s theory and practice, each written by one of our editors—interact and intertwine with one another. At times the observations interrupt one another; at other times they continue a thought, occasionally reiterating a particular point and occasionally reframing the issues. Their organization is modeled after a collectively written piece entitled "Feminism and Film: Critical Approaches" that appeared in the first issue of the journal.[2] This present essay thus embodies the history and original aims of *Camera Obscura*. We have, nevertheless, altered the organization of that earlier model by refining it to meet our current needs. In this way, what follows embodies the transformations—and even contradictions—that have been inherent to the journal from its beginnings. The original statement by the collective used the following section headings: context, text, methodology, production. We liked the simplicity of those titles, but we have added to them more descriptive subtitles. Furthermore, we have altered their original arrangement, which we feel better permits us to narrate the journal's history and its approach over the years. In this way, the idealistic and prescriptive nature of the original piece is transformed into the retrospective bent of this current essay—though we also clearly maintain the idealism of the original editors. Given our shared interests and history, similar points invariably emerge in all of the contributions here; yet given our differences, each contribution also gives specific emphases to select topics, calling attention to particular aspects of our theory and practice.

The first section, for example, tends to the journal's institutional history—or, perhaps more accurately, its anti-institutional history. Related to that is the history of the journal's editorial collective, and so the second section considers the complicated practice of collectivity that has defined not only the journal's operation but also its political orientation. There are some aspects of that orientation that have remained constant over the journal's history—most notably, a commitment to feminist theory and practice. Yet as section three elaborates, other aspects have shifted: no longer just interested in the question of sexual difference as originally formulated, *Camera Obscura* is also now interested in questions of difference more broadly defined, equally invested in analyses of race, ethnicity, nationality, sexuality, gender expression, and generation. In addition to broadening our political and theoretical scope to encompass such concerns, *Camera Obscura* has also enlarged the scope of the texts it addresses, moving beyond a consideration of cinema alone to other media formations and institutions (television, music, photography, medical imaging, digital productions, and so on), both in relation to and in distinction from those of film. However, despite these changes and the varied political, theoretical, and textual commitments that they represent, there is something that has always held (and continues to hold) the journal together: an ongoing intellectual verve—the epistemological excitement of active cultural engagement—that both initiated the *Camera Obscura* project and continues to fuel the journal today. The last section of the essay thus attempts to capture some of the flavor of this energy and to clarify how it has both directed and redirected the journal over the course of its history.

All of these issues overlap; the sections therefore overlap as well. In perhaps classic *Camera Obscura* fashion, this is a truly self-reflexive piece: one in which the current editors reflect on their own and the journal's concerns; one in which the various contributions reflect one another; and one that, we hope, reflects the theory and practice, intellectual and political engagements, and personal and professional motivations that define our work. Such reflexivity is an intrinsic part of that work: it undergirds both what we do (producing a text that situates and critically comments on other cultural texts that themselves can be read as commenting on our cultural situation) and how we do it (processing such critique through our editorial practice of collective processing itself). Our approach to this history and overview has thus been personal, anecdotal, collective, individual, and even sometimes contentious. It is a kind of living history that is as much about the present work of collectivity as it is about the journal and its original aims. We believe that it therefore not only describes but itself enacts the way in which *Camera Obscura* operates.

Context: A Brief History

Camera Obscura emerged as a collective feminist response to a paradoxical tension between the presence of the image of women on screen in mainstream film and the absence of women in both the fields of mainstream film production and the emerging disciplinary production of film theory. Issues of the representation of women in film were central to the journal's original project, foregrounded by an emphasis on alternative women's production and on psychoanalytic and ideological inquiries into commercial and avant-garde cinema.

The journal was founded by four women who were just beginning graduate school at University of California, Berkeley: Janet Bergstrom, Sandy Flitterman, Elisabeth Lyon, and Constance Penley. They met while working on the magazine *Women and Film*, which had moved from Los Angeles in 1973 to be somewhat informally housed in the Pacific Film Archive. The four founders left *Women and Film* after two years because they wanted to engage with theoretical issues that were beyond the scope of the magazine and to experiment with the ideals of collective work. *Camera Obscura*'s first issue was published in 1976 and featured discussions of Jackie Raynal's *Deux Fois*, the work of Yvonne Rainer, and Jean-Louis Baudry's theory of the cinematographic apparatus. Subsequent issues were produced sporadically for three years then largely were regularized at three issues per annum. Some key essays in this new venture were collectively written, and the production of the journal was also collectively engineered. Members of the editorial group sought and received small amounts of funding through UC Berkeley and the city of Berkeley for the first four issues. By the fifth issue, *Camera Obscura* was partially funded by a grant from the National Endowment for the Arts, which was renewed for almost two decades. The high level of design and production values was enabled by the large number of graphic artists and fine arts printing facilities in the Bay Area, many of them also receiving crucial support from the NEA.

In its later years, the universities affiliated with the editors have supported the journal in large and small ways, through minor grants as well as through housing the journal. These institutions include the University of Rochester's Susan B. Anthony Center (1985–1990) and UC Santa Barbara's Department of Film Studies (since 1991). After ten years of "do-it-yourself publishing," the move to the University of Rochester provided the journal with its first non-P.O.-box address. This move also coincided with a subsidy (from Johns Hopkins University Press) to publish the journal. *Camera Obscura* would later be published by Indiana University Press (from 1992 to 2000) and then by Duke University Press (2000 to present). These varied institutional affiliations mark the ways in which *Camera Obscura* has been tied to the broader development of film studies in colleges and universities, yet they have also allowed relative independence for its collective members and its production of ideas. They further display how the journal is a collective enterprise, not just in the makeup of its editorial board but also in the ways it brings together multiple organizations and institutions. Of course, the latter is true of most academic journals, but, in the case of *Camera Obscura*, every element of its production is sparked by the collective action of its editorial members.

Indeed, given its philosophical as well as material condition as a collective enterprise, *Camera Obscura* has been actively formed by its editorial members as individuals and as a body of feminists working together. An important theoretical scope of the journal—its commitment to continental philosophies like psychoanalysis, semiotics, and apparatus theory—was influenced by the journal's original editors who studied abroad in France with teachers like Christian Metz and Raymond Bellour. These theorists themselves were early contributors to the journal, and so *Camera Obscura* (alongside other journals such as *Screen*) became an early leader in the larger turn toward continental theories in the evolution of film studies in the 1970s. Psychoanalysis functioned as a tool of interpretation for many *Camera Obscura* authors as this approach provided a model for rigorous textual analysis to consider the intricate workings of gender relations and the concomitant oppression of women as manifest symptomatically in film.

This same form of analysis was an intimate part of women's alternative production, also emphasized in the journal. As noted, the first issue of the journal showcased films by Jackie Raynal and Yvonne Rainer;[3] the second included work on films by Chantal Akerman, Marguerite Duras, and Babette Mangolte;[4] the double third/fourth issue included an essay on Dorothy Arzner's *Christopher Strong*;[5] and the fifth contained work on Sally Potter.[6] Alongside this attention to women's filmmaking practices, the second issue of the journal inaugurated a section entitled "Women Working," which highlighted ongoing work by women theorists and historians alongside the films of women artists and activists. In this capacity, *Camera Obscura* early on documented such projects as *The Legend of Maya Deren* (which sought to collect all writings by the pioneer avant-garde filmmaker), published brief reviews of new work by a range of feminist filmmakers, and included reports on feminist conferences. Hence, "Women Working" offered an expansive definition of feminist work in film, combining creative and intellectual, cinematic, and written production.

Camera Obscura was also known through its presence in other critical spaces, which helped to underscore its theoretical and collective project. For instance, as the feminist journal was emerging, board members Constance Penley and Janet Bergstrom contributed an essay to *Screen* (1978), in which they were identified as members of the "*Camera Obscura* editorial collective."[7] This contribution revealed something of a shared position between the journals, however contentious the debates about theoretical production were in *Screen* during this time.[8] It also pointed to the complementary projects underway in *Camera Obscura* between psychoanalytic/semiotic analysis and women's filmmaking practices, as well as to the tensions and contestations between these projects within the journal itself. These tensions were largely borne out through the deep textual analysis that became the journal's signature style. As the editors described it in the first volume of the journal: "Textual analysis considers the text (the film) as a dynamic process of the production of meanings, inscribed within the larger context of social relations. The text is seen not as a closed work, but as a discourse, a play of signification, dynamism and contradiction. This definition of text displaces the spectator as a fixed receiver of meaning; and implies an unfixing and unsettling of the spectator-screen relationship."[9]

This early and historical pronouncement of a commitment to seeing the text—which ultimately includes the theoretical text as well as the filmic one—as a dynamic process is repeatedly enacted in the ensuing history of the journal, as it seeks new texts and new textual approaches, the latter of which are often borne of moving-image media. While the journal's original context "evolved from the recognition of a need for theoretical study of film in this country from a feminist and socialist perspective," these goals remain current not only in the face of the threat of "postfeminism" (a sense that our work has already been done) but also in the continually expanding spaces of feminist inquiry, especially in those efforts to make that space broader and more inclusive.

Production: A Collective Fate

Those of us who came of age in the 1960s and 1970s know that the range of possible fates for collectives is limited. These unwieldy organizations strain with tensions that can easily tip their fragile balances. A collective can implode, reducing its size to a tiny kernel that threatens total collapse; it can explode, either by reciprocal purging or by expanding so far that it loses all shape. Or, the collective can mutate as the comings and goings of members redefine the group. In the case of *Camera Obscura*, of course, we have been dealing with two overlapping entities: the editorial collective and the journal itself. For all but one of the current editors (Constance Penley, who was part of the original collective), discovering *Camera Obscura* in a library, bookstore, classroom, or friend's office had a distinct impact on our professional direction and development. Before we knew the members of the collective, or understood the editorial practice, we were readers excited by this forum who aspired to place our work there. Indeed, the journal seemed to us to be carving out exactly the terrain that we hoped to inhabit as scholars in film, media, and feminism. So *Camera Obscura* made our work possible before we were recruited to make its work possible. And just as we were drawn to the journal through our own evolving networks of identification—professional and personal—so a shifting collective identification has continued to reshape the journal's project.

Surely the biggest force haunting collectives and collective work is temporality, both in the sense of history—it is a way of organizing work that many consider anachronistic—and in the sense of time consumed in the collective process. But equally important, in *Camera Obscura*'s case, is that its collective has persisted for nearly thirty years while its membership has undergone numerous shifts. While members have departed and arrived one by one, the evolving collective has taken a palimpsest form, as the editors embody the journal's various historical stages. Each new editor helps to reshape and reanimate the group, whose respect for the legacy of previous collectives casts change against the memory of past experience and practices. As a result, *Camera Obscura*'s culture allows for continuity that accommodates differences.

Camera Obscura's current shape is intimately tied to its history. Founded as a feminist collective in the 1970s, it remains marked by the legacies of both the feminism of the period (this includes the perhaps dated practice of consciousness raising) and the basics of Left political organizing. The journal also profited incalculably from the cultural shift that women were producing within the university: more women were completing Ph.D.s and producing scholarship in the area of feminism, film, and media studies. The journal participated in this shift, as the founding collective took as part of its mission to encourage emerging feminist academics by providing a venue for their work. They also mentored these new scholars, some of whom went on to join the editorial group. Of course, the strongest mark of the journal's history has been its commitment to a collective editorial structure and process.

Most important to the journal's success has been the collective's commitment to lively and unbridled debate. As it launched its project, the journal participated enthusiastically, even aggressively, in the fierce contests that shaped the emerging fields of film studies and women's studies in the U.S. academy—along with the field of literary studies from which many of the original editors had migrated. *Camera Obscura* made its early marks in the field polemically, and its contentious nature resonated at the level of collective work. In contrast to many feminist enterprises of the period, *Camera Obscura* embraced dissent and contention. In our view, its commitment to thorough and vigorous debate leading to consensus has been its greatest strength, though this commitment has not been without casualties. This intellectually and often emotionally challenging process has proven to be too time consuming or overly demanding to some editors. And surely, at times, we have achieved consensus on a political or theoretical point at the cost of leaving other issues out of account. For example, looking over our history it becomes clear that the early centrality of theorizing sexual difference left little room for consideration of homo/heterosexual differences or of other compelling social differences. That central commitment, of course, gave way—not without struggle—as the collective's perspective shifted both through its changing members and in the context of ongoing debates in the field. Not least among the casualties of our process may also have been our publication schedule, whose historical irregularities stemmed in no small part from the cumbersome process of arriving at consensus on any given issue. At the same time, however, the insistence that serious intellectual exchange and discussion of political concerns must underlie both our editorial process and the shaping of each particular volume has given *Camera Obscura* the sharpness of profile that it maintains to this day. That is, while the journal reworks its theoretical and methodological commitments as the collective's membership evolves to represent new issues, approaches, and expertise, it continues striving to identify new intellectual currents and to intervene in ongoing debates.

Because *Camera Obscura* began as a feminist collective without any regular institutional support or endorsement, it has maintained an unusual degree of independence. *Camera Obscura*'s relative autonomy from institutions, departments, and professional organizations has significantly favored the collective organization. Indeed, many institutions would not have supported a journal that lacked (or refused) a hierarchical editorial structure. Only in 1985, when the journal was by any standard mature, did it find an institutional home at the University of Rochester when Constance Penley joined that institution's English Department and Film Studies Program. Still, we have consistently chosen to distribute labor and decision-making across the group and its diffuse geographies, preferring not to consolidate either authority or accountability in a single editor or place. This means, of course, that we work largely without the kind of individual credit that any one academic institution might reward, but it also means that the editorial process must provide its own internal satisfactions.

Primary among these satisfactions is regular intellectual exchange. But equally important to us and to our mission is the sense that contributors expect us to experiment and to take risks. Moreover, functioning as a collective has allowed us to perform all of the primary review processes ourselves, without using outside referees. While we have taken criticism for this policy from some of the membership of the Society for Cinema and Media Studies, it has allowed us to stay very close to developments in the field, and to keep the journal on a course that we continually renew without the policing of disciplinary or field-specific boundaries. Rather, the content of the journal more closely reflects the concerns of the collective and its readership, since this policy has kept us in close dialogue with one another and with our authors. Because at least two editors read every submission, and because the whole collective discusses acceptances and revisions, the commentary the author receives includes her or him in our conversation. This admittedly labor-intensive editorial process has produced at least three significant effects: it has allowed us to identify and promote the work of younger, emerging scholars, and it has generated a loyal readership eager to contribute their mature work to our pages and to encourage their students to submit some of their first scholarship to the journal. Thus, the editorial process has generated a scholarly community.

Our collective operates not by any exact calculation or completely equal distribution of labor or participation, but rather it allows us all some flexibility in organizing our working lives. This means that we take turns shouldering a little extra work, providing the final push we need to conclude a project, or assuming responsibility for the all-important timekeeping that holds us to schedule. But the tradeoff is that no one person provides the primary leadership or bears the primary burdens of the role of editor-in-chief. In short, we carry on through a sense of mutual responsibility to both the journal and the collective. And this is how *Camera Obscura* maintains some continuity of profile and practice across the differences introduced by changes in the collective. As the membership has evolved from the original collective, invariably attracting feminist scholars for whom the journal provided a formative influence, we find that our work is sustained by a shared—and perhaps idealized—vision of the journal and by shared aspirations for its future, which depend on identifications both with the collective and with *Camera Obscura* itself.

Texts: Broadening the Scope

Camera Obscura was introduced with the subtitle "A Journal of Feminism and Film Theory." As that title indicates, the journal focused on film as its object of analysis, using—and originating—new approaches in feminist, cultural, and critical theory to rethink cinema as well as, notably, using cinema to rethink feminism and critical theory. In particular, *Camera Obscura* was interested in the ways in which the film spectator is positioned and addressed by cinema's visual and narrative strategies. The journal thus became known for its rigorous deployment of semiotic and psychoanalytic theories of textuality and the subject, as *Camera Obscura* attempted to produce both a systematic description of film's modes of representation and an interrogation of the phantasmatic and ideological implications of the cinematic apparatus (especially its enunciation of and implications for relations of sexual difference). The great value of this approach was that it encouraged work that concentrated on the specific operations of cinema (particularly classical Hollywood cinema) and thus on the specific ways in which differences (primarily, at that time, sexual differences) might be constituted and defined—or, in some cases, reconstituted and redefined—through particular cultural apparatuses, including film and other popular media. That is, by attending closely to cinema's texts, institutions, and spectator relations, those affiliated with *Camera Obscura* (as editors, mentors, and contributors) emphasized how structures of desire and identification are formed, maintained, and reproduced—structures that are typically operative not only in the cinema but in phallocentric culture as a whole.

In this way, *Camera Obscura* aimed to avoid approaches to cinema that risked presuming the static existence of precisely those identifications, pleasures, and meanings that film and media studies scholars have taken as their objects of analysis.[10] Instead of assuming that women, as members of a unified group with certain qualities determined by gender norms, simply have a fixed status in relation to cinema—whether as subjects or objects of vision, as audience members, authors, or images on screen—*Camera Obscura* attempted to interrogate how categories like those of gender, spectatorship, or spectacle are constructed, and how subjects are made to see and to appear in particular (though not essential) sexed positions. Instead of treating popular cinema as a mode of escape from such social positions, the journal took seriously the way in which films have significant psychic, social, and ideological effects, how they—and those of us engaged with them—operate within delimited parameters. Instead of assuming that our responses to film are, in some way, our "own," it considered how larger dynamics of desire and knowledge are inscribed in films and how these engender meanings and pleasures of which we're not fully aware. In other words, *Camera Obscura*'s emphasis on the specificity of cinema helped the journal analyze formations of media and culture in a truly critical way, refusing approaches that might be faulted for being too volunteeristic or naively pluralistic—both a too-easy validation of viewers' experiences and enjoyments as well as an overly optimistic faith in filmmakers' and film critics' ability simply to make of films what they choose.[11]

Yet while avoiding those problems the journal, arguably, risked other pitfalls: some critiques of *Camera Obscura*'s project (including, importantly, self-critiques arising from journal editors and contributors themselves) suggested that in its emphasis on how film's strategies of representation and enunciation reproduce and reinforce those of phallocentric culture, *Camera Obscura* overlooked other possibilities for film, media, and culture. Critics claimed that in its attempt to avoid a naive pluralism, the journal tended to disavow the differences that do exist within media culture and our relationships to it — differences inscribed in texts through varying conventions and modes of address, as well as differences elicited in readings by varying intertexts, discourses, and audience engagements. However, charges that *Camera Obscura* promoted a universalizing and monolithic theory of film are belied by a look at the range of its actual contents. From the beginning of the journal's history, *Camera Obscura*'s editors and authors were interested in alternatives to the (relatively) closed form of classical Hollywood cinema, and a number of essays that considered texts from other traditions and institutions were published. In particular, as elaborated in other sections of this piece, there was great interest displayed in the work of feminist, independent, and avant-garde filmmakers, with journal authors looking to various countercinemas in order to consider how films might undermine classical structures, rework Hollywood's modes of looking and narration, and thus establish other terms of desire and identification — a different spectator/screen dynamic that might then correspond to the different psychic and social dynamics to which the journal was (and continues to be) committed.

There have also long been essays that considered texts other than films. Indeed, the journal's growing interest in a variety of media forms followed from the aforementioned interest in alternatives to Hollywood cinema and in the work of independent artists and producers. Several of those artists and producers (Chantal Akerman, Marguerite Duras, Valie Export, Laura Mulvey, Ulrike Ottinger, Sally Potter, and Yvonne Rainer, among others) worked not only in film but in other arenas as well (dance, performance, photography, video, writing), and that work intersected with their films in intriguing ways, raising questions of multi- and intermedia relations. And, of course, an interest in the ways in which image and narrative might be differently articulated in the work of different authors, operating with different codes and within different contexts, dovetails with an interest in the ways in which different media forms — even so-called dominant ones — might variously articulate modes of seeing and knowing. Thus, just as many filmmakers were also involved with other media, so were many film scholars. People who were trained in film theory began to consider how that theory applied — or failed to apply — to different media forms, thus leading to reconsiderations of both their objects and methods of analysis. Given that media forms are themselves often gendered in discourse (i.e., the history of seeing television as a "feminine" form or medical image technology as a "masculine" one), this question of inter- or cross-mediation opened, one might say, a "natural" area of inquiry for *Camera Ob-*

scura—something discussed, for example, by many contributors to *Camera Obscura*'s 1989 survey of work on "The Spectatrix."[12]

The institutional as well as textual links—and, importantly, the institutional and textual disjunctures—between film and other signifying/social formations (medical imaging, television, video, performance, urban space, advertising, etc.) therefore became a notable area of exploration for *Camera Obscura*, shifting its concerns from an exclusive focus on film to broader questions of media and culture. For example, in 1988, *Camera Obscura* published its first special issue on television studies, "Television and the Female Consumer," which included essays on soap operas, melodrama, and "new woman" genres; television and domestic space; TV stars and fans; and early television's treatment of class and ethnicity, in addition to providing source guides on television research and archives and reviews of other recent TV scholarship. Next was an issue on "Male Trouble" that included a dossier on the configurations of gender, generation, and sexuality in the television program *Pee-wee's Playhouse*; and an issue titled "Popular Culture and Reception Studies" with essays on, among other things, amusement parks, burlesque, film exhibition in African American communities, rap music, and Elvis soon followed.[13] Further indicating *Camera Obscura*'s far-ranging involvement in cultural studies, a two-part special issue titled "Imaging Technologies, Inscribing Science" was produced in 1992 with work covering such topics as x-ray and laser technologies, fetal imaging and reproductive politics, AIDS, breast cancer, cosmetic surgery, constructions of transgender bodies and identities, and health educational and activist video.[14] And many contributors to the special issue "The Spectatrix" indicated their interest in broadening *Camera Obscura*'s traditional focus on "the female spectator" of film to include considerations of spectators of other technological and media forms, as well as, indeed, "other" spectators in general—those not necessarily nor solely delimited by binary sexual difference in the way that the term "the female spectator" typically implies. These (and other) special issues and dossiers helped both to inaugurate and to demonstrate the developing interests of the journal, positioning it within the fields of visual and media studies quite expansively defined.[15] In that sense, the change in *Camera Obscura*'s subtitle almost two decades after its introduction—from "a journal of feminism and film theory" to "feminism, culture, and media studies"—only made more visible and official the changes that had already taken place in its editorial emphases and aims, as well as in the collective itself: the new subtitle first appeared, appropriately, in a 1994–95 special issue titled "Lifetime: A Cable Network 'For

Women,'"[16] but, as elaborated, clearly by that time *Camera Obscura* had already established itself as a journal devoted to the analysis of a wide variety of media texts.

With this move toward a broadly conceived object of analysis came a move toward varied means and methods of analysis. Although "feminism" remained in *Camera Obscura*'s subtitle as a primary political and theoretical commitment, the journal expanded its notion of differences beyond a supposedly singular "sexual difference" to include multiple, overlapping differences (of race, nationality, sexuality, gender expression, age, and so on), suggesting an implicit critique of the unifying tendencies of a narrowly conceived identity politics. Similarly, while semiotic and psychoanalytic theories have retained a place of importance in the journal, other approaches (industrial and historical analyses, genre and star studies, ethnographic and reception models, analyses of race and ethnicity, postcolonial theory and critiques of empire, queer and trans-sexuality studies, etc.) have also figured significantly in its contents. These approaches have been at times articulated in opposition to and at times articulated in concert with semiotic and psychoanalytic models, indicating the intellectual debates and academic shifts with which the journal has engaged. In this way, *Camera Obscura* has foregrounded and even helped to establish a scholarly interest in moving within and between both disciplinary and identity categories.

As suggested, such changes in the journal go hand in hand with the shift from "film" to "culture and media." Just as exploring a range of media texts meant considering how those texts may differ from the terms of classical cinematic ones, considering a range of subjects and categories of "difference" (aside from just that of "sexual difference") meant exploring, in various ways, other media that historically have been significant in terms of those differences. That is, though the initial work of *Camera Obscura* suggested that classical film emphasizes structures of binarized sexual difference that are perhaps best approached through a psychoanalytic lens, other media may bring other issues and methods to the fore: for instance, television's relationship to the domesticated family—and what that family disavows/excludes—may make sociologically inflected reception models of TV viewing contexts and/or queer theory models of TV textuality central concerns; likewise, the fraught history of U.S. popular music, urban entertainments, and/or youth subcultures may make approaches that emphasize class, race, ethnicity, nationality, and/or age a particular focus in studies of those formations. As *Camera Obscura* began to consider multiple media formations, it thus in a reciprocal and mutually dynamic relationship also began to consider issues, theories, and methodologies beyond the ones it initially emphasized.

In sum, then, *Camera Obscura*'s shift from "a journal of feminism and film theory" to a site for "feminism, culture, and media studies" is intimately connected to the other issues under discussion in this essay—the history of the journal, its theoretical and methodological development, its political and intellectual charge, and its basis in a theory and practice of collectivity. Offering not a "naive pluralism" but, rather, an informed and more radical one, *Camera Obscura*'s embrace of work on multiple media and subjects, from multiple perspectives and with multiple concerns, has allowed the journal to continue making an impact in film, media, and cultural studies without losing sight of either its initial vision or various options for the future. Indeed, in presaging and predicting many aspects of current work in film, media, feminist, and cultural studies (an interest in interdisciplinarity and intermediality, a critique of unified models of both textuality and subjectivity, a concern with media conventions in conjunction with media histories, an exploration of the ways in which various intertexts, discourses, and identifications intersect), *Camera Obscura* has provided, and will continue to present, a lens through which to view these fields.

Methodology: The Camera Obscura *Effect*

The heady appeal of the early years of *Camera Obscura*—a thrill elicited especially by essays written and signed by "the *Camera Obscura* collective"—lay, certainly for an undergraduate becoming infatuated with the fields of women's and film studies, in its double affiliation with the women's movement, on the one hand, and with French theory, on the other. The by-now clichéd but one-time improbable merger between feminism and poststructuralist theory epitomized the identity of the journal, became its cultural and intellectual legacy, and still shades its reputation today. I say "heady appeal," because the journal's passionate feminism pursued affairs of the head much more than those of the body: it fought on the academic front of the women's movement. The topicality demanded of the journal format heightened the urgency infusing the many books of French-inflected feminist theory appearing in the United States and Britain during that period—books such as Jane Gallop's *The Daughter's Seduction* and Juliet Mitchell and Jacqueline Rose's *Feminine Sexuality* (both 1982). At the same time, by publishing reports on women filmmakers (primarily avant-garde), film distributors, and conferences, *Camera Obscura* maintained close ties with feminist practice, with the groundswell of women's media organizations—production collectives, distributors, and festivals—that sprung up internationally during the 1970s. The journal's feel of militancy was exciting—despite, or because of, serving two mistresses. The French connection made the journal chic; its edge of dogmatism signified rigor in relation to a certain "crunchy" strain of U.S. women's culture of the time. But without a concurrent culture of women's media activism, reflected in the notes on contemporary activities headed "Women Working" and the short reviews of important films headed "Matrix," as well as in the ads for such sister publications as *Heresies* and *Jump Cut* and the small feminist distributor Serious Business, the journal's French fizz would have gone flat.

The journal's design, which remained consistent until the end of the twentieth century, balanced its two affiliations to the feminist movement and French theory: a plain white cover, fading to a shade of cream (quite similar to paperbacks from the French publisher Gallimard); a single black-and-white academy ratio film image on front and back covers; the title rendered always in lowercase. Feminist authenticity and antihierarchical convictions were served by the do-it-yourself minimalist look and lowercase logo, while the asceticism and suspiciousness of visual pleasure preached in the art and theory of the period was sweetened with just enough fetishism of form. Indeed, its two affiliations were counterpoised—or locked in dialectical tension—in most aspects of the journal. Something about this combination was compelling.

Primary to the seeming-contradictions that *Camera Obscura* posed was the status that the journal granted to "male theory," or, simply, to men. Unafraid to challenge the "bachelor machines" of male avant-garde filmmaking and masculinist theorizing, the journal nevertheless gave Christian Metz and Alfred Hitchcock exalted spots in its pantheon alongside such filmmakers as Laura Mulvey and Chantal Akerman. Raymond Bellour and Thierry Kuntzel, male gurus of the Paris Film Program, were also given pride of place in its pages. But the difficult prose and even the admittedly patriarchal premises of Lacanian theory only enhanced the journal's aura of rigor, rigor, rigor—apparent most notably in its close textual analyses of experimental feminist work. In *this* venue—translating, editing, framing, even contradicting male-generated ideas (notably Bellour's contention in a conversation with Janet Bergstrom that "I think that a woman can love, accept and give a positive value to [classical Hollywood] films only from her own masochism")—the sisters were doing it for themselves.[17]

It was this extravagant intellectualism—combined with the commitment to currency and wide relevance and with the always sexy subject matter of film and filmmaking—that made the journal emblematic of the moment of greatest consolidation of feminist film theory in the late 1970s and 1980s. Its American, rather than British or French, provenance probably gave it wider circulation as film studies programs and small bookstores proliferated in the United States, and certainly this feature tinged its polemicism since interdisciplinary women's studies programs frequently resisted "male theory" in favor of a political orientation built solidly on American pragmatism. As part of the legacy of its first years, *Camera Obscura* still has passionate defenders and detractors even after its politics, look, subtitle, and collective membership have altered notably. This aura of controversy does not diminish, but probably enhances, the intellectual high in discovering that *Camera Obscura*'s so-called dogmatism is a chimera— one that fades upon closer inspection of its contents. It is true that the journal, in conjunction with important writings in the late-1970s and early 1980s by such scholars as Annette Kuhn, E. Ann Kaplan, Teresa de Lauretis, Pam Cook, and Claire Johnston, helped establish a canon of feminist films and filmmakers that excluded most straight documentary and narrative films and included few women of color, with the experimental documentarian Trinh T. Minh-ha a notable exception. But it is important to note that *Camera Obscura*'s influence coincided with, and in part defined, a moment in feminist film culture in which a symbiotic relationship existed between production/distribution/exhibition and theorists. Work by independent women filmmakers, including women of color, mushroomed in the mid-1980s (see, for example, the enormous growth of Women Make Movies, the single U.S. independent feminist distributor that survived the decade), and mainstream successes increased as well. Indeed, there were more films than one journal could cover. Yet features of the journal in its current manifestation—including the revival of the "Women Working" feature—attest to the crucial role of this interdependence of theory and practice in "cinefeminism."

Another paradox alluded to above is *Camera Obscura*'s emblematic identification with the "sexual difference" paradigm of spectatorship—that is, with a psychoanalytic discourse that is fatally heteronormative, ahistorical, and abstract. An early kinship between the journal and the British journal *m/f* (whose psychoanalytically informed Marxism is profiled in *Camera Obscura* 3/4) made a significant impact on Constance Penley's 1988 edited volume *Feminism and Film Theory*, which defines the field almost exclusively in terms of psychoanalytic approaches to sexual difference.[18] Tania Modleski and Teresa de Lauretis, two feminist film scholars critical of the orthodoxies of "sexual difference," did not participate in *Camera Obscura*'s survey of the field—the special issue entitled "The Spectatrix." Yet in contradiction to the perception of the journal's "straight mind," not only have a significant number of queer women served as members of the editorial collective since the 1980s, but *Camera Obscura* has also published lesbian film theory extensively in more recent years. The inclusion of queer perspectives also opened the editorial offices and, for a time, the collective itself to male participation; gay men also joined straight male feminists on the advisory board. Concurrently, psychoanalysis, while engaged by many in the journal's pages, ceased to function as a master—or master's—discourse. Instead, it was wielded as part of queer theory or combined with, even contested by, other methodologies. In a context in which feminist criticism was being challenged to take on multiple axes of analysis, the critique of race and racism became central concerns of the editors and contributors, and the race-blind manner in which psychoanalysis had so often been used contributed to its loss of authority. Finally, as cinema yielded its dominance as object of study in the pages of the journal as in the field at large, cultural studies methodologies allowed lived social differences of race, class, nation, sexuality, and gender expression to become tangibly addressed.

The journal's shifts in emphases are illustrated by the books that *Camera Obscura* has issued. Volumes based on special issues on masculinity, television, and science and technology coincide with a long stretch of the journal's history in which all but Constance Penley from the original collective moved on to other things, and passionate new members (some of them still among us) came on board. The turn to history, which many commentators on the academic discipline of film studies saw as the "next big thing" after psychoanalytic feminism, is represented both in the most recent *Camera Obscura* book—an independently edited volume on women and early cinema—as well as throughout the journal. If we take the move to Duke University Press (2000) as marking the beginning of the journal's current period, we must also situate this as a retrospective period in order to distill some of the energies, orthodoxies, and intellectual adventures traced in this piece.

Today, we are in many ways far away from the seemingly unified editorial point of view represented in those early issues of the journal. A diversity of topics, methods, and approaches, particularly as these are fostered in an emphasis on emerging writers, is characteristic of the current period. But in other ways the journal remains consistent with its origins: *Camera Obscura* is passionate about ideas, about film and its sister media. And its editors are just utopian enough once again to sign the current contribution as

     —the *Camera Obscura* collective

Notes

The authors wish to thank Constance Penley for the valuable information and assistance that she provided us in writing this essay, as well as for the invaluable inspiration that she continues to provide us in working with the journal.

1. This essay was written on the invitation of the volume editors Lee Grieveson and Haidee Wasson and subsequently published in *Camera Obscura* to inaugurate the publication of a series of short pieces by feminist scholars imagining "An Archive for the Future," *Camera Obscura* 61 (2006): 1–25.
2. *Camera Obscura* collective (Janet Bergstrom, Sandy Flitterman, Elisabeth Hart Lyon, and Constance Penley), "Feminism and Film: Critical Approaches," *Camera Obscura* 1 (fall 1976): 3–10.
3. From *Camera Obscura* 1 (fall 1976), see *Camera Obscura* collective, "An Interrogation of the Cinematic Sign: Jackie Raynal's *Deux Fois*," 11–26; *Camera Obscura* collective, "*Deux Fois*: Shot Commentary, Shot Chart, Photogramme," 27–51; *Camera Obscura* collective, "Yvonne Rainer: Interview," 76–96; and Janet Bergstrom, "Yvonne Rainer: Introduction," 53–70.
4. From *Camera Obscura* 2 (fall 1997), see Janet Bergstrom, "*Jeanne Dielman, 23 Quai du Commerce, 1080 Bruxelles*," 114–21; Elisabeth Lyon, "*La Femme du Gange*," 122–29; and Constance Penley, "*What Maisie Knew*," 130–36.
5. Jacqueline Suter, "Feminine Discourse in *Christopher Strong*," *Camera Obscura* 3–4 (summer 1979): 135–50.
6. From *Camera Obscura* 5 (spring 1980), see Jane Weinstock, "She Who Laughs First Laughs Last," 100–10; and "Sally Potter on *Thriller*," 99.
7. Constance Penley and Janet Bergstrom (for the *Camera Obscura* collective), "The Avant-Garde: Histories and Theories," *Screen* 19.3 (autumn 1978): 113–28.
8. See, for instance, *Screen* 17.2 (summer 1976). This issue has a contribution entitled "Why We Have Resigned from the Board of *Screen*" by Edward Buscombe, Christine Gledhill, Alan Lovell, and Christopher Williams.
9. *Camera Obscura* collective, "Feminism and Film," 5.
10. Specifically, *Camera Obscura* attempted to go beyond the limitations of the "images of women" approach that was extremely common at the time of the founding of the journal, providing the basis for numerous courses on women and film, for educational films that attempted to counter media stereotypes, and for books such as Molly Haskell's *From Reverence to Rape: The Treatment of Women in the Movies* (New York: Holt, Rinehart and Winston, 1973) and Marjorie Rosen's *Popcorn Venus:*

Women, Movies, and the American Dream (New York: Avon Books, 1973). These early attempts to engage with the representation of women in film were certainly important and, indeed, often more complex than is typically acknowledged. However, as the phrase "images of women" suggests, such work tended to presume a fixed content to both "images" and "women." In its most reductive formulations, it thus risked implying that a film's meaning, defined through its content, is easily readable and that women, defined as a group, share certain traits indicative of an essential identity, such that one needs only to compare the two—film content and women's reality—in order to determine the implications of the portrayal.

11. This, for instance, might be said of a certain kind of cultural studies work that applauds audiences for their resistant readings of texts without always carefully considering the ways in which such "resistance" might itself be inscribed within, exploited, and/or recuperated by dominant media and consumer industries.

12. "The Spectatrix," edited by Janet Bergstrom and Mary Ann Doane, *Camera Obscura* 20–21 (May–September 1989). Not only is the question of the applicability of film theory to other media forms such as television raised in the issue's introduction ("The Female Spectator: Contexts and Directions" by Janet Bergstrom and Mary Ann Doane, particularly pages 14–15 and 21), but numerous contributors also discuss this in regard to a wide range of media and practices (television, video, performance, music and youth subcultures, pornography and sexual subcultures, fan communities, women's writing and reading, etc.). See, for example, the contributions by Jacqueline Bobo, Giuliana Bruno, Charlotte Brunsdon, Sandy Flitterman-Lewis, Mary Beth Haralovich, Christine Holmlund, Lynne Joyrich, E. Ann Kaplan, Marsha Kinder, Annette Kuhn, Julia Lesage, Gina Marchetti, Judith Mayne, Patricia Mellencamp, Meaghan Morris, Margaret Morse, Constance Penley, Ellen Seiter, Lynn Spigel, Lesley Stern, and Chris Straayer. Significantly, two of these contributors—Sandy Flitterman-Lewis and Constance Penley—were members of *Camera Obscura*'s founding group; their broadening interests thus stand as an interesting testament to the broadening interests of the journal as a whole. The same might be said of many of *Camera Obscura*'s later editors (such as Lynn Spigel, Denise Mann, Julie D'Acci, Sasha Torres, and Lynne Joyrich), who are as (if not more) known for their work on texts other than cinematic ones than for work within the discipline of film studies proper.

13. "Television and the Female Consumer," special issue edited by Lynn Spigel and Denise Mann, *Camera Obscura* 16 (January 1988); "Male Trouble," special issue edited by Constance Penley and Sharon Willis, *Camera Obscura* 17 (May 1988); and "Popular Culture and Reception Studies," special issue edited by Lynn Spigel, *Camera Obscura* 23 (May 1990).

14. "Imaging Technologies, Inscribing Science," special issue edited by Paula A. Treichler and Lisa Cartwright, *Camera Obscura* 28 (January 1992), and "Imaging Technologies, Inscribing Science 2," special issue edited by Paula A. Treichler and Lisa Cartwright, *Camera Obscura* 29 (May 1992).

15. *Camera Obscura*'s shift from "film" to "media" both reflected and helped to solidify a similar shift in the discipline as a whole; work in other journals also marked this general disciplinary expansion. For instance, television was featured early on in *Screen*, with a special issue on independent cinema and British TV and then one on TV more broadly in 1980 and 1981; see *Screen* 21.4 (1980–81) and *Screen* 22.4 (1981). Even earlier (in 1978, between its volumes 6 and 7) *The Journal of Popular Film* became *The Journal of Popular Film and Television*. And an early interest in video in other forums (for instance, in the journal *Afterimage*) also signaled work in the field that attempted to define moving image media in various ways, rather than just through film.

16. "Lifetime: A Cable Network 'For Women,'" special issue edited by Julie D'Acci, *Camera Obscura* 33–34 (May–September–January 1994–95).

17. Janet Bergstrom, "Alternation, Segmentation, Hypnosis: Interview with Raymond Bellour," *Camera Obscura* 3/4 (summer 1979): 70–103, 97.

18. Constance Penley, ed., *Feminism and Film Theory* (New York: Routledge/BFI, 1988).

Little Books

MARK BETZ

"The only exact knowledge there is," said Anatole France, "is the knowledge of the date of publication and the format of books." And indeed, if there is a counterpart to the confusion of a library, it is the order of its catalogue.
—Walter Benjamin, "Unpacking My Library"

I don't think there are big themes and little themes. The smaller a theme, the more you can treat it with grandeur.
—Claude Chabrol, "Big Subjects, Little Subjects"

■ By common consent, film studies as an academic discipline in Britain and North America is understood to have formed in the 1960s. Its protoforms, along with its subsequent developments, have received or are in the process of undergoing retrospective accounts. In this essay I propose that the rise, consolidation, and current position of academic film studies might be usefully charted and examined by concentrating on a specific site for the dissemination of film knowledge that has largely been held—and perhaps even has held itself—at arm's length from the discipline: the little book. By this I mean a small-format publication—usually around 18 cm × 13.5 cm (7 in × 5.25 in)—published in series, often by a trade publisher, and purchased more or less cheaply by an audience not primarily, or at least not exclusively, academic. Little books distinguish themselves from university press books by their smaller dimensions (often including thickness). Yet, importantly, they also share a mode of address, and a more expansive sense of film culture, that is different from academic work. In this sense, the word "little" here loosely designates not only a physical quality but also a disposition, a relationship to the formal constraints of university-based scholarship that is circumscribed by clear ideas and practices of disciplinarity.

In collecting these little books myself, I have become fascinated by the moments of eruption in little book publishing—periods of intense publication on film by houses introducing series on all manner of subjects. Such moments fall into two distinct waves, the first from the mid-1960s to the early 1970s and the second from the early 1970s until around 1980. From then on through the next decade and a half the little book was at ebb tide as the full force of academic research and publication crashed onto the scene in works of ever-increasing size and authority. Stamped by the imprimaturs of the first generation of university-trained film scholars and the academic presses that published them, the "bigger books" of the mid-1980s through the early 1990s tended toward the historical rather than the theoretical pole of the discipline, despite the usual characterizations of this as the era of "Grand Theory." These big books were also of an American rather than Continental cast, forging between the two geographies a seam that betrays their differing histories and attitudes toward the professionalization of film study. Nonetheless, the evidence of a discipline rather secure in its place in the academy lies in the weight of these tomes as much as it does in the increasingly stringent research methods and the detailed referencing of the claims held within them.

The appearance around the end of the 1990s of a number of essays and collections that argue for a "reconstruction" or "reinvention" of film studies is, however, a fresh symptom of a field in self-perceived crisis—a field giving way to interdisciplinary imperatives as the boundaries demarcating film studies erode by the force of powerful waves of new and emerging media and visual technologies. The rise of the Internet as a forum for film writing of all stripes, from chatroom salonspeak to online articles to blogs, by authors of varying relations to film studies as a profession, represents a different challenge to disciplinary definition and control of its object. In short, the repressed film culture that gave rise to film studies has returned with a vengeance. The resurgence of the little book at the same historical moment is thus a more than fortuitous indication of the place and function that publications of such size have had, and might continue to have, for academic film studies.

In this essay I undertake an overview of little books on film with an eye toward certain histories, geographies, and continuities/discontinuities as they pertain to academic film studies. On the one hand, I offer an overall picture of little book production—the periods in which such books rose and fell and rose again, the publishers that have proffered them to the reading public, and the patterns and features that have made them salient. On the other hand, I am putting forward a thesis that is polemical and driven by a certain logic of return: that little books encapsulate a film culture and study that were instrumental in the creation of academic film studies; that this culture and study were different in Britain than in America; that debates concerning the parts that theoretical and historical discourses have contributed in the shaping of Anglo-American film studies are ones deriving from differing geographic specificities and relations to the academy itself; and that the current crisis in academic film publication might be strategically addressed through a renewed engagement with the small-format monograph. A conspicuous line throughout the essay is the prominent role that the British Film Institute (BFI) has played in terms of not only the publication of little books but also the shaping and development of the discipline, both in Britain and America.[1] Little books serve in my essay not only as a register for the history of film studies but also more crucially for the abiding presence of film study itself, which I think is as healthy as it ever was.

First Wave, 1965–1971

Charles Barr, in his introductory essay to *All Our Yesterdays: 90 Years of British Cinema*, states: "The importance of the mid-1960s period can hardly be exaggerated: it saw the foundation of academic film study in Britain, and a huge expansion of published criticism, and it set new terms for approaching popular cinema, film authorship, and close textual analysis."[2] This foundation was laid in part by an outpouring of little book series publication that rose, crested, and fell during the years 1965 to 1971, when more than a dozen publishers in Britain and America produced nearly two hundred pocket-sized books well-illustrated with stills and designed to appeal to the general and cinephile market.

Some of these publishers preceded and exceeded this wave, but all had their highest levels of productivity in the middle of it. Before the first wave there were some thirty years of sporadic little book production that I would demarcate as falling into two periods. The first, from 1933 to 1958, is characterized by ripples from a few, largely British, publishers. London's Faber and Faber, at present the most prolific trade press for little books, was the first, with its release of Rudolf Arnheim's *Film* in 1933. Throughout the decade it released seven other titles, many by filmmakers, about the process of creation. George Allen and Unwin followed suit with a half dozen publications on British film and filmmaking. The distinctively blue-covered Pelican Books (the nonfiction imprint for Penguin) released a few surveys of its own edited by Roger Manvell beginning in 1950.[3] The BFI, too, entered the little book scene in 1950, and in so doing it inaugurated a publishing interest in the form that would be extended in key ways in the decades to come.[4] New York's Doubleday and Company and Simon and Schuster were in on the action in the 1950s as well; the latter's *Film: An Anthology*, edited by Daniel Talbot and released in 1959, effectively marked the transition to the next, more condensed period of little book protopublishing and the full emergence onto the scene of American publishing houses.

A rising tide began around 1959 when Grove Press, in cooperation with the American Federation of Film Societies, started publishing the Robert Hughes–edited small collections as well as selected film scripts. In the mid-1960s Pelican Books began releasing some key titles that appeared on some of the first film course outlines of that era and beyond, including Penelope Houston's *The Contemporary Cinema* (1963), Ralph Stephenson and J. R. Debrix's *The Cinema as Art* (1965), and V. F. Perkins's widely influential *Film as Film: Understanding and Judging Movies* (1970). Allen and Unwin, in partnership with Hill and Wang, published a clutch of titles in the mid-1960s as well, but with no perceivable coherence, and by 1968 it ceased being a player at all.

Not so Grove Press, which continued throughout the first wave to publish its Evergreen Book/Evergreen Original series and later its Evergreen Black Cat Books, the latter of which specialized in volumes on single films that included critical articles, full credits and film scripts, and interviews with directors, as well as generous collections of photographs and stills. The simpler published screenplays that it had started with were imitated by other publishers, and these two types pioneered by Grove—screenplays and film guides—have maintained a presence since their emergence as cornerstones of little book publishing. Of the 1,416 little books published between 1965 and 2005, 349 have been screenplays and 313 film guides; combined, they comprise close to half of all little book production. But while they are certainly important facets of the contemporary scene, neither was as significant a force in the first wave as they are today.[5]

More significant were the varied little books dedicated to other aspects of film culture and film study in Britain and in America. Raymond Durgnat had a monopoly on Faber and Faber's meager output (though from the late 1980s on this publisher would become the most prolific player in this market). E. P. Dutton and Co. released a small series of seven "Paperback Originals," which included much-used anthologies such as Richard Dyer MacCann's *Film: A*

Montage of Theories (1966) and one of the three most influential little books of the era (despite its greater-than-usual thickness): Andrew Sarris's *The American Cinema: Directors and Directions, 1929-1968* (1968). Another New York house, Crown Publishers, released between 1969 and 1971 a half dozen translations of director monographs that first appeared through Paris' Editions Seghers' Cinema d'Aujourd'hui series. And the Dover Books on Cinema and Stage, somewhat larger than pocket size but certainly slim enough to be sequestered on one's person, came out between 1970 and 1972 with ten titles as well, including key translations of film theory by Béla Balázs, Sergei Eisenstein, and Hugo Münsterberg.

But these were not the key players in the field at this time, of which I would name five: the studio vista/dutton pictureback series, 1963–73, which released fifteen titles; the International Film Guide series, 1963–74, thirty-three titles; the Screen series, 1969–79, twelve titles; the Movie Paperbacks/Praeger Film Library, 1967–71, seventeen titles; and the Cinema One series, 1967–76, twenty-eight titles. Across all of these I have found some common features of interest:

1. A prominent general editor or editors, none of whom was an academic (and only a couple of whom would later become so): Peter Cowie, Ian Cameron, Penelope Houston, Tom Milne, Christopher Williams, and Peter Wollen, preeminently. This suggests a mirroring of the creative control and consistency of vision generally associated with the penetration of auteurism during this period, as well as the authority of someone whose career resides in some form of habitual film criticism for a general (albeit informed) public, the intended audience for these publications.

2. A stable of authors for each series (with the exception of Cinema One) who would contribute two or more volumes to it.

3. A fairly circumscribed set of subjects as the focus for each volume. These are, in order of frequency: directors; nations/movements or the "new" cinema; theory or topics; American film genres; periods in American cinema, especially silent and/or comedy; and actors/actresses/character types.

4. The inclusion of a series blurb calling attention to the illustrations. Thus the studio vista/dutton picturebacks were "the first series of comprehensive pictorial surveys to appear in paperback form. Each volume contains well over 120 striking and informative pictures; and the text, written by experts primarily for laymen, is closely tied to these pictures, acting as a

direct commentary." And the Movie Paperbacks/Praeger Film Library offered volumes that were "lavishly illustrated with stills and frame enlargements closely integrated with the text and, where appropriate, . . . a full filmography."

5. A high degree of cooperation between British and U.S. publishing houses. Studio Vista Limited and E. P. Dutton and Co. were the most stable match and those for the Cinema One series were the least: it started out as an all-British affair between the BFI and Thames and Hudson but then over the years moved back and forth between Thames and Hudson and Secker and Warburg, Doubleday and Company, Viking Press, and, nearer the end, Indiana University Press. The involvement of the BFI was the only constant.

6. In two cases the stewardship of a film journal, both of them British: *Movie Magazine* for the Movie Paperbacks/Praeger Film Library and *Sight and Sound* for Cinema One.

This golden age of little books produced few that are still read for anything but historical interest in the discipline today. Nevertheless, their cumulative effect was instrumental in shaping academic film studies as it was forming in North America and later on in Britain. They made available to a growing young audience of cinephiles specialized studies of their favorite directors, national film movements, and genres. They also cemented the paradigms, methodologies, and critical terrain for the burgeoning academic discipline, and were pressed into service as course texts by the first generation of film scholars trained in other disciplines. Little books provided the mortar for film course organization, the building blocks for which—directors, genres, and national cinemas—were already in place in the 1940s. But the construction of academic film studies was nonetheless structurally affected by these little books' mortar, which was comprised of cinephilia, thematic and stylistic textual analysis, and the crucial linking of film culture with discourses of art and aesthetic maturity—one register of which is the number of volumes published on what was then dubbed the "new cinema," and what is now called art cinema. And these foci were often crystallized through studies of directors old and new, with Ingmar Bergman, Charlie Chaplin, Sergei Eisenstein, John Ford, Fritz Lang, Alain Resnais, Josef von Sternberg, and François Truffaut meriting two dedicated studies apiece; Samuel Fuller, Alfred Hitchcock, and Orson Welles each with three; and Jean-Luc Godard the front-runner at four.

In this sense I am not saying anything new about this period of nascent

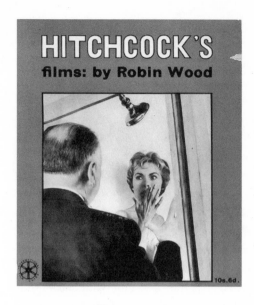

Front cover of Robin Wood's
Hitchcock's Films (London:
A. Zwemmer; New York:
A. S. Barnes, 1965).

academic film study, and I would hold up Robin Wood as the exemplar of the era. Wood wrote five books and coauthored two more in six years, five for the Movie Paperbacks/Praeger Film Library—which comes as no surprise, given its and his close relation to *Movie Magazine*. But it is his first book, *Hitchcock's Films*, published in 1965 for the International Film Guide series, that is the classic as well as the most prescient, taking as its subject the director who is still the most studied and written about figure in the history of the cinema. Wood's opening words of *Hitchcock's Films* are worth restating: "Why should we take Hitchcock seriously? It is a pity the question has to be raised; if the cinema were truly regarded as an autonomous art, not a mere adjunct of the novel or the drama—if we were able yet to *see* films instead of mentally reducing them to literature—it would be unnecessary."[6] Through his investment in film—whether it be art films from Europe or popular ones from Hollywood—as a form of artistic expression best analyzed under the sign of the auteur, Wood is the most representative and prolific of the little book authors of the first wave.[7]

And yet, something of a countertendency was presented by the Cinema One series, despite Wood's contribution to it in the form of a volume on Howard Hawks. Cinema One, like its neighbors, was heavy on the auteurs, with fully half of its twenty-eight volumes falling under this rubric. It too was wedded to a film journal, *Sight and Sound*. But Cinema One changed publishers frequently, eventually settling on a university press (Indiana). As well, only two authors, Richard Roud and Tom Milne, wrote more than one volume for it. This owes to the particularity of the series' stewardship, which was evenly split between *Sight and Sound* and the BFI Education Department and would witness in 1971 a struggle between these two branches of the BFI for editorial policy and control. Significantly, Roud and Milne were both in the *Sight and Sound* camp, with their books promoting what the Education Department staff would increasingly criticize as an "official film culture and a definite if unexamined critical line."[8] Colin McArthur has recalled the "particularly bitter battle" that ensued when the BFI directorate attempted to grant control entirely to *Sight and Sound*, marginalizing the critiques of those working at BFI Education.[9]

It is of the utmost importance, then, that Cinema One was a co-initiative of the Education Department at the BFI, as this cohort quickly became a significant player in the shaping of the Anglo-American academic discipline of film studies.[10] From the start, the volumes commissioned for Cinema One by the Education Department presented a countervailing strand in film publication: theory. This strand was activated on at least three fronts: the auteur, with Geoffrey Nowell-Smith's structuralist study of *Luchino Visconti* (1967); genre, with Jim Kitses's *Horizon's West* (1969); and semiotics, in the form of a key little book of the era, Peter Wollen's *Signs and Meaning in the Cinema* (1969), which along with Andrew Sarris's *The American Cinema* formed the bible for film studies in the early 1970s. Edward Buscombe has suggested that "the BFI, especially its education department under Paddy Whannel, had in the absence of university film studies taken on a vanguard role in forcing the intellectual development of the subject."[11] And Peter Wollen recalls: "Very soon after that book came out the first serious film courses in universities were developed. As a result of that I was invited to teach in a university for the first time, so in that sense, it changed things radically for me, at least. The immediate reaction to the book was one of polarization. You got people who supported it—'about time too, now we have a proper book of film theory in England,' and people who hated and loathed it—'what is all this garbage? We don't need all this to understand and appreciate film!' It certainly created some controversy."[12]

Indeed, one of those who "hated and loathed it"—or rather disagreed mightily with its account of the ways in which art has been and must be read, and then hated and loathed what he called "The Totalitarian Tendencies in Criticism" that were to follow in its wake—was Robin Wood.[13] His 1976 publication *Personal Views* offers a defense of his own critical position first formulated in a pair of articles for *Film Comment* a year earlier.[14] Having gone to Canada for three years, Wood returned to a British film scene that had changed dramatically at the hands of a small group of intellectuals who were nonetheless

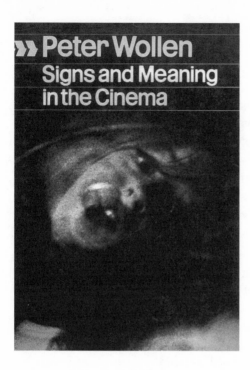

Front cover of Peter Wollen's
Signs and Meaning in the Cinema
(Bloomington: Indiana University
Press; London: British Film Insti-
tute, 1969).

"by far the most active, the most assertive, the most dogmatic, the most impressive and the most organized group currently operating."[15] In a word: *Screen*.

Second Wave, 1972–1980

I am positioning Cinema One as the necessary transitional little book series
between the first and second waves, for the particular theoretical inflections it
placed on the director/national movements/American genre paradigms that
preceded it and which it was at the same time maintaining. For the BFI from
the late 1960s on has always been of two minds on the academicization of
film study. On the one hand, the BFI was implicitly and literally invested in
it by educating a generation of film teachers through annual summer schools
and the three-to-four-year University of London extramural certificate and diploma course.[16] On the other hand, its motives for investment could be seen as
keeping its staff at arm's length from the academy, as Colin McArthur recalls:
"It had been a *quid pro quo* that the BFI Governors' precluding the Education Department from behaving—as they saw it—like a university department
would be accompanied by a new budget to pump prime lectureships in film
and television studies at British universities."[17] Nonetheless, by funding such

limited-term lectureships in film at Keele, Warwick, Essex, and Stirling, the BFI helped to establish a presence for the serious study of film in British higher education.

At the same time, and similarly unprogrammatically, the BFI also helped clear the way for some slightly bigger books in the early 1970s that increasingly were published by university presses. This was aided through its endorsement of the Cinema Two series of 1971–76, which, while initially retaining some familiar publishers from the previous phase, bound its sixteen titles in rather larger packages than its predecessor. Cinema Two would soon be published in turn by Indiana University Press and the University of California Press, the latter of which had offered a few film titles in the 1950s and early 1960s.[18] Of all of the university presses publishing on film in the late 1960s and early 1970s (Oxford being a notable one), California emerged as the strongest player by nailing some key contracts in parallel to the little books series of the era, such as the two-volume translation of André Bazin's *What Is Cinema?* (1967, 1971), Kevin Brownlow's *The Parade's Gone By . . .* (1968), translations of Georges Sadoul's *Dictionary of Films* and *Dictionary of Film Makers* (both 1972), and hitting a goldmine with Bill Nichols's collection of contemporary criticism and theory, *Movies and Methods: An Anthology* (1976).

These connections notwithstanding, BFI Education has always been wary of academics, or at least what the academy represents, and this is no less true of their key contribution to little book publication of the second wave, despite the mythology that now surrounds this period. This second wave is, as I have already indicated, as indebted to Sarris as it is to Wollen, and the American cinema history/director slant of little book publication is in evidence in four second wave series: Galahad Books/W. H. Allen's Pictorial Treasury of Film Stars (et al.), with its twelve titles on classic Hollywood stars; Prentice-Hall's Film Focus or *Focus on . . .* film guides, of which there were eighteen published between 1971 and 1976; the Tantivy Press/A. S. Barnes series The Hollywood Professionals, with seven collections on nineteen Hollywood directors between 1973 and 1980; and the Ungar Film Library, with its several titles on American writers and film among other subjects. The auteurist line was enthusiastically taken up by Twayne, which in two separately named series stretching from 1977 to 1998 published seventy titles, nearly all on directors, thus arguably forming a bridge between the still prevalent interest in auteur studies in the 1970s through its decline in the 1980s and early 1990s through to its present renewal. But in the history of the discipline, this period is more generally considered as the age of *Screen*, which pressed for a politicization of film study through a variety of theoretical discourses, particularly semiotics, Althusserian Marxism, psycho-analysis, and feminism.[19] *Screen*'s importance in turning the discipline toward theory is incontestable. It is incorrect, however, to consider *Screen* in isolation from the broader "debate culture" engaged by the BFI Education Department at this time. As defined and enacted by the Education Department, this "debate culture" was equally at odds with the "official culture" of the BFI at large, whose mandate has always been "to encourage the art of the film," as it was with the British university system. The BFI's response was to cut *Screen* loose, an action prefaced in August 1971 by the resignation of six members of the Education Department for a variety of reasons, not the least of which was a negative report on the department prepared by the vice-chancellor of Sussex University.[20]

Herein lies the reason that the most extensive little book series of the second wave, the fifty BFI (Television) Monographs, published between 1973 and 1982, is of primary interest for this period. These monographs are—equally as much as *Screen*—important touchstones for defining this phase of film studies as theoretical. The collectively authored *The Work of Dorothy Arzner: Towards a Feminist Cinema* (1975), *Gays and Film* (1977), and *Women in Film Noir* (1978), as well Sylvia Harvey's *May '68 and Film Culture* (1978), Richard Dyer's *Stars* (1979), and Steve Neale's *Genre* (1980), are all acknowledged as classics from the series, provocative publications that put forward new topics, or new means for considering familiar ones, that still consume many today. Slim but dense, these BFI Monographs are at times as obscurantist and theoretically dogmatic as anything published in *Screen* during these years. But they are not really representative of the series as a whole, which more significantly pushed into other directions—some old, some new. Directors were still a popular subject, with fourteen titles of the series dedicated to their study, albeit sometimes with different agendas and methodologies. In this context appeared Ivens, Rouch, Rivette, and Fassbinder. So did Europeans of the past, such as Dreyer, Ophüls, Powell/Pressburger, and the surrealists, as well as American popular genre directors like Don Siegel, Robert Aldrich, and—I think it's important to place her here—Dorothy Arzner.

But it is the subject of television that received the most titles, nineteen in all (thirteen as part of a special numbered series), covering such areas as football, the news, the program *Nationwide*, the popular ITV soap opera *Coronation Street*, and Channel Four, among others. This points to the degree to which television and media studies assumed a firm place in British film culture and higher education much earlier than it did in North America—a place due in part to the BFI's early interest in television generally and to publications like

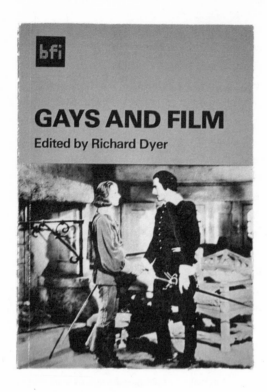

Front cover of Richard Dyer's
edited collection *Gays and
Film* (London: British Film
Institute, 1977).

these that were designed as teaching tools specifically. As television is perceived as less global than film, speaking in its host nations' tongues to concerns, narratives, myths, and characters of local interest, the selective reception and consumption of the BFI Monographs in North America — where very few university or college libraries hold the television titles — is perhaps unsurprising. Nonetheless, it points to the care that needs to be taken when drawing comparisons between the history of the British and American academic scenes with respect to moving image studies.

Another feature of the BFI Monographs that links them concretely to their time and place is the fact that several of them arose from, or were commissioned as interpretive documents for, National Film Theatre seasons. *Gays and Film* and *May '68 and Film Culture* are the most conspicuous examples, but others include Mark Nash's *Dreyer* (1977), the collections on surrealism (1978) and images of alcoholism (1979), and Rosalind Delmar's *Joris Ivens: 50 Years of Film-Making* (1979). Such close tie-ins are further indicators of the BFI Monographs' connections to a broader-based film cultural audience in London than the usual characterizations of the *Screen* era in Britain as a closed shop of triumphalist and elitist intellectuals might lead one to believe. In fact, the relationship between British little books and repertory moviegoing in London is one that extends both back to the first wave, wherein at least seven titles can be coupled with NFT seasons, and to the ebb tide of the 1980s, wherein three of the BFI Dossiers appear to be performing this duty.[21] The differences among the three eras on this front lay in the nature of the seasons themselves: all of the first wave NFT tie-ins are director monographs, less than half of the second wave ones deal with filmmakers, and only one ebb tide volume does so. Neither dogmatically theoretical nor auteurist in the *Cahiers* tradition, the BFI Monographs speak to audiences interested in a wider range of cinema programming and print interpretation than the little books that had preceded them only a few years before.

Importantly, these audiences were not wholly London based, as a strong presence was established in Scotland in the form of two other cultural organs: the BFI summer schools, and the Edinburgh Film Festival. Both of these contributed in important ways to the "debate culture" pursued by the BFI Education Department, not the least because of the publications that were read during them and/or grew out of them. The first summer schools from the late 1950s through the late 1960s, held at the University of Bangor in Wales, were comparatively star-studded affairs, with guest speakers comprising famous personnel from the industry—stars, directors, producers, cinematographers, etc.[22] The relocation geographically to Stirling and institutionally to BFI Education in the 1970s coincided with a decided shift in course presenters, content, and assigned readings. The syllabus for the 1971 course on "Realism: Theory and Practice" is just over four pages long and features a reading list of five texts (including André Bazin and Siegfried Kracauer in translation, and Elizabeth Sussex's 1969 Movie Paperbacks/Praeger Film Library little book on Lindsay Anderson) and nine short articles, almost all from *Sequence* and *Sight and Sound*. The twenty-three-page syllabus for the 1979 course "Realism, Cinema and Cultural Production" offers a five-page bibliography of readings (which includes the BFI Monographs *May '68 and Film Culture*, *The Work of Dorothy Arzner*, and *Women in Film Noir* alongside translations of Karl Marx, Georg Lukacs, and the Frankfurt school) and fourteen pages of "Contexting Notes for Seminars."[23] Clearly, the bar had been raised theoretically throughout the 1970s at these summer schools. But it is important to recognize as well that the target demographic was not *Screen* semiotots but those interested in pursuing in-depth coursework that addressed broad aspects of film and television culture—style, genre, textual analysis, audiences, realism, and the like. As stated in

Raoul Walsh

Front cover of Phil Hardy's
edited collection *Raoul Walsh*
(Edinburgh: Edinburgh Film
Festival, 1974).

the introduction to the 1979 course: "The School is exploratory and no special qualifications are required of students beyond a basic knowledge of film and television informed by the critical debates of the past ten years."[24]

While the summer schools at Stirling provided a forum for research undertaken by BFI Education staff, much of which was published in the form of BFI Monographs, the schools also served as a testing ground for new projects that would eventually become other little books. This was true in a more consistent way for the Edinburgh Film Festival (EFF), which published six little books between 1969 and 1975, all on American auteurs. These EFF monographs are extremely interesting for the way in which they pull in two directions at once—a *Cahiers*-inflected fascination with *enfant terrible* American directors but shot through with the "critical debates" of the age. In this sense they represent a consistent trend in second wave little books toward rethinking American auteurs in ways that might conform to the political and theoretical concerns of the BFI Education Department (and later *Screen*) in Britain. "The publications policy of the festival from 1969 onwards followed up a series of questions that *Signs and Meaning in The Cinema* raised. These books, studies of the works of individual directors, explored the structural configurations providing coherence of a given director's work."[25] The EFF's commitment to "structured programming"—something of a buzzword among film educators in Britain in the 1970s—was held up as a healthy alternative to the London Film Festival on the one hand, and "the limitations of both progressive (*Movie*) and dominant (*Sight and Sound*) trends in British criticism" on the other.[26]

Still, the tension between theoretical investigation and populist auteurism that wends its way through the EFF monographs would by mid-decade render their fragile coherence unsustainable. The EFF books offer here a clear line of continuity from Cinema One in not only content but also form, carrying on the prominent design influence of the series—the chevron slashes of the film clapper along their top borders—as a mark of the kind of cinephilia out of which these publications came and could never quite divest themselves, with their iconic reference to film production, and thus the very object "film." The introduction to the publication that superseded them in 1976, *Edinburgh '76 Magazine*, makes the point itself that "the positivist separation between film as an object of study and the politics of film culture" had become "progressively untenable. The contradictions contained within the books, particularly the last two on Walsh and Tourneur, though already discernible in earlier publications, forced the realization that the key issue at stake was film as an ideological practice rather than as a predetermined and self-sufficient object of study."[27] In this sense, Edinburgh's decision to move from monograph to magazine form in 1976 points to the increasing influence of the journal *Screen* on the film cultural scene. But the general interpenetration among cinémathèque/festival programming, extramural and summer school courses, and little book publishing in the age of *Screen* must equally be borne in mind in a consideration of British film study in the 1970s.

This second wave, then, set the foundations for a discipline in Britain where the study of film continued to take place largely in venues and forms outside the academic arena. But it also evidences the cementing of the discipline as a theoretical one in America (of which Bill Nichols's *Movies and Methods*, published by a university press in 1976, is a key marker).[28] Ironically, the BFI Monographs represent an apogee of the little book at the same time as they sowed the seeds for its decline. For the BFI Monographs were (selectively) consumed, along with *Screen*, by the first university-trained generation of American film studies scholars who would reach their terminal degrees in the late 1970s and then go on to publish much lengthier treatises with university presses in the early 1980s. In Britain they were intended for and purchased by a wider audience, as contributions to a "debate culture" not centered in the university but on its fringes and dealing with aspects of popular culture in Britain, whether that be American cinema or national television. I think we should see, then, that the transit from the little book to the thick academic text bearing the scholarly stamp of the university press in the late 1970s and early 1980s marks a geographic shift as much as it indicates a change of format and a move toward professionalization. Film culture was in the process of becoming increasingly separated from film study, and North America was at the forefront of this development.

Ebb Tide, 1981–1996

The period from around 1980 through to the late 1990s was the ebb tide for little book publication. It is the age of the scholarly study proper and the university presses, which washed little books onto the shelves of the used bookstore. The BFI would soon all but abandon little books, opting in the short term for a much cheaper, oversized BFI Dossier format for the quick turnout of twenty-two works between 1980 and 1984 on subjects remarkably similar to its previous pamphlets but with nowhere near the same print run, and establishing in the long term its publishing division in 1980. As Buscombe notes, "Publishing was detached from the education department and reorganised into a separate department and a new imprint, BFI Publishing, with Geoffrey Nowell-Smith as head. American distribution had been secured, the books looked more professional, and the number of titles was increased to about thirty a year."[29] True to form, the BFI introduced the BFI Cinema Series—another, no-longer-quite-so-little book series that was published in tandem with Macmillan Education in Britain and Indiana University Press in the United States. Buscombe has averred that the "BFI's objective has always been to improve the general level of film culture" and that publishing "was a key element in its strategy." While I do not disagree with these statements in principle, the formalization by the BFI of a publishing division quite separate from the Education Department nonetheless marked an in-house shift toward writing for and marketing toward an increasingly large and lucrative educational sector in Britain as opposed to a general film cultural audience. While the blurb for the Cinema Series implies continuity with past series in terms of audience address, the short and sporadic run of titles here—only seven appearing in a dozen years—suggests that BFI Publishing's investments lay elsewhere. Though there were occasional little books, at least in size, on the BFI list from the 1980s—reprints of Kaplan's *Women in Film Noir* (1980) and Dyer's *Stars* (1986), along with Charlotte Brundson's collection *Films for Women* (1986)—the dominant trend was toward releasing bigger, glossier, and more expensive books: notably, readers on realism, authorship, and the musical, in association with Routledge and

Kegan Paul, in 1980–81; and then Pam Cook's huge *The Cinema Book* in 1985, with its copious information on 16mm film clips recommended for teaching purposes and available for hire from the BFI Film Extracts Service.

Based on the publishing record of university presses alone, 1985 must be marked as the *annus mirabilis* for the academic film text as big book. The early 1980s were watershed years for the consolidation of film studies as an academic discipline in its own right, and it was North America that seized the reins. The *Journal of Film and Video* began publishing a section of "College Course Files" starting in 1984; the first syllabus was, significantly, "An Introduction to the American Film Industry." Barry Keith Grant's collection *Film Study in the Undergraduate Curriculum*, commissioned by the Modern Language Association of America, had appeared a year earlier and got down to the nuts and bolts of seventeen film studies programs in the United States and Canada.[30] A partial list of some of the more notable and/or influential books published in the middle 1980s would include, for example, for 1985: Robert C. Allen and Douglas Gomery, *Film History: Theory and Practice* (McGraw-Hill); Tino Balio, ed., *The American Film Industry*, rev. ed. (Wisconsin); David Bordwell, *Narration in the Fiction Film* (Wisconsin); David Bordwell, Janet Staiger, and Kristin Thompson, *The Classical Hollywood Cinema: Film Style and Mode of Production to 1960* (Columbia/Routledge and Kegan Paul); Jim Hillier, ed., *Cahiers du Cinéma, the 1950s: Neo-Realism, Hollywood, New Wave* (Routledge and Kegan Paul/BFI/Harvard); Gerald Mast and Marshall Cohen, eds., *Film Theory and Criticism: Introductory Readings*, 3rd ed. (Oxford); and Bill Nichols, ed., *Movies and Methods, Volume 2* (California). And for 1986: David Bordwell and Kristin Thompson, *Film Art: An Introduction*, 2nd ed. (Random House); Gilles Deleuze, *Cinema 1: The Movement-Image*, trans. Hugh Tomlinson and Barbara Habberjam (Athlone Press/Minnesota); Barry Keith Grant, ed., *Film Genre Reader* (Texas); Philip Rosen, ed., *Narrative, Apparatus, Ideology: A Film Theory Reader* (Columbia); and Robin Wood, *Hollywood from Vietnam to Reagan* (Columbia).

Some little books were still being published. And there were more than enough books to demonstrate the extent to which theory was of major concern, particularly in the form of the three identically sized readers that collected some of the more frequently taught articles on theory (Mast and Cohen, Nichols, Rosen). Fat as these anthologies are, however, they were competing in the marketplace with texts of equal or even larger formats dedicated to questions of film style, technology, and history: Balio's revised edition of *The American Film Industry* (22 cm × 15 cm); Bordwell's *Narration in the Fiction Film* (24 cm × 24 cm); and Bordwell, Staiger, and Thompson's *The Classical Hollywood Cinema* (24.5 cm × 18.6 cm). The American and historical dimensions of these books, and the authority by which they presented themselves, are part and parcel of their literal size. No coincidence, perhaps, that all three derived from a middle-American state, film studies program, and university press—Wisconsin—that have each demonstrated a penchant for large portions when it comes to food on the plate, graduate student intake, and book formats.[31]

Of all of these big books, Bordwell, Staiger, and Thompson's door-stopping *The Classical Hollywood Cinema* is the milestone—and, in some ways I think, a millstone. Acknowledged from the beginning as setting a new and imposing standard in scholarship and research, the book also put forward a different kind of "scientific rigor" than that pursued by the theoretical cohort of *Screen* from a decade earlier. *The Classical Hollywood Cinema* is itself the classical text for American film studies of the past twenty years. But it also, despite its multiple authors, inaugurated the era of the thick, single-authored scholarly tome that would serve as the benchmark for promotion and tenure in the American academic system. It presupposes a very different student of film than the little book, one less mobile and autodidactic, bound to a seat of higher learning, the university library, the college dorm room study desk—a student now, to put it plainly, "institutionalized." Film books could no longer be sequestered in a coat pocket to be read seated in a café or on a bus or train; bookbags or backpacks for their transport were now required, a table on which to unfold them, a highlighter pen with which to mark pertinent passages for the writing of essays and the studying of exams. Such was the context for my formal education in film: the thorough specialization of film study within the academy; and the demands for those who reach terminal degrees to publish work of a certain size and length for a certain audience—themselves.

Not all of the academic books that followed in the wake of *The Classical Hollywood Cinema* were as replete with such thick description. There was still room for film book series of more modest proportions—for example, the short run (1987–90) of color-coded Indiana University Press books dealing with various aspects of feminist film theory and practice. Indeed, series like these lend some credence to the characterization of the 1980s as years in which many film scholars were lost in the highlands of theory.

Few have been more invested than David Bordwell in setting up this semantic field so as to debunk it. His 1989 *Making Meaning: Inference and Rhetoric in the Interpretation of Cinema* (Harvard) is aimed at exposing the suppositions and weaknesses of symptomatic interpretation, which, in the form of post-1968 critical theory (including feminist film theory), "presents itself as a challenge to traditional criticism" but is revealed as doing no such thing.[32] Indeed, Bordwell aligns the very professionalization of film studies with what he calls here "Grand Theory": "The growth of film interpretation requires the sort of shared conventions I have described, but they have flourished chiefly because of the post-1960s consolidation of intellectual power within colleges and universities—a political development that is only now beginning to receive the analysis it warrants. The emergence of 'theory' is at once a symptom of this process and a powerful maneuver within it."[33] Apart from the fact that Bordwell is deploying precisely the rhetoric of "symptom" he is at pains to distance his own project from, in terms of actual books published and courses being taught in North America at the time this broadstroke portrait of film studies as perched precariously on theory does not bear up under scrutiny. In the late 1980s film studies had not simply taken hold in the American academic scene but was beginning to be analyzed as a subject in itself, with all that suggests for a discipline that had become stabilized—though not by theory.[34]

Two film book series launched in 1990—one sized in the now-standard range for the academic book, 23 cm × 15.5 cm, the other of the Mr. Big and Tall variety, 27 cm × 18.7 cm—usefully capture the timbre of the academic publishing scene. Routledge's AFI Film Readers have, in their seventeen volumes to date, offered collections of original essays by both young and established film scholars on all manner of topics. Early entries leaned on aspects of theory. Television, video, and the new media soon warranted titles as well, as did black moving image production and reception. So have the long-standing topics dear to film studies—classical Hollywood comedy, the Western, authorship. These readers effectively range over the terrains first covered by the first and second waves of the little book, thus extending their legacy into the 1990s and demonstrating the tenacity of the categories and topics they bequeathed to academic American film studies in its formative phases. The History of American Cinema series, however, is another (though related) story. Also launched in 1990, in hardcover format by Charles Scribner's Sons, the series offered scrupulously researched and footnoted decade-by-decade coverage of the history of American cinema. It was taken over by the University of California Press in 1994, which offered paperback editions. Each one is a fine piece of contemporary historical scholarship; some are exceptional. And yet I think as much is lost as is gained by this big book series. The sheer scale of the enterprise suggests a kind of authority and a particular kind of academic rigor that have become the *sine qua non* for acknowledgment and credibility for scholarship in film studies today. That the American cast of the series has no contemporary equivalent for another national cinema represents the migration of several forms of film study to a kind of final resting home: the American academy. As well, its emphasis on historical processes—be they industrial, economic, legal, aesthetic, or thematic—indicates the degree to which the historical turn has staked its claim as *the* methodological approach best equipped to cover the past and present of the discipline. But what might such a claim mean for the future for film studies, and for the little book, in both its North American and its British contexts?

Resurgence, 1997–2005

Academic scholars today increasingly face institutional pressures to produce work of a certain research model and length to gain tenure or promotion. But many in film studies perceive more particular pressures concerning the domain and the vitality of their field. Two collections published in the last decade, *Post-Theory: Reconstructing Film Studies* and *Re-Inventing Film Studies* typify what many have termed a crisis surrounding film studies' stability, disciplinary integrity, and scholarly standards.[35] A forum on publishing, which appeared in *Cinema Journal* in 2005, is particularly germane here.[36] Its editor and five respondents outline the reasons for the recent decline in university press contracts and print runs for scholarly books on film and media, the potential impact this decline might have on academic standards of research choices and rigor, and some possible tactics film studies scholars might consider in confronting the crisis. A nostalgia for the heyday of university press big book publishing and consumption is palpable in this discussion; that all of the respondents work in the American context merely heightens the geographic specificity of their views and fears.[37] As Kathleen Fitzpatrick puts it bluntly, "I am writing in a dying field. Or so it seems given the way academic presses treat the field of late."[38]

Are we writing in a dying field? If so, are university presses to blame for pulling out on us, or are we to blame for investing too much in their imprimatur? Certainly, the inroads of media studies, cultural studies, and visual culture in the academy, of Internet publishing of all sorts, from fanboy and fangirl celebrations of favorite films and stars, cult and extreme cinema sites, autodidact pages of all description, and online journals refereed or not, have marked the disciplinary boundaries of film studies as more porous than the 1980s and 1990s had led many to believe. And this return is felt no less by academic gatekeepers wringing their hands about how best to plug the dikes ringing the field as by university press editors who must now deal with a marketplace in which film books written,by scholars for the academic market alone no longer sell as well as they did in the 1980s and 1990s.

But film books do sell still. The last few years have witnessed a resurgence of the little book, and a resurgence of a scale and concentration not seen before in the history of Anglo-American film culture. By my reckoning, some 631 little film books in thirty-eight series offered by twenty-two separate publishing houses were released between 1997 and 2005 — an astounding 44.6 percent of all little book production since the onset of the first wave in 1965 (see the addendum). Of the twenty-two publishers involved in this phenomenon, only six are university presses. The bulk of these little book publishers are British, and the BFI is once again in the thick of it. Launched in 1992, the BFI Film Classics series was initially intended to support a program by the National Film and Television Archive (NFTVA) to strike and circulate new prints of classic feature films. In 1983, David Meeker, then keeper of films at the NFTVA, drew up a list of 360 films for this purpose. The supporting program that started in 1989, "Treasures from the National Film Archive," was hosted at the (now defunct) Museum of the Moving Image on the same site as the NFT, where the films were presented one film per day, year in and year out.[39] Although the program failed to draw the expected crowds, the BFI Classics have proven to be a solid performer for BFI Publishing, due at least in part to its commissioning of non-academic writers to author them. Edward Buscombe's assessment of the venture is telling: "In looking for authors surely here was an opportunity to move beyond the usual suspects, the professors of film, and try to get some non-academic enthusiasts to write. Not that the BFI had anything against cinema academics, but surely they shouldn't have a stranglehold on the subject. So the series has been written by the most diversified group of authors of any film book series: novelists such as Salman Rushdie, A. L. Kennedy, Simon Louvish, film-makers such as Taylor Downing, Michael Eaton, Nelly Kaplan, visual artists like Ian Breakwell, journalists like Richard Boston and Philip French, cultural critics like Marina Warner and Camille Paglia, an MP (Gerald Kaufman), a knight (Sir Christopher Frayling), a lord (Lord (Melvyn) Bragg [sic]) . . . It's been the BFI's most successful publishing venture. Imitation is the sincerest form of flattery, and other publishers such as Cambridge have been quick to launch similar series."[40]

The resurgence of the little book since 1997 rivals the quantity and penetration of the two waves from 1965 to 1980. And while many of the current titles are penned by academics, equally as many are not. Is this a return to the pre-academic film studies days in Britain? In some ways, yes. The BFI has been accompanied in the little book market since the mid-1990s by several other British trade publishers, most notably Faber and Faber, Methuen, Flicks Books, Screenpress Books, Pocket Essentials, Harlow, I. B. Tauris, and Wallflower Press. While each publisher is a significant presence in the little book scene, I find Wallflower Press to be the most cogent of the clutch, as it displays so many continuities with those of the first and second waves that I have presented here. Like many of these, Wallflower has linked British publishing houses with those in the United States, though this time from the start with a university press (Columbia) acting as the North American distributor. Its individual series, too, bear resemblance to those that have come before: genres and topics, national cinemas and movements, and directors. The sizes and formats of their series cut a swath between some of the much smaller little books in current publication and that of the standard university press monograph, denoting Wallflower's crossover address among those studying film within the educational sector and a new generation of the cineliterate fueling their passion from without. On the production end, there is room in its stable for both the academic scholar and the belletrist critic. Wallflower's constituency of writers and readers conforms especially to that of the second wave of little books.

Another important continuity is the predominance of the director as subject of study. Excluding the screenplays and film guides, of the remaining 258 little books published between 1997 and 2005, exactly half (129) are director monographs. As one might expect, the names have changed from those of the first wave, of whom only Orson Welles has remained a force today with more than one study. While the increasing popularity of film festivals and the availability of international cinema via satellite and cable movie channels as well as DVD unquestionably have affected which directors now receive monographs, are these outlets and platforms really so different in outcome from the art house and café cultures of the first and second waves? The names have changed, but have the structures of thought that they serve, the passion for film they fulfill?

I would say no. Two recently published collections on cinephilia demonstrate that the subject is not at all dead, though it has become dispersed across venues of consumption and production that could not have been predicted in its first great manifestation in the 1960s.[41] The academic study of film in both geographies has served a generative function for film culture as well as a fragmenting one. The current resurgence of little books has been in part enabled by the success of film studies as a discipline, of the persistence of core ideas about cinema that the field continues to support and develop — core ideas that issued, as I claim here, from film culture in the first place. But film studies must play a more active role in this complex film cultural network if it is to reconnect with the impulses and the pleasures, the enthusiasm and the excitement, that were functional in breathing life into it in the first place, and may equally revivify it now. We are writing not in a dying field but rather in one too in thrall with scholarly rules of completeness, of institutional verification, of order. It is time again for a little grandeur.

Notes

I would like to thank the British Academy for funding overseas conference presentations of drafts of this essay in 2004 and 2006.

1. The British Film Institute was registered by the Board of Trade as a private company in September 1933, following the recommendations of a report entitled *The Film in National Life*, which itself was the result of a conference held by the British Institute of Adult Education (The Commission on Educational and Cultural Films, *The Film in National Life: Being the Report of an Enquiry Conducted by the Commission on Educational and Cultural Films into the Service which the Cinematograph May Render to Education and Social Progress* [London: Allen and Unwin, 1932]). Finance was initially provided by a grant from the Cinematograph Fund. During its history the BFI has engaged in a range of activities, including film, television, and paper preservation; education (across all ages); film production and distribution (now video and DVD rentals and sales); theatrical presentation (including film festivals); and publishing (magazines, books, resources for teachers and students). Since 1965 the BFI has been funded by an annual government grant, and it was given a Royal Charter in July 1983. Its current mission statement is as follows: "The purpose of the BFI is to champion moving image culture in all its richness and diversity, across the UK, for the benefit of as wide an audience as possible and to create and encourage debate." The BFI's own Web site is replete with information concerning its histories and activities: see http://www.bfi.org.uk.

2. "Introduction," *All Our Yesterdays: 90 Years of British Cinema*, edited by Charles Barr (London: BFI/MOMA, 1986), 3.

3. The front cover of *The Cinema 1950* characterizes it as "the first volume of an annual publication, designed to take the place of the Penguin Film Review, this is a collection of essays on the Film in all its aspects, illustrated with over 120 Stills from the year's films." The nine volumes of the *Penguin Film Review* (1946–1949) were also collections.

4. The New Index Series that the BFI began in 1950 was an extension of a previous

series of numbered indexes (largely filmographies) that appeared as "special supplements" to its *Sight and Sound* magazine in the previous decade.

5. Of the first wave's 197 titles, there were sixty-two screenplays and only five film guides, making up just over one-third of the total. Screenplays and film guides dropped slightly in their output in the second wave, with the forty-two of the former and twenty-five of the latter comprising 29.8 percent of little book production. It is only during little books' ebb tide of the 1980s and their resurgence around the new millennium that these two forms demonstrated their dominance: 97 screenplays and 58 film guides in the ebb tide, or 42.7 percent; and 148 screenplays and 225 film guides in the resurgence, or 59.1 percent.

6. Robin Wood, *Hitchcock's Films* (London: A. Zwemmer; New York: A. S. Barnes, 1965), 7.

7. Wood's only competition, in terms of not only his output and influence but also his concentration on directors, is Peter Bogdanovich, who wrote six such studies between 1961 and 1971, three during what I am calling the rising tide. These three — *The Cinema of Orson Welles* (1961), *The Cinema of Howard Hawks* (1962), and *The Cinema of Alfred Hitchcock* (1962) — were published by the Museum of Modern Art (MOMA) Film Library and distributed by Doubleday and Co. I should mention here why I have not included them. In addition to Bogdanovich's titles, MOMA/Doubleday released similar volumes on Swedish films (1962) as well as the films of Carl Dreyer (1964), D. W. Griffith (1965), and Josef Von Sternberg (1966). But their large-format size and film-by-film credits and commentary mark them as high-quality MOMA film program accompaniments as opposed to the more critical-explicative tenor of the little books that are my subject here.

8. "Editorial," *Screen* 12.3 (1971): 11.

9. Colin McArthur, "Two Steps Forward, One Step Back: Cultural Struggle in the British Film Institute," *Journal of Popular British Cinema*, no. 4 (2001): 116. See also "An Open Letter to the Staff of the British Film Institute," *Screen* 12.3 (1971): 6.

10. In 1971, Ivan Butler explained the BFI's position of seeking publishing partners for Cinema One as emanating from *Sight and Sound*. The floating nature of these partnerships are as indicative of the internal tensions plaguing the BFI over issues of cultural policy as were the flurry of controversies and crises that Butler summarizes with such bemusement elsewhere in his book. See Butler, *"To Encourage the Art of the Film": The Story of the British Film Institute* (London: Robert Hale, 1971), especially 45–47, 49–53, 127, 135, 176.

11. Edward Buscombe, "21 Years of Films Studies," http://www.bfi.org.uk/bookvid/books/21/buscombe.html. My argument concerning the central role played by the BFI Education Department in the formation of film studies in Britain is adumbrated and fleshed out considerably by the conversation between Laura Mulvey and Peter Wollen that appears in this volume. They foreground how Paddy Whannel, through not only his departmental leadership but also his investments in workers' and adult education, the popular arts, and theoretical thought and writing, was

crucial in the establishment of both film studies and the rise of film theory in the United Kingdom.

12. Serge Guilbaut and Scott Watson, "From an Interview with Peter Wollen," January 13, 2001, Vancouver, http://www.belkin-gallery.ubc.ca/lastcall/current/page1.html. See also Mulvey and Wollen, "From Cinephilia to Film Studies," this volume.

13. Wood found Wollen's final chapter of *Signs and Meaning in the Cinema* "compounded of confusions, distortions and self-delusions in roughly equal measure: an extraordinary piece of frenzied mystification" (Wood, *Personal Views: Explorations in Film* [London: Gordon Fraser, 1976], 57).

14. See Wood's "In Defense of Art," *Film Comment* 11.4 (July–August 1975): 44–51, and his "Against Conclusions," *Film Comment* 11.5 (September–October 1975): 30–32.

15. Wood, *Personal Views*, 33.

16. For more on the extramural course, see Butler, *"To Encourage the Art of the Film,"* 85–86.

17. McArthur, "Two Steps Forward, One Step Back," 117. For an overview of the Education Department up to and around 1971, see Butler, *"To Encourage the Art of the Film,"* 83–89.

18. Although I have not thoroughly trawled the history of university press publishing on film before the 1960s, I have found little to suggest that interest was more than passing. Apart from the University of Chicago Press, which published a series of reports on film and mass communications in the 1930s and 1940s, as far as I can tell no university press put forth a concentrated series of publications on film with a coherent editorial policy until the 1970s. The first of these was Indiana, with its Filmguide series (1973–1975), which I suspect resulted from its experience distributing the British trade-led Cinema One and Cinema Two series.

19. On *Screen* and its legacy, see Philip Rosen's essay in this volume.

20. The resignees were Eileen Brock, Alan Lovell, Jennifer Norman, Gail Naughton, Jim Pines, and Paddy Whannel; see "An Open Letter to the Staff of the British Film Institute," "Editorial," and Alan Lovell's "The BFI and Film Education" all in *Screen* 12.3 (1971): 2–26.

21. Between 1986 and 1994, the National Film Theatre for its part released a dozen numbered "NFT Dossiers" as small-format publications coinciding with various film seasons, focusing on practitioners and national film movements especially.

22. See Butler, *"To Encourage the Art of the Film,"* 94–96.

23. Jim Cook and Nicky North, eds., *BFI Summer Schools 1971–1979: A Dossier* (London: BFI Education Department, 1981), 4–8, 116–39.

24. Cook and North, *BFI Summer Schools 1971–1979*, 116. Edward Buscombe has noted as well that "it soon became clear from the sales" of *Women in Film Noir* in 1978 "that it was being snapped up by teachers to be used as a course book" (Buscombe, "21 Years of Films Studies").

25. Phil Hardy, Claire Johnston, and Paul Willemen, "Introduction," *Edinburgh '76 Magazine: Psychoanalysis, Cinema, Avant-Garde*, no. 1 (1976): 3.

26. Ibid.

27. Ibid.

28. Another marker is the formation of *Camera Obscura* in the same year by a collective of American feminists dissatisfied with the sociological approach of the journal *Women and Film*. See the essay in this volume on the history of *Camera Obscura*.

29. Buscombe, "21 Years of Films Studies."

30. Barry Keith Grant, ed., *Film Study in the Undergraduate Curriculum* (New York: Modern Language Association, 1983).

31. To be fair, Wisconsin University Press did in the early 1980s produce little books in its Warner Bros. Screenplay Series; but I also think it is significant that the series completed its run in 1984, at which time the big books took over the terrain.

32. David Bordwell, *Making Meaning: Inference and Rhetoric in the Interpretation of Cinema* (Cambridge, Mass.: Harvard University Press, 1989), 95. See also his "Adventures in the Highlands of Theory," *Screen* 29.1 (winter 1988): 72–97.

33. Bordwell, *Making Meaning*, 220. The term "Grand Theory" appears in the first instance on page 96. Other phrases receive such capitalization in the book as well — Interpretation Unlimited, the Historical Turn — but not historical poetics. The difference is telling, for it highlights the degree to which the author proffers here, and indeed throughout his publications, the unassailable workings of what Robert B. Ray identifies as "normal science. . . . a single, persistently used method" (Ray, "The Bordwell Regime and the Stakes of Knowledge," *Strategies* 1 [Fall 1988]; reprinted in *How a Film Theory Got Lost and Other Mysteries in Cultural Studies* [Bloomington: Indiana University Press, 2001], 42).

34. Another publication from 1989 reflected on the practices and structures of film studies, in terms not of its modes of interpretation but its curricular organization, and it makes for interesting reading in light of Bordwell's claim that this was the era of grand theorizing: only two courses in the second volume contain a whiff of the usual theoretical suspects in their reading lists. See Erik S. Lunde and Douglas E. Noverr, eds., *Film History: Selected Course Outlines from American Colleges and Universities* and *Film Studies: Selected Course Outlines from American Colleges and Universities* (New York: Marcus Weiner, 1989).

35. David Bordwell and Noël Carroll, eds., *Post-Theory: Reconstructing Film Studies* (Madison: University of Wisconsin Press, 1996); and Christine Gledhill and Linda Williams, eds., *Reinventing Film Studies* (London: Arnold; New York: Oxford University Press, 2000).

36. "In Focus: The Crisis in Publishing," edited by Alexandra Juhasz, *Cinema Journal* 44.3 (spring 2005): 81–98.

37. The pressure to publish university press books in Britain certainly exists, but for very different reasons than in the United States and Canada, where nailing a first book contract with a university press is now essential to achieving tenure, and subsequent books are needed to move up the promotional ladder. In Britain, where many scholars are only tangentially connected to academe and where tenure does

not exist, publishing books of a recognized research standard is important at the departmental level and necessary because of the ongoing Research Assessment Exercise (RAE), which determines government allocations of funds to institutions and plays a major role in determining the national reputations (important for student intake) of departments, schools, colleges, and universities. In short, a research-active academic in Britain is expected to turn out a book every five years or so for the sake of the RAE; promotion depends on publishing books, too, but the carrot or stick of tenure does not come into play.

38. "From the Crisis to the Commons," *Cinema Journal* 44.3 (spring 2005): 92.

39. For a complete list of the films in the 360 Classic Feature Films Project (which actually consists of 362 films), as well as for background and critical commentary from filmmakers, reviewers, and scholars, see the pamphlet *360 Film Classics from the National Film and Television Archive*, edited by Nick James (London: BFI, 1998).

40. Buscombe, "21 Years of Films Studies."

41. Jonathan Rosenbaum and Adrian Martin, eds., *Movie Mutations: The Changing Face of World Cinephilia* (London: BFI Publishing, 2003); and Marijke de Valck and Malte Hagener, eds., *Movies, Love and Memory* (Amsterdam: Amsterdam University Press, 2005).

Addendum: Little Books, 1965-2005

FIRST WAVE, 1965–1971

1 Penguin Books Ltd., Harmondsworth, Middlesex, England
   Penguin Books, Baltimore, Maryland
   A Pelican Book / A Pelican Original (1965–1974) — 14 titles (on film)

2 Faber and Faber, London (1967–1976) — 4 titles on film

3 Grove Press, New York
   An Evergreen Book / Evergreen Original (1967–1969) — 3 titles (on film)
   Evergreen Black Cat Book (1968–1970) — 13 titles

4 Frederick Ungar Publishing Co., Inc., New York
   RKO Classic Screenplays (1959–1980) — 9 titles

5 Lorrimer Publishing Limited, London
   Simon and Schuster, New York
   Classic and Modern Film Scripts (1966–1972) — 36 titles (numbered)

6 Orion Press / Grossman Publishers, Inc., New York
   Screenplay series (1963–1973) — 16 titles

7 E. P. Dutton and Co., Inc., New York
   Dutton Paperback Original (1966–1968) — 7 titles (on film)

8   Crown Populishers, Inc., New York
    Editions Seghers' Cinéma d'Aujourd'hui in English (1969–1971)—6 titles

9   Dover Publications, Inc., New York
    Dover Books on Cinema and the Stage (1969–1976)—16 titles (on film)

10 Studio Vista Limited, London
    E. P. Dutton and Co., Inc., New York
    Studio vista / dutton pictureback / dutton vista pictureback (1965–1973)—15 titles

11 Tantivy Press, London; A. Zwemmer Limited, London
    A. S. Barnes and Co., New York; Paperback Library, New York
    International Film Guide series (1965–1974)—33 titles

12 Tantivy Press, London; A. Zwemmer Limited, London
    A. S. Barnes and Co., New York
    Screen series (1969–1979)—13 titles

13 Studio Vista Limited, London
    Frederick A. Praeger, Inc., Publishers, New York
    Movie Paperbacks/Praeger Film Library (1967–1971)—17 titles

14 Thames and Hudson, London / British Film Institute, London
    Secker and Warburg Limited, London / BFI
    Doubleday and Company, New York / BFI
    Viking Press, New York / BFI
    Indiana University Press, Bloomington / BFI
    Cinema One series (Cinema World with Doubleday) (1967–1976)—28 titles (numbered)

SECOND WAVE, 1972–1980

1   Secker and Warburg Limited, London; Thames and Hudson, London
    Various New York publishing houses
    Indiana University Press, Bloomington; University of California Press, Berkeley
    Cinema Two series (some distributed/published in the United States as Praeger Paperbacks) (1969–1978)—16 titles

2   Prentice-Hall, Inc., Englewood Cliffs, New Jersey
    Film Focus (A Spectrum Book) (1971–1976)—18 titles

3   Indiana University Press, Bloomington
    Filmguide series (1973–1975)—11 titles (numbered)

4   Grove Press, New York
    An Evergreen Book / Evergreen Original (1973–1976)—10 titles

5   Lorrimer Publishing Limited, London
    Frederick Ungar Publishing Co., Inc., New York
    Classic and Modern Film Scripts (1973–1975)—9 titles (numbered 37–45)

6   Galahad Books / W. H. Allen, New York
    The Pictorial Treasury of Film Stars / (Pyramid) Illustrated History of the
    Movies / A Star Book (1973)—12 titles

7   Tantivy Press, London
    A. S. Barnes and Co., New York
    The Hollywood Professionals (1973–1979)—7 titles (numbered)

8   Frederick Ungar Publishing Co., Inc., New York
    Ungar Film Library (1976–1983)—24 titles

9   Twayne Publishers, Boston, Massachusetts
    Twayne's Theatrical Arts Series (1977–1981)—30 titles

10 Edinburgh Film Festival (1969–1975)—6 titles

11 The Society for Education in Film and Television, London
    Screen Pamphlets (1972–1973)—2 titles (numbered)

12 British Film Institute / Educational Advisory Services, London
    BFI Monograph (1975–1982)—37 titles
    BFI Television Monograph (1973–1981)—13 titles (numbered)

EBB TIDE, 1981–1996

1   British Film Institute, London
    BFI Dossier (1980–1984)—22 titles (numbered)

2   Macmillan Education, Ltd. and the British Film Institute, London
    Indiana University Press, Bloomington (later: Da Capo Press, New York)
    British Film Institute Cinema Series (1980–1992)—7 titles

3   British Film Institute / National Film Theatre, London
    NFT Dossier (1986–1994)—12 titles (numbered)

4   BFI Publishing, London
    BFI Working Papers (1992–1995)—5 titles

5   Faber and Faber, London and Boston (1981–1987)—6 titles (on film)

6   Twayne Publishers, Boston, Massachusetts
    (from 1992 an imprint of Simon and Schuster Macmillan, New York)
    Twayne's Filmmakers Series (1981–1998) — 40 titles

7   Wisconsin Center for Film and Theatre Research / Wisconsin University Press
    Wisconsin / Warner Bros. Screenplay Series (1979–1984) — 21 titles

8   Rutgers University Press
    Rutgers Films in Print Series (1984–1995) — 22 titles

RESURGENCE, 1997–2005

1   Faber and Faber, London and Boston
    Screenplays (1987–2005) — 149 titles
    Film books (1988–2005) — 111 titles
    Faber Film ("Director on Director") (1989–2005) — 22 titles

2   BFI Publishing, London
    BFI Film Classics (1992–2004) — 76 titles
    BFI Modern Classics (1996–2005) — 47 titles
    BFI World Directors (2001–2004) — 8 titles
    BFI TV Classics (2005–) — 4 titles
    BFI Screen Guides (2005–) — 2 titles

3   Currency Press, Sydney and Strawberry Hills, New South Wales
    Screenplays (1992–2005) — 23 titles
    [with ScreenSound Australia, Canberra]
    Australian Screen Classics (2002–2005) — 5 titles

4   Cambridge University Press, Cambridge and New York
    Cambridge Film Classics (1993–2004) — 16 titles
    Cambridge Film Handbooks (1997–2004) — 17 titles

5   Methuen, London
    Screenplays (1996–2003) — 17 titles

6   Flicks Books, Trowbridge, Wiltshire, England
    Cinetek series (1996–2004) — 19 titles

7   Orion Media, London
    Director books (1997–1998) — 5 titles

8   Screenpress Books, Suffolk, England
    Screenplays (1997–2002) — 43 titles

9   Manchester University Press, Manchester
    French Film Directors (1998–2005) — 16 titles
    British Film Makers (1999–2005) — 9 titles

10 Bloomsbury Publishing, Plc, London
Bloomsbury Movie Guides (1998–1999) — 6 titles
Bloomsbury Pocket Movie Guides (2000) — 6 titles

11 Creation Books, London
Movie Top Ten (1999–2004) — 6 titles

12 Thunder's Mouth Press, New York
Close Up Series (1999–2005) — 6 titles (20 other titles on film)

13 Pocket Essentials, Harpenden, Hertfordshire, England
The Pocket Essentials (1999–2005) — 60 titles (on film)

14 Harlow, London; Longman, New York
York Film Notes (2000) — 20 titles
Ultimate Film Guides (2001) — 11 titles

15 I. B. Tauris and Co.; Ltd., London
KINOfiles Film Companions (2000–2003) — 10 titles
British Film Guides (2002–2005) — 13 titles
KINOfiles Filmmaker's Companions (2004) — 4 titles
Ciné-File French Film Guides (2005–) — 4 titles

16 Wallflower Press, London
short cuts (2000–2005) — 29 titles
directors cuts (2001–2004) — 13 titles
24 frames (2003–2005) — 8 titles

17 Cork University Press in association with the Film Institute of Ireland, Cork
Ireland into Film (2001–2004) — 10 titles

18 Virgin Books, Ltd., London
Virgin Film (2002–2004) — 7 titles (9 other titles on film)

19 Reaktion Books, London
Locations (2002–2004) — 3 titles (7 other titles on film)

20 Toronto International Film Festival Group, Toronto
Indiana University Press, Bloomington
Canadian Filmmakers (2002–2005) — 4 titles

21 University of Illinois Press, Urbana and Chicago
Contemporary Film Directors (2003–2005) — 6 titles

22 Hong Kong University Press
New Hong Kong Cinema (2003–2005) — 5 titles

MAKING AND REMAKING CINEMA STUDIES

Footstool Film School:

Home Entertainment as Home Education

ALISON TROPE

■ In 1999, when the director Michael Bay released on DVD his two mega-blockbusters *Armageddon* and *The Rock* through the prestige outlet the Criterion Collection, he commented that it was "a cool way for film students and filmphiles to see [a movie] in more depth."[1] Bay's use of the word "depth" may seem generous—especially in relation to his films. Nevertheless, his comment sheds light on a burgeoning trend in the home entertainment arena. Once viewed simply as an ancillary exhibition site used to recycle studio product, the home increasingly serves as a site to reinvent and reinterpret the film medium.[2] Home entertainment, particularly in the form of DVDs and to a lesser extent in their cable movie channel predecessors, situates the original film text within an often overloaded and overlooked extratextual arena. The extratextual content, including behind-the-scenes and making-of featurettes, documentaries, production exercises, and audio commentaries serves two functions. It offers media distributors an additional marketing arena for their products: one that suggests, even promises, a new experience—a film transformed and remade especially for the home. At the same time, this content can function as a form of popular education, offering the everyday viewer access to the production process, textual analysis of a film's formal elements, and in the case of classic titles, a look back at film history. These satellite texts potentially breed a new type of film student, a distinct form of cinephilia, and a unique apparatus of film acculturation. The home, in turn, becomes a key site in the popularization and mainstreaming of film study.

With home entertainment, the possibilities for film study are no longer limited to public educational institutions. Home entertainment, indeed, depends upon efforts to bring the public sphere of the archive, museum, theater, film school, and even the studio back lot into the domestic sphere. As such, DVDs represent an exemplary format in the contemporary home entertainment arena that both emulate and rearticulate these spheres. The DVDs that I explore below borrow the language and rhetoric of film study to transform the living room into a personal library or a comfy classroom, where knowledge is at the tip of one's remote control. In the process of this transformation, these home entertainment products often redefine and even reinvent the original film medium as well as potentially alter not only its market value but its cultural and pedagogical value as well.[3] The consumer is poised by the media distributor to gain cultural capital, practical know-how, and a cinephile's identity by participating in a film culture constructed around the regular viewing and ownership of status-laden DVDs. Many media distributors, in fact, use the promise of cultural capital as a means to create value around the purchase or viewing of home entertainment products. The promise is not altogether disingenuous. The extratextual content in many DVDs arguably breathes new life into film culture by offering new avenues and creating new audiences for film study.

Thus we need to look at the home entertainment arena, and DVDs in particular, as more than a mere delivery platform for film. Looking at how film crosses over and interacts with other media and their contexts (namely television's ancillary components such as DVDs) sheds light on the significant role that home entertainment plays in reshaping film culture and film education. By way of home entertainment, I am interested in examining the DVD not only as a technology, delivery platform, or exhibition site but also as a method by which the film text itself is constructed and potentially altered by the satellite texts and discourses that surround it. This reshaping and redefinition of cinema as home entertainment not only reflects a technological or programming shift but also marks a discursive and corporate transition that reframes film study and its texts simultaneously as products of mass consumerism and populist education.

Channeling Culture and Commerce in Home Entertainment

It is easy to be skeptical of the educational value of home entertainment. After all, ancillary media such as DVD are commodities packaged and sold by corporate conglomerates that function within a profit-driven arena where entertainment is valued over education. Within a traditional liberal critique of commodity culture, home entertainment dating from early television easily has fit the classification of "bad object" supporting a suspicion that commerce inevitably corrupts culture. Culture under capitalism, however, is more complicated.

Certainly there are limits to the educational value of home entertainment. Such media generally lack the intertextuality afforded by a course syllabus or a lecture. They do not promote the peer interaction and discussion elicited in a typical classroom setting. Furthermore, the rigor of such texts (e.g., DVD commentaries) may be compromised by a lack of scholarly peer review and editorial attention. At the same time, it is problematic to assume that the traditional classroom setting remains inherently superior to other environments, or that traditional academic gatekeeping structures are always effective. We generally accept other public nonprofit institutions as valuable educational outlets, so why not the home? And why not texts and "curriculum" produced by commercial entities such as Hollywood? In many respects, the study of film is inherently implicated in the commercial apparati that structure the medium and the industry that produces it. It is therefore crucial to consider the role of the home and home entertainment media in the context of film study despite and because of their ties to commerce.

Such questions not only require us to rethink the boundaries between education and commerce but also elucidate a historical tension and a familiar divide between culture and commerce—one that has troubled the film medium since its inception with attempts to define film's relationship to "Culture," writ large, in an Arnoldian tradition.[4] This enduring tension between film's artistic and industrial roots has played a defining role in the history of film studies. Just as film commerce has long depended on discourses of art, the field of film study often has relied on (and in some cases been driven by) the commercial arena. The crossover between industry and academy illustrates not only a historically rooted desire to mediate high and low culture but also an understanding of the mutual benefits that such mediation could offer.

The ideas and institutional structures that historically shaped the field of academic and amateur film study often have revolved around a distinction if not direct opposition to mainstream (namely Hollywood) cinema and its exhibition arenas. Since the early twentieth century, film culture, film study, and the idea of film as art have maintained a foothold in public nonprofit institutions, universities, and repertory theaters—a fairly contained, specialized, and even elitist arena. Many institutions, in turn, have used the distinction in relation to Hollywood in order to legitimate film as an object of study, art, and culture. Within some of these contexts, institutions intent on separating film culture from its industrial roots have balkanized Hollywood cinema in a conscious effort to privilege avant-garde and art cinema.[5] At the same time, however, other public institutions, curricula, and educational texts have explicitly relied upon mainstream cinema and Hollywood studios in very direct ways. As several essays in this anthology have shown, film study historically has had strong ties to the medium's entertainment side. Indeed, a populist strain of both film study and film culture has existed since the teens.[6]

From the earliest days of the academy's flirtation with film, universities including Columbia, Harvard, the University of Southern California, and Stanford clearly found advantages in aligning themselves with Hollywood. Some of Columbia's initial film courses in the teens, in fact, were designed and backed by Hollywood studios. The courses specifically focused on the development of original story material for the burgeoning industry. While such courses fulfilled a populist mission of closing the perceived gap between the ivory tower and the general public, they also served a more crucial function as professional training grounds for future industry employees. Students enrolled in these courses were promised direct access to film texts, lectures on how to "read" a film, industry guest speakers, and in the case of USC, visits to the lots of Hollywood studios.[7]

The crossover between industry and academy in these examples parallels the popularization of self-improvement courses and discourses on a rising middlebrow culture in which the once privileged arenas of high culture found themselves open to the masses, commodifed, and therefore potentially compromised.[8] When films first were screened at the Museum of Modern Art (MOMA) in the 1930s and 1940s, the institution struck a similarly delicate but always deliberate balance between Hollywood and a quickly developing canon of European art cinema. Universities, art houses, repertory theaters, and other nonprofit institutions increasingly relied on the museum's film collection to disseminate its brand of film history and film culture. The museum, therefore, not only afforded essential access to Hollywood films whose theatrical run had long expired but also provided a unique film experience—one of value because of an association with high art and culture endemic to the art museum.[9]

While the universities and museums clearly borrowed from Hollywood, the film industry likewise has borrowed from the nonprofit arena. As Barbara Wilinsky and others have argued, Hollywood studios have long exploited and appropriated elements from art cinema or alternative cinema, reframing them to appeal to mass audiences.[10] Barbara Klinger takes a similar perspective in her discussion of the home entertainment market by suggesting that the marketing of home theater often relies on references to high art. Klinger characterizes such references as strategies intended both to appeal to mass audiences, and also to distinguish potential consumers from their less technologically inclined peers. Both Wilinsky and Klinger foreground the need to examine the relationship between commerce and culture in their respective discussions of the discourses that define art cinema and home theater. While markedly different sites, the success of both theatrical art cinema in the postwar period and home theater since the 1980s and the 1990s directly stems from each exhibition arena's ability to work within and against mainstream Hollywood cinema.

Because home entertainment media cannot rely on the spectacle or authenticity of the theatrical experience or the prestige associated with the museum or art house cinema moniker, media distributors must find other ways to create value. While not directly referencing high art, the burgeoning home entertainment market (particularly on specialty DVDs like Criterion) often more subtly tap into a historical concept of high film culture.[11] Expanding the scope and site of traditional film culture beyond the exclusive arenas of art cinema, museum, and repertory exhibition, this populist and mass market shift in turn expands and alters the general audience of film students and cinephiles.

Studios and media distributors additionally pitch the value of DVDs as promoting a different, novel, and unique experience—one that holds sway not only because of easy-access viewing but also the access to extrafilmic materials and information. The educational nature and value of this extratextual content is not clear cut. On the one hand, it serves as a new form of film education; on the other hand, this education is steeped in commodification. The DVDs discussed below feature several different pedagogical tactics that can generate equally varied effects. Such variation in approach and quality necessarily complicates the very application of the term "education" to the home entertainment media that I am discussing.

The educational content in the supplemental material on DVDs discussed below can be divided into two general categories related to the history of film study. The elucidation of film history in audio commentaries and documentaries as well as in formal and generic analysis generally adheres to the conventions of scholarly film study common to universities and other nonprofit public institutions. The technical and production-oriented forms of instruction in director and other audio commentaries and behind-the-scenes featurettes, meanwhile, trace their roots both to contemporary professional film education and to the early industry training at universities like USC. This kind of practical instruction reflects a long-standing interest and cachet value in unearthing the trade secrets, mystique, and trivia behind the Hollywood production process, implicitly promising that the viewer too can be a filmmaker (or other crafts-person).[12] Coupled with this desire to go behind the Hollywood curtain is a steady and marked proliferation of camcorders and the more prevalent avail-ability of home desktop editing systems, as well as the popularity of behind-the-scenes and do-it-yourself television programs that further stimulate an interest in learning from Hollywood professionals.[13]

In attending to historical, formal, and genre analysis as well as technical and industrial instruction, much DVD content further reflects the negotiation between culture and commerce that fundamentally and historically has shaped the film industry as well as the history of film study. The value attached to such home entertainment instruction promises viewers easy accessibility and a do-it-yourself control over the film medium, its history, and distribution method. Both types of film study offered by these home entertainment products indeed implicitly celebrate a do-it-yourself and do-it-at-home education. In offering a bottom-up rather than top-down style of learning, the curriculum often re-volves around personal empowerment and self-improvement more than tradi-tional classroom instruction. These home entertainment media position their consumers as prospective students who retain mastery over a high-tech home theater. In this arena, the consumer-student ostensibly maintains control over the classroom and the curriculum; they are agents of their own education.

Such promises or perceptions of empowerment and mastery, of course, fail to take fully into account the industrial and institutional realities of home entertainment media. The institutions producing DVDs have complicated agen-das and missions. While celebrating a bottom-up, do-it-yourself accessibility tailored to the consumer, home entertainment distributors clearly create and market their products in an industrially and profit-driven top-down frame. Rethinking the site, institutions, and texts of film study in the context of home entertainment therefore necessitates revisiting a familiar high-low divide in a new framework. The industrial motives behind DVDs can easily and insidi-ously compromise the promise and pedagogical value of veritable instruction; however, in each of the cases discussed below, they also can offer valuable and quality instruction using materials and perspectives that are otherwise inac-cessible in the context of a traditional academic setting. Commercial motives therefore do not necessarily outweigh or taint the educational value in all DVDs.

The educational value of these products, then, rests in assessing how commercial and cultural interests intertwine in individual examples at the level of production and consumption.

DVDs and Home Schooling

The DVD offers a level of interactivity and consumer empowerment unmatched by previous home entertainment products such as cable television and VHS. Even more than classic cable channels such as American Movie Classics and Turner Classic Movies, DVDs present a new alternative to formal film study. The popular press has openly commented on the relationship between DVDs and film study. Frequently DVDs are called "film school in a can" or "film school in a box." In several stories celebrating what has been dubbed a DVD revolution, the *New York Times* highlighted the fact that the extra features on DVD can "illuminate and explain," "bring the medium close to a scholarly edition of a book," and that "even as amusements, the supplements impart a good deal of information."[14] According to industry estimates, the extra features or so-called "value-added material" largely drives DVD market sales. A 2003 survey, in fact, claimed that 63 percent of DVD owners name value-added materials as a determinant in their DVD purchases.[15] As the target audience for DVD or "digital versatile disc" has diversified since the late 1990s, DVD distributors have capitalized on the platform's versatility by widening the scope of supplemental materials and using them as a primary marketing tool. The ever-widening array of extra features found on DVDs includes audio commentaries from directors, actors, and crew members, behind-the-scenes featurettes and interviews, marketing materials (posters, trailers), correspondence, memorabilia, newsreels and other period shorts, outtakes, galleries of stills and conceptual drawings, production notes, storyboards, alternate endings, games, and film-it-yourself activities.

The question remains: What *value* does this "value-added material" offer to the consumer? Or, for that matter, the student, the fan, or cinephile? Early on, such value-added material was found primarily in two types of DVD product. The Criterion Collection, a nonstudio independent DVD production company, which had its roots in laser disc and educational CD-ROM production in the mid-1980s, has produced widely and critically celebrated supplemental material on over three hundred DVD titles since 1997. On the studio side, action and science fiction titles targeted at technophiles and male consumers tended

Gladiator, 3-disc Extended Edition: reinventing and rewriting the original film with "never before seen" content and hours of bonus features.

Alexander Director's Cut: resurrecting the original film through director's cut and commentary.

to represent the forerunners in DVD supplemental materials. In moving beyond technophiles and cinephiles, studios have successfully conquered the family and mainstream consumer market. Such a shift, in turn, notably parallels the broadening reach of film culture and its inevitable commodification.

According to Universal Home Entertainment President Craig Kornblau, "Our challenge is to bring [the movie] back into the culture, and make it an event."[16] For Kornblau, along with other studio executives, bringing the movie *back* into culture signals a further popularization of the film commodity as well as a mainstreaming of film culture. Kornblau clearly associates film culture not only with popular culture but with retail culture as well. In order to profit in the retail arena, studios market DVDs as equal if not superior to theatrical exhibition. The studio marketing around DVDs claims that the format offers a "new" reinvented and rewritten version of the original film not only through never-before-seen director's cuts but also outtakes, audio commentary, deleted scenes, and alternate endings.[17] One home entertainment executive further commented that DVDs are "even more exciting than the movie."[18] The idea that DVD is more, or better, than some original version of the film clearly works against the tenets of traditional film culture, which privileges the authenticity of the primary theatrical experience. With DVD, film culture more clearly and directly resides in film's extratextual materials, just as film study can more easily take place outside the classroom. In supporting film's commercial and cultural value as popular educator, the supplemental materials serve as crucial elements in defining the film text. In turn, DVD becomes an artifact worthy of film study in its own right.

Much of the popular journalism further works to align DVDs with traditional high culture, even high film culture, thereby echoing the industrial and editorial efforts to legitimate cinema in the teens and twenties. A *New York Times* review of a DVD collection of Griffith Masterworks, for example, claims that "the seven disc collection of his early work belongs on the shelf next to your Oxford Shakespeare—both as crucial reference and as endless source of pleasure."[19] Phil Alden Robinson, the director of *Field of Dreams* and *The Sum of All Fears*, further contends that the DVD is not realizing its full potential. He would like to involve more craftspeople in the commentaries and other features, because "it would be cubist in a way to show the film through different eyes."[20] In addition to these highbrow associations, the popular press often reverts to a more conventional high-low film divide, structuring a traditional art-house European film canon where Criterion produces the "gold standard" in comparison to Hollywood studios and smaller DVD production companies like Anchor Bay Entertainment, Synapse Films, and Grindhouse Releasing that feature cult classics and exploitation films.

Peter Becker, president of the Criterion Collection, upheld such a divide in a 1999 interview in which he aired his views on studio supplemental material. In distinguishing Criterion's DVDs from the average studio DVD, Becker made the following comment: "The attitude that you see represented very often in the sales material for studio DVDs refers to this stuff as 'added value' or 'bonus,' which gives you a sense that this is really being driven by the marketplace. That's not inherently bad, but it's different from what we're doing. We generally don't like to use those 'the making of' programs because they tend to be designed only to lure viewers into theaters or to convince exhibitors that they're going to make a lot of money."[21] Becker instead frames Criterion along the lines of a nonprofit film institution. Their mission, he claims, is to provide "a film archive for the home viewer." Criterion certainly has cornered the DVD market on high film culture, and even with titles like *Armageddon* it tries to frame the blockbuster "genre" as part of a "huge cultural cross-pollination" that influences tastes, shooting styles, and visual references in a wide range of media.[22] Despite Becker's outreach to blockbuster films, the average Criterion consumer remains a conventional film student or cinephile who likely will view a film numerous times and seek out an expert's interpretation of its meaning.

Following in Criterion's footsteps, those Hollywood studios with extremely well-stocked and critically lauded vaults, particularly Warner Bros., Twentieth Century–Fox, and Disney, have created distinctive lines and special editions for many of their classic titles since the early 2000s. Like Criterion, these studio home entertainment divisions amass a wide range of supplemental elements such as original source material, screen tests, storyboards, theatrical trailers, publicity stills, and poster art, as well as period newsreels, interviews, radio theater broadcasts based around the film, and Academy Awards footage in order to frame the titles in a broader historical context.[23] Since 2003, Twentieth Century–Fox has released over thirty titles that include restored versions of classic films as well as archival supplemental materials including their own Movietone newsreels under the banner label "Fox Studio Classics." Disney, meanwhile, has released special editions of many of its animated classics pairing a wealth of archival material with interactive games. With a far more extensive vault and higher production value on DVD packaging and menu design, Warner Bros., too, has released a substantial number of classic titles with similar archival sup-

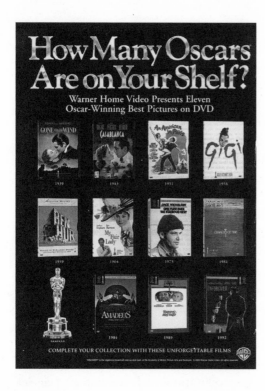

"How Many Oscars Are on Your Shelf? Warner Home Video Presents Eleven Oscar-Winning Best Pictures on DVD": borrowing legitimacy from the Academy and the Oscar statuette.

plements. Some DVDs like *Treasure of the Sierra Madre* further frame these supplements in the context of classical-era theatrical exhibition. Grouped together as a single supplement entitled "Warner Bros. Night at the Movies, 1948," the DVD features a trailer for *Key Largo* as well as a period newsreel, comedy short, and cartoon, thereby simulating the movie experience in the late 1940s. Educational value here is offered not only by the archival materials, but potentially in this case by their presentation as well. This DVD content exceeds classroom instruction by offering not simply a trip through time but a virtual field trip to the studio archive and library.

Like Criterion, studios releasing films from their vaults also typically will include audio commentaries by scholar-historians as well as contemporary documentaries.[24] The audio commentaries provided by professors and independent scholars such as David Bordwell, Donald Richie, Peter Cowie, Laura Mulvey, Dana Polan, Tom Gunning, Charles Musser, Robert Sklar, and Jim Kitses lend these DVDs legitimacy and, in turn, uphold the "film school in a box" moniker. These commentaries, however, tend to focus on one side of film studies based in formal analysis. Even Laura Mulvey, for example, who offers audio commentary on *Peeping Tom*, makes little mention of her own patented theoretical work.[25] And, while many of the historical titles offer much archival documentation and may even reference other films, the scope of film history necessarily gets compromised to some degree by the focus on a single film title.

Formal analysis, of course, remains a key feature of film studies, particularly in introductory courses where students are taught how to read and dissect a film text. Criterion as well as the mainstream studios offer products with supplemental material, particularly those featuring audio commentary focused on dissecting the film form. In addition to the focus on film's formal properties, the supplemental material on many DVD titles tends to highlight the film's director. Many DVD titles now include a release version of the film along with the director's cut. The director's cut as well as the almost de rigueur commentary on contemporary DVD titles fetishize the director and echo traditional auteur studies. Both the focus on formal analysis (through audio commentary as well as how-to production exercises) and the auteur suggest an approach to film education dating back to the earliest days of film studies as an academic discipline. They further suggest a particular approach to learning, one that historically resonates with a middlebrow commodification of high culture. In largely adhering to a film appreciation model, these formal and director-based analyses recycle a vision of film culture cultivated in and by both the art cinema arena as well as renowned institutions such as the Museum of Modern Art. When packaged on DVD, the focus on the creative process and on the technical feats of directors and other craftspeople additionally parallels the professional training and production-oriented courses that were introduced at major universities in the early decades of the twentieth century.

In extolling the educational value of such DVD materials, much of the popular press supports an alignment with, if not replacement of, formal film education. One *New York Times* article highlighted the Criterion DVD of *In the Mood for Love* as having enough supplemental material to "satisfy the most dedicated graduate student" of Wong Kar Wai's films. In another *New York Times* piece, the film critic Elvis Mitchell discussed the DVD's pedagogical predecessor, the laser disc, calling Martin Scorsese's audio commentary on *Taxi Driver*, "a master class" and describing Sydney Pollack's discussion of *Tootsie* as "just the kind of education one would hope to get at film school, without having to echo the professor's thoughts in a paper." Mitchell goes on to argue that "for a time, it seemed that Criterion's output might eliminate the need for film schools altogether, since their essential components, access to films and information about them, were packaged in two-disc sets."[26] A contemporaneous story in the

Los Angeles Times seemed to support these points, citing courses at the UCLA Film School that employ DVD extras in the classroom.[27]

The apparent antagonism toward formal education rests, in general, on a populist celebration of democratic, bottom-up, individual access. At the same time, and more specifically, this response echoes a discourse most recently tied to computers and the Internet (as well as increasingly critiqued in relation to them). In this vein, DVDs get framed as superior to formal film study because they promote interactivity and empowerment (assumed to exceed that of the typical classroom). One of the most sought-after DVD producers and menu designers contends that "interactivity empowers both the filmmaker and the consumer."[28] Not only can the "user" interact with the storytelling but also with the filmmaking process; in some cases this even includes the scholarly critique, such as in the "record your own commentary" feature available on a few DVD-ROM titles (e.g., *Spiderman: 3 Disc Deluxe Edition* and *Pulp Fiction: Collector's Edition, Jay and Silent Bob Strike Back*).[29]

As a reinvented medium that can "bring audiences backstage," "behind closed doors," and put viewers into the film world, studios also sell DVDs as new immersive experiences tailored to the home viewing arena.[30] Some titles, such as *The Lord of the Rings* trilogy, use a multitude of discs and supplemental features to literally walk the viewer through the filmmaking process from preproduction to postproduction. In these examples, film education largely revolves around film production and technical knowledge. Many DVDs convey this information through commentaries and other featurettes in order to frame a title's accessibility and value in terms of proximity to a film's craftspeople or cast.

In constructing an intimate connection between viewer and filmmaker, other titles offer video diaries or first-person accounts of the filmmaking process. The *Godfather* DVD, for example, includes a featurette in which Francis Ford Coppola sits on a sofa in an informal office setting, casually talking to viewers while thumbing through his original production notebook for the film. In this cozy exchange, Coppola excitedly shares how he made the notebook by pasting pages of Mario Puzo's novel onto loose-leaf notebook paper so he could jot down his impressions and ideas next to Puzo's text. The how-to featurette reveals close-ups of Coppola's extensive notes while also offering his nostalgic reminiscences of regularly toting his typewriter to a café in San Francisco's North Beach to work on the script. The use of such video diaries that mingle practical instruction alongside production trivia and nostalgia is typical of behind-the-scenes supplemental material. The line between education and entertainment may be blurred in such material, but the access to Coppola's copious documentation on this canonical film proves invaluable to both the budding filmmaker and the historian.

Highly structured in design and presentation, such content does not offer a radically new or particularly interactive experience. In fact, the technical language and complex explanations used in many features largely reaffirms a traditional top-down pedagogical approach. Indeed, in some of these cases it seems that the viewer must already possess a fundamental grasp of certain technical properties and vocabulary in order to understand the commentaries. This is especially true not only on some special effects and sound design featurettes, but also on those that have to do with computer animation. Some DVDs use "animatrics" (or animated moving storyboards) as a pedagogical device to help explain a technical process visually. On many titles, however, the purported educational aim in such features remains extremely rudimentary and often superficial (if not incomplete). Not surprisingly, given DVD sales figures, these features are often geared toward the mainstream consumer. While seemingly interactive and implicitly touting a film-it-yourself ethos on the surface, many of these features feel like play more than education.[31]

The idea that DVD extra features can somehow empower a viewer and further change the nature and meaning of the original film remains debatable. Not only is the level of interactivity still highly limited by virtue of technology and cost but these extra features are strictly controlled by the film's director, studio, DVD producer, and their views on target consumer groups. Other titles similarly promise industry access through editing exercises (*Men in Black*, the first *Star Wars, Scream 3*), multiple-angle viewing (*Fight Club, Moulin Rouge, Se7en, Speed, Pearl Harbor, Die Hard*), and audio track mixing (*Se7en, Die Hard*). The *Die Hard* DVD sets up each instructive exercise with a user-friendly explanation. These explanations function on two levels—to place the viewer in a privileged position, and at the same time, to address the viewer as a novice or layperson. The purported interactivity and in some cases educational value offered by the extra features on many DVDs, therefore, remains skewed and potentially compromised by the studios that produce and define their content. As Barbara Klinger argues, "viewers do not get the unvarnished truth about the production; instead, they are presented with the 'promotable' facts, behind-the-scenes information that supports and enhances a sense of the 'movie magic' associated with the Hollywood production machine."[32]

The *Die Hard* DVD admits as much in claiming before one of its exercises that "the actual process of mixing the soundtracks of a motion picture is, of course, much more complex and involved than this DVD-based workshop can allow, and requires talent and years of experience to master. It is hoped that this feature affords you a simple but entertaining experience of the craft." This unusually honest, if not self-conscious, declaration remains rare.[33] Most supplemental materials designed around production and technical instruction highlight the educational potential over the entertainment value. And, while many viewers nonetheless may learn from such exercises and commentary, real-life application requires not only talent, practice, and entrée to Hollywood but also a budget matching the exorbitant costs on the model feature film. Such details tend to get effaced in behind-the-scenes features, thereby complicating any real-life application of the instruction.

Much of the supplemental material as well as the studio marketing and rhetoric surrounding DVD titles must therefore be viewed in terms of their promotional intent. Most studio DVDs use a combination of Hollywood mystique paired with the authenticity and realism of a backstage pass to motivate sales. Any interest in training new professionals or teaching viewers how to understand or "read" a film by listening to a director's commentary remains a secondary consideration. Whether these titles truly educate or merely "edutain" depends not only on how the consumer uses them but on how they are produced. Beyond the nonprofit repertory image proffered by the Criterion collection, DVD production (even on some of the most thoroughly researched studio special editions) for the most part is motivated by economic return over the more altruistic goal of education or archival posterity.[34] The economics of the industry thus necessarily complicate the pedagogical potential of home entertainment.

With DVD production itself increasingly celebrated as an artistic endeavor in the popular press and trade papers, and the DVD producer hailed as "auteur," DVD design and supplemental material potentially gain legitimacy as independent objects of film study. At the same time, with profit potential determining the budget, design, and array of supplemental materials on the average studio DVD, the creative and pedagogical promise on most titles is invariably limited. The top-selling DVDs fall within genres that parallel the top-grossing box office releases, notably family films, action, and science fiction. These titles, in turn, seem to be the ones that Hollywood distributors devote the most time and money to as they develop value-added material. With such a narrow scope of genres, we must ask again about the value of these "value-added materials." Do these materials hold real pedagogical promise? Are they mere novelties and a new kind of attraction? Do they simply offer posterity for a director and revenue for a studio? Or are they, as the director Frank Darabont suggests, just "cultural white noise"?

The utopian discourse surrounding contemporary home entertainment and the lack of concrete statistics on how these media actually are used render questions pertaining to value difficult to address. Obviously, there is great demand for these supplemental materials both on DVD and even through cable channels and the Internet. Peter Staddon, a marketing executive at Twentieth Century–Fox, however, admits that despite the fact that the list of features on a DVD box (the more the better) will justify a DVD purchase, most consumers only spend ten or fifteen minutes exploring the many hours (ten or more on some titles) of value-added materials. It remains unclear, therefore, what drives film viewer-consumers, to what degree they are learning, and what results from expanding and relocating the site of film study.

On the one hand, then, supplemental materials serve as a marketing ploy, and the extra content being sold may have little value other than the economic one. At the same time, these extrafilmic materials, whether on DVD, cable, or the Internet, can offer insight into the way that film culture can be reimagined and can help reimagine film studies. The film itself may no longer play the starring role in film study. Indeed, within the home entertainment arena, the film text is simply one part of a larger ensemble of satellite texts. These satellite texts put the original film in a broader context that, depending on the home entertainment outlet or producer (DVD, cable television, video-on-demand, etc.), can impart scholarly insight, practical filmmaking tips, trivia, and nostalgia. The cultural value of these satellite texts and their potential place in the history of film studies nevertheless remains difficult to assess in any general way. It is safe to assume that more people are watching and learning from these satellite texts than are attending university film courses and museum or repertory screenings. What they take from these texts depends, of course, on the individual (consumer, student, cinephile, or fan), the products they choose to consume, as well as how and where they consume them.

While home viewing may lack the engagement offered by peer and instructor interaction and the curricular context offered by formal education, the site itself does not preclude critical engagement. Nor does the home and individual interaction necessarily negate the quality of the text or the instruction. It would be irresponsible and misleading nevertheless to claim that all home entertainment texts offer valuable educational experiences. Suggesting that the information presented by experts and Hollywood insiders who reveal trade secrets is useful and practical sidesteps the potentially limited scope of the access and learning, not to mention the economic motives driving much of the production. Like mainstream film, DVDs always will be produced within an industrial context. It is crucial, therefore, to assess each text individually with a twofold goal in mind. First, make visible and take into account the often highly regulated, constructed, and commodified exhibition context that is by nature home entertainment. Second, appreciate not only what is being archived by these home entertainment products but also the accessibility afforded by home exhibition. While the for-profit goals of the home entertainment industry may seem antithetical to traditional visions of film culture and film study, the products themselves nonetheless can open up the possibility to rethink the object of film studies, the site of film culture, and film's overall value in an ongoing and ever-complex negotiation between commerce and culture.

Notes

1. Susan King, "As DVD Popularity Grows, So Do Extras," *Los Angeles Times Calendar Weekend*, July 15, 1999, 50.
2. It would be limiting and misleading to claim that this renegotiation of home viewing is tied exclusively to the recent rise of DVD. Studios, using the VHS format, and television cable networks have been targeting the home entertainment arena aggressively for at least twenty years, bringing Hollywood (as well as other classic and foreign film fare) home to a viewer decidedly different from the theatrical filmgoer. Even earlier, there is evidence that classic (or at least older) films have long been screened on television through popular network programming such as *The Late Show, Hollywood Film Theater, Saturday Night at the Movies*, and *Warner Bros. Presents* in the 1950s and 1960s. See Douglas Gomery, *Shared Pleasures: A History of Movie Presentation in the United States* (Madison: University of Wisconsin Press, 1992), 247; see also Christopher Anderson, *Hollywood TV: The Studio System in the Fifties* (Austin: University of Texas Press, 1994). Film also entered the home much before the popularization of television with 16mm film libraries. For more on this early home archiving practice, see Haidee Wasson, *Museum Movies: The Museum of Modern Art and the Birth of Art Cinema* (Berkeley: University of California Press, 2005).
3. Here, my argument departs to some degree from what Barbara Klinger has argued with regard to home theater and the domestication of feature films. She focuses on a spatial difference to contextualize her argument. At the same time, her discussion of a changing spectator experience resonates with my own approach in discussing how viewing contexts have changed. See Barbara Klinger, "The New Media Aristocrats: Home Theater and the Domestic Film Experience," *Velvet Light Trap*, no. 42 (fall 1998): 4–19; see also Barbara Klinger, "The Contemporary Cinephile: Film

Collecting in the Post-Video Era," in *Hollywood Spectators: Changing Perceptions of Cinema Audiences*, edited by Melvyn Stokes and Richard Maltby (London: BFI Press, 2001).

4. Lawrence Levine, *Highbrow/Lowbrow: The Emergence of Cultural Hierarchy in America* (Cambridge, Mass.: Harvard University Press, 1988), 223–24.

5. As Barbara Wilinsky argues, art cinemas in the postwar period not only showed different film fare than mainstream commercial cinema but also created a distinctive filmgoing experience through theater decor, special programs, amenities, and promotions that suggested an air of sophistication. Wilinsky cites Thomas Elsaesser who contends that "without the European art and auteur cinema, film studies might not have found a home in American universities" (Elsaesser, "Putting on a Show: The European Art Movie," *Sight and Sound* [April 1994]: 25, quoted in Wilinsky, *Sure Seaters: The Emergence of Art House Cinema* [Minneapolis: University of Minnesota Press, 2001]). Further discussion of early art cinema and the avant-garde can be found in Jan Christopher Horak, ed., *Lovers of Cinema: The First American Film Avant-Garde, 1919–1945* (Madison: University of Wisconsin Press, 1998). See also David James's discussion of the Anthology Film Archive in David James, *Allegories of Cinema: American Film in the Sixties* (Princeton, N.J.: Princeton University Press, 1989), 18–28; and David James, ed., *To Free the Cinema* (Princeton, N.J.: Princeton University Press, 1992).

6. We can also see film history celebrated in populist histories of the 1920s and 1930s, e.g. Terry Ramsaye's *A Million and One Nights*, originally published in 1926; and Benjamin A. Hampton's *History of the Movies*, originally published in 1931.

7. Peter Decherney, "Inventing Film Study and Its Object at Columbia University, 1915–1938," *Film History* 12.4 (2000): 444. Decherney offers some interesting historical details that lend themselves to comparison with contemporary home entertainment. Victor Oscar Freeburg, one of the Columbia professors who taught photoplay composition in 1915, envisioned a time when films could be screened at home. Through repeated home viewing, Freeburg believed that one could learn about cinematic structure. Freeburg's early plan for home "film school" is remarkably similar to the actual design of some DVD supplemental materials, particularly those that include the screenplay and allow the user/consumer to move back and forth between the script and the film. Decherney has elaborated on this study in his book *Hollywood and the Culture Elite: How the Movies Became American* (New York: Columbia University Press, 2005). See also Dana Polan, *Scenes of Instruction: The Beginning of the United States Study of Film* (Berkeley: University of California Press, 2007).

8. Janice Radway claims that the idea of middlebrow culture first surfaced in the early 1920s. Her discussion of the Book of the Month Club and the commodification of highbrow literature offers an interesting parallel to film's entry into the academy. While there was much heated debate over the merits of the Book of the Month Club, the universities faced fewer obstacles in their acceptance of film. See Radway,

"The Scandal of the Middlebrow: The Book-of-the-Month Club, Class Fracture, and Cultural Authority," *South Atlantic Quarterly* 89.4 (fall 1990): 703–36.

9. See Wasson, *Museum Movies*.

10. See Wilinsky, *Sure Seaters*, 1–15.

11. Looking at the ownership of cable movie channels reveals the widespread power of multimedia conglomerates. Time Warner owns HBO and TCM; Viacom owns Showtime, The Movie Channel, Sundance (along with Robert Redford and NBC-Universal), and FLIX; and Rainbow Media, which previously owned Bravo, owns AMC and IFC among others. Bravo, meanwhile, rarely shows films anymore and is currently owned by NBC-Universal.

12. Barbara Klinger, in her "The Contemporary Cinephile," 140, discusses the appeal of behind-the-scenes information and comments on the way that video collectors are addressed as film industry "insiders" and reside in privileged positions of industry personnel, particularly the director. While Klinger claims that these collectors are addressed as already knowledgeable, I would contend that many of the DVD supplemental materials and cable programming are addressed not to the connoisseur but to the uninitiated, *potential* student of film.

13. *Project Greenlight*, Sundance Channel's *Anatomy of a Scene*, NBC's *Next Action Star*, and even James Lipton's *Inside the Actor's Studio*, which has aired on Bravo since 1994, are a few examples. *Project Greenlight* initially aired on HBO in 2000 and subsequently was shown on the Bravo network. *Next Action Star*, featuring producer Joel Silver, first aired on NBC in 2004. While Joel Silver partnered with NBC to produce the show and make the occasional appearance, the judges and supposed experts had far less Hollywood clout with mediocre credits including *Double Dragon*, *Fair Game*, *Bats*, and *Carnosaur 2*. The Independent Film Channel, meanwhile, airs several programs that offer behind-the-scenes access to film production outside the studio system—e.g. in film school and the festival circuit. They also offer shows such as *Film Fanatic* and *Dinner for Five* that are geared toward the serious cinephile.

14. Peter M. Nichols, "Producing DVDs with Lavish Extras," *New York Times*, August 27, 2000.

15. This statistic comes from a 2000 study done by the DVD Entertainment Group, an industry-supported trade coalition that was reprinted in the *Los Angeles Times* (Marc Saltzman, "The Behind-the-Scenes Art of Developing DVD Extras," *Los Angeles Times*, January 14, 2003, E12). The box office gross from these DVD titles also drives the increase in marketing (particularly print and television ads) for upcoming DVD releases.

16. John Horn, "How the Moguls Came to Love Retail," *Los Angeles Times*, April 17, 2005.

17. Thomas K. Arnold, "Special Features Boost DVD Sales," *Los Angeles Times*, December 5, 2000.

18. "Today DVDs Conquer the Movie," *USA Today*, October 18, 2002.

19. David Kehr, "Movies 'Deluxe': Definitely Bigger, Sometimes Better," *New York Times*, December 15, 2002.

20. "How Does Hollywood Spell the Future?" *Los Angeles Times*, April 7, 2002.

21. Gary Crowdus, "Providing a Film Archive for the Home Viewer: An Interview with Peter Becker of The Criterion Collection," *Cineaste* 25.1 (December 1999): 49.

22. Michael Sragow, "The Disc Master," http://salon.com/ent/col/srag/2000/03/23/criterion.

23. Other studios have not exploited the classic collection angle to the same degree, in large part because they don't have the sizable vaults owned by these studios. Although MGM created a Vintage Classics line, it does not offer extensive supplemental features. Universal released its horror cycle under a classic banner. Other studios like Paramount and Columbia Tri-Star tend to release classics collector's or limited editions.

24. Most of this content has previously aired on classic movie channels like AMC and TCM or on biographical and other historical programming from cable stations such as A&E and the History Channel.

25. Here I am referring to Laura Mulvey's "Visual Pleasure and Narrative Cinema" (*Screen* 16.3 [autumn 1975]: 6–18), which has become a staple in film theory courses and courses that deal with gender and media.

26. Elvis Mitchell, "Everyone's a Film Geek Now," *New York Times*, August 17, 2003, 2:1, 15.

27. Jon Matsumoto, "Class, Open Your DVDs to 'Extras,'" *Los Angeles Times Calendar* (April 7, 2002), 80.

28. Richard Natale, "Press Play to Access the Future," *Los Angeles Times Calendar*, April 7, 2002, 80.

29. There are restrictions on all of these titles that allow one to record commentary. For *Jay and Silent Bob*, Miramax owns the rights to the commentary. On *Pulp Fiction*, one can only comment over select scenes. On *Spiderman*, one can only play back the commentary on the computer used to record it. Another trend that got its start in 2001 involves film fans recording their own commentary as MP3 audio files and making them available to others via the Internet. This unregulated mode fits more within a veritable do-it-yourself ethos; however, as of this writing the site that used to store these files, "DVD Tracks," is no longer operational.

30. The Academy of Television Arts and Sciences took it upon itself to create, beginning in 2005, a DVD series devoted to behind-the-scenes instruction with titles such as "Journey Below the Line." The DVD uses popular television shows currently in production, such as *ER* and *24*, to examine individual below-the-line jobs including editing, props, and special effects.

31. Many of the interactive trends in DVD extra features use imbedded content such as New Line's Infinifilm, which allows the viewer access to supplemental material during the film through navigable pop-up menus. "Easter eggs" also can be found on hundreds of titles. These features tend to mimic the world of computer games,

another highly profitable arena in contemporary home entertainment. Some DVDs, particularly family, science fiction, action, and comedy titles, clearly imitate the highly profitable computer game market and, in many cases, advertise actual tie-ins for other ancillary game products. In turn, they transform film characters or stories into games, allowing users to revoice (or sing, Karaoke style) characters in the film (*Shrek, Austin Powers: Goldmember, Elf*), readalong on *Stuart Little 2* or *Elf*, learn about Egyptology on *The Mummy Returns*, take a quiz to see which Disney princess they most resemble, and study the art of hula dancing on *Lilo and Stitch*. Like the Infinifilm features, the level of interactive play on these games remains limited, especially in comparison to actual game platforms such as X Box and Playstation.

32. Klinger, "The Contemporary Cinephile," 140.

33. Other features on the *Die Hard* DVD reflect a similar degree of integrity and pedagogical value, including a "Why Letterbox?" segment that offers a detailed discussion of telecine transfer as well as a fairly extensive glossary of film terms.

34. The budget for supplemental materials generally correlates with the film's projected box office and home video revenues (with action-adventure and animation having the highest budgets of studio DVDs).

Dr. Strange Media, or How I Learned to
Stop Worrying and Love Film Theory
D. N. RODOWICK

■ Imagine you are a young sociologist working around 1907. In the course of
a year or two on your daily ride to the university you witness an explosion of
"nickelodeons" along the trolley route. They seem to operate continuously, day
and night, and it is rare not to see a queue outside their doors. Because your
children not only spend an extravagant amount of time and money unsupervised within their walls but also exhibit an extraordinary and sometimes incomprehensible fascination with the characters presented there and the people
who play them, perhaps you yourself have gone inside to see a "photoplay" or
two. How would it be possible to comprehend, despite the breadth and depth
of your knowledge, that an entirely new medium and an important industry
were being created that, in many respects, would define the visual culture of
the twentieth century?[1]

This is how I respond when friends and colleagues ask me why my critical
attention has in recent years turned so strongly to "new media" and computer-
mediated communications. My hypothetical social theorist may have been for-
tunate enough to participate in early studies of cinema or radio as mass cultural
phenomena. In retirement, this imaginary scholar's interest may again have
been piqued by the emergence of television. But the question remains: How
would it be possible to imagine in 1907 what cinema would become in the
course of the fifty years that followed? Or to imagine in 1947 what television
would become in just ten or fifteen years? As the twentieth century unfolded,
technological, economic, and cultural changes took place on the scale of a life-

time. This was already incomprehensibly fast from the perspective of the nine-teenth or eighteenth centuries. Now at the edge of the twenty-first century, these same changes are taking place in less than a generation.

The rapid emergence of new media as an industry and perhaps an art raises a more perilous question for cinema studies. The twentieth century was un-questionably the century of cinema, but is cinema's time now over? And if so, what is to become of its barely matured field, cinema studies?

Despite my interest in new technologies and the new media I have never given up, and indeed still insist on, my identity as a *film theorist*, much to the confusion of my family and the amusement of taxi drivers the world over. When feeling more pompous, I'll say that my principal interest is philosophy and contemporary visual culture with cinema as the decisively central element of study. Now, even in cinema studies itself this could be considered a marginal position. Film theory has fallen on hard times, even within the field of cinema studies itself. In the 1970s and early 1980s, many identified cinema studies en-tirely with film theory, especially its Franco-British incarnation represented by the journal *Screen* and its importation from France of the work of Christian Metz, Roland Barthes, and others. More currently, research in film history has for many, and with just cause, dominated the field. In addition, many of the questions that film theory raised in the heady days of political modernism concerning representation, ideology, subjectivity, and so on have evolved in the direction of cultural studies and media theory with their more sociological orientation. Thus, through the 1980s and 1990s one of the recurrent debates in the Society for Cinema Studies was how to represent the growing interest in television and electronic media. Was cinema studies disappearing and was film becoming less central? This was a hard pill to swallow for the prevideo cine-phile generation of which I am a card-carrying member. Not only do many feel that film theory is much less central to the identity of the field, within cinema studies itself the disappearance of "film" as a clearly defined aesthetic object anchoring our young discipline is also the cause of some anxiety.

So what becomes of cinema studies if "film" should disappear? Perhaps this is a question that only film theory can answer?

The Incredible Shrinking Medium

In May 1999 I took advantage of a bachelor weekend in New York to make the rounds of the new summer movies. Something was clearly afoot. Released earlier that spring, *The Matrix* was dominating the screens. Settling in to watch previews at a large downtown cineplex, nearly every big summer film seemed to follow its lead. This was the summer of digital paranoia. As part of a trend that began with *Dark City* the year before, films like *The Matrix*, *Thirteenth Floor*, and *eXistenZ* each played with the idea that a digitally created simulation could invisibly and seamlessly replace the solid, messy "analog" world of our everyday life. Technology had effectively become nature by wholly replacing our complex and chaotic world—too "smelly" according to the lead agent in *The Matrix*—with an imaginary simulation where social control was nearly complete. The digital versus the analog was the heart of narrative conflict in these films, as if cinema were fighting for its very aesthetic existence. The replacement of the analog "world" by a digital simulation functions here as an allegorical conflict wherein cinema struggles to reassert or redefine its identity in the face of a new representational technology that threatens to overwhelm it. The implicit and explicit references to computer gaming in these films are also significant.

As I took in previews for *The Mummy* and *Phantom Menace*, it was clear to me that at the level of representational technologies, the digital had in fact *already* supplanted the analog. Feature films comprised entirely of computer-generated images (CGI) such as *Toy Story* (1995) or *A Bug's Life* (1998) were not harbingers of a future world but rather *the* world of cinematic media as experienced today. Computer-generated images are no longer restricted to isolated special effects; they comprise in many sequences the whole of the mise-en-scène to the point where even major characters are, in whole or in part, computer generated.

The gradual replacement of the actor's recorded physical presence by computer-generated imagery signals a process of substitution that is occurring across the film industry. The successive stages of the history of this substitution might look something like this.[2]

> 1980s: *Digital image processing and synthesis* become increasingly prevalent in television advertising and music video production. Steven Jobs's Pixar and George Lucas's Industrial Light and Magic emerge as the most innovative producers of digital imaging for motion pictures.

> Late 1980s: *Digital nonlinear editing systems* begin rapidly replacing the mechanical Steenbeck and Moviola tables as the industry editing standard. From 1995 they begin to be perceived as a universal standard.

Late 1980s: successful trials of *digital cameras with resolution approximating that of 35mm film*.

1989: James Cameron's *The Abyss* produces the first convincing *digitally animated character* in a live-action film—the "pseudopod." The experiment is raised to a new level in 1991 with the use in *Terminator 2* of a character that morphs continually between human actors and computer-generated images—the T-1000 terminator.

1990: *Digital sound* was introduced with *Dick Tracy* and *Edward Scissorhands*. By the end of 1994 most studios are releasing prints with digital soundtracks.

1993: *Jurassic Park* makes prevalent and popular the possibility of generating *"photographically" believable synthesized images*. This trend continues with increasing success throughout the 1990s.

1995: Pixar releases *Toy Story*—the first fully *synthetic feature film*.

1998–2001: The increasing popularity of digital video cameras, whose use for fiction films is popularized in films of the Dogme movement, such as *Festen* (1998) and Mike Figgis's *Time Code* (2000).

1998: *Pleasantville* and then *O Brother Where Art Thou?* (2000) are among the first films whose negatives are digitized for treatment in postproduction. By 2004, *digital intermediates* are becoming standard practice.

June/July 1999: Successful test screenings in New Jersey and Los Angeles of *Star Wars I: The Phantom Menace* use *fully electronic and digital projection*.

June 2000: *Digital projection and distribution* come together as Twentieth Century–Fox and Cisco Systems collaborate in transmitting a feature film, *Titan A.E.*, over the Internet and then project it digitally in an Atlanta movie theater.

For the avid cinephile, it is tempting to think about the history of this substitution as a terrifying remake of *Invasion of the Body Snatchers*. In the course of a short decade, the long privilege of the analog image and the technology of analog image production have been almost completely replaced by digital simulations and digital processes. The celluloid strip with its reassuring physical passage of visible images, the noisy and cumbersome cranking of the mechanical film projector or the Steenbeck editing table, and the imposing bulk of the film canister are all disappearing one by one into a virtual space, along with the images they so beautifully recorded and presented.

What is left, then, of cinema as it is replaced, part by part, by digitization? Does cinema studies have a future in the twenty-first century? This is a problem I take personally because as I write this essay I am, for the fourth time in my career of twenty-five years, either creating or remodeling a film studies program. As I rethink yet again a possible curriculum for undergraduate and graduate students I find myself confronting a new disturbing question: Is this the end of film, and therefore the end of cinema studies?

Back to the Future

Periods of intense technological change are always extremely interesting for film theory, because the films themselves tend to stage its primary question: *What is cinema?* The emergent digital era poses this question in a new and interesting way because for the first time in the history of film theory the photographic process is challenged as the ontological basis of cinematic representation. If the discipline of film studies is anchored to a specific material object, then a real conundrum emerges with the arrival of digital technologies as a dominant aesthetic and social force. For 150 years the material basis of photography, and then cinema, has been defined by a process of the mechanical recording of images through the registration of reflected light on a photosensitive chemical surface. Moreover, most of the key debates on the representational nature of photographic and cinematic media—and indeed whether and how they could be defined as an art—were deduced from the basic photographic/cinematographic process.

As digital processes come more and more to displace analogical ones, what is the potential import for a photographic ontology of film? Unlike analogical representations, which have as their basis a transformation of substance isomorphic with an originating image, virtual representations derive all their powers from their basis in numerical manipulation. Timothy Binckley greatly clarifies matters when he reminds us that numbers, and the kinds of symbolization they allow, are the first "virtual reality."[3] The analogical arts are fundamentally arts of intaglio, or worked matter—a literal sculpting by light of hills and valleys in the raw film whose variable density produces a visible image. But the transformation of matter in the electronic and digital arts takes place on a different atomic register and in a different conceptual domain. Where analog media record traces of events, as Binckley puts it, digital media produce tokens of numbers: the constructive tools of Euclidian geometry are replaced by the computational tools of Cartesian geometry.

This transformation in the concept of materiality is the key to understanding some basic distinctions between the analog and the digital. Comparing computer-generated images with film reaffirms that photography's principal powers are those of analogy and indexicality. The photograph is a receptive substance literally etched or sculpted by light forming a mold of the object's reflected image. The image has both spatial and temporal powers that reinforce photography's designative function with an existential claim. As Roland Barthes explained, photography is an "emanation of the referent" whose *noeme* is *ça-a-été*: this thing was; that is, it had a spatial existence that endured in time.[4] Even film's imaginary worlds, say the moonscapes of *2001: A Space Odyssey*, are founded by these powers. Alternatively, CGI is wholly created from algorithmic functions. Analogy exists as a function of spatial recognition, of course, but it has loosed its anchors from both substance and indexicality. And it is not simply that visuality has been given a new mobility where any pixel in the electronic image can be moved or its value changed at will. Because the digital arts are without substance and therefore not easily identified as objects, no medium-specific ontology can fix them in place. The digital arts render all expressions as identical since they are all ultimately reducible to the same computational basis. The basis of all "representation" is virtuality: mathematic abstractions that render all signs as equivalent regardless of their output medium. Digital media are neither visual, textual, nor musical—rather they are pure simulation.

But here a first important objection can be raised. Is "film" in its most literal sense synonymous with "cinema"? To say that "film" is disappearing means only that photochemical celluloid is starting to disappear as the medium for registering, distributing, and presenting images. As celluloid with its satisfying substantiality and visibility available to the naked eye disappears into a virtual and electronic realm, is "cinema" itself disappearing? At a time when cinema studies—after a long battle for legitimation in the eyes of the academy that has only recently been won and even then not in all corners of the humanities—is finally enjoying unprecedented professional recognition and maturity, has it all been for naught?

One simple response is to say that digital cameras (or even "virtual" cameras creating wholly synthesized spaces on computers) are still based on the same optical geometry as traditional cameras and as such they rely on the same historically and culturally evolved mathematics of depth and light rendering that are descended from *perspectiva legittima*. Although digital processes have produced many fascinating stylistic innovations, there is a strong sense in which what counts intuitively as an "image" has changed very little for Western cultures for several centuries. Indeed, there is much to be learned from the fact that "photographic" realism remains the Holy Grail of digital imaging. If the digital is such a revolutionary process of image making, why is its technological and aesthetic goal to become perceptually indiscernible from an earlier mode of image production? A certain cultural sense of the "cinematic" and an unreflective notion of "realism" remain in many ways the touchstones for valuing the aesthetic innovations of the digital.

Nonetheless, I think there is a deeper and more philosophical way of discussing the "virtuality" of film and film studies. One consistent lesson from the history of film theory is that there has never been a general consensus concerning the answer to the question "What is cinema?" And for this reason the evolving thought on cinema in the twentieth century has persisted in a continual state of identity crisis. Despite its range and complexity, the entire classical period of film aesthetics can be understood as a genealogy of conflicting debates that sought to ground filmic ontology in a single medium-specific concept or technique: the *photogénie* of Louis Delluc and Jean Epstein; Béla Balázs's defense of the close-up; the rhythmic *cinégraphie* dear to French impressionist filmmakers; the montage debates during the Soviet golden age; Walter Benjamin on mechanical reproducibility and the decline of aura; Siegfried Kracauer's photographic affinities; Bazin's defense of the long take and composition in depth, etc.

In its historical efforts to define film as art, and thus to legitimate a new field of aesthetic analysis, never has one field so thoroughly debated, in such contradictory and interesting ways, the nature of its ontological grounding. The perceived necessity of defining the artistic possibilities of a medium by proving its unique ontological grounding in an aesthetic first principle derives from a long tradition in the history of philosophy. Deconstruction has not completely, or perhaps not even partially, purged our culture of the instinct to view and value art in this way. This same perspective produced a sort of aesthetic inferiority complex in both film theory and film studies where, if all of the above principles were true, cinema could only be defined as a mongrel medium that would never evolve in an aesthetically pure form. Hence the great paradox of classical film theory: intuitively, film seemed to have a material specificity with claims to self-identity; nonetheless, this specificity was notoriously difficult to pin down. There was something about the spatiality and the temporality of the medium that eluded, indeed confounded, hierarchies of value and concepts of judgment in modern aesthetics.

Therefore, the difficulty of placing film as an object grounding an area of study does not begin with the digital "virtualization" of the image. Indeed one might say that the entire history of the medium, and of the critical thought that has accompanied it, has returned incessantly to film's uncertain status. What accounts for this flux at the very heart of film studies, which has always seemed less of a *discipline* than a constantly shifting terrain for thinking about time-based spatial media? All disciplines evolve and change, of course. But I would argue, and I think this is a positive thing, that film studies has never congealed into a discipline in the same way that English literature or art history has done. Even today it is far more common to find university film studies in a wide variety of interdisciplinary contexts; the fully-fledged Department of Film Studies is rather the exception that proves the rule. There are reasons both economic and political for this, but I find the possible philosophical explanations more interesting to explore.

Cinema's overwhelming and enduring status as mostly though not exclusively a popular and industrial art has proved exclusionary from a certain snobbish perspective. But there is another, deeper reason why film studies has remained the much loved though bastard child of the humanities. From the standpoint of early modern aesthetic theory, the painting, the sculpture, or the book have a reassuring ontological stability—their status as objects, and therefore potentially *aesthetic* objects, seems self-evident. However, despite the apparent solidity of the celluloid strip rolled with satisfying mass and weight on reels and cores, and continuities in the experience of watching projected motion pictures, film studies has continually evolved as a field in search of its object.

Why is "film" so difficult to place as an "object" of aesthetic investigation? Perhaps because it was the first medium to challenge fundamentally the concepts on which the very idea of the aesthetic was founded. Up until the emergence of cinema, most of the fine arts remained readily classifiable and rankable according to Gotthold Ephraim Lessing's 1766 distinction between the arts of succession or time and simultaneity or space. As I have argued elsewhere, this distinction became the basis for defining an aesthetic ontology that anchored individual arts in self-identical mediums and forms.[5] Moreover, implied in Lessing's distinction is a valuation of the temporal arts for their immateriality and thus their presumed spirituality or closeness to both voice and thought.

Among the "new" media, the emergence of cinema, now over a hundred years old, unsettled this philosophical schema even if it did not successfully displace it. In the minds of most people cinema remains a "visual" medium. And more often than not cinema still defends its aesthetic value by aligning itself with the other visual arts and by asserting its self-identity as an image-making medium. Yet the great paradox of cinema, with respect to the conceptual categories of eighteenth- and nineteenth-century aesthetics, is that it is both a temporal and "immaterial" as well as spatial medium. The hybrid nature of cinematic expression—which combines moving photographic images, sounds, and music as well as speech and writing—has inspired equally cinema's defenders and detractors. For cinema's defenders, especially in the teens and twenties, film represented a grand Hegelian synthesis—the apogee of the arts. Alternatively, from the most conservative point of view cinema can never be an art because it is a mongrel medium that will never rest comfortably within the philosophical history of the aesthetic. The suspicion, or anxiety, that cinema could not be defined as art derived from its hybrid nature as both an art of space *and* an art of time. Indeed, some of the most compelling contributions of classical film theory recognized and valued this: Panofsky's definition of cinema as an art that dynamizes space and spatializes time; Eisenstein's discussion of the filmic fourth dimension; and Bazin's defense of an ontology of the image as a temporal as well as spatial realism or a unique spatial record of duration. The most philosophically elaborate discussion of this idea would be Gilles Deleuze's concepts of the movement-image and the time-image.

The difficult hybridity of film can be pushed even further. In early modern aesthetics there is a traditional privileging of what Nelson Goodman called the *autographic* arts.[6] These are the arts of signature. From hand-drafted manuscript to easel painting, autographic arts are defined by action—the physical contact of the artist's hand—and by a certain telos: they are concluded as aesthetic objects once the artist's hand has terminated its work. All autographic arts are therefore unique. There is only one original; any repeated manifestation must be either a copy or a forgery.

Alternatively, Goodman's criteria for *allographic* arts, of which music is his primary example, include the following. They are two-stage arts in which there is a spatial and temporal separation between composition and performance. More importantly, they are amenable to notation. Here the primary creative work is finished when the notation is complete. All performances are variants on this principal act. Thus musical composition is a kind of writing, as of course are literature or poetry, though painting and sculpture are not. And while the action of printing is allographic, literature—like painting—is an autographic art for Goodman in that the creative act flows from and terminates with the artist's hand. Repeated printings are simply instantiations, then, that are identical in all relevant aspects with the original notation.

Film shares with music a difficult status in the history of the aesthetic evaluation, and Goodman's concepts help us understand why. All two-stage arts are difficult to judge because the author is absent from the performance. No "signature" verifies their authenticity as art, even if the composer conducts his or her own work. The touchstone here is that temporal and allographic arts, of which music and cinema may be the best examples, lack a tactile substance that serves as the medium for a permanent and inalterable authorial inscription. And in fact, film shares with music a real Dionysian madness owing to its complex temporality.

However, in music the notational act of composition acts as the guarantee of the author's signature. And here film differentiates itself most clearly from music according to Goodman's criteria. Film is obviously a two-stage (and perhaps multistage) art, but where do we make the division between composition and performance? Paradoxically, making a photographic image would seem to be, like etching or lithography, both an autographic and a two-stage process. From Bazin to Barthes, the photographic act is understood as producing a unique record of a singular duration. But subsequent prints must be struck from an original, thus comprising the second stage of the photographic process. As in lithography, "The prints are the end-products; and although they may differ appreciably from one another, all are instances of the original work. But even the most exact copy produced otherwise than by printing from that plate counts not as an original but as an imitation or forgery."[7] Thus, in either photography or cinematography, producing an "original" may not serve as a notational act. Here technological reproducibility raises obvious problems. The original negative of *Citizen Kane* (1941) is lost. Are therefore all existing prints imitations? And this is to set aside the vexed question of who is the author of a film: the screenwriter? the director? the star actor? Do films have a primary notational origin, and is it the script? the storyboard? Is the film *Citizen Kane* simply the performance of Herman Mankiewicz and Orson Welles's written screenplay? Or is the film the unique preservation of the multiple creative acts performed both before the camera (not only of the actors and their direction but also the entire construction of the mise-en-scène and camera placement) and after in the postproduction processes of editing image and sound? In any case, as in musical composition, all are displaced in space and time from the actual performance of the film.

The digital image extends these problems in another direction. For two reasons CGIs are not autographic: as "synthetic" images they cannot be considered the physical act of the author's hand nor do they result in an "end product." Indeed, one of the great creative powers of digital images is their lack of closure: they are easily reworked, reappropriated, and recontextualized. Synthesis, sampling, and sequencing are the fundamental creative acts of the digital arts. In this they are the very antithesis of the autographic arts. Alternatively, they are a paradigm for allographic arts since any copy is fully identical to the "original." This is so for a specific reason. One can say that the sampling and reworking of a digital image is a new performance of it or even, indeed, that the new performance is a citation or paraphrase of the original. But even if films or live music can also cite or paraphrase precedent works, they are not allographic arts in the same way that computer-generated works are so. Why? Because these digital artifacts are produced by a rigorous notation: the algorithms, programs, or instruction sets according to which they are "computed." While *Toy Story* has as many "authors" as any big budget Hollywood movie, paradoxically it is fully notational in a way that no predigital-era film could be.

It is important to emphasize that Goodman's argument is not an "aesthetic" one since the criteria of signature and uniqueness are the grounds neither for valuing nor defining the ontological specificity of art forms. Nonetheless, *autographicality* and *notationality* would seem to function as concepts defining the "aesthetic" nature of creative acts. The clearest examples of autographic arts imply a unique author whose work is accomplished in a one-stage act. Two-stage arts require aesthetic grounding in a system of ideally inalterable notation. Film does not fully satisfy either criterion. Alternatively, the synthetic image presents a radical case: undoubtedly a two-stage image, it can also be considered fully notational. Reproducing the same program or algorithm will produce an image identical to the "original" if such an original can be said to exist.[8] Unlike other two-stage arts, each performance will be identical instantiations of the same instruction set. Neither music nor dance can make this claim. And, paradoxically, by this criterion the synthetic image would be aesthetic in a way that the film image is not. (And here is a most terrible conclusion: every art has aesthetic value except film.)

Film's difficult status with respect to concepts of notationality has been a key concept of film theory, especially the structuralist and semiological approaches of the postwar period. And here we can return to the film/cinema distinction with interesting consequences.

Film theory gained much from an awkward term when Etienne Souriau designated as *filmophanic* the film perceived as such by the spectator during projection. This effort to make precise the different analytical dimensions of film theory—*profilmic* space before the camera, *screen* space (photographic dimension), *film* space (temporal dimension), and *spectatorial* or psychological space—derived from a fundamental distinction coined by Gilbert Cohen-Séat in 1946: namely, that of cinematographic and filmic facts.[9] As Christian Metz noted in his commentary on this distinction in *Language and Cinema*, what we culturally define as "film" has a dizzying series of overlapping and often contradictory connotations: a physical object resting in film cans; an object of economic exchange; an aesthetic object defined both singularly and generally. For Metz, Cohen-Séat's original distinction had the value of putting film theory on a sound methodological basis, for "filmic facts" isolate film as a localizable signifying discourse with respect to its varying sociological, economic, techno-logical, and industrial contexts.[10] Here "film" comes into focus as an object of theory as a semiological fact that is distinguishable from the vaster social and historical terrain of cinematic phenomena, some of which intervene *before* production (economic and legislative infrastructure, studio organization, tech-nological invention and innovation, biographies of creative personnel); others *after* the film (audience and critical response, ideological and cultural impact of the film, star mythology); and still others *during* the film but *apart from* and *outside of it* (architectural and cultural context of projection of movie viewing, and so on).

Metz's goal here is not only to specify the object of film theory but also to delimit precisely the object of film semiology. And here, suddenly, is the bril-liance and difficulty of his book *Language and Cinema*. The distinction between film as actual (as a concrete discursive unity) and the virtuality of cinema as an ideal set launches us toward another sense of the virtuality of film theory. Cohen-Séat calls "cinema" the sum of phenomena surrounding the film while remaining external to it. But film theory cannot do without a certain concept of cinema, or at least a sense of the word "cinema" that in everyday parlance refers also to "the sum of films themselves, or rather the sum of traits which, in the films themselves, are taken to be characteristic of what is sensed to be a certain 'language.' . . . There is also the same relationship between cinema and films as between literature and books, painting and paintings, sculpture and sculptures, etc."[11] Thus, when one speaks of *cross-cutting* in the climactic sequence of *The*

Matrix, where the action of Neo's final confrontation with the Agents in the simulated world of the Matrix is alternated with an attack by the robotic Sentinels on the rebel ship Nebuchadnezzar in the "real" world, one refers to it both as a singular filmic figure while also saying that this figure is cinematographic; that is, it has the qualities of belonging to cinema or the semiological/aesthetic resources of cinema. By a curious dialectical turn, cinema in this sense reinscribes itself within the filmic fact as defined by Cohen-Séat.

Therefore, the semiological distinction between cinema and film requires a vertiginous dialectical circularity between two terms and two sets. Here film and cinema are contrasted as actual and ideal objects that in fact cannot be separated. This is the difference between an *énoncé*, or discrete utterance, and language, or *langue*, as a virtual system of differences; or more simply, that of an individual and concrete message and the abstract code that gives it sense. Thus the semiological status of film cannot be established without referring back to a specificity that is, paradoxically, cinematographic. But according to Metz this specificity is defined neither by the criterion of substantial self-similarity (the uniqueness of a medium or a material) nor by an aesthetic ontology. It can only be defined by the set of all possible films or filmic figures that could be derived from the possibilities of cinematic "language," and this language is in a continual state of innovation and change.

So now film theory confronts two kinds of ideal sets. One groups together all the potential messages of a certain perceptual or aesthetic order without necessarily coinciding with either a single and unique code or a homogeneous substance. These are all the actual films that have been or could be made, that is, aesthetic artifacts defined as "cinema" in the same sense that the novels of Henry James could be defined as "literature." But the sense or meaning of individual films would be impossible to analyze without a unity of another kind— that of code. Here Metz makes a definite break both with classical film theory and with classical aesthetics. Within the filmic, the cinematographic inscribes itself as a vast virtuality that is nonetheless specific and homogeneous—this is the notion of cinematic codes. The notion of codes could not be constructed without the possibility of regrouping, at least conceptually, "all messages of a certain sensory modality," that is, the totality of films that constitute cinema. But only the messages are concrete and singular; the codes are virtual and the quality of being cinematic in no way derives from the physical nature of the signifier. A code, then, "is *a constructed rather than inherent unity, and it does not exist prior to analysis.* . . . [They] are . . . units which aim at formalization.

Their homogeneity is not a sensory one, but rather one of logical coherence, of explanatory power, of generative capacity."[12]

Thus the quality of being cinematic, or even of defining, if we still dare, cinematographic specificity, rests on the analysis and definition of a code or codes immanent to the set of all films. But immanent does mean originating in either an ontology or the material specificity of the signifier. The materiality of the cinematic signifier, as Metz often insisted, is heterogeneous. Fundamentally, it is composed from five matters of expression: moving photographic images, speech, sound effects, music, and graphic traces. Moreover, any given narrative film will be comprised of a plurality of codes, both cinematic and noncinematic, whose very nature is to be conceptually heterogeneous. Here cinema presents an important lesson in philosophy to modern aesthetics, for it is useless to want to define the specificity of any medium according to criteria of ontological self-identification or substantial self-similarity. Heterogeneous and variable both in its matters of expression and the plurality of codes that organize them, the set of all films is itself an uncertain territory that is in a state of continual change. It is itself a conceptual virtuality, though populated with concrete objects, that varies unceasingly, and therefore to extract the codes that give this sense narrative and cultural meaning is a process that is, as Freud would have said, interminable.

Film, it would seem, is a very uncertain object. And it is this very instability that makes it so riveting and fascinating for some and yet for others a cultural scandal. The solid ontological anchoring of a worked substance is only difficultly grasped yielding an art that so far leans, more than any other, on an experience of the imaginary. On this basis the virtuality of film takes on yet a new sense. Raymond Bellour in a short but brilliant essay defines film as "*le texte introuvable*" or "the unfindable text." The difficulties of film semiology return implicitly here to the questions of notationality raised by Goodman. Literary texts may be cited critically and analytically in the same notation as their source. But film loses what is most specific to it once it is captured in a different analytic medium: the frame enlargement or film still absents the movement that defines its particular form of visuality: "On the one hand, [film] spreads in space like a picture; on the other it plunges into time, like a story which its serialization into writing approximates more or less to the musical work. In this it is peculiarly unquotable, *since the written text cannot restore to it what only the projector can produce*; a movement, the illusion of which guarantees the reality."[13] Here the curious paradox of film is that its materiality cannot be grasped because it *re-*

sists writing. And one of the curious consequences of structuralist film theory and narratology is their demonstration of film narration as a complex, highly elaborated, and codified system that nonetheless escapes notation. By the same token, the imbrication of spatiality with temporality in film, and the fact that it cannot be anchored in a system of notationality, leads to another idea: that of Metz's definition of film as the "Imaginary signifier." The passage in film semiology from the structuralist to the psychoanalytic conception of the signifier pushed Metz toward a redefinition of film as a sensory modality that is also a psychical structuring. Rather than a haptic object or a stable self-identical form, the film viewer is always in pursuit of an absent, indeed an *absenting*, object. In Metz's elegant description, psychologically the spectator is always in pursuit of a double absence: the hallucinatory projection of an absent referent in space as well as the slipping away of images in time. The inherent virtuality of the image is a fundamental condition of cinema viewing where the ontological insecurity of film as an "aesthetic" object is posed as both a spatial uncertainty and a temporal instability.

So, even the "filmophanic" definition, which identifies the singularity of film as a phenomenological event—the attended film projection—finds itself split by a certain virtuality. And in this respect I still hold that the experience of the imaginary signifier is something of a psychological constant in theatrical film viewing. Instead of an "aesthetic" analysis, cinematic specificity becomes the location of a variable constant, the instantiation of a certain form of desire that is at once semiological, psychological, technological, and cultural. Here film theory reconnects usefully with the historical argument above. Throughout the twentieth century, the technological processes of film production have innovated constantly, its narrative forms have evolved continuously, and its modes of distribution and exhibition have also varied widely. But what has persisted is a certain mode of psychological investment—a modality of desire if you will. Film theory, and the history of film theory, remain important for the range of concepts and methods it has developed for defining the "cinematic," no matter how variable the concept, and for evaluating both the spectatorial experience (perceptual, cognitive, affective) and the range of cultural meanings that devolve from films. Perhaps these theories are too "grand" for some. But what the turn to a rather vulgar philosophical empiricism (which confuses, as the Althusserians used to say, the real object with the object-in-thought) has gained in the knowledge of individual films, in their signifying processes, and in their social and historical contexts it has lost in a possible knowledge of the cinematic, of a generalizable theory, while relinquishing the bolder social task of cultural and even ideological evaluation. In an effort to become more "scientific," film theory risks, sadly, becoming more conservative and reductionist.

The Old and the New

Now that the Society for Cinema Studies has changed its name to the Society for Cinema and Media Studies, one might be tempted to conclude that this is a case of "if you can't beat 'em, join 'em." Or more conservatively, one could imagine an organization of archivists and antiquarians content with rehearsing and refining their understanding of a medium that had a good run but that is now simply "history." I want to conclude, however, by making a plea not only for the continuing relevance of film studies but also for the special significance of film theory in the electronic and digital era.

While historically many important debates in film theory have based themselves in a certain materiality, it is nonetheless a historical actuality that film has no persistent identity. Rather, its (variable) specificity lies elsewhere: a twofold virtuality defined by a vertiginous spatialization of time and temporalization of space as well as a peculiar perceptual and psychological instability wherein the spectator pursues a doubly absent object. Consequently, film studies can claim no ontological ground as a discipline, that is, if we continue to insist that the self-identity of an art be defined by medium specificity, or what I have called the criterion of substantial self-similarity. In fact the ontological ungroundedness of film from the standpoint of aesthetic philosophy offers an important object lesson for every discipline that seeks a stable frame or substance. That specificity, no matter how mobile, derives from and is legitimated by the wealth of its concepts. In this respect, institutional cinema studies has recently neglected to its peril the importance of theory and the history of theory: the invention, critique, and reassessment of the fundamental concepts that underlie the kinds of questions we ask—whether historical, sociological, or aesthetic—and the kinds of answers those questions allow.

So, cinema studies can stake no permanent claims on its disciplinary territories—its borders are in fact continually shifting. To state the matter in its most specific terms: there is no ontology that grounds film as an aesthetic medium and serves as an anchor for its claims to exist as a humanistic discipline. Now the same should be said for both the College Art Association and every section of the Modern Language Association. And it would be hard to find a humanities professor these days who wouldn't be willing to take the default decon-structive position that any claims for self-identity in their respective disciplines are just an illusion based on a faulty assumption—that is, until the time comes to argue for a new faculty position. At the same time, the study of literature or art history still enjoys a cultural prestige that is hardly secured for the study of film, much less digital and interactive media. The enduring quality of the book as an "interface," for example, as well as the social forms of its use enjoys a his-tory whose *durée* is long enough to be forgotten by many as *having* a history, and an embattled one. And this contributes to the ideological solidity of an idea of literature and its persistent cultural capital.

Contrariwise, the history of film and cinema has been lived in three or four short generations in which the medium's aesthetic and social form have evolved rapidly and varied considerably. However, the impermanence and mu-tability of film studies as a field should be seen as one of its great strengths: the self-consciousness of film theory about the uncertain ontological status of the medium and the conflictual nature of the debates that have defined the gene-alogy of film study mark it still as one of the most daring areas of intellectual inquiry of the last century. And this, I believe, is one of the persistent attrac-tions of film for intellectuals.

But what now of cinema studies and the "new" media?

In periods of intense economic and cultural competition from other media, cinema has always incorporated the image of its rival the better to remake the narrative and social image of its aesthetic identity and to differentiate itself eco-nomically. At the same time, the marketing of the new is also the reassertion of something already well established: the preservation and enhancement of the psychological structures that have informed the pleasures of cinema viewing throughout its history. Film history helps us cut through the dissemblances of digital paranoia to understand how theatrical cinema has entered a phase of technological innovation and accommodation where rather than fading away it is in fact renewing and renovating itself. Yet some things persist. In like man-ner, earlier periods of technological change involving sound, color, and wide screen can be seen not as revolutions but rather as additions or enhancements to the basic psychological and cultural experience of cinema. Despite structural adjustments on the level of technology, the organization of the work force, the structure of exhibition, and economic strategies of finance and distribution, the social and technological architecture of theatrical film viewing and the basic structure of classical Hollywood narrative have remained remarkably constant since 1917. While television and video certainly present different social and technological architectures of film viewing that compete directly with theatrical exhibition, economically they have functioned more as new and lucrative channels of distribution. Perceptually, cognitively, and psychologically, television, video, and now the Internet present very different ways of viewing the same kind of narrative structure in different technological contexts. Financially, however, they serve to feed the same system: the multinational entertainment industries. In Hollywood cinema, and in cinema studies, both the excitement and the anxiety fueled by the emergence of digital media are inspired by the possibility that they will *replace* and eventually *supercede* the cinematic experience. But again this paranoia is an old one. Hollywood has learned to coexist peacefully with, and to profit enormously from, radio, television, and video. It is undoubtedly learning to do the same with the leisure hours consumed by the Internet and computer gaming.

In the same breath I also want to emphasize that there is something fundamentally "new" emerging in the new media that challenges us to rethink the fundamental concepts of film theory. This is evident, for example, in the non-linear (though not necessarily nonteleological) narrative structure of multiuser and simulation gaming, whose interactive and collective nature also mobilizes the spectator's vision and desire in novel ways. Not only does online gaming require new ways of conceptualizing the placement of the spectator but multiuser domains, where users participate collectively in the creation and modification of the game/narrative space, also ask us to rethink notions of authorship. Interactive media promote a form of participatory spectatorship relatively unknown in other time-based spatial media. Webcams are promoting new forms of self-presentation and new modalities of pleasurable and even perverse looking. A certain concept of representation is also changing profoundly. As I have already argued, in digital imaging the criterion of "realism" remains a curious constant even as the indexical image is replaced by a computational simulation that enables new forms and modalities of creative activity. Finally, the various media that derive their power from distributed computing represent fundamentally new technological organizations of the time and space of spectatorship, both in its singular and collective forms. The collective audience organized in the unified space and linear time of the film projection has been dispersed into the serialized space and unified time of broadcast media. And in turn, the one-to-many model of broadcasting is yielding to the many-to-many model of distributed computing characterized by an atomized space and asynchronous time whose global reach is vaster yet more ephemeral.

It would be foolish to believe that we are encountering any of these media in their mature form. Part of the excitement of the critical study of digital culture is the possibility of recognizing that we are witnessing the birth of a medium or media whose future is as difficultly imagined as my sociologist at the nickelodeon in 1907. Despite or perhaps because of their rapid economic, cultural, and aesthetic emergence, new media lack concepts for critical and social assessment. The velocity of the changes taking place since the Internet entered into the popular view toward the end of the 1980s, and the even faster spread of the World Wide Web since 1994, have rapidly overtaken the capacity of academic disciplines to comprehend them. Nearly twenty-five years had to elapse after the emergence of cinema as a mass, popular medium and a major American industry before the first large-scale sociological inquiry—the Payne Fund Studies—took place. The academic and educational response to radio and television as new communication technologies was somewhat quicker but nonetheless can still be measured in decades. However, unlike my young sociologist at the nickelodeon, we are not bereft of critical resources for comprehending the broad outlines of these new media. For to the extent that they share common lines of descent with the history of film, there is nearly a hundred years of international film theory and historical enquiry to serve as a critical resource for their evaluation.

Here the old (cinematic) and the new (electronic and digital) media find themselves in a curious genealogical mélange whose chronology is by no means simple or self-evident. As "film" disappears in the successive substitutions of the digital for the analog, what persists is *cinema* as a narrative form and a psychological experience—a certain modality of imbricating visuality, signification, and desire. Indeed, while computer-generated imagery longs to be "photographic," many forms of interactive media long to be "cinematic." Nonetheless, watching a movie on broadcast television or video, much less the Internet, is arguably not a cinematic experience. At the same time, although there have been mutations in the forms of spectatorship, the fundamental narrative architecture of film persists, and, despite competition from video and the Internet, theatrical film viewing shows no signs of disappearing. The unity or homogeneity of the cinematic spectatorial experience peaked long ago in 1946 and since has fragmented and branched off into other distribution streams. Yet it remains the baseline for understanding and evaluating other spatial time-based media. For this reason, neither television nor digital *studies* has emerged with a coherence separate from a fundamental grounding in *film* studies, and, therefore, critically understanding the evolution of film narrative and new variations in "cinematic" spectatorial experience still relies on the core concepts of film *theory*. To understand critically what television, video, and interactive digital media are becoming means both defining their significant technological and aesthetic differences *and* understanding that they descend from similar genealogical roots with photography and film. This is defined in part by the twofold virtuality that breaches the Maginot line dividing the arts of time or discourse from the arts of space or image.

In this respect, we can see how the history of film and film theory reaches out to the larger concerns of visual studies. There is an obvious alliance here between film studies and media studies on the one hand, and the emerging field of visual studies on the other. But implicit in the idea of visual studies is either to return film studies to the history of art or to resituate it as an extension or part of a larger (multi)media studies. However, I would like to suggest a more radical idea.

While cultural conservatives consider film and CGI to be debased creative endeavors, from another point of view they may be understood as raising fascinating philosophical problems that are less evident, and less interesting, with respect to other more established arts. Moreover, despite their ostensible differences, film and CGI do so in similar ways. As I have argued in a previous book—*Reading the Figural, or Philosophy after the New Media*—cinema shares with new media a common line of descent characterized by their powers of the "figural." This is why I include film among the "new" media and claim that the concepts of film theory define the best horizon for assessing both what is new, and at the same time, very old, in the new media. In figural media, older distinctions of spatiality and temporality, visuality and expression, autographicality and notationality are collapsed or reconfigured in ways that require both the deconstruction of previous philosophical thought and the creation of new concepts. Thus I am quite serious in including photography and film in a history of "new media" that follows the same genealogical declension, no matter how complex, and this should be evident from my discussion of virtuality above.

For these reasons, I believe that twentieth-century culture is fundamentally an "audiovisual culture," the history of whose forms and concepts are concomitant with the history of film and film theory. Thus the history of cinema, and the concepts of film theory, become the most productive contexts for defining the audiovisuality of our past and current centuries. And in this manner cinema studies suddenly asserts its central role in any humanities curriculum once we relinquish an outmoded aesthetic argument and start to value figural media for the new thought they produce. At the same time, the new media also challenge film studies and film theory to reinvent themselves through reassessing and constructing anew their concepts. To reassert and renew the province of cinema studies also means defining and redefining what "film" signifies. Hence the apparent paradox of asserting the continuation and renewal of cinema studies in the face of the disappearance of what most self-evidently defines it — celluloid as a means of registering and projecting indexical/analogical images. I agree with Anne Friedberg that cinema studies now finds itself in a transitional moment wherein *screens* become display and delivery formats whose form and dimensions are variable (theatrical film, television, computer); *film* is relegated to a storage device variable as to its medium (celluloid, 1/2 inch tape, DVD, video servers, etc.); and *spectators* become "users" manipulating interfaces, either as simple as a remote control or as complex as data-gloves and head-mounted displays. The convergence of media that occurs in digital technologies also encourages us to widen considerably cinema's genealogy to include the telephone, radio, television, and the computer as parts of a broader audiovisual regime.[14] Equally interesting in Friedberg's observations is not only the concise expression of the variety and complexity of changes taking place, but also the resolute continuity of certain concepts — *screen, film, spectator* — that already have a long and complex history. In the best critical work on digital culture, then, one finds the recirculation, and indeed renovation, of certain key concepts and problems of film theory: how new forms of image emerge in relation to factors of movement and temporality; the shifting status of "'photographic' realism" as a cultural construct; how questions of signification are transformed by the narrative organization of time-based spatial media; and the question of technology in relation to art, not only in the production and dissemination of images but also in the technological delimitation and organization of the spatiality and temporality of spectatorial experience and desire.

Screen, film, spectator; image, movement, and time; representation and the problem of realism, or the relation of image to referent; signification and narrative; technology and art: the form and vocabulary in which these questions are posed has changed continuously in the history of film theory as a series of conflictual debates. Yet the basic set of concepts has remained remarkably constant. Moreover, the real accomplishment of cinema studies, I believe, is to have forged more than any other related discipline the methodological and philosophical bases for addressing the most urgent and interesting questions, both aesthetic and cultural, of modernity and visual culture. Only the history of film theory gives us the basis to understand and to judge the extent and nature of the changes taking place in photographic, cinematographic, electronic, and interactive digital media. Suddenly, the questions and debates of not just a hundred years of cinema but of nearly a hundred years of film theory become the baseline for comprehending both what is entirely new in the emergence of interactive digital media and computer-mediated communications *and* what endures as the core experience of narrative-representational cinema. Film has not died yet, though it may become thoroughly "remediated."[15] Nonetheless, the main questions and concepts of film theory persist, and we should pay careful attention to how they define a certain history of thought, how they can be used to reexamine that history, and how they form the basis for a critical understanding of both new media and old. And at the same time the core concepts of film theory are being recontextualized in ways that extend and render more complex their critical powers.

Both the academic and cultural status of university cinema studies still suffer from the time lag between the emergence of film and cinema and their serious academic study. As in my opening example, a whole new industry and art emerged in the early twentieth century without a philosophical or sociological context to imagine its social impact and consequences. Despite its richness and complexity, the history of film theory in the first half of the twentieth century was largely a matter of playing catch-up. Fortunately, the new digital culture is not emerging in a similar theoretical vacuum. For that same history positions us to better comprehend the complex genealogy defining both the technological and aesthetic possibilities of computer-generated imagery, as well as its commercial and popular exploitation. The history of film and film theory thus becomes the most productive conceptual horizon against which we can assess both what is new and yet very old in the new media. Film theory, then, is our best hope for understanding critically how digital technologies are serving, like television and video before them, to perpetuate the cinematic as the mature audiovisual culture of the twentieth century and, at the same time, how they are preparing the emergence of a new audiovisual culture whose broad and indiscernible outlines we are only just beginning to distinguish.

Notes

1. This is not unlike the case of Hugo Münsterberg, the preeminent psychologist of turn-of-the-century America, whose last book, *The Photoplay: A Psychological Study* (New York: Dover, 1970), is perhaps the first work of English-language film theory. Münsterberg was no longer young, however, and rumor has it that his fas-

cination derived from the image of a young actress, Annette Kellerman, in the 1915 film *Neptune's Daughter.*

2. For an interesting historical and aesthetic survey of these issues, see Andrew Darley, *Visual Digital Culture: Surface, Play and Spectacle in New Media Genres* (London: Routledge, 2000), as well as the anthologies *Culture, Technology, and Creativity in the Twentieth Century*, edited by Philip Hayward (London: John Libbey and Co., 1990), and *Future Visions: New Technologies of the Screen*, edited by Philip Hayward and Tana Wollen (London: BFI, 1993).

3. Timothy Binckley, "Refiguring Culture," in Hayward and Wollen, *Future Visions*, 93.

4. Roland Barthes, *Camera Lucida: Reflections on Photography*, translated by Richard Howard (New York: Hill and Wang, 1981), 80.

5. See my *Reading the Figural, or Philosophy after the New Media* (Durham, N.C.: Duke University Press, 2001), especially chapter 1.

6. See Nelson Goodman, *Languages of Art: An Approach to a Theory of Symbols* (Indianapolis: Hackett, 1976), especially the chapter "Art and Authenticity," 99–123. When reading the arguments that follow, we should note that Goodman in no way assumes hierarchies of value in presenting the distinction between autographic and allographic arts. His concern, rather, is with how the problem of discourse shifts with respect to different forms and strategies of notationality in nonlinguistic art practices.

7. Ibid., 114.

8. There is even a more unusual paradox here. As various "synesthetic" programs like Color Music and Text-to-Midi show, the same algorithm can be used to produce outputs in different media: a set of musical sounds may be transformed as color values or ASCII text as music. In this sense, from the perspective of notation the resultant color or sound is mathematically identical to its "source" even though perceptually their inputs and outputs are different.

9. Cohen-Séat develops this argument in his *Essai sur les principes d'une philosophie du cinéma* (Paris: PUF, 1958), esp. 54. Souriau's distinctions are outlined in his essay "Les grands caractères de l'univers filmique," in *L'Univers filmique*, edited by Etienne Souriau (Paris: Flammarion, 1953). For an overview in English of both thinkers, see Edward Brian Lowry, *The Filmology Movement and Film Study in France* (Ann Arbor: UMI Research Press, 1985).

10. Christian Metz, *Language and Cinema*, translated by Donna Jean Umiker-Sebeok (The Hague: Mouton, 1974), 12.

11. Ibid., 22.

12. Ibid., 28; my emphasis.

13. Raymond Bellour, "The Unattainable Text," *Screen* 16.3 (autumn 1975): 25; my emphasis.

14. Anne Friedberg, "The End of Cinema: Multimedia and Technological Change," in *Reinventing Film Studies*, edited by Christine Gledhill and Linda Williams (London:

Arnold, 2000), 440. Equally interesting is her suggestion that as film loses more and more its identity as a discrete object, the more the field has turned to film history as a way of reasserting its identity and continuity. However, the way in which this turn to history has taken place might miss the more radical consequences of filmic temporality.

15. On the genealogy of new media as a history of remediation, see Jay David Bolter and Richard Grusin, *Remediation: Understanding New Media* (Cambridge, Mass.: MIT Press, 1999).

Appendix:
Timeline for a History of Anglophone Film Culture and Film Studies

STEPHEN GROENING

In keeping with the spirit of this volume, the following timeline focuses on events and developments within film studies in the Anglophone context. By juxtaposing publications, film courses, film societies, and institutions in chronological fashion, this timeline presents the history of film studies as an assemblage of intersecting and overlapping developments located at various sites. Tempting as it may be to attribute an arc of progress or development to the information in this timeline, I hope the reader recognizes these entries as potential passages to explore within the history of film studies. Acknowledging that there are many histories of the discipline, this timeline is not exhaustive. It does not list every single event of relevance; rather, it contains information coinciding with and complementing the essays in this volume.

Much of the material contained in the timeline consists of journal publications, which are not necessarily events in the strict sense. Nonetheless, these journals are taken to be material manifestations of knowledge and debate, as well as indications of theoretical developments informing the discipline. Journals also constitute part of the institutional context that enables and shapes the discipline. In that same spirit, inaugural conferences sponsored by film studies organizations are included. Also contained is a survey of university course offerings, which began as early as the 1910s and proliferated in geometric proportions during the 1970s. These provide an index to the discipline's longevity and recent renaissance. Other entries, such as film festivals, the founding of archival institutions and associations, and the establishment of film societies indicate widespread interest in the cultural and social significance of the medium. Industrial and technological developments have been omitted, as these can be found in many histories regarding the development of media technology or the film industry in its various incarnations. The one exception to this rule is 16mm film. As a relatively inexpensive and nonflammable substandard gauge, 16mm enabled the medium's penetration into the classroom, assisted in the development of film societies, and made film a more democratic art even as it rendered it useful to new kinds of institutional control.

1895 *New York City*   William Kennedy-Laurie Dickson with Antonia Dickson wrote *The History of the Kinetograph, Kinetoscope, and Kinetophonograph*, an account of the early motion picture technology innovation.[1]

1907 *New York City*   Founding of *The Moving Picture World* (–1927), publication of the Moving Picture Exhibitors' Association and the leading trade journal in the United States. Merged with *Exhibitor's Herald* in 1928.

1909 *New York City*   National Board of Censorship established. Renamed National Board of Review (NBR) in 1915.

1909 *Chicago*   Founding of *Nickelodeon*, "America's leading journal of motography" (–1911). Retitled *Motography: Exploiting Motion Pictures* "for entertainment, education, science and advertising" (1911–1918).

1913 *New York City*   Founding of *Motion Picture News* (–1930). Merged with *Exhibitor's Herald World* in 1931 to form *Motion Picture News*.

1913 *Heidelberg, Germany*   Emilie Altenloh, at Ruprecht-Karls-Universität zu Heidelberg, completed her doctoral dissertation on the sociology of cinema.[2]

1915 *New York City*   Publication of Vachel Lindsay's *The Art of the Moving Picture*, the first book-length work on appreciating motion pictures as an art form, "intended, first of all, for the new art museums springing up all over the country."[3]

| 1915 | *New York City* | Columbia University introduced "Photoplay Composition," a course in screenwriting. |

| 1916 | *New York City* | Society of Motion Picture Engineers (SMPE) founded to develop technical standards for the motion picture industry. Monthly journal first published January 1930. |

| 1916 | *New York City* | Publication of Hugo Münsterberg's *The Film: A Psychological Study* (New York: D. Appleton and Company). First book-length work on the experience of the filmviewer. |

| 1919 | *New York City* | NBR first to pick "Ten Best" films of the year. |

| 1919 | *Chicago* | Founding of *Exhibitors Herald: The Independent Film Trade Paper* (–1927). Merged with *Moving Picture World* in 1928 to form *Exhibitors Herald and Moving Picture World*. |

| 1919 | | American Society of Cinematographers established as a professional society promoting the work and use of the motion picture camera. |

| 1920 | *Chicago* | Founding of *Visual Education* (–1923), published by the Visual Education Institute, Inc. Along with *Educational Screen* (see below), *Visual Education* was part of a series of progressive education journals concerned with integrating visual aids, including motion pictures, in public education in the United States. |

| 1920 | *Chicago* | Founding of *Educational Screen* (–1971), "a source freely accessible to all interested in the progress of the new, nation-wide movement which seeks to broaden and deepen, by the use of visual aids, our national education in school, church, club, and community center." Merged with *Visual Education* in 1923, *Visual Instruction News* in 1932, and *Audio-Visual Guide* in 1956. |

| 1922 | *Los Angeles* | Motion Picture Producers and Distributors of America (MPPDA) established "to restore a more favorable public |

image for the motion picture business," with former Post-master General Will H. Hays as president. Later renamed the Motion Picture Association of America (MPAA).[4]

1923 *Rochester, N.Y.*   Eastman Kodak introduced 16mm film.

1925 *London*   London Film Society established by Ivor Montagu and Hugh Miller, with Iris Barry, Adrian Brunel, Walter Mycroft, Sidney Bernstein, and Frank Dobson as council members. Anthony Asquith, Michael Balcon, John Gielgud, Julian Huxley, Ivor Novello, George Pearson, and John Strachey were also founding members.[5] Similar societies formed in other European cities.

1925 *New York City*   Film Associates, Inc. founded as part of the "Little Theatre" movement, with Gilbert Seldes as a chief proponent. Small exhibition spaces of only a few hundred seats (compared to contemporary movie palaces) with specialized fare, in this case foreign-language films, were dubbed "Little Theatres."[6]

1926 *Paris*   First International Motion Picture Congress held, under auspices of the League of Nations, in order to better spread the ideals of the League through film, which was assumed to have enormous potential for education and intellectual life.[7]

1926 *New York City*   Founding of *Amateur Movie Makers*, published by the Amateur Cinema League to "organize . . . the new art of amateur cinematography." Renamed *Movie Makers* in 1928.

1926 *Los Angeles*   Founding of *Film Spectator* (–1931), published by Welford Beaton, "the frankest and ablest periodical in America dealing with the American film."

1926 *Chicago*   Founding of *Visual Review* (–1938), published by the Society for Visual Education.

1927 *Los Angeles*   Academy of Motion Picture Arts and Sciences organized. Officially, the academy took on the task of rewarding and improving artistry in motion pictures.[8]

1927 *London* London Television Society established as a forum for television engineers and enthusiasts to share developments and achievements in television technology.

1927 *Cambridge, Mass.* Harvard University Business School offered a series of lectures on the film industry, organized by alumnus, banker, and industry executive Joseph P. Kennedy.[9]

1927 *Territet, Switzerland* Founding of *Close Up* (–1933), "the first to approach films from the angles of art, experiment and possibility," edited by Kenneth Macpherson, H.D. (Hilda Doolittle), and Bryher (Annie Winifred Ellerman). *Close Up* was an attempt by literary intellectuals to examine the aesthetic possibilities of film. In addition, it was an important English-language source of the writings of G.W. Pabst as well as Sergei Eisenstein and other Soviet filmmakers.

1928 *Rome* International Educational Cinematograph Institute (–1938) founded under the aegis of the League of Nations to bring together national participation to an international forum for discussing the role and circulation of the cinema, with an emphasis on its educative values.[10]

1928 *Cambridge, Mass.* Harvard University founded a short-lived film library. The Fine Arts Department promised, in conjunction with Hollywood studios, to "select every year the best films . . . and preserve them in a special film library," in conjunction with Hollywood studios.[11] The plan called for two prints of each film to be housed in the Fogg Museum. Foreign films were excluded from consideration.[12]

1928 *Cambridge, Mass.* The Anthropology and Geology Departments of Harvard University partnered with Pathé Exchange to produce and distribute educational films; the venture was called the University Film Foundation.[13]

1928 *Los Angeles* University of Southern California (USC) founded cinematograph museum, "established for a special course of training and record of the motion picture industry."[14]

1928	*New York City*	Founding of *Movie Makers* (–1954), formerly *Amateur Movie Makers*.
1929	*Rochester, N.Y.*	Kodak introduced color 16mm film.
1929	*New York City*	Museum of Modern Art (MOMA) founded.
1929	*Los Angeles*	USC established School of Cinema and announced bachelor of science degree in cinematography.
1929	*Rome*	Founding of *International Review of Educational Cinematography* (–1934), published by the League of Nations International Educational Cinematographic Institute, "to promote the production, circulation and exchange between various countries, of educational films."
1929	*New York City*	Payne Fund Studies (–1932) organized to assess the influence of motion pictures on children. The results were published in 1933 in twelve volumes as *Motion Pictures and Youth*. Henry J. Forman wrote a popularized version, *Our Movie Made Children*.[15]
1930	*Philadelphia*	Founding of *Experimental Cinema* (–1934) published by the Cinema Crafters of America. David Platt and Lewis Jacobs were editors, while Seymour Stern and H. A. Potamkin served as correspondents. The magazine emphasized primarily Soviet film and other experimental cinematic forms. Communist in politics, the editors claimed *Experimental Cinema* as "the advance guard of a new motion picture art," and hoped the journal would "be the nucleus of a profound and vital force toward the creation of a world-wide cinema ideology."
1931	*New York City*	*Motion Picture Herald* formed from the consolidation of *Exhibitor's Herald World* and *Motion Picture News*.
1932	*Venice, Italy*	The first film festival, founded by Count Giuseppe Volpi.
1932	*New York City*	At the New School for Social Research Harry Potamkin offered an evening film course that covered a broad range of topics, including animation, national cinemas, comedy,

and satire as well as the socioeconomics of the film industry.[16]

1932 *London* Founding of *Sight and Sound,* a monthly magazine of film reviews and criticism (taken over by the British Film Institute in 1933).

1933 *New York City* Irving Jacoby offered film course at the City College of New York that focused on the history of the motion picture and used films no longer exhibited as examples of important trends.[17]

1933 *London* British Film Institute founded, partly as a result of the Commission on Educational and Cultural Films report *The Film in National Life*. With its aim, in part, to combat the influence of Hollywood, to "encourage the art of the film," and to advocate for the "intelligent filmgoer," the institute's membership was initially dominated by educators and clergymen.[18]

1933 *London* Founding of *Film Art* (–1937), "an international review of avant-garde cinema."

1933 *New York City* New York City Film Forum established by Sidney Howard and Tom Brandon to exhibit workers' films from Germany, the Soviet Union, and Great Britain.[19]

1933 *New York City* New York City Film Society established with the purpose of screening "motion pictures of excellence" (often European) that would neither be under the purview of the censor nor bow to commercial pressures.[20]

1933 *New York City* Frederick Thrasher offered film course at New York University.

1934 *London* Founding of *Monthly Film Bulletin* (–1991), a journal of reviews of publicly exhibited films in Great Britain published by the British Film Institute.

1934 *Syracuse, N.Y.* Sawyer Falk offered a cinema appreciation course at Syracuse University.[21]

1935	*New York City*	MOMA established its Film Library.
1935	*London*	National Film Library (later renamed National Film Archive) established as the archival wing of the British Film Institute, in charge of collections.[22]
1935	*Berlin*	Reichsfilmarchiv established.
1935	*Ottawa*	Founding of the National Film Society of Canada. Proposed by Donald Buchanan after his visit to the British Film Institute, the society was to "encourage the study and appreciation of the technique and art of the motion picture through the private showing to its members of selected films of an artistic or experimental nature."[23]
1936	*Paris*	Cinémathèque Française established by Henri Langlois and Georges Franju.
1937	*Urbana-Champaign*	Ernest Bernbaum offered "Appreciation of Movies" course at the University of Illinois.[24]
1937	*New York City*	The National Council of Teachers of English published *Film and School: A Handbook in Moving-Picture Evaluation* by Helen Rand and Richard Lewis. Written partly in response to the Payne Fund Studies, the book attempted to set protocols and standards for judging and evaluating moving pictures.
1938	*New York City*	Columbia University inaugurated four-year film study unit offered through extension service in collaboration with MOMA.
1938	*New York City*	Founding of the American Film Center (–1948). Inspired by the British Film Institute and partly funded by the Rockefeller Foundation as a counterweight to Hollywood, the center aimed to establish better relationships between documentary filmmakers and distributors. Began to publish *Film News* in 1939.[25]
1938	*Paris*	Founding of the International Federation of Film Archives (FIAF). John Abbott (MOMA), Iris Barry (MOMA), Frank

Hensel (Reichsfilmarchiv), Henri Langlois (Cinémathèque Française), and Olwen Vaughan (BFI) were all founding members.

1938 *New York City* Association of School Film Libraries established, sponsored by the Rockefeller Foundation and the American Council on Education "as a clearing house for information on the production and distribution of educational films to schools and colleges."[26]

1939 *Ottawa* National Film Board of Canada founded by John Grierson, "a public agency that produces and distributes films and other audiovisual works which reflect Canada to Canadians and the rest of the world."[27]

1939 *New York City* Founding of *Film News* (–1981), an "International Review of AV materials and Equipment" published by the American Film Center until 1943 and then by the Educational Film Library Association.

1940 *Austin, Texas* Founding of NAVED News (–1945), published by the National Association of Visual Education Dealers.

1941 *New York City* *The Film Index: A Bibliography* published by the Museum of Modern Art Film Library. In the foreword, Iris Barry writes that the index "for the first time makes useful and accessible to the layman the enormous accumulation of information about films housed in the many libraries all over the country."[28]

1943 *New York City* Founding of the EFLA *Bulletin* (–1967), published by the Educational Film Library Association.

1945 *Los Angeles* Motion Picture Association (MPA) formed "to reestablish American films in the world market." Renamed Motion Picture Export Association (MPEA) in 1994.

1945 *Berkeley* Founding of *Hollywood Quarterly* (–1951), to gain "a clearer understanding, of current techniques of the film and radio, but also of the social, educational, and aesthetic functions" of film, radio, and television. Succeeded by *Quarterly of Film, Radio and Television* in 1951.

1946 *Cannes* First Cannes Film Festival, originally scheduled for 1939, but canceled due to the outbreak of war.

1946 *Washington, D.C.* Film Council of America founded (–1957) as the civilian outgrowth of the Office of War information, whose mission was to function as a central collector and dispenser of information about film and its use in classrooms and community centers.[29]

1946 *New York City* Founding of *Film Forum Review* (–1949), "devoted to the use of motion pictures in adult education," published by Columbia University and the National Committee of Film Forums.

1946 *London* Founding of *Penguin Film Review* (–1949), edited by Roger Manville, to "survey the field of cinema from a wide and international standpoint." Contributors included Hans Richter, Siegfried Kracauer, Anthony Asquith, Ivor Montagu, and Sergei Eisenstein.

1946 *New York City* Cinema 16 founded as "a cultural, non-profit organization devoted to the presentation of outstanding 16mm documentary, educational, scientific and experimental films."[30]

1947 *Rochester, N.Y.* George Eastman House Museum began its motion picture collection.

1947 *Chicago* Founding of *The Film Counselor* (–1953), published by the Film Council of America.

1947 *Edinburgh* First Edinburgh International Film Festival founded by the Edinburgh Film Guild. Advisory committee included Basil Wright, Paul Rotha, and H. Forsyth Hardy.

1950 *Ottawa* The National Film Society of Canada reorganized as the Canadian Film Institute (CFI) in order to serve as "the central coordinating body for non-theatrical film in Canada."

The film societies established a separate group, the Canadian Federation of Film Societies (CFFS), in 1954.[31]

1950 *Harmonds-worth, Middle-sex, U.K.* Founding of *The Cinema* (–1952), an annual that replaced *Penguin Film Review*. Contained film stills, reviews of "important foreign films of the year," and longer essays on "the Cinema in all its aspects" than could be published in *Film Review*.[32]

1951 *Berkeley* Founding of the *Quarterly of Film, Radio and Television* (–1958). Formerly the *Hollywood Quarterly*, the journal was renamed because the editors found the original title misleading as the journal's audience and subject material were increasingly located outside of Hollywood.

1951 *Berlin* Berlin International Film Festival founded by Alfred Bauer.

1952 *Olinda, Australia* First Australian Film Festival held in the Melbourne suburb of Olinda, sponsored by the Australian Council of Film Societies. By 1953, the festival had split into the Melbourne Festival and the Sydney Festival.

1953 *Washington, D.C.* Founding of *Audio Visual Communication Review* (–1977), published by the National Education Association to promote the use of film, television, and other audiovisual apparatuses in learning, training, and the classroom.

1954 American Federation of Film Societies established.

1955 *New York City* Founding of *Film Culture* (–1999) as "a meeting ground for outspoken discussion and constructive analysis of ideas, achievements and problems in the domain of film."

1955 *Berkeley* Founding of *Film Quarterly*, formerly *Quarterly of Film, Radio and Television*, as "a journal dedicated to the hypothesis that a body of serious critical thought about films is possible."[33]

1956 *Kingston, Ontario* Gerald Pratley offered a summer film course at Queen's University.[34]

1959 *New York City*   Society of Cinematologists founded by John Driscoll, Jack Ellis, Robert Gessner, and Gerald Noxon. Renamed the Society for Cinema Studies in 1969.[35]

1959 *London*   Founding of *Screen Education* (–1969), published by the Society for Education in Film and Television and aimed at investigating the relationships between children and cinema and television.

1960 *New York City*   Society of Cinematologists held its first national meeting at New York University with featured speaker Erwin Panofsky.[36]

1962 *New York City*   Founding of *Film Comment*, published by the Film Society of Lincoln Center for those with a "sincere interest in the unlimited scope of the motion picture." This journal was primarily concerned with, and arose out of, the New American Cinema movement. The first two issues were published under the title *Vision: A Journal of Film Comment.*

1962 *New York City*   Filmmakers' Cooperative established as the distribution center for filmmakers associated with the New American Cinema Group partly in reaction to Cinema 16's rejection of Stan Brakhage's *Anticipation of the Night.*

1962 *London*   Founding of *Movie*, edited by Ian Cameron, which focused on film criticism inflected by auteur theory. First issue included a chart of British and American directors rated as "great," "talented," or "competent."

1963 *New York City*   First New York Film Festival, founded by Amos Vogel.

1966 *New York City*   National Society of Film Critics founded, partly in response to the New York Film Critics Circle's refusal to extend membership to magazine writers. Today there is overlap in membership.

1966 *Los Angeles*   Arthur Friedman, Ruth Schwartz, and Robert Lewine announced the National Television Library at UCLA, which later became the UCLA Film and Television Archive.

1966	*New York City*	Founding of *Cineaste* a quarterly, independent film magazine aimed at "focusing on both the art and the politics of the cinema."
1966	*Melbourne*	Swinburne Technical College (now Swinburne University of Technology) established diploma of art program in film and television, the first of its kind in Australia.[37]
1966	*New York City*	A short-lived venture to publish *Cahiers du Cinéma* in English lasted only a year. The influential French-language journal began publication in 1951.
1967	*Washington, D.C.*	The National Endowment for the Arts established the American Film Institute (AFI). In 1965, Lyndon Johnson proclaimed: "We will create an American Film Institute, bringing together leading artists of the film industry, outstanding educators, and young men and women who wish to pursue this 20th century art form as their life's work."[38]
1967	*Washington, D.C.*	AFI listed approximately 200 colleges and universities in the United States offering courses in film.
1967	*Champaign, Ill.*	Founding of *Cinema Journal*, published by the Society of Cinematologists.
1967	*Greenwich, Conn.*	Founding of *Film Library Quarterly* (–1984), published by the Film Library Information Council "to promote better film librarianship."
1968	*London*	Founding of *Screen: The Journal of the Society for Education in Film and Television*, which replaced *Screen Education*.
1969	*Washington, D.C.*	The AFI listed 68 colleges and universities with film majors and nearly 300 colleges and universities offering film courses.
1969	*Toronto*	York University created the first Department of Film offering an undergraduate film degree in Canada.[39]

1970	*New York City*	The Anthology Film Archives opened as a museum for avant-garde film.
1970	*Madison, Wisc.*	Founding of *Velvet Light Trap*, a journal of film history and criticism published for the Madison film community by the Arizona Jim Co-op. Members and contributors included Russell Campbell, Joseph McBride, Gerald Peary, and Michael Wilmington.
1970	*Washington, D.C.*	The AFI listed 233 colleges and universities offering courses in film and 68 institutions with a degree program in film or a related field, including 11 with Ph.D. programs.[40]
1970	*Newark, N.J.*	Founding of *Film and History: An Interdisciplinary Journal of Film and Television*, a semi-annual journal published by the Historians Film Committee of the American Historical Association to "study how history is being shaped by media as well as how media are being shaped by history."[41]
1971	*Berkeley*	Founding of *Camera Obscura: A Journal of Feminism and Film Theory*, published in "recognition of a need for theoretical study of film in this country from a feminist and socialist perspective."
1972	*Berkeley*	Founding of *Women and Film* (–1975), published by the Women's History Research Center, Inc.
1974	*Berkeley*	Founding of *Jump Cut*, a quarterly on contemporary film "committed to presenting and developing film criticism which recognizes theories often unfamiliar to Americans, such as structuralism, semiology, and Marxism."
1974	*East Anglia, U.K.*	Founding of *Framework* (–1992), an open and diverse film journal attendant to the cinemas of Latin America, Hollywood, Asia, Europe, as well as various aspects of film culture including film festivals and other forms of film exhibition. Implicitly against *Screen*'s attempts at a general theory of film. Relaunched in 1999 as *Framework: The Journal of Cinema and Media*, published by Wayne State University (Detroit).

1974 *Athens, Ohio*   First Annual Athens International Film Festival, organized by Giulio Scalinger, then an undergraduate at Ohio University. The journal *Wide Angle* would later be established by some of the conference organizers and attendees.

1976 *Québec City*   Film Studies Association of Canada established at the Conference of Learned Societies "to foster and advance scholarship in the history and art of film and related fields as well as to aid those teaching film and video production at Canadian colleges and universities."[42]

1976 *Athens, Ohio*   Founding of *Wide Angle*, "a quarterly journal of film history, theory, criticism and practice," which grew out of the Athens, Ohio, First International Film Festival.

1976 *Montréal*   Founding of *Ciné-tracts* (–1983), edited by Ron Burnett. Aimed to bring "together the issues of self-reflexivity, subjective positioning and hegemonic social structures, [and to] propose the outline of a possible theory of culture which embraces both the critique of ideology and the problematic of praxis."[43]

1976 *Edinboro, Pa.*   Founding of *Film Criticism*, initially published as a call to "arise" against film censorship and the suppression of filmic content. The journal became increasingly interested in film theory but still maintained a focus on film criticism proper.

1977 *New York*   James Monaco wrote *How to Read a Film: The Art, Technology, Language, History and Theory of Film and Media*, "because the media so very closely mimic reality, we apprehend them much more easily than we comprehend them. Film and electronic media have drastically changed the way we perceive the world—and ourselves—during the last eighty years."[44]

1978 *Ottawa*   The Canadian Film Index (cfi) listed 18 colleges and universities offering a bachelor's degree in film (or related) studies, and over 80 offering film courses in Canada (with most of the remainder offering a two-year technical diploma).[45]

1978	*Washington, D.C.*	The AFI listed over 1,000 colleges and universities offering courses in film and over 300 institutions with a degree program in film or a related field: 12 offer Ph.D.s and 45 offer master's programs. The guide also listed addresses for "film schools," which are defined as colleges or universities offering courses in film or television, in Australia (1), Canada (41) and Great Britain (15).[46]
1978	*Brighton, U.K.*	The International Federation of Film Archivists conference included a symposium entitled "Fiction Film, 1900–1906," which leads to a revisionist history of early film and new attention to alternate historiographic methods.[47]
1979	*Madison, Wisc.*	David Bordwell and Kristin Thompson wrote *Film Art: An Introduction*, aimed at introducing students to film aesthetics: "This book seeks to isolate those basic features of film which can constitute it as an art. The book therefore directs itself at the person interested in how the film medium may give us experiences akin to those offered by painting, sculpture, music, literature, theater, architecture, or dance."[48]
1985	*London*	The British Film Institute published *The Cinema Book*, edited by Pam Cook. Originally intended as a supplement for the BFI Film Library's extract collection, the book combined close readings of films with introductions to various theoretical approaches to film and film history.[49]
1987	*Los Angeles*	The Film Foundation created by Martin Scorcese, Woody Allen, Francis Ford Coppola, Stanley Kubrick, George Lucas, Sydney Pollack, Robert Redford, and Steven Spielberg to assist in the task of preserving and archiving films and raising money for film archives and museums.[50]
1987	*New York City*	Founding of *Film History: An International Journal*, which focuses on primary research into "the historical development of the motion picture, and the social, technological, and economic context in which this has occurred." The journal also published primary documentation of historical interest.

1990	*Ottawa*	The Film Studies Association of Canada began to publish the *Canadian Journal of Film Studies* "to promote scholarship on Canadian film and television."
1990	*Washington, D.C.*	The AFI listed over 500 schools in the United States offering degrees in film, television, or related fields, with over 100 offering bachelor's degrees and ten with doctoral programs in film. The AFI also listed four "film schools" (defined as colleges or universities offering courses in film or television) in Australia, 21 in Canada, and 14 in Great Britain.[51]
1990	*Los Angeles*	The Association of Moving Image Archivists (AMIA) established. Began publishing *Moving Image: The Journal of the Association of Moving Image Archivists* in 2001.
1991	*Glasgow*	First Screen Studies Conference, University of Strathclyde.
1996	*Washington, D.C.*	National Film Preservation Foundation (NFPF) created by an act of the U.S. Congress to give film preservation grants to museums, archives, and libraries.[52]
1996	*London*	Founding of *Film-Philosophy*, a free, publicly available online journal "dedicated to philosophically reviewing film studies, philosophical aesthetics, and world cinema."[53]
1997	*Melbourne*	Founding of *Screening the Past*, a free, publicly available online journal "concerned with: the history of photography, film, television and multimedia; the representation of history on/in these media; the role of these media in social history."[54]
2002	*Norman, Okla.*	Members of the Society of Cinema Studies voted via mail-in ballot to rename the organization the Society of Cinema and Media Studies. In the words of SCMS President Lucy Fischer, "Our new moniker clearly signals our organization's breadth of interest in the history and analysis of the moving image."[55]

Notes

I would like to thank William J. Buxton, Jane Dye, Oksana Dykyj, Rochelle Elstein, and Douglas Gomery for their valuable assistance with this research. I have also benefited enormously from the support and guidance of Haidee Wasson and Lee Grieveson, to whom I owe a debt of thanks.

Note: for journal entries, all quotations are from the editorial statement of volume 1, issue 1 (unless otherwise noted).

1. W. K.-L. Dickson and Antonia Dickson, *History of the Kinetograph, Kinetoscope and Kinetophonograph* (New York: A. Bunn, 1895).

2. Emilie Altenloh, *Zur Soziologie des Kino; die Kino-Unternehmung und die sozialen Schichten ihrer Besucher* (*Toward a Sociology of the Cinema: The Film Industry and the Social Strata of Filmgoers* [my translation]). Published in book form in 1914 by Diederichs in Jena.

3. Vachel Lindsay, *The Art of the Motion Picture* (New York: Macmillan Company, 1922 [1915]).

4. See http://www.mpaa.org/about.

5. Jamie Sexton, "The Film Society and the Creation of an Alternative Film Culture in Britain in the 1920s," in *Young and Innocent? The Cinema in Britain: 1896–1930*, edited by Andrew Higson (Exeter, U.K.: University of Exeter Press, 2002).

6. Douglas Gomery, *Shared Pleasures: A History of Movie Presentation in the United States* (Madison: University of Wisconsin Press, 1992), 172–80.

7. See Zoë Druick, "'Reaching the Multimillions': Liberal Internationalism and the Establishment of Documentary Film," this volume.

8. Tino Balio, *Grand Design: Hollywood as a Modern Business Enterprise, 1930–1939* (New York: Charles Scribner's Sons, 1993), 77.

9. Joseph P. Kennedy, *The Story of the Films* (New York: A. W. Shaw Company, 1927).

10. See Druick, "'Reaching the Multimillions.'"

11. Kennedy, *The Story of the Films*.

12. The current Harvard Film Archive was founded in 1979 with assistance from the Henry Luce Foundation and the National Endowment of the Arts (see http://www.harvardfilmarchive.org/history.php).

13. "Harvard Films at the Summer Schools," *Educational Screen* 7 (June 1928): 148–51; "The Movies Have Come to Harvard," *Educational Screen* 8 (December 1928): 260.

14. The museum curator J. Tarbotton Armstrong, quoted in "A Cinematograph Museum on Campus," *Educational Screen* 8 (October 1928): 191.

15. Lee Grieveson, "Cinema Studies and the Conduct of Conduct," this volume; Mark Anderson, "Taking Liberties: The Payne Fund Studies and the Creation of the Media Expert," this volume; and Henry James Forman, *Our Movie Made Children* (New York: Macmillan, 1935).

16. "Writer to Conduct Cinema Course," *Educational Screen* 11 (September 1932): 209.

17. "College Plans Course in Study of Motion Picture," *Educational Screen* 12 (March 1933): 78.

18. Penelope Houston, *Keepers of the Frame: The Film Archives* (London: BFI Publishing, 1994).

19. Haidee Wasson, *Museum Movies: The Museum of Modern Art and the Birth of Art Cinema* (Berkeley: University of California Press, 2005), 42.

20. Ibid., 41–43.

21. "Film Courses at Universities," *Educational Screen* 16 (April 1937): 122.

22. Houston, *Keepers of the Frame*, 23–37.

23. Yvette Hackett, "The National Film Society of Canada, 1935–1951: Its Origins and Development," in *Flashback: People and Institutions in Canadian Film History*, edited by Gene Walz (Montréal: Mediatexte, 1986).

24. "Film Courses at Universities," 122.

25. William Buxton, "Rockefeller Support for Projects on the Use of Motion Pictures for Educational and Public Purposes, 1935–1954," in "A Research Report for the Rockefeller Archive Center," 2001.

26. "Association of School Film Libraries," *Educational Screen* 17 (September 1938): 226.

27. Gary Evans, *In the National Interest: A Chronicle of the National Film Board of Canada from 1949 to 1989* (Toronto: University of Toronto Press, 1991), 4.

28. *The Film Index: A Bibliography. Volume 1: The Film as Art* (New York: Museum of Modern Art Film Library; H. W. Wilson Company, 1941).

29. See Charles Acland, "Classrooms, Clubs, and Community Circuits: Reconstructing Cultural Authority and the Film Council Movement, 1946–1957," this volume.

30. From the "Statement of Purpose" as reprinted in *Wide Angle* 19.1 (1997): 11.

31. Hackett, *The National Film Society of Canada*.

32. Roger Manvell, ed., *The Cinema 1950* (London: Penguin, 1950).

33. "Editorial Notebook," *Film Quarterly* 12.3 (spring 1959).

34. Peter Morris, "From Film Club to Academy: The Beginnings of Film Education in Canada," in *Québec Canada: L'enseignement du cinéma et de l'audiovisuel*, edited by Réal La Rochelle (Condé-sur-Noireau: Corlet-Télérama; Montréal: Cinémathèque québécoise, 1991).

35. Jack C. Ellis, "The Society for Cinema Studies: A Personal Recollection of the Early Days," *Cinema Journal* 43.1 (fall 2003), 105–12.

36. Ellis, "The Society for Cinema Studies."

37. Barbara Paterson, *Renegades: Australia's First Film School from Swinburne to VCA* (Victoria: Helicon Press, 1996).

38. William Horrigan and Greg Beal, eds., *The American Film Institute Guide to College Courses in Film and Television* (New York: Prentice Hall, 1990).

39. Morris, "From Film Club to Academy."

40. Linda B. Greensfelder, ed., *The American Film Institute's Guide to College Film Courses* (Chicago: American Library Association, 1970).
41. *Film and History*, http://www.h-net.org/~filmhis/about_us.htm, October 31, 2005.
42. Film Studies Association of Canada, http://www.filmstudies.ca, 2004–2005.
43. Ron Burnett, ed., *Explorations in Film Theory: Selected Essays from Ciné-tracts*. Bloomington: Indiana University Press, 1991.
44. James Monaco, "Preface," in *How to Read a Film: The Art, Technology, Language, History, and Theory of Film and Media* (New York: Oxford University Press, 1977), vii.
45. Marie-Claude Hecquet and David McNicoll, *A Guide to Film and Television Courses in Canada, 1978–1979* (Ottawa: Canadian Film Institute, 1978).
46. "Film School" is the term used by AFI, although it seems clear that these are not solely institutions offering a degree in production (as the term often connotes). *The American Film Institute Guide to College Courses in Film and Television*, edited by Dennis R. Bohnenkamp and Sam L. Grogg (New York: Prentice Hall, 1978).
47. See *Quarterly Review of Film Studies* 4.4 (1979).
48. David Bordwell and Kristin Thompson, "Preface," in *Film Art: An Introduction* (Menlo Park, Calif.: Addison-Wesley, 1979), iii.
49. Pam Cook, "Introduction to the First Edition," in *The Cinema Book* (London: BFI, 1985).
50. See http://www.film-foundation.org.
51. Greg Beal et al., *The American Film Institute Guide to College Courses in Film and Television*, 8th ed. (New York: Arco, 1990).
52. See http://www.filmpreservation.org.
53. *Film-Philosophy*, http://www.film-philosophy.com, 2005.
54. "Editorial Policy," *Screening the Past*, http://www.latrobe.edu.au/screeningthepast/policy.html, July 27, 2000.
55. "Letter from the President," SCMS Newsletter, October 2002 (as e-mailed to me by Jane Dye).

Selected Bibliography

Abel, Richard. *French Film Theory and Criticism: A History/Anthology, 1907–1939*. Princeton, N.J.: Princeton University Press, 1988.

Acland, Charles R. "The Film Council of America and the Ford Foundation: Screen Technology, Mobilization, and Adult Education in the 1950's." In *Patronizing the Public: American Philanthropic Support for Communication, Culture, and the Humanities*, edited by William J. Buxton. Lanham, Md.: Lexington Books, Critical Communication Series, forthcoming, 2009.

———. "Mapping the Serious and the Dangerous: Film and the National Council of Education." *Cinemas* 6.1 (1995): 101–18.

———. "Patterns of Cultural Authority: The National Film Society of Canada and the Institutionalization of Film Education, 1938–41." *Canadian Journal of Film Studies* 10.1 (2001): 2–27.

Addams, Jane. *The Spirit of Youth and the City Streets*. New York: Macmillan, 1909.

Adler, Mortimer. *Art and Prudence: A Study in Practical Philosophy*. New York: Longmans Green, 1937.

Altenloh, Emilie. "A Sociology of the Cinema: the Audience." Translated by Kathleen Cross. *Screen* 42.3 (2001 [1914]): 249–93.

Altman, Rick. "Film Studies, Inc.: Lessons from the Past about the Current Institutionalization of Film Studies." *Film Criticism* 17.2–3 (1992–3): 22–30.

American Film Institute's Guide to College Film Courses. 2nd ed. Chicago: American Film Institute/American Library Association, 1970.

Andrew, Dudley. *Concepts in Film Theory*. Oxford: Oxford University Press, 1984.

———. "The 'Three Ages' of Cinema Studies and the Age to Come." *PMLA* 115.3 (2000).

Arnheim, Rudolph. *Film*. Translated by L. M. Sievenking and Ian F. D. Morrow. London: Faber and Faber, 1933.

Auerbach, Jonathan. "American Studies and Film, Blindness and Insight." *American Quarterly* 58.1 (2006).

Bazin, André. *What Is Cinema?* Translated by Hugh Gray. 2 vols. Berkeley: University of California Press, 1967.

Blumer, Herbert. *Movies and Conduct*. New York: Macmillan, 1933.

Blumer, Herbert, and Philip Hauser. *Movies, Delinquency, and Crime*. New York: Macmillan, 1933.

Bohnenkamp, Dennis R., and Sam L. Grogg, eds. *The American Film Institute Guide to College Courses in Film and Television*. New York: Prentice Hall, 1978.

Bordwell, David. *Making Meaning: Inference and Rhetoric in the Interpretation of Cinema*. Cambridge, Mass.: Harvard University Press, 1989.

Bordwell, David, and Kristin Thompson. *Film Art: An Introduction*. Reading, Mass.: Addison-Wesley, 1979.

Bordwell, David, and Noël Carroll. *Post-Theory: Reconstructing Film Studies*. Madison: University of Wisconsin Press, 1996.

Browne, Nick, ed. *Cahiers du Cinéma 1969–1972: The Politics of Representation*. Cambridge, Mass.: Harvard University Press, 1990.

Butler, Ivan. *"To Encourage the Art of the Film": The Story of the British Film Institute*. London: Robert Hale, 1971.

Chicago Motion Picture Commission Hearings, Report. Chicago: Chicago Historical Society, 1920.

Chow, Rey. "A Phantom Discipline." PMLA 116.5 (2001): 1386–95.

Commission on Educational and Cultural Films. *The Film in National Life: Being the Report of an Enquiry Conducted by the Commission on Educational and Cultural Films into the Service Which the Cinematograph May Render to Education and Social Progress*. London: Allen and Unwin, 1932.

Cook, Jim, and Nicky North, eds. BFI *Summer Schools 1971–1979: A Dossier*. London: BFI Education Department, 1981.

Dale, Edgar. *Audio-Visual Methods in Teaching*. Rev. ed. New York: Dryden Press, 1954.

———. *How to Appreciate Motion Pictures: A Manual of Motion-Picture Criticism Prepared for High School Students*. New York: Macmillan, 1933.

———. "Methods for Analyzing the Contents of Motion Pictures." *Journal of Educational Sociology* 6.4 (1932): 244–50.

Dale, Edgar, Fannie W. Dunn, Charles F. Hoban Jr., and Etta Schneider. *Motion Pictures in Education: A Summary of the Literature*. New York: H. W. Wilson Company, 1937.

Decherney, Peter. *Hollywood and the Culture Elite: How the Movies Became American*. New York: Columbia University Press, 2005.

Donald, James, Anne Friedberg, and Laura Marcus, eds. *Close up, 1927–33: Cinema and Modernism*. Princeton, N.J.: Princeton University Press, 1998.

Dupin, Christophe. "The Postwar Transformation of the British Film Institute and Its Impact on the Development of a National Film Culture in Britain." *Screen* 47.4 (2006): 443–51.

Dysinger, Wendell S., and Christian A. Ruckmick. *The Emotional Responses of Children to the Motion Picture Situation*. New York: Macmillan, 1933.

Eisenstein, Sergei. *Film Form: Essays in Film Theory*. Translated by Jay Leyda. New York: Harcourt Brace Jovanovitch, 1949.

———. *The Film Sense*. Translated by Jay Leyda. New York: Harcourt Brace Jovanovitch, 1942.

Ellis, Jack C. "Film Societies and Film Education." *Film Culture* 4.3 (1958); 29–31.

———. "The Society of Cinema Studies: A Personal Recollection from the Early Days." *Cinema Journal* 43.1 (2003): 105–12.

Feinstein, Peter. *The Independent Film Community: A Report on the Status of Independent Film in the United States*. New York: Committee on Film and Television Resources and Services, 1977.

Fensch, Thomas. *Films on the Campus*. South Brunswick, N.J.: A. S. Barnes, 1970.

Fielding, Raymond. "Second Bibliographic Survey of Theses and Dissertations on the Subject of Film at U.S. Universities, 1916–1969." *Journal of the University Film Association (JUFA)* 21.4 (1969): 111–13.

Forman, Henry. *Our Movie Made Children*. New York: Macmillan, 1933.

Freeburg, Victor. *The Art of Photoplay Making*. New York: Macmillan, 1918.

Fuller, Kathryn H. *At the Picture Show: Small-Town Audiences and the Creation of Movie Fan Culture*. Washington, D.C.: Smithsonian Institution Press, 1996.

Gledhill, Christine, and Linda Williams, eds. *Reinventing Film Studies*. New York: Oxford, 2000.

Graff, Gerald. *Professing Literature: An Institutional History*. Chicago: University of Chicago Press, 1987.

Grant, Barry Keith, ed. *Film Study in the Undergraduate Curriculum*. New York: Modern Language Association, 1983.

Harley, John Eugene. *World-Wide Influences of the Cinema: A Study of Official Censorship and the International Cultural Aspects of Motion Pictures*. Los Angeles: University of Southern California, 1940.

Hecquet, Marie-Claude, and David McNicoll. *A Guide to Film and Television Courses in Canada, 1978–1979*. Ottawa: Canadian Film Institute, 1978.

Hillier, Jim, ed. *Cahiers du Cinema. Volume 1: The 1950's: Neo-Realism, Hollywood, the New Wave*. Cambridge, Mass.: Harvard University Press, 1985.

———, ed. *Cahiers du Cinema. Volume 2: 1969–1968: New Wave, New Cinema, Re-evaluating Hollywood*. Cambridge, Mass.: Harvard University Press, 1986.

Hoban, Charles F. Jr. *Focus on Learning: Motion Pictures in the School.* Washington, D.C.: American Council on Education, 1942.

Holaday, Perry W., and George D. Stoddard. *Getting Ideas from the Movies.* New York: Macmillan, 1933.

Jacobs, Lea. "Reformers and Spectators: The Film Education Movement in the 1930's." *Camera Obscura* (January 1990): 29–49.

Jacobs, Lewis. *Rise of the American Film: A Critical History.* New York: Harcourt Brace, 1939.

Jowett, Garth, Ian C. Jarvie, and Kathryn H. Fuller. *Children and the Movies: Media Influence and the Payne Fund Controversy.* Cambridge: Cambridge University Press, 1996.

Kennedy, Joseph P. *The Story of the Films, as Told by Leaders of the Industry to the Students of the Graduate School of Business Administration, George F. Baker Foundation, Harvard University.* Chicago: A. W. Shaw, 1927.

Klinger, Barbara. "In Retrospect: Film Studies Today." *Yale Journal of Criticism: Interpretation in the Humanities* 2.1 (1988): 129–51.

Kracauer, Siegfried. *From Caligari to Hitler: A Psychological History of the German Film.* Princeton N.J.: Princeton University Press, 1947.

Landy, Marcia. "Film and English/American Studies: What Are We Doing in an English Department?" *Critical Quarterly* 39.1 (1997): 42–50.

Leonard, Harold, ed. *The Film Index: A Bibliography. Volume 1, The Film as Art.* New York: Museum of Modern Art; H. W. Wilson Company, 1941.

Lindsay, Vachel. *The Art of the Moving Picture.* New York: Macmillan, 1915.

Lipton, Lenny. *Independent Filmmaking.* San Francisco: Straight Arrow Books, 1972.

Lowry, Edward. *The Filmology Movement and Film Study in France.* Ann Arbor, Mich.: UMI Research Press, 1985.

Lunde, Erik S., and Douglas A. Noverr, eds. *Film History.* Selected Course Outlines From American Colleges and Universities series. New York: Marcus Weiner, 1989.

MacCann, Richard Dyer, and Jack C. Ellis. *Cinema Examined: Selections from Cinema Journal.* New York: E. P. Dutton, 1982.

MacDonald, Scott, ed. *Cinema 16: Documents toward a History of the Film Society.* Philadelphia: Temple University Press, 2002.

Macgowan, Kenneth. "Film in the University." In *Ideas on Film: A Handbook for the 16mm User,* edited by Cecile Starr. New York: Funk and Wagnalls, 1951.

Marchant, James, ed. *The Cinema in Education.* New York: Arno Press, 1978 [1925].

McArthur, Colin. "Two Steps Forward, One Step Back: Cultural Struggle in the British Film Institute." *Journal of Popular British Cinema* 4 (2001): 112–27.

Mitchell, Alice Miller. *Children and Movies*. Chicago: University of Chicago Press, 1929.

Moley, Raymond A. *Are We Movie Made?* New York: Macy-Masius, 1938.

Morey, Anne. *Hollywood Outsiders: The Adaptation of the Film Industry, 1913–1934*. Minneapolis: University of Minnesota Press, 2003.

Morris, Peter. "From Film Club to Academy: The Beginnings of Film Education in Canada." In *Québec, Canada: L'enseignement du cinéma et de l'audiovisuel*, edited by Réal La Rochelle. Condé-sur-Noireau; Montréal: Corlet-Télérama and Cinémathèque québécoise, 1991.

Münsterberg, Hugo. "The Photoplay: A Psychological Study, 1916." In *Hugo Münsterberg on Film. "The Photoplay: A Psychological Study" and Other Writings*, edited by Allan Langdale. New York: Routledge, 2002.

Nowell-Smith, Geoffrey. "The 1970 Crisis at the BFI and Its Aftermath." *Screen* 47.4 (2006): 453–59.

Paterson, Barbara. *Renegades: Australia's First Film School from Swinburne to VCA*. Victoria: Helicon Press, 1996.

Patterson, Frances Taylor. *Cinema Craftsmanship: A Book for Photoplaywrights*. New York: Harcourt Brace and Company, 1920.

Perkins, Victor. *Film as Film: Understanding and Judging Movies*. Harmondsworth, U.K.: Penguin, 1972.

Peters, Charles C. *Motion Pictures and Standards of Morality*. New York: Macmillan, 1933.

Peterson, Ruth C., and L. L. Thurstone. *Motion Pictures and the Social Attitudes of Children: A Payne Fund Study*. New York: Macmillan, 1933.

Phelan, John J. "Motion Pictures as a Phase of Commercialized Amusement in Toledo, Ohio." *Film History* 13.3 (2001 [1919]): 234–328.

Polan, Dana. *Scenes of Instruction: The Beginnings of the U.S. Study of Film*. Berkeley: University of California Press, 2007.

Renshaw, Samuel, Vernon L. Miller, and Dorothy P. Marquis. *Children's Sleep*. New York: Macmillan, 1933.

Rodowick, D. N. *The Crisis of Political Modernism: Criticism and Ideology in Contemporary Film Theory*. Urbana: University of Illinois Press, 1988.

Rotha, Paul. *The Film till Now: A Survey of the Cinema*. London: J. Cape, 1930.

Sarris, Andrew. *The American Cinema: Directors and Directions, 1929–1968*. New York: Dutton, 1968.

Seabury, William Marston. *Motion Picture Problems: The Cinema and the League of Nations*. New York: Arondale Press, 1929.

Sheridan, Marion C., Harold H. Owen Jr., Ken Macrorie, and Fred Marcus, eds. *The Motion Picture and the Teaching of English*. New York: Appleton-Century-Crofts, 1965.

Short, William H. *A Generation of Motion Pictures: A Review of Social Values in Recreational Films.* New York: National Committee for Study of Social Values in Motion Pictures, 1928.

Shuttleworth, Frank K., and Mark A. May. *The Social Conduct and Attitudes of Movie Fans.* New York: Macmillan, 1933.

Sklar, Robert. "Oh! Althusser!: Historiography and the Rise of Cinema Studies." *Radical History Review* 41 (1988): 10–35.

Smoodin, Eric. *Regarding Frank Capra: Audience, Celebrity, and American Film Studies, 1930–1960.* Durham, N.C.: Duke University Press, 2004.

Starr, Cecile, ed. *Ideas on Film: A Handbook for the 16mm User.* New York: Funk and Wagnalls, 1951.

Stewart, David C. *Film Study in Higher Education.* Washington, D.C.: American Council on Education, 1966.

Taylor, Greg. *Artists in the Audience: Cults, Camp, and American Film Criticism.* Princeton, N.J.: Princeton University Press, 1999.

Uriccio, William. "German University Dissertations with Motion Picture Related Topics: 1910–1945." *Historical Journal of Film, Radio and Television* 7.2 (1987): 175–90.

Wagner, Robert W. "Cinema Education in the United States." *Journal of the University Film Producers Association (JUFPA)* 13.3 (1961): 8–10, 12–14.

Wasson, Haidee. *Museum Movies: The Museum of Modern Art and the Birth of Art Cinema.* Berkeley: University of California Press, 2005.

Whannel, Paddy and Peter Harcourt, eds. *Studies in the Teaching of Film within Formal Education: Four Courses Described.* London: British Film Institute, 1968.

Wilinsky, Barbara. *Sure Seaters: The Emergence of Art House Cinema.* Minneapolis: University of Minnesota Press, 2001.

Wilson, David, ed. *Cahiers du Cinéma Volume 4 1973–1978: History, Ideology, Cultural Struggle.* Cambridge, Mass.: Harvard University Press, 1995.

Wollen, Peter. *Signs and Meaning in the Cinema.* London: Secker and Warburg; British Film Institute, 1969.

Writers' Program, New York. *The Film Index: A Bibliography. Volume 2, The Film As Industry.* White Plains, N.Y.: Kraus International Publications, n.d.

———. *The Film Index: A Bibliography. Volume 3, The Film in Society.* White Plains, N.Y.: Kraus International Publications, n.d.

Yoshimoto, Mitsuhiro. *Kurosawa: Film Studies and Japanese Cinema.* Durham, N.C.: Duke University Press, 2000.

Young, Colin. "University Film Teaching in the United States: A Survey." *Film Quarterly* 16.3 (1963): 37–47.

Zryd, Michael. "The Academy and the Avant-Garde: A Relationship of Dependence and Resistance." *Cinema Journal* 45.2 (2006): 17–42.

About the Contributors

CHARLES R. ACLAND is the Concordia Research Chair and Professor of Communications at Concordia University in Montreal. His most recent books are *Screen Traffic* (2003) and the edited collection *Residual Media* (2007). His current research on the history of vernacular media critique will be published by Duke University Press.

MARK LYNN ANDERSON is an Assistant Professor in the Film Studies Program at the University of Pittsburgh. He is the author of *Twilight of the Idols: Hollywood and the Human Sciences in 1920s America* (forthcoming).

MARK BETZ is a Senior Lecturer in the Film Studies Department at King's College, London. He is the author of *Beyond the Subtitle: Remapping European Art Cinema* (forthcoming 2009).

ZOË DRUICK is an Associate Professor in the School of Communication at Simon Fraser University. She is the author of *Projecting Canada: Government Policy and Documentary Film at the National Film Board of Canada* (2007) and coeditor of *Programming Reality: Perspectives on English-Canadian Television* (2008). She has published numerous essays on cultural policy and media history.

LEE GRIEVESON is a Reader in Film Studies and the Director of the Graduate Programme in Film Studies at University College London. He is the author of *Policing Cinema: Movies and Censorship in Early Twentieth Century America* (2004) and coeditor of *The Silent Cinema Reader* (2003) and *Mob Culture: Hidden Histories of the American Gangster Film* (2005).

STEPHEN GROENING is a Ph.D. candidate in the Comparative Studies in Discourse and Society Program at the University of Minnesota. He is currently working on his dissertation, "Connected Isolation: Screens, Mobility, and Globalized Media Culture."

HADEN GUEST is the Director of the Harvard Film Archive. He is currently working on a critical history of film study in the United States between 1945 and 1968 and an anthology of unpublished and uncollected writings by Sam Fuller.

AMELIE HASTIE is an Associate Professor of Film and Digital Media at the University of California, Santa Cruz. She is the author of *Cupboards of Curiosity: Women, Recollection, and Film History* (2007) and numerous essays on feminist film history, television studies, and ephemera. She has been a member of the *Camera Obscura* editorial collective since 2001.

LYNNE JOYRICH is an Associate Professor of Modern Culture and Media at Brown University. She is the author of *Re-viewing Reception: Television, Gender, and Postmodern Culture* (1996) and numerous essays on television, film, gender, and sexuality studies. She has been a member of the *Camera Obscura* editorial collective since 1996.

LAURA MULVEY is a Professor in the Department of History of Art, Film and Visual Media at Birkbeck College, University of London. She is the author of *Visual and Other Pleasures* (1989), *Citizen Kane* (1992), *Fetishism and Curiosity* (1996), and *Death Twenty-four Times a Second: Reflections on Stillness in the Moving Image* (2005).

DANA POLAN is a Professor of Cinema Studies at New York University. His most recent book is *Scenes of Instruction: The Beginnings of the U.S. Study of Film* (2007). He has Duke University Press volumes forthcoming on the television shows *The Sopranos* (2009) and *The French Chef*.

D. N. RODOWICK is a Professor of Visual and Environmental Studies and the Director of Graduate Studies for Film and Visual Studies at Harvard University. He is the author of *Reading the Figural, or, Philosophy after the New Media* (2001), *Gilles Deleuze's Time Machine* (1997), *The Difficulty of Difference: Psychoanalysis, Sexual Difference, and Film Theory* (1991), *The Crisis of Political Modernism: Criticism and Ideology in Contemporary Film Theory* (1989, 1994), and most recently, *The Virtual Life of Film* (2007).

PHILIP ROSEN is a Professor of Modern Culture and Media at Brown University. He has published numerous articles on film, media and theory. His books include *Change Mummified: Cinema, Historicity, Theory* (2001) and, as editor, *Narrative, Apparatus, Ideology: A Film Theory Reader* (1986).

ALISON TROPE received her Ph.D. in Critical Studies from the School of Cinema-Television at the University of Southern California in 1999. She has taught in the Critical Studies Department in the School of Cinema-Television and currently teaches a range of courses at the Annenberg School for Communication at USC. She also serves on the editorial board and as book review editor for *The Moving Image*.

HAIDEE WASSON is an Associate Professor of Cinema at Concordia University in Montreal. She has previously taught at the University of Minnesota and in the Visual and Environmental Studies Department at Harvard University. She is author of *Museum Movies* (2005) and has published numerous essays on film history, cultural institutions, and emergent media.

PATRICIA WHITE is an Associate Professor and Chair of Film and Media Studies at Swarthmore College. She is the author of *Uninvited: Classical Hollywood Cinema and Lesbian Representability* (1999), coauthor of *The Film Experience: An Introduction* (2004), and editor of *Figures of Resistance: Essays in Feminist Theory* (2007) by Teresa de Lauretis. She has been a member of the *Camera Obscura* editorial collective since 1997.

SHARON WILLIS is a Professor of French and Visual and Cultural Studies at the University of Rochester. She is the author of *High Contrast: Race and Gender in Contemporary Hollywood Film* (1997) and *Marguerite Duras: Writing on the Body* (1987) as well as coeditor, with Constance Penley, of *Male Trouble* (1993). She has been a member of the *Camera Obscura* editorial collective since 1991.

PETER WOLLEN is a Professor Emeritus at UCLA. He is the author of numerous books and articles, including *Signs and Meaning in the Cinema* (1969), *Singin' in the Rain* (1993), *Raiding the Icebox: Reflections on Twentieth-Century Culture* (1996), and *Paris Hollywood: Writings on Film* (2002).

MICHAEL ZRYD is an Associate Professor in cinema and media studies in the Department of Film at York University in Toronto and past president of the Film Studies Association of Canada. He has published essays on experimental and documentary cinema in *Cinema Journal, October, Public*, and *The Moving Image*.

Index

American Museum of Natural History, 57

American Social Hygiene Association, 57

American Society of Cinematographers, 401

Amery, Leo S., 72

Anderson, Florence, 167, 169

Anderson, Joseph L., 187, 194, 199

Anderson, Lindsay, 331

Anderson, Mark Lynn, 106

Anderson, Perry, 223

Andrew, Dudley, xv

Anger, Kenneth, 197, 206

animation, 57, 137; computer, 366, 376–77

Anthology Film Archives, 412

Anticipation of the Night (1958), 410

Archer, Eugene, 220, 222–23, 230n8

archives, 76–77, 79–80, 87, 414–15

Armageddon (1998), 353

Arnheim, Rudolf, 67, 75, 321

Around the World in Eighty Minutes (1931), 138

art cinema, 324

art, 94, 97–98, 110–11, 140, 188, 378, 380, 382, 414

Arthur, Paul, 193

Arzner, Dorothy, 303, 329

Asquith, Anthony, 402, 408

Association of Moving Image Archivists, 415

Association of School Film Libraries, 154, 407

Athens International Film Festival, 413

Attenborough, Richard, 219

audience, 10, 15, 60; adult, xx; children, xix, 16–18, 42; as hypnotized subjects, 3–37; mass, 46–47; nickelodeon, 11

Audio Visual Communication Review, 409

Augsburger, Michael, 112–13

Australia: film studies programs, 411

Australian Council of Film Societies, 409

Australian Film Festival, 409

auteurism, 218, 225, 229, 269, 323, 325–26, 328, 333, 340, 364

avant-garde film, xxii, 26, 69, 87, 98, 138, 182–208, 228–30, 252–54, 257, 269; definition of, 183; literature on, 207; museum of, 412

Bachmann, Gideon, 239–40, 242, 250–52

Baillie, Bruce, 255

Baird, Thomas, 164

Balázs, Béla, 67, 323, 380

Balcon, Michael, 402

Baldwin, James Mark, 5, 8–9

Balio, Tino, 335

Ballet mécanique (1924), 206

Banes, Sally, 200

Barr, Alfred, 125, 127

Barr, Charles, 321

Barrett, Wilton, 57

Barry, Iris, 57, 67, 126–28, 130–32, 136, 162, 164, 167, 402, 406–7

Barthes, Roland, 276, 375, 379

Bartlett, Scott, 198–9

Basso, Leilio, 224

Bauchau, Patrick, 220–21, 230n7

Baudry, Jean-Louis, 24, 282, 302

Bay, Michael, 353

Bazin, André, 67, 220, 225, 227, 270, 282, 328, 331, 380, 382

Becker, Peter, 362

Beckett, Alan, 224

Bellour, Raymond, 25, 227, 276, 303, 313, 387

Bender, Thomas, 186, 188, 192

Benjamin, Walter, 319, 380

Benoit-Levy, Jean, 251

Benveniste, Emile, 278–79

Bergman, Ingmar, 324

Dovzhenko, Aleksander, 72
Downing, Taylor, 339
Dreyfus-Barney, Laura, 75
Driscoll, John, 410
Dulmac, Germaine, 79
Dumazedier, Joffre, 86
Durand, Jean, 137
Duras, Marguerite, 303, 309
Durgnat, Raymond, 322
DVDs: educational value of, 357–59,
    363–64, 366; extra features of, 353–73;
    interactivity with, 365–66, 372n31;
    marketing of, 357, 361, 367; production
    of, 367
Dyer, Richard, 329–30, 334
Dysinger, Wendell, 19

early film, 182, 256–59, 414. *See also*
    silent film
Eastman Kodak, 402, 404
Eaton, Michael, 339
Eckhart, Charles, 268
Edinburgh International Film Festival,
    83, 171, 202, 229, 292, 296n33, 331–33,
    408
Edison, Thomas, 109, 244
educational film, xxii, 69, 72, 75–78,
    80–82, 86–87, 126, 137, 150–51, 155, 158,
    160, 171, 403; catalogues of, 79. *See also*
    documentary film
Educational Film Library Association
    (EFLA), 154, 171–72, 407
Educational Screen, 401
Edward Scissorhands (1990), 377
Eikhenbaum, Boris, 270
Einstein, Albert, 70
Eisenstein, Sergei, 128, 130–31, 248, 290;
    as director, 72, 324; as theorist, 109,
    220, 282, 323, 403, 408
Eisner, Lotte, 239, 243
Eley, Geoff, 172
Ellerman, Annie Winifred, 403

Ellis, Jack, 170, 191, 206, 410
Empire Marketing Board, 72
Emshwiller, Ed, 198
Encyclopedia Britannica Films, 169
Epstein, Jean, 250–52, 380
Epstein, Marie, 251
ethnographic film, 84
Eureka (1974), 256
Everson, William K., 240, 243, 246–47
Exhibitor's Herald, 400–401, 404
eXistenZ (1999), 376
Experimental Cinema, 131, 404
experimental film, 57, 133, 182–208; defi-
    nition of, 183; feminist, 313
exploitation film, 362
Export, Valie, 309
extra-theatrical exhibition. *See* non-
    theatrical exhibition

Fairbanks, Douglas, 138
Falk, Sawyer, 97–98, 114, 405
fascism, 77
Fassbinder, Rainer Werner, 329
Fellini, Federico, 239
feminism, xxv–xxvi, 202, 290, 298–
    318, 412; and film production, 303,
    331; French influence, 312–13; post-
    feminism, 304; psychoanalytic theory,
    287–89, 296n30; theory, 25, 182, 202,
    312, 314, 337, 412
Ferguson, Otis, 236
Festen (1998), 377
Fiering, Alvin, 186
Figgis, Mike, 37
Film and History, 412
Film Art, 405
Film Associates, Inc., 402
Film Comment, 268, 326, 410
Film Council of America (FCA), xx–xxii,
    149–73, 408; affiliated organizations,
    156; conferences, 166–67; events,
    164–66; Film Preview Project, 164;

filmmaking, xix–xx; dominant codes, 285–86; feminist, 314; oppositional, 286, 288; political, 68; process, 365; as self-expression, 105–6, 193, 195, 199; student, 194–97, 199–203; techniques, 96; women's, 303

filmography, xxiv, 246–48, 255, 258

filmology, xii

Films in Review, xxiv, 235–37, 241–49, 253, 255

Fischer, Lucy, 415

Fisher, Morgan, 259

Fit to Win (1919), 13–14

Fitzpatrick, Kathleen, 338

Flaherty, Robert, 67, 129, 164

Fleischer, Max, 57

Fleming, Victor, 138

Fletcher, Scott, 169

Flitterman, Sandy, 301

Florey, Elizabeth, 163

folk art, 108–9

Ford Foundation, 168–69

Ford, John, 223, 225, 228, 324

Forman, Henry, 21, 44, 404

Fortune, 112–13

Foucault, Michel, 17n14, 38–39, 67, 268–69

Fox, William, 99

Framework, 412

Frampton, Hollis, 256

France, xii, 77, 84, 133, 272, 291; and American films, 236; and the League of Nations, 70, 75; feminism, 312–13; film societies, 149; national film academy, 192; New Wave, 186

Franju, Georges, 406

Frankfurt school, 331

Frayling, Sir Christopher, 339

Freeburg, Victor Oscar, 97, 102–4, 370n7

French, Philip, 339

Freud, Sigmund, 7, 24–25, 35n115, 279–80, 298

Friedberg, Anne, 394

Friedman, Arthur, 410

Friend, Bernard, 149

Fuller, Katherine, 44–45

Fuller, Samuel, 223, 228–29, 324

Gallop, Jane, 312

Gance, Abel, 13, 251

Gehr, Ernie, 256–57

General Agreement on Trade and Tariffs, 83

genre, 66, 326

George Eastman House Museum, 408

Germany, 77, 128, 133

Germany: and the League of Nations, 75; and propaganda, 137

Gerstein, Evelyn, 57

Gessner, Robert, xii, 60, 116, 410

Gidal, Peter, 274

Gieger, Joseph Roy, 16

Gielgud, John, 402

Gish, Lillian, 239

Gladiator (2000), 360

Gledhill, Christine, 290

Godard, Jean-Luc, 223, 239, 274, 324

Godfather, The (1972), 365

Golden Reel Film Festival, 170–71

Gomery, Douglas, 335

Good Housekeeping, 12

Goodman, Nelson, 382–84, 387

Gough-Yates, Kevin, 266

governance, xix, 5, 8, 10, 12, 14–15, 20–23, 17n14, 42, 69

Graff, Gerald, 100–101, 107, 114

Gramsci, Antonio, 66–67, 152–53

Grant, Barry Keith, 335

Great Books curriculum, 95–96

Greed (1925), 250

Greenburg, Clement, 23, 114

Grenauer, Emily, 121

Griebsch, John, 187, 194

Grierson, John, 67, 71, 81, 130, 161, 407

Jacobs, Lewis, 128, 239, 245, 404

Jakobson, Roman, 226

James, David, 193

James, William, 8–9

Jarvie, Ian, 44–5

Jazz Singer, The (1927), 18

Jefferson Park study, 45–46, 50–51, 54–55, 59

Job, Steven, 376

Johnson, Lyndon B., 411

Johnston, Claire, 229, 290, 314

Joll, James, 151

Jongbloed, H. J. L, 86

Journal of Film and Video, 335

Journal of the Society of Cinematologists, xiii

journals, xxiv–xxv, 87, 235–59, 265, 399; and little books, 324; on film education, 401; online, 415; survey of, 240–41. *See also individual titles*

Jowett, Garth, 44

Jump Cut, 313, 412

Jump, Rev H. A., 12

Jurassic Park (1993), 377

Juvenile Protective Association, 11

Kael, Pauline, 238–39

Kaplan, E. Ann, 314, 334

Kaplan, Nelly, 339

Kaufman, Gerald, 339

Kellerman, Annette, 396n1

Kennedy, A. L., 339

Kennedy, Joseph P., 94, 110, 112–14, 403

Kibbons, Gary, 183

Kitses, Jim, 326, 363

Klein, George, 15

Klinger, Barbara, 357

Knight, Arthur, 67, 198, 206

Kornblau, Craig, 361

Kracauer, Siegfried, 67, 251, 331, 380, 408

Kristeva, Julia, 275

Kroll, Jack, 193

Kruse, William F., 156, 165

Kubelka, Peter, 254

Kubrick, Stanley, 414

Kuhn, Annette, 290, 314

Kuntzel, Thierry, 276, 313

L'Herbier, Marcel, 251

Lacan, Jacques, 25–26, 279–81, 282–83, 313

Lady Eve (1941), 245

Landy, Marcia, 152

Lang, Fritz, 239, 250, 324

Langlois, Henri, 251, 406–7

laser disc, 364

Lashley, Karl, 13–15

Lasky, Jesse, 99, 110

Lasky, Joseph, 67

Lasswell, Harold, 15

Le Bon, Gustave, 7–8, 20–21

Leacock, Richard, 196–97

League of Nations, xix, 67, 78; conferences, 72–73, 75, 79; and film policy, 71; film production, 76; founding of, 69; International Educational Cinematograph Institute (IECI), 68, 74–77, 79, 403–4; International Institute of Intellectual Cooperation (IIEC), 70, 73, 75, 79–80; motion picture congress, 402; and the United States, 70, 74. *See also* United Nations

Lears, T. J. Jackson, 105, 112

Leavis, F.R., 267

Lebensphilosophie, 41

lecture film, 154

Lee, Rohama, 168

Lee, Spike, 200

Leger, Fernand, 206

Lessing, Gotthold Ephraim, 381

Lester, Elenor, 194, 196

Lévi-Strauss, Claude, 225–26, 268

Levine, Lawrence, 100

Levy, Benoit, 129

Library of Congress Cataloging-in-Publication Data
Grieveson, Lee, 1969–
Inventing film studies / Lee Grieveson and Haidee
Wasson, editors.
p. cm.
Includes bibliographical references and index.
ISBN 978-0-8223-4289-2 (cloth : alk. paper) —
ISBN 978-0-8223-4307-3 (pbk. : alk. paper)
1. Motion pictures—Study and teaching—United States.
2. Motion pictures—Study and teaching—Great Britain.
3. Film criticism—United States—History.
4. Film criticism—Great Britain—History.
I. Wasson, Haidee, 1970– II. Title.
PN1993.8.U5G75 2008
791.43071'073—dc22
2008013870